American Politics

American Politics

Classic and Contemporary Readings

Seventh Edition

Allan J. Cigler
University of Kansas

Burdett A. Loomis
University of Kansas

Houghton Mifflin Company   Boston   New York

Publisher: Suzanne Jeans
Senior Sponsoring Editor: Traci Mueller
Marketing Manager: Edwin Hill
Development Editor: Christina Lembo
Associate Project Editor: Deborah Berkman
Cover Design Director: Tony Saizon
Senior Photo Editor: Jennifer Meyer Dare
Composition Buyer: Chuck Dutton
New Title Project Manager: Susan Brooks-Peltier
Marketing Assistant: Erin Timm

Cover Image: Smithsonian American Art Museum, Washington, DC;
Hemphill/Art Resource, NY

Printed in the U.S.A.

Library of Congress Control Number: 2007925759

Instructor's examination copy
  ISBN-10: 0-618-83392-7
  ISBN-13: 978-0-618-83392-4

For orders, use student text ISBNs
  ISBN-10: 0-618-80289-4
  ISBN-13: 978-0-618-80289-0

23456789-MV-11 10 09 08 07

CONTENTS

TOPIC CORRELATION CHART

Although the chapters of this book of readings have been organized to mesh with the coverage of most American government textbooks, many subjects receive attention in more than one chapter. The following chart permits students and instructors to locate relevant readings for twenty-four subjects, ranging (in alphabetical order) from bureaucracy to the Washington establishment.

Topic:	Covered In:
Bureaucracy	Chapter 12; 2.3, 2.4, 14.1, 14.5
Campaigns and Elections	Chapter 7; 4.3, 5.4, 6.2, 6.3, 10.5
Bush Administration	2.3, 2.4, 3.6, 4.3, 11.3, 14.4, 14.5
Congress	Chapter 10; 6.3, 7.3, 9.4, 14.3
Constitution	Chapters 1, 3, 13; 2.1, 2.2, 7.2, 9.1, 11.3, 13.2
Domestic Policy	Chapter 14; 2.3, 2.4, 3.9, 3.10, 4.1, 9.4, 10.4, 10.5, 11.3, 12.1, 13.4, 14.2, 14.3
Federalism	Chapter 2; 1.1, 9.1, 12.4
Interest Groups	Chapter 9; 14.1, 14.2, 14.3
Leadership	Chapter 11; 8.1, 10.3, 10.4, 10.5, 13.4, 14.1
Money and Politics	7.2, 9.2, 9.4, 10.3, 10.4, 10.5
Participation	Chapter 5; 4.2, 6.2, 9.3, 10.1
Policy Making Process	Chapter 14; 2.3, 2.4, 3.8, 7.3, 9.4, 10.3, 10.4, 10.5, 12.3
Political Culture	3.5, 5.2, 5.3, 5.4, 6.3, 9.3, 10.1, 12.1
Political Parties	Chapter 6; 5.1, 5.4, 7.1, 7.2, 7.3, 10.3, 10.5, 12.1
Post 9/11 and the War on Terrorism	3.6, 4.3, 8.2, 8.3, 11.3, 14.4, 14.5
Presidency	Chapter 11; 8.1, 14.4, 14.5
Public Opinion	Chapter 4; 3.6, 5.4, 8.3, 9.4, 12.1
Reform	5.2, 6.3, 7.1, 7.2, 9.3, 10.4, 14.5
Representation	Chapter 9; 4.2, 5.1, 6.3, 7.3, 10.1, 10.2, 10.3, 10.4, 13.4
Separation of Powers	1.4, 10.2, 10.4, 11.1, 11.3, 12.1, 13.1
Supreme Court and the Judiciary	Chapters 3 and 13; 7.2
Washington Establishment	1.3, 9.2, 10.3, 10.4, 10.5, 11.1, 12.4, 14.5

PREFACE

Over the course of seven editions of this book, we have sought to balance coverage of the powerful consistencies in American politics with the equally powerful tendencies toward change. In this text, as in our classroom teaching, we hark back to the founding and to the Constitution, time after time, even as we struggle to explain the most contemporary of events. Indeed, the presidency of George W. Bush continues to test constitutional strictures on executive power. And several readings in this new edition focus on this source of tension in the wake of the September 11, 2001, terrorist attacks and our reactions to them.

In addition, the essential checks-and-balances fragmentation of American politics has come under real challenge by the growth of strong, centralized political parties. The 2006 elections produced an almost parliamentary confrontation between the president's Republican party and the out-of-power Democrats, with the results turning largely on how voters felt about George Bush and his administration's Iraq policies. Such polarization is far different from the dominant political context of the twentieth century, when conservative Democrats and liberal Republicans exercised real power within the bipartisan coalitions that often dominated on Capitol Hill. If this edition of *American Politics: Classic and Contemporary Readings* appears to emphasize the role of the president within a constitutional government, it is because this issue represents the most important intellectual and political conflict of our time. The president, the Congress, and the Supreme Court will wrestle with the role of the executive as we confront an international "war on terror" for many years to come.

Still, even as we move further into the twenty-first century, 220 years removed from the writing of the Constitution, there are great continuities in American politics. The framers would have easily understood the roles played by today's interest groups, the current state of electoral politics, and recent controversies regarding the Supreme Court. They might not have predicted the lasting strength of political parties, but they would have understood the implications of former Majority Leader Tom DeLay creating a dominant (and dangerous?) "majority faction" within the House of Representatives.

Readings in the Seventh Edition

In light of the simultaneous continuity and change that characterize American politics, we remain committed to assembling a mix of articles that combines well-established classics with the best of contemporary analysis. The fifty-nine articles of this edition include nineteen new pieces. As always, it has been extremely difficult to settle on a limited number of articles to reflect the entirety of the American political experience; in the end, any collection must be a sample, and we are confident that this set offers a robust array of the new and the familiar, with a few unexpected pieces to spice up the mix.

Aside from various *Federalist* papers, our classics include key Supreme Court cases, such as *Marbury v. Madison* and *Brown v. Board of Education*, although we do, in this edition, reprint an article that questions the substantive significance of *Brown*. We also rely on John Roche's classic discussion of the framers as a "Reform Caucus" and Richard Neustadt's essential analysis of presidential power—the latter all the more important given its implicit testing by George W. Bush. In a related vein, we continue to emphasize some "modern classics" that have illuminated the politics of our era. For example, articles like Kenneth Shepsle's "The Changing Textbook Congress" and Richard Posner's reflections on judicial activism in "What Am I? A Potted Plant?" provide valuable commentary that links modern politics to the past.

Of course, we include a large number of new articles, which place contemporary events within broad scholarly contexts for understanding the nature of American politics. For example, Thomas Mann and Norman Ornstein examine today's Congress within an historical framework and find it seriously flawed, as their article's title, "The Broken Branch," suggests.

Framework of the Text

This edition of *American Politics* consists of fourteen chapters that correspond to the organization of most American government texts. Each chapter starts with an essay that lays out the major themes of the particular subject and links the readings to those themes. And each article begins with a headnote that introduces it and provides some context for its selection. Following each article are questions for discussion. As with past editions, this one also includes two other valuable features: a series of annotations that provide clarifications of difficult terms and obscure historical references and an extensive correlation chart that follows the table of contents. This chart allows students and professors to connect themes and issues in American politics beyond the order imposed by the fourteen chapters. For example, the categories of "war on terrorism" and "money in politics" direct readers to articles across several chapters.

Ancillary Materials for Instructors

Complementing the text readings are an *Instructor's Resource Manual* and a *Test Bank*, both ably prepared by Professor Joel Paddock of Missouri State University. The *Instructor's Manual* is available online at http://college.hmco.com/pic/cigler7e (please contact your Houghton Mifflin sales representative for the site's user name and password) and the Test Bank questions, provided as Word files, are available from your sales representative upon request.

Acknowledgments

Over the years, Houghton Mifflin has recruited excellent reviewers for this book, and they have made many first-rate suggestions for articles and organization. Once again, we acknowledge our debt to these scholars, including:

Donald C. Baumer, Smith College
Stefanie Chambers, Trinity College
Mitchel Gerber, Southeast Missouri State University
Ted Bueter, DePauw University
Jeremy Walling, Southeast Missouri State University

Once again, our Houghton Mifflin editors have proven invaluable to producing the best book possible. Our deep thanks go to Christina Lembo, Tom Finn, and the godmother of them all, Jean Woy.

Finally, after almost twenty years, we continue to try to get it right. A thousand miles from our western Pennsylvania roots, we still favor the Steelers and long for the good old days of the Pirates. Beth Cigler and Michel Loomis are still our strongest supporters and our most insightful critics. And it's all for the best.

A.J.C.
B.A.L.

American Politics

 # Chapter 1

THE CONSTITUTION AND FOUNDING

The framing of the Constitution serves as one of the anchors of American politics. The Constitution was written, under pressure, by an extraordinary band of political leaders, whose accomplishments at the Philadelphia convention have proven so workable and lasting that it is difficult not to see them as mythical figures. Still, with the possible exception of George Washington, these were people, not demigods. And Washington's elevated status proved useful to the framers: As they devised the presidency and later pushed for ratification, they, along with the great body of citizens, could easily envision Washington as the first incumbent of the office.

It is difficult to exaggerate the scope of the problems the framers faced. They confronted a system of government under the Articles of Confederation that emphasized the sovereignty of the individual states at the expense of a coherent national identity and that hindered the development of the nation. An armed insurrection in Massachusetts (Shays's Rebellion) demonstrated the weakness of the states in coming to terms with problems of commerce, currency, and credit. In addition, this uprising brought home the supposed dangers of the masses within a democratic state. The possible "tyranny of the majority" was a real fear. Domestic challenges were no greater than those from abroad. The United States may have won its war of independence, but European powers certainly did not see American sovereignty as immutable. Throughout the country's first few decades, there were numerous plots to compromise American independence, such as the XYZ Affair and Aaron Burr's plan for a separatist state in the Southwest.

In writing the Constitution and securing its ratification, the framers proved themselves skillful political engineers and propagandists. As Jack Rakove points out, the framers had to "reconstitute" the government of the new nation by the very act of writing a constitution, and Rakove argues that they learned well from the Massachusetts experience of including "broad statements on the first principles of government" within the document. John P. Roche sees these individuals as a "reform caucus," a label that aptly captures the essentially political nature of their task. Nevertheless, their purposes were more radical than merely carrying out a set of reforms. As Roche notes, "The Constitutionalists went forth to subvert the Confederation," not to enact some modest changes.

Just as the American Revolution has been characterized as conservative, the same can be said of the writing of the Constitution. As historian Richard Hofstadter emphasizes, protecting property rights played a central role in the framers' thinking. Given their status as part of the new nation's elite, this is understandable. Still, protecting property rights represented more than a simple appeal to self-interest; for the framers, such safeguards were important guideposts in assessing the reach of governmental power. Property rights could best be protected by the creation of a central government that was strong enough to ensure orderly commerce but not so strong that it impinged on the rights of the minority.

A governmental structure that could protect property rights without becoming oppressive would not only have to make sense theoretically; it would have to win the approval of the states in the ratification process. To address these necessities, the framers created a series of checks and balances, most notably federalism (see Chapter 2) and the separation of powers. In *The Federalist*, No. 51, James Madison argues that liberty can be protected only where the executive, legislative, and judicial functions are divided. The division, however, need not be, and cannot be, complete; there will always be some sharing of powers. Indeed, Madison notes in *The Federalist*, No. 47, "where the *whole* power of one department is exercised by the same hands which possess the *whole* power of another department, the fundamental principles of a free constitution are subverted."

One test of a "fundamental principle" of any constitution is its staying power. The separation of powers has not gone unchallenged over the course of the American republic. The most common conflict has arisen between the executive and the legislature, with critics often arguing that the executive branch needs more power to carry out its electoral mandate and to implement a coherent foreign policy.

In the 2000 election between Vice President Al Gore and Governor George W. Bush of Texas, the staying power of one fundamental element of the American political system—the Electoral College—was challenged by the closest election in more than a century. This jerrybuilt system, the product of political compromises in the 1787 convention, survived and produced a legitimate winner, even though Gore received about 500,000 more votes than Bush.

Still, as we proceed well into our third century as a nation, eighteenth-century solutions developed by the framers may require re-evaluation, especially in highly partisan times. The impeachment of Bill Clinton, the contentiousness of Senate judicial confirmations, and the lack of effective legislative deliberation all demonstrate the costs of seeking partisan advantage, which often overwhelms the willingness of national politicians to work together. Much as the Supreme Court continues to reassess the meaning of federalism in the twenty-first century, so too must legislators and presidents wrestle with the fundamental issues of governance addressed by the framers almost 220 years ago.

A Tradition Born of Strife

Jack N. Rakove

When the framers decided to write a new constitution rather than attempt to re-structure the Articles of Confederation, they were setting out for unknown terri-tory. Some of them, however, had experience with state constitutions that had been written after 1776. In addition, the framers could reflect on how well these documents had done in establishing a balance of liberty and order. In particular, the Massachusetts delegates to the 1787 Constitutional Convention benefited from their four years of efforts to craft a suitable constitution.

In this article, Jack N. Rakove argues that in writing a new constitution the framers concluded that the Union needed to be completely reconstituted and that the states' constitution-building experiences offered a series of practical lessons for them to draw on. Most important, the state experiences taught the framers to think of a constitution as specifying the broad nature and powers of government, an integral step to making it the supreme law of the land. Their pre-liminary efforts at writing state documents gave the framers a base of under-standing for their more difficult task of constructing a national constitution.

Traditions, by nature conservative, may sometimes have revolutionary origins. So it is with America's constitutional tradition. It was shaped not only by the decade of controversy that carried Americans to inde-pendence, but also—and more importantly—by the process of writing a series of innovative governing documents for the states and observing their effective-ness over the decade that followed.

For much of the 18th century, the American colonies and Great Britain had shared a constitutional tradition, though each emphasized different aspects. England, of course, had no single written constitutional document; its "consti-tution" was the totality of its governing laws and customs. The British held that the Glorious Revolution of 1688–89, which limited the King's authority over Parliament and confirmed that he was bound by constitutional principles, had

Jack N. Rakove is the Coe Professor of History and American Studies at Stanford University.

"A Tradition Born of Strife" by Jack Rakove. From *Constitution*, Volume 7, Number 1, pp. 4–10. Reprinted by permission from Jack Rakove.

also made parliament the supreme source of law within the British Empire. But during the Stamp Act crisis of 1765, when Parliament took the position that it had the power to legislate for America "in all cases whatsoever," a grave and prophetic constitutional dispute erupted between the two countries.

In the American view, the Glorious Revolution restrained all arbitrary power, Parliament's as well as the King's. Americans were seeking for their own legislative assemblies the same rights and privileges that Parliament had secured for itself—including the exclusive power to enact laws and taxes for the people whom these bodies represented. That right rested on an ancient and hallowed constitutional principle: that law was binding only when enacted through popular consent.

Each crisis that followed the Stamp Act brought Britain's and the colonies' views of their rights and obligations toward each other into greater conflict. In Massachusetts in 1768, for example, the colony's General Court denied Parliament's authority to impose the Townshend duties. Britain's movement of troops into Boston that year was denounced as an occupation by a standing army. It begat the Boston Massacre in 1770. After the 1773 Tea Party, Parliament closed Boston's port, restructured the General Court, forbade town meetings without the governor's consent and decreed that Americans might be taken to England to stand trial. These actions brought on the convocation of the First Continental Congress and, eventually, the open hostilities at Lexington and Concord.

In the aftermath of these events, Americans were forced to think creatively about constitutionalism. Legal government collapsed in nearly every colony. Governors and officials acting under royal commission could hardly allow the colonial assemblies to enact laws mobilizing arms and men to defy Parliament and the King; colonists, on the other hand, had to reconsider their allegiance to a crown that made war on them. In the traditional view, government meant a contract under which subjects pledged fealty in exchange for the King's protection. Many Americans thus felt they were now absolved of any obligation to George III.

These colonists concluded that war and the collapse of lawful government had placed them in something like the state of nature described by the philosophers Thomas Hobbes and John Locke. It was impossible simply to restore the old colonial government: The judges, councillors and governors who ran it had resigned or fled. Government itself must be reconstituted. Americans had to replace elements of the monarchy under which they'd lived with new institutions appropriate to a republican people.

But how does one reconstitute government? Obviously a new executive must replace the old imperial governors, but the enterprise did not stop there. In the months preceding and after the Declaration of Independence, then, 11 of the 13 colonies decided to write constitutions that would bring their citizens out of the state of nature and give them the benefits of government by consent. These constitutions were revolutionary not only because of the circumstances that gave them birth, but also because the process of writing them enabled Americans to break from the constitutional tradition inherited from England. No longer did the colonists think of a constitution as a set of norms and customs descended from a distant past, or use the word to describe the current practices of a government. Americans gave the concept an entirely new meaning. As they now defined it, *constitution* referred to a single document that specified the nature and powers of the government, written and adopted at a specific moment in time. A later innovation would give the document revolutionary authority: It would be adopted under conditions establishing it as the supreme and fundamental law of the land, limiting government and unalterable by it.

In reconstituting government through written constitutions, the colonists did not consider how to distinguish an act establishing government from statutes or ordinary legislative acts. Although several states had held new elections so that the drafters of these constitutions could come with fresh authority from their citizenry, some observers—notably in Massachusetts—began to think that more might be needed.

In the often contentious Bay State, the legislature's efforts to draft a constitution under its own authority sparked a popular revolt that led to a critical constitutional breakthrough. For a constitution to become supreme law, a number of communities insisted, two conditions had to be met. First, the document had to be drafted by a body appointed for that purpose alone; and second, the proposed constitution then had to be submitted to the people for approval. It took the citizens of Massachusetts four years to reach agreement on these points, but when they adopted the constitution of 1780 on this basis, they had discovered a principle that would be of critical importance to the framers of the federal Constitution.

The precise legal authority of the other state constitutions was in doubt. These constitutions and their accompanying declarations of rights were more than statutes but less than supreme, fundamental law. To a modern reader, these declarations of rights are strange but exciting documents. They are not merely compendiums of legally enforceable rights; they also include broad statements on the first principles of government, the moral obligations and political rights of citizens and the importance of freedom of the press and religious conscience, as well as rules relating to specific issues such as search-and-seizure and compensation for property taken for public use. But rather than compel government to follow their dictates, these statements typically said that such rights "ought to" (not "shall") be respected.

But it is one thing to declare rights and another to set them beyond the reach of politics. To observers like Thomas Jefferson and James Madison, the experience of the states after 1776 offered a continuing lesson in the errors of the "compilers"—as Madison called them—of the first constitutions. Two errors were critical. First, the defective procedures used to adopt those constitutions prevented the documents from becoming fundamental law, unalterable by later legislatures. And second, the real danger to balanced government that a well-constructed constitution should guard against came from the people's own legislative representatives. As Jefferson observed in his *Notes on the State of Virginia* (1785), "An elective despotism was not the government we fought for."

Madison kept these problems in mind as he worked to bring about the Constitutional Convention of 1787. The Articles of Confederation, America's first governing document, had often been denounced as an "imbecility" because of its want of power. Its single-chambered Congress had no authority to legislate or tax in its own right; instead it proposed measures that the state legislatures were expected to carry out. The failure of the states to do so had convinced Madison and others that the national government had to be given the authority to enact, execute and adjudicate law in its own right, without relying on the intermediary authority of the states.

Had the framers simply wished to give the existing Congress a few modest additional powers, the convention could have wrapped up its business in a fortnight or so and headed home. But many of them realized that the Union must be reconstituted as a government in the full sense of the term, and with this insight they embarked on a more ambitious and difficult project. Now they could ask what a well-constructed republican government should look like. And in answering this question, they drew time and again on the past decade of constitutional experience within the states. There were many sources for the framers' ideas of government—from the writers of classical antiquity to the luminaries of the European Enlightenment—but the lessons that mattered most were those they had learned on native ground.

The framers were expected to present the results of the convention's work to the Confederation Congress, which presumably would submit the Constitution to the states for approval. Under the Articles of Confederation, all 13 legislatures had to accept any amendments; but one of those states, Rhode Island, had not even sent a delegation to Philadelphia. Nor were the framers at all confident that the other 12 states, as net losers of power, would comply with so radical a restructuring of the Union and sanction the Constitution.

Obviously, the rule of unanimity had to go. But even if the Constitution won approval, how was its supremacy over state constitutions to be confirmed? Now Madison, James Wilson and other nationalists invoked the Massachusetts discovery, which became a guiding rule of American constitutionalism. They asked Congress to suggest that the state legislatures lay the proposed Constitution before special, popularly elected ratification conventions. Approval by these conventions would establish grounds for making the Constitution the supreme and fundamental law of the land. Ratification by the people would create a Constitution superior in authority to the constitutions and laws of the states, and would give the federal government a persuasive argument for countermanding state measures that ran contrary to national law. Popular ratification would also convey this benefit within the national government. Each of the three federal branches—particularly the weaker executive and the judiciary—would have a rationale for opposing the "encroachments" of the others, especially Congress's.

The possibility, however, that a powerful national government would run roughshod over the states alarmed anti-Federalists, who opposed the Constitution. One of the most vociferous, Maryland Attorney General Luther Martin, left the convention early to organize opposition to the new government. In his view, and those of many states'-rights advocates since, no national constitution can abridge the immutable sovereignty of the Union's original members—the states. This tension between national supremacy and state sovereignty has been a continuing part of America's constitutional tradition. It dominated constitutional discourse for much of the 19th century, and has been revived periodically in the 20th, most recently in the wake of the 1994 congressional elections.

George Mason of Virginia, a delegate to the convention who would refuse to sign the Constitution, opposed it for other reasons. High on his list of objections was his colleagues' refusal to add a declaration of rights such as the one he had drafted for Virginia in 1776. Their failure to do so is often regarded as a political error—and perhaps it was. But the omission also reflected the reexamination of constitutionalism that was going on. Before 1787, a bill of rights recognized those rights existing from time immemorial that had become part of the social contract, a pact formed in some mythic past when people first agreed to live in society. But Americans were writing real compacts of government, and this process raised disturbing questions: Must rights be explicitly stated in these new constitutions to retain their authority? Or would fundamental rights remain intact whether stated or not?

Anti-Federalists had a plain answer to these questions: adopt a bill of rights no matter what. But Federalists were less certain. Suppose you wrote a bill of rights, Madison asked, and failed to enumerate all rights worth protecting? Would those unenumerated rights lose influence? Or suppose you used an ambiguous or watered-down text to secure adoption of an unpopular right. Wouldn't you risk weakening the authority of that right?

Despite these concerns, Madison conceded that a bill of rights should be added to the Constitution—more to allay the fears of moderate anti-Federalists than because he believed it important in itself. In 1789, at the first session of the new Congress, he persuaded his colleagues to propose 12 amendments; of these, the 10 we know as the Bill of Rights were ratified by the states. For more than a century afterward, the seeming irrelevance of these amendments suggested that Madison's doubts about their utility were well founded. Only early in the 20th century did the courts begin to interpret parts of the Bill of Rights to protect individual rights and liberties from abuse by both state and national governments. In the past 50 years, the interpretation and reinterpretation of the Bill of Rights and its great descendant, the 14th Amendment, have generated many of the serious controversies of law and politics that have shaped the American constitutional tradition.

Despite two centuries of debate, urgent political or legal questions repeatedly call the meaning of one or another constitutional provision into doubt. That the Constitution can be continually enlarged and invigorated in this way tells us something important. When Americans began writing constitutions, they did not foresee that these texts—especially the national charter—would acquire such profound authority. Constitutionalism was an experiment; even its greatest adherents—men like Madison, Jefferson and Alexander Hamilton—brooded about its likely success. Both Madison and Hamilton were privately skeptical whether the federal Constitution would last, and Jefferson mused that constitutions should be replaced every generation. Each would be surprised by how deep a hold the Constitution has acquired and retained over our political culture. Revolutionary in its origins, the American constitutional tradition may have grown more conservative in its workings—yet what is most striking about it is its vitality.

Questions for Discussion

1. How did the framers' experiences within the colonies and states (under the Articles of Confederation) shape their approaches to constructing a new constitution?

2. Why did Madison oppose the listing of a particular "Bill of Rights"? You might return to this question in light of the reasoning in *Griswold* v. *Connecticut* (see selection 3.4), which establishes a "right of privacy."

1.2

The Founding Fathers: An Age of Realism

Richard Hofstadter

If the framers were, in John P. Roche's words (see selection 1.3), "a reform caucus," they were also realists who had witnessed more than a decade of severe
economic, social, and political turbulence. They wanted some greater certainty
for themselves and their new nation. At the same time, they remained steadfast
in their desire to retain the liberty they had so recently won.

Historian Richard Hofstadter examines the interplay among liberty, stability,
and property rights in this brief essay. As the framers saw it, the key to the long-
term success of a democratic state (if it was to be possible) was to ensure that
substantial numbers of citizens had a stake in the government and in the state. If
that were so, people's "rapacious self-interest" might well be reconciled with
freedom. This tenuous balance of self-interest and property rights seems an
unlikely brace for a government, but it has proven adequate for more than two
hundred years.

It is ironical that the Constitution, which Americans venerate so deeply, is
based upon a political theory that at one crucial point stands in direct an-
tithesis to the main stream of American democratic faith. Modern American folklore assumes that democracy and liberty are all but identical, and when
democratic writers take the trouble to make the distinction, they usually assume that democracy is necessary to liberty. But the Founding Fathers thought
that the liberty with which they were most concerned was menaced by democracy. In their minds liberty was linked not to democracy but to property.

What did the Fathers mean by liberty? What did Jay mean when he spoke of
"the charms of liberty"? Or Madison when he declared that to destroy liberty in
order to destroy factions would be a remedy worse than the disease? Certainly
the men who met at Philadelphia were not interested in extending liberty to

Probably the pre-eminent American historian of his time, Richard Hofstadter (1916–1970) was
DeWitt Clinton Professor of American History at Columbia University.

"The Founding Fathers: An Age of Realism" in *The Moral Foundations of the Republic*, edited by Robert H.
Horwitz (Kenyon Public Affairs Conference Center Series, University of Virginia, 1986), pp. 79–85. Copyright ©
1986 by Kenyon College. Reprinted by permission.

those classes in America, the Negro slaves and the indentured servants, who were most in need of it, for slavery was recognized in the organic structure of the Constitution and indentured servitude was no concern of the Convention. Nor was the regard of the delegates for civil liberties any too tender. It was the opponents of the Constitution who were most active in demanding such vital liberties as freedom of religion, freedom of speech and press, jury trial, due process, and protection from "unreasonable searches and seizures." These guarantees had to be incorporated in the first ten amendments because the Convention neglected to put them in the original document. Turning to economic issues, it was not freedom of trade in the modern sense that the Fathers were striving for. Although they did not believe in impeding trade unnecessarily, they felt that failure to regulate it was one of the central weaknesses of the Articles of Confederation, and they stood closer to the mercantilists than to Adam Smith.* Again, liberty to them did not mean free access to the nation's unappropriated wealth. At least fourteen of them were land speculators. They did not believe in the right of the squatter to occupy unused land, but rather in the right of the absentee owner or speculator to pre-empt it.

The liberties that the constitutionalists hoped to gain were chiefly negative. They wanted freedom from fiscal uncertainty and irregularities in the currency, from trade wars among the states, from economic discrimination by more powerful foreign governments, from attacks on the creditor class or on property, from popular insurrection. They aimed to create a government that would act as an honest broker among a variety of propertied interests, giving them all protection from their common enemies and preventing any one of them from becoming too powerful. The Convention was a fraternity of types of absentee ownership. All property should be permitted to have its proportionate voice in government. Individual property interests might have to be sacrificed at times, but only for the community of propertied interests. Freedom for property would result in liberty for men—perhaps not for all men, but at least for all worthy men. Because men have different faculties and abilities, the Fathers believed, they acquire different amounts of property. To protect property is only to protect men in the exercise of their natural faculties. Among the many liberties, therefore, freedom to hold and dispose property is paramount. Democracy, unchecked rule by the masses, is sure to bring arbitrary redistribution of property, destroying the very essence of liberty.

The Fathers' conception of democracy, shaped by their practical experience with the aggressive dirt farmers in the American states and the urban mobs of the Revolutionary period, was supplemented by their reading in history and po-

---

*Mercantilist theory emphasized state control of the economic process to accumulate as much of value as possible. Achieving positive trade balances became a principal element of national policy. Scottish economist Adam Smith, in *The Wealth of Nations* and other writings, opposed this theory and developed his own ideas on the division of labor, laissez-faire (free market) economics, and the ultimate increase in value as more labor is expended in the production process.

litical science. Fear of what Madison called "the superior force of an interested and overbearing majority" was the dominant emotion aroused by their study of historical examples. The chief examples of republics were among the city-states of antiquity, medieval Europe, and early modern times. Now, the history of these republics—a history, as Hamilton said, "of perpetual vibration between the extremes of tyranny and anarchy"—was alarming. Further, most of the men who had overthrown the liberties of republics had "begun their career by paying an obsequious court to the people; commencing demagogues and ending tyrants."

All the constitutional devices that the Fathers praised in their writings were attempts to guarantee the future of the United States against the "turbulent" political cycles of previous republics. By "democracy," they meant a system of government which directly expressed the will of the majority of the people, usually through such an assemblage of the people as was possible in the small area of the city-state.

A cardinal tenet in the faith of the men who made the Constitution was the belief that democracy can never be more than a transitional stage in government, that it always evolves into either a tyranny (the rule of the rich demagogue who has patronized the mob) or an aristocracy (the original leaders of the democratic elements). "Remember," wrote the dogmatic John Adams in one of his letters to John Taylor of Carolina, "democracy never lasts long. It soon wastes, exhausts, and murders itself. There never was a democracy yet that did not commit suicide." Again:

> If you give more than a share in the sovereignty to the democrats, that is, if you give them the command or preponderance in the . . . legislature, they will vote all property out of the hands of you aristocrats, and if they let you escape with your lives, it will be more humanity, consideration, and generosity than any triumphant democracy ever displayed since the creation. And what will follow? The aristocracy among the democrats will take your place, and treat their fellows as severely and sternly as you have treated them.

Government, thought the Fathers, is based on property. Men who have no property lack the necessary stake in an orderly society to make stable or reliable citizens. Dread of the propertyless masses of the towns was all but universal. George Washington, Gouverneur Morris, John Dickinson, and James Madison spoke of their anxieties about the urban working class that might arise some time in the future—"men without property and principle," as Dickinson described them—and even the democratic Jefferson shared this prejudice. Madison, stating the problem, came close to anticipating the modern threats to conservative republicanism from both communism and fascism:

> In future times, a great majority of the people will not only be without landed but any other sort of property. These will either combine, under the influence of their common situation—in which case the rights of property and the public liberty will not be secure in their hands—or, what is more probable, they will become the tools of opulence and ambition, in which case there will be equal danger on another side.

What encouraged the Fathers about their own era, however, was the broad dispersion of landed property. The small landowning farmers had been troublesome in recent years, but there was a general conviction that under a properly made Constitution a *modus vivendi* could be worked out with them. The possession of moderate plots of property presumably gave them a sufficient stake in society to be safe and responsible citizens under the restraints of balanced government. Influence in government would be proportionate to property; merchants and great landholders would be dominant, but small property-owners would have an independent and far from negligible voice. It was "politic as well as just," said Madison, "that the interest and rights of every class should be duly represented and understood in the public councils," and John Adams declared that there could be "no free government without a democratical branch in the constitution."

The farming element already satisfied the property requirements for suffrage in most of the states, and the Fathers generally had no quarrel with their enfranchisement. But when they spoke of the necessity of founding government upon the consent of "the people," it was only these small property-holders that they had in mind. For example, the famous Virginia Bill of Rights, written by George Mason, explicitly defined those eligible for suffrage as all men "having sufficient evidence of permanent common interest with and attachment to the community"—which meant, in brief, sufficient property.

However, the original intention of the Fathers to admit the yeoman into an important but sharply limited partnership in affairs of state could not be perfectly realized. At the time the Constitution was made, Southern planters and Northern merchants were setting their differences aside in order to meet common dangers—from radicals within and more powerful nations without. After the Constitution was adopted, conflict between the ruling classes broke out anew, especially after powerful planters were offended by the favoritism of Hamilton's policies to Northern commercial interests. The planters turned to the farmers to form an agrarian alliance, and for more than half a century this powerful coalition embraced the bulk of the articulate interests of the country. As time went on, therefore, the mainstream of American political conviction deviated more and more from the antidemocratic position of the Constitution-makers. Yet, curiously, their general satisfaction with the Constitution together with their growing nationalism made Americans deeply reverent of the founding generation, with the result that as it grew stronger, this deviation was increasingly overlooked.

There is common agreement among modern critics that the debates over the Constitution were carried on at an intellectual level that is rare in politics, and that the Constitution itself is one of the world's masterpieces of practical statecraft. On other grounds there has been controversy. At the very beginning contemporary opponents of the Constitution foresaw an apocalyptic destruction of local government and popular institutions, while conservative Europeans of the old regime thought the young American Republic was a dangerous leftist experiment. Modern critical scholarship, which reached a high point in Charles A. Beard's *An Economic Interpretation of the Constitution of the United States*, started a new turn in the debate. The antagonism, long latent, between the philosophy of the Constitution and the philosophy of American democracy again came into the open. Professor Beard's work appeared in 1913 at the peak of the Progressive Era, when the muckraking fever was still high;* some readers tended to conclude from his findings that the Fathers were selfish reactionaries who do not deserve their high place in American esteem. Still more recently, other writers, inverting this logic, have used Beard's facts to praise the Fathers for their opposition to "democracy" and as an argument for returning again to the idea of a "republic."

In fact, the Fathers' image of themselves as moderate republicans standing between political extremes was quite accurate. They were impelled by class motives more than pietistic writers like to admit, but they were also controlled, as Professor Beard himself has . . . emphasized, by a statesmanlike sense of moderation and a scrupulously republican philosophy. Any attempt, however, to tear their ideas out of the eighteenth-century context is sure to make them seem starkly reactionary. Consider, for example, the favorite maxim of John Jay: "The people who own the country ought to govern it." To the Fathers this was simply a swift axiomatic statement of the stake-in-society theory of political rights, a moderate conservative position under eighteenth-century conditions of property distribution in America. Under modern property relations this maxim demands a drastic restriction of the base of political power. A large portion of the modern middle class—and it is the strength of this class upon which balanced government depends—is propertyless; and the urban proletariat, which the Fathers so greatly feared, is almost one half the population. Further, the separation of ownership from control that has come with the corporation deprives Jay's maxim of twentieth century meaning even for many propertied people. The six hundred thousand stockholders of the American Telephone & Telegraph Company not only do not acquire political power by virtue of their stock-ownership, but they do not even acquire economic power; they cannot control their own company.

From a humanistic standpoint there is a serious dilemma in the philosophy of the Fathers, which derives from their conception of man. They thought man was a creature of rapacious self-interest, and yet they wanted him to be free— free, in essence, to contend, to engage in an umpired strife, to use property to get property. They accepted the mercantile image of life as an eternal battleground, and assumed the Hobbesian war of each against all; they did not propose to put an end to this war, but merely to stabilize it and make it less murderous. They had no hope and they offered none for any ultimate organic change in the way men conduct themselves. The result was that while they thought self-interest the most dangerous and unbrookable quality of man, they necessarily underwrote it in trying to control it. They succeeded in both respects: under the competitive capitalism of the nineteenth century America

---

*The Progressive era, from roughly 1900 to 1920, was marked by reformist movements against governmental corruption and political machines. Crusading journalists (muckrakers) and insurgent mayors and governors attempted to inject professionalism and merit into government.

continued to be an arena for various grasping and contending interests, and the federal government continued to provide a stable and acceptable medium within which they could contend; further, it usually showed the wholesome bias on behalf of property which the Fathers expected. But no man who is as well abreast of modern science as the Fathers were of eighteenth-century science believes any longer in unchanging human nature. Modern humanistic thinkers who seek for a means by which society may transcend eternal conflict and rigid adherence to property rights as its integrating principles can expect no answer in the philosophy of balanced government as it was set down by the Constitution-makers of 1787.

Questions for Discussion

1. What is the connection between property and liberty? Does it still hold true today?
2. How would widespread property ownership contribute to the stability of government?

 1.3

The Founding Fathers: A Reform Caucus in Action

John P. Roche

After two hundred years, the American Constitution remains a vital document, subject to continuing reinterpretation in the courts. At the same time, its status in American mythology has become more firmly enshrined. A balance between tangible and symbolic elements has been central to the success of the Constitution, but we need to put down our rose-colored glasses to view its creation in

John P. Roche was formerly a professor of political science at Tufts University.

From *American Political Science Review* 55 (1961): 799–816. Copyright © 1961 by the American Political Science Association. Reprinted with permission.

ways that contribute to both our contemporary and our historic understanding of it.

In this selection, John P. Roche argues that the framers of the Constitution were above all "superb democratic politicians" who constituted an elite—but a democratic elite. Roche objects to viewing the framers solely through the lens of *The Federalist*, the collection of articles in support of ratification, which he regards as a brilliant set of post hoc rationalizations. Instead, James Madison should be seen as a clever tactical politician and an "inspired propagandist," whose writing in *The Federalist* only incidentally emerges as brilliant political theory. We might well wonder what our political system would have looked like, absent the framers' political acumen.

◆ ◆ ◆ The Convention has been described picturesquely as a counter-revolutionary junta and the Constitution as a *coup d'état*, but this has been accomplished by withdrawing the whole history of the movement for constitutional reform from its true context. No doubt the goals of the constitutional elite were "subversive" to the existing political order, but it is overlooked that their subversion could only have succeeded if the people of the United States endorsed it by regularized procedures. Indubitably they were "plotting" to establish a much stronger central government than existed under the Articles, but only in the sense in which one could argue equally well that John F. Kennedy was, from 1956 to 1960, "plotting" to become President. In short, on the fundamental *procedural* level, the Constitutionalists had to work according to the prevailing rules of the game. . . .

I

The history of the United States from 1786 to 1790 was largely one of a masterful employment of political expertise by the Constitutionalists against bumbling, erratic behavior by the opponents of reform. Effectively, the Constitutionalists had to induce the states, by democratic techniques of coercion, to emasculate themselves. To be specific, if New York had refused to join the new Union, the project was doomed; yet before New York was safely in, the reluctant state legislature had . . . to take the following steps: (1) agree to send delegates to the Philadelphia Convention; (2) provide maintenance for these delegates . . . ; (3) set up the special *ad hoc* convention to decide on ratification; and (4) concede to the decision of the *ad hoc* convention that New York should participate. New York admittedly was a tricky state, with a strong interest in a *status quo* which permitted her to exploit New Jersey and Connecticut, but the same legal hurdles existed in every state. . . . [T]he *only* weapon in the Constitutionalist arsenal was an effective mobilization of public opinion.

The group which undertook this struggle was an interesting amalgam of a few dedicated nationalists with the self-interested spokesmen of various parochial bailiwicks. The Georgians, for example, wanted a strong central authority to provide military protection for their huge, underpopulated state . . . ; Jerseymen and Connecticuters wanted to escape from economic bondage to New York; the Virginians hoped to establish a system which would give that great state its rightful place in the councils of the republic. . . . There was, of course, a large element of personality in the affair: There is reason to suspect that Patrick Henry's opposition to the Convention and the Constitution was founded on his conviction that Jefferson was behind both, and a close study of local politics elsewhere would surely reveal that others supported the Constitution for the simple (and politically quite sufficient) reason that the "wrong" people were against it.

To say this is not to suggest that the Constitution rested on a foundation of impure or base motives. It is rather to argue that in politics there are no immaculate conceptions, and that in the drive for a stronger general government, motives of all sorts played a part. Few men in the history of mankind have espoused a view of the "common good" or "public interest" that militated against their private status; even Plato with all his reverence for disembodied reason managed to put philosophers on top of the pile. Thus it is not surprising that a number of diversified private interests joined to push the nationalist public interest; what would have been surprising was the absence of such a pragmatic united front. And the fact remains that, however motivated, these men did demonstrate a willingness to compromise their parochial interests on behalf of an ideal which took shape before their eyes and under their ministrations.

As Stanley Elkins and Eric McKitrick have suggested in a perceptive essay, what distinguished the leaders of the Constitutionalist caucus from their enemies was a "Continental" approach to political, economic and military issues. To the extent that they shared an institutional base of operations, it was the Continental Congress (thirty-nine of the delegates to the Federal Convention had served in Congress), and this was hardly a locale which inspired respect for the state governments. . . . "Continental" ideology developed which seems to have demanded a revision of our domestic institutions primarily on the ground that only by invigorating our general government could we assume our rightful place in the international arena. Indeed, an argument with great force—particularly since Washington was its incarnation—urged that our very survival in the Hobbesian* jungle of world politics depended upon a reordering and strengthening of our national sovereignty. . . .

The great achievement of the Constitutionalists was their ultimate success in convincing the elected representatives of a majority of the white male popula-

---

*Thomas Hobbes (1588–1679) was an English philosopher who viewed human nature as brutish and self-seeking to the point of anarchy. The state, with an absolute ruler, thus becomes an agency for maintaining peace and order.

tion that change was imperative. A small group of political leaders with a Continental vision and essentially a consciousness of the United States' *international* impotence, provided the matrix of the movement. To their standard other leaders rallied with their own parallel ambitions. Their great assets were (1) the presence in their caucus of the one authentic American "father figure," George Washington, whose prestige was enormous; (2) the energy and talent of their leadership (in which one must include the towering intellectuals of the time, John Adams and Thomas Jefferson, despite their absence abroad), and their communications "network," which was far superior to anything on the opposition side; (3) preemptive skill which made "their" issue The Issue and kept the locally oriented opposition permanently on the defensive; and (4) the subjective consideration that these men were spokesmen of a new and compelling credo: *American* nationalism, that ill-defined but nonetheless potent sense of collective purpose that emerged from the American Revolution. . . .

The Constitutionalists got the jump on the "opposition" (a collective noun: oppositions would be more correct) at the outset with the demand for a Convention. Their opponents were caught in an old political trap: They were not being asked to approve any specific program of reform, but only to endorse a meeting to discuss and recommend needed reforms. If they took a hard line at the first stage, they were put in the position of glorifying the *status quo* and of denying the need for *any* changes. Moreover, the Constitutionalists could go to the people with a persuasive argument for "fair play"—"How can you condemn reform before you know precisely what is involved?" Since the state legislatures obviously would have the final say on any proposals that might emerge from the Convention, the Constitutionalists were merely reasonable men asking for a chance. Besides, since they did not make any concrete proposals at that stage, they were in a position to capitalize on every sort of generalized discontent with the Confederation.

Perhaps because of their poor intelligence system, perhaps because of overconfidence generated by the failure of all previous efforts to alter the Articles, the opposition awoke too late to the dangers that confronted them in 1787. Not only did the Constitutionalists manage to get every state but Rhode Island . . . to appoint delegates to Philadelphia, but when the results were in, it appeared that they dominated the delegations. Given the apathy of the opposition, this was a natural phenomenon: In an ideologically nonpolarized political atmosphere those who get appointed to a special committee are likely to be the men who supported the movement for its creation. Even George Clinton, who seems to have been the first opposition leader to awake to the possibility of trouble, could not prevent the New York legislature from appointing Alexander Hamilton—though he did have the foresight to send two of his henchmen to dominate the delegation. Incidentally, much has been made of the fact that the delegates to Philadelphia were not elected by the people; some have adduced this fact as evidence of the "undemocratic" character of the gathering. But put in the context of the time, this argument is wholly specious:

The central government under the Articles was considered a creature of the component states and in all the states but Rhode Island, Connecticut and New Hampshire, members of the national Congress were chosen by the state legislatures. This was not a consequence of elitism or fear of the mob; it was a logical extension of states'-rights doctrine to guarantee that the national institution did not end-run the state legislatures and make direct contact with the people.

II

With delegations safely named, the focus shifted to Philadelphia. While waiting for a quorum to assemble, James Madison got busy and drafted the so-called Randolph or Virginia Plan with the aid of the Virginia delegation. This was a political master-stroke. Its consequence was that once business got underway, the framework of discussion was established on Madison's terms. There was no interminable argument over agenda; instead the delegates took the Virginia Resolutions—"just for purposes of discussion"—as their point of departure. And along with Madison's proposals, many of which were buried in the course of the summer, went his major premise: a new start on a Constitution rather than piecemeal amendment. This was not necessarily revolutionary—a little exegesis could demonstrate that a new Constitution might be formulated as "amendments" to the Articles of Confederation—but Madison's proposal that this "lump sum" amendment go into effect after approval by nine states (the Articles required unanimous state approval for any amendment) was thoroughly subversive. . . .

Basic differences of opinion emerged, of course, but these were not ideological; they were *structural*. If the so-called "states'-rights" group had not accepted the fundamental purposes of the Convention, they could simply have pulled out and by doing so have aborted the whole enterprise. Instead of bolting, they returned day after day to argue and to compromise. An interesting symbol of this basic homogeneity was the initial agreement on secrecy: These professional politicians did not want to become prisoners of publicity; they wanted to retain that freedom of maneuver which is only possible when men are not forced to take public stands in the preliminary stages of negotiation. There was no legal means of binding the tongues of the delegates: At any stage in the game a delegate with basic principled objections to the emerging project could have taken the stump (as Luther Martin did after his exit) and denounced the convention to the skies. Yet Madison did not even inform Thomas Jefferson in Paris of the course of the deliberations and available correspondence indicates that the delegates generally observed the injunction. Secrecy is certainly uncharacteristic of any assembly marked by strong ideological polarization. This was noted at the time: The *New York Daily Advertiser*, August 14, 1787, commented that the ". . . profound secrecy hitherto observed by the Convention [we consider] a happy omen, as it demonstrates that the spirit of party on any great and essential point cannot have arisen to any height."

Commentators on the Constitution who have read *The Federalist* in lieu of reading the actual debates have credited the Fathers with the invention of a sublime concept called "Federalism." Unfortunately *The Federalist* is probative evidence for only one proposition: that Hamilton and Madison were inspired propagandists with a genius for retrospective symmetry. Federalism, as the theory is generally defined, was an improvisation which was later promoted into a political theory. . . .

It is indeed astonishing how those who have glibly designated James Madison the "father" of Federalism have overlooked the solid body of fact which indicates that he shared Hamilton's quest for a unitary central government.* Tobe specific, they have avoided examining the clear import of the Madison-Virginia Plan, and have disregarded Madison's dogged inch-by-inch retreat from the bastions of centralization. The Virginia Plan envisioned a unitary national government effectively freed from and dominant over the states. The lower house of the national legislature was to be elected directly by the people of the states with membership proportional to population. The upper house was to be selected by the lower, and the two chambers would elect the executive and choose the judges. The national government would be thus cut completely loose from the states.

The structure of the general government was freed from state control in a truly radical fashion, but the scope of the authority of the national sovereign as Madison initially formulated it was breathtaking. . . . The national legislature was to be empowered to disallow the acts of state legislatures, and the central government was vested, in addition to the powers of the nation under the Articles of Confederation, with plenary authority wherever ". . . the separate States are incompetent or in which the harmony of the United States may be interrupted by the exercise of individual legislation." Finally, just to lock the door against state intrusion, the national Congress was to be given the power to use military force on recalcitrant states. This was Madison's "model" of an ideal national government, though it later received little publicity in *The Federalist*.

The interesting thing was the reaction of the Convention to this militant program for a strong autonomous central government. Some delegates were startled, some obviously leery of so comprehensive a project of reform, but nobody set off any fireworks and nobody walked out. Moreover, in the two weeks that followed, the Virginia Plan received substantial endorsement *en principe*; the initial temper of the gathering can be deduced from the approval "without debate or dissent," on May 31, of the Sixth Resolution which granted Congress the authority to disallow state legislation ". . . contravening *in its opinion* the

---

*Unitary governments such as that of Great Britain minimize the importance of local or regional units. Most major decisions are made at the national level.

Articles of Union." Indeed, an amendment was included to bar states from contravening national treaties.

The Virginia Plan may therefore be considered, in ideological terms, as the delegates' Utopia, but as the discussions continued and became more specific, many of those present began to have second thoughts. After all, they were not residents of Utopia or guardians in Plato's Republic who could simply impose a philosophical ideal on subordinate strata of the population. They were practical politicians in a democratic society, and no matter what their private dreams might be, they had to take home an acceptable package and defend it—and their own political futures—against predictable attack. On June 14 the breaking point between dream and reality took place. Apparently realizing that under the Virginia Plan, Massachusetts, Virginia and Pennsylvania could virtually dominate the national government—and probably appreciating that to sell this program to "the folks back home" would be impossible—the delegates from the small states dug in their heels and demanded time for a consideration of alternatives. One gets a graphic sense of the inner politics from John Dickinson's reproach to Madison: "You see the consequences of pushing things too far. Some of the members from the small States wish for two branches in the General Legislature, and are friends to a good National Government; but we would sooner submit to a foreign power than . . . be deprived of an equality of suffrage in both branches of the Legislature, and thereby be thrown under the domination of the large States."

. . . Now the process of accommodation was put into action smoothly—and wisely, given the character and strength of the doubters. Madison had the votes, but this was one of those situations where the enforcement of mechanical majoritarianism could easily have destroyed the objectives of the majority: The Constitutionalists were in quest of a qualitative as well as a quantitative consensus. This was hardly from deference to local Quaker custom; it was a political imperative if they were to attain ratification.

III

According to the standard script, at this point the "states'-rights" group intervened in force behind the New Jersey Plan, which has been characteristically portrayed as a reversion to the *status quo* under the Articles of Confederation with but minor modifications. A careful examination of the evidence indicates that only in a marginal sense is this an accurate description. It is true that the New Jersey Plan put the states back into the institutional picture, but one could argue that to do so was a recognition of political reality rather than an affirmation of states' rights. A serious case can be made that the advocates of the New Jersey Plan, far from being ideological addicts of states' rights, intended to substitute for the Virginia Plan a system which would both retain strong national power and have a chance of adoption in the states. The leading spokesman for the project asserted quite clearly that his views were based more on counsels of expediency than on principle; said Paterson on June 16: "I came here not to speak my own sentiments, but the sentiments of those who sent me. Our object is not such a Governmt. as may be best in itself, but such a one as our Constituents have authorized us to prepare, and as they will approve." This is Madison's version; in Yates' transcription, there is a crucial sentence following the remarks above: "I believe that a little practical virtue is to be preferred to the finest theoretical principles, which cannot be carried into effect." . . .

This was a defense of political acumen, not of states' rights. In fact, Paterson's notes of his speech can easily be construed as an argument for attaining the substantive objectives of the Virginia Plan by a sound political route, *i.e.*, pouring the new wine in the old bottles. With a shrewd eye, Paterson queried:

> Will the Operation and Force of the [central] Govt. depend upon the mode of Representn.—No—it will depend upon the Quantum of Power lodged in the leg. ex. and judy. Departments—Give [the existing] Congress the same Powers that you intend to give the two Branches [under the Virginia Plan], and I apprehend they will act with as much Propriety and more Energy. . . .

In other words, the advocates of the New Jersey Plan concentrated their fire on what they held to be the *political liabilities* of the Virginia Plan—which were matters of institutional structure—rather than on the proposed scope of national authority. Indeed, the Supremacy Clause of the Constitution first saw the light of day in Paterson's Sixth Resolution; the New Jersey Plan contemplated the use of military force to secure compliance with national law; and finally Paterson made clear his view that under either the Virginia or the New Jersey systems, the general government would ". . . act on individuals and not on states." From the states'-rights viewpoint, this was heresy: the fundament of that doctrine was the proposition that any central government had as its constituents the states, not the people, and could only reach the people through the agency of the state government.

Paterson then reopened the agenda of the Convention, but he did so within a distinctly nationalist framework. Paterson's position was one of favoring a strong central government in principle, but opposing one which in fact *put the big states in the saddle.* (The Virginia Plan, for all its abstract merits, did very well by Virginia.) As evidence for this speculation, there is a curious and intriguing proposal among Paterson's preliminary drafts of the New Jersey Plan:

> Whereas it is necessary in Order to form the People of the U.S. of America in to a Nation, that the States should be consolidated, by which means all the Citizens thereof will become equally intitled to and will equally participate in the same Privileges and Rights . . . it is therefore resolved, that all the Lands contained within the Limits of each state individually, and of the U.S. generally be considered as constituting one Body or Mass, and be divided into thirteen or more integral parts.
>
> Resolved, That such Divisions or integral Parts shall be styled Districts.

This makes it sound as though Paterson was prepared to accept a strong unified central government along the lines of the Virginia Plan if the existing states were eliminated. He may have gotten the idea from his New Jersey colleague Judge David Brearley, who on June 9 had commented that the only remedy to the dilemma over representation was ". . . that a map of the U.S. be spread out, that all the existing boundaries be erased, and that a new partition of the whole be made into 13 equal parts." According to Yates, Brearley added at this point, ". . . then a government on the present [Virginia Plan] system will be just."

This proposition was never pushed—it was patently unrealistic—but one can appreciate its purpose: It would have separated the men from the boys in the large-state delegations. How attached would the Virginians have been to their reform principles if Virginia were to disappear as a component geographical unit (the largest) for representational purposes? Up to this point, the Virginians had been in the happy position of supporting high ideals with that inner confidence born of knowledge that the "public interest" they endorsed would nourish their private interest. Worse, they had shown little willingness to compromise. Now the delegates from the small states announced that they were unprepared to be offered up as sacrificial victims to a "national interest" which reflected Virginia's parochial ambition. Caustic Charles Pinckney was not far off when he remarked sardonically that ". . . the whole [conflict] comes to this"[:] "Give N. Jersey an equal vote, and she will dismiss her scruples, and concur in the Natil. system." What he rather unfairly did not add was that the Jersey delegates were not free agents who could adhere to their private convictions; they had to take back, sponsor and risk their reputations on the reforms approved by the Convention—and in New Jersey, not in Virginia. . . .

IV

On Tuesday morning, June 19, . . . James Madison led off with a long, carefully reasoned speech analyzing the New Jersey Plan which, while intellectually vigorous in its criticisms, was quite conciliatory in mood. "The great difficulty," he observed, "lies in the affair of Representation; and if this could be adjusted, all others would be surmountable." (As events were to demonstrate, this diagnosis was correct.) When he finished, a vote was taken on whether to continue with the Virginia Plan as the nucleus for a new constitution: seven states voted "Yes"; New York, New Jersey, and Delaware voted "No"; and Maryland, whose position often depended on which delegates happened to be on the floor, divided. Paterson, it seems, lost decisively; yet in a fundamental sense he and his allies had achieved their purpose: From that day onward, it could never be forgotten that the state governments loomed ominously in the background and that no verbal incantations could exorcise their power. Moreover, nobody bolted the convention: Paterson and his colleagues took their defeat in stride and set to work to modify the Virginia Plan, particularly with respect to its provisions on representation in the national legislature. Indeed, they won an immediate rhetorical bonus; when Oliver Ellsworth of Connecticut rose to move that the word "national" be expunged from the Third Virginia Resolution ("Resolved that a *national* Government ought to be established consisting of a *supreme* Legislative, Executive and Judiciary"), Randolph agreed and the motion passed unanimously. The process of compromise had begun.

For the next two weeks, the delegates circled around the problem of legislative representation. The Connecticut delegation appears to have evolved a possible compromise quite early in the debates, but the Virginians and particularly Madison (unaware that he would later be acclaimed as the prophet of "federalism") fought obdurately against providing for equal representation of states in the second chamber. There was a good deal of acrimony and at one point Benjamin Franklin—of all people—proposed the institution of a daily prayer; practical politicians in the gathering, however, were meditating more on the merits of a good committee than on the utility of Divine intervention. On July 2, the ice began to break when through a number of fortuitous events—and one that seems deliberate—the majority against equality of representation was converted into a dead tie. The Convention had reached the stage where it was "ripe" for a solution (presumably all the therapeutic speeches had been made), and the South Carolinians proposed a committee. Madison and James Wilson wanted none of it, but with only Pennsylvania dissenting, the body voted to establish a working party on the problem of representation.

The members of this committee, one from each state, were elected by the delegates—and a very interesting committee it was. Despite the fact that the Virginia Plan had held majority support up to that date, neither Madison nor Randolph was selected (Mason was the Virginian) and Baldwin of Georgia, whose shift in position had resulted in the tie, was chosen. From the composition, it was clear that this was not to be a "fighting" committee: The emphasis in membership was on what might be described as "second-level political entrepreneurs." On the basis of the discussions up to that time, only Luther Martin of Maryland could be described as a "bitter-ender." Admittedly, some divination enters into this sort of analysis, but one does get a sense of the mood of the delegates from these choices—including the interesting selection of Benjamin Franklin, despite his age and intellectual wobbliness, over the brilliant and incisive Wilson or the sharp, polemical Gouverneur Morris, to represent Pennsylvania. His passion for conciliation was more valuable at this juncture than Wilson's logical genius, or Morris' acerbic wit.

. . . It should be reiterated that the Madison model had no room either for the states or for the "separation of powers": Effectively *all* governmental power was vested in the national legislature. The merits of Montesquieu did not turn up until *The Federalist*; and although a perverse argument could be made that Madison's ideal was truly in the tradition of John Locke's *Second Treatise of Government*, the Locke whom the American rebels treated as an honorary president was a pluralistic defender of vested rights, not of parliamentary supremacy.*

It would be tedious to continue a blow-by-blow analysis of the work of the delegates; the critical fight was over representation of the states and once the Connecticut Compromise† was adopted on July 17, the Convention was over the hump. . . . Moreover, once the compromise had carried (by five states to four, with one state divided), its advocates threw themselves vigorously into the job of strengthening the general government's substantive powers—as might have been predicted, indeed, from Paterson's early statements. It nourishes an increased respect for Madison's devotion to the art of politics, to realize that this dogged fighter could sit down six months later and prepare essays for *The Federalist* in contradiction to his basic convictions about the true course the Convention should have taken. . . .

VI

Drawing on their vast collective political experience, utilizing every weapon in the politician's arsenal, looking constantly over their shoulders at their constituents, the delegates put together a Constitution. It was a makeshift affair; some sticky issues (for example, the qualification of voters) they ducked entirely; others they mastered with that ancient instrument of political sagacity, studied ambiguity (for example, citizenship), and some they just overlooked. In this last category, I suspect, fell the matter of the power of the federal courts to determine the constitutionality of acts of Congress. When the judicial article was formulated (Article III of the Constitution), deliberations were still in the stage where the legislature was endowed with broad power under the Randolph formulation, authority which by its own terms was scarcely amenable to judicial review. In essence, courts could hardly determine when ". . . the separate States are incompetent or . . . the harmony of the United States may be interrupted"; the National Legislature, as critics pointed out, was free to define its own jurisdiction. Later the definition of legislative authority was changed into the form we know, a series of stipulated powers, *but the delegates never seriously reexamined the jurisdiction of the judiciary under this new limited formulation.* All arguments on the intention of the Framers in this matter are thus deductive and *a posteriori*, though some obviously make more sense than others.

---

*John Locke (1632–1704) was an English philosopher whose writings served as a basis for government rooted in a social contract between citizens and their rulers. Montesquieu (1689–1755) was a French political philosopher whose work emphasized checks and balances in the exercise of authority.

†The Connecticut Compromise advanced the solution of a two-chamber legislature, with each state receiving two senators and House representation in proportion to its population.

The Framers were busy and distinguished men, anxious to get back to their families, their positions, and their constituents, not members of the French Academy devoting a lifetime to a dictionary. They were trying to do an important job, and do it in such a fashion that their handiwork would be acceptable to very diverse constituencies. No one was rhapsodic about the final document, but it was a beginning, a move in the right direction, and one they had reason to believe the people would endorse. In addition, since they had modified the impossible amendment provisions of the Articles (the requirement of unanimity which could always be frustrated by "Rogues [Rhode] Island") to one demanding approval by only three-quarters of the states, they seemed confident that gaps in the fabric which experience would reveal could be rewoven without undue difficulty. . . .

Madison, despite his reservations about the Constitution, was the campaign manager in ratification. His first task was to get the Congress in New York to light its own funeral pyre by approving the "amendments" to the Articles and sending them on to the state legislatures. Above all, momentum had to be maintained. The anti-Constitutionalists, now thoroughly alarmed and no novices in politics, realized that their best tactic was attrition rather than direct opposition. Thus they settled on a position expressing qualified approval but calling for a second Convention to remedy various defects (the one with the most demagogic appeal was the lack of a Bill of Rights). Madison knew that to accede to this demand would be equivalent to losing the battle, nor would he agree to conditional approval (despite wavering even by Hamilton). This was an all-or-nothing proposition: national salvation or national impotence with no intermediate positions possible. Unable to get congressional approval, he settled for second best: a unanimous resolution of Congress transmitting the Constitution to the states for whatever action they saw fit to take. . . .

VII

. . . Victory for the Constitution meant simultaneous victory for the Constitutionalists; the anti-Constitutionalists either capitulated or vanished into limbo—soon Patrick Henry would be offered a seat on the Supreme Court and Luther Martin would be known as the Federalist "bull-dog." And irony of ironies, Alexander Hamilton and James Madison would shortly accumulate a reputation as the formulators of what is often alleged to be our political theory, the concept of "federalism." Also, on the other side of the ledger, the arguments would soon appear over what the Framers "really meant"; while these disputes have assumed the proportions of a big scholarly business in the last century, they began almost before the ink on the Constitution was dry. One of the best early ones featured Hamilton versus Madison on the scope of presidential power, and other Framers characteristically assumed positions in this and other disputes on the basis of their political convictions.

Probably our greatest difficulty is that we know so much more about what the Framers *should have meant* than they themselves did. We are intimately acquainted with the problems that their Constitution should have been designed to master; in short, we have read the mystery story backward. If we are to get the right "feel" for their time and their circumstances, we must, in Maitland's phrase, ". . . think ourselves back into a twilight." Obviously, no one can pretend completely to escape from the solipsistic web of his own environment, but if the effort is made, it is possible to appreciate the past roughly on its own terms. The first step in this process is to abandon the academic premise that because we can ask a question, there must be an answer.

Thus we can ask what the Framers meant when they gave Congress the power to regulate interstate and foreign commerce, and we emerge, reluctantly perhaps, with the reply that . . . they may not have known what they meant, that there may not have been any semantic consensus. The Convention was not a seminar in analytic philosophy or linguistic analysis. Commerce was *commerce*—and if different interpretations of the word arose, later generations could worry about the problem of definition. The delegates were in a hurry to get a new government established; when definitional arguments arose, they characteristically took refuge in ambiguity. If different men voted for the same proposition for varying reasons, that was politics (and still is); if later generations were unsettled by this lack of precision, that would be their problem. . . .

The Constitution, then, was not an apotheosis of "constitutionalism," a triumph of architectonic genius; it was a patch-work sewn together under the pressure of both time and events by a group of extremely talented democratic politicians. They refused to attempt the establishment of a strong, centralized sovereignty on the principle of legislative supremacy for the excellent reason that the people would not accept it. They risked their political fortunes by opposing the established doctrines of state sovereignty because they were convinced that the existing system was leading to national impotence and probably foreign domination. For two years, they worked to get a convention established. For over three months, in what must have seemed to the faithful participants an endless process of give-and-take, they reasoned, cajoled, threatened, and bargained amongst themselves. The result was a Constitution which the people, in fact, by democratic processes, did accept, and a new and far better national government was established. . . .

To conclude, the Constitution was neither a victory for abstract theory nor a great practical success. Well over half a million men had to die on the battlefields of the Civil War before certain constitutional principles could be defined—a baleful consideration which is somehow overlooked in our customary tributes to the farsighted genius of the Framers and to the supposed American talent for "constitutionalism." The Constitution was, however, a vivid demonstration of effective democratic political action, and of the forging of a national elite which literally persuaded its countrymen to hoist themselves by their own boot straps. American pro-consuls would be wise not to translate the Constitution into Japanese, or Swahili, or treat it as a work of semi-Divine origin; but when students of comparative politics examine the process of nation-building in countries newly freed from colonial rule, they may find the American experience instructive as a classic example of the potentialities of a democratic elite.

Questions for Discussion

1. How does Roche's approach to the framers affect our contemporary understanding of the Constitution? How might the framers have confronted difficult problems such as abortion and affirmative action?
2. What does Roche mean by a "democratic elite"? Is this phrase a contradiction in terms, or does it have real meaning?

 1.4

The Federalist, No. 51

James Madison

As we have seen, among the formidable tasks the framers faced in writing the Constitution was establishing a strong central government while minimizing the possibility that this authority would be abused. The resulting system of checks and balances relies heavily on the separation of powers and a multiple-level, federal relationship between the states and the national government.

James Madison, Alexander Hamilton, and John Jay led the fight for ratification through a series of newspaper articles, *The Federalist*. In the following selection from these papers, Madison articulates a sophisticated understanding of the actual operation of central authority divided into legislative, executive, and judicial branches. Madison observes that regardless of the formal separations embodied within a constitution, the different branches in fact will share powers. Such a realistic assessment is reflected today in continuing arguments over the

---

James Madison, who was the chief drafter of the Constitution, became the fourth president of the United States.

legislature's role in foreign policy (for example, passing legislation to implement the North American Free Trade Agreement) and the Supreme Court's willingness to range beyond narrow constitutional interpretations, as in its 1973 *Roe* v. *Wade* abortion decision.

To the People of the State of New York: To what expedient, then, shall we finally resort for maintaining in practice the necessary partition of power among the several departments as laid down in the Constitution? The only answer that can be given is, that as all these exterior provisions are found to be inadequate, the defect must be supplied by so contriving the interior structure of the government as that its several constituent parts may, by their mutual relations, be the means of keeping each other in their proper places. Without presuming to undertake a full development of this important idea, I will hazard a few general observations, which may perhaps place it in a clearer light, and enable us to form a more correct judgment of the principles and structure of the government planned by the convention.

In order to lay a due foundation for that separate and distinct exercise of the difficult powers of government, which to a certain extent is admitted on all hands to be essential to the preservation of liberty, it is evident that each department should have a will of its own; and consequently should be so constituted that the members of each should have as little agency as possible in the appointment of the members of the others. Were this principle rigorously adhered to, it would require that all the appointments for the supreme executive, legislative, and judiciary magistracies should be drawn from the same fountain of authority, the people, through channels having no communication whatever with one another. Perhaps such a plan of constructing the several departments would be less difficult in practice than it may in contemplation appear. Some difficulties, however, and some additional expense would attend the execution of it. Some deviations, therefore, from the principle must be admitted. In the constitution of the judiciary department in particular, it might be inexpedient to insist rigorously on the principle: first, because peculiar qualifications being essential in the members, the primary consideration ought to be to select that mode of choice which best secures these qualifications; secondly, because the permanent tenure by which the appointments are held in that department must soon destroy all sense of dependence on the authority conferring them.

It is equally evident, that the members of each department should be as little dependent as possible on those of the others for the emoluments annexed to their offices. Were the executive magistrate or the judges not independent of the legislature in this particular, their independence in every other would be merely nominal.

But the great security against a gradual concentration of the several powers in the same department, consists in giving to those who administer each de-

partment the necessary constitutional means and personal motives to resist encroachments of the others. The provision for defence must in this, as in all
other cases, be made commensurate to the danger of attack. Ambition must be
made to counteract ambition. The interest of the man must be connected with
the constitutional rights of the place. It may be a reflection on human nature,
that such devices should be necessary to control the abuses of government.
But what is government itself, but the greatest of all reflections on human nature? If men were angels, no government would be necessary. If angels were to
govern men, neither external nor internal controls on government would be
necessary. In framing a government which is to be administered by men over
men, the great difficulty lies in this: you must first enable the government to
control the governed; and in the next place oblige it to control itself. A dependence on the people is, no doubt, the primary control on the government;
but experience has taught mankind the necessity of auxiliary precautions.

The policy of supplying, by opposite and rival interests, the defect of better
motives might be traced through the whole system of human affairs, private as
well as public. We see it particularly displayed in all the subordinate distributions of power, where the constant aim is to divide and arrange the several offices in such a manner as that each may be a check on the other—that the private interest of every individual may be a sentinel over the public rights. These
inventions of prudence cannot be less requisite in the distribution of the
supreme powers of the state.

But it is not possible to give to each department an equal power of self-defence.
In republican government the legislative authority necessarily predominates. The
remedy for this inconveniency is to divide the legislature into different branches;
and to render them, by different modes of election and different principles of
action, as little connected with each other as the nature of their common functions and their common dependence on the society will admit. It may even be
necessary to guard against dangerous encroachments by still further precautions.
As the weight of the legislative authority requires that it should be thus divided,
the weakness of the executive may require, on the other hand, that it should be
fortified. An absolute negative on the legislature [i.e., veto] appears, at first view,
to be the natural defence with which the executive magistrate should be armed.
But perhaps it would be neither altogether safe nor alone sufficient. On ordinary
occasions it might not be exerted with the requisite firmness, and on extraordinary occasions it might be perfidiously abused. May not this defect of an absolute
negative be supplied by some qualified connection between this weaker department and the weaker branch of the stronger department, by which the latter may
be led to support the constitutional rights of the former, without being too much
detached from the rights of its own department?

If the principles on which these observations are founded be just . . . and
they be applied as a criterion to the several state constitutions and to the federal Constitution, it will be found that if the latter does not perfectly correspond with them, the former are infinitely less able to bear such a test.

There are, moreover, two considerations particularly applicable to the federal system of America, which place that system in a very interesting point of view.

First. In a single republic, all the power surrendered by the people is submitted to the administration of a single government; and the usurpations are guarded against by a division of the government into distinct and separate departments. In the compound republic of America,* the power surrendered by the people is first divided between two distinct governments, and then the portion allotted to each subdivided among distinct and separate departments. Hence a double security arises to the rights of the people. The different governments will control each other, at the same time that each will be controlled by itself.

Second. It is of great importance in a republic not only to guard the society against the oppression of its rulers, but to guard one part of the society against the injustice of the other part. Different interests necessarily exist in different classes of citizens. If a majority be united by a common interest, the rights of the minority will be insecure. There are but two methods of providing against this evil: the one by creating a will in the community independent of the majority—that is, of the society itself; the other by comprehending in the society so many separate descriptions of citizens as will render an unjust combination of a majority of the whole very improbable, if not impracticable. The first method prevails in all governments possessing an hereditary or self-appointed authority. This, at best, is but a precarious security; because a power independent of the society may as well espouse the unjust views of the major, as the rightful interests of the minor party, and may possibly be turned against both parties. The second method will be exemplified in the federal republic of the United States. Whilst all authority in it will be derived from and dependent on the society, the society itself will be broken into so many parts, interests and classes of citizens, that the rights of individuals or of the minority will be in little danger from interested combinations of the majority. In a free government the security for civil rights must be the same as that for religious rights.† It consists in the one case in the multiplicity of interests and in the other in the multiplicity of sects. The degree of security in both cases will depend on the number of interests and sects; and this may be presumed to depend on the extent of country and number of people comprehended under the same government. This view of the subject must particularly recommend a proper federal system to all the sincere and considerate friends of republican government, since it shows that in exact proportion as the territory of the Union may be

---

*For the framers, a republic was essentially a representative democracy. A compound republic placed representative authority at two levels, state and national.

†Madison and his colleagues did not incorporate a separate bill of rights into the Constitution; rather, they relied on the "multiplicity of interests" to protect these rights. In part, a guarantee that a bill of rights would be passed was essential to ratification, especially at New York's convention, where the document won a narrow 30-to-27 victory.

formed into more circumscribed confederacies or states, oppressive combinations of a majority will be facilitated; the best security under the republican forms for the rights of every class of citizens will be diminished; and consequently the stability and independence of some member of the government, the only other security, must be proportionally increased. Justice is the end of government. It is the end of civil society. It ever has been and ever will be pursued until it be obtained, or until liberty be lost in the pursuit. In a society under the forms of which the stronger faction can readily unite and oppress the weaker, anarchy may as truly be said to reign as in a state of nature, where the weaker individual is not secured against the violence of the stronger; and, as in the latter state even the stronger individuals are prompted, by the uncertainty of their condition, to submit to government which may protect the weak as well as themselves; so, in the former state will the more powerful factions or parties be gradually induced by a like motive to wish for a government which will protect all parties, the weaker as well as the more powerful. It can be little doubted that if the state of Rhode Island was separated from the Confederacy and left to itself, the insecurity of rights under the popular form of government within such narrow limits would be displayed by such reiterated oppressions of factious majorities that some power altogether independent of the people would soon be called for by the voice of the very factions whose misrule had proved the necessity of it. In the extended republic of the United States and among the great variety of interests, parties, and sects which it embraces, a coalition of a majority of the whole society could seldom take place on any other principles than those of justice and the general good; and there being thus less danger to a minor from the will of a major party, there must be less pretext, also, to provide for the security of the former, by introducing into the government a will not dependent on the latter, or, in other words, a will independent of the society itself. It is no less certain than it is important, notwithstanding the contrary opinions which have been entertained, that the larger the society, provided it lie within a practical sphere, the more duly capable it will be of self-government. And happily for the *republican cause*, the practicable sphere may be carried to a very great extent by a judicious modification and mixture of the *federal principle*.

Questions for Discussion

1. Could governmental powers ever be completely separated into three distinct branches?
2. Madison claims that the legislative branch will be the strongest. Why would this be so? Does such a contention hold true today?

# Chapter 2

FEDERALISM AND INTERGOVERNMENTAL RELATIONS

Federalism is a way of organizing a political system so that authority is shared between a central government and state or regional governments. Individuals living in Pennsylvania, for example, are citizens of both that state and the United States, are under the legal authority of both governments, and have obligations (such as paying taxes) to each government.

A country is federal only if the subnational units exist independently of the national government and can make some binding decisions on their own. Some nations, like Britain and France, have unitary forms of government, in which regional and local units exist only to aid the national administration. Such subnational units can be abolished or altered at any time by the national government. In contrast, the central government in the United States (commonly referred to as the federal government) can never abolish a state. Also, the U.S. Constitution protects states by providing for two senators and at least one member of the House of Representatives from each state.

The United States embraced the concept of federalism in the Constitution more than two hundred years ago, amid much debate. The Articles of Confederation had proved inadequate because of the weakness of the central government and the almost total autonomy of the states. The nation's domestic economy was chaotic, as individual states' trade restrictions, tariff barriers, and currency weaknesses led to local depressions and encouraged citizens to move from state to state to escape debt obligations. At the same time, neither the central government nor the states could protect citizens from foreign threats or even from domestic insurrection. At the Constitutional Convention in 1787, the founders agreed that the existing government was inadequate; debate arose over the amount of power the central government should be given and how certain aspects of state autonomy could be ensured.

Federalism resulted from a compromise between those seeking a more powerful and efficient central government and those who feared such a government and valued state independence. The founders hoped the national government would act on matters concerning the common good, such as defense, trade, and financial stability, yet not become so strong that it threatened individual liberty and reduced diversity among the states. Federalism as it was understood then, and as it operated until the twentieth century, essentially meant dual federalism: Governmental functions were divided between the state and the national government, each of which was autonomous in its own sphere. For example, the national government had a monopoly on delivering the mail and conducting foreign relations, whereas state governments were in charge of education and law enforcement.

The framers tried to be as clear as possible in defining the powers possessed by the national government (Article I, Section 8 of the Constitution). But with some exceptions, such as state control of the conduct of elections, they said little about state powers or about what should happen when national and state authorities collide.

In general, the trend has been to expand the central government's powers beyond those enumerated in the Constitution and thus to erode state power and independence. Supreme Court decisions have played a crucial role here, opening the door for the federal government's involvement in many traditionally state functions. In the landmark case of *McCulloch* v. *Maryland* (1819), the Court affirmed the supremacy of the national government over the states and introduced the notion of implied powers. The Court ruled that the purpose of the Constitution is not to prevent Congress from carrying out the enumerated powers; Congress has the authority to use all means "necessary and proper" to fulfill its obligations. For example, broad interpretations of the commerce clause not only have given Congress the authority to regulate commerce with foreign nations and among the states but also have provided it with a basis for intervention within state boundaries on matters such as racial relations.

The variety and scale of the federal government's actions have changed over the years. Since the Civil War (which definitively settled the question of national supremacy), the relationships between the states and the federal government have become increasingly characterized by cooperative federalism, in which governmental powers and policies are shared. Cooperative federalism often involves sharing the costs of needed programs or projects, which requires state and local officials to adhere to federal guidelines. Franklin Roosevelt's New Deal, with its expanded national economic and social agenda, had an especially marked impact on intergovernmental relations. Both states and citizens became dependent on the federal government for aid, for many states were incapable of dealing with poverty on their own. In addition, the problems of an industrial society that did not stop at state boundaries, such as water and air pollution, necessitated federal government action.

By the 1960s, American citizens seemed unwilling to let states and localities thwart the national will, and the central government was viewed as an entity to be encouraged rather than feared. Perhaps the greatest cost of federalism has been the systematic oppression of African Americans by localities and states, first as slaves and then as a separate class. The Great Society programs of the Lyndon Johnson years attempted to eliminate racism and poverty through national initiatives, and federal aid to the states rose greatly during the 1960s and 1970s. By 1980, Daniel Elazar, a leading scholar of federalism, concluded that

> we have moved to a system in which it is taken as axiomatic that the federal government shall initiate policies and programs, shall determine their character, shall delegate their administration to the states and localities according to terms that it alone determines, and shall provide for whatever intervention on the part of its administrative agencies it deems necessary to secure compliance with those terms.

Still, the boundaries between state and national authority, originally inspired by a fear of a strong central government, have never been fixed, and political conflict between national and state governments has existed since the nation's founding.

There is a great deal of evidence to support the notion that the role of the states was enhanced during the 1980s. But forces such as the mass media and economic interdependence among nations are leading to an increasingly national culture. Further, it is unlikely that the states will have the protection of the courts in defending their rights, as has often been the case in the past. In *Garcia v. San Antonio Metropolitan Transit Authority* (1985), the Supreme Court ruled that no constitutional limits contained in the Tenth Amendment or any other section of the Constitution may limit the national government's power over commerce. States' rights, therefore, are to be found only in the structure of the government, such as equal state representation in the Senate. In a sense, states are now considered equivalent to other special-interest groups asking for favors and protection from the national government in Washington.

By the 1990s, however, the political winds were blowing in favor of returning power on many matters back to the states, and "devolution" became the rage among Washington policymakers. The Clinton administration sought to "reinvent" federalism, while congressional Republican majorities aggressively pursued a states'-rights agenda. One consequence was that in a number of program areas, such as welfare, states became more influential.

The new century has again brought the subject of federalism to the forefront of national debate. Especially controversial have been responses of various units of government to the terrorist attacks of 9/11 and the devastation suffered by the Mississippi and Louisiana Gulf coasts as a result of Hurricane Katrina. A national debate continues over the role of intergovernmental actors in responding to disasters and how recovery should be managed. At issue is whether American government is capable of dealing with the challenge of catastrophe, and the proper role of governmental units in the federal system when faced with such a challenge.

The four readings in this chapter illustrate various aspects of the controversy over the meaning and changing nature of federalism. *The Federalist*, No. 39, reflects James Madison's views on the relations between states and the national government under the new Constitution and on the importance of the governmental structure as an American innovation. The landmark case

McCulloch v. *Maryland* resolved two key issues left open by the Constitution: which level of government is supreme when state and national policies clash and whether the federal government is limited by the Tenth Amendment to those powers explicitly enumerated in the Constitution.

The last two selections look at the current debate over federalism in practice. Jonathan Walters and Donald Kettl examine the Katrina disaster in an effort to understand why intergovernmental cooperation broke down and how similar problems can be prevented in the future. In the final selection, Robert Gordon explores the implications of the increasing role of national government policy in public education, a policy area long dominated by state and local governments. His focus is on the No Child Left Behind Act, which attempted to establish national proficiency standards for school performance and accountability.

2.1

The Federalist, No. 39

James Madison

At the time of the framing of the Constitution, the founders were aware of two basic forms of government: a national government, with total central domination, and a confederation, a loose alliance of states in which the central government has virtually no power. When the Constitution and *The Federalist* were written, a "federal" government and a "confederation" were synonymous. The governmental form that has come to be called *federalism*, in which authority is divided between two independent levels, was the invention of the founders, though the label came later.

Critics of the Constitution believed the document gave so much power to the central government that it was in fact "national" in character. In *The Federalist*, No. 39, James Madison rebuts this charge and asserts that the new government is "neither a national nor a federal Constitution, but a composition of both." Being a politician, Madison took great pains to point out that the national government's powers are strictly limited to those enumerated in the Constitution and that the residual sovereignty of the states is greater than that of the national government. The first part of this paper can also be regarded as an elegant statement of what Madison meant by the term *republic*.

To the People of the State of New York: The first question that offers itself is, whether the general form and aspect of the government be strictly republican?* It is evident that no other form would be reconcilable with the genius of the people of America; with the fundamental principles of the revolution; or with that honorable determination, which animates every votary [devotee] of freedom, to rest all our political experiments on the capacity of mankind for self-government. If the plan of the Convention therefore be found to depart from the republican character, its advocates must abandon it as no longer defensible.

What then are the distinctive characters of the republican form? Were an answer to this question to be sought, not by recurring to principles, but in the

---

*A *republican* form of government is one in which power resides in the people but is formally exercised by their elected representatives.

application of the term by political writers, to the constitutions of different States, no satisfactory one would ever be found. Holland, in which no particle of the supreme authority is derived from the people, has passed almost universally under the denomination of a republic. The same title has been bestowed on Venice, where absolute power over the great body of the people, is exercised in the most absolute manner, by a small body of hereditary nobles. Poland, which is a mixture of aristocracy and of monarchy in their worst forms, has been dignified with the same appellation. The government of England, which has one republican branch only, combined with a hereditary aristocracy and monarchy, has with equal impropriety been frequently placed on the list of republics. These examples, which are nearly as dissimilar to each other as to a genuine republic, show the extreme inaccuracy with which the term has been used in political disquisitions.

If we resort for a criterion, to the different principles on which different forms of government are established, we may define a republic to be, or at least may bestow that name on, a government which derives all its powers directly or indiectly from the great body of the people; and is administered by persons holding their offices during pleasure, for a limited period, or during good behaviour. It is *essential* to such a government, that it be derived from the great body of the society, not from an inconsiderable proportion, or a favored class of it; otherwise a handful of tyrannical nobles, exercising their oppressions by a delegation of their powers, might aspire to the rank of republicans, and claim for their government the honorable title of republic. It is *sufficient* for such a government, that the persons administering it be appointed, either directly or indirectly, by the people; and that they hold their appointments by either of the tenures just specified; otherwise every government in the United States, as well as every other popular government that has been or can be well organized or well executed, would be degraded from the republican character. According to the Constitution of every State in the Union, some or other of the officers of government are appointed indirectly only by the people. According to most of them the chief magistrate himself is so appointed. And according to one, this mode of appointment is extended to one of the coordinate branches of the legislature. According to all the Constitutions also, the tenure of the highest offices is extended to a definite period, and in many instances, both within the legislative and executive departments, to a period of years. According to the provisions of most of the constitutions, again, as well as according to the most respectable and received opinions on the subject, the members of the judiciary department are to retain their offices by the firm tenure of good behaviour.

On comparing the Constitution planned by the Convention, with the standard here fixed, we perceive at once that it is in the most rigid sense conformable to it. The House of Representatives, like that of one branch at least of all the State Legislatures, is elected immediately by the great body of the people. The Senate, like the present Congress, and the Senate of Maryland, derives its appointment indirectly from the people.* The President is indirectly derived from the choice of the people, according to the example in most of the States. Even the judges, with all other officers of the Union, will, as in the several States, be the choice, though a remote choice, of the people themselves. The duration of the appointments is equally conformable to the republican standard, and to the model of the State Constitutions. The House of Representatives is periodically elective as in all the States: and for the period of two years as in the State of South-Carolina. The Senate is elective for the period of six years; which is but one year more than the period of the Senate of Maryland; and but two more than that of the Senates of New-York and Virginia. The President is to continue in office for the period of four years; as in New-York and Delaware, the chief magistrate is elected for three years, and in South-Carolina for two years. In the other States the election is annual. In several of the States, however, no constitutional provision is made for the impeachment of the Chief Magistrate. And in Delaware and Virginia, he is not impeachable till out of office. The President of the United States is impeachable at any time during his continuance in office. The tenure by which the Judges are to hold their places, is, as it unquestionably ought to be, that of good behaviour. The tenure of the ministerial offices generally will be a subject of legal regulation, conformably to the reason of the case, and the example of the State Constitutions.

Could any further proof be required of the republican complexion of this system, the most decisive one might be found in its absolute prohibition of titles of nobility, both under the Federal and the State Governments; and in its express guarantee of the republican form to each of the latter.

But it was not sufficient, say the adversaries of the proposed Constitution, for the Convention to adhere to the republican form. They ought, with equal care, to have preserved the *federal* form, which regards the union as a *confederacy* of sovereign States; instead of which, they have framed a *national* government, which regards the union as a *consolidation* of the States. And it is asked by what authority this bold and radical innovation was undertaken. The handle which has been made of this objection requires, that it should be examined with some precision.

Without enquiring into the accuracy of the distinction on which the objection is founded, it will be necessary to a just estimate of its force, first to ascertain the real character of the government in question; secondly, to enquire how far the Convention were authorised to propose such a government; and thirdly, how far the duty they owed to their country, could supply any defect of regular authority.

First. In order to ascertain the real character of the government it may be considered in relation to the foundation on which it is to be established; to the

---

*The Seventeenth Amendment, adopted in 1913, changed the election procedure for U.S. senators from indirect election by state legislatures to direct election by the people of each state.

sources from which its ordinary powers are to be drawn; to the operation of those powers; to the extent of them; and to the authority by which future changes in the government are to be introduced.

On examining the first relation, it appears on one hand that the Constitution is to be founded on the assent and ratification of the people of America, given by deputies elected for the special purpose; but on the other, that this assent and ratification is to be given by the people, not as individuals composing one entire nation; but as composing the distinct and independent States to which they respectively belong. It is to be the assent and ratification of the several States, derived from the supreme authority in each State, the authority of the people themselves. The act therefore establishing the Constitution, will not be a *national* but a *federal* act.

That it will be a federal and not a national act, as these terms are understood by the objectors, the act of the people as forming so many independent States, not as forming one aggregate nation, is obvious from this single consideration that it is to result neither from the decision of a *majority* of the people of the Union, nor from that of a *majority* of the States. It must result from the *unanimous* assent of the several States that are parties to it, differing no other wise from their ordinary assent than in its being expressed, not by the legislative authority, but by that of the people themselves. Were the people regarded in this transaction as forming one nation, the will of the majority of the whole people of the United States would bind the minority; in the same manner as the majority in each State must bind the minority; and the will of the majority must be determined either by a comparison of the individual votes; or by considering the will of a majority of the States, as evidence of the will of a majority of the people of the United States. Neither of these rules has been adopted. Each State in ratifying the Constitution, is considered as a sovereign body independent of all others, and only to be bound by its own voluntary act. In this relation then the new Constitution will, if established, be a *federal* and not a *national* Constitution.

The next relation is to the sources from which the ordinary powers of government are to be derived. The house of representatives will derive its powers from the people of America, and the people will be represented in the same proportion, and on the same principle, as they are in the Legislature of a particular State. So far the Government is *national* not *federal*. The Senate on the other hand will derive its powers from the States, as political and co-equal societies; and these will be represented on the principle of equality in the Senate, as they now are in the existing Congress. So far the government is *federal*, not *national*. The executive power will be derived from a very compound source. The immediate election of the President is to be made by the States in their political characters. The votes allotted to them are in a compound ratio, which considers them partly as distinct and co-equal societies; partly as unequal members of the same society. The eventual election again is to be made by that branch of the Legislature which consists of the national representatives; but in this particular act, they are to be thrown into the form of individual delegations from so many distinct and co-equal bodies politic. From this aspect of the Government, it appears to be of a mixed character presenting at least as many *federal* as *national* features.

The difference between a federal and national Government as it relates to the *operation of the Government* is supposed to consist in this, that in the former, the powers operate on the political bodies composing the confederacy, in their political capacities: In the latter, on the individual citizens, composing the nation, in their individual capacities. On trying the Constitution by this criterion, it falls under the *national*, not the *federal* character; though perhaps not so compleatly, as has been understood. In several cases and particularly in the trial of controversies to which States may be parties, they must be viewed and proceeded against in their collective and political capacities only. So far the national countenance of the Government on this side seems to be disfigured by a few federal features. But this blemish is perhaps unavoidable in any plan; and the operation of the Government on the people in their individual capacities, in its ordinary and most essential proceedings, may on the whole designate it in this relation a *national* Government.

But if the Government be national with regard to the *operation* of its powers, it changes its aspect again when we contemplate it in relation to the *extent* of its powers. The idea of a national Government involves in it, not only an authority over the individual citizens; but an indefinite supremacy over all persons and things, so far as they are objects of lawful Government. Among a people consolidated into one nation, this supremacy is compleatly vested in the national Legislature. Among communities united for particular purposes, it is vested partly in the general, and partly in the municipal Legislatures. In the former case, all local authorities are subordinate to the supreme; and may be controuled, directed or abolished by it at pleasure. In the latter the local or municipal authorities form distinct and independent portions of the supremacy, no more subject within their respective spheres to the general authority, than the general authority is subject to them, within its own sphere. In this relation then the proposed Government cannot be deemed a *national* one; since its jurisdiction extends to certain enumerated objects only, and leaves to the several States a residuary and inviolable sovereignty over all other objects. It is true that in controversies relating to the boundary between the two jurisdictions, the tribunal which is ultimately to decide is to be established under the general Government.* But this does not change the principle of the case. The decision is to be impartially made, according to the rules of the Constitution; and all the usual and most effectual precautions are taken to secure this impartiality. Some such tribunal is clearly essential to prevent an appeal to the sword, and a disso-

---

*The tribunal to resolve boundary disputes became the Supreme Court (see *McCulloch* v. *Maryland*, which follows this selection).

lution of the compact; and that it ought to be established under the general rather than under the local Governments; or to speak more properly, that it could be safely established under the first alone, is a position not likely to be combated.

If we try the Constitution by its last relation, to the authority by which amendments are to be made, we find it neither wholly *national*, nor wholly *federal*. Were it wholly national, the supreme and ultimate authority would reside in the *majority* of the people of the Union; and this authority would be competent at all times, like that of a majority of every national society, to alter or abolish its established Government. Were it wholly federal on the other hand, the concurrence of each State in the Union would be essential to every alteration that would be binding on all. The mode provided by the plan of the Convention is not founded on either of these principles. In requiring more than a majority, and particularly, in computing the proportion by *States*, not by *citizens*, it departs from the *national*, and advances towards the *federal* character: In rendering the concurrence of less than the whole number of States sufficient, it loses again the *federal*, and partakes of the *national* character.

The proposed Constitution therefore is in strictness neither a national nor a federal constitution; but a composition of both. In its foundation, it is federal, not national; in the sources from which the ordinary powers of the Government are drawn, it is partly federal, and partly national; in the operation of these powers, it is national, not federal; in the extent of them again, it is federal, not national. And finally, in the authoritative mode of introducing amendments, it is neither wholly federal, nor wholly national.

Questions for Discussion

1. According to Madison, why was the new U.S. Constitution neither a "national" nor a "federal" document? Which of its features were designed to curb the national government's domination of the states?
2. Madison believed the Constitution set up a republican rather than a democratic form of government. What features of the document were designed to give the people an indirect rather than a direct influence on public policy?

McCulloch v. Maryland (1819)

In many areas, the framers of the Constitution were explicit about the powers granted to the national government and to the states. In other areas, however, such as the power to tax, the two were given many of the same responsibilities. The Constitution leaves open the relationship of state and national authority when their policies conflict. In 1819, *McCulloch* v. *Maryland* settled the issue in favor of the national government.

In 1791 Congress created a national bank to print money, make loans, and engage in a variety of banking activities. The bank was deeply resented by a number of state legislatures, which held that Congress did not have the authority to charter a bank, and in 1818 Maryland passed a law that taxed its Baltimore branch $15,000. James McCulloch, a cashier at the bank, refused to pay and was sued in state court. The state's tax was upheld, and the bank appealed to the U.S. Supreme Court.

Chief Justice John Marshall delivered a landmark opinion for the Court with a decision that markedly expanded the powers of the national government over those explicitly stated in the Constitution and affirmed the supremacy of the national government over the states. According to the Court, Congress had the power to charter a national bank because it had been granted the power "to make all laws which shall be necessary and proper for carrying into execution" the expressed powers. In short, Congress has a number of implied powers in addition to its enumerated powers. Further, because the power to tax could be used to destroy an institution that is necessary for the operations of the national government, Maryland's attempt to levy a tax on the national bank was unconstitutional. The Court upheld the supremacy of the national government when policies collide.

M r. Chief Justice Marshall* delivered the opinion of the Court.
In the case now to be determined, the defendant, a sovereign State, denies the obligation of a law enacted by the legislature of the Union, and the plaintiff, on his part, contests the validity of an act which has been

---

*John Marshall became chief justice of the United States in 1801. He is probably most famous for his opinion in *Marbury* v. *Madison* (see selection 13.2), which established the principle of judicial review—the power of the Court to declare laws unconstitutional.

passed by the legislature of that State. The constitution of our country, in its most interesting and vital parts, is to be considered; the conflicting powers of the government of the Union and of its members, as marked in that constitution, are to be discussed; and an opinion given, which may essentially influence the great operations of the government. . . .

The first question made in the case is, has Congress power to incorporate a bank? . . .

The power now contested was exercised by the first Congress elected under the present constitution. The bill for incorporating the bank of the United States did not steal upon an unsuspecting legislature, and pass unobserved. Its principle was completely understood, and was opposed with equal zeal and ability. After being resisted, first in the fair and open field of debate, and afterward in the executive cabinet, with as much persevering talent as any measure has ever experienced, and being supported by arguments which convinced minds as pure and as intelligent as this country can boast, it became a law. The original act was permitted to expire; but a short experience of the embarrassments to which the refusal to revive it exposed the government, convinced those who were most prejudiced against the measure of its necessity, and induced the passage of the present law. It would require no ordinary share of intrepidity to assert that a measure adopted under these circumstances was a bold and plain usurpation, to which the constitution gave no countenance. . . .

In discussing this question, the counsel for the State of Maryland have deemed it of some importance, in the construction of the constitution, to consider that instrument not as emanating from the people, but as the act of sovereign and independent States. The powers of the general government, it has been said, are delegated by the States, who alone are truly sovereign; and must be exercised in subordination to the States, who alone possess supreme dominion.

It would be difficult to sustain this proposition. The Convention which framed the constitution was indeed elected by the State legislatures. But the instrument, when it came from their hands, was a mere proposal, without obligation, or pretensions to it. It was reported to the then existing Congress of the United States, with a request that it might "be submitted to a Convention of Delegates, chosen in each State by the people thereof, under the recommendation of its Legislature, for their assent and ratification." This mode of proceeding was adopted; and by the Convention, by Congress, and by the State Legislatures, the instrument was submitted to the people. They acted upon it in the only manner in which they can act safely, effectively, and wisely, on such a subject, by assembling in Convention. It is true, they assembled in their several States—and where else should they have assembled? No political dreamer was ever wild enough to think of breaking down the lines which separate the States, and of compounding the American people into one common mass. Of consequence, when they act, they act in their States. But the measures they adopt do not, on that account, cease to be the measures of the people themselves, or become the measures of the State governments.

From these Conventions the constitution derives its whole authority. The government proceeds directly from the people; is "ordained and established" in the name of the people; and is declared to be ordained, "in order to form a more perfect union, establish justice, ensure domestic tranquillity, and secure the blessings of liberty to themselves and to their posterity." The assent of the States, in their sovereign capacity, is implied in calling a Convention, and thus submitting that instrument to the people. But the people were at perfect liberty to accept or reject it; and their act was final. It required not the affirmance, and could not be negatived, by the State governments. The constitution, when thus adopted, was of complete obligation, and bound the State sovereignties.

It has been said, that the people had already surrendered all their powers to the State sovereignties, and had nothing more to give. But, surely, the question whether they may resume and modify the powers granted to government does not remain to be settled in this country. Much more might the legitimacy of the general government be doubted, had it been created by the States. The powers delegated to the State sovereignties were to be exercised by themselves, not by a distinct and independent sovereignty, created by themselves. To the formation of a league, such as was the confederation, the State sovereignties were certainly competent. But when, "in order to form a more perfect union," it was deemed necessary to change this alliance into an effective government, possessing great and sovereign powers, and acting directly on the people, the necessity of referring it to the people, and of deriving its powers directly from them, was felt and acknowledged by all.

The government of the Union, then (whatever may be the influence of this fact on the case) is, emphatically, and truly, a government of the people. In form and in substance it emanates from them. Its powers are granted by them, and are to be exercised directly on them, and for their benefit.

This government is acknowledged by all to be one of enumerated powers. The principle, that it can exercise only the powers granted to it, would seem too apparent to have required to be enforced by all those arguments which its enlightened friends, while it was depending before the people, found it necessary to urge. That principle is now universally admitted. But the question respecting the extent of the powers actually granted, is perpetually arising, and will probably continue to arise, as long as our system shall exist. . . .

If any one proposition could command the universal assent of mankind, we might expect it would be this—that the government of the Union, though limited in its powers, is supreme within its sphere of action. This would seem to result necessarily from its nature. It is the government of all; its powers are delegated by all; it represents all, and acts for all. Though any one State may be willing to control its operations, no State is willing to allow others to control them. The nation, on those subjects on which it can act, must necessarily bind its component parts. But this question is not left to mere reason: the people have, in express terms, decided it, by saying, "this constitution, and the laws of the United States, which shall be made in pursuance thereof, . . . shall be the supreme law of the land," and by requiring that the members of the State legis-latures, and the officers of the executive and judicial departments of the States, shall take the oath of fidelity to it.

The government of the United States, then, though limited in its powers, is supreme; and its laws, when made in pursuance of the constitution, form the supreme law of the land, "any thing in the constitution or laws of any State to the contrary notwithstanding."

Among the enumerated powers, we do not find that of establishing a bank or creating a corporation. But there is no phrase in the instrument which, like the articles of confederation, excludes incidental or implied powers; and which re-quires that every thing granted shall be expressly and minutely described. Even the 10th amendment, which was framed for the purpose of quieting the exces-sive jealousies which had been excited, omits the word "expressly," and declares only that the powers "not delegated to the United States, nor prohibited to the States, are reserved to the States or to the people"; thus leaving the question, whether the particular power which may become the subject of contest has been delegated to the one government, or prohibited to the other, to depend on a fair construction of the whole instrument. The men who drew and adopted this amendment had experienced the embarrassments resulting from the insertion of this word in the articles of confederation, and probably omitted it to avoid those embarrassments. A constitution, to contain an accurate detail of all the subdivisions of which its great powers will admit, and of all the means by which they may be carried into execution, would partake of the prolixity of a legal code, and could scarcely be embraced by the human mind. It would probably never be understood by the public. Its nature, therefore, requires, that only its great outlines should be marked, its important objects designated, and the minor ingredients which compose those objects be deduced from the nature of the objects themselves. That this idea was entertained by the framers of the American constitution, is not only to be inferred from the nature of the instru-ment, but from the language. Why else were some of the limitations, found in the ninth section of the 1st article, introduced?* It is also, in some degree, war-ranted by their having omitted to use any restrictive term which might prevent its receiving a fair and just interpretation. In consideration of this question, then, we must never forget, that it is a *constitution* we are expounding.

Although, among the enumerated powers of government, we do not find the word "bank" or "incorporation," we find the great powers to lay and collect taxes; to borrow money; to regulate commerce; to declare and conduct a war; and to raise and support armies and navies. The sword and the purse, all the ex-ternal relations, and no inconsiderable portion of the industry of the nation,

---

*Article I, Section 9, follows the provision enumerating the national government's powers and is a broad list of specific prohibitions that restrain the national government, including the inability to levy taxes or duties on articles from any state or to give preferential treatment to the ports of one state at the expense of another.

are entrusted to its government. It can never be pretended that these vast powers draw after them others of inferior importance, merely because they are inferior. Such an idea can never be advanced. But it may with great reason be contended, that a government, entrusted with such ample powers, on the due execution of which the happiness and prosperity of the nation so vitally depends, must also be entrusted with ample means for their execution. The power being given, it is the interest of the nation to facilitate its execution. It can never be their interest, and cannot be presumed to have been their intention, to clog and embarrass its execution by withholding the most appropriate means. Throughout this vast republic, from the St. Croix to the Gulf of Mexico, from the Atlantic to the Pacific, revenue is to be collected and expended, armies are to be marched and supported. The exigencies of the nation may require that the treasure raised in the north should be transported to the south, *that* raised in the east conveyed to the west, or that this order should be reversed. Is that construction of the constitution to be preferred which would render these operations difficult, hazardous, and expensive? Can we adopt that construction, (unless the words imperiously require it), which would impute to the framers of that instrument, when granting these powers for the public good, the intention of impeding their exercise by withholding a choice of means? If, indeed, such be the mandate of the constitution, we have only to obey; but that instrument does not profess to enumerate the means by which the powers it confers may be executed; nor does it prohibit the creation of a corporation, if the existence of such a being be essential to the beneficial exercise of those powers. It is, then, the subject of fair inquiry, how far such means may be employed. . . .

But the constitution of the United States has not left the right of Congress to employ the necessary means, for the execution of the powers conferred on the government, to general reasoning. To its enumeration of powers is added that of making "all laws which shall be necessary and proper, for carrying into execution the foregoing powers, and all other powers vested by this constitution, in the government of the United States, or in any department thereof." . . .

We admit, as all must admit, that the powers of the government are limited, and that its limits are not to be transcended. But we think the sound construction of the constitution must allow to the national legislature that discretion, with respect to the means by which the powers it confers are to be carried into execution, which will enable that body to perform the high duties assigned to it, in the manner most beneficial to the people. Let the end be legitimate, let it be within the scope of the constitution, and all means which are appropriate, which are plainly adapted to that end, which are not prohibited, but consist with the letter and spirit of the constitution, are constitutional. . . .

It being the opinion of the Court, that the act incorporating the bank is constitutional; and that the power of establishing a branch in the State of Maryland might be properly exercised by the bank itself, we proceed to inquire—

Whether the State of Maryland may, without violating the constitution, tax that branch?

That the power of taxation is one of vital importance; that it is retained by the States; that it is not abridged by the grant of a similar power to the government of the Union; that it is to be concurrently exercised by the two governments: are truths which have never been denied. But, such is the paramount character of the constitution, that its capacity to withdraw any subject from the action of even this power, is admitted. The States are expressly forbidden to lay any duties on imports or exports, except what may be absolutely necessary for executing their inspection laws. If the obligation of this prohibition must be conceded—if it may restrain a State from the exercise of its taxing power on imports and exports; the same paramount character would seem to restrain, as it certainly may restrain, a State from such other exercise of this power, as is in its nature incompatible with, and repugnant to, the constitutional laws of the Union. A law, absolutely repugnant to another, as entirely repeals that other as if express terms of repeal were used.

On this ground the counsel for the bank place its claim to be exempted from the power of a State to tax its operations. There is no express provision for the case, but the claim has been sustained on a principle which so entirely pervades the constitution, is so intermixed with the materials which compose it, so interwoven with its web, so blended with its texture, as to be incapable of being separated from it, without rending it into shreds.

This great principle is, that the constitution and the laws made in pursuance thereof are supreme; that they control the constitution and laws of the respective States, and cannot be controlled by them. From this, which may be almost termed an axiom, other propositions are deduced as corollaries, on the truth or error of which, and on their application to this case, the cause has been supposed to depend. These are, 1st. that a power to create implies a power to preserve. 2nd. That a power to destroy, if wielded by a different hand, is hostile to, and incompatible with these powers to create and to preserve. 3d. That where this repugnancy exists, that authority which is supreme must control, not yield to that over which it is supreme.

These propositions, as abstract truths, would, perhaps, never be controverted. Their application to this case, however, has been denied; and, both in maintaining the affirmative and the negative, a splendor of eloquence, and strength of argument, seldom, if ever, surpassed, have been displayed.

The power of Congress to create, and of course to continue, the bank, was the subject of the preceding part of this opinion; and is no longer to be considered as questionable.

That the power of taxing it by the States may be exercised so as to destroy it, is too obvious to be denied. . . .

The Court has bestowed on this subject its most deliberate consideration. The result is a conviction that the States have no power, by taxation or otherwise, to retard, impede, burden, or in any manner control, the operations of the constitutional laws enacted by Congress to carry into execution the powers vested in the general government. This is, we think, the unavoidable consequence of that supremacy which the constitution has declared.

We are unanimously of opinion, that the law passed by the legislature of Maryland, imposing a tax on the Bank of the United States, is unconstitutional and void. . . .

Questions for Discussion

1. Why did the Court believe that the national government possessed powers beyond those enumerated in the Constitution?
2. Does Marshall's view in this case seem consistent with the view of national-state relations expressed by James Madison in *The Federalist*, No. 39?

 2.3

The Katrina Breakdown

Jonathan Walters and Donald Kettl

Federalism as a form of government offers many advantages, especially the potential capacity to respond to the needs and wishes of a diverse population. One disadvantage of a federal system is that it may encourage extreme complexity; the division of power among national, state, and local authorities makes government liable to contradictions and confusions. Developing the capacity to respond to a large-scale catastrophe, which demands communication and coordination among all levels of government, is especially challenging.

In early September 2005, the Gulf coast of Mississippi and Louisiana was battered by Hurricane Katrina, a category 4 storm. New Orleans was particularly hard hit after the levees designed to protect the city were breached and por-

Jonathan Walters is a staff correspondent for *Governing* magazine. Don Kettl is Director of the Fells Institute of Government.

"The Katrina Breakdown." From *Governing*, December 2005, pp. 20–25. Reprinted with permission of the authors.

tions of the city flooded. Besides the immediate death and destruction, hundreds of thousands of people were displaced, many without the resources to take care of themselves; businesses were forced to shut down or were compelled to relocate elsewhere; and crime and unemployment soared. Oil and gas production was suspended, contributing to a rise in fuel prices nationally. Mississippi River commerce was disrupted for an extended period. Government at all levels was slow to respond. Politicians, regardless of political stripe, were in agreement that the public sector's handling of the Katrina disaster represented an example of government failure at the most basic level—ensuring the safety and security of citizens.

In this selection, Jonathan Walters and Donald Kettl examine some reasons for the failure; they explore the tensions inherent among levels of government as decision makers try to sort out "who should do what—and how to make sure the public sector is ready to act when the unexpected but inevitable happens." While the history of disaster response and recovery has witnessed an ever-increasing federal role because of a bigger funding base, and while there was much pressure after Katrina to further increase the effort, the authors remind readers that "all emergencies are initially at least, local—or local and state—events." As a consequence, disaster responses necessitate well-planned, coordinated efforts that include all levels of government.

When Hurricane Katrina hit New Orleans, only one thing disintegrated as fast as the earthen levees that were supposed to protect the city, and that was the intergovernmental relationship that is supposed to connect local, state and federal officials before, during and after such a catastrophe.

In sifting through the debris of the disaster response, the first question is why intergovernmental cooperation broke down so completely. While it's hard even at this point to get an official accounting of exactly what happened, clearly there were significant communication and coordination problems at all levels of government. At the moment, much time and effort is being spent assigning culpability—for a lack of preparation, delayed decision making, bureaucratic tie-ups and political infighting—to individuals and agencies. . . .

What is more critical, and has significant implications for the future of emergency management in the United States, is the need to explicitly and thoroughly define governments' roles and responsibilities so that officials in other jurisdictions don't suffer the same sort of meltdown in the next natural or man-made disaster. The lurching tactical responses to the terrorist attacks of 2001 and this year's rash of major hurricanes only underline the truly fundamental issue: how to sort out who should do what—and how to make sure the public sector is ready to act when the unexpected but inevitable happens.

It won't be easy. Some in the federal government clearly feel that if they're going to be blamed for failures—failures that they ascribe at least in part to state and local officials—then they'd prefer a system where the federal government has the option of being much more preemptive in handling large-scale domestic disasters. States as a whole, though, are not going to go along with any emergency management plan that involves the feds declaring something like martial law. They would much prefer that existing protocols be continued and the Federal Emergency Management Agency regain its independence from the Department of Homeland Security and be led by experienced professionals rather than political appointees.

A Growing Federal Role

In fact, the history of disaster response and recovery in the United States has witnessed an ever-increasing federal role. On April 22, 1927, President Calvin Coolidge named a special cabinet-level committee headed by Commerce Secretary Herbert Hoover to deal with the massive flooding that was ravaging communities up and down the Mississippi River Valley that year. . . . It . . . represents the first clear attempt to politicize federal disaster response, with Hoover consciously riding his performance during the disaster all the way to the White House.

In 1950, the federal government began trying to formalize intergovernmental roles and responsibilities through the Federal Civil Defense Act, which defined the scope and type of assistance that the federal government would extend to states and localities after certain kinds of disasters or emergencies (although Congress had been offering financial aid to states and localities in a piecemeal fashion since the early 1800s). In 1979, President Jimmy Carter created the Federal Emergency Management Agency, largely in response to governors' complaints about the fragmented nature of federal disaster planning and assistance. And in 1988, Congress passed the Robert T. Stafford Disaster Relief Act, which outlined the protocols for disaster declaration and what sort of intergovernmental response would follow.

From 1989 to 1992, a succession of disasters, including the Loma Prieta earthquake in California and hurricanes Hugo in South Carolina and Andrew in Florida put the whole issue of intergovernmental emergency response in the public hot seat. . . . In particular, the disasters highlighted the federal government's slow-footed and bureaucratic response in the wake of such catastrophic events. . . . That, in turn, led to a major turnaround at FEMA, with the appointment of James Lee Witt, the first FEMA director to arrive on the job with actual state emergency management experience.

In general, two things were going on around the increasing federal role in emergency readiness and response. . . . States and localities were getting hooked on federal money—especially for recovery. But American presidents were also discovering the political benefits of declaring disasters, which allowed them to liberally sprinkle significant amount of cash around various states and localities in distress. . . . [According to one expert it] created the expectation of federal government largesse. Federal spending, however, was always meant to supplement and not supplant state and local spending.

Local Response

But if the federal role in disaster response and recovery has increased—along with expectations of federal help—emergency management experts at all levels still agree on the basics of existing emergency response protocol: All emergencies are, initially at least, local—or local and state—events. . . .

The extent to which the local-state-federal response ramps up depends on a host of factors, including the size of the incident and what plans and agreements are in place prior to any event. It also very much depends on the capacity of the governments involved. Some local and state governments have the ability to deal with disasters on their own and seem less inclined to ask for outside help. Others seem to hit the intergovernmental panic button more quickly. But whichever it is, say those on the front line of emergency response, how various governmental partners in emergency response and recovery are going to respond shouldn't be a surprise-filled adventure. Key players at every level of government should have a very good idea of what each will be expected to do or provide when a particular disaster hits.

Most important to the strength of the intergovernmental chain are solid relationships among those who might be called upon to work closely together in times of high stress. "You don't want to meet someone for the first time while you're standing around in the rubble," says Jarrod Bernstein, spokesman for the New York City Office of Emergency Management. "You want to meet them during drills and exercises." In New York, says Bernstein, the city has very tight relationships with state and federal officials in a variety of agencies. "They're involved in all our planning and all our drills. They have a seat at all the table-top exercises we do."

During those exercises, says Bernstein, federal, state and local officials establish and agree on what their respective jobs will be when a "big one" hits. Last summer, for example, the city worked with FEMA, the U.S. Department of Health and Human Services, the Federal Bureau of Investigation and New York State health and emergency response officials on an exercise aimed at collecting 8 million doses of medicine and distributing them throughout the city in a 48-hour window. "What we were looking at is how we'd receive medical stockpiles from the federal government, break them down and push them out citywide. There is a built-in federal component to that plan," Bernstein says.

No Plan B

While pre-plans and dry runs are all well and good, they're not much use if not taken seriously, however. In 2004, FEMA and Louisiana's Office of Homeland Security and Emergency Preparedness conducted a tabletop exercise, called Hurricane Pam, that simulated a Category 3 storm hitting and flooding New Orleans. It identified a huge gap in disaster planning: An estimated 100,000 people wouldn't be able to get out of the city without assistance. As is standard in emergency management practice, it is the locality's responsibility—at least initially—to evacuate residents, unless other partners are identified beforehand.

Critics of Mayor Ray Nagin say he failed to follow up aggressively on the finding. Last spring, the city floated the notion that it would rely primarily on the faith-based community to organize and mobilize caravans for those without cars or who needed special assistance getting out of the city. The faith-based community balked, however, citing liability issues. The city never came up with a Plan B.

Meanwhile, the Department of Homeland Security had great confidence in its 426-page "all-hazards" National Response Plan. Unveiled last January, it "establishes standardized training, organization and communications procedures for multi-jurisdictional interaction; clearly identifies authority and leadership responsibilities; enables incident response to be handled at the lowest possible organizational and jurisdictional level; ensures the seamless integration of the federal government when an incident exceeds state or local capabilities; and provides the means to swiftly deliver federal support in response to catastrophic incidents."

Katrina was its first test. And in the wake of the Category 4 storm and subsequent flooding, the city's vital resources—communications, transportation, supplies and manpower—were quickly overwhelmed. But DHS Secretary Michael Chertoff waited until 24 hours after the levees were breached to designate the hurricane as an "incident of national significance—requiring an extensive and well-coordinated response by federal, state, local tribal and nongovernmental authorities to save lives, minimize damage and provide the basis for long-term community and economic recovery."

The nation—indeed the world—bore painful witness to its failure. "There are mechanisms and protocols set up as part of the National Response Plan, and those were not followed," says John R. Harrald, director of the Institute for Crisis, Disaster and Risk Management at George Washington University. Harrald notes that under the response plan, one of the first things that's supposed to happen is the rapid activation of a joint operations center to coordinate the intergovernmental response. In Louisiana, that didn't happen quickly enough, he says.

Calling in the Troops

As a result of Katrina, and to a lesser extent hurricanes Rita and Wilma, the general citizenry and elected leaders at all levels of government, as well as emergency responders up and down the chain of command, are demanding a comprehensive review of how local, state and federal governments work (or don't work) together.

Part of that discussion has to include what to do when a state or local government's ability to prepare, respond or to ask for help is either impaired or wiped out altogether. "The question is what do you do when state and local capacity fails for one reason or another, either because they're overwhelmed or they're incompetent," says GWU's Harrald. "Do we have a system that allows us to scale up adequately or do we need a system where we can bring the military in sooner but that doesn't give away state and local control?"

Bill Leighty, Virginia Governor Mark Warner's chief of staff, who volunteered to spend two weeks in Louisiana helping manage the state response to Katrina, says he thinks there needs to be a serious intergovernmental discussion about when, for example, it might be appropriate to involve the military more directly in a domestic crisis. It is a position born of watching FEMA in action, versus what he saw of the military while he was in New Orleans. FEMA's bureaucratic approach to every item it provided or action it took was, at times, brutally exasperating, says Leighty. "But when you tell the 82nd Airborne, 'Secure New Orleans,' they come in and they know exactly what to do and it gets done."

Even some long-time New Orleans residents, who watched helplessly as looters rampaged through parts of the city, say they wouldn't have minded at all if the military had stepped in to restore order. "There are times when people are overwhelmed," says Frank Cilluffo, director of the Homeland Security Policy Institute at George Washington University, "and they don't care what color uniform is involved in coming to the rescue—red, blue or green."

However, both Kathleen Babineaux Blanco, the Democratic governor of Louisiana, and Haley Barbour, the Republican governor of Mississippi, strenuously objected to requests from the White House to give the Pentagon command over their states' National Guard troops. And President George W. Bush's suggestion of a quick resort to the military in future disasters stunned many observers, including those in his own party. In a television address from New Orleans, he argued that only the armed forces were "capable of massive logistical operations on a moment's notice."

But governors were aghast at the idea that the military would become America's first responders. In a USA Today poll, 36 of 38 governors (including brother Jeb Bush) opposed the plan. Michigan governor Jennifer Granholm put it bluntly: "Whether a governor is a Republican or Democrat, I would expect the response would be, 'Hell no.'" For one blogger, the worry was "How long before a creek flooding in a small town in Idaho will activate the 82nd Airborne Division?"

Bush grabbed the military option partly because of the poor performance of state and local governments. Indeed, everyone breathed a sigh of relief when Coast Guard Admiral Thad Allen arrived to assume command.

Part of the explanation also lies in public opinion polls. A Pew Research Center survey just after the storm revealed that nearly half of those surveyed believed state and local governments had done a fair or poor job—and there was no partisan difference on that conclusion. That meant the smart political play for Bush, although he didn't fare much better in the poll, was to suggest that the military might have to do what state and local governments could not.

That idea, of course, could scarcely be further from the strategy the Republicans had spent a generation building. The Richard Nixon–Ronald Reagan model of new federalism revolved around giving the states more autonomy and less money. But faced with the need to do something—and lacking any alternative—Bush reached back to Lyndon Johnson's Great Society philosophy of an expanded role for the federal government. . . .

Control and Contention

Some believe there is a middle ground when it comes to issues of authority and autonomy. James A. Stever, director of the Center for Integrated Homeland Security and Crisis Management at the University of Cincinnati, says he and colleagues had forwarded a paper to the former head of Homeland Security, Tom Ridge, outlining the concept of "homeland restoration districts." The idea is to have established criteria for when a more robust federal disaster response might be appropriate. Recovery districts would allow for ad hoc federal takeovers of specific geographic areas when appropriate, says Stever, rather than creating some new, overriding national response protocol that calls for broad federal preemption of local and state authority.

But sifting through such ideas—and the others that are sure to surface—is going to mean rekindling the sort of conversation about intergovernmental coordination and cooperation that Washington hasn't seen in a long time. . . . [S]uch sessions have frequently had the familiar ring of both state and local tensions over who controls federal funding, as well as a little tin-cup rattling.

For example, in testimony before the House Homeland Security Committee, David Wallace, mayor of Sugar Land, Texas, argued that the first lesson learned in the wake of Katrina is that local governments should have more control over how federal homeland security first-responder money should be spent. "There was a real concern from the beginning that an over-reliance by the federal government on a state-based distribution system for first responder resources and training would be slow and result in serious delays in funding reaching high-threat, high-risk population areas." Wallace concluded his testimony with a request for federal funding for what he describes as Regional Logistics Centers, designed to bring local regional resources to bear in the immediate aftermath of disasters.

Nor is it only touchy issues of funding and control related to readiness and response that need discussing, points out Paul Posner, who spent years as a

GAO intergovernmental affairs analyst. "There's other knotty issues that cause a lot of intergovernmental friction, like federal insurance policies, local building codes and state land use policies." These are key issues that Posner points out all influence how vulnerable certain places are to disasters in the first place.

From hurricanes and pandemics and to earthquakes and terrorism, the United States is grappling with the prospect of a host of cataclysmic events. Taken individually, most communities face a small chance of being hit, but experts agree that it's not a matter of "if" but "when" another large-scale disaster will occur somewhere in the United States. As Katrina so powerfully illustrated, a fragmented intergovernmental response can be disastrous.

Questions for Discussion

1. What factors led to the failure of various levels of government to respond adequately in the Katrina catastrophe? How can such obstacles be overcome in the future?
2. Should the role of the federal government expand as the nation plans how to deal with future catastrophes? What objections might be raised about an increased federal role?

The Federalism Debate: Why the Idea of National Education Standards Is Crossing Party Lines

Robert Gordon

During the last half century, beginning with the landmark Supreme Court decision in *Brown* v. *Board of Education* in 1954 (see selection 3.7), the role of the federal government in matters of public education has been controversial. Traditionally, both public school financing and the setting of educational standards have been state and local prerogatives. But as egalitarian concerns have increasingly come to the forefront of policymaking, elected and appointed federal officials have been pressured to ensure that students from varying backgrounds can succeed in the public schools, even if that means infringing on state and local autonomy.

In 2001, Congress passed the No Child Left Behind Act, legislation advocated by President George W. Bush, who had used accountability in public education as a major campaign issue in 2000. The act was designed to create incentives for public school systems to make extra efforts to guarantee that all students, especially certain minorities and those from low-income areas, would achieve "proficiency" in subjects like mathematics and reading by 2014. Amidst much optimism, the act was passed by a bipartisan coalition from across the political spectrum.

Implementing the act has been contentious, raising concerns that are at the core of the debate over the proper role of various levels of government. State autonomy has been limited by requiring testing and defining adequate yearly progress, but, because states can still set their own unique standards and design their own tests, it is impossible to compare the performance of schools across states—or of states against each other.

In this selection, Robert Gordon argues that a national standard of proficiency and a uniform national test are essential if No Child Left Behind is to achieve its lofty intent. In Gordon's view, national standards would encourage competition among states to achieve excellence. In his words, "if the federal government

Robert Gordon is a senior vice president at the Center for American Progress, a Washington-based think tank.

"The Federalism Debate." From *Education Week*, March 15, 2006. Reprinted by permission of the author.

rewards states that improved their performance, states would seek to outbid each other to recruit teachers and offer extracurricular enrichment. That's the race to the top we want."

The debate over federalism in education once followed a simple storyline: Liberals wanted a strong federal role, and conservatives supported "states' rights." The No Child Left Behind Act scrambled those sides. A Republican president championed massive new federal demands on schools, and some Democrats, like Howard Dean, derided the federal invasion of local authority.

The confusion will continue, as attention moves to another controversial idea: revising the No Child Left Behind law to establish national standards and tests. The loudest proponents of this idea are conservative accountability advocates. . . . But the progressive Center for American Progress, where I work, also supports national standards.

It isn't only education that has mixed up the teams. The Bush administration has recently tried to override state prerogatives on issues as diverse as end-of-life medical treatment, the definition of marriage, and tort law. Many liberals have sharply criticized all of these efforts in the terms conservatives once used: Washington is "overreaching" on "state issues."

Emerson said that a "foolish consistency is the hobgoblin of little minds." Is consistency in federalism the hobgoblin of little policy wonks? Or, more to the point, is federalism a ploy rather than a principle, invoked in service of other ends rather than valued for its own sake?

No to both. Details matter. There are good reasons for assigning some roles, but not others, to each layer of government. The right results depend on a complex of moral, legal, and practical judgments. Those judgments support national standards in education—even as they undercut many of President Bush's other nationalization initiatives.

The Values Dimension

When the nation is divided on a controversial moral question, state control can satisfy local majorities. If most Oregonians believe in euthanasia, for example, that's an argument for letting them have euthanasia—without imposing the same law in Alabama. But it is hard to imagine that different state education standards reflect different state attitudes. . . .

National definition makes more sense for non-negotiable aspects of national citizenship. While it is hard to get too worked up if different states want different standards for barbershop licensure, Southern states' Jim Crow laws clashed with America's constitutional commitment to equal citizenship.

Education, too, is at the center of national citizenship. As the constitutional-law specialist Goodwin Liu has argued, the place of education in our national identity was recognized in Reconstruction and reaffirmed when *Brown v. Board of Education* called education "the very foundation of good citizenship." In the half-century since *Brown*, education has become only more important in a global economy driven by knowledge and skills. More than ever, the basic skills needed in Maine are also needed in Montana. Education also matters for national greatness: The more individuals learn, the more wealth they can create for America. So it is right for our national leaders to define core goals for public schools and to hold them accountable for achieving them. (And as part of the same conversation, it would also be right to reconsider a school financing regime that leads to vast funding inequities both within states and between states.)

The Practical Dimension

State control makes some sense when states compete to provide the best possible services. Such competition occurs when, for example, states modify their laws to prevent doctors from leaving for better practice environments. . . .

But the No Child Left Behind law has created downward pressure on states. It demands that states enable virtually all students to achieve "proficiency" by 2014, but then fails to define what "proficiency" means. This is like a parent demanding that her child get a 95 percent on her next math test, but then saying she can take the test in calculus, or algebra, or arithmetic. States have maximized their scores by defining proficiency down. That foils the law's core goals of encouraging excellence and holding schools accountable for achieving it.

National standards could encourage the right kind of competition. If the federal government rewarded states that improved their performance, states would seek to outbid each other to recruit teachers and offer extracurricular enrichment. That's the race to the top we want.

State control also makes sense when states can teach us new things as "laboratories of democracy." Many people in principle support a broad right to die, but worry that legalizing assisted suicide will bring terrible pressure on sick patients to end their own lives. Oregon is testing that proposition.

The No Child Left Behind law has already limited state variation by requiring testing and defining adequate yearly progress. That reduction in experimentation is a loss that can only be justified by better outcomes and more transparency. But the law hasn't achieved its own promise of transparency: Because of different state standards, policymakers, administrators, and parents aren't able to compare the performance of schools across states—or states against each other. National standards could produce *more* learning than federalism.

Without yielding many of federalism's benefits, the No Child Left Behind law still has its typical cost: waste. We now spend more than half a billion dollars a year on tests required by the federal legislation. Much of that money is spent on variations of the same test. Yet a new report from Education Sector finds that even $500 million is not nearly enough to ensure that 50 states' tests measure high-level skills rather than memorization (Feb. 1, 2006). The weakness of the current tests fuels the most serious objections to No Child Left Behind. The same $500 million could help fund a single set of national tests far better than any we now have.

The biggest practical concern about national standards is also the simplest: that the federal government will blow it. . . . A bad testing regime in Utah ruins standards in Utah, but a bad national system can ruin them for everyone.

But this practical concern should be met by practical responses, of the sort our government has regularly used. Although states should be encouraged through financial incentives to adopt standards, there should remain an opportunity to opt out. An apolitical institution like the National Academies should be responsible for developing standards and tests. Generous funding should be provided to develop standards and tests that measure the high-level capacities we want schools to foster. And any standards should be tested locally before being implemented nationally. Under enormous public scrutiny, the standards-setting process can succeed.

The Political Issue

If the risk of uniformity is the biggest practical concern, the biggest political problem is a sound bite: National standards means a "national school board." But already today, establishing standards isn't a local school board function. It is a state function—and must be, if the standards are to be uniform statewide. Keeping the definition of standards in an out-of-touch state capital, rather than an out-of-touch national capital, hardly adds to community involvement.

There is no contradiction between setting broad goals nationally and giving communities more freedom to achieve those goals. So if we want to foster genuine local control of schools, there is plenty we could do—from expanding charter schools, to encouraging more parental involvement, to bringing more decisionmaking about personnel within the schoolhouse. Today, one obstacle to sound community engagement is the shortage of good information about how educators are performing. National standards and tests would help supply that information. If national standards can facilitate community control, there may be something here for everybody.

Questions for Discussion

1. In your view, should there be national proficiency standards and one national test to measure if the standards are being achieved?
2. The author asserts that national standards would create a competition among states to achieve excellence in public education. Can you think of any other instances where competition among states has created a "race to the top"? Are there instances of state competition where a "race to the bottom" has resulted from having no national standards?

# Chapter 3

CIVIL LIBERTIES AND CIVIL RIGHTS

Abortion. Prayer in public schools. Libel and slander. School integration and vouchers. Affirmative action and racial quotas. The right to legal counsel. These often-emotional issues strike at the core of the relationship between the citizen and the state. The framers understood the central position of individual rights, seeing them as inalienable—that is, as God-given, neither handed down nor taken away by rulers or the government as a whole. Still, the government serves as the chief agency for protecting individual rights, even though it can effectively deny them as well (for example, through the long history of legal segregation). The framers and subsequent generations of policymakers have thus performed a pair of balancing acts with civil liberties and civil rights issues.

First, they have strived to balance the rights of individuals with the needs of the community at large. On many occasions, the individual and the community are best served by the same policy. For example, the court decision in *Gideon* v. *Wainwright* (see selection 3.3) that guarantees indigents the right to counsel was a victory both for individual poor people and for society as a whole. Frequently, however, the interests of the community and the individual are, or appear to be, at odds. Does the right to freedom of speech and assembly extend to Nazis who wish to march through a predominantly Jewish community like Skokie, Illinois? The list of troubling and important questions in this area is endless and has produced a river of cases for the Supreme Court to wade through.

The second balance policymakers must maintain lies in the relative amounts of power accorded the government and its citizens. The government stands as the ultimate protector of individual liberties, such as the Constitution's enumerated rights of speech, religion, petition, and so forth. At the same time, the government can adopt policies and procedures that deny rights. The actions of an overzealous FBI or CIA have infringed on privacy rights, and many legislative initiatives have overstepped the bounds of propriety in seeking to regulate political organizations and speech. The Supreme Court's willingness to curb the government's assertion of power has varied. The Supreme Court of the 1990s was probably more likely to decide in favor of the government—whether national, state, or local—than it had been at any time since Earl Warren became chief justice in 1953.

More recently, the terrorist attacks of 2001 have prompted a broad re-evaluation of the balance between security and liberty. The hastily written and passed

Patriot Act provided the federal government with many more tools to address terrorism within domestic settings. Civil libertarians have predictably objected to many federal initiatives, including more freedom to gather personal information and to hold those suspected of terror-related activities. Stuart Taylor (see selection 3.6) argues that this rebalancing of security and liberty has not eroded fundamental freedoms while addressing legitimate concerns for national security.

What makes the study of civil rights and civil liberties so fascinating is the simultaneous timelessness and immediacy of the issues. For example, the notion of freedom of speech is as important today as it was in the eighteenth century, and contemporary controversies place basic issues, such as the potential defamation of a public figure, in new contexts. Likewise, civil rights and civil liberties issues hold our interest because their implications are extensive. Millions of individuals are directly affected by the Supreme Court's ruling in abortion or desegregation cases.

Although the legislative and executive branches play important roles in making and implementing rights policies, it is the judiciary that stands at center stage in this arena. At first such a responsibility may seem incongruous, since the courts are insulated from the influence of most citizens. In the end, however, this very independence from the popular will and the daily intrigues of politics is what renders the judicial branch, especially in its upper reaches, well suited to consider questions of rights. Protecting rights is frequently an unpopular business. In the 1940s and 1950s, for instance, Congress shied away from legislation that challenged racial separation, and the Supreme Court ruled on a series of desegregation cases, culminating in *Brown* v. *Board of Education*.

The direction of the Court is influenced by precedent and societal context as well as by individual justices. Although the membership of the Court during the last twenty-five years has become more conservative, its decisions have not dramatically turned away from the expansive civil liberties positions under Chief Justice Earl Warren (1953–1969). For example, the Burger (1969–1986) and Rehnquist (1986–2005) courts have gradually expanded the flexibility of the police in carrying out searches and seizures. But their decisions have not overturned any of the key Warren Court precedents, such as *Mapp* v. *Ohio* (1961), which limited the use of evidence from an illegal search, or *Miranda* v. *Arizona* (1966), which guaranteed that the accused be made aware of their right to counsel and protection from self-incrimination. Still, the increasing willingness of the Rehnquist Court of the 1990s to limit or overturn previous decisions may indicate that some fundamental changes (such as overturning *Roe* v. *Wade*) remain possible, though unlikely. A single change in the Court's personnel might shift the balance of power and the content of important rulings. Indeed, the recent additions of Chief Justice John Roberts and Justice Samuel Alito, to replace Justices Rhenquist and O'Connor, respectively, will almost certainly lead to a more conservative Court, overall.

The following selections show the variety of civil rights and civil liberties issues. The first two address the conflict over the possibility of limiting free speech. In *Near* v. *Minnesota* (1931), the Supreme Court refused to bar the publication of an irresponsible newspaper that had mounted vicious anti-Semitic attacks on Minneapolis public officials. This decision reflects the Court's great reluctance to order the prior restraint of any publication, even the most despicable. The *Near* decision was notable not for its immediate impact, which was next to nothing, but for the precedent it set. In 1971, the Court ruled in *New York Times* v. *United States* that the government could not suppress the publication of the Pentagon Papers, a highly critical history of U.S. involvement in Vietnam. The Defense Department had commissioned the extensive study and distributed it internally (though not widely). As Fred Friendly notes (see selection 3.2), the justices relied heavily on *Near* in their reasoning. That obscure Minnesota case thus had a major impact on an issue of great national importance.

One contested area of civil liberties is the so-called right to privacy. Unlike enumerated rights, which protect speech, religion, assembly, and so on, the right to privacy is not acknowledged in the Constitution. Such a right has evolved, however, becoming explicit in *Griswold* v. *Connecticut* (1965) (see selection 3.4). The *Griswold* ruling was a focal point in the 1987 confirmation hearings of Robert Bork, President Reagan's unsuccessful nominee for a Supreme Court seat. Moreover, the 1973 *Roe* v. *Wade* abortion decision relied heavily on the "right of privacy" that Griswold began to establish. More recently, the Court ruled in *Lawrence and Garner* v. *Texas* (see selection 3.5) that privacy rights extend to consenting adults who were convicted of a crime (sodomy) under a Texas statute that made "it a crime for two persons of the same sex to engage in certain intimate sexual conduct."

Much as the right of privacy has evolved, so too has antidiscrimination policy. Although many civil rights cases preceded *Brown* v. *Board of Education* (see selection 3.7), this 1954 decision proved a watershed in our willingness to address past discrimination. Although *Brown* eventually put an end to *de jure* (in law) segregation, it did relatively little to address *de facto* (in fact) separation. Indeed, as Gerald Rosenberg argues (see selection 3.8), much of *Brown*'s power may be more symbolic than substantive, in that the decision went unimplemented for at least a decade, and desegregation came about mainly in the wake of the extensive civil rights legislation of the 1960s.

In the wake of *Brown*, affirmative action policies have sought to address inequities in both opportunity and outcome on racial, gender, and ethnic grounds. The Court has ruled numerical quotas to be unconstitutional, but has allowed some consideration of race as a criterion for admission to law school (see selection 3.10, "Reaffirming Diversity").

Still, as Peter Schuck argues in "Affirmative Action: Don't Mend It or End It— Bend It" (see selection 3.9), an active affirmative action plan in the public sector may produce unintended negative consequences, with preferences producing skepticism about the merit of those who receive them. At present, the Court has laid out narrow guidelines under which race may be considered in providing opportunities. Sandra Day O'Connor, in the Michigan affirmative action cases (see selection 3.10), expressed the hope that preferences will not be needed in twenty-five years. But given the fifty-year record of *Brown* and continuing segregation in many school systems, one can scarcely be too optimistic.

Near v. Minnesota (1931)

Among the rights guaranteed in the Constitution, perhaps the most fundamental is the freedom of expression. Without unfettered speech and a free press, the idea of democracy loses its meaning. Freedom of expression issues emerge in many forms, including controversies over libel, obscenity, and political speech. Even a very large number of articles could not capture the range of questions that courts regularly face in deciding freedom of expression cases.

In *Near* v. *Minnesota*, the central question revolves around prior restraint of the press. In 1931, the Supreme Court ruled 5 to 4 that Minnesota could not muzzle the publisher of a newspaper that was attacking various Minneapolis public officials. Although any public official who is the subject of a "malicious, scandalous, and defamatory" article can sue for libel, the state could not halt publication of a newspaper merely because it expected that paper to defame public officials.

M r. Chief Justice Hughes delivered the opinion of the Court. . . .
Under this statute, [section one, clause (b)], the County Attorney of Hennepin County brought this action to enjoin the publication of what was described as a "malicious, scandalous and defamatory newspaper, magazine and periodical," known as "The Saturday Press," published by the defendants in the city of Minneapolis. The complaint alleged that the defendants, on September 24, 1927, and on eight subsequent dates in October and November, 1927, published and circulated editions of that periodical which were "largely devoted to malicious, scandalous and defamatory articles" concerning Charles G. Davis, Frank W. Brunskill, the *Minneapolis Tribune*, the *Minneapolis Journal*, Melvin C. Passolt, George E. Leach, the Jewish Race, the members of the Grand Jury of Hennepin County impaneled in November 1927, and then holding office, and other persons, as more fully appeared in exhibits annexed to the complaint, consisting of copies of the articles described and constituting 327 pages of the record. While the complaint did not so allege, it appears from the briefs of both parties that Charles G. Davis was a special law enforcement officer employed by a civic organization, that George E. Leach was Mayor of Minneapolis, that Frank W. Brunskill was its Chief of Police, and that Floyd B. Olson (the relator in this action) was County Attorney.

Without attempting to summarize the contents of the voluminous exhibits attached to the complaint, we deem it sufficient to say that the articles charged in substance that a Jewish gangster was in control of gambling, bootlegging and racketeering in Minneapolis, and that law enforcing officers and agencies were not energetically performing their duties. Most of the charges were directed against the Chief of Police; he was charged with gross neglect of duty, illicit relations with gangsters, and with participation in graft. The County Attorney was charged with knowing the existing conditions and with failure to take adequate measures to remedy them. The Mayor was accused of inefficiency and dereliction. One member of the grand jury was stated to be in sympathy with the gangsters. A special grand jury and a special prosecutor were demanded to deal with the situation in general, and, in particular, to investigate an attempt to assassinate one Guilford, one of the original defendants, who, it appears from the articles, was shot by gangsters after the first issue of the periodical had been published. There is no question but that the articles made serious accusations against the public officers named and others in connection with the prevalence of crimes and the failure to expose and punish them. . . .

If we cut through mere details of procedure, the operation and effect of the statute in substance is that public authorities may bring the owner or publisher of a newspaper or periodical before a judge upon a charge of conducting a business of publishing scandalous and defamatory matter—in particular that the matter consists of charges against public officers of official dereliction—and unless the owner or publisher is able and disposed to bring competent evidence to satisfy the judge that the charges are true and are published with good motives and for justifiable ends, his newspaper or periodical is suppressed and further publication is made punishable as a contempt. This is of the essence of censorship.

The question is whether a statute authorizing such proceedings in restraint of publication is consistent with the conception of the liberty of the press as historically conceived and guaranteed. In determining the extent of the constitutional protection, it has been generally, if not universally, considered that it is the chief purpose of the guaranty to prevent previous restraints upon publication. The struggle in England, directed against the legislative power of the licenser, resulted in renunciation of the censorship of the press. The liberty deemed to be established was thus described by Blackstone.* "The liberty of the press is indeed essential to the nature of a free state; but this consists in laying no *previous* restraints upon publications, and not in freedom from censure for criminal matter when published. Every freeman has an undoubted right to lay what sentiments he pleases before the public; to forbid this, is to destroy the freedom of the press; but if he publishes what is improper, mischievous or illegal, he must take the consequence of his own temerity." . . . The distinction

---

*Sir William Blackstone (1723–1780) was an English jurist and legal scholar whose writings served as the core of legal education in the United States during the nineteenth century.

was early pointed out between the extent of the freedom with respect to censorship under our constitutional system and that enjoyed in England. Here, as Madison said, "the great and essential rights of the people are secured against legislative as well as against executive ambition. They are secured, not by laws paramount to prerogative, but by constitutions paramount to laws. This security of the freedom of the press requires that it should be exempt not only from previous restraint by the Executive, as in Great Britain, but from legislative restraint also." . . .

The objection has . . . been made that the principle as to immunity from previous restraint is stated too broadly, if every such restraint is deemed to be prohibited. That is undoubtedly true; the protection even as to previous restraint is not absolutely unlimited. But the limitation has been recognized only in exceptional cases: "When a nation is at war many things that might be said in time of peace are such a hindrance to its effort that their utterance will not be endured so long as men fight and that no Court could regard them as protected by any constitutional right." . . . No one would question but that a government might prevent actual obstruction to its recruiting service or the publication of the sailing dates of transports or the number and location of troops. On similar grounds, the primary requirements of decency may be enforced against obscene publications. The security of the community life may be protected against incitements to acts of violence and the overthrow by force of orderly government. The constitutional guaranty of free speech does not "protect a man from an injunction against uttering words that may have all the effect of force. . . ." These limitations are not applicable here. Nor are we now concerned with questions as to the extent of authority to prevent publications in order to protect private rights according to the principles governing the exercise of the jurisdiction of courts of equity.

The exceptional nature of its limitations places in a strong light the general conception that liberty of the press, historically considered and taken up by the Federal Constitution, has meant, principally although not exclusively, immunity from previous restraints or censorship. The conception of the liberty of the press in this country had broadened with the exigencies of the colonial period and with the efforts to secure freedom from oppressive administration. That liberty was especially cherished for the immunity it afforded from previous restraint of the publication of censure of public officers and charges of official misconduct. . . . Madison, who was the leading spirit in the preparation of the First Amendment of the Federal Constitution, thus described the practice and sentiment which led to the guaranties of liberty of the press in state constitutions.[1]

"In every State, probably, in the Union, the press has exerted a freedom in canvassing the merits and measures of public men of every description which has not been confined to the strict limits of the common law. On this footing the freedom of the press has stood; on this footing it yet stands. . . . Some degree of abuse is inseparable from the proper use of everything, and in no

instance is this more true than in that of the press. It has accordingly been decided by the practice of the States, that it is better to leave a few of its noxious
branches to their luxuriant growth, than, by pruning them away, to injure the
vigour of those yielding the proper fruits. And can the wisdom of this policy be
doubted by any who reflect that to the press alone, chequered as it is with
abuses, the world is indebted for all the triumphs which have been gained by
reason and humanity over error and oppression; who reflect that to the same
beneficent source the United States owe much of the lights which conducted
them to the ranks of a free and independent nation, and which have improved
their political system into a shape so auspicious to their happiness? Had 'Sedition Acts,' forbidding every publication that might bring the constituted agents
into contempt or disrepute, or that might excite the hatred of the people
against the authors of unjust or pernicious measures, been uniformly enforced
against the press, might not the United States have been languishing at this
day under the infirmities of a sickly Confederation?* Might they not, possibly,
be miserable colonies, groaning under a foreign yoke?"

The fact that for approximately one hundred and fifty years there has been
almost an entire absence of attempts to impose previous restraints upon publications relating to the malfeasance of public officers is significant of the deep-
seated conviction that such restraints would violate constitutional right. Public
officers, whose character and conduct remain open to debate and free discussion in the press, find their remedies for false accusations in actions under libel
laws providing for redress and punishment, and not in proceedings to restrain
the publication of newspapers and periodicals. The general principle that the
constitutional guaranty of the liberty of the press gives immunity from previous
restraints has been approved in many decisions under the provisions of state
constitutions.

The importance of this immunity has not lessened. While reckless assaults
upon public men . . . exert a baleful influence and deserve the severest condemnation in public opinion, it cannot be said that this abuse is greater, and it is
believed to be less, than that which characterized the period in which our institutions took shape. Meanwhile, the administration of government has become
more complex, the opportunities for malfeasance and corruption have multiplied, crime has grown to most serious proportions, and the danger of its protection by unfaithful officials and of the impairment of the fundamental
security of life and property by criminal alliances and official neglect, emphasizes the primary need of a vigilant and courageous press, especially in great
cities. The fact that the liberty of the press may be abused by miscreant purveyors
of scandal does not make any the less necessary the immunity of the press

---

*The fear of such legislation was scarcely idle. In 1798 Congress passed the Alien and Sedition
Acts, which provided for indicting those who conspired against the administration or who spoke
or wrote "with intent to defame" the government. The Sedition Act was enforced against a few
individuals before being repealed during the Jefferson administration.

from previous restraint in dealing with official misconduct. Subsequent punishment for such abuses as may exist is the appropriate remedy, consistent with constitutional privilege.

In attempted justification of the statute, it is said that it deals not with publication *per se*, but with the "business" of publishing defamation. If, however, the publisher has a constitutional right to publish, without previous restraint, an edition of his newspaper charging official derelictions, it cannot be denied that he may publish subsequent editions for the same purpose. He does not lose his right by exercising it. If his right exists, it may be exercised in publishing nine editions, as in this case, as well as in one edition. If previous restraint is permissible, it may be imposed at once; indeed, the wrong may be as serious in one publication as in several. Characterizing the publication as a business, and the business as a nuisance, does not permit an invasion of the constitutional immunity against restraint. Similarly, it does not matter that the newspaper or periodical is found to be "largely" or "chiefly" devoted to the publication of such derelictions. If the publisher has a right, without previous restraint, to publish them, his right cannot be deemed to be dependent upon his publishing something else, more or less, with the matter to which objection is made.

Nor can it be said that the constitutional freedom from previous restraint is lost because charges are made of derelictions which constitute crimes. With the multiplying provisions of penal codes, and of municipal charters and ordinances carrying penal sanctions, the conduct of public officers is very largely within the purview of criminal statutes. The freedom of the press from previous restraint has never been regarded as limited to such animadversions as lay outside the range of penal enactments. Historically, there is no such limitation; it is inconsistent with the reason which underlies the privilege, as the privilege so limited would be of slight value for the purposes for which it came to be established.

The statute in question cannot be justified by reason of the fact that the publisher is permitted to show, before injunction issues, that the matter published is true and is published with good motives and for justifiable ends. If such a statute, authorizing suppression and injunction on such a basis, is constitutionally valid, it would be equally permissible for the legislature to provide that at any time the publisher of any newspaper could be brought before a court, or even an administrative officer (as the constitutional protection may not be regarded as resting on mere procedural details) and required to produce proof of the truth of his publication, or of what he intended to publish, and of his motives, or stand enjoined. If this can be done, the legislature may provide machinery for determining in the complete exercise of its discretion what are justifiable ends and restrain publication accordingly. And it would be but a step to a complete system of censorship. The recognition of authority to impose previous restraint upon publication in order to protect the community against the circulation of charges of misconduct, and especially of official misconduct, necessarily would carry with it the admission of the authority of the censor against which the constitutional barrier was erected. The preliminary freedom, by virtue of the very reason for its existence, does not depend, as this Court has said, on proof of truth. . . .

Equally unavailing is the insistence that the statute is designed to prevent the circulation of scandal which tends to disturb the public peace and to provoke assaults and the commission of crime. Charges of reprehensible conduct, and in particular of official malfeasance, unquestionably create a public scandal, but the theory of the constitutional guaranty is that even a more serious public evil would be caused by authority to prevent publication. "To prohibit the intent to excite those unfavorable sentiments against those who administer the Government, is equivalent to a prohibition of the actual excitement of them; and to prohibit the actual excitement of them is equivalent to a prohibition of discussions having that tendency and effect; which, again, is equivalent to a protection of those who administer the Government, if they should at any time deserve the contempt or hatred of the people, against being exposed to it by free animadversions on their characters and conduct."[2] There is nothing new in the fact that charges of reprehensible conduct may create resentment and the disposition to resort to violent means of redress, but this well-understood tendency did not alter the determination to protect the press against censorship and restraint upon publication. As was said in *New Yorker Staats-Zeitung* v. *Nolan* . . . : "If the township may prevent the circulation of a newspaper for no reason other than that some of its inhabitants may violently disagree with it, and resent its circulation by resorting to physical violence, there is no limit to what may be prohibited." The danger of violent reactions becomes greater with effective organization of defiant groups resenting exposure, and if this consideration warranted legislative interference with the initial freedom of publication, the constitutional protection would be reduced to a mere form of words.

For these reasons we hold the statute, so far as it authorized the proceedings in this action under clause (b) of section one, to be an infringement of the liberty of the press guaranteed by the Fourteenth Amendment. We should add that this decision rests upon the operation and effect of the statute, without regard to the question of the truth of the charges contained in the particular periodical.* The fact that the public officers named in this case, and those associated with the charges of official dereliction, may be deemed to be impeccable, cannot affect the conclusion that the statute imposes an unconstitutional restraint upon publication.

Notes

1. Report on the Virginia Resolutions, Madison's Works, vol. iv, p. 544.
2. Madison, *op. cit.*, p. 549.

---

*Note the strength of this declaration. The falsity of a statement does not constitute adequate grounds for imposing prior restraint.

Questions for Discussion

1. Why should public figures be treated differently when libel or slander is alleged? Is it possible to libel someone as public as the president?
2. In what instances might prior restraint of a publication be appropriate? In wartime? In the case of a consistently obscene magazine?

 3.2

From the *Saturday Press* to the *New York Times*

Fred Friendly

Fred Friendly notes the importance of the *Near* decision in the Pentagon Papers case of 1971. In this instance the publisher was not a purveyor of sensational accusations but the *New York Times* and the *Washington Post*, which were printing long extracts of the Pentagon's classified history of American involvement in Vietnam. The only common thread between the Pentagon Papers case (*New York Times Co.* v. *United States*) and *Near* was the issue of prior restraint. But that thread held fast, demonstrating the importance of maintaining freedom of speech both in distasteful circumstances (*Near*) and when the national interest is at stake.

Although his name is hardly a household word, the ghost of Jay M. Near still stalks most U.S. courtrooms. There exists no plaque that bears his name, and even Colonel McCormick's marble memorial to Chief Justice Hughes's opinion omits the name of the case.* Near is truly the unknown

Fred Friendly, formerly president of CBS News (1964–1966), was the Edward R. Murrow Professor of Journalism at Columbia University.

From *Minnesota Rag* by Fred W. Friendly, copyright © 1981 by Fred W. Friendly and Ruth Friendly. Used by permission of Random House, Inc.

*Robert R. McCormick was an owner and publisher of the *Chicago Tribune* who attacked a host of public officials and took on various crusades.

soldier in the continuing struggle between the powers of government and the power of the press to publish the news.

Near v. *Minnesota* placed freedom of the press "in the least favorable light"; as Minnesota and New York newspapers and lawyers viewed the litigation, it was the worst possible case. But perhaps it is just because Near's cause did not at first appear to be significant, except to Colonel McCormick and Roger Baldwin,* that it created such sturdy law. So indestructible has it proved that its storied progeny, the Pentagon Papers case, was able to survive the political firestorms of 1971. If "great cases like hard cases make bad law," as the [Justice Oliver Wendell] Holmes proverb warns, it may follow that since few knew or cared about Near's cause, freedom of the press was transformed successfully from an eighteenth- and nineteenth-century ideal into a twentieth-century constitutional bulwark.

By his admonition, Holmes meant that volatile national confrontations which appeal to prejudices and distort judgment can be counterproductive in shaping the law of the future. Such emotional conflicts as slavery, as in the Dred Scott decision, and minimum-wage laws, as in *Adkins*, Holmes suggested seventy-seven years ago, "exercise a kind of hydraulic pressure which makes what previously was clear seem doubtful, and before which even well-settled principles of law will bend." In 1931 an American public plagued by economic panic, unemployment, Prohibition and the likes of Al Capone cared little about the civil rights of a scandalmonger from Minnesota. To paraphrase Holmes, Near's case embodied all the underwhelming interests required to shape the grand law of the future. His success was based not in frenzied national debate, but in quirks-of-fate delays in the Minnesota courts, the deaths of two conservative Justices, and Hoover's subsequent appointments.[†] It was the new Chief Justice who made the difference, not simply because he added one more vote to Near's side, but because of his unexpected passion for the First Amendment and his intellectual capacity to lead others, especially Justice Roberts.

The precedent of *Near* v. *Minnesota* has withstood onslaughts from Presidents, legislatures and even the judiciary itself in its attempts to enforce basic rights which seemed to clash with the First Amendment. It demonstrated the latent strengths for an amendment which had gone untested for 150 years. That five-to-four decision achieved far more than simply asserting Near's rights. . . . It marked the beginning of a concerted process "to plug the holes punched in the Bill of Rights," and what [Baltimore Sun writer George] Mencken had called in 1926 "the most noble opportunity that the Supreme Court, in all its history, ever faced." . . .

There have been hundreds of other press cases before the Court since 1931—some won, some lost. Perhaps the seminal judgment was the 1964 decision

---

*Roger Baldwin founded the American Civil Liberties Union.

†Justices William H. Taft and Edward T. Sanford died. President Herbert Hoover appointed Charles E. Hughes and Owen J. Roberts to replace them.

in *New York Times Co. v. Sullivan*, which prevented Southern courts from using the law of libel to thwart national news coverage of the civil rights battle. Although not a prior-restraint case, *Sullivan* freed the press from the threat of chilling damages in reporting the conduct of public officials in Alabama in the explosive sixties. Associate Justice William Brennan's majority opinion established that officials, and later public figures, could not recover libel damages for reports concerning their official actions without proving "malice," that is, deliberate lying or "reckless disregard for the truth."

But *Near*'s ultimate legacy was finally realized forty years later, almost to the day, in the clash between the power of the presidency of the United States and two powerful newspapers, the *New York Times* and the *Washington Post*. Its official name was *New York Times Co. v. United States*, but it is remembered as the Pentagon Papers case. It began when the *New York Times* obtained a forty-seven-volume secret history of the Vietnam war from Daniel Ellsberg, a former analyst of the Rand Corporation; it ended with a major victory for the press in the Supreme Court. On June 13, 1971, the *New York Times* began publishing its synopsis and analysis of the secret documents, and two days later the Nixon Administration began legal efforts to restrain it. Later that week the government also sought to enjoin the *Washington Post* from publishing the same classified material. In a "frenzied train of events," as one Justice described it, the cases bobbed back and forth between district and appeals courts until, eleven days later, the Supreme Court agreed to try to untangle the conflicting and confusing opinions.

What dominated all the arguments in all briefs and opinions, from district court to Supreme Court, was the theory of no previous restraint, codified by Blackstone and incorporated by Madison, but made concrete in *Near*.

The Court met hastily on Saturday morning, June 25, and five days later announced its six-to-three decision. Leaning heavily on *Near v. Minnesota*, the Court held that the heavy burden of justifying the imposition of prior restraint had not been met by the government. It required nine opinions for the Supreme Court to explain its votes, and *Near* was cited ten times.

Justice William O. Douglas, in an opinion joined by Justice Hugo Black, quoted long passages from Chief Justice Hughes's majority opinion in *Near*. Believing that the government had no power to punish or restrain "material that is embarrassing to the powers-that-be," Douglas and Black reiterated Hughes's opinion: "The fact that liberty of the press may be abused . . . does not make any less necessary the immunity of the press." But it was Douglas' concluding statement that emphasized the tremendous strength of *Near*: "The stays in these cases that have been in effect for more than a week constitute a flouting of the principles of the First Amendment as interpreted in *Near v. Minnesota*."

Justice Black's language, in an opinion joined by Justice Douglas, also echoed some of the discussion during oral arguments in *Near*:

> Both the history and language of the First Amendment support the view that the press must be left free to publish news, whatever the source, without censorship, in-

junctions or prior restraints. . . . Only a free and unrestrained press can effectively expose deception in government. . . . [T]he *New York Times*, the *Washington Post*, and other newspapers should be commended for serving the purpose that the Founding Fathers saw so clearly. In revealing the workings of government that led to the Vietnam War, the newspapers did precisely what the founders hoped and trusted they would do.

Even in the dissents in the Pentagon Papers case, *Near* was ubiquitous. Chief Justice Warren Burger, Justice John Harlan and Justice Harry Blackmun in their dissenting opinions also cited Hughes's exceptions to the prohibitions against prior restraint such as interfering with recruiting during wartime and publishing troopship sailing dates. As in *Near*, the Court's judgment in the Pentagon Papers case did not establish the absolutism of the First Amendment (as some journalists still contend) against *all* prior restraints. Justice Byron White wrote: "I do not say that in no circumstances would the First Amendment permit an injunction against publishing information about government plans and operations."

Although it was the judgment of the divided Court that lifted the prior restraint on the *New York Times*, the *Washington Post* and twenty other newspapers, which were prepared to publish sections of the Pentagon Papers, five sentences by District Court Judge Murray Gurfein endure. It is the kind of quotation Colonel McCormick might have had chiseled in his hall:

> The security of the Nation is not at the ramparts alone. Security also lies in the value of our free institutions. A cantankerous press, an obstinate press, a ubiquitous press must be suffered by those in authority in order to preserve the even greater values of freedom of expression and the right of the people to know. . . . These are troubled times. There is no greater safety valve for discontent and cynicism about the affairs of Government than freedom of expression in any form.

. . . *Near* was a perilously close case, but "a morsel of genuine history," as Jefferson described such events, "a thing so rare as to be always valuable." . . .

Questions for Discussion

1. In light of the ruling in *New York Times Co.* v. *United States*, can you imagine any circumstances that would justify prior restraint of the press?
2. Does libel law adequately guard against an irresponsible and overaggressive press, or should there be other safeguards, such as an independent review board?

3.3

Gideon v. Wainwright (1963)

Clarence Gideon, an indigent, was accused of breaking and entering a pool-room, a felony under Florida law. He proclaimed his innocence and requested that he be provided with a lawyer. The trial judge refused this request, Gideon was found guilty, and he was sentenced to a five-year term in the state peniten-tiary. In a handwritten statement Gideon appealed his case to the Supreme Court, which took the case and appointed Abe Fortas, a prominent Washington attorney and later Supreme Court justice, to represent him.

The Supreme Court had frequently ruled in specific circumstances that the Sixth Amendment guaranteed a right to counsel and that this right was incorpo-rated by the Fourteenth Amendment and was thus applicable to the states. Still, before *Gideon* v. *Wainwright* (1963), the Court had not ruled that there was any general right to counsel. Indeed, the governing rule was that of *Betts* v. *Brady*, a 1942 decision that the right to counsel was not a "fundamental" right. The Court's reconsideration of the *Betts* rule after only twenty-one years was un-usual.

After the decision in this case, Gideon was retried in Florida, with counsel, and found innocent. Subsequently, thousands of prisoners in Florida and else-where won their release on the grounds that they had not been represented by counsel at their trials.

M r. Justice Black delivered the opinion of the Court. . . .
. . . Since 1942, when *Betts* v. *Brady* . . . was decided by a divided Court, the problem of a defendant's federal constitutional right to counsel in a state court has been a continuing source of controversy and litiga-tion in both state and federal courts. To give this problem another review here, we granted certiorari. Since Gideon was proceeding *in forma pauperis*, we ap-pointed counsel to represent him and requested both sides to discuss in their briefs and oral arguments the following: "Should this Court's holding in *Betts* v. *Brady* be reconsidered?" . . .

We think the Court in *Betts* had ample precedent for acknowledging that those guarantees of the Bill of Rights which are fundamental safeguards of lib-erty immune from federal abridgment are equally protected against state inva-sion by the Due Process Clause of the Fourteenth Amendment. This same principle was recognized, explained, and applied in *Powell* v. *Alabama* . . . , a case upholding the right of counsel, where the Court held that despite sweeping language to the contrary in *Hurtado* v. *California* . . . , the Fourteenth Amendment "embraced" those " 'fundamental principles of liberty and justice which lie at the base of all our civil and political institutions,' " even though they had been "specifically dealt with in another part of the federal Constitution." . . . In many cases other than *Powell* and *Betts*, this Court has looked to the fundamental nature of original Bill of Rights guarantees to decide whether the Fourteenth Amendment makes them obligatory on the States. . . .

We accept *Betts* v. *Brady*'s assumption, based as it was on our prior cases, that a provision of the Bill of Rights which is "fundamental and essential to a fair trial" is made obligatory upon the States by the Fourteenth Amendment. We think the Court in *Betts* was wrong, however, in concluding that the Sixth Amendment's guarantee of counsel is not one of these fundamental rights. Ten years before *Betts* v. *Brady*, this Court, after full consideration of all the historical data examined in *Betts*, had unequivocally declared that "the right to the aid of counsel is of this fundamental character." *Powell* v. *Alabama*. . . . While the Court at the close of its *Powell* opinion did by its language, as this Court frequently does, limit its holding to the particular facts and circumstances of that case, its conclusions about the fundamental nature of the right to counsel are unmistakable. . . .

In light of . . . many other prior decisions of this Court, it is not surprising that the *Betts* Court, when faced with the contention that "one charged with crime, who is unable to obtain counsel, must be furnished counsel by the State," conceded that "[e]xpressions in the opinions of this court lend color to the argument. . . . " The fact is that in deciding as it did—that "appointment of counsel is not a fundamental right, essential to a fair trial"—the Court in *Betts* v. *Brady* made an abrupt break with its own well-considered precedents. In returning to these old precedents, sounder we believe than the new, we but restore constitutional principles established to achieve a fair system of justice. Not only these precedents but also reason and reflection require us to recognize that in our adversary system of criminal justice, any person haled into court, who is too poor to hire a lawyer, cannot be assured a fair trial unless counsel is provided for him. This seems to us to be an obvious truth. Governments, both state and federal, quite properly spend vast sums of money to establish machinery to try defendants accused of crime. Lawyers to prosecute are everywhere deemed essential to protect the public's interest in an orderly society. Similarly, there are few defendants charged with crime, few indeed, who fail to hire the best lawyers they can get to prepare and present their defenses. That government hires lawyers to prosecute and defendants who have the money hire lawyers to defend are the strongest indications of the widespread belief that lawyers in criminal courts are necessities, not luxuries. The right of one charged with crime to counsel may not be deemed fundamental and essential to fair trials in some countries, but it is in ours. From the very beginning, our state and national constitutions and laws have laid great emphasis on procedural and substantive safeguards designed to assure fair trials before impartial tribunals in which every defendant stands equal before the law. This noble ideal cannot be realized if the poor man charged with crime has to face his accusers without a lawyer to assist him. . . . The Court in *Betts* v. *Brady* departed from the sound wisdom upon which the Court's holding in *Powell* v. *Alabama* rested. Florida, supported by two other states, has asked that *Betts* v. *Brady* be left intact. Twenty-two States, as friends of the Court,* argue that *Betts* was "an anachronism when handed down" and that it should now be overruled. We agree.

The judgment is reversed and the cause is remanded to the Supreme Court of Florida for further action not inconsistent with this opinion.

Mr. Justice Harlan, concurring:

I agree that *Betts* v. *Brady* should be overruled, but consider it entitled to a more respectful burial than has been accorded, at least on the part of those of us who were not on the Court when that case was decided.

I cannot subscribe to the view that *Betts* v. *Brady* represented "an abrupt break with its own well-considered precedents." In 1932, in *Powell* v. *Alabama* . . . , a capital case, this Court declared that under the particular facts there presented—"the ignorance and illiteracy of the defendants, their youth, the circumstances of public hostility . . . and above all that they stood in deadly peril of their lives"—the state court had a duty to assign counsel for the trial as a necessary requisite of due process of law. It is evident that these limiting facts were not added to the opinion as an afterthought; they were repeatedly emphasized, and were clearly regarded as important to the result.

Thus when this Court, a decade later, decided *Betts* v. *Brady*, it did no more than to admit of the possible existence of special circumstances in noncapital as well as capital trials, while at the same time insisting that such circumstances be shown in order to establish a denial of due process. The right to appointed counsel had been recognized as being considerably broader in federal prosecutions, see *Johnson* v. *Zerbst* . . . , but to have imposed these requirements on the States would indeed have been "an abrupt break" with the almost immediate past. The declaration that the right to appointed counsel in state prosecutions, as established in *Powell* v. *Alabama*, was not limited to capital cases was in truth not a departure from, but an extension of, existing precedent.

The principles declared in *Powell* and in *Betts*, however, have had a troubled journey throughout the years that have followed first the one case and then the other. Even by the time of the *Betts* decision, dictum in at least one of the Court's opinions had indicated that there was an absolute right to the services

---

*Various organizations and individuals, such as interest groups or state attorneys general, offer *amicus curiae* (friend of the court) briefs on major cases. Since the 1950s, *amicus* briefs as practiced by groups such as the National Association for the Advancement of Colored People (NAACP) and the American Civil Liberties Union (ACLU) have become a major tool for promoting social change.

of counsel in the trial of state capital cases. Such dicta continued to appear in subsequent decisions and any lingering doubts were finally eliminated by the holding of *Hamilton* v. *Alabama*. . . .

In noncapital cases, the "special circumstances" rule has continued to exist in form while its substance has been substantially and steadily eroded. In the first decade after *Betts*, there were cases in which the Court found special circumstances to be lacking, but usually by a sharply divided vote. However, no such decision has been cited to us, and I have found none, after *Quicksall* v. *Michigan* . . . , decided in 1950. At the same time, there have been not a few cases in which special circumstances were found in little or nothing more than the "complexity" of the legal questions presented, although those questions were often of only routine difficulty. The Court has come to recognize, in other words, that the mere existence of serious criminal charge constituted in itself special circumstances requiring the services of counsel at trial. In truth the *Betts* v. *Brady* rule is no longer a reality.

This evolution, however, appears not to have been fully recognized by many state courts, in this instance charged with the front-line responsibility for the enforcement of constitutional rights. To continue a rule which is honored by this Court only with lip service is not a healthy thing and in the long run will do disservice to the federal system.

The special circumstances rule has been formally abandoned in capital cases, and the time has now come when it should be similarly abandoned in noncapital cases, at least as to offenses which, as the one involved here, carry the possibility of a substantial prison sentence. (Whether the rule should extend to *all* criminal cases need not now be decided.) This indeed does no more than to make explicit something that has long since been foreshadowed in our decisions. . . .

Questions for Discussion

1. At what point does having access to counsel become a constitutional right? Is it a right for any felony? What about for a serious misdemeanor?
2. *Gideon* paved the way for the *Miranda* case, which required the police to inform a suspect of his or her constitutional rights, including the right to counsel. Should the police be able to question a suspect without counsel present?
3. Has *Gideon* completely closed the gap between the wealthy and the poor when it comes to obtaining adequate counsel?

3.4

Griswold v. Connecticut (1965)

Since the 1960s, one of the most interesting and controversial fields of constitutional law has involved the alleged right of privacy. The Constitution nowhere explicitly spells out any such right, yet preserving privacy is of paramount concern in an increasingly intrusive society.

One key case (not presented here) is *Roe* v. *Wade* (1973), which declared abortion laws in almost all states unconstitutional. Justice Harry A. Blackmun held that the constitutional right to privacy allowed women to determine whether to go ahead with an abortion, although the rights of the mother were to be balanced against the potential right to life of the fetus (which was not a person in a constitutional sense). *Roe* v. *Wade* set off almost ceaseless attempts by prolife activists to ban abortions. It also became a turning point in the Senate's defeat of Ronald Reagan's Supreme Court nominee, Appeals Court Judge Robert Bork, in 1987.

Griswold v. *Connecticut* (1965) laid the groundwork for *Roe* by giving the right of privacy formal constitutional protection. The decision grew from a challenge to Connecticut's restrictive but rarely enforced birth control laws. Estelle Griswold, executive director of the Planned Parenthood League of Connecticut, was convicted of dispensing birth control information to married people. The Supreme Court overturned the lower court's decision.

Mr. Justice Douglas delivered the opinion of the Court. . . .

Coming to the merits, we are met with a wide range of questions that implicate the Due Process Clause of the Fourteenth Amendment. Overtones of some arguments suggest that *Lockner* v. *State of New York* . . . should be our guide. But we decline that invitation. . . . We do not sit as super-legislature to determine the wisdom, need, and propriety of laws that touch economic problems, business affairs, or social conditions. This law, however, operates directly on an intimate relation of husband and wife and their physician's role in one aspect of that relation.

The association of people is not mentioned in the Constitution nor in the Bill of Rights. The right to educate a child in a school of the parents' choice—whether public or private or parochial—is also not mentioned. Nor is the right to study any particular subject or any foreign language. Yet the First Amendment has been construed to include certain of those rights.

By *Pierce* v. *Society of Sisters* . . . , the right to educate one's children as one chooses is made applicable to the States by the force of the First and Fourteenth Amendments. By *Meyer* v. *State of Nebraska* . . . , the same dignity is given the right to study the German language in a private school. In other words, the State may not, consistently with the spirit of the First Amendment, contract the spectrum of available knowledge. The right of freedom of speech and press includes not only the right to utter or to print, but the right to distribute, the right to receive, the right to read (*Martin* v. *City of Struthers* . . .) and freedom of inquiry, freedom of thought, and freedom to teach (see *Wieman* v. *Updegraff* . . .)—indeed the freedom of the entire university community. . . . Without those peripheral rights the specific rights would be less secure. And so we reaffirm the principle of the *Pierce* and the *Meyer* cases.

In *NAACP* v. *State of Alabama* . . . we protected the "freedom to associate and privacy in one's associations," noting that freedom of association was a peripheral First Amendment right. Disclosure of membership lists of a constitutionally valid association, we held, was invalid "as entailing the likelihood of a substantial restraint upon the exercise by petitioner's members of their right to freedom of association." In other words, the First Amendment has a penumbra where privacy is protected from governmental intrusion.* In like context, we have protected forms of "association" that are not political in the customary sense but pertain to the social, legal, and economic benefit of the members. In *Schware* v. *Board of Bar Examiners,* . . . we held it not permissible to bar a lawyer from practice, because he had once been a member of the Communist Party. The man's "association with that Party" was not shown to be "anything more than a political faith in a political party" and was not action of a kind proving bad moral character.

Those cases involved more than the "right of assembly"—a right that extends to all irrespective of their race or ideology. The right of "association," like the right of belief is more than the right to attend a meeting; it includes the right to express one's attitudes or philosophies by membership in a group or by affiliation with it or by other lawful means. Association in that context is a form of expression of opinion; and while it is not expressly included in the First Amendment its existence is necessary in making the express guarantees fully meaningful.

The foregoing cases suggest that specific guarantees in the Bill of Rights have penumbras, formed by emanations from those guarantees that help give them life and substance. Various guarantees create zones of privacy. The right of association contained in the penumbra of the First Amendment is one, as we have seen. The Third Amendment in its prohibition against the quartering of

---

*Justice William O. Douglas developed the analogy to a penumbra, "the partial shadow surrounding a complete shadow (as in an eclipse)." Douglas found a right to privacy in the "penumbras" of the First, Third, Fourth, Fifth, and Ninth Amendments. Most scholars of the Constitution agree that some right to privacy does exist, but the extension of that right is open to debate.

soldiers "in any house" in time of peace without the consent of the owner is another facet of that privacy. The Fourth Amendment explicitly affirms the "right of the people to be secure in their persons, houses, papers, and effects, against unreasonable searches and seizures." The Fifth Amendment in its Self-Incrimination Clause enables the citizen to create a zone of privacy which government may not force him to surrender to his detriment. The Ninth Amendment provides: "The enumeration in the Constitution, of certain rights, shall not be construed to deny or disparage others retained by the people."

The Fourth and Fifth Amendments were described in *Boyd* v. *United States* . . . as protection against all governmental invasions "of the sanctity of a man's home and the privacies of life." We recently referred in *Mapp* v. *Ohio* . . . to the Fourth Amendment as creating a "right to privacy, no less important than any other right carefully and particularly reserved to the people." . . .

The present case, then, concerns a relationship lying within the zone of privacy created by several fundamental constitutional guarantees. And it concerns a law which, in forbidding the use of contraceptives rather than regulating their manufacture or sale, seeks to achieve its goals by means having a maximum destructive impact upon that relationship. Such a law cannot stand in light of the familiar principle, so often applied by this Court, that a "governmental purpose to control or prevent activities constitutionally subject to state regulation may not be achieved by means which sweep unnecessarily broadly and thereby invade the area of protected freedoms." *NAACP* v. *Alabama*. . . . Would we allow the police to search the sacred precincts of marital bedrooms for telltale signs of the use of contraceptives? The very idea is repulsive to the notions of privacy surrounding the marriage relationship.

We deal with a right to privacy older than the Bill of Rights—older than our political parties, older than our school system. Marriage is a coming together for better or for worse, hopefully enduring, and intimate to the degree of being sacred. It is an association that promotes a way of life, not causes; a harmony in living, not political faiths; a bilateral loyalty, not commercial or social projects. Yet it is an association for as noble a purpose as any involved in our prior decisions.

Mr. Justice Goldberg, whom the Chief Justice and Mr. Justice Brennan join, concurring:

I agree with the Court that Connecticut's birth-control law unconstitutionally intrudes upon the right of marital privacy, and I join in its opinion and judgment. Although I have not accepted the view that "due process" as used in the Fourteenth Amendment includes all of the first eight Amendments . . . I do agree that the concept of liberty protects those personal rights that are fundamental, and is not confined to the specific terms of the Bill of Rights. My conclusion that the concept of liberty is not so restricted and that it embraces the right of marital privacy though that right is not mentioned explicitly in the Constitution is supported both by numerous decisions of this Court, referred to in the Court's opinion, and by the language and history of the Ninth Amendment. In reaching the conclusion that the right of marital privacy is protected, as being within the protected penumbra of specific guarantees of the Bill of Rights, the Court refers to the Ninth Amendment. I add these words to emphasize the relevance of that Amendment to the Court's holding. . . . The Framers did not intend that the first eight amendments be construed to exhaust the basic and fundamental rights which the Constitution guaranteed to the people.

While this Court has had little occasion to interpret the Ninth Amendment "[i]t cannot be presumed that any clause in the constitution is intended to be without effect." *Marbury v. Madison.* . . . In interpreting the Constitution, "real effect should be given to all the words it uses." *Myers v. United States.* . . . The Ninth Amendment to the Constitution may be regarded by some as a recent discovery but since 1791 it has been a basic part of the Constitution which we are sworn to uphold. To hold that a right so basic and fundamental and so deep-rooted in our society as the right of privacy in marriage may be infringed because that right is not guaranteed in so many words by the first eight amendments to the Constitution is to ignore the Ninth Amendment and to give it no effect whatsoever. Moreover, a judicial construction that this fundamental right is not protected by the Constitution because it is not mentioned in explicit terms by one of the first eight amendments or elsewhere in the Constitution would violate the Ninth Amendment, which specifically states that "[t]he enumeration in the Constitution, of certain rights shall not be *construed* to deny or disparage others retained by the people." (Emphasis added.) . . . [T]he Ninth Amendment simply lends strong support to the view that the "liberty" protected by the Fifth and Fourteenth Amendments from infringement by the Federal Government or the States is not restricted to rights specifically mentioned in the first eight amendments. . . .

In sum, I believe that the right of privacy in the marital relation is fundamental and basic—a personal right "retained by the people" within the meaning of the Ninth Amendment. Connecticut cannot constitutionally abridge this fundamental right, which is protected by the Fourteenth Amendment from infringement by the States. I agree with the Court that petitioners' convictions must therefore be reversed.

Mr. Justice Black, with whom Mr. Justice Stewart joins, dissenting: . . .

The Court talks about a constitutional "right of privacy" as though there is some constitutional provision or provisions forbidding any law ever to be passed which might abridge the "privacy" of individuals. But there is not. . . .

One of the most effective ways of diluting or expanding a constitutionally guaranteed right is to substitute for the crucial word or words of a constitutional guarantee another word or words, more or less flexible and more or less restricted in meaning. This fact is well illustrated by the use of the term "right of privacy" as a comprehensive substitute for the Fourth Amendment's guarantee against "unreasonable searches and seizures." "Privacy" is a broad, abstract and ambiguous concept which can easily be shrunken in meaning but which can also, on the other hand, easily be interpreted as a constitutional ban against many things other than searches and seizures. I have expressed the view many times that First Amendment freedoms, for example, have suffered from a failure of the courts to stick to the simple language of the First Amendment in construing it, instead of invoking multitudes of words substituted for those the Framers used. For these reasons I get nowhere in this case by talk about a constitutional "right of privacy" as an emanation from one or more constitutional provisions. I like my privacy as well as the next one, but I am nevertheless compelled to admit that government has a right to invade it unless prohibited by some specific constitutional provision. For these reasons I cannot agree with the Court's judgment and the reasons it gives for holding this Connecticut law unconstitutional. . . .

My Brother Goldberg has adopted the recent discovery that the Ninth Amendment as well as the Due Process Clause can be used by this Court as authority to strike down all state legislation which this Court thinks violates "fundamental principles of liberty and justice," or is contrary to the "traditions and [collective] conscience of our people." He also states, without proof satisfactory to me, that in making decisions on this basis judges will not consider "their personal and private notions." One may ask how they can avoid considering them. Our Court certainly has no machinery with which to take a Gallup Poll. And the scientific miracles of this age have not yet produced a gadget which the Court can use to determine what traditions are rooted in the "[collective] conscience of our people." Moreover, one would certainly have to look far beyond the language of the Ninth Amendment to find that the Framers vested in this Court any such awesome veto powers over lawmaking, either by the States or by the Congress. Nor does anything in the history of the Amendment offer any support for such a shocking doctrine. The whole history of the adoption of the Constitution and Bill of Rights points the other way, and the very material quoted by my Brother Goldberg shows that the Ninth Amendment was intended to protect against the idea that "by enumerating particular exceptions to the grant of power" to the Federal Government, "those rights which were not singled out, were intended to be assigned into the hands of the General Government [the United States], and were consequently insecure." That Amendment was passed, not to broaden the powers of this Court or any other department of "the General Government," but, as every student of history knows, to assure the people that the Constitution in all its provisions was intended to limit the Federal Government to the powers granted expressly or by necessary implication. If any broad, unlimited power to hold laws unconstitutional because they offend what this Court conceives to be the "[collective] conscience of our people" is vested in this Court by the Ninth Amendment, the Fourteenth Amendment, or any other provision of the Constitution, it was not given by the Framers, but rather has been bestowed on the Court by the Court. This fact is perhaps responsible for the peculiar phenomenon that for a period of a century and a half no serious suggestion was ever made that the Ninth Amendment, enacted to protect state powers against federal invasion, could be used as a weapon of federal power to prevent state legislatures from passing laws they consider appropriate to govern local affairs. Use of any such broad, unbounded judicial authority would make of this Court's members a day-to-day constitutional convention. . . .

Questions for Discussion

1. Can a right be fundamental yet not enumerated in the Constitution?
2. Should the state ever have an interest in the relationships and actions between consenting adults? In what instances?

 3.5

Lawrence and Garner v. Texas (2003)

Although the 1965 *Griswold* decision provided a basis for claiming a constitutional right to privacy, and the 1973 *Roe* v. *Wade* holding built on that foundation, such a "right" remains a matter of contention. In 1986, the Supreme Court ruled, in *Bowers* v. *Hardwick*, that the "Federal Constitution confers [no] fundamental right upon homosexuals to engage in sodomy." Bowing to precedent, the Court rarely reverses itself after only seventeen years, but societal changes and the widespread (though scarcely unanimous) opinion that *Bowers* had been wrongfully decided led the justices to reconsider this decision in 2003. In the decision excerpted here, Justice Anthony Kennedy concludes that the Court failed to "appreciate the extent of the liberty at stake." In other words, it was the privacy to act within a personal relationship that was at stake, not the more limited question of sexual relations. He continues, "When sexuality finds overt expression in intimate conduct with another person, the conduct can be but one element in a personal bond that is more enduring. The liberty provided by the Constitution allows homosexual persons the right to make this choice."

At least three justices, various interests, and many other people disagree with the conclusion reached here. Justice Antonin Scalia's dissent is also excerpted below. In 2004 a movement was undertaken to revisit not only *Roe* and this case, but also to overturn the long-standing decision of *Griswold*, which remains the underpinning of the Court's interpretation of a core right of privacy.

J ustice Kennedy delivered the opinion of the Court.
        Liberty protects the person from unwarranted government intrusions into a dwelling or other private places. In our tradition the State is not omnipresent in the home. And there are other spheres of our lives and existence, outside the home, where the State should not be a dominant presence. Freedom extends beyond spatial bounds. Liberty presumes an autonomy of self that includes freedom of thought, belief, expression, and certain intimate conduct. The instant case involves liberty of the person both in its spatial and more transcendent dimensions.

I

The question before the Court is the validity of a Texas statute making it a crime for two persons of the same sex to engage in certain intimate sexual conduct.

In Houston, Texas, officers of the Harris County Police Department were dispatched to a private residence in response to a reported weapons disturbance. They entered an apartment where one of the petitioners, John Geddes Lawrence, resided. The right of the police to enter does not seem to have been questioned. The officers observed Lawrence and another man, Tyron Garner, engaging in a sexual act. The two petitioners were arrested, held in custody over night, and charged and convicted before a Justice of the Peace.

The complaints described their crime as "deviate sexual intercourse, namely anal sex, with a member of the same sex (man)." The applicable state law is Tex. Penal Code Ann. §21.06(a) (2003). It provides: "A person commits an offense if he engages in deviate sexual intercourse with another individual of the same sex." The statute defines "[d]eviate sexual intercourse" as follows:

> (A) any contact between any part of the genitals of one person and the mouth or anus of another person; or
> (B) the penetration of the genitals or the anus of another person with an object.

§21.01 (1).

The petitioners exercised their right to a trial *de novo* in Harris County Criminal Court. They challenged the statute as a violation of the Equal Protection Clause of the Fourteenth Amendment and of a like provision of the Texas Constitution. Tex. Const., Art. 1, §3a. Those contentions were rejected. The petitioners, having entered a plea of *nolo contendere*, were each fined $200 and assessed court costs of $141.25.

The Court of Appeals for the Texas Fourteenth District considered the petitioners' federal constitutional arguments under both the Equal Protection and Due Process Clauses of the Fourteenth Amendment. After hearing the case en banc the court, in a divided opinion, rejected the constitutional arguments and affirmed the convictions. The majority opinion indicates that the Court of Appeals considered our decision in *Bowers* v. *Hardwick* to be controlling on the federal due process aspect of the case. *Bowers* then being authoritative this was proper. . . .

II

We conclude the case should be resolved by determining whether the petitioners were free as adults to engage in the private conduct in the exercise of their liberty under the Due Process Clause of the Fourteenth Amendment to the Constitution. For this inquiry we deem it necessary to reconsider the Court's holding in *Bowers*. . . .

In *Griswold* the Court invalidated a state law prohibiting the use of drugs or devices of contraception and counseling or aiding and abetting the use of contraceptives. The Court described the protected interest as a right to privacy and placed emphasis on the marriage relation and the protected space of the marital bedroom.

After *Griswold* it was established that the right to make certain decisions regarding sexual conduct extends beyond the marital relationship. In *Eisenstadt* v. *Baird*, the Court invalidated a law prohibiting the distribution of contraceptives to unmarried persons. . . .

> It is true that in *Griswold* the right of privacy in question inhered in the marital relationship. . . . If the right of privacy means anything, it is the right of the *individual*, married or single, to be free from unwarranted governmental intrusion into matters so fundamentally affecting a person as the decision whether to bear or beget a child.

The opinions in *Griswold* and *Eisenstadt* were part of the background for the decision in *Roe* v. *Wade*. As is well known, the case involved a challenge to the Texas law prohibiting abortions, but the laws of other States were affected as well. Although the Court held the woman's rights were not absolute, her right to elect an abortion did have real and substantial protection as an exercise of her liberty under the Due Process Clause. . . .

In *Carey* v. *Population Services Int'l*, the Court confronted a New York law forbidding sale or distribution of contraceptive devices to persons under 16 years of age. Although there was no single opinion for the Court, the law was invalidated. Both *Eisenstadt* and *Carey*, as well as the holding and rationale in *Roe*, confirmed that the reasoning of *Griswold* could not be confined to the protection of rights of married adults. This was the state of the law with respect to some of the most relevant cases when the Court considered *Bowers* v. *Hardwick*. . . .

The Court began its substantive discussion in *Bowers* as follows: "The issue presented is whether the Federal Constitution confers a fundamental right upon homosexuals to engage in sodomy and hence invalidates the laws of the many States that still make such conduct illegal and have done so for a very long time." That statement, we now conclude, discloses the Court's own failure to appreciate the extent of the liberty at stake. To say that the issue in *Bowers* was simply the right to engage in certain sexual conduct demeans the claim the individual put forward, just as it would demean a married couple were it to be said marriage is simply about the right to have sexual intercourse. The laws involved in *Bowers* and here are, to be sure, statutes that purport to do no more than prohibit a particular sexual act. Their penalties and purposes, though, have more far-reaching consequences, touching upon the most private human conduct, sexual behavior, and in the most private of places, the home. The statutes do seek to control a personal relationship that, whether or not entitled to formal recognition in the law, is within the liberty of persons to choose without being punished as criminals. . . .

The policy of punishing consenting adults for private acts was not much discussed in the early legal literature. We can infer that one reason for this was the very private nature of the conduct. Despite the absence of prosecutions, there may have been periods in which there was public criticism of homosexuals as such and an insistence that the criminal laws be enforced to discourage their practices. But far from possessing "ancient roots," American laws targeting same-sex couples did not develop until the last third of the 20th century. The reported decisions concerning the prosecution of consensual, homosexual sodomy between adults for the years 1880–1995 are not always clear in the details, but a significant number involved conduct in a public place.

It was not until the 1970's that any State singled out same-sex relations for criminal prosecution, and only nine States have done so. . . .

In summary, the historical grounds relied upon in *Bowers* are more complex than the majority opinion and the concurring opinion by Chief Justice Burger indicate. Their historical premises are not without doubt and, at the very least, are overstated.

It must be acknowledged, of course, that the Court in *Bowers* was making the broader point that for centuries there have been powerful voices to condemn homosexual conduct as immoral. The condemnation has been shaped by religious beliefs, conceptions of right and acceptable behavior, and respect for the traditional family. For many persons these are not trivial concerns but profound and deep convictions accepted as ethical and moral principles to which they aspire and which thus determine the course of their lives. These considerations do not answer the question before us, however. The issue is whether the majority may use the power of the State to enforce these views on the whole society through operation of the criminal law. "Our obligation is to define the liberty of all, not to mandate our own moral code." *Planned Parenthood of Southeastern Pa. v. Casey.* . . .

In our own constitutional system the deficiencies in *Bowers* became even more apparent in the years following its announcement. The 25 States with laws prohibiting the relevant conduct referenced in the *Bowers* decision are reduced now to 13, of which 4 enforce their laws only against homosexual conduct. In those States where sodomy is still proscribed, whether for same-sex or heterosexual conduct, there is a pattern of nonenforcement with respect to consenting adults acting in private. The State of Texas admitted in 1994 that as of that date it had not prosecuted anyone under those circumstances. . . .

The rationale of *Bowers* does not withstand careful analysis. In his dissenting opinion in *Bowers* Justice Stevens came to these conclusions:

> Our prior cases make two propositions abundantly clear. First, the fact that the governing majority in a State has traditionally viewed a particular practice as immoral is not a sufficient reason for upholding a law prohibiting the practice; neither history nor tradition could save a law prohibiting miscegenation from constitutional attack. Second, individual decisions by married persons, concerning the intimacies of their physical relationship, even when not intended to produce offspring, are a form of "liberty" protected by the Due Process Clause of the Fourteenth Amendment. Moreover, this protection extends to intimate choices by unmarried as well as married persons.

Justice Stevens' analysis, in our view, should have been controlling in *Bowers* and should control here.

Bowers was not correct when it was decided, and it is not correct today. It ought not to remain binding precedent. *Bowers* v. *Hardwick* should be and now is overruled.

The present case does not involve minors. It does not involve persons who might be injured or coerced or who are situated in relationships where consent might not easily be refused. It does not involve public conduct or prostitution. It does not involve whether the government must give formal recognition to any relationship that homosexual persons seek to enter. The case does involve two adults who, with full and mutual consent from each other, engaged in sexual practices common to a homosexual lifestyle. The petitioners are entitled to respect for their private lives. The State cannot demean their existence or control their destiny by making their private sexual conduct a crime. Their right to liberty under the Due Process Clause gives them the full right to engage in their conduct without intervention of the government. "It is a promise of the Constitution that there is a realm of personal liberty which the government may not enter." *Casey*. The Texas statute furthers no legitimate state interest which can justify its intrusion into the personal and private life of the individual.

Had those who drew and ratified the Due Process Clauses of the Fifth Amendment or the Fourteenth Amendment known the components of liberty in its manifold possibilities, they might have been more specific. They did not presume to have this insight. They knew times can blind us to certain truths and later generations can see that laws once thought necessary and proper in fact serve only to oppress. As the Constitution endures, persons in every generation can invoke its principles in their own search for greater freedom.

The judgment of the Court of Appeals for the Texas Fourteenth District is reversed, and the case is remanded for further proceedings not inconsistent with this opinion.

It is so ordered.

Justice Scalia, with whom The Chief Justice and Justice Thomas join, dissenting.

. . . Texas Penal Code Ann. §21.06(a) (2003) undoubtedly imposes constraints on liberty. So do laws prohibiting prostitution, recreational use of heroin, and, for that matter, working more than 60 hours per week in a bakery. But there is no right to "liberty" under the Due Process Clause, though today's opinion repeatedly makes that claim. ("The liberty protected by the Constitution allows homosexual persons the right to make this choice"); ("'These matters . . . are central to the liberty protected by the Fourteenth Amendment'"); ("Their right to liberty under the Due Process Clause gives them the full right to engage in their conduct without intervention of the government"). The Fourteenth Amendment *expressly allows* States to deprive their citizens of "liberty," *so long as "due process of law" is provided:*

> No state shall . . . deprive any person of life, liberty, or property, *without due process of law*. Amdt. 14 (emphasis added).

Our opinions applying the doctrine known as "substantive due process" hold that the Due Process Clause prohibits States from infringing *fundamental* liberty interests, unless the infringement is narrowly tailored to serve a compelling state interest. We have held repeatedly, in cases the Court today does not overrule, that *only* fundamental rights qualify for this so-called "heightened scrutiny" protection—that is, rights which are " 'deeply rooted in this Nation's history and tradition.' " All other liberty interests may be abridged or abrogated pursuant to a validly enacted state law if that law is rationally related to a legitimate state interest.

Bowers held, first, that criminal prohibitions of homosexual sodomy are not subject to heightened scrutiny because they do not implicate a "fundamental right" under the Due Process Clause. Noting that "[p]roscriptions against that conduct have ancient roots," that "[s]odomy was a criminal offense at common law and was forbidden by the laws of the original 13 States when they ratified the Bill of Rights," and that many States had retained their bans on sodomy, *Bowers* concluded that a right to engage in homosexual sodomy was not "'deeply rooted in this Nation's history and tradition.'"

The Court today does not overrule this holding. Not once does it describe homosexual sodomy as a "fundamental right" or a "fundamental liberty interest," nor does it subject the Texas statute to strict scrutiny. Instead, having failed to establish that the right to homosexual sodomy is "'deeply rooted in this Nation's history and tradition,'" the Court concludes that the application of Texas's statute to petitioners' conduct fails the rational-basis test, and overrules *Bowers'* holding to the contrary. "The Texas statute furthers no legitimate state interest which can justify its intrusion into the personal and private life of the individual." . . .

Today's opinion is the product of a Court, which is the product of a law-profession culture, that has largely signed on to the so-called homosexual agenda, by which I mean the agenda promoted by some homosexual activists directed at eliminating the moral opprobrium that has traditionally attached to homosexual conduct. I noted in an earlier opinion the fact that the American Association of Law Schools (to which any reputable law school *must* seek to belong) excludes from membership any school that refuses to ban from its job-interview facilities a law firm (no matter how small) that does not wish to hire as a prospective partner a person who openly engages in homosexual conduct.

One of the most revealing statements in today's opinion is the Court's grim warning that the criminalization of homosexual conduct is "an invitation to subject homosexual persons to discrimination both in the public and in the private spheres." It is clear from this that the Court has taken sides in the culture war, departing from its role of assuring, as neutral observer, that the democratic rules of engagement are observed. Many Americans do not want persons who openly engage in homosexual conduct as partners in their business, as scout-masters for their children, as teachers in their children's schools, or as boarders in their home. They view this as protecting themselves and their families from a lifestyle that they believe to be immoral and destructive. The Court views it as "discrimination" which it is the function of our judgments to deter. So imbued is the Court with the law profession's anti-anti-homosexual culture, that it is seemingly unaware that the attitudes of that culture are not obviously "mainstream"; that in most States what the Court calls "discrimination" against those who engage in homosexual acts is perfectly legal; that proposals to ban such "discrimination" under Title VII have repeatedly been rejected by Congress; that in some cases such "discrimination" is *mandated* by federal statute, see 10 U. S. C. §654(b)(1) (mandating discharge from the armed forces of any service member who engages in or intends to engage in homosexual acts); and that in some cases such "discrimination" is a constitutional right.

Let me be clear that I have nothing against homosexuals, or any other group, promoting their agenda through normal democratic means. Social perceptions of sexual and other morality change over time, and every group has the right to persuade its fellow citizens that its view of such matters is the best. That homosexuals have achieved some success in that enterprise is attested to by the fact that Texas is one of the few remaining States that criminalize private, consensual homosexual acts. But persuading one's fellow citizens is one thing, and imposing one's views in absence of democratic majority will is something else. I would no more *require* a State to criminalize homosexual acts—or, for that matter, display *any* moral disapprobation of them—than I would *forbid* it to do so. What Texas has chosen to do is well within the range of traditional democratic action, and its hand should not be stayed through the invention of a brand-new "constitutional right" by a Court that is impatient of democratic change. It is indeed true that "later generations can see that laws once thought necessary and proper in fact serve only to oppress"; and when that happens, later generations can repeal those laws. But it is the premise of our system that those judgments are to be made by the people, and not imposed by a governing caste that knows best.

One of the benefits of leaving regulation of this matter to the people rather than to the courts is that the people, unlike judges, need not carry things to their logical conclusion. The people may feel that their disapproval of homosexual conduct is strong enough to disallow homosexual marriage, but not strong enough to criminalize private homosexual acts—and may legislate accordingly. The Court today pretends that it possesses a similar freedom of action, so that that we need not fear judicial imposition of homosexual marriage, as has recently occurred in Canada (in a decision that the Canadian Government has chosen not to appeal). At the end of its opinion—after having laid waste the foundations of our rational-basis jurisprudence—the Court says that the present case "does not involve whether the government must give formal recognition to any relationship that homosexual persons seek to enter." Do not believe it. More illuminating than this bald, unreasoned disclaimer is the progression of thought displayed by an earlier passage in the Court's opinion, which notes the constitutional protections afforded to "personal decisions relating to *marriage*, procreation, contraception, family relationships, child rearing, and education," and then declares that "[p]ersons in a homosexual relationship may seek autonomy for these purposes, just as heterosexual persons do." Today's opinion dismantles the structure of constitutional law that has permitted a distinction to be made between heterosexual and homosexual unions, insofar as formal recognition in marriage is concerned. If moral disapprobation of homosexual conduct is "no legitimate state interest" for purposes of proscribing that conduct; and if, as the Court coos (casting aside all pretense of neutrality), "[w]hen sexuality finds overt expression in intimate conduct with another person, the conduct can be but one element in a personal bond that is more enduring"; what justification could there possibly be for denying the benefits of marriage to homosexual couples exercising "[t]he liberty protected by the Constitution"? Surely not the encouragement of procreation, since the sterile and the elderly are allowed to marry. This case "does not involve" the issue of homosexual marriage only if one entertains the belief that principle and logic have nothing to do with the decisions of this Court. Many will hope that, as the Court comfortingly assures us, this is so.

The matters appropriate for this Court's resolution are only three: Texas's prohibition of sodomy neither infringes a "fundamental right" (which the Court does not dispute), nor is unsupported by a rational relation to what the Constitution considers a legitimate state interest, nor denies the equal protection of the laws. I dissent.

Questions for Discussion

1. Conservatives often desire that government not expand its powers to affect the lives of ordinary citizens. Why would they not embrace a "right of privacy" that had achieved constitutional status?
2. How does the decision in this case flow from *Griswold*? Some legislators have suggested that *Griswold* should be overturned. What implications would such a ruling have for this case?

 3.6

Rights, Liberties, and Security: Recalibrating the Balance After September 11

Stuart Taylor Jr.

Since the 9/11 terrorist attacks, both governmental officials and the public at large have had to reassess the proper balancing point between two core values—security and liberty. Americans prize freedom and individual liberty, to be sure, but they also understand that, in Harvard Law professor Lawrence Tribe's words, "the Constitution is not a suicide pact." That is, when faced with real dangers to society, the government must restrike the balance between liberty and security. To some extent, this is unexceptionable. We all put up with more inconvenience at airports, and few object when security is tightened at ports or nuclear plants.

At the same time, civil libertarians have grown increasingly uneasy over various data-collecting provisions in the Patriot Act, which contains few limits on federal investigations of "national security" matters, and which would open up various records (such as library checkouts) to scrutiny.

In this article, Stuart Taylor Jr. calmly assesses the tradeoffs between enhancing security and protecting individual liberties. He rejects alarmism over the loss of rights, relative to the government's need to protect its citizens. Taylor argues that civil libertarians will be better off by welcoming more stringent security measures, which may well prevent another major attack—an event that might produce far more aggressive restraints on Americans' freedoms. No alarmist, Taylor addresses central issues of how a nation can protect itself, while retaining as many liberties as possible.

When dangers increase, liberties shrink. That has been our history, especially in wartime. And today we face dangers without precedent: a mass movement of militant Islamic terrorists who crave martyrdom, hide in shadows, are fanatically bent on slaughtering as many of us as possible and—if they can—using nuclear truck bombs to obliterate New York or Washington or both, without leaving a clue as to the source of the attack.

How can we avert catastrophe and hold down the number of lesser mass murders? Our best hope is to prevent al-Qaida from getting nuclear, biological, or chemical weapons and [smuggling] them into this country. But we need be unlucky only once to fail in that. Ultimately we can hold down our casualties only by finding and locking up (or killing) as many as possible of the hundreds or thousands of possible al-Qaida terrorists whose strategy is to infiltrate our society and avoid attention until they strike.

The urgency of penetrating secret terrorist cells makes it imperative for Congress—and the nation—to undertake a candid, searching, and systematic reassessment of the civil liberties rules that restrict the government's core investigative and detention powers. Robust national debate and deliberate congressional action should replace what has so far been largely ad hoc presidential improvisation. While the USA-PATRIOT Act—no model of careful deliberation—changed many rules for the better (and some for the worse), it did not touch some others that should be changed.*

Carefully crafted new legislation would be good not only for security but also for liberty. Stubborn adherence to the civil liberties status quo would probably damage our most fundamental freedoms far more in the long run than would judicious modifications of rules that are less fundamental. Considered congressional action based on open national debate is more likely to be sensitive to civil liberties and to the Constitution's checks and balances than unilateral expansion of executive power. Courts are more likely to check executive excesses if Congress sets limits for them to enforce. Government agents are more likely to respect civil liberties if freed from rules that create unwarranted obstacles to doing their jobs. And preventing terrorist mass murders is the best way of avoiding a panicky stampede into truly oppressive police statism, in which measures now unthinkable could suddenly become unstoppable. . . .

Stuart Taylor writes a regular column on public affairs, often focusing on legal issues, for *National Journal*.

Stuart Taylor Jr. "Rights, Liberties, and Security: Recalibrating the Balance After September 11, 2001," *The Brookings Review* 21, no. 1 (Winter 2003): 25–31. Reprinted by permission of The Brookings Institution.

*The Patriot Act was signed into law on October 26, 2001, forty-five days after the 9/11 terrorist attacks.

Recalibrating the Liberty-Security Balance

The courts, Congress, the president, and the public have from the beginning of this nation's history demarcated the scope of protected rights "by a weighing of competing interests . . . the public-safety interest and the liberty interest," in the words of Judge Richard A. Posner of the U.S. Court of Appeals for the Seventh Circuit. "The safer the nation feels, the more weight judges will be willing to give to the liberty interest."

During the 1960s and 1970s, the weight on the public safety side of the scales seemed relatively modest. The isolated acts of violence by groups like the Weather Underground and Black Panthers—which had largely run their course by the mid-1970s—were a minor threat compared with our enemies today. Suicide bombers were virtually unheard of. By contrast, the threat to civil liberties posed by broad governmental investigative and detention powers and an imperial presidency had been dramatized by Watergate and by disclosures of such ugly abuses of power as FBI Director J. Edgar Hoover's spying on politicians, his wiretapping and harassment of the Rev. Martin Luther King, Jr., and the government's disruption and harassment of antiwar and radical groups.

To curb such abuses, the Supreme Court, Congress, and the Ford and Carter administrations placed tight limits on law enforcement and intelligence agencies. . . . Congress barred warrantless wiretaps and searches of suspected foreign spies and terrorists—a previously untrammeled presidential power—in the 1978 Foreign Intelligence Surveillance Act. And Edward Levi, President Ford's attorney general, clamped down on domestic surveillance by the FBI.

As a result, today many of the investigative powers that government could use to penetrate al-Qaida cells—surveillance, informants, searches, seizures, wiretaps, arrests, interrogations, detentions—are tightly restricted by a web of laws, judicial precedents, and administrative rules. Stalked in our homeland by the deadliest terrorists in history, we are armed with investigative powers calibrated largely for dealing with drug dealers, bank robbers, burglars, and ordinary murderers. We are also stuck in habits of mind that have not yet fully processed how dangerous our world has become or how ill-prepared our legal regime is to meet the new dangers.

Rethinking Government's Powers

Only a handful of the standard law-enforcement investigative techniques have much chance of penetrating and defanging groups like al-Qaida. The four most promising are: infiltrating them through informants and undercover agents; finding them and learning their plans through surveillance, searches, and wiretapping; detaining them before they can launch terrorist attacks; and interrogating those detained. All but the first (infiltration) are now so tightly restricted by Supreme Court precedents (sometimes by mistaken or debatable readings of them), statutes, and administrative rules as to seriously impede terrorism investigators. Careful new legislation could make these powers more flexible and useful while simultaneously setting boundaries to minimize overuse and abuse.

Searches and Surveillance

The Supreme Court's caselaw involving the Fourth Amendment's ban on "unreasonable searches and seizures" does not distinguish clearly between a routine search for stolen goods or marijuana and a preventive search for a bomb or a vial of anthrax. . . .

Federal agents and local police alike need more specific guidance than the Supreme Court can quickly supply. Congress should provide it, in the form of legislation relaxing for terrorism investigations the restrictions on searching, seizing, and wiretapping, including the undue stringency of the burden of proof to obtain a search warrant in a terrorism investigation.

Search and seizure restrictions were the main (if widely unrecognized) cause of the FBI's famous failure to seek a warrant during the weeks before September 11 to search the computer and other possessions of Zacarias Moussaoui, the alleged "20th hijacker." He had been locked up since August 16, technically for overstaying his visa, based on a tip about his strange behavior at a Minnesota flight school. The FBI had ample reason to suspect that Moussaoui—who has since admitted to being a member of al-Qaida—was a dangerous Islamic militant plotting airline terrorism.

Congressional and journalistic investigations of the Moussaoui episode have focused on the intelligence agencies' failure to put together the Moussaoui evidence with other intelligence reports that should have alerted them that a broad plot to hijack airliners might be afoot. Investigators have virtually ignored the undue stringency of the legal restraints on the government's powers to investigate suspected terrorists. Until these are fixed, they will seriously hobble our intelligence agencies no matter how smart they are.

From the time of FDR until 1978, the government could have searched Moussaoui's possessions without judicial permission, by invoking the president's inherent power to collect intelligence about foreign enemies. But the 1978 Foreign Intelligence Security Act (FISA) barred searches of suspected foreign spies and terrorists unless the attorney general could obtain a warrant from a special national security court (the FISA court). The warrant application has to show not only that the target is a foreign terrorist, but also that he is a member of some international terrorist "group." . . .

[I]t is clear that FISA—even as amended by the USA-PATRIOT Act—would not authorize a warrant in any case in which the FBI cannot tie a suspected foreign terrorist to one or more confederates, whether because his confederates have escaped detection or cannot be identified or because the suspect is a lone wolf.

Congress could strengthen the hand of FBI terrorism investigators by amending FISA to include the commonsense presumption that any foreign terrorist who comes to the United States is probably acting for (or at least inspired by) some international terrorist group. Another option would be to lower the burden of proof from "probable cause" to "reasonable suspicion." A third option—which could be extended to domestic as well as international terrorism investigations—would be to authorize a warrantless "preventive" search or wiretap of anyone the government has reasonable grounds to suspect of preparing or helping others prepare for a terrorist attack. To minimize any temptation for government agents to use this new power in pursuit of ordinary criminal suspects, Congress could prohibit the use in any prosecution unrelated to terrorism of any evidence obtained by such a preventive search or wiretap. . . .

Exaggerated Fear of Big Brother

Proposals to increase the government's wiretapping powers awaken fears of unleashing Orwellian thought police to spy on, harass, blackmail, and smear political dissenters and others. Libertarians point out that most conversations overheard and e-mails intercepted in the war on terrorism will be innocent and that the tappers and buggers will overhear intimacies and embarrassing disclosures that are none of the government's business.

Such concerns argue for taking care to broaden wiretapping and surveillance powers only as much as seems reasonable to prevent terrorist acts. But broader wiretapping authority is not all bad for civil liberties. It is a more accurate and benign method of penetrating terrorist cells than the main alternative, which is planting and recruiting informers—a dangerous, ugly, and unreliable business in which the government is already free to engage without limit. The narrower the government's surveillance powers, the more it will rely on informants. . . .

To keep the specter of Big Brother in perspective, it's worth recalling that the president had unlimited power to wiretap suspected foreign spies and terrorists until 1978 (when FISA was adopted); if this devastated privacy or liberty, hardly anyone noticed. It's also worth noting that despite the government's already-vast power to comb through computerized records of our banking and commercial transactions and much else that we do in the computer age, the vast majority of the people who have seen their privacy or reputations shredded have not been wronged by rogue officials. They have been wronged by media organizations, which do far greater damage to far more people with far less accountability.

Nineteen years ago, in *The Rise of the Computer State*, David Burnham wrote: "The question looms before us: Can the United States continue to flourish and grow in an age when the physical movements, individual purchases, conversations and meetings of every citizen are constantly under surveillance by private companies and government agencies?" It can. It has. And now that the computer state has risen indeed, the threat of being watched by Big Brother or smeared by the FBI seems a lot smaller than the threat of being blown to bits or poisoned by terrorists.

The Case for Coercive Interrogation

. . . We all know the drill. Before asking any questions, FBI agents (and police) must warn the suspect: "You have a right to remain silent." And if the suspect asks for a lawyer, all interrogation must cease until the lawyer arrives (and tells the suspect to keep quiet). This seems impossible to justify when dealing with people suspected of planning mass murder. But it's the law, isn't it?

Actually, it's not the law, though many judges think it is, along with most lawyers, federal agents, police, and cop-show mavens. You do *not* have a right to remain silent. The most persuasive interpretation of the Constitution and the Supreme Court's precedents is that agents and police are free to interrogate any suspect without *Miranda** warnings; to spurn requests for a lawyer; to press hard for answers; and—at least in a terrorism investigation—perhaps even to use hours of interrogation, verbal abuse, isolation, blindfolds, polygraph tests, death-penalty threats, and other forms of psychological coercion short of torture or physical brutality. Maybe even truth serum.

The Fifth Amendment self-incrimination clause says only that no person "shall be compelled in any criminal case to be a witness against himself." The clause prohibits forcing a defendant to testify at his trial and also making him a witness against himself indirectly by using compelled pretrial statements. It does not prohibit compelling a suspect to talk. *Miranda* held only that in determining whether a defendant's statements (and information derived from them) may be used against him at his trial, courts must treat all interrogations of arrested suspects as inherently coercive unless the warnings are given. . . .

Fortunately for terrorism investigators, the Supreme Court said in 1990 that "a constitutional violation [of the Fifth Amendment's self-incrimination clause] occurs only at trial." It cited an earlier ruling that the government can obtain court orders compelling reluctant witnesses to talk and can imprison them for contempt of court if they refuse, if it first guarantees them immunity from prosecution on the basis of their statements or any derivative evidence. These decisions support the conclusion that the self-incrimination clause "does not forbid the forcible extraction of information but only the use of informa-

---

*In 1963, Ernesto Miranda was accused of kidnapping and rape. He subsequently confessed, but was not informed of his right to counsel. The Supreme Court ruled his conviction unconstitutional in 1966, but the circumstances of receiving a *Miranda* warning remain under scrutiny by the Supreme Court in the post-2000 era.

tion so extracted as evidence in a criminal case," as a federal appeals court ruled in 1992.

Of course, even when the primary reason for questioning a suspected terrorist is prevention, the government could pay a heavy cost for ignoring *Miranda* and using coercive interrogation techniques, because it would sometimes find it difficult or impossible to prosecute extremely dangerous terrorists. But terrorism investigators may be able to get their evidence and use it too, if the Court—or Congress, which unlike the Court would not have to wait for a proper case to come along—extends a 1984 precedent creating what the justices called a "public safety" exception to *Miranda*. That decision allowed use at trial of a defendant's incriminating answer to a policeman's demand (before any *Miranda* warnings) to know where his gun was hidden. . . .

Congress should neither wait for the justices to clarify the law nor assume that they will reach the right conclusions without prodding. It should make the rules as clear as possible as soon as possible. Officials . . . need to know that they are free to interrogate suspected terrorists more aggressively than they suppose. While a law expanding the public safety exception to *Miranda* would be challenged as unconstitutional, it would contradict no existing Supreme Court precedent and—if carefully calibrated to apply only when the immediate purpose is to save lives—would probably be upheld. . . .

Bringing Preventive Detention Inside the Law

Of all the erosions of civil liberties that must be considered after September 11, preventive detention—incarcerating people because of their perceived dangerousness even when they are neither convicted nor charged with any crime—would represent the sharpest departure from centuries of Anglo-American jurisprudence and come closest to police statism.

But the case for some kind of preventive detention has never been as strong. Al-Qaida's capacity to inflict catastrophic carnage dwarfs any previous domestic security threat. Its "sleeper" agents are trained to avoid criminal activities that might arouse suspicion. So the careful ones cannot be arrested on criminal charges until it is too late. And their lust for martyrdom renders criminal punishment ineffective as a deterrent. . . .

What should the government do when it is convinced of a suspect's terrorist intent but lacks admissible evidence of any crime? Or when a criminal trial would blow vital intelligence secrets? Or when ambiguous evidence makes it a tossup whether a suspect is harmless or an al-Qaidan? What should it do with suspects like Jose Padilla, who was arrested in Chicago and is now in military detention because he is suspected of (but not charged with) plotting a radioactive "dirty-bomb" attack on Washington, D.C.? Or with a (hypothetical) Pakistani graduate student in chemistry, otherwise unremarkable, who has downloaded articles about how terrorists might use small planes to start an anthrax epidemic and shown an intense but unexplained interest in crop-dusters?

Only four options exist. Let such suspects go about their business unmoni-tored until (perhaps) they commit mass murders; assign agents to tail them until (perhaps) they give the agents the slip; bring prosecutions without solid evidence and risk acquittals; and preventive detention. The latter could theo-retically include not only incarceration but milder restraints such as house ar-rest or restriction to certain areas combined with agreement to carry (or to be implanted with) a device enabling the government to track the suspect's move-ments at all times. . . .

As Alan Dershowitz notes, "[N]o civilized nation confronting serious danger has ever relied exclusively on criminal convictions for past offenses. Every country has introduced, by one means or another, a system of preventive or ad-ministrative detention for persons who are thought to be dangerous but who might not be convictable under the conventional criminal law." . . .

[T]he dangers of punishing dissident speech, guilt by association, and overuse of preventive detention could be controlled by careful legislation. This would not be the first exception to the general rule against preventive detention. The others have worked fairly well. They include pretrial detention without bail of criminal defendants found to be dangerous, civil commitment of people found dangerous by reason of mental illness, and medical quarantines, a practice that may once again be necessary in the event of bioterrorism. All in all, the danger that a preventive detention regime for suspected terrorists would take us too far down the slippery slope toward police statism is simply not as bad as the danger of letting would-be mass murderers roam the country.

In any event, we already have a preventive detention regime for suspected international terrorists—three regimes, in fact, all created and controlled by the Bush administration without congressional input. First, two U.S. citizens—Jose Padilla, the suspected would-be dirty bomber arrested in Chicago, and Yaser Esam Hamdi, a Louisiana-born Saudi Arabian captured in Afghanistan and taken first to Guantanamo—have been in military brigs in this country for many months without being charged with any crime or allowed to see any lawyer or any judge. The administration claims that it never has to prove any-thing to anyone. It says that even U.S. citizens arrested in this country—who may have far stronger grounds than battlefield detainees for denying that they are enemy combatants—are entitled to no due process whatever once the gov-ernment puts that label on them. This argument is virtually unprecedented, wrong as a matter of law, and indefensible as a matter of policy.

Second, Attorney General John Ashcroft rounded up more than 1,100 mostly Muslim noncitizens in the fall of 2001, which involved preventive de-tention in many cases although they were charged with immigration violations or crimes (mostly minor) or held under the material witness statute. This when-in-doubt-detain approach effectively reversed the presumption of inno-cence in the hope of disrupting any planned followup attacks. We may never know whether it succeeded in this vital objective. But the legal and moral bases for holding hundreds of apparently harmless detainees, sometimes without access to legal counsel, in conditions of unprecedented secrecy, seemed less and less plausible as weeks and months went by. Worse, the administration treated many (if not most) of the detainees shabbily and some abusively. (By mid-2002, the vast majority had been deported or released.)

Third, the Pentagon has incarcerated hundreds of Arab and other prisoners captured in Afghanistan at Guantanamo, apparently to avoid the jurisdiction of all courts—and has refused to create a fair, credible process for determining which are in fact enemy combatants and which of those are "unlawful."

These three regimes have been implemented with little regard for the law, for the rights of the many (mostly former) detainees who are probably innocent, or for international opinion. It is time for Congress to step in—to authorize a regime of temporary preventive detention for suspected international terrorists, while circumscribing that regime and specifying strong safeguards against abuse.

Civil Liberties for a New Era

It is senseless to adhere to overly broad restrictions imposed by decades-old civil-liberties rules when confronting the threat of unprecedented carnage at the hands of modern terrorists. In the words of Harvard Law School's Laurence H. Tribe, "The old adage that it is better to free 100 guilty men than to imprison one innocent describes a calculus that our Constitution—which is no suicide pact—does not impose on government when the 100 who are freed belong to terrorist cells that slaughter innocent civilians, and may well have access to chemical, biological, or nuclear weapons." The question is not whether we should increase governmental power to meet such dangers. The question is how much.

Questions for Discussion

1. Should the rules for pursuing terrorists be different from those for pursuing drug dealers or bank robbers? Why or why not? What are the dangers in taking a more aggressive approach, even when it may be essential?
2. Taylor advocates the limited use of "preventive detention" for suspected international terrorists. Can this extreme measure be squared with the ordinary constitutional guarantees of a speedy trial, due process, and protection against self-incrimination?

3.7

Brown v. Board of Education (1954; 1955)

No single contemporary court case has had more widespread impact than *Brown* v. *Board of Education* (1954; 1955). The 1954 case consolidated four suits, from Kansas, South Carolina, Virginia, and Delaware; each state mandated the separate schooling of children by race. The lead case was brought by Oliver Brown, whose daughter Linda attended an all-black school twenty-one blocks from her Topeka home, each day passing by an all-white school five blocks away. In *Brown*, the Court unanimously ruled that such legalized practices were unconstitutional.

The 1954 decision promised so much social change that the justice reheard the case a year later to consider how it should be implemented. In the process, Chief Justice Earl Warren coined the ambiguous phrase "with all deliberate speed" to describe how desegregation should be ended. Warren was sensitive to the fact that the Court cannot easily enforce its decisions, especially when they are controversial and require substantial changes in both laws and patterns of behavior.

1954

Mr. Chief Justice Warren delivered the opinion of the Court.

These cases come to us from the States of Kansas, South Carolina, Virginia, and Delaware. They are premised on different facts and different local conditions, but a common legal question justifies their consideration together in this consolidated opinion.

In each of the cases, minors of the Negro race, through their legal representatives, seek the aid of the courts in obtaining admission to the public schools of their community on a nonsegregated basis. In each instance, they had been denied admission to schools attended by white children under laws requiring or permitting segregation according to race. This segregation was alleged to deprive the plaintiffs of the equal protection of the laws under the Fourteenth Amendment. In each of the cases other than the Delaware case, a three-judge federal district court denied relief to the plaintiffs on the so-called "separate but equal" doctrine announced by this Court in *Plessy* v. *Ferguson*. . . . Under that doctrine, equality of treatment is accorded when the races are provided substantially equal facilities even though these facilities be separate. In the Delaware case, the Supreme Court of Delaware adhered to that doctrine, but ordered that the plaintiffs be admitted to the white schools because of their superiority to the Negro schools.

The plaintiffs contend that segregated public schools are not "equal" and cannot be made "equal," and that hence they are deprived of the equal protection of the laws. Because of the obvious importance of the question presented, the Court took jurisdiction. Argument was heard in the 1952 Term, and reargument was heard this Term on certain questions propounded by the Court.

Reargument was largely devoted to the circumstances surrounding the adoption of the Fourteenth Amendment in 1868. It covered exhaustively consideration of the Amendment in Congress, ratification by the states, then existing practices in racial segregation, and the views of proponents and opponents of the Amendment. This discussion and our own investigation convince us that, although these sources cast some light, it is not enough to resolve the problem with which we are faced. At best, they are inconclusive. The most avid proponents of the post-War Amendments undoubtedly intended them to remove all legal distinctions among "all persons born or naturalized in the United States." Their opponents, just as certainly were antagonistic to both the letter and the spirit of the Amendments and wished them to have the most limited effect. What others in Congress and the state legislatures had in mind cannot be determined with any degree of certainty.

An additional reason for the inconclusive nature of the Amendment's history, with respect to segregated schools, is the status of public education at that time. In the South, the movement toward free common schools, supported by general taxation, had not yet taken hold. Education of white children was largely in the hands of private groups. Education of Negroes was almost nonexistent, and practically all of the race were illiterate. In fact, any education of Negroes was forbidden by law in some states. Today, in contrast, many Negroes have achieved outstanding success in the arts and sciences as well as in the business and professional world. It is true that public education had already advanced further in the North, but the effect of the Amendment on Northern States was generally ignored in the congressional debates. Even in the North, the conditions of public education did not approximate those existing today. The curriculum was usually rudimentary; ungraded schools were common in rural areas; the school term was but three months a year in many states; and compulsory school attendance was virtually unknown. As a consequence, it is not surprising that there should be so little in the history of the Fourteenth Amendment relating to its intended effect on public education.

In the first cases in this Court construing the Fourteenth Amendment, decided shortly after its adoption, the Court interpreted it as proscribing all state-imposed discriminations against the Negro race. The doctrine of "separate but equal" did not make its appearance in this court until 1896 in the case of *Plessy*

v. *Ferguson*, *supra*, involving not education but transportation. American courts have since labored with the doctrine for over half a century. In this Court, there have been six cases involving the "separate but equal" doctrine in the field of public education. In *Cumming* v. *County Board of Education* . . . and *Gong Lum* v. *Rice* . . . , the validity of the doctrine itself was not challenged. In more recent cases, all on the graduate school level, inequality was found in that specific benefits enjoyed by white students were denied to Negro students of the same educational qualifications. *Missouri* ex rel. *Gaines* v. *Canada*; *Sipuel* v. *Oklahoma*; *Sweatt* v. *Painter*; *McLaurin* v. *Oklahoma State Regents*. In none of these cases was it necessary to reexamine the doctrine to grant relief to the Negro plaintiff. And in *Sweatt* v. *Painter*, *supra*, the Court expressly reserved decision on the question whether *Plessy* v. *Ferguson* should be held inapplicable to public education.

In the instant cases, that question is directly presented. Here, unlike *Sweatt* v. *Painter*, there are findings below that the Negro and white schools involved have been equalized, or are being equalized, with respect to buildings, curricula, qualifications and salaries of teachers, and other "tangible" factors. Our decision, therefore, cannot turn on merely a comparison of these tangible factors in the Negro and white schools involved in each of the cases. We must look instead to the effect of segregation itself on public education.

In approaching this problem, we cannot turn the clock back to 1868 when the Amendment was adopted, or even to 1896 when *Plessy* v. *Ferguson* was written. We must consider public education in the light of its full development and its present place in American life throughout the Nation. Only in this way can it be determined if segregation in public schools deprives these plaintiffs of the equal protection of the laws.

Today, education is perhaps the most important function of state and local governments. Compulsory school attendance laws and the great expenditures for education both demonstrate our recognition of the importance of education to our democratic society. It is required in the performance of our most basic public responsibilities, even service in the armed forces. It is the very foundation of good citizenship. Today it is a principal instrument in awakening the child to cultural values, in preparing him for later professional training, and in helping him to adjust normally to his environment. In these days, it is doubtful that any child may reasonably be expected to succeed in life if he is denied the opportunity of an education. Such an opportunity, where the state has undertaken to provide it, is a right which must be made available to all on equal terms.

We come then to the question presented: Does segregation of children in public schools solely on the basis of race, even though the physical facilities and other "tangible" factors may be equal, deprive the children of the minority group of equal educational opportunities? We believe that it does.

In *Sweatt* v. *Painter*, *supra*, in finding that a segregated law school for Negroes could not provide them equal educational opportunities, this Court relied in large part on "those qualities which are incapable of objective measurement but which make for greatness in a law school." In *McLaurin* v. *Oklahoma State*

Regents, supra, the Court, in requiring that a Negro admitted to a white graduate school be treated like all other students, again resorted to intangible considerations: ". . . his ability to study, to engage in discussions and exchange views with other students, and, in general, to learn his profession." Such considerations apply with added force to children in grade and high schools. To separate them from others of similar age and qualifications solely because of their race generates a feeling of inferiority as to their status in the community that may affect their hearts and minds in a way unlikely ever to be undone. The effect of this separation on their educational opportunities was well stated by a finding in the Kansas case by a court which nevertheless felt compelled to rule against the Negro plaintiffs:

> Segregation of white and colored children in public schools has a detrimental effect upon the colored children. The impact is greater when it has the sanction of the law; for the policy of separating the races is usually interpreted as denoting the inferiority of the Negro group. A sense of inferiority affects the motivation of a child to learn. Segregation with the sanction of law, therefore, has a tendency to retard the educational and mental development of Negro children and to deprive them of some of the benefits they would receive in a racially integrated school system.

Whatever may have been the extent of psychological knowledge* at the time of *Plessy* v. *Ferguson,* this finding is amply supported by modern authority. Any language in *Plessy* v. *Ferguson* contrary to this finding is rejected.

We conclude that in the field of public education the doctrine of "separate but equal" has no place. Separate educational facilities are inherently unequal. Therefore, we hold that the plaintiffs and others similarly situated for whom the actions have been brought are, by reason of the segregation complained of, deprived of the equal protection of the laws guaranteed by the Fourteenth Amendment. This disposition makes unnecessary any discussion whether such segregation also violates the Due Process Clause of the Fourteenth Amendment.

Because these are class actions, because of the wide applicability of this decision, and because of the great variety of local conditions, the formulation of decrees in these cases presents problems of considerable complexity. On reargument, the consideration of appropriate relief was necessarily subordinated to the primary question—the constitutionality of segregation in public education. We have now announced that such segregation is a denial of the equal protection of the laws. In order that we may have the full assistance of the parties in formulating decrees, the cases will be restored to the docket, and the parties are requested to present further argument. . . .

---

*The decision in *Brown* v. *Board of Education* was justified in part on psychological and sociological grounds. This line of argument helped Chief Justice Warren obtain a unanimous decision, but it did not provide the strongest legal foundation for attacking desegregation.

1955

Mr. Chief Justice Warren delivered the opinion of the Court.

These cases were decided on May 17, 1954. The opinions of that date, declaring the fundamental principle that racial discrimination in public education is unconstitutional, are incorporated herein by reference. All provisions of federal, state, or local law requiring or permitting such discrimination must yield to this principle. There remains for consideration the manner in which relief is to be accorded.

Because these cases arose under different local conditions and their disposition will involve a variety of local problems, we requested further argument on the question of relief. In view of the nationwide importance of the decision, we invited the Attorney General of the United States and the Attorneys General of all states requiring or permitting racial discrimination in public education to present their views on that question. The parties, the United States, and the States of Florida, North Carolina, Arkansas, Oklahoma, Maryland, and Texas filed briefs and participated in the oral argument.

These presentations were informative and helpful to the Court in its consideration of the complexities arising from the transition to a system of public education freed of racial discrimination. The presentations also demonstrated that substantial steps to eliminate racial discrimination in public schools have already been taken, not only in some of the communities in which these cases arose but in some of the states appearing as *amici curiae*, and in other states as well. Substantial progress has been made in the District of Columbia and in the communities in Kansas and Delaware involved in this litigation. The defendants in the cases coming to us from South Carolina and Virginia are awaiting the decision of this Court concerning relief.

Full implementation of these constitutional principles may require solution of varied local school problems. School authorities have the primary responsibility for elucidating, assessing, and solving these problems; courts will have to consider whether the action of school authorities constitutes good faith implementation of the governing constitutional principles. Because of their proximity to local conditions and the possible need for further hearings, the courts which originally heard these cases can best perform this judicial appraisal.* Accordingly, we believe it appropriate to remand the cases to those courts.

In fashioning and effectuating the decrees, the courts will be guided by equitable principles. Traditionally, equity has been characterized by a practical flexibility in shaping its remedies and by a facility for adjusting and reconciling public and private needs. These cases call for the exercise of these traditional attributes of equity power. At stake is the personal interest of the plaintiffs in admission to public schools as soon as practicable on a non-discriminatory basis. To effectuate this interest may call for elimination of a variety of obstacles

---

*The emphasis on local interpretation of the Court's decision makes sense, but it allowed for great variation in implementation well into the 1970s.

in making the transition to school systems operated in accordance with the constitutional principles set forth in our May 17, 1954, decision. Courts of equity may properly take into account the public interest in the elimination of such obstacles in a systematic and effective manner. But it should go without saying that the vitality of these constitutional principles cannot be allowed to yield simply because of disagreement with them.

While giving weight to these public and private considerations, the courts will require that the defendants make a prompt and reasonable start toward full compliance with our May 17, 1954, ruling. Once such a start has been made, the courts may find that additional time is necessary to carry out the ruling in an effective manner. The burden rests upon the defendants to establish that such time is necessary in the public interest and is consistent with good faith compliance at the earliest practicable date. To that end, the courts may consider problems related to administration, arising from the physical condition of the school plant, the school transportation system, personnel, revision of school districts and attendance areas into compact units to achieve a system of determining admission to the public schools on a nonracial basis, and revision of local laws and regulations which may be necessary in solving the foregoing problems. They will also consider the adequacy of any plans the defendants may propose to meet these problems and to effectuate a transition to a racially nondiscriminatory school system. During this period of transition, the courts will retain jurisdiction of these cases.

The judgments below, except that in the Delaware case, are accordingly reversed and the cases are remanded to the District Courts to take such proceedings and enter such orders and decrees consistent with this opinion as are necessary and proper to admit to public schools on a racially nondiscriminatory basis with all deliberate speed the parties to these cases. The judgment in the Delaware case—ordering the immediate admission of the plaintiffs to schools previously attended only by white children—is affirmed on the basis of the principles stated in our May 17, 1954, opinion, but the case is remanded to the Supreme Court of Delaware for such further proceedings as that Court may deem necessary in light of this opinion.

Questions for Discussion

1. What is wrong with the idea of "separate but equal" facilities? Could this notion ever have some merit?
2. Could the Court have speeded the process of desegregation by handing down a more detailed ruling on how the *Brown* decision was to be implemented? What kinds of problems would such a ruling have faced?
3. *Brown v. Board of Education* concerned legal (*de jure*) desegregation. Have the courts been as capable of dealing with segregation in practice (*de facto*), such as that produced by housing patterns? Why or why not?

3.8

Substituting Symbol for Substance: What Did *Brown* Really Accomplish?

Gerald Rosenberg

No single civil rights decision, at least within the twentieth century, approaches the stature of *Brown* v. *Topeka Board of Education*. Indeed, it has stood for more than a half-century as testimony to the Supreme Court's willingness to address a societal wrong, and, without question, the impact of this seminal case has ranged far past judicial decisions and school desegregation. Yet *Brown*, both in its original 1954 ruling and in the 1955 followup decision, did not produce much concrete change for school integration in the South. Rather, southern politicians and southern school districts strongly and successfully resisted the Court's ruling that desegregation should end; in fact, many of them drew encouragement from *Brown's* words, which stated that desegregation proceed with "all deliberate speed."

  In this iconoclastic article, drawn from a more detailed book, Gerald Rosenberg states that *Brown* v. *Board* produced little change on its own; rather, the *Brown* victory was symbolic, above all. Given its great stature within the history of the civil rights movement, *Brown* has been accorded far more influence than it actually merits, Rosenberg argues. In particular, the continuing existence of *de facto* segregation throughout the United States illustrates the continuing limitations in *Brown*. Happy to confront the conventional wisdom (and willing to give *Brown* some credit), Rosenberg concludes that the historic decision should be addressed without blinders and that scholarship, not sentiment, should dictate our understanding of *Brown's* impact.

On May 17th, 1954, the Supreme Court issued perhaps the twentieth century's most celebrated decision. Fifty years later, the importance of *Brown* is unquestionable, as . . . countless fiftieth anniversary conferences, panels, and symposia, attest. For decades commentators have celebrated *Brown* as "a revolutionary statement of race relations law" through which the

Gerald Rosenberg is a professor of law and political science at the University of Chicago.

Gerald Rosenberg, "Substituting Symbol for Substance: What Did *Brown* Really Accomplish?" *PS: Political Science & Politics*, April 2004, pp. 205–209. Reprinted with the permission of Cambridge University Press.

Supreme Court "blazed the trail" of civil rights. Being "nothing short of a recon-secration of American ideals," *Brown*, it is claimed, "profoundly affected national thinking and has served as the principal ideological engine" of the civil rights movement. *Brown* has long served as the "symbol" of the courts' ability to pro-duce significant social reform, the "principal inspiration to others who seek change through litigation." As [Harvey J.] Wilkinson puts in, "*Brown* may be the most important political, social, and legal event in America's twentieth-century history." It has served, Robert Cover tells us, as a "paradigmatic event."

Despite its enduring importance, major claims made about *Brown* are highly questionable: that the decision made a difference in ending race-based segrega-tion in public schools in particular, and racial discrimination more broadly, or that it had the effects claimed by the authors quoted above. These are emphat-ically empirical questions, not matters of ideology, or fervent wishes for a better world. Nor are they questions of whether the decision *should have* found racial segregation in public schools unconstitutional. They are questions about what *Brown* actually accomplished. And the answer is, "not very much."

In asking these questions, I don't mean to slight the dedication and commit-ment of the civil rights lawyers of the twentieth century. Thurgood Marshall, Jack Greenberg, and others, dedicated their careers, and sometimes their lives, to a principled belief in justice for all. I challenge neither their commitment nor their principles. One may ask, however, whether litigation was the right strate-gic choice to further their goals, and whether their understanding of the strengths and weaknesses of courts as agents of social change was subtle enough to guide them to the best strategy for change.

Underlying these questions about *Brown* is a broader one about the role of the Supreme Court in the larger society. Since the mid-twentieth century, there has been a prevalent belief that courts can further the interests of the relatively dis-advantaged. Starting with civil rights and spreading to issues raised by women's groups, environmental advocates, political reformers, and others, American courts seemingly have become important producers of political and social change. Indeed, for many, part of what makes American democracy exceptional is that it includes the world's most powerful judicial system protecting minori-ties and defending liberty, sometimes in the face of opposition from the demo-cratically elected branches.

In this short article I can only sketch out the briefest of answers to the ques-tion of whether *Brown* made a major contribution to civil rights and, more gen-erally, whether U.S. courts can produce significant social reform. . . .

Measuring *Brown's* Efficacy

The *Brown* decision may have made a major contribution to furthering civil rights in two ways. First, and most straightforward, it could have directly ended race-based segregation in public schools. Second, perhaps more subtly, the decision could have indirectly contributed to change. *Brown* could have inspired individuals to act or persuaded them to examine and change their opinions about racial discrimination. The decision might have given salience to civil rights, in effect placing it on the political agenda. It might have provided legitimization to the civil rights movement and created pressure for government action. In other words, *Brown* might have served as a powerful symbol and resource for change.

Given the praise accorded to the *Brown* decision, examining its actual effect produces quite a surprise. The surprise is that a decade after *Brown* virtually nothing had changed for African-American students living in the 11 states of the former Confederacy that required race-based school segregation by law. For example, in the 1963–1964 school year, barely one in 100 (1.2%) of these African-American children was in a non-segregated school. That means that for nearly 99 of every 100 African-American children in the South a decade after *Brown*, the finding of a constitutional right changed nothing.

By the 1972–1973 school year, however, change did occur. In that school year over 91% of African-American children in the South attended an integrated school. Change came to Southern school systems in the wake of congressional and executive branch action. Title VI of the 1964 Civil Rights Act permitted the cut-off of federal funds to programs that practiced racial discrimination and the 1965 Elementary & Secondary Education Act provided a great deal of federal money to poor school districts, many in the South. By the 1971–1972 school year, for example, federal funds comprised from between 12% and 27.8% of Southern state school budgets, up from between 4.6% and 11.1% in the 1963–1964 school year. This combination of federal funding and Title VI gave the executive branch a tool to induce desegregation when it chose to do so. When the U.S. Department of Health, Education, and Welfare threatened to cut off federal funds from school districts that refused to desegregate, dramatic change occurred. By the 1972–1973 school year, over 91% of African-American school children in the 11 Southern states were in integrated schools, up from 1.2% in the 1963–1964 school year. With only the constitutional right in force in the 1963–1964 school year, no more that 5.5% of African-American children in any Southern state were in school with whites. By the 1972–1973 school year, when economic incentives were offered for desegregation and costs imposed for failure to desegregate, in no Southern state were fewer than 80% of African-American children in integrated schools. It was the actions of the Congress and the executive branch and not the courts that led to desegregation.

Regarding indirect effects, little or no evidence supports the claims that *Brown* gave civil rights salience, pressed political elites to act, pricked the consciences of whites, legitimated the grievances of blacks, or inspired the activists of the civil rights movement. For example, press coverage of civil rights did not increase in a sustained way until the 1960s. In passing civil rights legislation Congress responded not to *Brown* but to electoral concerns in the 1950s, enhanced by the civil rights movement of the 1960s. Similarly, presidential action responded to credible threats of violence, not constitutional statements of principle. There is no evidence that *Brown* influenced public opinion nor, surprisingly, is there much evidence supporting the claim that *Brown* instigated the civil rights movement. That movement, particularly the courageous actions of the Student Non-Violent Coordinating Committee, the Southern Christian Leadership Conference (Dr. [Martin Luther] King's organization), and the Congress of Racial Equality was independent of *Brown*, spurred on by the Montgomery bus boycott, Dr. King's Gandhi-inspired Christian non-violent movement, and emerging African liberation movements. Indeed, all three groups were hostile to litigation as a strategy for change, a position that often brought them into conflict with the National Association for the Advancement of Colored People (NAACP) and its litigation-based strategy. The evidence suggests that *Brown*'s major positive impact was limited to reinforcing the belief in a legal strategy for change of those already committed to it.

Why Wasn't *Brown* Implemented?

These findings raise two questions. First, why was the *Brown* decision not implemented? Second, why, given the lack of implementation, do we hold *Brown* in such high regard? The answer to the first question, in a nutshell, is that there was no political pressure to implement the decision and a great deal of pressure to resist it. On the executive level, there was little support for desegregation until the Johnson presidency. President Eisenhower steadfastly refused to commit his immense popularity or prestige in support of desegregation in general or *Brown* in particular. As Roy Wilkins, executive secretary of the NAACP put it, "if he had fought World War II the way he fought for civil rights, we would all be speaking German today." Although President Kennedy was openly and generally supportive of civil rights, he, too, took little concrete initiative in school desegregation and other civil rights matters until pressured by events.

Civil rights were not supported by other national leaders until late in the Kennedy administration. In March 1956, Southern members of Congress, virtually without exception, signed a document entitled a "Declaration of Constitutional Principles," also known as the Southern Manifesto. Its 101 signers attacked the *Brown* decision as an exercise of "naked power" with "no legal basis." They pledged themselves to "use all lawful means to bring about a reversal of this decision which is contrary to the Constitution and to prevent the use of force in its implementation." This unprecedented attack on the Court, coupled with presidential inaction, signaled that pressure from Washington to implement the Court's decisions in civil rights would not be forthcoming.

On the state and local level, there was even less support. A study of the 250 gubernatorial candidates in the Southern states from 1950 to 1973 revealed that after *Brown* "ambitious politicians, to put it mildly, perceived few incentives to advocate compromise." This perception was reinforced by Arkansas Governor

Orval Faubus's landslide re-election in 1958, after he repeatedly defied court orders and acted to prevent the desegregation of Central High School in Little Rock, demonstrating the "political rewards of conspicuously defying national authority." Throughout the South, governors and gubernatorial candidates called for defiance of court orders. Political support for desegregation was virtually non-existent.

At the prodding of state leaders, state legislatures throughout the South passed a variety of pro-segregation laws. By 1957, only three years after *Brown*, at least 136 new laws and state constitutional amendments designed to preserve segregation had been enacted. In 1960–1961 alone, the Louisiana legislature met in one regular and five extraordinary sessions to pass 92 laws and resolutions to maintain segregated public schools. As the Southern saying went, "as long as we can legislate, we can segregate." Similarly, school boards refused to follow *Brown*. In the five Deep South states of Alabama, Georgia, Louisiana, Mississippi, and South Carolina, not one school-board member or superintendent openly advocated compliance with the Supreme Court decision. And despite *Cooper* v. *Aaron*, and the sending of federal troops to Little Rock in 1957, as of June 1963, only 69 out of 7,700 students at the supposedly desegregated, "formerly" white, junior and senior high schools of Little Rock were black. Public resistance, supported by local political action, can almost always effectively defeat court-ordered civil rights.

Along with opposition to desegregation from political leaders at all levels of government, there was hostility from many white Americans. For example, in December 1958, when Gallup asked its usual question about the most-admired men in the world, Governor Orval Faubus of Arkansas, who had repeatedly defied court orders a year earlier was among the 10 most frequently named. Law and legal decisions operate in a given cultural environment and the norms of that environment influence the decisions that are made and the impact they have. In the case of *Brown* and civil rights, decisions were announced in a culture in which slavery had existed and apartheid did exist. Institutions and social structures throughout America reflected a history of, if not a present commitment to, racial discrimination. Cultural barriers to civil rights had to be overcome before change could occur. And courts do not have the tools to tear down these barriers.

One of the important cultural barriers to civil rights was the existence of private groups supportive of segregation. One type, represented by the Ku Klux Klan, White Citizens' Councils, and the like, existed principally to fight civil rights. Either through their own acts, or the atmosphere these groups helped create, violence against blacks and civil rights workers was commonplace throughout the South. Spectacular cases such as the murder of Medgar Evers, the attacks on the freedom riders, the Birmingham Church bombing that killed four black girls, and the murder of three civil rights workers near Philadelphia, Mississippi, are well known. But countless bombings and numerous murders occurred throughout the South. During the summer of 1964 in Mississippi alone there were 35 shootings, 65 bombings (including 35 churches), 80 beatings, and 6 murders. It was a brave soul indeed who worked to end segregation or implement court decisions amidst so much segregationist opposition.

To make matters worse, while there is little evidence that *Brown* helped produce positive change, there is some evidence that it hardened resistance to civil rights among both elites and the white public. In the wake of *Brown* white groups intent on using coercion and violence to prevent change grew. Resistance to change increased in all areas, not merely in education but also in voting, transportation, public places, and so on. *Brown* "unleashed a wave of racism that reached hysterical proportions." By stiffening resistance and raising fears before the activist phase of the civil rights movement was in place, *Brown* may actually have delayed the achievement of civil rights.

In sum, *Brown*'s constitutional mandate that racial segregation in public schools end confronted a culture opposed to that change. The American judicial system, constrained by the need for both elite and popular support, was unable to overcome that culture.

Critics

Brown has become a sacred cow and my finding of its lack of efficacy has troubled some and incensed others. For example, some critics allege that the impact of the Court can't be measured, and that the data I present are merely suggestive, at best. While there is some truth to this, it is mostly wrong, and partly misleading. It is mostly wrong because a variety of impacts are empirical and thus measurable. These include the actual number and rate of African-American children in school with whites, the actual number and content of media stories about *Brown* and civil rights, the number and timing of civil rights demonstrations, and so forth. What social scientists cannot do is understand precisely what people are thinking and why. Thus, it is possible that even though there is no evidence supporting the claim that *Brown* had important, positive effects, the fault is with the measurement, not the effect. This is possibly correct, but not without its own problems that make the criticism misleading. First, in all the most obvious places to find such evidence, the evidence that can be found either does not support the claim of *Brown*'s causal influence, or cuts against it. This suggests that any unmeasured effects, at the very best, are quite weak. Second, because some of the data are merely suggestive and not definitive, it does not follow that *Brown* had an important impact. The argument seems to go something like this: (1) *Brown* had inspirational impact; (2) we cannot measure that impact because we lack sufficiently honed measures; (3) therefore *Brown* had inspirational impact. But this is argument by assertion, with point 3 (conclusion) being merely a particularized restatement of point 1 (the thesis) with no support from point 2 (evidence). That kind of logic dismisses empirical investigation by fiat. It is ideology, not social science.

Some critics have also alleged that Supreme Court decisions like *Brown* are only one resource among many and to expect major change to follow from them is to create a straw person argument. Perhaps this is correct, but it is not I who have made the claim of judicial efficacy! The Supreme Court in general, and *Brown* in particular, is credited with enormous power and influence. The quotations that fill the first paragraph of this essay could be replicated many times over. The straw person argument against the findings presented here often amounts to little more than post hoc rationalization for judicial inefficacy.

Yet another criticism deals with timing. *Brown* said desegregate and sometime later some desegregation occurred. As Erwin Chemerinsky puts it, "Change is often a long-term process." Thus, the argument goes, it is immaterial that no change occurred over the first decade or more. But this is problematic for several reasons. First, given enough time lots of things are bound to occur that do not result from the event in question. There was a substantial time lag between the decision and more than token desegregation. This allowed all sorts of other influences independent of *Brown* to play a role. In the case of desegregation and civil rights, the principal factor was the civil rights movement. Second, this argument is made entirely at a macro level. It lacks the micro connections that show how *Brown* influenced people to act and how those acts led to school desegregation and civil rights more generally. Arguments that change takes time explain nothing because they explain everything.

Overall, a general notion that many critiques of my argument seem to have goes something like this: "Look, *Brown* happened; it had to matter." The problem with this critique is that many events happen in the world that exert little or no causal influence on later events. Of course law matters, and of course people reacted to *Brown*, but it doesn't automatically or necessarily follow that *Brown* furthered the cause of civil rights. Such a claim assumes the importance of a particular institution, and particular outcomes of that institution, rather than treating the importance of that institution and outcomes as a question for empirical investigation. In the case of *Brown*, this argument uncritically credits the Supreme Court with a degree of influence and power that it lacks.

Substituting Symbol for Substance

Given *Brown*'s lack of impact, why is it widely held in such high regard? We celebrate *Brown* for two reasons. The first is that since the mid-1960s the U.S. has become officially committed to a non-segregated society. *Brown* stands as a constitutional symbol of that commitment. This is a noble vision, one of which Americans can be proud. The second reason is much less noble. The celebration of *Brown* serves an ideological function of assuring Americans that they have lived up to their constitutional principles without actually requiring them to do so. Today, *Brown* and *de facto* segregation live side-by-side. The danger of celebrating a symbol is that it can lead to a sense of self-satisfaction and an unwillingness to examine practice. *Brown*, then, can be seen as "little more than an ornament, or golden cupola, built upon the roof of a structure found rotting and infested, assuring the gentlefolk who only pass by without entering that all is well inside." So, in the end we celebrate *Brown* not because of what it did but because of what we officially state it should have done. And this celebration relieves us of the obligation to confront the systematic racial biases that permeate American society. It encourages us to look to legal solutions for political and cultural problems. In this way, *Brown* serves a deeply conservative function of diverting resources away from substantive political battles, where success is possible, to symbolic legal ones where it is not.

None of this means that *Brown* was wrongly decided. In a nation built on slavery, degraded by Jim Crow, and based on deep-seated belief in white racial superiority, racial segregation denies equal protection. Nor does it mean that law is irrelevant or that courts can never further the goals of the relatively disadvantaged. For the civil rights movement, for example, courts played an important role in keeping the sit-in movement going, ending the Montgomery bus boycott by providing the boycotters with leverage they could use, and threatening to cut off federal funds under Title VI. But in each case courts were effective because a political movement was forcing change. The analysis does mean that courts acting alone, as in *Brown*, are structurally constrained from furthering the goals of the relatively disadvantaged.

American courts are not all-powerful institutions. They were designed with severe limitations and placed in a political system of divided powers. To celebrate decisions such as *Brown* uncritically misunderstands both the limits of courts and the lessons of history, clouding our vision with a naive and romantic belief in the triumph of rights over politics. And while romance and even naiveté have their charms, they are best exhibited neither in courtrooms, nor in scholarship.

Questions for Discussion

1. *Brown* v. *Board of Education* stands as an historic Supreme Court case and a racial landmark in the United States. Can it be both those things and yet not be effective in attacking segregated schools, especially in the South? Explain.
2. Rosenberg emphasizes the symbolic impact of the *Brown* decision. If something is symbolic, is it real? Do symbolic victories matter over the long run? How so?

Affirmative Action: Don't Mend It or End It—Bend It

Peter H. Schuck

Since the mid-1970s, no civil rights issue has generated more heat and light within the American public than that of "affirmative action." In the wake of *Brown v. Board of Education* and the civil rights legislation of the 1960s, many activists came to believe that racial equality could result only from some "affirmative" assistance that would help minorities climb the educational and vocational ladders of opportunity in the United States. Conversely, opponents of affirmative action argued that such a policy explicitly violated the vision of a color-blind, nondiscriminatory society that stood at the heart of the civil rights movement of the 1950s and 1960s.

Peter Schuck's article comes to the affirmative action debate at a very mature stage. That is, the Supreme Court limited affirmative action with its 1978 *Bakke* decision that ruled numerical quotas (for medical school admission) unconstitutional. Subsequently, the Court has walked a fine line in limiting affirmative action in some employment cases, but allowing it as a consideration in admissions to some university programs (see the interpretation of the 2003 University of Michigan cases in selection 3.10).

Schuck argues that there may be a place for affirmative action, but that place is not embedded in laws and regulations. Indeed, he embraces the principle of "nondiscrimination" for all public institutions, although he does not tease out all of its implications (for instance, should a large university care only about academic records, and not about one's ability to shoot a basketball, play the flute, or write for a newspaper?). At the same time, he would encourage private entities, such as Notre Dame or Stanford, to engage in affirmative action practices, as long as they clearly stated their intent. Given that most universities accept federal funds (and thus fall under federal rules on discrimination), this solution is problematic. Still, Schuck provides a thoughtful approach to a thorny problem.

Peter H. Schuck is professor of law at Yale University and New York University.

Peter H. Schuck, "Affirmative Action: Don't Mend It or End It—Bend It," *The Brookings Review* 20, no. 1 (Winter 2002): 24–27. Reprinted by permission of The Brookings Institution.

Affirmative action policy—by which I mean ethno-racial preferences in the allocation of socially valuable resources—is even more divisive and unsettled today than at its inception more than 30 years ago.

Affirmative action's policy context has changed dramatically since 1970. One change is legal. Since the Supreme Court's 1978 *Bakke* decision, when Justice Lewis Powell's pivotal fifth vote endorsed certain "diversity"-based preferences in higher education, the Court has made it increasingly difficult for affirmative action plans to pass constitutional muster unless they are carefully designed to remedy specific past acts of discrimination. Four other changes— the triumph of the nondiscrimination principle; blacks' large social gains; evidence on the size, beneficiaries, and consequences of preferences; and new demographic realities—persuade me that affirmative action as we know it should be abandoned even if it is held to be constitutional.

"As we know it" is the essential qualifier in that sentence. I propose neither a wholesale ban on affirmative action ("ending" it) nor tweaks in its administration ("mending" it). Rather, I would make two structural changes to curtail existing preferences while strengthening the remaining ones' claim to justice. First, affirmative action would be banned in the public sector but allowed in the private sector. Second, private-sector institutions that use preferences would be required to disclose how and why they do so. These reforms would allow the use of preferences by private institutions that believe in them enough to disclose and defend them, while doing away with the obfuscation, duplicity, and lack of accountability that too often accompany preferences. Affirmative action could thus be localized and customized to suit the varying requirements of particular contexts and sponsors.

Triumph of the Nondiscrimination Principle

Why is change necessary? To explain, one must at the outset distinguish affirmative action entailing preferences from nondiscrimination, a principle that simply requires one to refrain from treating people differently because of their race, ethnicity, or other protected characteristics. Although this distinction can blur at the edges, it is clear and vital both in politics and in principle.

When affirmative action became federal policy in the late 1960s, the nondiscrimination principle, though fragile, was gaining strength. Preferences, by contrast, were flatly rejected by civil rights leaders like Hubert Humphrey, Ted Kennedy, and Martin Luther King, Jr. In the three decades that followed, more and more Americans came to embrace nondiscrimination and to oppose affirmative action, yet . . . federal bureaucrats extended affirmative action with little public notice or debate. Today, nondiscrimination, or equal opportunity, is a principle questioned by only a few bigots and extreme libertarians, and civil rights law is far-reaching and remedially robust. In contrast, affirmative action is widely seen as a demand for favoritism or even equal outcomes.

Social Gains by Blacks

Blacks, the intended beneficiaries of affirmative action, are no longer the insular minority they were in the 1960s. Harvard sociologist Orlando Patterson shows their "astonishing" progress on almost every front. "A mere 13% of the population," he notes, "Afro-Americans dominate the nation's popular culture. . . . [A]t least 35 percent of Afro-American adult, male workers are solidly middle class." The income of young, intact black families approaches that of demographically similar whites. On almost every other social index (residential integration is a laggard), the black-white gap is narrowing significantly; indeed, the income gap for young black women has disappeared.

Even these comparisons understate black progress. Much of racism's cruel legacy is permanently impounded in the low education and income levels of older blacks who grew up under Jim Crow; their economic disadvantages pull down the averages, obscuring the gains of their far better-educated children and grandchildren. These gains, moreover, have coincided with the arrival of record numbers of immigrants who are competing with blacks. To ignore this factor, economist Robert Lerner says, is like analyzing inequality trends in Germany since 1990 without noting that it had absorbed an entire impoverished country, East Germany. In addition, comparisons that fail to age-adjust social statistics obscure the fact that blacks, whose average age is much lower than that of whites, are less likely to have reached their peak earning years.

My point, emphatically, is not that blacks have achieved social equality—far from it—but that the situation facing them today is altogether different than it was when affirmative action was adopted. . . .

Size, Beneficiaries, and Consequences of Preferences

When we weigh competing claims for scarce resources—jobs, admission to higher education, public and private contracts, broadcast or other spectrum licenses, credit, housing, and the like—how heavy is the thumb that affirmative action places on the scales? This is a crucial question. The larger the preference, the more it conflicts with competing interests and values, especially the ideal of merit—almost regardless of how one defines merit.

The best data concern higher education admissions where (for better or for worse) schools commonly use standardized test scores as a proxy for aptitude, preparation, and achievement. William Bowen and Derek Bok, the former presidents of Princeton and Harvard, published a study in 1999 based largely on the academic records of more than 80,000 students who entered 28 highly selective institutions in three different years. Affirmative action, they claimed, only applies to these institutions, although a more recent study suggests that the practice now extends to some second- and even third-tier schools.

Selective institutions, of course, take other factors into account besides race. Indeed, some whites who are admitted have worse academic credentials than the blacks admitted under preferences. Still, Bowen and Bok find a difference of almost 200 points in the average SAT scores of the black and white applicants, and even this understates the group difference. First, the deficit for black applicants' high school grade point average (GPA), the other main admission criterion, is even larger. Thomas Kane finds that black applicants to selective schools "enjoy an advantage equivalent to an increase of two-thirds of a point in [GPA]—on a four-point scale—or [the equivalent of] 400 points on the SAT." Second, although the SAT is often criticized as culturally biased against blacks, SAT (and GPA) scores at every level actually overpredict their college performance. Third, the odds were approximately even that black applicants with scores between 1100 and 1199 would be admitted, whereas the odds for whites did not reach that level until they had scores in the 1450–1499 range. With a score of 1500 or above, more than a third of whites were rejected while every single black gained admission. The University of Michigan . . . weighs race even more heavily than the average school in the Bowen and Bok sample.* At Michigan, being black, Hispanic, or Native American gives one the equivalent of a full point of GPA; minority status can override any SAT score deficit. And a recent study of 47 public institutions found that the odds of a black student being admitted compared to a white student with the same SAT and GPA were 173 to 1 at Michigan and 177 to 1 at North-Carolina State.

These preferences, then, are not merely tie-breakers; they are huge. . . .

How much of blacks' impressive gains is due to reduced discrimination resulting from changing white attitudes and civil rights enforcement, as distinct from preferences? How would they have fared had they attended the somewhat less prestigious schools they could have attended without preferences? What would the demographics of higher education be without those preferences? We cannot answer these vital questions conclusively. We know that black gains were substantial even before preferences were adopted, that preference beneficiaries are overwhelmingly from middle- and upper-class families, and that most black leaders in all walks of life did not go to elite universities. We also know that many institutions are so committed to affirmative action that they will find ways to prefer favored groups—legacies, athletes, and others—no matter what the formal rules say. . . .

New Demographic Realities

The moral case for affirmative action rests on the bitter legacy of black slavery, Jim Crow, and the violent dispossession of Native Americans. Yet the descendants of slaves and Native Americans constitute a shrinking share of affirmative

---

*The Supreme Court ruled these standards unconstitutional. (See selection 3.10.)

action's beneficiaries. Political logrolling has extended preferential treatment to the largest immigrant group, Hispanics, as well as to blacks from Africa, the Caribbean, and elsewhere, Asians and Pacific Islanders, and in some programs to women, a majority group.

Some affirmative action advocates acknowledge this problem and want to fix it. Orlando Patterson, for example, would exclude "first-generation persons of African ancestry" but not "their children and later generations—in light of the persistence of racist discrimination in America." He would also exclude all Hispanics except for Puerto Ricans and Mexican Americans of second or later generations and would exclude "all Asians except Chinese-Americans descended from pre-1923 immigrants. . . ." With due respect for Patterson's pathbreaking work on race, his formula resembles a tax code provision governing depreciation expenses more than a workable formula for promoting social justice.

Centuries of immigration and intermarriage have rendered the conventional racial categories ever more meaningless. The number of Americans who consider themselves multiracial and who wish to be identified as such (if they must be racially identified at all) was 7 million in the 2000 census, including nearly 2 million blacks (5 percent of the black population) and 37 percent of all Native Americans. This is why advocacy groups who are desperate to retain the demographic status quo lobbied furiously to preempt a multiracial category.

In perhaps the most grimly ironic aspect of the new demographic dispensation, the government adopted something like the one-drop rule that helped enslave mulattos and self-identifying whites before Emancipation. Under OMB's rules, any response combining one minority race and the white race must be allocated to the minority race. This, although 25 percent of those in the United States who describe themselves as both black and white consider themselves white, as do almost half of Asian-white people and more than 80 percent of Indian-white people. The lesson is clear: making our social policy pivot on the standard racial categories is both illogical and politically unsustainable.

Alternatives

Even a remote possibility that eliminating affirmative action would resegregate our society deeply distresses almost all Americans. Nothing else can explain the persistence of a policy that, contrary to basic American values, distributes valuable social resources according to skin color and surname. But to say that we must choose between perpetuating affirmative action and eliminating it entirely is false. To be sure, most suggested reforms—using social class or economic disadvantage rather than race, choosing among minimally qualified students by lottery, and making preferences temporary—are impracticable or would make matters worse. Limiting affirmative action to the descendants of slaves and Native Americans would minimize some objections to the policy but, as Patterson's proposal suggests, would be tricky to implement and would still violate the nondiscrimination and merit principles.

Most Americans who favor affirmative action would probably concede that it fails to treat the underlying problem. Black applicants will continue to have worse academic credentials until they can attend better primary and secondary schools and receive the remediation they need. A root cause of their disadvantage is inferior schooling, and affirmative action is simply a poultice. We must often deal with symptoms rather than root causes because we do not know how to eliminate them, or consider it too costly to do so, or cannot muster the necessary political will. If we know which social or educational reforms can substantially improve low-income children's academic performance, then we should by all [means] adopt them. But this does not mean that we should preserve affirmative action until we can eliminate the root causes of inequality.

I propose instead that we treat governmental, legally mandated preferences differently than private, voluntary ones. While prohibiting the former (except in the narrow remedial context approved by the Supreme Court), I would permit the latter—but only under certain conditions discussed below. A liberal society committed to freedom and private autonomy has good reasons to maintain this difference; racial preferences imposed by law are pernicious in ways that private ones are not. [T]o most Americans (including many minorities), affirmative action is not benign. [R]ace is perhaps the worst imaginable category around which to organize political and social relations. The social changes I have described only reinforce this lesson. A public law that affirms our common values should renounce the distributive use of race, not perpetuate it.

There are other differences between public and private affirmative action. A private preference speaks for and binds only those who adopt it and only for as long as they retain it. It does not serve, as public law should, as a social ideal. [L]egal rules tend to be cruder, more simplistic, slower to develop, and less contextualized than voluntary ones, which are tailored to more specific needs and situations. Legal rules reflect interest group politics or the vagaries of judicial decision; voluntary ones reflect the chooser's own assessment of private benefits and costs. Legal rules are more difficult to reform, abandon, or escape. Voluntary ones can assume more diverse forms than mandated ones, a diversity that facilitates social learning and problem solving.

Still, many who believe in nondiscrimination and merit and who conscientiously weigh the competing values still support affirmative action. If a private university chooses to sacrifice some level of academic performance to gain greater racial diversity and whatever educational or other values it thinks diversity will bring, I cannot say—nor should the law say—that its choice is impermissible. Because even private affirmative action violates the nondiscrimination principle, however, I would permit it only on two conditions: transparency and protection of minorities. First, the preference—its criteria, weights, and reasons—must be fully disclosed. If it cannot withstand public criticism, it should be scrapped. The goal is to discipline preferences by forcing institutions to reveal their value choices. This will trigger market, reputational, and other informal mechanisms that make them bear more of the policy's costs rather than just shifting them surreptitiously to nonpreferred applicants, as they do now. Second, private affirmative action must not disadvantage a group to which the Constitution affords heightened protection. A preference favoring whites, for example, would violate this condition.

The Commitment to Legal Equality

For better *and* for worse, American culture remains highly individualistic in its values and premises, even at some sacrifice (where sacrifice is necessary) to its goal of substantive equality. The illiberal strands in our tangled history that en-slaved, excluded, and subordinated individuals as members of racial groups should chasten our efforts to use race as a distributive criterion. Affirmative ac-tion in its current form, however well-intended, violates the distinctive, deeply engrained cultural and moral commitments to legal equality, private autonomy, and enhanced opportunity that have served Americans well—even though they have not yet served all of us equally well.

Questions for Discussion

1. In this piece, Peter Schuck differentiates between public institutions, such as Indiana University, and private ones, such as Notre Dame. Is this a legiti-mate distinction when it comes to permitting affirmative action to affect decisions (in admissions or hiring)?
2. The notion of "colorblind" admissions and advancement sounds more than reasonable. Why might universities, corporations, and other organizations desire *not* to be colorblind? Is the society at large colorblind?

 3.10

Reaffirming Diversity: A Legal Analysis of the University of Michigan Affirmative Action Cases

Joint Statement of Constitutional Law Scholars

The 2003 Supreme Court decisions in two related affirmative action cases provided some clarity on how far public institutions can go in weighing diversity in their admissions decisions. The Court adopted a relatively expansive view of affirmative action in promoting diversity for the University of Michigan Law School (*Grutter*), while opting for substantial limitations on affirmative action in undergraduate admissions (*Gratz*); still, the justices did rule that race could continue to be a consideration in admissions policies, a line of reasoning that was expressed in 1978 by Justice Lewis Powell, even as he ruled against a quota system for minorities in *Bakke* v. *California*.

Affirmative action remains a hot-button issue in many quarters because it juxtaposes two different ways of addressing the broad value of equality—a value that Americans frequently see through different lenses. Those who oppose affirmative action view equality through the lens of nondiscrimination at any given point where advantage might occur, such as admission to college, or to law school, or in obtaining a job. Equality here means simply that the process does not discriminate against any individual. Advocates of affirmative action, in whatever form, argue that a lack of discrimination does not equate to real equality of opportunity. Life situations create all kinds of inequalities that affect actual opportunity. Affirmative action advocates have relied less and less on such arguments, however, in large part because Americans find equality a less compelling value than those of freedom and merit. Rather, as "Reaffirming Diversity" demonstrates, the idea of diversity within an institution has become the foundation for contemporary support for affirmative action policies.

Effective participation by members of all racial and ethnic groups in the civic life of our Nation is essential if the dream of one Nation, indivisible, is to be realized.
—GRUTTER V. BOLLINGER

Introduction

On June 23, 2003, the United States Supreme Court upheld the constitutionality of race-conscious admissions policies designed to promote diversity in higher education. In a 5-to-4 decision in *Grutter v. Bollinger*, the Supreme Court, drawing on Justice Powell's opinion in the 1978 case of *Regents of the University of California v. Bakke*, held that student body diversity is a compelling governmental interest that can justify the use of race as a "plus" factor in a competitive admissions process. Applying its "strict scrutiny" standard of review within the context of higher education, the Supreme Court upheld the University of Michigan Law School admissions policy as constitutional. However, in a 6-to-3 decision in *Gratz v. Bollinger*, the Supreme Court held that the University's current undergraduate admissions policy was not narrowly tailored to advance an interest in diversity because it was not sufficiently flexible and did not provide enough individualized consideration of applicants to the University.

In ruling that the promotion of student body diversity is a compelling interest, the Supreme Court's decisions resolve a disagreement among the lower federal courts and allow selective colleges and universities throughout the country to employ race in admissions. The decisions reject the absolute race-blind approach to higher education admissions advanced by the *Grutter* and *Gratz* plaintiffs and by the U.S. government and others as *amici curiae*. The Court's decisions also effectively overrule major portions of the 1996 ruling of the U.S. Court of Appeals for the Fifth Circuit in *Hopwood v. Texas*, and will allow colleges and universities in the states of Texas, Louisiana, and Mississippi to use race-conscious admissions policies designed to advance diversity. State universities in California, Washington, and Florida are still prohibited under their state laws from employing race-conscious admissions policies; however, private universities in those states can employ properly designed race-conscious policies consistent with their obligations under Title VI of the Civil Rights Act of 1964 and other federal laws.

Taken together, the Court's opinions in the *Grutter* and *Gratz* cases reinforce the importance of flexible and holistic admissions policies that employ a limited use of race. The Court's opinion in the law school case, *Grutter v. Bollinger*, confirms that admissions programs which consider race as one of many factors in the context of an individualized consideration of all applicants can pass constitutional muster. The Court's decision to strike down the undergraduate admissions policy in *Gratz* as unconstitutional also makes clear that policies which automatically and inflexibly assign benefits on the basis of race, such as the

University's undergraduate point system that allocated a fixed number of points for underrepresented minority group members, are constitutionally suspect. Universities that employ systems which lack sufficient individualized review will need to re-examine their current admissions policies to determine whether their policies require adjustment or revision in light of the Court's decision in *Gratz*. Institutions that have adopted more restrictive policies than the Court's decisions allow may wish to re-examine their policies to ensure that they are not "overcorrecting" out of a misplaced fear of being held legally liable. . . .

Although the Supreme Court has yet to address the constitutionality of diversity-based affirmative action programs outside of higher education admissions, language in the *Grutter* decision acknowledges the importance of diversity in other contexts, including K-12 education, government, and private employment and business. For instance, the Court states expressly that the benefits of affirmative action "are not theoretical but real, as major American businesses have made clear that the skills needed in today's increasingly global marketplace can only be developed through exposure to widely diverse people, cultures, ideas, and viewpoints." This and other statements by the Court imply that diversity may be a constitutional predicate for race-conscious affirmative action programs in areas outside of higher education. . . .

I. *Grutter*, *Gratz*, and the Constitutional Boundaries of Race-Conscious Admissions

The University of Michigan cases reaffirm the Supreme Court's fundamental requirement that race-conscious policy making—even if designed to benefit racial minority groups—is subject to "strict scrutiny," the highest standard of review used by the courts to evaluate the constitutionality of policies under the Equal Protection Clause of the Fourteenth Amendment. Under strict scrutiny, the courts ask two questions to assess the ends and the means that underlie race-conscious policy making: (1) Is the goal of a race-conscious policy sufficiently important to constitute a "compelling governmental interest"? and (2)If so, is the policy "narrowly tailored" to advance that interest?

Strict scrutiny is exacting but it is not rigid. As the Supreme Court made clear in *Grutter v. Bollinger*, "[c]ontext matters when reviewing race-based governmental action under the Equal Protection Clause" and "strict scrutiny must take 'relevant differences' into account." Applying strict scrutiny within the context of evaluating an inclusive higher education policy, the Supreme Court ruled in *Grutter v. Bollinger* that colleges and universities do have a compelling interest in obtaining a diverse student body. Employing a multi-factor test of narrow tailoring, the Court upheld the University of Michigan Law School's admissions policy in *Grutter*, but struck down the University's undergraduate policy in *Gratz* for lacking the necessary flexibility and individualized consideration required under narrow tailoring.

A. The Compelling Interest in Diversity

Like hundreds of selective colleges and universities throughout the country, the University of Michigan relied on Justice Powell's opinion in *Regents of the University of California* v. *Bakke* as the legal underpinning for its diversity-based admissions policies. In *Bakke*, a fragmented Supreme Court struck down the race-conscious special admissions policy at the medical school of the University of California, Davis, but reversed a lower court's ruling that race could never be considered a factor in admissions. Justice Powell provided the fifth vote for a majority of the Court which found that the medical school's special admissions policy—a plan that set aside 16 out of 100 seats in the entering class for disadvantaged minority applicants—was illegal because it precluded white applicants from competing for those special admissions seats. But Justice Powell, as part of a different five-member majority, also held that the use of race as one of many factors in a competitive admissions process would be constitutionally permissible.

Justice Powell's pivotal opinion stated that a university's interest in promoting broad diversity—and not just racial diversity—within its student body is grounded partly in the academic freedoms historically accorded to institutions of higher education and constitutes a compelling governmental interest that can justify the limited use of race in admissions. Relying on the undergraduate admissions policy at Harvard College as a case in point, Justice Powell went on to distinguish an illegal policy such as the Davis medical school plan, in which white applicants could not compete for specified seats in an entering class, from a legal policy such as the Harvard plan, in which race is employed as a "plus" factor in a competitive process in which all applicants are eligible to compete for the same seats in the entering class. Under a plus-factor admissions policy, an applicant's race could "tip the balance" in an admissions decision, but race would be only one of many factors under consideration. . . .

The *Grutter* opinion offers a ringing endorsement of the value of student body diversity in promoting numerous benefits, including:

◆ concrete educational benefits;
◆ assisting in the breakdown of racial and ethnic stereotypes; and
◆ the development of a diverse, racially integrated leadership class

Citing expert reports in the trial record and research studies documenting the educational benefits of diversity, the *Grutter* opinion recognizes that student body diversity leads to substantial educational benefits for *all* students, including the promotion of cross-racial understanding, improved classroom discussions and other positive learning outcomes, and enhanced preparation for an increasingly diverse workforce and society. Moreover, according to the Court, student body diversity "helps to break down racial stereotypes" and "diminishing the force of such stereotypes is both a crucial part of [an institution's] mission, and one that it cannot accomplish with only token numbers of minority students. Just as growing up in a particular region or having particular professional experiences is likely to affect an individual's views, so too is one's own, unique experience of being a racial minority in a society, like our own, in which race unfortunately still matters."

Citing *Sweatt* v. *Painter*,* the *Grutter* Court also recognized that institutions of higher learning, and law schools in particular, provide the training ground for many of our Nation's leaders. Individuals with law degrees, for instance, occupy large numbers of the nation's state governorships, seats in both houses of Congress, and federal judgeships. According to the Court, "[i]n order to cultivate a set of leaders with legitimacy in the eyes of the citizenry, it is necessary that the path to leadership be visibly open to talented and qualified individuals of every race and ethnicity." Access to higher education "must be inclusive of talented and qualified individuals of every race and ethnicity, so that all members of our heterogeneous society may participate in the educational institutions that provide the training and education necessary to succeed in America." . . .

One of the Court's most powerful statements thus underscores the compelling interest in promoting diversity in higher education and the importance of racial integration and diversity in civic life more generally: "'[E]nsuring that public institutions are open and available to all segments of American society, including people of all race and ethnicities, represents a paramount government objective.' . . . And, '[n]owhere is the importance of such openness more acute than in the context of higher education.' . . . Effective participation by members of all racial and ethnic groups in the civic life of our Nation is essential if the dream of one Nation, indivisible, is to be realized."

B. Narrow Tailoring: A Bakke+ Test

Under the narrow tailoring prong of strict scrutiny, the courts evaluate the "fit" between a compelling interest and the policy adopted to advance that interest. The Supreme Court has not developed a uniform test of narrow tailoring in equal protection cases, but the Court has offered various guidelines in its earlier cases addressing race-conscious policies; the analyses employed in *Grutter* and *Gratz* draw on several of these guidelines. In *Bakke*, Justice Powell discussed two elements of narrow tailoring specific to admissions policies designed to promote diversity in higher education: First, an admissions policy must not rely on separate tracks or quotas that insulate racial minorities from competitive review. Second, race must be employed as a "plus"

---

*In 1950, the Supreme Court overturned a state supreme court decision and ordered the integration of the University of Texas School of Law.

factor that serves as only one of many factors being weighed in a competitive process that evaluates the particular qualifications of each individual applicant. . . .

Stating that the narrow tailoring test "must be calibrated to fit the distinct issues raised by the use of race to achieve student body diversity in public higher education," the Supreme Court's articulation of the narrow tailoring test in *Grutter* combines elements from *Bakke* and the Court's remedial cases into five basic inquiries:

♦ Does the program offer a competitive review of all applications (i.e., no quotas or separate tracks to insulate minorities)?

♦ Does the program provide flexible, individualized consideration of applicants so that race is only one of several factors being considered?

♦ Has the institution considered workable race-neutral alternatives to its program?

♦ Does the program unduly burden non-minority applicants?

♦ Is the program limited in time, so that it has a logical end point?

The *Grutter* Court applied all five of these inquiries in upholding the University of Michigan Law School's admissions policy. The *Gratz* Court focused on the second inquiry and found that the University's undergraduate admissions policy lacked the necessary flexibility and individualized review to satisfy narrow tailoring.

The *Grutter* Court stressed that context is critical in strict scrutiny analysis, and the Court may be more inclined to uphold race-conscious policies in employment contexts that closely parallel the higher education context, where the benefits of diversity in the workplace are well documented and race is used as a "plus" factor in a non-mechanical hiring or promotion process that also considers non-racial factors and allows applicants to compete for jobs on an equal footing.

Conclusion

The *Grutter* and *Gratz* decisions have affirmed the underlying values of diversity in higher education and of racial integration in American society, and the cases provide clear guidelines for institutions to use in designing inclusive admissions policies. Yet, as the Court stated in *Grutter*, "race unfortunately still matters," and affirmative action will continue to be an issue that divides much of our country, notwithstanding our nation's broad commitment to equal educational opportunity. The University of Michigan decisions have settled one set of legal questions, but we can expect many more to arise in our courts and legislatures with the passage of time.

In *Brown* v. *Board of Education*, the Supreme Court observed that education is "the very foundation of good citizenship." Those words ring as true today as they did nearly fifty years ago. Considerable progress has been made in the past fifty years, but the University of Michigan cases remind us that progress has been slow and much remains to be done. The Court's more recent words, echoing *Brown*, are thus worth repeating: "Effective participation by members of all racial and ethnic groups in the civic life of our Nation is essential if the dream of one Nation, indivisible, is to be realized."

Questions for Discussion

1. Why did the U.S. Supreme Court broadly accept the idea of affirmative action for the University of Michigan Law School while rejecting any such interpretation for undergraduates at the same institution?
2. Does a university have a "compelling interest" in diversity? If so, should race be one of the categories that make up the working definition of "diversity"? Why?

Chapter 4

Public Opinion

At base, politics is the relationship between those who govern and those who are governed. Public opinion plays a crucial role in this relationship. Governments—even totalitarian states—must take into account the attitudes and perspectives of the public, because without the people's support no government can endure.

In modern democracies, the idea that governments should consider the wishes of the governed can be traced to the late seventeenth and eighteenth centuries, particularly to the egalitarian and majoritarian ideas of John Locke and Thomas Jefferson. Governing authority had previously been based on an aristocratic ideology that defended social and legal inequality as a proper and permanent fact of life. The various classes had fixed places in society, and the ruling class devised elaborate justifications for the exclusion of others from politics. But the dissemination of radically different social ideas, plus changes in economic circumstances, broadened the base of political participation. What the growing middle class thought became important, and in the early 1800s the term *public opinion* became commonplace.

In countries that boast democratic forms of government, like the United States, it appears virtually mandatory that the "will of the people" prevail. The difficulty is in determining what the will of the people is—or indeed, whether it exists at all. "To speak with precision of public opinion," wrote political scientist V. O. Key, "is a task not unlike coming to grips with the Holy Ghost," partly because the distinction between "public" and "private" opinion is not easy to make and is constantly changing. For example, thirty-five years ago cigarette smoking was a private matter, unregulated by government and absent from the agenda of political debate. By the 1970s, however, when smoking had been identified as a major public health hazard, advertising by tobacco companies was severely curtailed and movements to ban smoking in all public places were afoot. Today smoking is a public matter, and interest groups on both sides of the issue are involved in legislative deliberations. Questions about smoking now are a routine component of national public opinion polls.

The meaning of *opinion* is similarly vague. Opinions, beliefs, and attitudes are often treated as if they were the same, but scholars increasingly make distinctions among these terms. One social scientist, Bernard Hennessy, defines opinions as "immediate orientations toward contemporary controversial political objects," whereas attitudes are "more diffused and enduring orientations toward political objects not necessarily controversial at the moment."

For most purposes, however, it is preferable to think of public opinion in the broadest sense—in Key's definition, as "those opinions held by private persons which governments find it prudent to heed." Public opinion may be expressed in a letter (or many letters) to an elected official or to the editor of a newspaper, turnout at a protest march, the statements of a special interest group, the results of an election, or the findings of survey research. Often public opinion is gathered by impressions—legislators' sense of their districts, what their political intimates tell them, or the number of interest group representatives they see or hear. More and more often, however, public opinion is being derived scientifically from efforts to poll citizens.

Survey research is now a major element of political life, and citizens are constantly bombarded with poll results. Besides independent polling concerns such as the Gallup Organization, which periodically release information concerning public attitudes, the three television networks have joined with major newspapers to create polling groups. Other efforts abound, and it seems fair to say that polling has become a major way of interpreting public opinion at the state, local, and national levels. Virtually all issues on the public agenda have generated public opinion data.

As opinion-gathering devices, polls are powerful vehicles for those who believe in majoritarian democracy. Unlike other methods of discovering public opinion, polls can represent the entire public, not just those elements with political resources or well-organized interest groups. Polls can be superior even to elections, because they report what everyone thinks rather than only what those who bother to vote think. Since poll results can make politicians aware of citizens' wishes, polls have the capacity to make government more responsible.

But not everyone believes poll-measured public opinion serves democratic ideals well. Often polls solicit opinions (and get them) on subjects on which little or no real opinion exists, such as on foreign policy. Not all polls are accurate, but their scientific aura lends them some credibility. Because all opinions count equally, polls tend to underrepresent intense opinion and give extra influence to the apathetic. Critics tend to believe that polls actually inhibit responsible government by forcing politicians to respond to public wishes that may be ill informed. Political leaders, in their quest for office, may follow poll results even when the long-term interests of the public are not well served.

Overall, both defenders and critics of opinion polls can point to convincing evidence for their views. Politicians are probably somewhat constrained by poll data and are restrained from taking action of which the public would disapprove. Programs such as Social Security, for example, are retained in their current form largely because the public strongly supports them. But it is also true that consistent, overwhelming majorities in the polls do not necessarily dictate public policy. This can be seen in the case of gun control; as early as 1938 the national polls showed that more than 80 percent of the public favored handgun registration, but the organized efforts of the National Rifle Association have thwarted the passage of such a law.

The selections in this chapter were chosen to explain public opinion through the instrument of political polling. In the first selection, Larry Bartels argues that survey questions on policy matters typically are so prone to "framing effects" that it is virtually impossible to discern public preferences. He questions whether the idealized notion of "popular rule," where decision makers translate citizen wishes into government policy, is possible, given the current state of opinion polling. In the second selection, Michael Traugott raises a number of issues concerning the survey design quality of many polling efforts. Technological advances have increased the numbers of those in the polling business, particularly at the local level, but it has become more difficult to separate "good" polls from "bad" ones. Response rates are down as well, raising issues about the representative nature of many polls. The final selection discusses an interpretation of polls on a substantive issue. John Mueller explores the parallels in public support for the Korean War, the Vietnam War, and the conflict in Iraq that began in 2003. He suggests that support in each case mounted as casualties rose and that mass public opinion acts as a constraint on decision makers in their foreign policymaking, limiting their options.

4.1

Is "Popular Rule" Possible?

Larry M. Bartels

Many believe an essential component of modern democracy is the ability of elected representatives to convert public preferences into public policy. An assumption underlying this premise is that such preferences exist and that tools such as public opinion polls can help discover such information.

In this provocative piece, Larry Bartels argues that the notion of "popular rule" is at odds with what researchers have found concerning the electorate's attitudes and preferences. Evidence suggests that although citizens may have meaningful beliefs and values, survey-gathered information often identifies vague and fluid attitudes rather than clear, meaningful public preferences on issues of public policy. A major problem is that survey questions are susceptible to "framing effects"— situations in which different ways of posing a policy issue produce distinctly different public responses. The way a question is worded, the order of the question in the survey, and the context in which the survey is administered may all cause great variation in citizen responses on policy matters. As a consequence, inferences from polls claiming to discern the policy preferences of the public must be viewed with extreme caution.

The celebrated political philosopher H. L. Mencken once characterized democracy as "the theory that the common people know what they want, and deserve to get it good and hard." Democratic theorists have mostly focused on the latter issue, without taking seriously the complexities lurking beneath the notion that "the common people know what they want." The ubiquity of opinion polls probing every conceivable aspect of modern politics and government both reflects and reinforces the notion that the primary problem of modern democracy is to translate definite public preferences into

Larry M. Bartels is the Donald Stokes Professor of Public and International Affairs and the Director of the Center for the Study of Democratic Politics, Woodrow Wilson School of Public and International Affairs, Princeton University.

Larry M. Bartels, "Is 'Popular Rule' Possible? Polls, Political Psychology, and Democracy," *The Brookings Review* 21, no. 3 (Summer 2003): 12–15. Reprinted by permission of The Brookings Institution.

policy. Leaders may ignore the dictates of public opinion, but they are assumed to do so only with good reason—and at their electoral peril.

My aim here is to suggest that this conventional view of democracy is fundamentally unrealistic. Whether it would be desirable to have a democracy based on public opinion is beside the point, because public opinion of the sort necessary to make it possible simply does not exist. The very idea of "popular rule" is starkly inconsistent with the understanding of political psychology provided by the past half-century of research by psychologists and political scientists. That research offers no reason to doubt that citizens have meaningful values and beliefs, but ample reason to doubt that those values and beliefs are sufficiently complete and coherent to serve as a satisfactory starting point for democratic theory. In other words, citizens have attitudes but not preferences—a distinction directly inspired by the work of psychologists Daniel Kahneman and Amos Tversky. My argument extends [certain research,] which challenges the behavioral assumptions underlying conventional economic theory, to the realm of politics and emphasizes particularly the challenge it poses to the most fundamental assumptions of democratic theory.

"Framing Effects"

Kahneman and Tversky have called attention to "framing effects"—situations in which different ways of posing, or "framing," a policy issue produce distinctly different public responses. Framing effects are hard to accommodate within a theory built on the assumption that citizens have definite preferences to be elicited; but they are easy to reconcile with the view that any given question may tap a variety of more or less relevant attitudes. The problem for democratic theory is that the fluidity and contingency of attitudes make it impossible to discern meaningful public preferences on issues of public policy, because seemingly arbitrary variations in choice format or context may produce contradictory expressions of popular will.

Survey researchers have been generating examples of framing effects for several decades in experimental work on question wording and question ordering. But only recently have they begun to think of them as manifestations of more general psychological phenomena—especially of the fundamental context-dependency of attitudes. The normative implications of question-wording and question-ordering effects for our understanding of democracy remain virtually unexplored.

Framing effects can be demonstrated most simply by noting the impact on survey responses of prompting respondents to consider some particular aspect of an issue that might otherwise have been overlooked. In a classic 1950 study by Herbert Hyman and Paul Sheatsley, half of a national sample was asked, "Do you think the United States should let Communist newspaper reporters from other countries come in here and send back to their papers the news as they see it?" To that question, 36 percent said yes. The other half of the sample was asked the same question, but only after being asked whether "a Communist country like Russia should let American newspaper reporters come in and send back to America the news as they see it." In this second group, 90 percent agreed that American reporters should be allowed in Russia, and 73 percent—twice the share in the first half-sample—said that communist reporters should be allowed to work in the United States. Clearly, asking first about American reporters in Russia prompted respondents in the second group to apply a norm of reciprocity that blunted (though it did not entirely supplant) strong anti-communist attitudes. . . .

What's in a Name?

Even more perplexing issues arise when the original question is not merely elaborated but altered. Some of the most striking framing effects on record come from question-wording experiments conducted as part of the 1984, 1985, and 1986 General Social Surveys. Respondents were asked whether "we" are spending "too much, too little, or about the right amount" on each of a variety of government programs. Separate random subsamples evaluated essentially similar sets of programs, but with more or less subtle differences in how each was denoted. Some of these subtle differences produced large differences in apparent public opinion. Most spectacularly, while only 20–25 percent of the respondents each year said that too little was being spent on "welfare," 63–65 percent said that too little was being spent on "assistance to the poor."

"Welfare" clearly has deeply unpopular connotations for significant segments of the American public and evokes rather different mental images than does "assistance to the poor." But these different images are attached to the same set of programs and policies; any effort to make subtle distinctions of substance between "welfare" and "assistance to the poor" seems fruitlessly tendentious. Nevertheless, one frame suggests that a substantial majority of the public supports spending more on those programs, while the other—equally legitimate on its face—suggests that the same programs are deeply unpopular. What should a democratic theorist make of this perplexing situation? How might either question—or either outcome—be judged more appropriate than the other?

Sometimes even more arbitrary choices of question wording can produce large differences in opinion. Most people, for example, would presumably acknowledge that "forbidding" an action is substantively equivalent to "not allowing" it. But as Howard Schuman and Stanley Presser have noted, in three separate split-sample experiments in the mid-1970s, between 44 percent and 48 percent of the American public would "not allow" a communist to give a speech, while only about half that share would "forbid" him or her to do so. Substantively identical questions produce markedly different results. Which result reflects the public's "true" opinion? I can suggest no sensible way to answer that question.

I interpret these framing effects as evidence for the thesis that citizens have attitudes rather than preferences. The contrasting patterns of responses documented in a variety of opinion surveys and experiments reflect real attitudes. The attitudes are neither meaningless nor whimsical nor—at least in any common-language sense—irrational. But neither are they the solid bedrock of comprehensive, logically consistent preferences that most liberal political theorists have taken as a starting point for democratic theory.

No Issue Is Immune

How ubiquitous are these framing effects? Are the examples cited here simply carefully selected anomalies, or are they the tips of icebergs? There is good reason to be wary of overgeneralization, given the wide variety of political issues and choice contexts in any functioning democracy, as well as the striking variation in information, motivation, and cognitive capacity in any mass public. But if these framing effects reflect fundamental aspects of the psychology of attitudes, they should appear with some frequency even in situations that seem ripe for the assumption that citizens have complete and consistent preferences over policy outcomes. This point may be dramatized by drawing examples from two issue areas often seen as prime exceptions to the generally disorganized and fluid character of American public opinion—abortion and affirmative action. The vagaries of survey responses evident even in these realms of unusual salience and concreteness reinforce the notion that public opinion is inherently sensitive to arbitrary aspects of how political issues are framed and political objects denoted.

Some of the complexities running beneath the surface of public opinion even on abortion are suggested by Paul Freedman and Ken Goldstein's analysis of responses to two questions on the topic in American National Election Study surveys. In response to a general question about abortion in the 1996 survey, about 40 percent of respondents said that "by law, a woman should always be able to obtain an abortion as a matter of personal choice." However, in response to a different abortion question posed in 1997, 39 percent of these same 1996 pro-choice respondents favored "a proposed law to ban certain types of late-term abortions, sometimes called partial birth abortions." (Of the remaining pro-choice respondents, 49 percent opposed a ban on partial birth abortions; 12 percent were undecided.) That is, a substantial fraction of those who believed that abortions should "always" be permitted "as a matter of personal choice" also believed that "partial birth abortions" should be banned. While it might be possible to render these two positions logically consistent (for example, by stipulating the availability of some practical alternative to partial birth abortions in situations where they are now being chosen), it seems more straightforward simply to acknowledge that when it comes to public opinion, "always" never means always. . . .

Nor is it obvious how one could clarify public preferences regarding abortion policy through more careful question writing. Some of the ambiguities inherent in any such attempt at clarification are suggested by another analysis of data from the 1997 National Election Study survey, this one by Virginia Sapiro. Half the respondents were asked to rate "opponents of abortion" and "supporters of abortion" on a 100-point "feeling thermometer"; the other half were asked to rate "pro-life people" and "pro-choice people."* It seems fruitless to deny that these are, in essence, alternative ways of tapping exactly the same substantive attitudes. Nevertheless, Sapiro found that they produced significantly different results, with both "pro-life" and "pro-choice" people being rated much more favorably than abortion "opponents" or "supporters," respectively. The differences appeared consistently among men and women, among more and less politically informed respondents, and among those who were themselves opponents and supporters of abortion. While these differences testify to the success of the rhetorical strategies adopted by abortion partisans in labeling themselves as "pro-choice" and "pro-life," they do nothing to justify one's faith in the reality of public attitudes toward them independent of the particular words by which they are denoted.

From Opinion Polls to Referenda

One might still object that questions in opinion surveys are a far cry from real political decisions and that peculiar responses to survey questions even about an issue as salient and fundamental as abortion have little genuine relevance for democratic theory. That objection seems to me misguided in both its aspects. Although most consequential decisions in democracies are made by representatives, and not directly by citizens in policy referenda, theories of representation are almost invariably grounded in analogous choices of policies by representatives, or of representatives by citizens, or both. As long as we continue to evaluate democracy in terms of the correspondence between citizens' preferences and policy outcomes, all the same theoretical problems will reappear when we attempt to specify what kind of representation is most democratic. . . .

The practical reality of these conceptual problems is illustrated by a 1997 referendum on affirmative action programs in Houston. As reported on November 6 in the *New York Times* by Sam Howe Verhovek, "the future of affirmative action may depend more than anything else on the language in which it is framed."

---

*A "feeling thermometer" is a device used to access a respondent's feelings (affective orientation) toward groups, political figures, countries, etc. Respondents are given a ratings scale ranging from 0 to 100 degrees in the form of a thermometer, where a rating of 0 degrees represents maximum "coldness" toward the object being assessed, 50 degrees represents a neutral point, and 100 degrees represents maximum "warmth" toward the object.

> The vote Tuesday came only after a tumultuous debate in the City Council over the wording of the measure. Rather than being asked whether they wanted to ban discrimination and "preferential treatment," to which voters said a clear "yes" in California last year and to which polls showed Houston voters would also say "yes," residents were instead asked whether they wished specifically to ban affirmative action in city contracting and hiring.
>
> The legal effect was the same under either wording, but to this revised question they answered "no" by 55 percent to 45 percent. . . .
>
> Affirmative-action proponents around the nation hailed not just the result of Houston's vote, but the phrasing of the referendum as a straight up-or-down call on affirmative action, and they said that is the way the question should be put to voters elsewhere.
>
> Its opponents, meanwhile, who are already in court challenging the City Council's broad rewording as illegal, denounced it as a heavy-handed way of obscuring the principles that were really at stake.

Who is to decide what principles are "really at stake" in such a policy choice? If we accept, for the sake of argument, that a referendum using the original wording "taken almost directly from the Civil Rights Act of 1964" would have passed, as most observers seem to have believed, would that result have been more or less legitimate than the actual result? These questions are of a piece with those raised by the research of psychologists and public opinion researchers. Political elites who pose referendum questions must frame complex, difficult political issues in specific, concrete language. If citizens had definite, preexisting preferences regarding the underlying issues, any reasonable choice of language might elicit those preferences equally well. But democracy with attitudes requires some more detailed, normatively compelling account of what makes one frame more appropriate than another as a basis for democratic choice. In the absence of such an account, political debate and policy choice become a rhetorical free-for-all—a practical art in which, at best, the ends justify the means. . . .

Popular Rule—Or Popular Veto?

The realization that attitude expressions are powerfully (and, in my view, intrinsically and unavoidably) context-dependent should spur democratic theorists to specify more clearly how political issues ought to be framed. Theoretical work along these lines may be inspired and informed by relevant empirical research, but first and foremost it will require a more subtle specification of the moral grounds on which one political context or institution might be deemed superior to another. It will not be sufficient to evaluate contexts or institutions by reference to their success or failure in reflecting citizens' preferences, since that is merely to beg the question.

The most obvious alternative to theoretical progress along these lines is a much-diluted version of democratic theory in which the ideal of "popular rule" is replaced by what William Riker once characterized as "an intermittent, sometimes random, even perverse, popular veto" on the machinations of political elites. If that sort of democracy is the best we can hope for, we had better reconcile ourselves to the fact. On the other hand, if we insist on believing that democracy can provide some attractive and consistent normative basis for evaluating policy outcomes, we had better figure out more clearly what we are talking about.

Questions for Discussion

1. In his conclusion, Bartels questions whether it would ever be possible to achieve the idealized notion of "popular rule" that some believe is essential for democracy. What do you think?
2. How might questions on a public opinion survey on the Iraq War be "framed" to show broad public support for the efforts of the Bush administration? To show opposition to the Bush administration's efforts?

 4.2

Can We Trust the Polls?

Michael W. Traugott

Public opinion polls—frequently conducted, and with results that are widely disseminated—are considered to be an essential feature of modern American democracy. But how much confidence should we place in the polls? In this selection, Michael Traugott suggests that poll consumers should be cautious in assigning meaning to many of the surveys that are reported; extra attention should be placed on how individual polls are conducted. In his view, although

Michael W. Traugott is a professor of communications studies and political science at the University of Michigan and senior research scientist at the Institute for Social Research.

Michael W. Traugott, "Can We Trust the Polls? It All Depends," *The Brookings Review* 21, no. 3 (Summer 2003): 8–11. Reprinted by permission of The Brookings Institution.

there has been an increase in the availability of polls, in some respects their quality may have declined.

Traugott identifies a number of serious problems. Thanks to technology and the falling costs of computers, phone service, and statistical software, it is inexpensive for almost anyone to get into the polling business. One consequence is that there has been a huge proliferation of polls being conducted at the local level. Such polls, in particular, may not be well administered and it is often difficult to determine if they meet the rigorous standards of the polling profession. According to Traugott, "The problem is exacerbated because journalists and others who report on public opinion are not generally well trained in assessing poll results and thus cannot always weed out 'bad' poll results before they enter the news stream and become 'fact.' "

Even the national-level polling industry faces challenges in designing surveys representative of the population under study. Response rates have been declining and new technologies (such as the increasing use of cell phones and caller ID) make it difficult for all members of the population to be included in the frame from which a sample is drawn. Pre-election pollsters must now contend with the fact that many Americans vote well before Election Day (early voting, absentee voting, vote-by-mail, etc.), and in some states citizens can decide at the last minute that they want to vote, even if they were not registered previously. Predictions on turnout and preferences may be muddled as a result. Such problems can be managed, but it takes a major commitment of resources and much more sophisticated survey designs.

Can we trust the polls? Under the best of circumstances, the answer is "Not necessarily without a fair amount of detailed information about how they were conducted." This general note of caution applies at any time to any poll consumer. But today, with polls proliferating in the media and with methodological concerns increasing within the polling industry, caution is even more warranted. This is not to suggest that the general quality of polling data is declining or that the problems facing pollsters have no answers. Still, consumers of polling data need to be more careful than ever.

Proliferating Polls

In a period of rapidly advancing technology and falling costs for computers, long-distance telephone service, and statistical software, it is easier than ever for start-up companies to get into the polling business. Because most polling now takes place on the telephone, it is cheap and easy for someone who wants to get into the polling business to buy a sample, write a short questionnaire for a Computer Assisted Telephone Interviewing (CATI) application, buy interviewing services from a field house, and receive a report based on the marginals for each question and a limited set of cross-tabulations.

As a consequence, the opportunity to see the results of a poorly conducted poll has become more frequent, even if we can't assess exactly whether the probability of seeing one has changed. The problem is exacerbated because journalists and others who report on public opinion are not generally well trained in assessing poll results and thus cannot always weed out "bad" poll results before they enter the news stream and become "fact." So the risk is growing that local polls on national or local issues may be less well conducted or less well reported than those conducted by major national organizations.

Neither poll consumers nor journalists who write about polls have access to quality-control criteria or certification processes by which to assess specific firms or individuals. As a result, all must rely on news organizations to evaluate polls on the basis of the standards of disclosure of poll results adopted by organizations like the American Association for Public Opinion Research (AAPOR) and the National Council of Public Polls (NCPP). And they should report any concerns they have about such items. Information thus made available on details such as sampling, question wording, field dates, and response rates is useful for the few informed poll consumers who can interpret it.

Declining Response Rates

Falling response rates are a concern for the entire survey research industry, whether academic researchers, political consultants who work for candidates, or news organizations. Recent compilations of response rates in telephone surveys by the Council for Marketing and Opinion Research suggest that studies with short field periods are now averaging about 10 percent, although most media polls have response rates in the 30–45 percent range. Although analysts have identified many factors behind this long-term trend—such as the negative impacts of telemarketers posing as pollsters and the increased use of various call-screening devices—we don't yet understand well how much each contributes to the overall decline. Researchers are also beginning to understand that declining participation rates probably affect different kinds of political polls in different ways.

For preelection polls that project the outcome of a race, preliminary research suggests that the same factors that may lower participation in surveys may also lower participation in elections. Declining response rates thus do not seem to pose dangers to the accuracy of estimates of the outcome of recent presidential elections. More research will help clarify whether declining participation will affect preelection estimates in lower-turnout elections held in nonpresidential years or whether over time it will have different effects on future preelection estimates.

Preelection polls are unusual in that their accuracy can be checked against the outcome of the election itself. (That characteristic may create a misplaced confidence in polling generally, since similar external validations do not apply in many other polling situations.) When it comes to polling on issues of general government policy, we do not know the potential impact of declining survey participation rates because we have no way to check the accuracy of the polls. For example, when polls assess the public's response to or appraisal of policies such as military action in Iraq or a proposed tax cut, there is no equivalent independent way to measure the validity of the measurements. There is, however, some suggestion that policy polling results may reflect more conservative or Republican views than are present in the population as a whole—a bias that would not be surprising because Republicans have long been known to be more likely to vote than Democrats (a fact accounted for in the likelihood estimators used by most polling firms).

Emerging Technology

Many polling organizations embrace new technology as a way to cut costs and speed data collection. Some new technologies also make it possible to collect more types of data. Web-based surveys, for example, can employ visual or audio stimuli that are not possible with other questionnaire designs, making them an excellent way to evaluate political commercials, especially when applied in a full experimental design. Many organizations have also turned to Web-based surveys to reduce the turnaround time between the design of a questionnaire and the start of data analysis and production of a first report of results.

Applied inappropriately, however, this technology offers several potential pitfalls for data quality. First and foremost are sampling issues related to respondent selection. Pollsters obtain respondents in three ways. They take "volunteers" who self-select themselves to answer generally available questionnaires on a Web site. They recruit volunteers, sometimes for a single survey and sometimes for a panel from which subsequent samples will be drawn. And they use a probability sample to select respondents on the telephone and supply Internet access to those who need it.

Because the availability of Web connections is not uniformly or randomly distributed in society, the existence of a "digital divide" can introduce one source of bias in volunteer samples.* This technique, for example, tends to produce samples that are more Republican and with more conservative leanings, as we have seen in such varied circumstances as post-debate polls in 2000 and more general public policy assessments since. The resulting bias tends to favor the current Bush administration and could work against a Democratic administration. Other possi-

---

*As a group, individuals with access to computers and the Internet tend to be of higher socioeconomic and educational status and reflect a different racial and ethnic profile from those without such access, creating what is known as the "digital divide." One consequence is that samples based on Web users tend to be unrepresentative of the population at large, typically undersampling those with liberal attitudes and Democratic preferences.

ble problems include fatigue from the requirement to respond to periodic and frequent surveys to maintain panel status—a requirement that could even lead, in some circumstances, to "professional" respondents. More research needs to be done on these issues, but at a minimum a poll consumer ought to know about respondent recruitment and selection for Web-based surveys.

Pollsters must also contend with the rise of cell phones. Despite the increasing penetration of these devices in the United States (approaching 75 percent), fewer than 5 percent of Americans rely solely on a cell phone. But that share is growing—and presenting pollsters with a new set of problems. First, cell phone exchanges have no general directory, and they are excluded from samples that most public polling firms can buy. Second, people who rely on cell phones are more mobile than the rest of the population, and many use phones provided by their business. If, as is likely, the geographical correspondence between the phones' assigned area codes and their owners' place of residence is poor, it may or may not be an issue for firms conducting surveys with national samples, but it could be for those conducting state or local surveys and effectively dialing out of their target area.

One further problem linked to new technology is telephone caller ID. This screening device, which alerts households to who is calling, makes it possible to avoid calls from "out of their area" or from unfamiliar numbers. In response to citizens' pleas for protection from telemarketers, the federal government is moving to develop a "do not call" list. Pollsters need not honor such list membership now, but future abuses by pollsters or telemarketers could change that. This technology too is exerting downward pressure on response rates.

New Voting Methods and Preelection Pollsters

Preelection pollsters face two relatively new problems, both of which they can manage by devoting more financial resources to their work. Whether firms will be willing to pay more to collect data with less error or bias remains to be seen.

For almost 10 years, new administrative procedures have been allowing Americans to change the way they cast their ballots. Increasingly, citizens are voting before election day—or rather, as it is coming to mean, "Vote Counting Day."

Through procedures such as "early voting" (where machines are set up in convenient locations such as malls or shopping centers as early as three weeks before election day), voting by mail (where every registered voter is sent a ballot up to 20 days before election day), and permanent absentee registration (where voters can ask to be mailed a ballot in advance of election day without indicating that they will be out of town), more and more voters are casting ballots early. In the 2000 election, about one-sixth of the national electorate voted early, and the share is growing. In selected states, the proportion can be much greater. This trend is also facilitated by other administrative changes, such as election day registration, whereby citizens can decide at the last minute that they want to vote, even if they have not previously registered.

These developments do not mean that preelection telephone polls are outmoded or will fade away. They do suggest that telephone pollsters will have to use hybrid designs that include different screening questions (Have you voted yet? Are you registered to vote in the upcoming election?). Voter News Service used such techniques in past elections, as did firms in large states—such as California, Texas, and Florida—with many early voters. Eventually telephone polls may be supplemented by exit polls of voters leaving early voting sites. Such problems are not insurmountable, but they imply added expense as well as the need for more sophisticated designs, which will likely complicate modeling the outcome of elections based on more and more disparate data sources.

A second issue for preelection pollsters—one that cropped up in the 2002 election—is the development by the Republican Party of 24-Hour Task Forces to counter union-based get-out-the-vote campaigns. Volunteer recruits were solicited on the Internet to make at least three calls in the final 72 hours of the campaign to encourage likely Republican voters to get to the polls. The effectiveness of these efforts has not been analyzed systematically, but they may have been of use in at least some states, especially in the South. The difficulty is that preelection pollsters, especially those linked to newspapers, traditionally poll up through Friday or Saturday to produce a story for Sunday's paper. Because their polling typically ends just as these mobilization efforts get under way, their polls could underestimate the Republican share of the vote. Pollsters could counter the problem by extending the period for preelection polling, even through Monday evening, but that would defy a set of news-making norms about the best time to publish stories about the campaign to reach the largest audience. And it also would increase data collection costs. . . .

The Internationalization of Polling

The recent military action in Iraq has increased news organizations' interest in what foreign publics, especially those in the Middle East or in states such as Afghanistan and Pakistan, think about the United States and its policies. But the polling industry in these regions is not yet well developed and typically relies on samples drawn from a few major urban areas rather than countrywide. The National Council of Public Polls has recently suggested that the issue may often be a pragmatic one for the data collection firm. In addition to cutting travel costs, these simpler designs may also reduce translation and language problems. But the resulting data also require journalists wishing to report about what others think of Americans to be careful about the level and type of generalizations they draw.

More Polls, More Problems

Public opinion polls, frequently conducted and with results that are widely disseminated, are one distinguishing feature of a healthy democracy. They provide a means for citizens to communicate with their elected representatives, and vice versa. But their value in this regard depends on the collection of high-quality data, well analyzed and appropriately interpreted.

Of late there has been a step-function increase in the availability of polls, accompanied by issues of potential reductions in quality. Such developments are not unprecedented. New technologies have, before, and will again, become available to produce data faster and cheaper, while the resulting savings are not devoted to reducing various kinds of error. No one yet fully understands what the consequences might be of the various problems outlined above. Poll consumers, as ever, have no recourse but to pay as much attention as they can to where the data came from and how they were analyzed.

Questions for Discussion

1. What factors underlie the proliferation of polling efforts, on one hand, and the potential for the decreased quality of polling results on the other? Why is the problem most pronounced at the local level?
2. Technological changes, from the Web to cell phones, appear to have the potential to bias many poll results. What political perspectives might be overrepresented? Underrepresented?

4.3

The Iraq Syndrome

John Mueller

In most instances when dealing with foreign affairs, elected officials feel relatively unconstrained by the views of the public. International issues are not a high priority for most citizens; such issues seem remote compared to matters that affect them directly such as the health of the domestic economy. But when the nation commits American troops to a foreign venture, public opinion can become a crucial driving force shaping foreign policy decisions.

In this selection, John Mueller examines the public's support for the war in Iraq, comparing patterns of support to those found during the Korean and Vietnam wars. In all three cases initially public support for war was exceptionally high, as Americans "rallied around the flag," but enthusiasm soon started to erode. In each case support decreased as the number of dead and wounded U.S. soldiers increased. Wars, as Mueller sees it, "hurt the war-initiating party not because the opposition comes up with a clashing vision . . . but because the discontent over the war translates into vague distrust of the capacities of the people running the country."

Mueller suggests than an "Iraq syndrome" is emerging, where the public is developing an aversion to U.S. involvement in future military endeavors abroad, and that American foreign policy may be affected long after the military presence has ended. Mueller speculates that one of the consequences of the Iraq syndrome is that public officials may feel constrained from taking unilateral military action and become more inclined to seek more international cooperation.

The War and the Public

American troops have been sent into harm's way many times since 1945, but in only three cases—Korea, Vietnam, and Iraq—have they been drawn into sustained ground combat and suffered more than 300 deaths

John Mueller is Woody Hayes Chair of National Security Studies, Mershon Center, and Professor of Political Science at Ohio State University.

John Mueller, "The Iraq Syndrome," *Foreign Affairs* 84, no. 6 (November/December 2005): 44–54. Reprinted by permission of *Foreign Affairs*. Copyright 2005 by the Council on Foreign Relations, Inc.

in action. American public opinion became a key factor in all three wars, and in each one there has been a simple association: as casualties mount, support decreases. Broad enthusiasm at the outset invariably erodes.

The only thing remarkable about the current war in Iraq is how precipitously American public support has dropped off. Casualty for casualty, support has declined far more quickly than it did during either the Korean War or the Vietnam War. And if history is any indication, there is little the Bush administration can do to reverse this decline.

More important, the impact of deteriorating support will not end when the war does. In the wake of the wars in Korea and Vietnam, the American public developed a strong aversion to embarking on such ventures again. A similar sentiment—an "Iraq syndrome"—seems to be developing now, and it will have important consequences for U.S. foreign policy for years after the last American battalion leaves Iraqi soil.

Drowning by Numbers

The public gave substantial support to the military ventures in Korea, Vietnam, and Iraq as the troops were sent in. In all cases, support decreased as casualties— whether of draftees, volunteers, or reservists—mounted. In each case, the increase in the number of people who considered the venture to be a mistake was steep during the war's early stages, as reluctant supporters were rather quickly alienated; the erosion slowed as approval was reduced to the harder core. (The dramatic early drop in support for the war in Korea reflected the large number of casualties suffered in the opening phase of that war.)

The most striking thing about the comparison among the three wars is how much more quickly support has eroded in the case of Iraq. By early 2005, when combat deaths were around 1,500, the percentage of respondents who considered the Iraq war a mistake—over half—was about the same as the percentage who considered the war in Vietnam a mistake at the time of the 1968 Tet offensive,* when nearly 20,000 soldiers had already died.

This lower tolerance for casualties is largely due to the fact that the American public places far less value on the stakes in Iraq than it did on those in Korea and Vietnam. The main threats Iraq was thought to present to the United

---

*The Tet offensive refers to a series of coordinated military attacks by North Vietnam and Vietcong forces upon major South Vietnamese cities and U.S. military bases starting on the evening of January 30 and the early morning of January 31, 1968 (a time chosen to correspond to lunar New Year celebrations). The attacks continued until June of that year. While the Tet offensive was a tactical defeat for the communist forces, the activity is usually credited as marking a turning point in the war. Press coverage, especially on television, of the large number of U.S. casualties and the devastation visited upon the cities and U.S. installations is credited with helping form public opinion that the war could not be won, eventually leading to U.S. withdrawal from South Vietnam.

States when troops went in—weapons of mass destruction and support for international terrorism—have been, to say the least, discounted. With those justifications gone, the Iraq war is left as something of a humanitarian venture. . . . Given the evaporation of the main reasons for going to war and the unexpectedly high level of American casualties, support for the war in Iraq is, if anything, higher than one might expect—a reflection of the fact that many people still connect the effort there to the "war" on terrorism, an enterprise that continues to enjoy huge support. In addition, the toppling of Saddam Hussein remains a singular accomplishment—something the American people had wanted since the 1991 Persian Gulf War.

When one shifts from questions about whether the war was a "mistake" or "worth it" to ones about whether the United States should get out, much the same pattern holds for Korea, Vietnam, and Iraq: relatively steep declines in support for continuing the war in the early stages, slower erosion later. However, it is close to impossible to judge how many people want to get out or stay the course at any given time because so much depends on how the question is worded. For example, there is far more support for "gradual withdrawal" or "beginning to withdraw" than for "withdrawing" or "immediate withdrawal." Thus in August 2005, *The Washington Post* found that 54 percent of respondents favored staying and 44 percent favored withdrawing when the options were posed this way: "Do you think the United States should keep its military forces in Iraq until civil order is restored there, even if that means continued U.S. military casualties, or, do you think the United States should withdraw its military forces from Iraq in order to avoid further U.S. military casualties, even if that means civil order is not restored there?" But in the same month, a Harris poll tallied only 36 percent in support of staying and 61 percent in support of withdrawing when it asked, "Do you favor keeping a large number of U.S. troops in Iraq until there is a stable government there or bringing most of our troops home in the next year?" Still, no matter how the questions are phrased, all the polls have logged increases in pro-withdrawal sentiment over the course of the war.

Many analysts have tried to link declining support to factors other than accumulating combat deaths. For example, the notion that public opinion sours as casualties increase has somehow turned into "support drops when they start seeing the body bags"—a vivid expression that some in the Bush administration have apparently taken literally. As a result, the military has worked enterprisingly to keep Americans from seeing pictures of body bags or flag-draped coffins in the hope that this will somehow arrest the decline in enthusiasm for the war effort. But such pictures are not necessary to drive home the basic reality of mounting casualties.

Growing opposition to the war effort also has little to do with whether or not there is an active antiwar movement at home. There has not been much of one in the case of the Iraq war, nor was there one during the war in Korea. . . .

Moreover, support for the war declines whether or not war opponents are able to come up with specific policy alternatives. Dwight Eisenhower never seemed

Figure 1

U.S. Public Opinion on the Wars in Iraq, Korea, and Vietnam

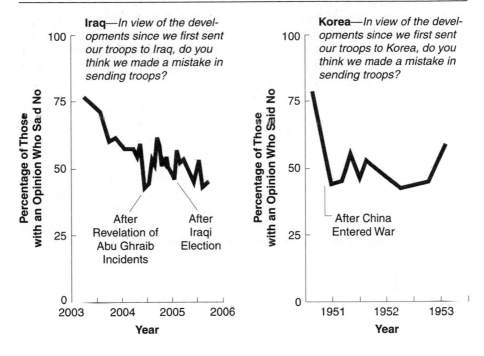

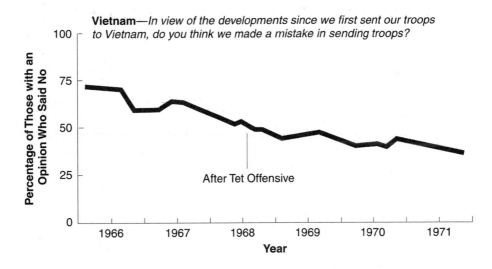

to have much of a plan for getting out of the Korean War—although he did say that, if elected, he would visit the place—but discontent with the war still worked well for him in the 1952 election; Richard Nixon's proposals for fixing the Vietnam mess were distinctly unspecific, although he did from time to time mutter that he had a "secret plan." Wars hurt the war-initiating political party not because the opposition comes up with a coherent clashing vision . . . but because discontent over the war translates into vague distrust of the capacities of the people running the country. . . .

Damage Control

President George W. Bush, like Lyndon Johnson before him, has made count-less speeches explaining what the effort in Iraq is about, urging patience, and asserting that progress is being made. But as was also evident during Woodrow Wilson's campaign to sell the League of Nations to the American public, the efficacy of the bully pulpit is much overrated. The prospects for reversing the erosion of support for the war in Iraq are thus limited. The run-ups to the two wars in Iraq are also instructive in this regard: even though both Presidents Bush labored mightily to sell the war effort, the only thing that succeeded in raising the level of enthusiasm was the sight of troops actually heading into action, which triggered a predictable "rally round the flag" effect.

Although the impact of official rhetoric is limited, favorable occurrences in the war itself can boost support from time to time. In the case of the war in Iraq, for example, there were notable upward shifts in many polls after Saddam was captured and elections were held. These increases, however, proved to be tem-porary, more bumps on the road than permanent changes in direction. Support soon fell back to where it had been before and then continued its generally downward course. The same is true of negative occurrences: a drop in support after the disclosure of abuses at Abu Ghraib in 2004 was in time mostly reversed.

Some scholars have argued that support for war is determined by the prospects for success rather than casualties. Americans are "defeat-phobic" rather than "casualty-phobic," the argument goes; they do not really care how many casualties are suffered so long as their side comes out the winner. . . .

There never were periods of continuous good news in the wars in Korea or Vietnam, so there is no clear precedent here. But should good news start coming in from Iraq—including, in particular, a decline in American casualty rates—it would more likely cause the erosion in public support to slow or even cease rather than trigger a large upsurge in support. For support to rise notably, many of those now disaffected by the war would need to reverse their position, and that seems rather unlikely: polls that seek to tap intensity of feeling find that more than 80 percent of those opposed to the war "strongly" feel that way. If you purchase a car for twice what it is worth, you will still consider the deal to have been a mistake even if you come to like the car.

Also relevant is the fact that despite the comparatively mild-mannered behavior of Democratic leaders in the run-up to the Iraq war, partisan differences regarding this war, and this president, are incredibly deep. . . . [T]he partisan divide over the war in Iraq is considerably greater than for any military action over the last half century and . . . the partisan split on presidential approval ratings, despite a major narrowing after the attacks of September 11, 2001, is greater than for any president over that period—greater than for Clinton, Reagan, or Nixon. This means that Bush cannot look for increased Republican support because he already has practically all of it; meanwhile, Democrats are unlikely to budge much. There may be some hope for him among independents, but their war-support patterns more nearly track those of the almost completely disaffected Democrats than those of the steadfast Republicans.

Moreover, it is difficult to see what a spate of good news would look like at this point. A clear-cut victory, like the one scored by George H. W. Bush in the Gulf in 1991, is hugely unlikely—and the glow even of that one faded quickly as Saddam continued to hold forth in Iraq. From the start of the current Iraq war, the invading forces were too small to establish order, and some of the early administrative policies proved fatally misguided. In effect, the United States created an instant failed state, and clambering out of that condition would be difficult in the best of circumstances. If the worst violence diminishes, and Iraq thereby ceases to be quite so much of a *bloody* mess, the war will attract less attention. But there is still likely to be plenty of official and unofficial corruption, sporadic vigilantism, police misconduct, militia feuding, political backstabbing, economic travail, regional separatism, government incompetence, rampant criminality, religious conflict, and posturing by political entrepreneurs spouting anti-American and anti-Israeli rhetoric. Under such conditions, the American venture in Iraq is unlikely to be seen as a great victory by those now in opposition, over half of whom profess to be not merely dissatisfied with the war, but angry over it.

In all of this, what chiefly matters for American public opinion is American losses, not those of the people defended. By some estimates, the number of Iraqis who have died as a result of the invasion has reached six figures—vastly more than have been killed by all international terrorists in all of history. . . . Yet the only cumulative body count that truly matters in the realm of American public opinion, and the only one that is routinely reported, is the American one. There is nothing new about this: although there was considerable support for the wars in Korea and Vietnam, polls made clear that people backed the wars because they saw them as vital to confronting the communist threat; defending the South Koreans or the South Vietnamese per se was never thought of as an important goal.

The Politics of Debacle

In Iraq, as they did in Vietnam, U.S. troops face an armed opposition that is dedicated, resourceful, capable of replenishing its ranks, and seemingly determined to fight as long as necessary. In Vietnam, the hope was that after suffering enough punishment, the enemy would reach its "breaking point" and then either fade away or seek accommodation. Great punishment was inflicted, but the enemy never broke; instead, it was the United States that faded away after signing a face-saving agreement. Whether the insurgents in Iraq have the same determination and fortitude is yet to be seen. The signs thus far, however, are not very encouraging: the insurgency does not appear to be weakening.

Many people, including President Bush, argue that the United States must slog on because a precipitous exit from Iraq would energize Islamist militants, who would see it as an even greater victory that the expulsion of the Soviet Union from Afghanistan. A quick exit would confirm, the thinking goes, Osama bin Laden's basic theory: that terrorists can defeat the United States by continuously inflicting on it casualties that are small in number but still draining. A venture designed and sold as a blow against international terrorists would end up emboldening and energizing them.

The problem is that almost any exit from Iraq will have this effect. Bin Laden, as well as huge majorities in Muslim countries and in parts of Europe, believe that the United States invaded Iraq as part of its plan to control oil supplies in the Middle East. Although Washington has no intention of doing that, at least not in the direct sense that bin Laden and others mean, U.S. forces will inevitably leave Iraq without having accomplished what many consider to be Washington's real goals there—and the terrorist insurgents will claim credit for forcing the United States out before it fulfilled these key objectives. Iraq has also, of course, become something of a terrorist training—and inspiration—zone.

When the United States was preparing to withdraw from Vietnam, many Americans feared that there would be a bloodbath if the country fell to the North Vietnamese. And indeed, on taking control, the Communists executed tens of thousands of people, sent hundreds of thousands to "reeducation camps" for long periods, and so mismanaged the economy that hundreds of thousands fled the country out of desperation, often in barely floating boats. . . .

There is a similar concern this time around: Iraq could devolve into a civil war after the Americans leave. Thus, U.S. officials have updated "Vietnamization" and applied it to Iraq. They are making strenuous efforts to fabricate a reasonably viable local government, police, and military that can take over the fight, allowing U.S. forces to withdraw judiciously. In Vietnam, of course, communist forces took over less than two years after the United States installed a sympathetic government. Although the consequences of a U.S. withdrawal from Iraq are likely to be messy, they may be less dire. The insurgency in Iraq, albeit deadly and dedicated, represents a much smaller, less popular, and less organized force than the Vietcong did, and it does not have the same kind of international backing. Moreover, many of the insurgents are fighting simply to get U.S. troops out of the country and can be expected to stop when the Americans leave. The insurgency will likely become more manageable without the U.S. presence, even if there is a determined effort by at least some of the rebels to go after a government that, in their eyes, consists of quislings and collaborators. It is also impressive that efforts by the insurgents to stoke a civil war between the Shiites and the Sunnis have not been very successful thus far; most Shiites have refused to see the insurgents as truly representative of the Sunni population.*

Even if Iraq does turn out to be a foreign policy debacle—by declining into a hopeless quagmire or collapsing into civil chaos—history suggests that withdrawing need not be politically devastating (unless, perhaps, failure in Iraq leads directly to terrorism in the United States). As it happens, the American people have proved quite capable of taking debacle in stride; they do not seem to be terribly "defeat-phobic." They supported the decision to withdraw U.S. troops from Lebanon in 1984 after a terrorist bomb killed 241 Americans in the civil war there; the man who presided over that debacle, Ronald Reagan, readily won reelection a few months later. Something similar happened to Bill Clinton when he withdrew troops from Somalia in 1994: by the time the next election rolled around, people had largely forgotten the whole episode.

The most remarkable, and relevant, precedent is the utter collapse of the U.S. position in Vietnam in 1975. The man who presided over that debacle, Gerald Ford, actually tried to use it to his advantage in his reelection campaign the next year. As he pointed out, when he came into office the United States was "still deeply involved in the problems of Vietnam, [but now] we are at peace. Not a single young American is fighting or dying on any foreign soil tonight." His challenger, Jimmy Carter, apparently did not think it good politics to point out the essential absurdity of Ford's declaration.

Moreover, even if disaster follows a U.S. withdrawal—as it did in Vietnam, Lebanon,[†] and Somalia[††]—the people dying will be Iraqis, not Americans. And the deaths of foreigners, as noted earlier, are not what move the public.

---

*The relationship between Shiites and Sunnis has clearly eroded since Mueller first published this article, and most observers now believe that the insurgency has evolved into a virtual sectarian civil war. Militias organized around various Shiite and Sunni religious figures have been playing a prominent role in the conflict; domestic casualties on both sides have continued to rise.

[†]On October 22,1983, a suicide bomber left hundreds of American servicemen dead and numerous others wounded in an attack on a military compound and barracks in Beirut, Lebanon. The soldiers, mostly Marines, were part of a United Nations international contingent on a peacekeeping mission. In February 1984, President Reagan withdrew American personnel from the UN force.

[††]In 1993, a United Nations contingent was involved in an effort to help alleviate extreme famine conditions in the context of a civil war in Somalia. U.S. military personnel were part of the UN force, eighteen of whom lost their lives after a helicopter was shot down. Some of the Americans were then shown on American TV being dragged through the streets by an angry, shouting mob. President Clinton soon withdrew American forces from Somalia.

Indispensable Nation?

. . . No matter how the war in Iraq turns out, an Iraq syndrome seems likely. A poll in relatively war-approving Alabama earlier this year [2005], for example, asked whether the United States should be prepared to send troops back to Iraq to establish order there in the event a full-scale civil war erupted after a U.S. withdrawal. Only a third of the respondents favored doing so.

Among the casualties of the Iraq syndrome could be the Bush doctrine. . . . Specifically, there will likely be growing skepticism about various key notions: that the United States should take unilateral military action to correct situations or overthrow regimes it considers reprehensible but that present no immediate threat to it, that it can and should forcibly bring democracy to other nations not now so blessed, that it has the duty to rid the world of evil, that having by far the largest defense budget in the world is necessary and broadly beneficial, that international cooperation is of only very limited value, and that Europeans and other well-meaning foreigners are naive and decadent wimps. The United States may also become more inclined to seek international cooperation, sometimes even showing signs of humility.

In part because of the military and financial overextension in Iraq (and Afghanistan), the likelihood of any coherent application of military power or even of a focused military threat against the remaining entities on the Bush administration's once-extensive hit list has substantially diminished. In the meantime, any country that suspects it may be on the list has the strongest incentive to make the American experience in Iraq as miserable as possible. Some may also come to consider that deterring the world's last remaining superpower can be accomplished by preemptively and prominently recruiting and training a few thousand of their citizens to fight and die in dedicated irregular warfare against foreign occupiers.

Evidence of the Iraq syndrome is emerging. Already, Bush has toned down his language. When North Korea abruptly declared in February [2005] that it actually possessed nuclear weapons, the announcement was officially characterized as "unfortunate" and as "rhetoric we've heard before." Iran has already become defiant, and its . . . president has actually had the temerity to suggest—surely the unkindest cut—that he does not consider the United States to be the least bit indispensable. Ultimately, the chief beneficiaries of the war in Iraq may be Iraq's fellow members of the "axis of evil."

Questions for Discussion

1. This article appeared in late 2005. Have some of Mueller's speculative predictions about the direction of public opinion on the Iraq War and potential

constraints on foreign policy decision makers come true? Defend your position with examples.

2. Mueller suggests that American's tolerance for war casualties has been far less in the Iraq War than during previous military conflicts in Korea and Vietnam, where the casualties were far greater. What explanations might be offered to explain such a difference?

Chapter 5

PARTICIPATION AND CIVIC ENGAGEMENT

In a democracy, political participation may take many forms, ranging from efforts by citizens merely to inform themselves about politics to running for and holding public office. Some citizens may even attempt to bypass more conventional modes of participation altogether by engaging in political protest marches or acts of civil disobedience—the nonviolent violation of laws that they believe to be unjust. For most citizens, however, political participation centers around the act of voting in an election.

Participation in free elections provides citizens with many benefits. When people believe they can communicate their needs and wants to those who govern, government becomes both stable and legitimate. Elections teach civic virtues and give citizens a sense of responsibility and personal satisfaction.

The key role of elections, however, is to provide a check on power. As James Madison wrote in *The Federalist*, No. 51, "If Angels were to govern men, neither external nor internal controls on the government would be necessary," but in the absence of heavenly guidance government must be restrained, and "a dependence on the people is, no doubt, the primary control." The ballot box offers the public a way to control those who govern, since people seeking election must further citizens' interests to achieve public office. The public does not rule, but it influences those who do.

Although most Americans probably would be hard-pressed to give a sophisticated answer to the question "Why vote?" most firmly believe that democracy is "rule by the people" and that the cornerstone of popular democracy is free elections. Students are taught that everyone "ought to vote," and voting for the first time is a political rite of passage that serves as a powerful symbol of adulthood and allegiance to the American system. Many Americans hold the view that anyone who doesn't vote has forfeited the right to criticize the government.

In spite of these beliefs and feelings, however, many citizens do not participate in contemporary elections, a fact that could challenge the validity of popular democracy. The United States ranks near the bottom of Western democracies in voter turnout. Furthermore, current turnout rates do not compare favorably with those of past elections. For example, in presidential elections in the last half of the 1800s, about 75 percent of eligible voters turned out (nearly 82 percent in the election of 1876), whereas in most recent presidential elections turnout hovered at around 50 percent. Turnout rates in off-year state and local elections are often less than 30 percent. President Reagan, who beat President Carter by an overwhelming margin in 1980, was elected by just a little more than 27 percent of the age-eligible voters in that year.

Comparisons to our own voting rates of years past and the voting rates of other countries are fraught with difficulties. A century ago, the electorate included neither women nor blacks. Ballots were not secret, and there were few registration barriers to restrict participation by white males. This created a strong incentive for political parties to mobilize voters, sometimes by herding citizens to the polls and giving them ballots containing only one party's candidates. The eastern cities, in particular, were dominated by political machines. Consequently, some of the high-turnout figures undoubtedly resulted from political corruption.

Some countries impose a fine for not voting—a policy that would raise turnout rates in the United States but would be interpreted as undemocratic by most Americans. Many Western democracies calculate turnout as the percentage of those on the electoral rolls who actually participate in an election, whereas in the United States turnout is calculated by dividing the number who vote by the total potential electorate—all persons of voting age, as determined by the U.S. Bureau of the Census. If this method were applied by other countries, U.S. voting rates would differ little from those of Canada, Great Britain, and Japan.

Surprisingly, voter turnout in the United States has constantly declined since the 1960 presidential election. This period has been marked by rising educational levels, increasingly prominent issues, and the removal of many voting barriers, such as poll taxes and registration and residency requirements. In addition, tremendous amounts of political information have been provided by the mass media, and campaigns have grown enormously in terms of cost and candidate exposure. Newspapers often chastise citizens for being lazy and uninterested in exercising their right to vote, but explanations for the turnout decline are much more complex.

One widely held belief is that, beginning in the mid-1960s, citizens developed mistrust of government officials and a diminished sense that their participation would make a difference. In 1966, about a quarter of the public believed the "people running the country don't care what happens to people like me." By 1977, 60 percent felt this way. By 1978, only 30 percent of Americans believed they could trust the government in Washington "to do what's right." In 1958, a similar poll revealed that 55 percent trusted the government.

Such disillusionment grew from the social disruptions of the 1960s, the assassinations of John F. Kennedy, Robert Kennedy, and Martin Luther King Jr., the unpopular Vietnam War, the Watergate scandal, and the subsequent resignation of President Nixon. Huge increases in consumer prices in the 1970s and the perceived ineffectiveness of the Carter administration in dealing with the energy crisis and with the Iranian hostage situation also contributed to citizens' perception that leaders were neither trustworthy nor competent. Some scholars suggest that television played a role, too. According to the theory of "video malaise," TV tends to overwhelm viewers with the complexities of political controversies, which convinces the public that individuals are politically ineffective and that problems may be too difficult to solve. Further, the tone of the TV medium has been generally critical of authorities, highlighting the human weaknesses and mistakes of political leaders. Many voters thus question the value of political participation.

A second widely accepted explanation for decreasing turnout relies on demographic factors. The arrival of the baby boomers at voting age during the mid-1960s, and constitutional changes that enfranchised eighteen- to twenty-year-olds, dramatically expanded the potential electorate between 1960 and 1972. Young voters made up an increasingly high proportion of the total electorate in the 1960s, 1970s, and early 1980s, yet this group participated less than older Americans did. Few saw politics as relevant to their lives. First-time eligible voters have had the lowest participation rates of any age group, perhaps because politics has to compete with schooling, social events, and dating.

The articles in this chapter have been chosen to encourage students to think about political involvement from a broad perspective, not just voting. In the first selection, Micah L. Sifry challenges the notion that apathy is largely responsible for low voter turnout. He argues that party candidates with a populist or progressive message have the potential to greatly enlarge the active electorate. The second selection deals with the role of the citizen in contemporary politics. Michael Schudson argues that our current concept of citizenship, based on the Progressive model, needs revision. He asserts that we need a new concept of citizenship, one that makes demands on us but is not burdened with impossible expectations. The third selection, by Robert D. Putnam, posits a linkage between the broad involvement of citizens in the associational life of their community and the health of American democracy. Putnam is dismayed by the decline of "social capital" that seems to have characterized American politics over the past quarter of a century. But there may be room for optimism. In the final selection, Scott Keeter profiles the political orientations of the most recent generation of young voters. Voter turnout of this age group rose markedly in the 2004 elections and may presage more political engagement in the future.

5.1

Finding the Lost Voters

Micah L. Sifry

Few subjects engender more heated discussion during and after an election than the nation's low voter-turnout rate. Although voter registration barriers have been virtually eliminated and party and candidate expenditures have been setting records in efforts to reach voters, turnout typically involves barely half of the age-eligible voters in presidential elections and usually well less than a third in sub-presidential races.

In this selection, Micah L. Sifry suggests that growing alienation from the major parties lies at the heart of why many people choose not to participate in elections. Besides the rise in the number of registered independents, who tend to vote less than partisans, poll data indicates that roughly a third of nonvoters aren't apathetic about voting, but are unhappy with the choices typically offered by Republicans and Democrats. Sifry believes the best way to enlarge the active electorate would be for parties to choose candidates committed to running progressive and populist campaigns, appealing to "potential voters" rather than solely concentrating on turning out "likely voters."

A l Garcia is one frustrated Democratic campaign manager. A criminal defense lawyer by trade and a 20-year veteran of Minnesota politics, he ran two candidates for the state assembly in 1998. Both were in Anoka County, ground zero of the Jesse Ventura vote.* One candidate, Jerry Newton, a decorated Vietnam veteran and small-business owner, fiscally conservative but very supportive of public schools and the environment, lost badly to a far-right pro-lifer as the voters who turned out for Ventura voted for Republican state representatives down the ballot. Garcia's other candidate, Luanne Kos-

Micah L. Sifry is a senior analyst for Public Campaign, a public-interest group focusing on campaign finance.

"Finding the Lost Voters" by Micah L. Sifry. Reprinted with permission from *The American Prospect*, Volume 11, Number 6: January 21, 2000. The American Prospect, 11 Beacon Street, Suite 1120, Boston, MA 02108. All rights reserved.

*Jesse Ventura, a former professional wrestler, was elected in 1998 as governor of Minnesota running on the Reform Party ticket.

kinen, an incumbent with strong labor backing, barely held onto her office. Garcia's problems were hardly unique: Ventura voters across the state ended up costing Democrats control of the state assembly.

Over lunch last winter at Billie's, a popular Anoka County restaurant, Garcia delivered his postmortem: Democrats had gotten whipped because they hadn't reached out to new voters—and there had been a lot of them. . . .

And why had his candidates fared so poorly? "We were too focused on the regular voters," Garcia said. "If you hadn't voted in two out of the last four elections, you didn't get anything from Luanne or Jerry." Targeting likely voters, of course, is standard practice in most campaigns these days. But Garcia said he'd known that strategy wouldn't be enough.

"I could sense it coming," he said. "My wife told me early on that she would support Ventura, and she hates politics. All my legal clients were supporting Jesse, from the first-time DWI offenders to the major dope dealers! And he was pulling at me, in my gut. I'm a blue-collar guy who grew up in north Minneapolis. My dad's a dockworker, my mother's a waitress. Like the folks in Anoka. And he was saying things that average people could connect with."

Garcia said he'd wanted his candidates to do the same thing. "The number-one issues in Anoka are taxes, wages, and traffic. That's what we wanted to focus on." But he'd been hamstrung by a centralized campaign effort run out of the House Democratic Caucus. "They had a $15,000 mail program—half of our budget—that we were forced to buy into or lose our field worker and party funds. Six out of the nine pieces they mailed were on education, even though we said that wasn't our top concern. And they mailed to too small a target group, and they wouldn't let us change it."

Campaigns at all levels of American politics these days are focused narrowly on "likely voters," people who vote regularly. Eric Johnson, campaign manager to Hubert "Skip" Humphrey, the losing Democratic candidate for governor, admitted as much after the election. "We didn't see Ventura coming because our polling screened out unlikely voters," he told *The Wall Street Journal.* All four of Minnesota's major polling organizations also failed to predict Ventura's victory because they factored out these voters.

The assumption governing the typical political campaign is that the American electorate is a stable, predictable mass—or, worse, that they're apathetic and easily manipulated. Ventura's victory is just the latest and loudest explosion of that piece of conventional wisdom.

Indeed, politicians are making a huge mistake when they focus only on "likely voters." A large subset of the "unlikely voters" filtered out by pollsters and left out of campaign targeting efforts might be better described as *discouraged* voters—potential participants who have been turned off or pushed out by an increasingly money-driven and manipulative electoral process.

Many of these citizens, people who are disproportionately downscale and correspondingly attracted to working-class issues and symbols, can be remotivated to turn out. A central question is whether more Democrats will take their campaigns to these voters or, by failing to do so, will continue to create opportunities for outsiders ranging from Jesse Ventura to Bernie Sanders to Patrick Buchanan.

Apathy or Independence?

Public trust in government has been declining steadily over the past four decades. The authoritative surveys conducted biennially since the 1950s by the University of Michigan's National Election Studies (NES) have found that large majorities of Americans, across all demographic groups, don't believe "you can trust the government in Washington to do what is right just about always [or] most of the time." Similarly, most people think "the government is pretty much run by a few big interests looking out for themselves." According to the NES, the percentage agreeing that "people like me don't have any say about what the government does" rose from 31 percent in 1952 to 53 percent in 1996. This is a strong statement of disaffection.

But some Americans still feel better represented than others. People are more likely to believe that they "don't have any say" if they are black rather than white, are poor rather than well-off, have a limited education compared to a college diploma or postgraduate degree, or work in blue-collar jobs rather than white-collar or professional fields. For example, 62 percent of people with a high school diploma said they don't have any say in what government does, compared to 40 percent of those with more education. And about 56 percent of those in the bottom two-thirds of the national income distribution felt left out, compared to 38 percent in the top twentieth.

A similar pattern applies to how Americans think about the major political parties. In general, polls find that between 50 and 60 percent of the population believes there are "important differences in what the Republicans and Democrats stand for." But in 1996, while most people in the top income brackets believed that there were significant differences between the parties, 50 percent of people in the bottom sixth of income distribution thought there was no difference. Similarly, 59 percent of those with less than a high school education and 40 percent of those with a high school diploma said there was no difference between the parties, compared to just 25 percent of those with at least some college education. Overall, blue-collar workers were almost twice as likely as professionals to believe party distinctions were meaningless.

Among active voters, the trend is away from the major parties and toward independence. From 1990 to 1998, while the number of voters registered as independent or third-party increased approximately 57 percent, the number of registered Republicans dropped by almost 5 percent and the number of Democrats by almost 14 percent, according to data collected from state agencies by the Committee for the Study of the American Electorate. Voters' political preferences—a looser definition than party registration—showed the same trend.

The proportion of people identifying themselves as independents increased from 23 percent in 1952 to an average of 35 percent in the 1990s, according to the NES. Independent voters are somewhat more likely to be of lower income, education, age, and occupational status than hard-core party partisans (though this variation is tempered by the strong Democratic loyalties of many blacks). And 41 percent of people under the age of 29 self-identify as independents, according to a 1999 Gallup poll.

Independents are the most volatile of active voters, with a marked tendency to support candidates who come from "outside the box." All the exit polls going back to George Wallace's 1968 presidential candidacy show that voters who identify themselves as independents are about twice as likely as other voters to support third-party candidates. In Minnesota in 1998, Ventura won with 37 percent overall, but got 52 percent of independents.

As the National Voter Registration Act of 1993 (known as the motor-voter law) brings more voters onto the registration rolls, this trend toward electoral volatility seems likely to strengthen. In Florida, the numbers of registered Republicans, Democrats, and nonaffiliates/third-party registrants each rose by about 500,000 in the first two years of the law's implementation. Since 1996, however, the number of major party registrants has declined slightly, while the number of non-major party registrants has risen another 250,000. The same thing has happened in California, where the number of major party registrants has held steady since 1996, while the number of non-major party registrants has risen about 300,000.

Of course, rising voter alienation and disaffection from the two major parties does not prove that a different kind of political engagement is possible. After all, as measures of political alienation have risen, turnout in national and state elections has declined. But are citizens really just signaling their apathy when they fail to vote? Or are they more specifically alienated from the Democratic and Republican establishments and their candidates? In fact, a significant number of nonvoters look a lot like politically active independent voters.

It is difficult to find data that distinguishes those abstainers who are principled or angry and those who are merely indifferent, but it does exist. In May of 1996, the League of Women Voters released a poll that showed nonvoters were no more distrustful of the federal government than regular voters. Active voters were, however, far more likely to see significant differences between the parties on major issues, to believe that elections mattered and that their votes made a difference. The poll also suggested that efforts to mobilize voters were highly important: About three-quarters of voters said they had been contacted by a candidate or party, compared with less than half of the nonvoters.

But this says little about the actual political preferences of nonvoters. More answers can be found in two little-noticed surveys, one conducted in the summer of 1983 by ABC News, and the second done after the election of 1996 by Republican pollster Kellyanne Fitzpatrick. ABC News polled more than 2,500 voting-age Americans and then compared highly likely voters (people who were registered to vote who said they always vote) with very unlikely voters (people who were not registered to vote and gave little inclination that they were planning to vote in the next election). The Fitzpatrick poll compared a sample of 800 voters with one of 400 nonvoters. Together, the two surveys reveal some telling points.

First, about a third of nonvoters aren't apathetic. Rather, they're angry and feel shut out by the choices offered. When asked by ABC why they didn't vote in the 1980 presidential election, 36 percent of the nonvoters gave a political reason such as "None of the candidates appealed to me." Thirty-eight percent of the nonvoters in the Fitzpatrick poll didn't vote in 1996 because they "did not care for any of the candidates" or were "fed up with the political system" or "did not feel like candidates were interested in people like me."

Second, nonvoters tilt toward liberalism. In the ABC News poll, 60 percent of the nonvoters who said they had voted in 1980 recalled choosing either Jimmy Carter or John Anderson;* only 30 percent said they had voted for Ronald Reagan. Considering that after an election, voters tend to "recall" voting for the winner, this is a striking finding. Sixty-seven percent of nonvoters said they had voted for the Democratic candidate for the House of Representatives, compared to 52 percent of regular voters. In the Fitzpatrick poll, just 38 percent of nonvoters identified as conservatives, compared to 48 percent of the voting public. And while 17 percent of voters called themselves liberals, 22 percent of nonvoters chose that label. (A *New York Times*/CBS News poll found that those who were not planning to vote in the 1998 election preferred Democrats for Congress by 49 percent to 27 percent; likely voters, on the other hand, were evenly split between Republicans and Democrats.)

How to Reach Discouraged Voters

"Low turnout is the compound consequence of legal and procedural barriers intertwined with the parties' reluctance to mobilize many voters, especially working-class and minority voters," says Frances Fox Piven, who along with her husband Richard Cloward wrote *Why Americans Don't Vote* and built the movement that passed the motor-voter law. "I've come to the conclusion that party competition takes the form of demobilizing, not mobilizing, voters, because new voters threaten incumbents, raise new issues, or create the incentive to raise new issues," she adds. "You need mavericks, outsiders to try to mobilize new voters—nobody else wants to take the risk."

"Nonvoters matter a lot," agrees pollster Stanley Greenberg, "though most candidates act as if they don't. . . . There's no question that you can change the

---

*John Anderson, a Republican congressman who failed to receive his party's nomination for president, ran in the 1980 general election as an Independent. He received 6.7 percent of the votes cast.

shape and size of the electorate, though that is more true for presidential elections than for individual, even statewide, campaigns." For example, turnout increased by 5.5 percent in the three-way presidential race of 1992. "There's reason to believe that the populist economic issues that Clinton was raising and the independent-libertarian issues that Perot was raising were at work there," Greenberg argues. "By comparison, in 1994, conservative definitions of the issues brought in more rural, conservative portions of the electorate while the health care reform failure led many noncollege women to drop out." Pollster John Zogby agrees: "If there's a strong independent candidate in the race, you begin to see the numbers of undecided voters in those groups who often don't vote—younger voters, registered independents—start to decline in our surveys, a sign they are planning to vote."

Representative Jesse Jackson Jr. points to his father's 1984 and 1988 campaigns as proof that discouraged voters can be effectively mobilized. Indeed, the number of Democratic primary voters rose from 18 million in 1984 to nearly 23 million in 1988, with Reverend Jackson's total share rising by 3.4 million. "If you're able to tap into the people who aren't consciously involved in politics or following it," the younger Jackson says, "and show how everything they do has something to do with politics—that shirt they wear, the stop sign, the taxes they pay, the schools they attend, the police officer on their street . . . you can inspire them and give them reason to participate."

It takes a certain kind of candidate, message, and campaign to reach these voters. "You're not going to be able to cater to traditional economic forces that have significant influence," says Jackson. "You have to have some relationship to them, but you can't be seen as beholden to them. You have to be seen as a real American; you have to be someone who can look the press right in the face and tell them exactly how it is. You have to be Beattyite, almost Bulworthian."

Not many American politicians are trying to run this kind of campaign or can convincingly pull it off. However, there are a number of successful examples that predate Jesse Ventura. What seems to matter most is that the candidate have a populist message and style—someone who wants to empower ordinary people versus the establishment, who is blue collar as opposed to buttoned-down, who favors effective government on behalf of the interests of average working people, and who supports sweeping efforts to clean up politics and reform the electoral process itself.

Those were Paul Wellstone's attributes in 1990, when he came from nowhere—he had been a college professor and progressive activist—to win the Minnesota Senate race. Not only did Wellstone draw more votes than the Democratic candidate in the previous Senate contest; more voters came out in 1990 than did in 1988, a presidential election year. (According to Francis Fox Piven, Wellstone attributed his victory in part to the increased number of poorer voters on the rolls, thanks to the earlier passage of a state-level, agency-based voter registration system.) Something similar happened in 1998 with Iowan Tom Vilsack, who waged a successful underdog run for governor and raised the Democratic vote total nearly 20 percent over the previous gubernatorial race. And activists in Washington State argue that their 1998 ballot initiative to raise the state minimum wage to the highest level in the country had a similar effect—drawing more votes than any other item or candidate on the ballot and bringing in enough new voters to swing control of both houses of the state legislature back to the Democratic column.

In 1990, Bernie Sanders, the former socialist mayor of Burlington, won Vermont's lone seat in Congress as an independent. He ran on issues like national health care, tax fairness, environmental activism, addressing the needs of the poor, and involving working people in the political process. In his first try for Congress in 1988, he came close, drawing 37.5 percent of the vote. Two years later, he won a solid victory with 56 percent of the vote. In both races, the total vote was way up—13 percent higher—compared to the previous election cycle.

And while Sanders did well in his breakthrough victory in 1990 with the college-educated, alternative life-style types who have moved up to Vermont in the past generation, his strongest support actually came from the poor conservative hill towns and farm communities of the state's "Northeast Kingdom." For example, Sanders's strongest showing statewide came in the county of Orleans, where he pulled 62 percent of the vote. A rural county on the border of Canada that voted solidly for George Bush in 1988, Orleans had a median household income in 1990 of $22,800, about $7,000 less than the state average. Only 14.2 percent of Orleans's residents were college graduates. The standard of living was low, with homes worth on average just $66,500, compared to $95,600 statewide. Nearly 15 percent of Orleans's residents were living under the official poverty line, 4 percent more than in the rest of the state.

And then there is Jesse Ventura, a socially liberal, fiscally conservative, pro-campaign finance reform, anti-establishment candidate with a working-class style, who hit discouraged voters—as well as disaffected Democrats and Republicans—on the bull's-eye. His campaign deliberately targeted "unlikely voters" by focusing his public appearances in an "Independent Belt" of bedroom communities to the north and west of Minnesota's Twin Cities, and by placing his offbeat TV ads not on the nightly news shows but on FOX programs like *The Simpsons* and *The X-Files*, and on cable TV wrestling programs. Helped by same-day voter registration, his candidacy drastically boosted turnout, and most of those new voters pulled his lever. He won a near-majority of 18- to 44-year-olds, the heart of political independents.

In several other ways, Ventura's vote corresponded with those groups least satisfied with the existing political choices. Far more self-identified liberals than conservatives voted for him. Women voted for him almost as much as men. In the high-income professional suburbs, Ventura did poorly. In the less affluent suburbs, he did very well. Turnout in many of these blue-collar districts was over 70 percent, with as many as 20 percent of the total registering on Election Day. Many rank-and-file union members swung to Ventura as well. "I could tell going into the election," said Doug Williams, head of an electrical workers' union. "I was getting requests for information on him from my members. People were wearing his T-shirts and bumper stickers—people who hadn't really participated before."

People think Ventura won because he was a celebrity. But his early name recognition in Minnesota, while high for a third-party candidate, only gave him a chance to get the voters' attention. It's what he said and how he said it that made him a contender. "The voters saw Jesse as someone who's an outsider who's going to change things," says Ed Gross, who worked on voter targeting for the Ventura campaign. "Watching the TV debates, they saw two 'suits' and one 'nonsuit'—and most of them don't wear suits. Not only that, one of the 'suits' had worked for the other, and they both were owned by big money."

Gross recognized the dynamic from the 1990 and 1996 Wellstone campaigns for Senate, on which he had also worked. "I told Ventura, in a lot of ways, to the voters, you are a Wellstone. And voters went for Wellstone because they want to have a connection. They've felt disconnected for a long time. They want to feel like the guy up there knows how they live." In the end, they latched onto Ventura with enthusiasm. And the strength of his campaign—which succeeded in a state with one of the lowest unemployment rates in the country—stands as a warning to both of the major parties: This could happen to you.

Raising Turnout, Reviving Politics

As the barriers to voter registration have fallen with the gradual implementation of motor-voter, the pool of potential voters has grown. According to the Federal Election Commission, the total number of registered voters rose from 129 million in 1994 to 151 million in 1998, an increase of 8 percent of the total voting-age population. But politicians haven't caught on. "Candidates aren't yet campaigning to those voters," says Linda Davidoff, the former executive director of Human SERVE, the nonprofit organization set up by Piven and Cloward to spearhead the motor-voter drive. "[But] motor-voter is laying the groundwork for poorer people to participate differently. There's an enormous opportunity here for candidates who get the picture and campaign to the potential voter," she says.

Jesse Jackson, Jr., is one politician who understands very well the new potential of reaching out to discouraged voters. One of the keys to his first race, in which he beat a veteran Democratic legislator backed by the Daley political machine in a special election to fill Mel Reynolds's seat, was his energetic campaign to register young voters. "He set up voter registration tables during local college registration," says Frank Watkins, his press secretary, "and we kept a record of those people and sent them a personal letter just before the election." Jackson registered about 6,500 new voters—5,000 of whom lived in his district. It's likely that many of them made up his winning margin of 6,000 votes.

Despite Jackson's evident success and personal energy (even though he's in a safe district, he's continued to work to turn out more voters, winning more votes than almost any other member of Congress), there's been little interest from the Democratic Party establishment in helping him spread his message of increasing political participation. "We went to the DNC and showed them how we did it," Watkins says, "and they sat there and looked at us like we were crazy. They'd rather focus on raising more and more money to spend on advertising to fewer and fewer people."

Obviously, going after the discouraged voters involves taking some risks, and it may be especially hard to do so in states that close their registration rolls weeks before Election Day. And there is a deeper challenge: convincing these citizens that voting really can matter again. Noting that outward expressions of populist anger seem to have declined in recent years, pollster John Zogby points to despair about politics as the explanation. "In one of my focus groups, a guy in Cleveland said, 'I'm now in the third of a series of lousy jobs. I lost my good job in '85. I was angry before. But now it's not going to happen. Government can't do anything. And my vote doesn't matter at all.' He had downsized his expectations," Zogby concludes. Piven agrees: "The sense that politics is so corrupt, combined with neoliberal rhetoric that argues that government can't do anything, tends to demobilize people."

The ultimate challenge then for anyone seeking to connect with discouraged voters is to restore their hope while not denying that they have good reason to be cynical. What is fascinating and exciting about each of the handful of populist victories of the last decade—by Jackson, Sanders, Wellstone, and Ventura—is that in every case, their success raised expectations about politics across the country. Hope, it seems, can be contagious; we need to keep it alive.

Questions for Discussion

1. Why does Micah L. Sifry believe so few people choose to vote in American elections, despite massive campaign efforts by competing candidates? What other factors do you believe play a role in the nation's poor record for voter turnout?

2. Sifry argues that voter turnout would increase if party candidates ran progressive and populist campaigns. Is it likely that parties in the future will take his advice? Do you have any additional suggestions that might help to increase voter participation?

5.2

Voting Rites: Why We Need a New Concept of Citizenship

Michael Schudson

In the face of voter turnout far less than that found in other countries or even in our own country's early history, a common response of political observers such as the mass media is to chastise the electorate for its failure to exercise the most basic of all citizen responsibilities. According to the common wisdom, well supported by public opinion surveys, many American voters are uninformed, are disengaged from politics, and participate at a level that, in the eyes of many, is an embarrassment to a country that prides itself on "rule by the people."

In this provocative essay, Michael Schudson suggests that the lack of electoral participation "may not be individual failure so much as our contemporary conception of how democratic citizenship ought to work." He finds that the Progressive ideal of citizenship, with its expectations that each citizen possess a high level of political information and pay constant attention to public affairs, sets an unrealistic standard in the contemporary political world.

In Schudson's view, citizens flourish in an environment that encourages worthwhile citizenship activities in the broadest sense, and we should be intent on creating such an environment, not on turning every voter into an expert.

I f recent trends hold up, only about one of every three eligible voters will show up at the polls this fall. Inevitably, many will conclude that Americans have once again failed as citizens. The problem, however, may not be individual failure so much as our contemporary conception of how democratic citizenship ought to work. Nothing puts that conception into clearer perspective than changes in the act of voting over the past 200 years.

Imagine yourself a voter in the world of colonial Virginia where George Washington, Patrick Henry, and Thomas Jefferson learned their politics. As a

Michael Schudson is Professor of Communication and Sociology at the University of California, San Diego.

matter of law, you must be a white male owning at least a modest amount of property. Your journey to vote may take several hours since there is probably only one polling place in the county. As you approach the courthouse, you see the sheriff supervising the election. Two candidates for office stand before you, both of them members of prominent local families. You watch the most prominent members of the community, the leading landowner and clergyman, cast their votes, and you know whom they have supported because they announce their votes in loud, clear voices. You do the same and then step over to the candidate for whom you have voted, and he treats you to a glass of rum punch. Your vote has been an act of restating and reaffirming the social hierarchy of a community where no one but a local notable would think of standing for office.

Now imagine you are in eighteenth-century Massachusetts rather than Virginia. The model of voting is different, as you elect town selectmen and representatives at a town meeting. But, like Virginia, the New England model reflects an organic view that the polity has a single common good and that the leaders of locally prominent, wealthy, and well-established families can be trusted to represent it. Dissent and conflict are no more acceptable in New England than in Virginia.

Move the clock ahead to the nineteenth century, as mass political parties cultivate a new democratic order. Now there is much more bustle around the polling place. The area is crowded with the banners and torches of rival parties. Election day is not set off from other days but is the culmination of a campaign of several months. You must still be a white male but not necessarily of property. During the campaign, you have marched in torchlight processions in military uniform with a club of like-minded men from your party. They may accompany you to the polls. If you were not active in the campaign, you may be roused on election day by a party worker to escort you on foot or by carriage. On the road, you may encounter clubs or groups from rival parties, and it would not be unusual if fisticuffs or even guns were to dissuade you from casting a ballot after all.

If you do proceed to the ballot box, you may step more lively with the encouragement of a dollar or two from the party—less a bribe than an acknowledgment that voting is a service to your party. A party worker hands you a colored ballot with the printed names of the party's candidates. You may also receive a slightly smaller ballot with the same names on it that can be surreptitiously placed inside the other so that you can cast two ballots rather than one. You are willing to do so not out of a strong sense that your party offers better public policies but because your party is your party, just as, in our own day, your high school is your high school. In any event, parties tend to be more devoted to distributing offices than to advocating policies.

Now turn to the early twentieth century as Progressive era reforms cleanse voting of what made it both compelling and, by our standards, corrupt. Reformers find the emphasis in campaigns on spectacle rather than substance much too emotional. They pioneer what they term an "educational campaign" that stresses the distribution of pamphlets on the issues rather than parades of soli-darity. They pass legislation to ensure a secret ballot. They enact voter registra-tion statutes. They help create an atmosphere in which it becomes more common for traditionally loyal party newspapers to "bolt" from party-endorsed candidates. They insist on official state ballots rather than party ballots and in some states develop state-approved voter information booklets rather than leaving education up to the parties themselves. At the same time, civil service reform limits the rewards parties can distribute to loyal partisans.

The world we experience today at the polls has been handed down to us from these reforms. What does voting look like and feel like today?

I asked my students at the University of California, San Diego to write about their experience of voting in 1992. Many of them had never voted before; hardly any had voted in a presidential election. It is something they looked for-ward to doing, especially those who supported Clinton. Still, some students felt a let-down in the act of voting:

> As I punched in the holes on my voting card, a slight sense of disappointment clouded my otherwise cheerful mood. First of all, the building behind Revelle Bargain Books was not what I had always imagined as a polling place. How could a location this close to the all-you-can-eat cafeteria be the site of a vote to choose the leader of our nation? Second, I could not understand why there were no curtains around my booth. As a child I can always remember crawling under curtains in voting booths to spy on my parents. Why couldn't I have those curtains to hide all of my important, private decisions?

Or listen to this student, a Filipino-American who voted for Bush:

> The more I tried to be aware of the political goings-on, through television mainly, the more I became aggravated with the whole situation. Perot represented the evil of a one-man monopoly, while Clinton was a man who knew how to manipulate an audi-ence and use the media. In addition, Hillary reminded me of the stories and com-ments my parents made about Imelda Marcos. Taxes came to mind every time I considered Bush, but I decided he might be the best qualified candidate.
>
> My Dad was an influential part of my decision to go; not because he urged me to do so, but so that after the election I would finally be able to tell him that I voted.
>
> Needless to say, no one at the polling site seemed to talk politics, at least not when I was there. The silence did not bother me, though, since I am definitely not confi-dent enough to talk politics to anyone outside of my family!

Or this immigrant Russian:

> My Mom went to vote with me that day (at the polling place in a neighbor's garage). The night before, I had marked my mother's sample ballot with circles around "yes" and "no" on particular propositions and checked the boxes next to "Feinstein" and "Boxer" so she would not forget. The sample ballot is very convenient. The propositions

are especially grueling to read. They disguise themselves in legal/state jargon and refuse to give way to meaning.

I felt distantly connected to other voters in other garages who would be making the same vote for change as I would. Nevertheless, I went through my ballot, standing in that cardboard cubicle, in a very ordinary way, feeling that I was, most likely, insignificant and that my views would find no representation. I remember guessing on some local offices, like county supervisor, and trying not to pick a "Christian right" candidate.

The individuality and jealously guarded privacy of voting today contrasts dramatically with the *viva voce* process of eighteenth-century Virginia or the colorful party ticket voting of the nineteenth century. So do the indecision and uncertainty. The students felt inadequate to the election—and why not? The list of propositions and complex voter information pamphlets in California were overwhelming. My voter information pamphlet for the June 1994 primary ran forty-eight pages—and that was just for city and county offices and referenda. For state offices and ballot measures, a separate publication ran sixty-four pages. The obscurity of many candidates and issues encouraged mass preelection mailings of leaflet slates of candidates produced by profit-making organizations with no connection to political parties. I received, for instance, "Voter Information Guide for Democrats" and "Crime Fighters '94" produced by "Democratic Choice '94." The weary voter had to read the fine print to learn that neither slate was endorsed by the Democratic party.

Whatever else we learn from elections, we are tutored in a sense of helplessness and fundamental inadequacy to the task of citizenship. We are told to be informed but discover that the information required to cast an informed vote is beyond our capacities. We are reminded that the United States has the lowest voter turnout of any democracy but rarely told that we have more elections for more levels of government with more elective offices at each level than any other country in the world. . . .

The Burden of Progressivism

We need a new concept of citizenship, one that asks something from us but is not burdened with the impossible expectations of the Progressive model. Contrast what we implicitly expect of ourselves today and what Thomas Jefferson hoped for citizens 200 years ago. In the preamble of Bill 79 to establish universal elementary instruction in Virginia, Jefferson observed that the people normally elect men of standing in the community. The community needs especially to educate these leaders. As for the citizenry at large, Jefferson sought to inculcate through the study of history knowledge that "they may be enabled to know ambition under all its shapes, and prompt to exert their natural powers to defeat its purposes." That was the whole of the citizen's job—watchfulness to defeat ambition.

Citizens were decidedly not to undertake their own evaluation of issues before the legislature. That was the job of representatives. The Founding Fathers assumed that voters would and should choose representatives on the basis of character, not issues. Representatives would have enough in common with the people they represented to keep their "interests" in mind. For the Founding Fathers, elected representatives—not parties, not interest groups, not newspapers, not citizens in the streets—were to make policy.

We have come to ask more of citizens. Today's dominant views about citizenship come from the Progressives' rationalist and ardently individualist worldview. The Progressive impulse was educational—to bring science to politics and professional management to cities, to substitute pamphlets for parades and parlors for streets. The practice of citizenship, at least in campaigning and voting, became privatized, more effortful, more cognitive, and a lot less fun.

In the eighteenth and nineteenth centuries, there was no concern about the people who did not vote. Political science and public discourse began to worry about nonvoters only after World War I when voting rates had declined to a low not reached again until the 1970s. . . .

The Progressive ideal requires citizens to possess a huge fund of political information and a ceaseless attentiveness to public issues. This could never be. Even at the Constitutional convention of 1787 a delegate observed that people grew "listless" with frequent elections. Fifty years later Tocqueville lamented, "Even when one has won the confidence of a democratic nation, it is a hard matter to attract its attention." . . .

. . . Perhaps television or party decline exacerbates it. But public inattention has been a fact of political life, with only momentary escapes, through our history. If this is so, what is a reasonable expectation for citizens, a reasonable standard of citizen competence?

A Practical Citizenship

Under democratic government, as the Founding Fathers constituted it, the representatives of the people could carry on the business of governing without individual citizens becoming experts on the questions of policy placed before the Congress. . . .

Citizens are not to be created one by one, pouring into each of them enough newspapers, information, or virtuous resolve for them to judge each issue and each candidate rationally. That is where the Progressive vision went wrong. Citizens flourish in an environment that supports worthwhile citizenship activities. We should be intent on creating such an environment, not on turning every voter into an expert.

If, like the Progressives, we take citizenship to be a function of the individual, we are bound to be discouraged. A classical model of citizenship asks that people seek the good of the general, the public. But this is either utopian—

people just do not pay that kind of attention—or else undesirable because it honors public life to the exclusion of work-a-day labor or inner spiritual pursuits. A more Lockean, modern, realistic version is that citizens should be moved in public life by self-interest and so should acquire a fair understanding of their own interests and which public policies best serve them. But people's knowledge of public affairs fails even by this standard. Even self-interest in politics is a surprisingly weak reed since the gratifications of private life—getting home on time rather than stopping at the polls to vote, spending seven or eight dollars for a movie rather than for a campaign contribution—are more visible and immediate than the marginal contribution one might make to determining policy by voting, signing a petition, or writing a letter.

How low can we go? We can seek to build a political system where individuals will perform the right actions for their own or the public's interest without knowing much at all. People will do the right thing in general ignorance. User-friendly technology works this way; almost anyone can drive a car while knowing scarcely anything about what makes it run.

In *The Reasoning Voter*, Samuel Popkin suggests we are pretty close to this user-friendly politics already. Relatively little of what voters know, Popkin argues, comes to them as abstract political intelligence. They make intelligent voting decisions based only in small measure on their attending to campaign issues. People have little of the propositional knowledge that models of citizenship demand, but they have more background knowledge than they may realize. They know about economic issues because they have savings accounts, home mortgages, or mutual funds. They have views about health care reform because they know someone personally who has been denied health insurance because of a pre-existing condition. They have enough "by-product information" from daily life to make the broad, either-or choice of a presidential candidate in ways consistent with their own interests and views. . . .

In elections for school boards and other local contests, however, where public information about candidates is more limited and there are often no party labels (again, thanks to Progressive reforms), voters may find themselves in the polling booth without a clue about whom to support. . . .

The Citizens' Trustees

Citizens have to find trustees for their citizenship. Identifying adequate trustees and holding them responsible, I submit, is where we should focus attention. There are three main sets of trustees: politicians, lobbyists, and journalists. Elected officials are our primary trustees. Their obligation is to act with the public in view. They act not so much in response to deliberative public opinion—which rarely exists—but in anticipation of future reward or punishment at the polls. The politicians may not always perceive public opinion accurately. They may not judge well just how much they can lead and shape and how much they must follow and bow to public sentiment. But the motivational structure of elective office demands that they must always be sensitive on this point.

Lobbyists are a second set of trustees. If you believe in the individual's right to bear arms unrestrained by federal legislation, send your annual dues to the National Rifle Association. If you believe that the environment needs aggressive protection, send your dues to an environmental action group. If you do not know what you believe—and this is the common condition for most people on most issues before the nation—you will do better at expressing your will if you at least know that you tend to favor one party over another. Partisanship is a still useful cue. . . .

Two mechanisms keep politician-trustees responsible. The first is the election, fallible as it is. If the representative does not satisfy the citizens, they have a regularly scheduled opportunity to throw the bum out. The second constraint on the politician is the party system. Of course, the party is a more effective discipline on wayward politicians in strong parliamentary systems than in the United States. Here parties are relatively weak, and entrepreneurial politicians relatively independent of them. Still, a politician's party affiliation is a check on his or her policy views and a useful piece of information for voters.

The demands citizens make on lobbyists are much narrower than those placed on politicians—lobbyists are expected to be advocates rather than judges, suppliers of information and resources to sympathetic politicians rather than builders of politically viable solutions to public problems. They are the instructed agents of their organizations rather than Burkean independent-minded representatives. As individuals, they are easy to hold responsible. The question of responsibility with lobbyists is how to hold the whole system responsible since the balance of lobbying power tilts heavily toward the richest and most powerful groups in society. If the system works, it facilitates expression for intensely felt interests from the far corners of the country; if it works badly, it twists and clogs up the primary system of political representation.

The usual answer is to seek to limit the influence of lobbies through campaign finance reform and other restrictions on lobbying activities. An alternative approach seeks to grant lobbyists more authority rather than less influence. Instead of closing down access where the rich and powerful have the resources to guarantee their over-representation, can entree be opened in settings where a broad array of interest groups are assured a voice? In decision making in some federal administrative agencies, interest groups have been granted quasi-public standing. The Negotiated Rulemaking Act of 1990 enables agencies like the Environmental Protection Agency and the Occupational Safety and Health Administration to create committees of private organizations to write regulatory rules.

For instance, EPA arranged for the Sierra Club and the Natural Resources Defense Council to sit down with the American Petroleum Institute and the National Petroleum Refiners Association to work out rules to carry out the

Clean Air Act. Millions of Americans belong to organizations that employ paid lobbyists; the lobbies are not about to disappear nor should they. But controlling them may be a delicate balance of restraining some kinds of influence while orchestrating other public opportunities for special interests to take on responsibility for governing.

The third set of trustees—the media—is the most difficult to hold accountable. The market mechanism does not serve well here. People buy a newspaper or watch a television network for many purposes besides gathering political information. The quality or quantity of political intelligence does not correlate well with the rise and fall of newspaper circulations or television news ratings.

There are, as the French press critic Claude-Jean Bertrand suggests, a variety of "media accountability systems"—nongovernmental mechanisms to keep the news media responsible to public interests and opinions. These include codes of ethics, in-house critics, media reporters, and ombudsmen, as well as liaison committees that news institutions have sometimes established with social groups they may report on or clash with. There are also letters to the editor, journalism reviews, journalism schools, awards for good news coverage, and libel suits or the threat of libel. . . .

The Overworked Citizen

William James said nearly a century ago that our moral destiny turns on "the power of voluntarily attending." But, he added, though crucial to our individual and collective destinies, attention tends to be "brief and fitful." This is the substantial underlying reality of political life that any efforts at enlarging citizenship must confront. Can we have a democracy if most people are not paying attention most of the time? The answer is that this is the only kind of democracy we will ever have. Our ways of organizing and evoking that brief and fitful attention are different but not necessarily any worse from those in our past.

One response could be to harness the rare moments of attentiveness. Social movements and the occasional closely fought, morally urgent election have sometimes done that. When political scientists have looked at intensively fought senatorial campaigns, for instance, and compared them to run-of-the-mill campaigns, they find much more information in the news media about candidates' policy positions, increased knowledge among voters about those positions, and apparently increased inclination of voters to make decisions on the issues. At the level of presidential politics and occasionally in senatorial or gubernatorial politics, there is enough information available for voter rationality to have a chance; but for other offices, . . . our elections say much more about the supply of candidates than the demands of voters.

An alternate response would be to build a society that makes more of situations that build citizenship without taxing attentiveness. In an environment that supports worthwhile citizenship activity, there is intrinsic reward for doing the right thing. If we interpret citizenship activity to mean taking unpaid and uncoerced responsibility for the welfare of strangers or the community at large, examples of good citizenship abound. I think of the people who serve as "room parents" in the schools or coach Little League. Why do they do it? Their own children would do just as well if someone else took on the job. Coaching Little League or serving in the Parent-Teachers Association are activities or practices rather than cognitive efforts; they are social and integrated into community life. They make citizenship itself into a "by-product" effect. Their success suggests that citizenship may be harder to instill when it involves burdens beyond daily life than to engineer it as an everyday social activity. The volunteers may not enjoy every minute, but they find intrinsic social reward in having friends, neighbors, and strangers praise and admire them.

Our common language for a better public life seems impoverished. We think of politicians with distrust rather than thinking of ways to enforce their trust-worthiness. We think of lobbyists with disdain instead of thinking of ways to recognize and harness their virtues. We think of journalists alternately as he-roes or scoundrels. And we think of our own citizenship too often with either guilt at our ignorance and lack of participation or with a moral pat on the back for having sacrificed more than our neighbors. We must think more about building a democratic environment that will make us smarter as a people than we are as individuals.

Questions for Discussion

1. What does Schudson mean by the "burden of Progressivism"? Does the Progressive model of citizenship seem unrealistic when applied to today's voters? Have you personally experienced the "burden of Progressivism"?
2. What components does Schudson believe should underlie a new concept of citizenship? In your view, how practical is Schudson's viewpoint?

5.3

Bowling Alone: America's Declining Social Capital

Robert D. Putnam

Political behavior is learned behavior. Although individual freedoms and rights provide the fundamental underpinnings of the nation, citizens learning by experience to act collectively in pursuit of shared goals has long been thought crucial to the success of American democracy. More than 150 years ago, Alexis de Tocqueville in *Democracy in America* acknowledged the critical role played by associational life in supporting democratic values.

In this selection, Robert D. Putnam questions whether the United States has retained the characteristics of civil society. He suggests that there is an important linkage between "citizen engagement" in community affairs and government performance. Civic engagement refers to people's associational connections to the life of their communities in the broadest sense, from going to church to participating in a bowling league to becoming involved in a political group. Experience in a wide array of such activities develops what Putnam calls "social capital": "features of social organization such as networks, norms, and social trust that facilitate coordination and cooperation for mutual benefit."

M any students of the new democracies that have emerged over the past decade and a half have emphasized the importance of a strong and active civil society to the consolidation of democracy. Especially with regard to the postcommunist countries, scholars and democratic activists alike have lamented the absence or obliteration of traditions of independent civic engagement and a widespread tendency toward passive reliance on the state. To those concerned with the weakness of civil societies in the developing or postcommunist world, the advanced Western democracies and above all the United States have typically been taken as models to be emulated. There is

Robert D. Putnam is Malkin Professor of Public Policy at Harvard University.

From "Bowling Alone: America's Declining Social Capital" by Robert D. Putnam. From *Journal of Democracy*, January 1995, Vol. 6, No. 1, pp. 65–78. Reprinted by permission from The Sagalyn Literary Agency.

striking evidence, however, that the vibrancy of American civil society has notably declined over the past several decades.

Ever since the publication of Alexis de Tocqueville's *Democracy in America*, the United States has played a central role in systematic studies of the links between democracy and civil society. Although this is in part because trends in American life are often regarded as harbingers of social modernization, it is also because America has traditionally been considered unusually "civic" (a reputation that, as we shall later see, has not been entirely unjustified).

When Tocqueville visited the United States in the 1830s, it was the Americans' propensity for civic association that most impressed him as the key to their unprecedented ability to make democracy work. "Americans of all ages, all stations in life, and all types of disposition," he observed, "are forever forming associations. There are not only commercial and industrial associations in which all take part, but others of a thousand different types—religious, moral, serious, futile, very general and very limited, immensely large and very minute. . . . Nothing, in my view, deserves more attention than the intellectual and moral associations in America."[1]

Recently, American social scientists of a neo-Tocquevillean bent have unearthed a wide range of empirical evidence that the quality of public life and the performance of social institutions (and not only in America) are indeed powerfully influenced by norms and networks of civic engagement. Researchers in such fields as education, urban poverty, unemployment, the control of crime and drug abuse, and even health have discovered that successful outcomes are more likely in civically engaged communities. Similarly, research on the varying economic attainments of different ethnic groups in the United States has demonstrated the importance of social bonds within each group. These results are consistent with research in a wide range of settings that demonstrates the vital importance of social networks for job placement and many other economic outcomes. . . .

No doubt the mechanisms through which civic engagement and social connectedness produce such results—better schools, faster economic development, lower crime, and more effective government—are multiple and complex. . . . Social scientists in several fields have recently suggested a common framework for understanding these phenomena, a framework that rests on the concept of *social capital*.[2] By analogy with notions of physical capital and human capital—tools and training that enhance individual productivity—"social capital" refers to features of social organization such as networks, norms, and social trust that facilitate coordination and cooperation for mutual benefit.

For a variety of reasons, life is easier in a community blessed with a substantial stock of social capital. In the first place, networks of civic engagement foster sturdy norms of generalized reciprocity and encourage the emergence of social trust. Such networks facilitate coordination and communication, amplify reputations, and thus allow dilemmas of collective action to be resolved. When economic and political negotiation is embedded in dense networks of social interaction, incentives for opportunism are reduced. At the same time, networks of civic engagement embody past success at collaboration, which can serve as a cultural template for future collaboration. Finally, dense networks of interaction probably broaden the participants' sense of self, developing the "I" into the "we," or (in the language of rational-choice theorists) enhancing the participants' "taste" for collective benefits. . . .

Whatever Happened to Civic Engagement?

We begin with familiar evidence on changing patterns of political participation, not least because it is immediately relevant to issues of democracy in the narrow sense. Consider the well-known decline in turnout in national elections over the last three decades. From a relative high point in the early 1960s, voter turnout had by 1990 declined by nearly a quarter; tens of millions of Americans had forsaken their parents' habitual readiness to engage in the simplest act of citizenship. Broadly similar trends also characterize participation in state and local elections.

It is not just the voting booth that has been increasingly deserted by Americans. A series of identical questions posed by the Roper Organization to national samples ten times each year over the last two decades reveals that since 1973 the number of Americans who report that "in the past year" they have "attended a public meeting on town or school affairs" has fallen by more than a third (from 22 percent in 1973 to 13 percent in 1993). Similar (or even greater) relative declines are evident in responses to questions about attending a political rally or speech, serving on a committee of some local organization, and working for a political party. By almost every measure, Americans' direct engagement in politics and government has fallen steadily and sharply over the last generation, despite the fact that average levels of education—the best individual-level predictor of political participation—have risen sharply throughout this period. Every year over the last decade or two, millions more have withdrawn from the affairs of their communities.

Not coincidentally, Americans have also disengaged psychologically from politics and government over this era. The proportion of Americans who reply that they "trust the government in Washington" only "some of the time" or "almost never" has risen steadily from 30 percent in 1966 to 75 percent in 1992.

These trends are well known, of course, and taken by themselves would seem amenable to a strictly political explanation. Perhaps the long litany of political tragedies and scandals since the 1960s (assassinations, Vietnam, Watergate, Irangate, and so on) has triggered an understandable disgust for politics and government among Americans, and that in turn has motivated their withdrawal. I do not doubt that this common interpretation has some merit, but its limitations become plain when we examine trends in civic engagements of a wider sort.

Our survey of organizational membership among Americans can usefully begin with a glance at the aggregate results of the General Social Survey, a scientifically conducted, national-sample survey that has been repeated 14 times over the last two decades. Church-related groups constitute the most common type of organization joined by Americans; they are especially popular with women. Other types of organizations frequently joined by women include school-service groups (mostly parent-teacher associations), sports groups, professional societies, and literary societies. Among men, sports clubs, labor unions, professional societies, fraternal groups, veterans' groups, and service clubs are all relatively popular.

Religious affiliation is by far the most common associational membership among Americans. Indeed, by many measures America continues to be (even more than in Tocqueville's time) an astonishingly "churched" society. For example, the United States has more houses of worship per capita than any other nation on Earth. Yet religious sentiment in America seems to be becoming somewhat less tied to institutions and more self-defined.

How have these complex crosscurrents played out over the last three or four decades in terms of Americans' engagement with organized religion? The general pattern is clear: The 1960s witnessed a significant drop in reported weekly churchgoing—from roughly 48 percent in the late 1950s to roughly 41 percent in the early 1970s. Since then, it has stagnated or (according to some surveys) declined still further. Meanwhile, data from the General Social Survey show a modest decline in membership in all "church-related groups" over the last 20 years. It would seem, then, that net participation by Americans, both in religious services and in church-related groups, has declined modestly (by perhaps a sixth) since the 1960s.

For many years, labor unions provided one of the most common organizational affiliations among American workers. Yet union membership has been falling for nearly four decades, with the steepest decline occurring between 1975 and 1985. Since the mid-1950s, when union membership peaked, the unionized portion of the nonagricultural work force in America has dropped by more than half, falling from 32.5 percent in 1953 to 15.8 percent in 1992. By now, virtually all of the explosive growth in union membership that was associated with the New Deal has been erased. The solidarity of union halls is now mostly a fading memory of aging men.

The parent-teacher association (PTA) has been an especially important form of civic engagement in twentieth-century America because parental involvement in the educational process represents a particularly productive form of social capital. It is, therefore, dismaying to discover that participation in parent-teacher organizations has dropped drastically over the last generation, from more than 12 million in 1964 to barely 5 million in 1982 before recovering to approximately 7 million now.

Next, we turn to evidence on membership in (and volunteering for) civic and fraternal organizations. These data show some striking patterns. First, membership in traditional women's groups has declined more or less steadily since the mid-1960s. For example, membership in the national Federation of Women's Clubs is down by more than half (59 percent) since 1964, while membership in the League of Women Voters (LWV) is off 42 percent since 1969.[3]

Similar reductions are apparent in the numbers of volunteers for mainline civic organizations, such as the Boy Scouts (off by 26 percent since 1970) and the Red Cross (off by 61 percent since 1970). But what about the possibility that volunteers have simply switched their loyalties to other organizations? Evidence on "regular" (as opposed to occasional or "drop-by") volunteering is available from the Labor Department's Current Population Surveys of 1974 and 1989. These estimates suggest that serious volunteering declined by roughly one-sixth over these 15 years, from 24 percent of adults in 1974 to 20 percent in 1989. The multitudes of Red Cross aides and Boy Scout troop leaders now missing in action have apparently not been offset by equal numbers of new recruits elsewhere.

Fraternal organizations have also witnessed a substantial drop in membership during the 1980s and 1990s. Membership is down significantly in such groups as the Lions (off 12 percent since 1983), the Elks (off 18 percent since 1979), the Shriners (off 27 percent since 1979), the Jaycees (off 44 percent since 1979), and the Masons (down 39 percent since 1959). . . .

The most whimsical yet discomfiting bit of evidence of social disengagement in contemporary America that I have discovered is this: more Americans are bowling today than ever before, but bowling in organized leagues has plummeted in the last decade or so. Between 1980 and 1993 the total number of bowlers in America increased by 10 percent, while league bowling decreased by 40 percent. (Lest this be thought a wholly trivial example, I should note that nearly 80 million Americans went bowling at least once during 1993, *nearly a third more than voted in the 1994 congressional elections* and roughly the same number as claim to attend church regularly. Even after the 1980s' plunge in league bowling, nearly 3 percent of American adults regularly bowl in leagues.) The rise of solo bowling threatens the livelihood of bowling-lane proprietors because those who bowl as members of leagues consume three times as much beer and pizza as solo bowlers, and the money in bowling is in the beer and pizza, not the balls and shoes. The broader social significance, however, lies in the social interaction and even occasionally civic conversations over beer and pizza that solo bowlers forgo. Whether or not bowling beats balloting in the eyes of most Americans, bowling teams illustrate yet another vanishing form of social capital.

Countertrends

At this point, however, we must confront a serious counterargument. Perhaps the traditional forms of civic organization whose decay we have been tracing have been replaced by vibrant new organizations. For example, national environmental organizations (like the Sierra Club) and feminist groups (like the National Organization for Women) grew rapidly during the 1970s and 1980s and now count hundreds of thousands of dues-paying members. An even more dramatic example is the American Association of Retired Persons (AARP), which grew exponentially from 400,000 card-carrying members in 1960 to 33 million in 1993, becoming (after the Catholic Church) the largest private organization in the world. The national administrators of these organizations are among the most feared lobbyists in Washington, in large part because of their massive mailing lists of presumably loyal members.

These new mass-membership organizations are plainly of great political importance. From the point of view of social connectedness, however, they are sufficiently different from classic "secondary associations" that we need to invent a new label—perhaps "tertiary associations." For the vast majority of their members, the only act of membership consists in writing a check for dues or perhaps occasionally reading a newsletter. Few ever attend any meetings of such organizations, and most are unlikely ever (knowingly) to encounter any other member. The bond between any two members of the Sierra Club is less like the bond between any two members of a gardening club and more like the bond between any two Red Sox fans (or perhaps any two devoted Honda owners): they root for the same team and they share some of the same interests, but they are unaware of each other's existence. Their ties, in short, are to common symbols, common leaders, and perhaps common ideals, but not to one another. The theory of social capital argues that associational membership should, for example, increase social trust, but this prediction is much less straightforward with regard to membership in tertiary associations. From the point of view of social connectedness, the Environmental Defense Fund and a bowling league are just not in the same category.

If the growth of tertiary organizations represents one potential (but probably not real) counterexample to my thesis, a second countertrend is represented by the growing prominence of nonprofit organizations, especially nonprofit service agencies. This so-called third sector includes everything from Oxfam and the Metropolitan Museum of Art to the Ford Foundation and the Mayo Clinic. In other words, although most secondary associations are nonprofits, most nonprofit agencies are not secondary associations. To identify trends in the size of the nonprofit sector with trends in social connectedness would be another fundamental conceptual mistake.[4]

A third potential countertrend is much more relevant to an assessment of social capital and civic engagement. Some able researchers have argued that the last few decades have witnessed a rapid expansion in "support groups" of various sorts. Robert Wuthnow reports that fully 40 percent of all Americans claim to be "currently involved in [a] small group that meets regularly and provides support or caring for those who participate in it."[5] Many of these groups are religiously affiliated, but many others are not. For example, nearly 5 percent of Wuthnow's national sample claim to participate regularly in a "self-help" group, such as Alcoholics Anonymous, and nearly as many say they belong to book-discussion groups and hobby clubs.

The groups described by Wuthnow's respondents unquestionably represent an important form of social capital, and they need to be accounted for in any serious reckoning of trends in social connectedness. On the other hand, they do not typically play the same role as traditional civic associations. As Wuthnow emphasizes,

> Small groups may not be fostering community as effectively as many of their proponents would like. Some small groups merely provide occasions for individuals to focus on themselves in the presence of others. The social contract binding members together asserts only the weakest of obligations. Come if you have time. Talk if you feel like it. Respect everyone's opinion. Never criticize. Leave quietly if you become dissatisfied. . . . We can imagine that [these small groups] really substitute for families, neighborhoods, and broader community attachments that may demand lifelong commitments, when, in fact, they do not.[6]

All three of these potential countertrends—tertiary organizations, nonprofit organizations, and support groups—need somehow to be weighed against the erosion of conventional civic organizations. One way of doing so is to consult the General Social Survey.

Within all educational categories, total associational membership declined significantly between 1967 and 1993. Among the college-educated, the average number of group memberships per person fell from 2.8 to 2.0 (a 26-percent decline); among high-school graduates, the number fell from 1.8 to 1.2 (32 percent); and among those with fewer than 12 years of education, the number fell from 1.4 to 1.1 (25 percent). In other words, at *all* educational (and hence social) levels of American society, and counting *all* sorts of group memberships, *the average number of associational memberships has fallen by about a fourth over the last quarter-century.* Without controls for educational levels, the trend is not nearly so clear, but the central point is this: *more Americans than ever before are in social circumstances that foster associational involvement (higher education, middle age, and so on), but nevertheless aggregate associational membership appears to be stagnant or declining.*

Broken down by type of group, the downward trend is most marked for church-related groups, for labor unions, for fraternal and veterans' organizations, and for school-service groups. Conversely, membership in professional associations has risen over these years, although less than might have been predicted, given sharply rising educational and occupational levels. Essentially the same trends are evident for both men and women in the sample. In short, the available survey evidence confirms our earlier conclusion: American social capital in the form of civic associations has significantly eroded over the last generation.

Good Neighborliness and Social Trust

I noted earlier that most readily available quantitative evidence on trends in social connectedness involves formal settings, such as the voting booth, the union hall, or the PTA. One glaring exception is so widely discussed as to require little comment here: the most fundamental form of social capital is the family, and the massive evidence of the loosening of bonds within the family (both extended and nuclear) is well known. This trend, of course, is quite consistent with—and may help to explain—our theme of social decapitalization.

A second aspect of informal social capital on which we happen to have reasonably reliable time-series data involves neighborliness. In each General Social Survey since 1974 respondents have been asked, "How often do you spend a social evening with a neighbor?" The proportion of Americans who socialize with their neighbors more than once a year has slowly but steadily declined over the last two decades, from 72 percent in 1974 to 61 percent in 1993. (On the other hand, socializing with "friends who do not live in your neighborhood" appears to be on the increase, a trend that may reflect the growth of workplace-based social connections.)

Americans are also less trusting. The proportion of Americans saying that most people can be trusted fell by more than a third between 1960, when 58 percent chose that alternative, and 1993, when only 37 percent did. The same trend is apparent in all educational groups; indeed, because social trust is also correlated with education and because educational levels have risen sharply, the overall decrease in social trust is even more apparent if we control for education.

Our discussion of trends in social connectedness and civic engagement has tacitly assumed that all the forms of social capital that we have discussed are themselves coherently correlated across individuals. This is in fact true. Members of associations are much more likely than nonmembers to participate in politics, to spend time with neighbors, to express social trust, and so on. . . .

Why Is U.S. Social Capital Eroding?

As we have seen, something has happened in America in the last two or three decades to diminish civic engagement and social connectedness. What could that "something" be? Here are several possible explanations, along with some initial evidence on each.

The Movement of Women into the Labor Force

Over these same two or three decades, many millions of American women have moved out of the home into paid employment. This is the primary, though not the sole, reason why the weekly working hours of the average American have increased significantly during these years. It seems highly plausible that this social revolution should have reduced the time and energy

Figure 2
Party Identification by Age

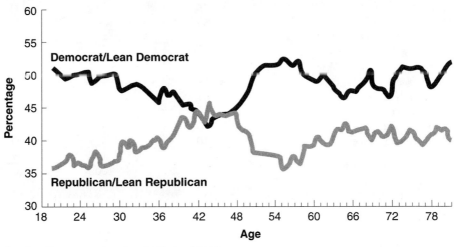

Based on Pew surveys from Jan. 2005–April 2006.

In fact, the partisan leanings of DotNets today mirror their parents' generation—many of whom are in the first half of the Baby Boomer cohort. Among Baby Boomers who came of age during the late 1960s and early 1970s—those roughly ages 50–59 now—party identification is nearly the same as among the DotNets: 51% Democratic or leaning, 38% Republican.

The youngest generation is most distinctive on social issues, notably questions about gay marriage and interracial dating. For example, a Pew poll in March found 58% of those ages 18–29 favor allowing gays and lesbians to adopt children. Among no other age group did as many as half favor this. Similarly, 48% in a July 2005 Pew poll supported gay marriage, significantly more than in any other age group.

Young people are also much more comfortable with diversity. In a 2003 Pew survey, 68% "completely" agreed that it's "all right for blacks and whites to date each other." Just 42% of respondents 30 and older felt that way.

But the social liberalism of the young does not extend to one of the signal issues of our day: abortion. Just 31% of people ages 18–19 told Pew that they believed abortion should be "generally available." Among those 30 and older, 37% said that abortion should be generally available.

Younger Americans are generally more positive than older Americans regarding the efficiency of government and the job it does in regulating business and helping the disadvantaged. Yet they are also more favorable toward business on some questions. Younger Americans were also substantially more likely than

Table 2

Young People More Liberal on Some, Not All Issues and Values

	All %	18–29 %	30+ %
Opinion about gay marriage[a]			
Favor	36	48	33
Oppose	53	48	54
Don't know	11	4	13
	100	100	100
OK for blacks & whites to date[b]			
Completely agree	47	68	42
Mostly agree	30	23	32
Mostly disagree	10	3	12
Completely disagree	10	5	11
Don't know	3	1	3
	100	100	100
Abortion should be . . .[c]			
Generally available	35	31	37
More limited	20	24	19
Illegal except rape/incest/save mother	31	30	31
Never permitted	11	13	10
Don't know	3	2	3
	100	100	100
Government is . . .[d]			
Wasteful and inefficient	47	32	52
Better than given credit for	45	64	40
Don't know	8	4	8
	100	100	100
Opinion of business corps.[b]			
Favorable	49	60	45
Unfavorable	40	32	42
Don't know	11	8	13
	100	100	100
Private retirement accounts[e]			
Favor	47	61	44
Oppose	40	24	43
Don't know	13	15	13
	100	100	100

All data based on surveys conducted by Pew Research Center.
[a] July 2005.
[b] July–Aug. 2003.
[c] Dec. 2005.
[d] Dec. 2005.
[e] May 2005.

other age groups to favor President Bush's proposal to create private accounts in the Social Security system.

Of course, there's no guarantee that opinions held today by young people will still be their views when they are older. People do change. But many fundamental values and political orientations are likely to be much the same as they grow older—for example, we can still clearly see the imprint of the 1960s and 1970s on the Baby Boomer generation's party identification—and thus it's worth considering what the future might look like when this group of younger Americans finally takes its turn running the country.

Based on the uptick in voter turnout among DotNets in 2004, their relatively high levels of civic engagement, and their willingness to express their opinions to political leaders, the media, and their peers, this cohort of Americans is not likely to be a silent generation.

Questions for Discussion

1. The voter turnout of young voters dramatically rose in the 2004 presidential election. What factors do you believe played a role in the change? Since eighteen-year-olds were given the right to vote in 1972, the highest turnout of young voters occurred in the 1972 and 2004 elections. What common factors in those years may have inspired a higher proportion of young voters to go to the polls? (Hint: See selection 4.2.)
2. In terms of policy viewpoints, how distinctive is the DotNet generation from previous generations? Which of the two major parties is likely to benefit from increased participation by those in the DotNet generation?

Chapter 6

POLITICAL PARTIES

The word *party* does not appear in the U.S. Constitution. The nation's founders, suspicious of special interests, viewed parties as devices to organize factions—"to put in the place of the delegated will of the nation the will of party," as George Washington put it. Yet within a generation of the nation's founding, parties had emerged as instruments for structuring political conflict and encouraging mass participation.

In retrospect, the development of political parties seems almost inevitable. The United States has always harbored a diverse political culture, and the practical necessity of governing demands that majorities be forged among contending interests. Political parties evolved as the only solution to the problem of reconciling individual diversity with majority rule.

The American political party functions as an intermediary between the public and the government. A party can combine citizens' demands into a manageable number of issues, thus enabling the system to focus on society's most crucial problems. The party performs its mediating function primarily through coalition building—in the words of journalist David Broder, "the process of constructing majorities from the broad sentiments and interests that can be found to bridge the narrower needs and hopes of separate individuals and communities."

For example, Franklin Roosevelt's New Deal, forged in the 1930s in the face of deep economic depression, brought about a Democratic coalition that essentially dominated national policymaking for thirty years. Generally speaking, socioeconomic divisions shaped politics in the 1930s. Less affluent citizens tended to support the Roosevelt administration's provisions for social and economic security and government regulation of private enterprise. Those who were better off usually took the opposite position. By and large, the New Deal coalition came to represent northern urban workers, immigrants and ethnic minorities, blacks, Catholics, Jews, and many southerners.

Such coalition building has contributed greatly to the stability of American political life, but the parties also serve as the major vehicle for political change. Political coalitions are never permanent. Old issues are dealt with or decrease in importance, while new issues move onto the agenda. New voters enter the electorate, older ones die, and the economic and social circumstances of groups and regions change.

Confronted with a new political environment, parties may realign—that is, rearrange the bases of their coalitions to reflect new issues and public concerns.

Critical realignments usually occur in the midst of an economic crisis such as a depression. Such an event causes sharp and durable changes in voter perceptions and identities because of the parties' differing positions on how to handle the situation. Scholars have concluded that party realignment has taken place a number of times since the early 1800s as the party system has adjusted to the changing issues in politics.

There is a general consensus among political observers that the American party system today is again in the midst of change, but there is little consensus as to its direction. Throughout the system's first 150 years, political realignment took place roughly every thirty-two to thirty-six years, but after the transforming election of 1932, the "expected" rearrangement did not occur by the early 1970s. New Deal political issues had faded in importance by the late 1960s, yet neither party appeared able or willing to build stable coalitions around the new issues.

Civil rights and the Vietnam War deeply divided the dominant Democrats in the 1960s, and divisions among constituent elements intensified in the 1970s as the governing system addressed such questions as women's rights, affirmative action, and consumer and environmental protection. As the party's agenda moved from guaranteeing equality of opportunity to pushing for equality of circumstance, the old coalition became impossible to sustain. Similarly, the Republican Party, though experiencing a variety of successes (especially at the presidential level), did not develop a stable electoral and governing coalition. During the Nixon years, the Watergate scandal stopped what many viewed as a long-term shift in the balance of power toward the Republican Party. Ronald Reagan's popularity caused some voters to shift party allegiance and may have enticed increasing numbers of young voters to identify with the Republican Party, but economic, cultural, and social divisions among Republicans remained a barrier to coalition unity.

The lack of a critical realignment by the party system has caused some political analysts to claim that the system is undergoing "dealignment"—the movement of voters away from both parties. This viewpoint holds that "candidate politics" is more prevalent than "party politics." Some observers even suggest that party politics is not possible in the age of high technology, mass media dominance, and a highly educated electorate that engages in split-ticket voting. Those who believe in dealignment point to the decline of the importance of party identification in voting, to the growth of independence among older voters, and to the nonalignment of young voters entering the electorate. They also note the great stress on the American political system over the past forty years. The Vietnam War, the energy crisis, the hyperinflation of the 1970s, and scandals and/or corruption in the highest places in government have heightened citizen awareness of political affairs and increased mistrust of public officials and political institutions, including parties. In the twenty-first century, the conduct of the war on terror and the Iraq War have further caused citizens to question political leadership generally in both parties.

Much of the decline in the importance of parties has been blamed on their inability to perform their traditional functions in the electoral process. For example, post-1968 reforms in both parties (but particularly in the Democratic Party) mean that delegates to presidential nomination conventions are selected largely in primaries rather than in caucuses and state conventions, thus increasing the number of narrow-issue activists and decreasing the number of elected officials and party professionals. Some believe the parties have lost their ability to set the political agenda in the nomination process as well. Candidates no longer have to spend years working within the party hierarchy to become contenders; today fresh faces quickly emerge, thanks to the role played by the media, particularly television, in determining who is or is not a "serious" candidate.

Changes in campaigning and finances have also reduced the parties' traditional role in campaign organization. Campaigns are now largely run by candidate organizations rather than by the parties. The ever-increasing importance of money and the growth of political action committees (PACs) since the Campaign Reform Acts of 1971 and 1974 (which mandated financial reporting by candidate committees) have enabled individuals to rely less on traditional party sources of funds and more on funds made available by special interests. Not surprisingly, those interests play a major role in recruiting candidates, setting issue agendas, and, in some cases, actually mobilizing voters.

Campaigns have also become more oriented toward the media than toward personal contact with voters in recent decades, and independent political consultants are now more likely than party professionals to run campaigns. Candidates for most national or statewide offices routinely place their campaigns in the hands of a comprehensive political consulting firm, which is charged with raising funds, polling, advertising, and designing campaign strategy. One consequence is that officeholders in most instances now owe little allegiance either to party organizations or to party leaders; they are elected by their own efforts and are accountable to no one but themselves.

In spite of these trends, some political scientists assert that the two major parties have adjusted to the challenge of money politics, high technology, and mass media and have staged a resurgence, especially at the national level. Both, for example, have taken advantage of the PAC phenomenon by forming loose alliances with some prominent groups. In their role as brokers and conduits of funds to their candidates, the national parties assist PACs in directing contributions to particular campaigns. Likewise, they aid candidates by soliciting contributions from PACs. In addition, the national parties provide professional assistance to candidates in the form of direct mail and polling services.

During the 1990s the national parties clearly renewed their ability to influence campaign politics. Taking advantage of a loophole in the campaign finance laws, both national parties raised and spent large amounts of so-called soft money, funds collected from individuals and organized interests outside the contribution limits of federal election law. The money was originally intended for "party-building" purposes, especially at the state and local level; some contributors gave over $1 million. However, beginning in the mid-1990s the parties typically used such funds for campaign advertising on behalf of party candidates. In the 2000 federal elections, party spending on campaign advertising outstripped that spent by candidate campaign committees or interest groups.

In 2002, however, Congress passed and President George W. Bush signed a new campaign finance law, the Bipartisan Campaign Reform Act (BCRA). A major provision banned soft money contributions to national party committees. Some observers believe that the influence of parties compared to interest groups in elections will again decline as the parties, particularly the Democrats, are strapped for funds.

The readings that follow were chosen to give readers insight into the sometimes misunderstood role of parties in the American political system. John H. Aldrich discusses why parties were created by "ambitious politicians" after the nation's founding, and the influence they have both inside and outside government in making democracy function. Paul Allen Beck looks at the party in the electorate, particularly efforts by each of the major parties to build a majority coalition of partisans in the years since the collapse of the New Deal party system. He finds the contemporary party system to be highly polarized, though neither party can depend on the loyalty of a majority of the voters. Beck believes that a large group of dedicated nonpartisan voters hold the balance of power in contemporary elections. In the final selection, Pietro Nivola examines some of the factors underlying partisan political polarization in contemporary American politics. Recognizing that some degree of polarization may be essential if the electorate is to have a meaningful choice in elections, he suggests several institutional reforms that might lessen what he believes is an exaggeration of the existing divisions in the party system.

6.1

The Case for the Importance of Political Parties

John H. Aldrich

Political parties, as they have been for more than a century and a half, are prominent features of U.S. politics both inside and outside government. Parties are most conspicuous when they are nominating candidates and contesting elections or are organizing and managing political conflict in the policy process.

In this selection, John H. Aldrich offers a theory of political parties based upon the central actors in the party—those who seek or hold public office. Political parties did not exist at the nation's founding, but they soon emerged when ambitious politicians came to realize that certain fundamental problems had to be solved if leaders were to achieve their goals. For politicians, parties reduce uncertainty and offer valuable resources. They regulate access to public office by their control of the nomination process, and they help mobilize the electorate on behalf of their candidates. Parties help manage the career advancement of officials once they are elected by providing leadership opportunities within institutions such as legislatures. Further, the party in government helps structure decision making in the government itself; it is important in proposing alternatives, shaping the agenda, passing (or rejecting) legislation, and implementing what is enacted.

In Aldrich's view, parties are essential to democracy. They help both public officials and the mass public make sense of a political system that is fragmented, multilayered, and complex.

The path to office for nearly every major politician begins today, as it has for over 150 years, with the party. Many candidates emerge initially from the ranks of party activists, all serious candidates seek their party's nomination, and they become serious candidates in the general

John H. Aldrich is the Pfizer-Pratt University Professor of Political Science at Duke University.

John H. Aldrich, *Why Parties? The Origin and Transformation of Political Parties in America* (Chicago: University of Chicago Press, 1995), pp. 14–27. Reprinted by permission of the publisher, The University of Chicago Press, and the author.

election only because they have won their party's endorsement. Today most partisan nominations are decided in primary elections—that is, based on votes cast by self-designated partisans in the mass electorate. Successful nominees count on the continued support of these partisans in the general election, and for good reason. At least since surveys have provided firm evidence, all presidential nominees have won the support of no less than a majority of their party in the electorate, no matter how overwhelming their defeat may have been.

This is an age of so-called partisan dealignment in the electorate.* Even so, a substantial majority today consider themselves partisans. The lowest percentage of self-professed (i.e., "strong" and "weak") partisans yet recorded in National Election Studies (NES) surveys was 61 percent in 1974, and another 22 percent expressed partisan leanings that year. Evidence from panel surveys demonstrates that partisanship has remained as stable and enduring for most adults after dealignment as it did before it, and it is often the single strongest predictor of candidate choice in the public.

If parties have declined recently, the decline has not occurred in their formal organizations. Party organizations are if anything stronger, better financed, and more professional at all levels now. Although its importance to candidates may be less than in the past, the party provides more support—more money, workers, and resources of all kinds—than any other organization for all but a very few candidates for national and state offices.

Once elected, officeholders remain partisans. Congress is organized by parties. Party-line votes elect its leadership, determine what its committees will be, assign members to them, and select their chairs. Party caucuses remain a staple of congressional life, and they and other forms of party organizations in Congress have become stronger in recent years. Party voting in committee and on the floor of both houses, though far less common in the United States than in many democracies, nonetheless remains the first and most important standard for understanding congressional voting behavior, and it too has grown stronger, in this case much stronger, in recent years.

Relationships among the elected branches of government are also heavily partisan. Conference committees to resolve discrepancies between House and Senate versions of legislation reflect partisan as well as interchamber rivalries. The president is the party's leader, and his agenda is introduced, fought for, and supported on the floor by his congressional party. His agenda becomes his party's congressional agenda, and much of it [sic] finds its way into law.

---

*Partisan dealignment describes the movement of voters away from identity with either of the parties. This may involve voters leaving one party and not affiliating with the other or entering the electorate without any party identification and never acquiring it. Issues and candidate attractiveness, rather than party identification, dominate such voters' decisions.

The Case for Weak and Weakening Parties

As impressive as the scenario above may be, not all agree that parties lie at the heart of American politics, at least not anymore. The literature on parties over the past two decades is replete with accounts of the decline of the political party. Even the choice of titles clearly reflects the arguments. David Broder perhaps began this stream of literature with *The Party's Over* (1972). Since then, political scientists have written extensively on this theme: for example, Crotty's *American Political Parties in Decline* (1984), Kirkpatrick's *Dismantling the Parties* (1978), Polsby's *Consequences of Party Reform* (1983 . . .), Ranney's thoughtful *Curing the Mischiefs of Faction* (1975), and Wattenberg's *The Decline of American Political Parties* (1990).

Those who see larger ills in the contemporary political scene often attribute them to the failure of parties to be stronger and more effective. In "The Decline of Collective Responsibility" (1980), Fiorina argued that such responsibility was possible only through the agency of the political party. Jacobson concluded his study of congressional elections (1992) by arguing that contemporary elections induce "responsiveness" of individual incumbents to their districts but do so "without [inducing] responsibility" in incumbents for what Congress does. As a result, the electorate can find no one to hold accountable for congressional failings. He too looked to a revitalized party for redress. These themes reflect the responsible party thesis, if not in being a call for such parties, at least in using that as the standard for measuring how short the contemporary party falls.

The literature on the presidency is not immune to this concern for decaying parties. Kernell's account of the strategy of "going public" (1986)—that is, generating power by marshaling public opinion—is that it became more common as the older strategy of striking bargains with a small set of congressional (and partisan) power brokers grew increasingly futile. The earlier use of the president's power to persuade (Neustadt 1960, 1990) failed as power centers became more diverse and fragmented and brokers could no longer deliver. Lowi argued this case even more strongly in *The Personal President* (1985). America, he claimed, has come to invest too much power in the office of the president, with the result that the promise of the presidency and the promises of individual presidents go unfulfilled. Why? Because the rest of government has become too unwieldy, complicated, and fragmented for the president to use that power effectively. His solution? Revitalize political parties.

Divided partisan control over government, once an occasional aberration, has become the ordinary course of affairs. Many of the same themes in this literature are those sounded above—fragmented, decentralized power, lack of coordination and control over what the government does, and absence of collective responsibility. Strong political parties are, among other things, those that can deliver the vote for most or all of their candidates. Thus another symptom of weakened parties is regularized divided government, in the states as well as in the nation.

If divided government is due to weakened parties, that condition must be due in turn to weakened partisan loyalties in the electorate. Here the evidence is clear. The proportions and strength of party attachments in the electorate declined in the mid-1960s. There was a resurgence in affiliation twenty years later, but to a lower level than before 1966. The behavioral consequences of these changes are if anything even clearer. Defection from party lines and split-ticket voting are far more common for all major offices at national, state, and local levels today than before the mid-1960s. Elections are more candidate centered and less party centered, and those who come to office have played a greater role in shaping their own more highly personalized electoral coalitions. Incumbents, less dependent on the party for winning office, are less disposed to vote the party line in Congress or to follow the wishes of their party's president. Power becomes decentralized toward the individual incumbent and, as Jacobson argues, individual incumbents respond to their constituents. If that means defecting from the party, so be it.

Is the Debate Genuine?

Some believe that parties have actually grown stronger over the past few decades. This position has been put most starkly by Schlesinger: "It should be clear by now that the grab bag of assumptions, inferences, and half-truths that have fed the decline-of-parties thesis is simply wrong" (1985, p. 1152). Rather, he maintains, "Thanks to increasing levels of competition between the parties, then, American political parties are stronger than before" (p. 1168). More common is the claim that parties were weakened in the 1960s but have been revitalized since then. Rohde pointed out that "in the last decade, however, the decline of partisanship in the House has been reversed. Party voting, which had been as low as 27 percent in 1972, peaked at 64 percent in 1987" (1989, p. 1). Changes in party voting in the Senate have been only slightly less dramatic, and Rohde has also demonstrated that party institutions in the House strengthened substantially in the same period (1991). If, as Rohde says, parties in the government are stronger, [and if] . . . the others are correct that party organizations are stronger, a thesis of decline with resurgence must be taken seriously. The electorate's partisan affiliations may be a lagging rather than a leading indicator, and even they have rebounded slightly.

A Theory of Political Parties

. . . How is it that such astute observers of American politics and parties, writing at virtually the same time and looking at much the same evidence, come to such diametrically opposed conclusions about the strength of parties? Eldersveld provided an obvious answer. He wrote that "political parties are complex institutions and processes, and as such they are difficult to understand and evaluate" (1982, p. 407). As proof, he went on to consider the decline of parties thesis. At one point he wrote, "The decline in our parties, therefore, is difficult to demonstrate, empirically or in terms of historical perspective" (p. 417). And yet he then turned to signs of party decline and concluded his book with the statement: "Despite their defects they continue today to be the major instruments for democratic government in this nation. With necessary reforms we can make them even more central to the governmental process and to the lives of American citizens. Eighty years ago, Lord James Bryce, after studying our party system, said, 'In America the great moving forces are the parties. The government counts for less than in Europe, the parties count for more. . . .' If our citizens and their leaders wish it, American parties will still be the 'great moving forces' of our system" (1982, pp. 432–33).

The "Fundamental Equation" of the New Institutionalism* Applied to Parties

That parties are complex does not mean they are incomprehensible. Indeed complexity is, if not an intentional outcome, at least an anticipated result of those who shape the political parties. Moreover, they are so deeply woven into the fabric of American politics that they cannot be understood apart from either their own historical context and dynamics or those of the political system as a whole. Parties, that is, can be understood only in relation to the polity, to the government and its institutions, and to the historical context of the times.

The study of political parties, second, is necessarily a study of a major pair of political *institutions*. Indeed, the institutions that define the political party are unique, and as it happens they are unique in ways that make an institutional account especially useful. Their establishment and nature are fundamentally extralegal; they are nongovernmental political institutions. Instead of statute, their basis lies in the actions of ambitious politicians that created and maintain them. . . .

. . . I mean it was the actions of political actors that created political parties in the first place, and it is the actions of political actors that have shaped and altered them over time. And political actors have chosen to alter their parties dramatically at several times in our history, reformed them often, and tinkered with them constantly. Of all major political bodies in the United States, the political party is the most variable in its rules, regulations, and procedures—that is to say, in its formal organization—and in its informal methods and traditions. It is often the same set of actors who write the party's rules and then choose the

---

New institutionalism is a broad term used to describe a movement beginning in the early 1980s to refocus the attention of political scientists on the role played by informal and formal institutions in the political process. Within this approach, a political party would be considered an extralegal institution rather than an "official" government institution like a legislature.

party's outcomes, sometimes at nearly the same time and by the same method. Thus, for example, one night national party conventions debate, consider any proposed amendments, and then adopt their rules by a majority vote of credentialed delegates. The next night these same delegates debate, consider any proposed amendments, and then adopt their platform by majority vote, and they choose their presidential nominee by majority vote the following night.

Who, then, are these critical political actors? Many see the party-in-the-electorate as comprising major actors. To be sure, mobilizing the electorate to capture office is a central task of the political party. But America is a republican democracy. All power flows directly or indirectly from the great body of the people, to paraphrase Madison's definition. The public elects its political leaders, but it is that leadership that legislates, executes, and adjudicates policy. The parties are defined in relation to this republican democracy. Thus it is political leaders, those Schlesinger (1975) has called "office-seekers"—*those who seek and those who hold elective office*—who are the central actors in the party.

Ambitious office seekers and holders are thus the first and most important actors in the political party. A second set of important figures in party politics comprises those who hold, or have access to, critical resources that office seekers need to realize their ambitions. It is expensive to build and maintain the party and campaign organizations necessary to compete effectively in the electoral arena. Thomas Ferguson, for example, has made an extended argument for the "primary and constitutive role large investors play in American politics" (1983, p. 3 . . .). Much of his research emphasizes this primary and constitutive role in party politics in particular, such as in partisan realignments. The study of the role of money in congressional elections has also focused in part on concentrations of such sources of funding, such as from political action committees which political parties are coming to take advantage of. Elections are also fought over the flow of information to the public. The electoral arm of political parties in the eighteenth century was made up of "committees of correspondence," which were primarily lines of communication among political elites and between them and potential voters, and one of the first signs of organizing of the Jeffersonian Republican party was the hiring of a newspaper editor. The press was first a partisan press, and editors and publishers from Thomas Ritchie to Horace Greeley long were critical players in party politics. Today those with specialized knowledge relevant to communication, such as pollsters, media and advertising experts, and computerized fund-raising specialists, enjoy influence in party, campaign, and even government councils that greatly exceeds their mere technical expertise.

In more theoretical terms, this second set of party actors include those Schlesinger (1975) has called "benefit seekers," those for whom realization of their goals depends on the party's success in capturing office. Party activists shade from those powerful figures with concentrations of, or access to, money and information described above to the legions of volunteer campaign activists who ring doorbells and stuff envelopes and are, individually and collectively, critical to the first level of the party—its office seekers. All are critical because they command the resources, whether money, expertise, and information or merely time and labor, that office seekers need to realize their ambitions. As a result, activists' motivations shape and constrain the behavior of office seekers, as their own roles are, in turn, shaped and constrained by the office seekers. . . . I argue that the changed incentives of party activists have played a significant role in the fundamentally altered nature of the contemporary party, but the impact of benefit seekers will be seen scattered throughout this account.

Voters, however, are neither office seekers nor benefit seekers and thus are not a part of the political party at all, even if they identify strongly with a party and consistently support its candidates. Voters are indeed critical, but they are critical as the targets of party activities. Parties "produce" candidates, platforms, and policies. Voters "consume" by exchanging their votes for the party's product (see Popkin et al. 1976). Some voters, of course, become partisans by becoming activists, whether as occasional volunteers, as sustained contributors, or even as candidates. But until they do so, they may be faithful consumers, "brand name" loyalists [as] it were, but they are still only the targets of partisans' efforts to sell their wares in the political marketplace.

Why, then, do politicians create and recreate the party, exploit its features, or ignore its dictates? The simple answer is that it has been in their interests to do so. That is, this is a *rational choice* account of the party, an account that presumes that rational, elective office seekers and holders use the party to achieve their ends.

I do not assume that politicians are invariably self-interested in a narrow sense. This is not a theory in which elective office seekers simply maximize their chances of election or reelection, at least not for its own sake. They may well have fundamental values and principles, and they may have preferences over policies as means to those ends. They also care about office, both for its own sake and for the opportunities to achieve other ends that election and reelection make possible. . . . Just as winning elections is a means to other ends for politicians (whether career or policy ends), so too is the political party a means to these other ends.

Why, then, do politicians turn to create or reform, to use or abuse, partisan institutions? The answer is that parties are designed as attempts to solve problems that current institutional arrangements do not solve and that politicians have come to believe they cannot solve. These problems fall into three general and recurring categories.

The Problem of Ambition and Elective Office Seeking

Elective office seekers, as that label says, want to win election to office. Parties regulate access to those offices. If elective office is indeed valuable, there will be more aspirants than offices, and the political party and the two-party system are means of regulating that competition and channeling those ambitions. Major party nomination is necessary for election, and partisan institutions have been developed—and have been reformed and re-reformed—for regulating competition. Intra-institutional leadership positions are also highly valued and therefore potentially competitive. There is, for example, a fairly well institutionalized path to the office of Speaker of the House. It is, however, a Democratic party institution. Elective politicians, of course, ordinarily desire election more than once. They are typically careerists who want a long and productive career in politics. Schlesinger's ambition theory (1966) . . . is precisely about this general problem. Underlying this theory, though typically not fully developed, is a problem. The problem is that if office is desirable, there will be more, usually many more, aspirants than there are offices to go around. . . . And it is a problem that can adversely affect the fortunes of a party. In 1912 the Republican vote was split between William Howard Taft and Theodore Roosevelt. This split enabled Woodrow Wilson to win with 42 percent of the popular vote. Not only was Wilson the only break in Republican hegemony of the White House in this period, but in that year Democrats increased their House majority by sixty-five additional seats and captured majority control of the Senate. Thus failure to regulate intraparty competition cost Republicans dearly.

For elective office seekers, regulating conflict over who holds those offices is clearly of major concern. It is ever present. And it is not just a problem of access to government offices but is also a problem internal to each party as soon as the party becomes an important gateway to office.

The Problem of Making Decisions for the Party and for the Polity

Once in office, partisans determine outcomes for the polity. They propose alternatives, shape the agenda, pass (or reject) legislation, and implement what they enact. The policy formation and execution process, that is, is highly partisan. The parties-in-government are more than mere coalitions of like-minded individuals, however; they are enduring institutions. Very few incumbents change their partisan affiliations. Most retain their partisanship throughout their career, even though they often disagree (i.e., are not uniformly like-minded) with some of their partisan peers. When the rare incumbent does change parties, it is invariably to join the party more consonant with that switcher's policy interests. This implies that there are differences between the two parties at some fundamental and enduring level on policy positions, values, and beliefs. Thus, parties are institutions designed to promote the achievement of collective choices—choices on which the parties differ and choices reached by majority rule. As with access to office and ambition theory, there is a well-developed theory for this problem: *social choice theory*.* Underlying this theory is the well-known problem that no method of choice can solve the elective

---

*Social choice theory is a formal theory, typically abstract and mathematical, concerned with how a group of voters or public officials with varying opinions and faced with a range of choices makes decisions.

officeholders' problem of combining the interests, concerns, or values of a polity that remains faithful to democratic values, as shown by the consequences flowing from Arrow's theorem (Arrow 1951).* Thus, in a republican democracy politicians may turn to partisan institutions to solve the problem of collective choice. In the language of politics, parties may help achieve the goal of attaining policy majorities in the first place, as well as the often more difficult goal of maintaining such majorities.

The Problem of Collective Action

The third problem is the most pervasive and thus the furthest-ranging in substantive content. The clearest example, however, is also the most important. To win office, candidates need more than a party's nomination. Election requires persuading members of the public to support that candidacy and mobilizing as many of those supporters as possible. This is a problem of collective action. How do candidates get supporters to vote for them—at least in greater numbers than vote for the opposition—as well as get them to provide the cadre of workers and contribute the resources needed to win election? The political party has long been the solution.

As important as wooing and mobilizing supporters are, collective action problems arise in a wide range of circumstances facing elective office seekers. Party action invariably requires the concerted action of many partisans to achieve collectively desirable outcomes. Jimmy Carter was the only president in the 1970s and 1980s to enjoy unified party control of government. Democrats in Congress, it might well be argued, shared an interest in achieving policy outcomes. And yet Carter was all too often unable to get them to act in their shared collective interests. In 1980 not only he but the Democratic congressional parties paid a heavy price for failed cooperation. . . .

The Elective Office Seekers' and Holders' Interests Are to Win

Why should this crucial set of actors, the elective office seekers and officeholders, care about these three classes of problems? The short answer is that these concerns become practical problems to politicians when they adversely affect their chances of winning. Put differently, politicians turn to their political party—that is, use its powers, resources, and institutional forms—when they believe doing so increases their prospects for winning desired outcomes, and they turn from it if it does not.

---

*Kenneth Arrow was an economist who gained fame for his mathematical proof demonstrating that the "ideal" voting system does not exist.

Ambition theory is about winning per se. The breakdown of orderly access to office risks unfettered and unregulated competition. The inability of a party to develop effective means of nomination and support for election therefore directly influences the chances of victory for the candidates and thus for their parties. The standard example of the problem of social choice theory, the "paradox of voting,"* is paradoxical precisely because all are voting to win desired outcomes, and yet there is no majority-preferred outcome. Even if there happens to be a majority-preferred policy, the conditions under which it is truly a stable equilibrium are extremely fragile and thus all too amenable to defeat. In other words, majorities in Congress are hard to attain and at least as hard to maintain. And the only reason to employ scarce campaign resources to mobilize supporters is that such mobilization increases the odds of victory. Its opposite, the failure to act when there are broadly shared interests—the problem of collective action—reduces the prospects of victory, whether at the ballot box or in government. . . .

So why have politicians so often turned to political parties for solutions to these problems? Their existence creates incentives for their use. It is, for example, incredibly difficult to win election to major office without the backing of a major party. It is only a little less certain that legislators who seek to lead a policy proposal through the congressional labyrinth will first turn to their party for assistance. But such incentives tell us only that an ongoing political institution is used when it is useful. Why form political parties in the first place? . . .

First, parties are institutions. This means, among other things, that they have some durability. They may be endogenous institutions, yet party reforms are meant not as short-term fixes but as alterations to last for years, even decades. Thus, for example, legislators might create a party rather than a temporary majority coalition to increase their chances of winning not just today but into the future. Similarly, a long and successful political career means winning office today, but it also requires winning elections throughout that career. A standing, enduring organization makes that goal more likely.

Second, American democracy chooses by plurality or majority rule. Election to office therefore requires broad-based support wherever and from whomever it can be found. So strong are the resulting incentives for a two-party system to emerge that the effect is called Duverger's law (Duverger 1954). It is in part the need to win vast and diverse support that has led politicians to create political parties.

---

*"The paradox of voting" refers to the possibility that simple majority rule voting may fail to give an unambiguous choice between alternatives. Consider the situation where, when choosing among at least three alternatives, a majority of voters may prefer each alternative over the others in head-to-head competition. In essence, the voter's paradox is that each alternative is the majority winner in head-to-head competition. This is not because the voters change their individual preferences, but because aggregating all their preferences does not always lead to a stable group preference ordering.

Third, parties may help officeholders win more, and more often, than alternatives. Consider the usual stylized model of pork barrel politics. All winners get a piece of the pork for their districts. All funded projects are paid for by tax revenues, so each district pays an equal share of the costs of each project adopted, whether or not that district receives a project. Several writers have argued that this kind of legislation leads to "universalism," that is, adoption of a "norm" that every such bill yields a project to every district and thus passes with a "universal" or unanimous coalition. Thus everyone "wins." . . . As a result, expecting to win only a bit more than half the time and lose the rest of the time, all legislators prefer consistent use of the norm of universalism. But consider an alternative. Suppose some majority agree to form a more permanent coalition, to control outcomes now and into the future, and develop institutional means to encourage fealty to this agreement. If they successfully accomplish this, they will win regularly. Members of this institutionalized coalition would prefer it to universalism, since they always win a project in either case, but they get their projects at lower cost under the institutionalized majority coalition, which passes fewer projects. Thus, even in this case with no shared substantive interests at all, there are nonetheless incentives to form an enduring voting coalition—to form a political party. And those in the excluded minority have incentives to counterorganize. United, they may be more able to woo defectors to their side. If not, they can campaign to throw those rascals in the majority party out of office.

In sum, these theoretical problems affect elective office seekers and officeholders by reducing their chances of winning. Politicians therefore may turn to political parties as institutions designed to ameliorate them. In solving these theoretical problems, however, from the politicians' perspective parties are affecting who wins and loses and what is won or lost. And it is to parties that politicians often turn, because of their durability as institutionalized solutions, because of the need to orchestrate large and diverse groups of people to form winning majorities, and because often more can be won through parties. Note that this argument rests on the implicit assumption that winning and losing hang in the balance. Politicians may be expected to give up some of their personal autonomy only when they face an imminent threat of defeat without doing so or only when doing so can block opponents' ability to build the strength necessary to win. . . .

The political party has regularly proved useful. Their permanence suggests that the appropriate question is not When parties? but How much parties and how much other means? . . . [P]arties are but a (major) part of the institutional context in which current historical conditions—the problems—are set, and solutions are sought with permanence only by changing that web of institutional arrangements. Of these the political party is by design the most malleable, and thus it is intended to change in important ways and with relatively great frequency. But it changes in ways that have, for most of American history, retained major political parties and, indeed, retained two major parties.

References

Arrow, Kenneth J. 1951. *Social choice and individual values*. New York: Wiley.

Broder, David S. 1972. *The party's over: The failure of politics in America*. New York: Harper and Row.

Crotty, William. 1984. *American political parties in decline*. 2d ed. Boston: Little, Brown.

Duverger, Maurice. 1954. *Political parties: Their organization and activities in the modern state*. New York: Wiley.

Eldersveld, Samuel J. 1982. *Political parties in American society*. New York: Basic Books.

Ferguson, Thomas. 1983. Party realignment and American industrial structures: The investment theory of political parties in historical perspective. In *Research in political economy*, vol. 6, ed. Paul Zarembka, pp. 1–82. Greenwich, Conn.: JAI Press.

Fiorina, Morris P. 1980. The decline of collective responsibility in American politics. *Daedalus* 109 (summer): 25–45.

Kernell, Samuel. 1986. *Going public: New strategies of presidential leadership*. Washington D.C.: CQ Press.

Kirkpatrick, Jeane J. 1978. *Dismantling the parties: Reflections on party reform and party decomposition*. Washington, D.C.: American Enterprise Institute of Public Policy Research.

Lowi, Theodore. 1985. *The personal president: Power invested, promise unfulfilled*. Ithaca, N.Y.: Cornell University Press.

Neustadt, Richard E. 1960. *Presidential power: The politics of leadership*. New York: Wiley.

Polsby, Nelson W. 1983. *Consequences of party reform*. Oxford: Oxford University Press.

Popkin, Samuel, John W. Gorman, Charles Phillips, and Jeffrey A. Smith. 1976. Comment: What have you done for me lately? Toward an investment theory of voting. *American Political Science Review* 70 (September): 779–805.

Ranney, Austin. 1975. *Curing the mischiefs of faction: Party reform in America*. Berkeley and Los Angeles: University of California Press.

Rohde, David W. 1989. "Something's happening here: What it is ain't exactly clear": Southern Democrats in the House of Representatives. In *Home style and Washington work: Studies of congressional politics*, ed. Morris P. Fiorina and David W. Rohde, pp. 137–163. Ann Arbor: University of Michigan Press.

Schlesinger, Joseph A. 1966. *Ambition and politics: Political careers in the United States*. Chicago: Rand McNally.

———. 1975. The primary goals of political parties: A clarification of positive theory. *American Political Science Review* 69 (September): 840–49.

———. 1985. The new American political party. *American Political Science Review* 79 (December): 1152–69.

Wattenberg, Martin P. 1990. *The decline of American political parties: 1952–1988*. Cambridge: Harvard University Press.

Questions for Discussion

1. What factors necessitated the rise of political parties in the United States? What problems do parties solve for those who seek to serve in public office?
2. What role do voters play in Aldrich's theory of political parties? If voters move away from the political parties, how will "ambitious politicians" respond? What alternatives to the parties exist for office seekers and holders in contemporary American politics?

6.2

A Tale of Two Electorates: The Changing American Party Coalitions, 1952–2000

Paul Allen Beck

Those interested in the long-term fortunes of American parties typically focus their attention on how the loyalties of components of the party coalitions change. In this selection, Paul Allen Beck examines how the partisan identities and voting behavior of categories of voters have been altered over the past half century. He finds that although there have been some distinct shifts in partisan loyalties between the parties since the 1950s (when the Democrats were the majority party), neither party can currently claim majority status.

Today's electorate, according to Beck, has two distinct components that are at odds. In the 2000 election, roughly 60 percent of the electorate was highly partisan and ideologically oriented. The followers of the two major parties represented more polar opposites in terms of political values and orientations than they did in the 1950s; the Democrats have become a more homogeneous party of the left, the Republicans of the right. But the other 40 percent of the electorate are nonpartisan in orientation and resistant to any long-term commitment to a political party. According to Beck, these nonpartisan voters "are moved by the candidates and issues of the moment" and are disgusted by the divisive partisan politics they often observe.

With virtual parity between the two major parties, nonpartisan voters now hold the balance of power in contemporary American politics. "The dilemma for the major parties and their candidates is that what mobilizes their partisan core voters repels the nonpartisan electorate, potentially costing them the election or, if victorious, a mandate to govern."

Paul Allen Beck is Professor of Political Science and Department Chair at Ohio State University.
Paul Allen Beck, "A Tale of Two Electorates: The Changing American Party Coalitions, 1952–2000," in *The State of the Parties: The Changing Role of Contemporary American Parties*, 4/e, edited by John C. Green and Rick Farmer (Lanham, MD: Rowman and Littlefield, 2003): 38–53. Copyright © 2003. Reprinted by permission of Rowman & Littlefield.

For several decades, the party loyalties of the American electorate have been undergoing contrasting changes. On the one hand, there has been a slow but steady change in the composition of the Democratic and Republican Party coalitions—what V. O. Key (1959) originally referred to as a "secular realignment."* Some see the realignment as beginning as early as the 1960s. . . . On the other hand, fewer Americans now claim party loyalties than did prior to the mid-1960s (Wattenberg 1998). Even though this partisan "dealignment" appears to have been concentrated in the late 1960s and early 1970s, and an overwhelming majority of Americans remain identified with a party, it has left a larger portion of the electorate as nonpartisans than at any time since the development of the American two-party system.† The story of recent American electoral politics revolves around this confluence of realignment and dealignment. It is a tale of two electorates.

One electorate is partisan and ideologically polarized. It has been shaped since the 1950s, which is a convenient benchmark for comparison, by a steady erosion of Democratic loyalists and recent gains in Republican identifiers that have recovered the Republican Party's 1950s share of the electorate. By 2000, these two party electorates were essentially equal in electoral influence, with the smaller GOP group attaining parity through its somewhat higher rates of turnout. The two parties' coalitions also have been reshuffled to a significant degree since the 1950s. By the beginning of the twenty-first century, Democratic loyalists were more dominant among blacks, women were more Democratic than men, and Catholics were less Democratic than they had been fifty years before. By contrast, Republican identifiers now outnumber Democrats among the overlapping groups of white Southerners and white fundamentalist Protestants. These changes have transformed the nature of the two parties and have made them more ideological opposites than they were in the 1950s.

The other electorate is independent and nonpartisan, sometimes even fiercely antipartisan. More inclined to respond to short-term factors involving the candidates and their campaigns, it is available for temporary mobilization on behalf of either a major party candidate or a third-party or independent candidate—or for demobilization into nonvoting. . . . In 2000 this pool of nonpartisan potential voters was more numerous than either self-identified

---

*"Secular realignment" involves the shift in a population category of voters from one party to the other over an extended period of time. An example would be the change in the partisan identities and voting behavior of white voters in the American South, a core component of the Democratic New Deal coalition first formed in the 1930s, to become a key element of the Republican Party base by the latter half of the twentieth century.

†"Dealignment" describes the movement of voters away from identity with either of the parties. This may involve voters leaving one party and not affiliating with the other or entering the electorate without any party identification and never acquiring it. Issues and candidate attractiveness, rather than party identification, dominate such voters' decisions.

Democrats or Republicans. With parity in party strength within the partisan electorate, this nonpartisan electorate now holds the balance of power between the parties, and election outcomes depend even more than before on short-term factors.

Theoretical Considerations

Detailing the story of the development of these two contrasting electorates and their effect on American politics is the task of this [selection]. Before providing the details of this story, though, the ideas on which it depends need to be made more explicit. The vote outcome of any election is best seen as the joint product of long-term predispositions of the electorate toward the parties and short-term orientations toward the issues and candidates of the day. Long-term predispositions are embodied in enduring party loyalties. Most voters possess these loyalties, even amidst today's largely unprecedented dealignment. Voters holding these loyalties seem to be readily aware of them, because they report them more reliably than any other political orientations in responding to survey questions.

When the distribution of these enduring party loyalties changes in a significant way, so that the coalitions of party loyalists are transformed or the balance between the parties is altered . . . , we speak of the electorate as having "realigned." Analyses of aggregate vote patterns suggest that the American electorate has realigned at regular thirty- to forty-year intervals throughout much of American history. When the share of the electorate professing party loyalties declines and more voters are basing electoral decisions necessarily on election-specific factors, the process is described as a "dealignment." . . .

This theoretical perspective focuses attention on the distribution of party loyalties, including their presence or absence, as the fundamental characteristic of an electorate at any particular time and on changes in these distributions as the principal dynamic in electoral politics. It relegates actual votes to the background—as consequences of enduring partisanship and immediate, and temporary, candidate or issue-specific forces. . . .

Changing American Partisanship: Realignment Amidst Dealignment

Since the mid-1960s, two important changes have taken place in the party loyalties of the American electorate. First came a decay or dealignment of partisan loyalties, especially within the Democratic Party coalition that had dominated American electoral politics since the 1930s. It was followed, most noticeably in the early 1980s but foreshadowed somewhat earlier, by the reshuffling of the major party coalitions and a slight growth of Republican Party loyalists after their dealignment-era decline. Together these two changes have altered the social composition of the American parties in significant ways.

Figure 1 reports the party identifications of the electorate from 1952 to 2000. From relatively stable levels during the 1950s and early 1960s, with Democrats outnumbering Republicans by a five to three margin, the partisan strength of both parties eroded, starting after 1962 for the Republicans and 1964 for the Democrats. The GOP had recovered its 1950s level of party loyalty in 1994, only to fall slightly from that apex for the rest of the decade. In 2000, even after winning both houses of Congress and the presidency, albeit by razor-thin margins in the most controversial election since 1876, the Republicans still were unable to attract more loyalists than either their Democratic opposition or nonpartisan independents. Indeed, they began the twenty-first century with no more loyalists as a percentage of the American electorate than they had in 1952.

That Republican identifiers are no larger a portion of the electorate today than they were in the 1950s is ignored by those who have seen the recent years as a time of pro-GOP realignment. The Republicans are better positioned electorally than in the 1950s and early 1960s. But the reasons are Democratic decay, Republicans' higher turnout rates at the polls, and the disappearance of the solid South as a dependably Democratic voting block—rather than any nationwide realignment to Republicanism. The current GOP hold on the House and the presidency, as well as on many of the state governments, consequently rests on shaky foundations.

It has been the Democratic Party that has borne the major brunt of the changes since the early 1960s. Erosion in its loyalist base first became visible in

Figure 1

Party Loyalties of Americans, 1952–2000

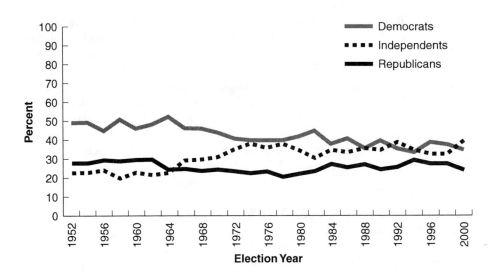

1966 and, despite a few temporary surges, typically in midterm elections, has continued through 2000. The beneficiary of these declines in partisanship has been the amorphous category called "independents." After being outnumbered by both Democrats and Republicans through 1964, independents have become more numerous than Republican loyalists ever since. They came close to comprising a plurality of the electorate in the mid-1970s and again in the mid-1980s, and, beginning in 1992, they attracted a plurality of the electorate in three of the following six election years. Within the range of sampling error these changes can be said to have produced an electorate almost evenly balanced among Democrats, Republicans, and independents by the turn of the century.

Partisan Changes in Key Groups Within the Electorate

To gain a better appreciation for how changes in partisan loyalties have transformed the American party system, it is necessary to disaggregate the movements of the entire electorate into the behavior of particular groups. Table 1 contains the divisions among Democrats, Republicans, and independents of seven groups that were divided noticeably along partisan lines either in the New Deal party system in place in the 1950s or in the system that replaced it.

As it is with many dominant coalitions, the roots of the post-1964 Democratic decay are found to a considerable degree within the political tensions of its original formulation. At its core, the New Deal Democratic majority was based on an alliance of white Southerners and liberal Northerners. Such an alliance could remain intact only so long as economic issues dominated the political agenda and the South was left alone to pursue its traditional segregation of blacks and whites. Once Southern autonomy was challenged over civil rights, the loyalties of both white Southerners and African Americans were put in motion. New Deal politics were largely organized around economic policy and social class issues. As the agenda of American politics shifted to embrace new social and moral issues, the partisanship of other key groups in the American population was challenged. The success of the New Deal welfare state in overcoming the problems of the Great Depression in the 1930s and lifting ethnic minorities and workers into the middle class undermined the subsequent attraction of the Democratic Party to many of its beneficiaries, especially their children and grandchildren. Moreover, the new issue agenda that emerged, like newly electrified poles of an electromagnet, yielded different party coalition clusters than before.

The Countermovements of White Southerners and African Americans

By the 1950s, the Democratic alliance between white Southerners and liberal Northerners was beginning to fray. Southern autonomy on matters of racial

Table 1

Changing Partisan Loyalties of Key Groups, 1952–2000

Year	White Southerners			African Americans			Catholic			Union Households			Men			Women			White Fundamentalists		
	Dems	Inds	Reps	Dems	Inds	Reps	Dems	Inds	Reps	Dems	Inds	Reps	Dems	Inds	Reps	Dems	Inds	Reps	Dems	Inds	Reps
1952	77	12	11	64	21	16	56	26	18	55	23	22	48	26	26	49	21	30			
1954	68	16	16	62	20	19	53	27	21	59	20	21	51	24	25	48	22	30			
1956	68	17	15	61	16	23	52	27	21	52	27	21	46	28	26	44	22	34			
1958	60	18	21	62	18	21	58	25	17	63	20	17	49	23	28	52	18	30			
1960	57	22	21	50	31	18	61	23	16	57	28	15	43	29	28	49	19	32	48	22	30
1962				70	14	16							50	24	26	47	20	32			
1964	66	20	15	77	15	7	58	25	17	64	23	13	50	26	24	54	21	26	55	18	27
1966	55	29	16	62	28	9	55	29	17	56	25	18	46	24	24	47	26	26	46	28	26
1968	50	37	13	88	10	2	53	32	15	51	30	19	43	32	25	48	28	24	42	31	27
1970	43	38	19	78	18	4	52	31	17	54	31	15	42	34	23	45	29	26	42	33	26
1972	47	34	19	69	23	8	51	35	14	46	39	15	37	39	23	44	32	24	38	36	26
1974	47	34	19	68	29	3	48	36	16	45	42	13	35	43	22	43	34	23	40	36	24
1976	45	34	21	71	24	4	50	35	15	47	40	12	37	42	20	42	32	26	36	36	28
1978	41	38	20	68	27	5	50	36	14	50	36	14	38	44	18	42	34	23	37	39	24
1980	43	34	23	75	20	5	43	38	19	46	39	14	38	40	22	44	32	24	42	34	24
1982	49	29	22	79	19	2	55	29	16	50	32	18	39	35	26	50	27	23	40	32	28
1984	37	38	24	65	31	4	43	36	21	46	35	19	34	39	28	41	32	28	33	34	32
1986	40	34	26	74	22	4	45	33	22	47	34	20	37	38	25	44	30	26	37	32	32
1988	34	40	26	64	30	6	38	36	26	43	37	20	30	42	29	40	32	28	32	37	30
1990	37	42	20	64	31	5	45	33	23	50	31	20	36	36	27	43	34	23	35	36	29
1992	32	42	26	66	29	4	41	39	20	45	38	17	32	40	28	40	37	23	28	39	33
1994	32	33	35	62	33	6	40	36	24	44	36	20	30	38	33	39	32	29	30	32	39
1996	36	34	30	66	31	3	43	33	24	43	39	18	34	34	32	44	32	24	37	29	34
1998	33	34	33	73	23	4	40	33	27	43	37	20	35	37	28	41	34	25	28	36	36
2000	24	40	36	68	29	3	35	40	25	46	36	18	30	41	29	39	38	23	23	38	39

Note: Entries are percentages of the group members who identify as Democrats, independents (pure + leaners), and Republicans, respectively. Within each group, these percentages sum to within rounding error of 100 percent across the (three) columns.

policy had become untenable to many Northern Democrats, and a movement to secure equal rights for blacks was emerging in the South. Once the national Democratic Party moved to champion civil rights for Southern blacks in the early 1960s and the GOP took the opposite position in 1964, the die was cast. White Southerners began to desert their traditional party's candidates as early as the 1950s. This desertion was manifested first in voting Republican for president. As long as Democratic candidates for state and local offices continued to reflect their region's mores, they retained the support of its white voters. Over the years, however, Republicanism steadily penetrated down the ballot as old-time Democratic officeholders retired and new, more mainstream party candidates replaced them.

It was not too long before the civil rights revolution in the South and the opposing postures of the parties toward it began to affect party loyalties. As the first columns of table 1 show, Democratic loyalties already were declining within the white Southern electorate in the 1950s; the reasons at first had little to do with race. As race became the most salient regional issue, though, this erosion of the solidly Democratic South continued with only occasional and partial reversals through the early 1990s. By 2000, Democratic loyalists among white Southerners had fallen to what undoubtedly is their lowest point in the history of the party. The Democratic share of this group is less than one-third of what it was fifty years before. The days of a solid South, built upon the Democratic commitments of its white electorate, are gone.

The GOP has been able to capitalize upon this Democratic decay to a considerable degree. Steadily, with only occasional slight reversals in the mid-1960s, 1990, and 1996, it gained a stronger base of party loyalists among white Southerners. By the 1990s, there were roughly equal numbers of Republicans and Democrats within this group. By 2000, with another surge in GOP loyalists and decline in Democratic loyalists, white Southerners had become significantly more Republican than Democratic. Republican advances have been especially pronounced within the new generations of white Southerners, many of whom have rejected inherited Democratic loyalties. . . .

It took several decades for the Republicans to outnumber Democrats among white Southerners, and they remain far short of dominance. At first, in the 1960s, the breakup of the solid South featured a surge of independents, reaching levels that were to be more or less sustained over the next twenty years. In their flight from Democratic loyalties, many white Southerners seemed to take refuge in nonpartisanship. Perhaps this shift is a phase in the natural journey of partisan realignment for a group. Older members first defect in their voting, as many white Southern Democrats did in presidential contests in the 1950s. Next they desert their traditional party identifications, but cannot bring themselves to convert to the other party, even if they are consistently voting for its candidates, as easily as newer members of the electorate can. Over time as the inexorable process of population replacement works it way, the group's partisan loyalties are brought into line with their votes.

The undeniable consequence of the changes in partisanship among white Southerners through 2000 is a realigned Southern party system—more Republican than ever before yet still competitive. . . . Many Southern whites have changed partisan loyalties due to racial issues, yet many others are drawn to the Republican Party for reasons that have little to do with race. Large numbers of Northerners moved to the South, bringing their traditional GOP loyalties with them. With the modernization of the Southern economy has come an expanding middle class, which as early as the 1950s was drawn to the GOP for many of the same reasons that middle-class Northerners were. The return of religious fundamentalism to the political arena, with its focus on moral and social conservatism, also has been a part of the Southern equation in recent years. More than elsewhere in the nation, it has further eroded the white working-class base of the Democratic Party in the South.

The changes in the South have had enormous consequences for party politics at the national level. Without a solid South, which had comprised the most loyal share of its vote since the 1870s and given it a regional "lock" in the Electoral College, the Democratic Party is no longer dominant in American politics. Important changes have occurred in the party coalitions outside of the South to be sure, but they pale in comparison to the changes wrought in the South.

The movement away from the Democratic Party by white Southerners is paralleled, and has been inextricably linked, to a consolidation of African American support for the Democrats, as shown in the next three columns of table 1. Since 1952, African Americans inside and outside of the South have become the most dependable Democratic loyalists. . . . They began the era with widespread Democratic loyalties, although they were not nearly as devoted to the party as white Southerners. Moreover, the early figures are somewhat illusory, for more than one-half of all African Americans lived in the South in the 1950s, and few of them were permitted to participate in elections because of the state registration laws and practices of that era. Not only were Southern blacks mobilized into politics in the 1960s, so that their Democratic loyalties became more consequential, but the positioning of the parties on opposite sides of the civil rights divide by the mid-1960s pushed most of the remaining black Republicans out of the GOP.

Discussions of possible growth in black Republicanism in recent years ignore the fact that the "party of Lincoln" enjoyed much more support in the African American community a generation ago than it does today. . . . No group within the modern American electorate contains proportionately fewer GOP adherents. . . .

Democratic Decay Among Catholics and Labor and Their Contrasting Consequences

Like Southern whites, Catholics and labor unions were core constituencies of the Democratic majority established in the 1930s. Catholics had long been attracted to the Democratic Party in the nation's cities, where they were heavily concentrated, but it took the events of the 1920s—the party's choice of a Catholic as its presidential nominee in 1928, the Great Depression, and Roosevelt's policies of the 1930s—to consolidate their loyalties. Labor unions were empowered by New Deal legislation in the 1930s, which secured the Democratic loyalties of their members. As the next two sets of columns in table 1 show, the legacy of these partisan commitments was present in the 1950s and 1960s, when Catholics and people in households containing a union member favored the Democrats over the Republicans by margins of about three to one.

From these parallel baselines, the partisan loyalties of Catholics and union families followed a familiar spiral for a while, and then diverged. Beginning in the late 1960s, the two groups joined in the general dealignment of the American electorate. They contributed to the declines in Democratic and Republican loyalists and the increases in independents through the 1970s. The dealignment of these two groups seems to have halted by 1980—a bit later than it had ended for the electorate as a whole. For union families, the ensuing period was a time of little net change in partisanship. By contrast, Catholics turned in a Republican direction beginning in 1980, and their movement came at the expense of Democratic loyalties. The net exchange of Democratic for Republican loyalties among Catholics is not large, but it is noticeable.

These changes in partisan loyalties leave Catholics and union families still more Democratic than Republican by the beginning of the twenty-first century. Union households now are over two to one Democratic, down from what they were in the 1950s and 1960s, but nonetheless decisively unbalanced. It is dealignment, rather than realignment, that best characterizes their movement. By contrast, Catholics underwent elements of first dealignment, then realignment, to the point that they show an almost equal balance between Democrats and independents, and a Republican minority that has grown to almost rival them. Union families are no more Republican, on net, at the end of the period than they were at the beginning, but more Catholics are supportive of the GOP than was the case a half-century ago. The emergence of religious issues as powerful shapers of partisan loyalties, it seems fair to surmise, has affected many Catholics just as it has affected many Protestant fundamentalists.

An Emerging Gender Gap in Partisan Loyalties

After years of no differences between men and women in partisan preferences, scholars and commentators have identified a consistent gender gap in recent decades in both partisanship and voting. The next six columns in table 1 show the extent of the gender gap in partisanship. The partisan loyalties of men and women began to diverge in the 1970s and had become significantly different by the 1980s and 1990s, especially where Democratic loyalties were concerned.

Comparison of the party loyalties of men and women over time yields insight into what has happened, although exactly why it has happened defies simple explanation. Both groups joined in the post-1964 dealignment. Republican loyalties eroded to about the same extent between both groups. Democratic loyalties declined between both as well, albeit at different rates, with the decline coming earlier and reaching deeper among men. This shift left women somewhat more Democratic than men by the mid-1970s. Beginning in the 1980s, Democratic loyalties among women stabilized, with no further losses or Republican gains for the most part; but the decline in Democratic loyalties and growth of Republicanism continued among men. By the turn of the twenty-first century, men were equally likely to be Republican or Democrat, while almost twice as many women were Democrats as were Republicans.

The gender gap, then, is the work of a substantial pro-GOP shift in the partisan orientations of men in the 1980s and 1990s at the same time most women were resisting the movement away from the Democrats. Scholars have been unable to attribute these changes to so-called women's issues and now consider them a result of different expectations about the role of government as well as myriad other forces. The gender changes are modest compared to those of Southern whites and even African Americans, but what makes them important is the size of the groups involved.

The Delayed Realignment of White Fundamentalist Protestants

Another important change in group party loyalties since the 1950s is a result of the growing importance of religion in American politics. Rather than the Protestant versus Catholic conflict of earlier times, contemporary religious politics has revolved more around the importance of religion in one's life. The GOP has been the traditional home for Protestants, especially in the North before the 1960s, but the party in earlier times represented middle-class "high church" Protestants better than their more fundamentalist and lower-status brethren. Recent years have witnessed the ascendancy of white Protestant fundamentalists in Republican nomination politics and its party organizations and policy-making circles. This new influence of fundamentalists is typically attributed to the group's growing Republicanism.

The changes in party loyalties of white Protestant fundamentalists, presented in the last columns of table 1, however, do not quite fit these first impressions. The group has become more Republican than Democratic, but only *after* it became more influential in GOP circles. Early on, white fundamentalists joined in the dealignment of the broader electorate, with its deeper erosion of Democratic than Republican loyalties. As the axis of American politics turned to religious and social questions, though, the Democratic loyalties of fundamentalists continued to decline—reaching their lowest point in the series (slightly more than 20 percent of the electorate) in 2000. The decline was not as steady or as sharp as that of Southern whites, particularly Southern white fundamentalists, but it has been persistent. During the time of dealignment, Republican loyalties among white fundamentalists fell off as well. They did not regain their 1960 high point (occasioned because the 1960 Democratic nominee was a Catholic) until 1984. The sharpest growth in Republican loyalties in this group, though, came recently—in the last decade of the twentieth century. By 2000, it had left Republicans tied with independents as the identification of choice for white Protestant fundamentalists.

What is surprising, given their considerable weight in the inner circles of Republican politics for some years, is the delay of a Republican surge in partisan loyalties among white fundamentalists. Strongly courted by GOP candidates since Richard Nixon in 1968, for two decades white fundamentalists seemed to resist becoming Republicans. Only in the early 1990s, then again in 1998 and 2000, have they been significantly more Republican than Democratic in professed party identifications. By 2000, this gap had widened considerably, with continued decline in Democratic identifications, but its significance is challenged by a recent surge of independents. What began as a story of Democratic dealignment seems only of late to have become a story of pro-Republican realignment among white Protestant fundamentalists.

Putting Everything Together

An important part of the story of partisan change in the American electorate during the past half-century can be told by the overall trends in party identification and the patterns for the seven groups discussed above. Overall the electorate has dealigned, becoming less partisan and more independent since the 1950s and early 1960s. The dealignment occurred during the ten-year period between Lyndon Johnson's reelection in 1964 and the immediate aftermath of the departure of Richard Nixon from the White House in 1974 under the threat of impeachment. The percentage of independents in the American electorate at the turn of the century is little different than it was in 1974, but they now may be more numerous than either Democrats or Republicans.

The seven groups I analyze . . . present a more variegated picture. White Southerners and white Protestant fundamentalists (and many Americans are both) have realigned from being overwhelmingly Democratic to marginally more Republican by century's end. At the same time, African Americans have become even more attached to the Democratic Party. Two other key groups within the Democratic coalition that emerged from the 1930s, Catholics and labor union households, remain more Democratic than Republican, but their loyalties to the party of Franklin Roosevelt and John Kennedy have eroded, contributing to the dealignment. Democratic (and Republican) loyalties among women have eroded as well, while those of men were realigning to the point that they are now as Republican as they are Democratic.

In describing these changes, I addressed in passing the question of why they took place. In a nutshell, changes in the political world—chief among them the Democrats' support for integration in the South, the traumas of Vietnam and urban riots, the replacement of class-based economic conflict by divisions over civil rights, social policy, and religion—tore the majority Democratic coalition apart. . . .

Although some scholars resist calling the result in this case a realignment, when seen in all of its complexity it certainly possesses key realignment characteristics—changes in the nature of the party coalitions, new issues dominating the political agenda, and differences in who exercises governmental power. It also exhibits signs of realignment in yet another way. The hallmark of a newly aligned party system, one may logically surmise, is that ideology and partisanship are more strongly linked than they have been before. As measured straightforwardly by the correlation (r) between respondents' self-locations on seven-point ideology and party identification scales, the connection between ideology and party loyalty has strengthened between 1960 and 2000. What we used to describe in 1960 as a remarkably nonideological party system now appears to have been only a snapshot of an electorate at the end of one party system and the beginning of another. Today's highly polarized parties in Washington and the state capitals are now paralleled by more ideologically polarized party electorates than we have experienced in decades.

What we miss here to complete a realignment scenario are two important ingredients. First, this "realignment" is not as broadly encompassing as past realignments have been. More than one-third of the electorate, virtually 40 percent in 2000, is unwilling to join the new two-party arrangement by choosing a major party as the object of their loyalty. Second, for all of its successes since 1968 at the presidential level and from 1994 to 2000 with the Congress, the Republican Party has not been able to become the party choice of a majority of Americans. Through 2000 at least, the GOP has fallen far short of achieving the gains expected for the ascendant party in realignment. Nor have more voters been mobilized into politics by the realignment, as they were in past realignments. Rather, with the exception of the Perot-induced boost in 1992, turnout has declined to where only half of the American electorate casts a presidential ballot and far fewer participate below the presidential level.

Instead of a decisive realignment, then, partisan changes in recent years have yielded a Democratic Party no longer in command of the loyalties of the dominant share of the electorate, and an enlarged group of political independents who are not dependable supporters of either party. There has been some recent Republican growth to be sure, but it has not been sufficient to recapture the levels of Republicanism of the 1950s, hardly a halcyon era for the GOP in terms of party loyalties.

Conclusion

The result of the 2000 presidential election—with George W. Bush's Electoral College victory turning on a U.S. Supreme Court decision about how to count votes in Florida's "dead heat" contest amid Bush's popular vote defeat nation-wide—reflects the state of Americans' partisan loyalties as they entered the new century. It is indeed a tale of two electorates—the one partisan, the other nonpartisan.

By 2000, about 60 percent of the electorate was composed of Democratic and Republican partisans, somewhat below the mid-60s average percentage from 1992 to 2000. Like the 2000 results in Florida, the partisan battle comes close to being a "dead heat." With the realignment of the party coalitions, these partisans also have become more ideologically polarized than in earlier times. Such polarization was evident in the 2000 presidential contest and especially its contentious aftermath, from the partisan warfare over the Florida vote through the first eight months of the Bush presidency. The tragic events of September 11 and the "rally around the flag" politics of a nation under attack temporarily muted partisan divisions, but the political battle between two parties with opposing policy dispositions and ideologically polarized partisans has reappeared.

The other electorate, about 35 percent of eligible voters from 1992 to 2000 and up to 40 percent in 2000, is nonpartisan. It opts out of Democratic or Republican identification when asked and, even where it may vote rather consistently for one party's candidates, it is unwilling to commit to that party for the long term. Not only is this electorate less involved in politics than its partisan counterpart, it also seems inclined to withdraw from the political fray as the major parties become more polarized—unless an attractive non–major party alternative is on the ballot. These nonpartisan voters are moved by the candidates and issues of the moment, not by the long-term positioning of the parties, and they add a considerable element of volatility to the electoral arena.

It is a combination of realignment and dealignment that most aptly characterizes contemporary electoral politics in the United States. The realignment has changed the major parties, reshuffling their loyalists along more ideological lines. But the dealignment has prevented either of these more ideological parties from dominating the political world—as is evidenced by persistent divided government, fluctuations in presidential voting from election to election, and slender margins of party control over governmental institutions. Nonpartisans hold the balance of power in the contemporary electorate between equally balanced major parties and provide fertile ground for non–major party candidates. The dilemma for the major parties and their candidates is that what mobilizes their partisan core voters repels the nonpartisan electorate, potentially either costing them the election or, if victorious, a mandate to govern. . . .

. . . The story of our current party system can best be told in terms of the relative sizes, compositions, and electoral tendencies of its two electorates—one partisan and about evenly divided, the other estranged from party politics. They shape the prime characteristics of party politics and American politics in our time.

References

Key, V. O., Jr. "Secular Realignment and the Party System." *Journal of Politics* 21: 198–210.
Wattenberg, Martin P. 1998. *The Decline of American Political Parties, 1952 1996.* Cambridge, Mass.. Harvard University Press.

Questions for Discussion

1. What factors have contributed to the realignment of key components of the Democratic and Republican Party coalitions since the 1950s? What categories of voters have been most affected? Why does Beck believe that realignment, in the classic sense, is still "incomplete"?
2. Do you consider yourself a partisan voter or a nonpartisan voter? Is there anything that might change your orientation?
3. Are third-party and independent candidacies likely to become more common in the contemporary electoral environment? What kinds of partisan presidential candidates are most likely to fare well in the current environment?

Thinking About Political Polarization

Pietro S. Nivola

The transformation of partisan conflict in American politics discussed in selection 6.2 has been led by the increasing rise of cultural issues on the political agenda, at least partially displacing the economic and class divisions that characterized the New Deal era. High-profile wedge issues like abortion, minority rights, gun control, and the teaching of evolution, to name a few, continue to divide the electorate and the parties into two rather distinct camps, at least stereotypically. One side, associated with the Democrats, advocates secular modernism, emphasizes equality, and represents a challenge to long-practiced norms of social behavior. The opposition, identified with Republican Party interests, is associated with the culture of traditionalism, arguing for preserving or reasserting traditional roles and standards of behavior.

The depth and extensiveness of contemporary political polarization, and its consequences, is a matter of considerable debate. Compared to some earlier periods of American history, today's political polarization seems rather tame. Battles between slavery and abolitionist advocates in the mid-nineteenth century or between agrarian and industrial/manufacturing interests at the turn of that century were far more intense and disruptive than contemporary conflicts.

In this selection, Pietro Nivola, while not convinced that the degree of polarization is as deep and widespread as many suggest, explores some of the potential causes of contemporary divisions. Religious factors and a news media that exaggerate the intensity of political warfare no doubt play a key role. Structural forces such as congressional redistricting, the primary nomination system, the Electoral College, and united government all potentially contribute to political polarization. Nivola suggests a number of structural reforms that might mitigate the excesses of conflict, and believes it is time "to take a critical look at unnecessary aggressive practices that have come to be standard operating procedure—at both ends of Pennsylvania Avenue, and in both chambers of Congress."

Pietro S. Nivola is Vice President and Director of Government Studies at the Brookings Institution. He also holds the Douglas Dillon Chair at Brookings.

Pietro S. Nivola, "Thinking About Political Polarization," *The Brookings Institution Policy Brief*, no. 139, January 2005. Reprinted with permission of the Brookings Institution.

    ◆ ◆ ◆ ontrary to a misapprehension purveyed by more than a few casual commentators, the bulk of the U.S. electorate continues to share moderate political persuasions, and is not increasingly split by wedge issues like abortion or gay rights. Moderate voters were hardly sidelined in the 2004 election. Both presidential candidates amassed support from them. Fifty-four percent of them went to Kerry, 45 percent to Bush. About 38 percent of those who thought abortion should be legal in most cases voted for Bush. So did 52 percent of those who favored civil unions.

"Moral values" (however defined) appeared to be the leading concern of slightly more than a fifth of the electorate. For the overwhelming majority of voters a combination of other issues such as the Iraq war, the terrorist threat, and the state of the economy were more salient. Roughly one out of five voters were self-described evangelicals. One of four in this fabled group voted for Senator Kerry.

What about the TV maps that depict "red" America clashing with "blue"?* They are colorful but misleading. Most of the country ought to be painted purple. There are plenty of red states—Oklahoma, Kansas, North Carolina, and Virginia, to name a few—that have Democratic governors. The bright blue states of California, New York, and even Massachusetts have Republican governors. Some red states such as Tennessee, North Carolina, and Mississippi send at least as many Democrats as Republicans to the House of Representatives. Michigan and Pennsylvania—two of the biggest blue states—send more Republicans than Democrats. North Dakota is blood red (Bush ran off with 63 percent of the vote there). Yet that state's entire congressional delegation remains composed of Democrats. On election night, Bush also swept all but a half-dozen counties in Montana. But that didn't prevent the Democrats from winning control of the governor's office and state legislature.†

The actual political geography of the United States, in short, bears little resemblance to the simplistic picture of a nation divided between solidly partisan states or regions.

---

*The nation's press typically characterizes contemporary party and electoral politics as a clash of values and cultures, with the country divided between socially conservative, red-state Republicans and socially liberal, blue-state Democrats. On the political map, blue states are concentrated on the West Coast, the upper Midwest, and the Northeast, while the rest of the nation represents red-state strongholds, with particular strength in the Heartland, the South, and the Southwest.

†The results of the 2006 election rendered the political landscape even more purple, with Democrats, in particular, gaining some impressive victories in what are usually considered red-state strongholds. A good example is the state of Kansas, where Democrats now hold half of the congressional seats and where Democratic incumbent governor Kathleen Sebelius won re-election with 58 percent of the vote. Overall, the 2006 election results suggest that many voters in both blue and red states are willing to split their tickets in the voting booth, voting for Democrats for some offices and Republicans for others.

A Problem?

Today's social conflicts and partisan strife pale in comparison with much of the nation's past. Recall the racial apartheid that scarred America for a century after the end of slavery, and the urban riots and anti-war protests that inflamed the country during the 1960s. Properly defined, polarization of U.S. politics reflects a sorting of political convictions by either the mass public or ruling elites, or both, into roughly two distinct camps: persons inclined to support the Democratic or the Republican parties' policies and candidates for elective office. Exactly how much of this sorting process is in fact taking place is hard to tell. But even granting that some has been underway, the upshot probably has virtues as well as liabilities.

Sharper ideological separation between Democrats and Republicans offers voters "a choice, not an echo," to borrow Barry Goldwater's phrase.* Surely, there is something to be said for that clarification. Was the public philosophy of the Democratic party more intelligible in the days when it had to accommodate the likes of Southern segregationists under its big tent? For years political scientists had lamented the lack of a "responsible" party system in the United States. Now, with our political parties somewhat more centralized, unified, cohesive, and disciplined—in sum, a bit more reminiscent of the style in European parliamentary regimes—analysts and pundits rhapsodize about the days of incongruous ad hoc coalitions, weaker party leadership, and often sloppy bipartisan compromises.

In any event, whether the present postures of the political parties are consistently more distinctive than they used to be is by no means obvious. There was a time when "smaller" government was a distinguishing aspiration of Republican presidents and congressional leaders. That no longer seems to be the case. Witness the GOP's role in the largest expansion of an entitlement program (Medicare drug benefits) in forty years, the free spending by the Republican-controlled Congress, and the Bush administration's efforts to federalize key aspects of local education policy, marriage law, and more.

The Democrats, to be sure, have differentiated themselves on certain matters—conserving the status quo for Social Security, for instance. But more than was commonly acknowledged in the 2004 election cycle, the two parties converged considerably on a number of key issues. On fighting terrorism, the Democratic platform sounded tough: the government should "take all needed steps." On Iraq, the Democratic presidential candidate (in his words) was "not talking about leaving," but "about winning." On fiscal policy, the party effectively embraced much of Bush's tax reduction. True, the Democrats proposed to raise the top tax rate on incomes above $200,000 back up to 39.6 percent—but that

---

*Barry Goldwater was the Republican nominee for president in 1964.

would still have been a far cry from the 70 percent rate that President Reagan had slashed.

In sum, just how politically polarized Americans really are, and precisely what the supposed dysfunctional consequences might be, remain unsettled questions that beckon for empirical research.

Root Causes

Assuming, though, that a degree of "polarization" has occurred, what has contributed to it?

Exogenous Forces

Plausible determinants of the phenomenon include both exogenous [external] and endogenous [internal] factors. On the exogenous list are considerations such as:

Historical Circumstances   As noted earlier, there have been long stretches of American history in which ruptures in society were far worse than they are now. Epic struggles were waged between advocates of slavery and abolitionists, between agrarian populists and urban manufacturing interests at the end of the nineteenth century, and between industrial workers and owners of capital well into the first third of the twentieth century. Yet, what modern observers remember nostalgically are the more recent intervals of relative political consensus, such as the bipartisan cooperation on foreign policy in the immediate post–World War II period. . . .

Any serious exploration of today's political polarities has to be placed in historical context. We have to ask: Compared to what?

Sectional Realignment of the Electorate   The Democrats' loss of their old Southern base consolidated the party's strength among liberal constituencies dominant in much of the Northeast. At the same time, as the traditional foothold of Republican moderates in regions such as New England diminished, so did the party's internal ballast against harder-line conservatives. The GOP, now anchored in the South and West, became more orthodox.

Party Parity   America's political parties are colliding because they are competing for power almost in a dead heat. Unusually small margins now make the difference between winning or losing the presidency, the House, or the Senate. With so much riding on marginal changes in political support, it is not surprising to see both sides battling to gain an edge by whatever means are deemed effective.

So, for instance, if the GOP sees that redrawing district lines in Texas can add a few seats to its majority in the House, the opportunity is seized without hesitation. When the Democratic opposition gets a chance to trip up a Republican president's judicial nominees, it frequently doesn't seem to hesitate either. The perpetually quarrelsome atmosphere sows ever more resentment and distrust.

Role of Religion   Some writers contend that religiosity is a stronger correlate of party preference and voting behavior than it was a number of years ago. Presumably church-goers are gravitating to the Republicans, secular voters to the Democrats. Others contend, however, that the story is oversimplified. Religious traditionalists of all kinds seem to tilt to the GOP, but other religious voters (for example, centrist Catholics and "modernist" evangelicals), not just "secularists," often lean Democratic. If the distinction is valid, it could imply that neither party, at least at the national level, can afford to embrace a strictly secular agenda.

Role of the Media   Some critics argue that the "culture war" in American society is substantially an artifact of extensive but non-systematic coverage by the media, including flawed reportage by respectable news outlets. According to these skeptics, the press's selective accounts do not square with scientific opinion surveys that find the general public less, not more, divided on a wide range of social, economic, and political issues.

In part, news stories exaggerate the intensity of our political warfare because acrimony and strident rhetoric make good copy, whereas footage of people getting along or reaching consensus doesn't sell. But if that is the case, which side—the media or the audience—is the principal agent? Amid the modern proliferation of news outlets, growing segments of the public are able to select their sources of information on the basis of partisan proclivities. Republican-leaning viewers and listeners choose talk radio, the Fox News Channel, and the *Wall Street Journal* editorial page; Democratic-leaners prefer National Public Radio, the three old-line broadcast networks, and the *New York Times*. This partitioning of audiences might suggest that increasingly the media are becoming hostages to partisan markets, rather than the other way around.

The Role of Technology   An even more fundamental force seemingly reshaping political patterns is technology. The revolution in communications—direct mail, cable TV, the Internet—has enabled ideological soul mates to seek each other out, organize, pool resources, and proselytize.

Endogenous Forces

A second assortment of explanations focuses on internal changes in the country's governing institutions. This emphasis posits that, at bottom, it is the political class—elected officials, political professionals, the party faithful, issue advocates, talking heads, as distinct from the electorate at large—that is the trouble-maker. The elites, in other words, are presenting voters with polar choices, and are resorting to increasingly confrontational rules of engagement. Among the developments worth considering here are these:

Congressional Redistricting   If there is an institutional practice that can be polarizing in its effect, it is the way congressional district lines are being drawn. In the first 15 House elections following World War II, one party or the other gained an average of 29 seats. In the past 15 elections the average switch was 12 seats. Competitive districts are in sharp decline. In 2004, as little as six percent of the House appeared to be in play.

Increasingly sophisticated computer software has further refined the ability of political cartographers to map with pin-point precision the spatial distribution of voters needed to maximize partisan advantage. In such precisely gerrymandered districts, seats are safe. There, candidates appeal primarily to their base, only concerning themselves with possible primary challenges from the extremes, and seldom needing to reach out to voters across party lines.

Apparently making matters worse is the recent precedent (in Texas and elsewhere) of mid-course redistricting—that is, the redesigning of districts when a state governorship and legislature change hands, rather than only after each decennial census.* A practice of rolling gerrymanders seems likely to prevent more districts from ever shifting from safe to marginal. Not only has the profusion of one-party districts directly driven centrists out of the House of Representatives; one-party politics further undercuts general voter turnout, the indirect effect of which is to further empower extreme electoral constituencies at the expense of the median voter.

The Dominance of Primaries   In theory, in a simple two-party electoral system the natural tendency of candidates competing for single member districts is to move toward the center of the political spectrum. But the balloting in direct primaries may discourage this convergence. The electorates in these contests tend to be small (under 18 percent even in the recent presidential primaries) and often unrepresentative. Hence, candidates are frequently forced to protect their flanks by moving away from the center—positioning themselves further to the left or right of the general public on issues that small but intense factions regard as litmus tests.

---

*Typically, congressional district lines have been redrawn to reflect population changes once every ten years, by a collaborative effort of a state's legislature and governor, usually during the first state legislative session after the new U.S. Census is released. Redistricting after the 2000 Census was released took place as usual, with new congressional districts in place in time for the 2002 election. After that election, however, a number of states, Texas being the most prominent, redistricted again, the aim being to increase the number of safe Republican seats. The legality of mid-decade redistricting was challenged in court by Democrats, but the principle was upheld.

The number of Democratic party primaries for House elections has remained about the same since 1964, but on the Republican side, the number of primaries has risen steeply since then. The unintended consequences of the direct primary as an institutional mainstay in American elections have given pause to political scientists since V. O. Key began calling attention to its risks some fifty years ago. The subject still merits revisiting.

The Electoral College   For the fourth time in U.S. history, a president who had lost a plurality of the popular vote was elected in 2000. Doubts and controversy were bound to follow this outcome.

Obviously, a president chosen in this questionable fashion could not claim an unambiguous mandate. On the other hand, what was such a leader supposed to do—summarily ditch his campaign commitments and, in essence, spend four years as a lame duck cohabiting benignly with his partisan adversaries? President Bush inevitably became perceived as an uncompromising figure when he opted to act decisively rather than "triangulate." Perhaps his style would have been regarded as less divisive, however, if a clear majority of voters—not merely the idiosyncratic Electoral College—had anointed him.

In 2004, Bush did obtain that popular majority. But notice how close the system came to malfunctioning again. A shift of only 60,000 votes in Ohio could have handed that state to John Kerry. Then, he would have joined the inauspicious ranks of presidents elected under circumstances of dubious legitimacy.

New Institutional Norms   Habits of civility and collegial deference that used to be generally recognized and respected in institutions like the U.S. Senate have changed. Abrasive adversarialism seems more often on display. And the slash-and-burn tactics are used even when they appear to offer few electoral advantages. Thus, the level of discord is artificially heightened. . . .

Unified or Divided Government?   A case can be made that the recent experiences with unified party control of the government—as in the past two years of the Bush presidency or the first two of the Clinton presidency—permitted partisans to move their political agendas further to the left or right than would otherwise have been possible. With the opposition more marginalized than is customary in the American system of separated powers, its grievances are more loudly voiced. As in many parliamentary regimes, relations with the ruling majority inevitably turn more rancorous.

Divided government, on the other hand, forces accommodation. The GOP's victory in 1994, for example, helped Clinton shift toward the center.* Similarly,

---

*In 1994 Republicans wrested control of Congress from the Democrats by picking up fifty-four House seats and eight Senate seats, making it impossible for Clinton to pursue his liberal policy agenda.

if the Democrats had regained control of at least one chamber of the legislative branch this year [2005], the result might have been to nudge the Bush administration a bit further toward middle ground in its second term. Arguably, divided party control makes "polarizing" presidents look more centrist.*

Possible Remedies

To the extent that polarization is real, troublesome, and significantly induced by systemic malfunctions (rather than here, so to speak, by popular demand), potential gains from various institutional reforms ought to be weighed. What might be worth considering?

Restraining Gerrymanders   A number of states (Iowa, Arizona, Montana, Maine, New Jersey, Washington) have delegated the mapping of congressional districts to special commissions. How do these innovations work in practice? Can they spread, and if so, how? Because this, like so many other aspects of electoral law, engages questions of state politics and federal-state relations, scholars knowledgeable about federalism can contribute importantly here. Also, few democracies abroad delineate legislative districts in the American fashion. Students of comparative government may well be able to tell us whether any foreign models might be emulated.

Further, in the United States, the federal courts have intervened aggressively in many of the nation's electoral practices (for example, on equality of representation), but ritually defer to the state legislatures and political parties on the issue of abusive gerrymandering. What would it take, legal scholars might ask, to bring the courts more constructively to the defense of democratic principles in this realm?

Primary Reorganization   Despite their setbacks in the courts, it still may be useful to take a closer look at particular state experiments, such as California's "blanket" primary,[†] to see whether such arrangements dilute the influence of hyper-partisans. Also, further adjustment of the presidential primary schedule, front-loading larger states that have a more diverse electorate, makes sense. [See selection 7.1.] (California's recent decision, reverting that state's presidential primary to a late date, is not helpful.)

---

*The 2006 federal election results created a divided government, with Democratic majorities controlling the House and Senate, and Republicans in charge of the executive branch.

†In a blanket primary voters may vote for a candidate of one party for one office and a candidate from a different party for another office. A voter, for example, might vote in the Republican contest for the nomination for governor, while casting a ballot in the Democratic race for the state treasurer nomination.

Voter Participation   Higher voter turnouts in U.S. elections could conceivably exert a moderating influence. When turnout sags, each party's energized base tends to gain leverage. Inasmuch as this tendency gives disproportionate voice to the extremes at the expense of mainstream preferences, efforts to greatly increase voter participation are in order. Easing voter registration and voting procedures could boost turnout markedly. Investment in improved technologies could help.

So might a reduction in the frequency of U.S. elections. What Oscar Wilde said about socialism ("it takes too many evenings") is in some ways the trouble with American democracy: to have any influence on it demands inordinate time, energy, and resources. Arguably, Americans are called upon to vote too often. In no other major democracy does the national legislature face reelection so frequently. At a minimum, if federal, state, and local balloting coincided more regularly and at somewhat longer intervals ("combining up"), the public might regard the overall stakes in each cycle as more significant—and might tire of the process a bit less.

The Electoral College   If the 2004 election again had instated a president who failed to win the popular vote, a reassessment of the Electoral College would have been inevitable. Although another crisis was (narrowly) avoided, the merits of this problematic institution still ought to be debated.

The Electoral College invites targeted appeals to a limited selection of states (the "battlegrounds"). That result may be of special interest to factions therein, but not necessarily to the wider public. A presidential electoral process with so localized a focus is cause for concern.

Further, the Electoral College can depress voter participation in much of the nation. Overall, the percentage of voters who participated in last fall's election was almost 5 percent higher than the turnout in 2000. Yet, most of the increase was limited to the battleground states. Because the electoral college has effectively narrowed elections like the last one to a quadrennial contest for the votes of a relatively small number of states, people elsewhere are likely to feel that their votes don't matter.

Revising the Rules of Engagement   Finally, the time has come to take a critical look at unnecessarily aggressive practices that have come to be considered standard operating procedure—at both ends of Pennsylvania Avenue, and in both chambers of Congress. Obstructionist antics have always been part of the Senate's repertoire. These days, however, their exercise—in deliberations over judicial selection, for example—sometimes seems indiscriminate and unrestrained. Of particular benefit would be further research examining the distinct possibility that members of Congress frequently overestimate the electoral payoff from "going negative."

Questions for Discussion

1. According to Nivola, how do various "structural" factors such as the current primary election system, Electoral College rules, and congressional redistricting affect the level and intensity of political polarization? Do you believe reform of such structures would have a marked impact on political polarization?
2. How have the proliferation of media outlets and changes in communications technology impacted political polarization? All things considered, have the changes been positive or negative for the political system?
3. Nivola believes that divided government has a tendency to lessen political polarization in Washington, making a "polarizing" president look more centrist. Does Nivola's generalization hold true for the second term of the Bush presidency?

Chapter 7

Campaigns and Elections

Few aspects of American politics have changed as much in recent decades as the ways in which candidates campaign for national office. A half century ago, electioneering was dominated by political parties, which were the main means of communication between candidates and voters. Party parades, mailings, rallies, and door-to-door canvassing were the essential ingredients of campaigns. Party affiliation, based on strong bonds of ethnic, class, regional, or religious identity, was the key factor in determining how voters cast their ballots. Ticket splitters who voted for a president from one party and Senate or House members from another were a small minority.

Today's campaigns are candidate centered. An individual politician's campaign organization raises funds, mobilizes activists, advertises on television, conducts sophisticated direct-mail operations, and polls voters, all largely independent of party organization. Political consultants, pollsters, and outside strategists have replaced the party bosses as central figures in campaigns. Candidates' issue positions and personal attractiveness have challenged party loyalties as key factors in voters' decisions. Split-ticket voting is now quite common.

The new style of campaigning is especially apparent in presidential elections. Prior to the 1970s, candidates were nominated by party professionals who were usually chosen through state conventions or caucuses tightly controlled by the party organization. The eventual nominee typically had worked his way up the party hierarchy over a long period, had served in a number of elected positions in government, and was able to put together a coalition of state party delegations to win the nomination. Once such a person was nominated, the presidential campaign was usually run by the national party organization. Between 1952 and 1968, for example, at least one of the party campaigns was run by the national committee staff in each election; in 1956 and 1964, both campaigns were run by the national party organizations.

The contemporary route to the presidency is quite different. Nominations are often won or lost on the basis of the personal appeal of candidates on television and their ability to put together effective campaign organizations. Traditional party factors are far less influential, as candidates with commanding media presence can gain recognition and stature almost overnight. Having held elected political office is now no longer a prerequisite to becoming a serious candidate, as demonstrated by the campaigns of television evangelist Pat Robertson and preacher/activist Jesse Jackson in 1988. Moreover, the nominating delegates are often amateurs in politics, motivated more by issues than by party loyalty. After the nomination, the presidential campaign is run by the candidate's organization rather than by the national party. (Since 1972, no general election campaign has been run by either the Republican or the Democratic national committee staffs.)

A number of factors have contributed to the new style of campaign politics. Some reflect social changes, such as rising levels of education, which have created an electorate far more independent and unwilling to follow party labels blindly. Others have resulted from reforms in the political parties, especially the Democratic Party, which are now far more open and democratic. New people have the opportunity to enter politics despite little partisan background. Perhaps most important has been the emergence of television as the primary political communications medium and of technological improvements in direct-mail techniques, polling, and other practices.

In general, there has been a shift in the nature of key campaign resources. The skill and labor of party functionaries, who are often volunteers, are less important; financial resources, so necessary in purchasing the services and skills of the new campaign operatives, consultants, pollsters, and media specialists, have become crucial. Expensive campaign travel by jet is now the norm, and the cost of network television advertising is exorbitant.

Not surprisingly, the costs of running national campaigns have risen tremendously. The 2004 presidential election campaign was by far the most expensive in history. According to Federal Election Commission data, George W. Bush raised more than $373 million in funds from all sources for his campaign, and his Democratic counterpart John Kerry was the recipient of more than $342 million of such funds. Bush raised more than $271 million from private sources alone; Kerry raised more than $224 million.

Senate and House races have been affected by the new style of campaigning as well. Senate contests are often highly competitive, typically attracting wealthy, prominent challengers and inspiring huge expenditures of funds, particularly for television advertising. Senate races that cost between $10 million and $20 million are common. In a 1996 U.S. Senate race in California, the two candidates together spent more than $45 million. Four years later, the New York U.S. Senate contest between Democrat Hillary Clinton and Republican Rick Lazio cost nearly $93 million all told. In the 2000 U.S. Senate race in New Jersey, Democrat John Corzine spent more than $60 million of his own money to win the seat!

House races are far less competitive than their Senate counterparts. Challengers are often relatively unknown, and they find it difficult to get funding and free media attention. Incumbents, in contrast, stay in the public eye through their work in Congress and their actions to help constituents. Also, their large victory margins in elections attract contributions for future campaigns. Despite the fact that incumbent safety in the House appears to be greater than at any time in history, House elections have not escaped huge campaign expenditures. According to Federal Election Commission figures, in 1974 the average House incumbent spent about $56,000, the average challenger $40,000. By 1992 incumbents were outspending challengers on the average of three-and-a-half-to-one, with the average incumbent spending over $560,000. By the 2004 elections, House incumbents were raising an average of more than $1.1 million and outspending challengers by greater than a four-and-three-quarters-to-one margin. Open-seat congressional contests, which tend to be the most competitive, are especially expensive.

In 2004, for the first time in more than a quarter of a century, federal elections were conducted under the rules of a new campaign law, the 2002 Bipartisan Campaign Reform Act (BCRA). The act was primarily directed at two loopholes that had emerged under the then-existing campaign finance regulations, the use of "soft money" raised and spent by the national parties and "issue advocacy electioneering" by organized interests. Throughout the 1990s, ever-larger amounts of money were spent in federal elections outside the constraints of the Federal Election Commission (FEC), which was charged with enforcing the campaign finance laws.

Soft money, which was originally intended to be money contributed to the national parties for nonfederal election purposes, such as strengthening local parties, had become a tool for influencing federal elections as well. Most bothersome to reformers was that contributions to the national parties were unlimited in size (and until the 1992 election contributors were undisclosed); businesses, unions, and wealthy individuals in some cases contributed over $1 million per donation to the national parties.

Much of the money was used by the national parties for "issue advocacy electioneering," spending large amounts of soft money to influence federal elections by circumventing campaign laws that drastically limited the funds parties could directly use to support their candidates. As long as the party advertisers avoided "express advocacy," or the use of words like "vote for" or "elect" or "cast a ballot for," which were spelled out in a 1976 Supreme Court decision, large amounts could be spent. Interest groups had even greater flexibility, with no limits at all on how much they could spend to influence elections with their broadcast messages, as long as they avoided direct "express advocacy" terminology. With such broadcast advertising by organized interests, the sources of funds used to pay for the ads did not even have to be disclosed. The ads were often negative in tone, and it was sometimes difficult to identify the sponsor of the ad.

The BCRA prohibits party soft money. National party committees may now spend only "hard money," funds subject to the contribution and source limits of federal law. Some observers believe the influence of parties on campaigns will diminish as a consequence of the law. The Democrats, who had relied heavily on soft money, may be the party most hurt.

The new law also bans broadcast advertising by organized interests, such as corporations and unions, in support of or in opposition to a candidate close to a federal election. Future elections may see groups spending less time on "air wars" and more time on "ground wars," especially grassroots get-out-the-vote (GOTV) efforts. But if the 2004 elections foretell the future, it does not appear that BCRA will lessen the trend of ever-increasing campaign costs. New loopholes to get around the law have already been found.

The selections in this chapter examine campaigns and elections from a variety of perspectives. In the first selection, William G. Mayer critically examines the way in which political parties nominate their candidates for president every four years. The process has been highly criticized for undermining the quality of voter participation and for being unrepresentative of the electorate. Mayer is skeptical of some of the comprehensive reforms that have been suggested and prefers that a number of incremental changes be considered, including making more funds available so candidates can remain in the race beyond the first few nomination contests. The second selection examines the Supreme Court's decision in *McConnell* v. *The Federal Election Commission* (2003), a 5-to-4 decision that upheld the Bipartisan Campaign Reform Act of 2002. The act is likely to greatly affect the role of political parties and interest groups in future federal campaigns, perhaps decreasing the impact of parties and increasing the impact of interest groups that can adapt to some of the new limitations. The third piece, by David Mark, looks at the role played by negative ads in election campaigns. Mark argues that negative advertising, much scorned by the press and the public, may give the electorate information that enhances voters' abilities to evaluate candidates and help hold officials accountable.

7.1

Race for the Nomination: In Search of Reform

William G. Mayer

The rules and practices governing the presidential nomination process have become especially controversial over the past several decades. There is nothing in the Constitution dealing with the party nomination process (parties were not in existence when the document was written), and prior to the 1970s the guidelines governing the selection of delegates who went to the national party conventions to choose the nominees were the exclusive prerogative of state party organizations. In many cases, delegates were simply appointed by party officials and/or party state committees, and rank-and-file party members were excluded from the process. Although presidential primary elections were held in a number of states, they were often simply "popularity" contests, registering support for particular candidates, but votes garnered were not generally translated into the selection of committed delegates.

Under pressure to make delegate selection more democratic and open, the Democratic Party in the early 1970s undertook a series of reforms that gave the national party organization much more control over the process. Later, the Republican Party, though to a lesser degree, also limited total state autonomy in delegate selection. The result has been more rank-and-file citizen participation in the nomination process in both parties, but also a weakened role for party officials, a much longer and expensive process, and a disproportionate influence by two very unrepresentative states (Iowa and New Hampshire).

In this selection, William Mayer presents a brief overview of how the current system works, outlines some of the problems with it, and discusses some proposed reforms, such as having a national primary or a series of regional primaries. He suggests that each of the comprehensive reforms "would probably make the system worse," and puts forth a number of incremental reforms that might make the existing system work better.

William G. Mayer is an associate professor of political science at Northeastern University.

William G. Mayer, "Race for the Nomination: In Search of Reform, *The National Voter*, September/October 2003, pp. 8–12. Reprinted by permission of the author.

The Current System

The American presidential nomination contest is a highly complex system, including a multitude of distinct rules and procedures, nearly all of which have generated some measure of controversy and a lengthy academic literature describing their alleged effects. What follows, then, is clearly not an exhaustive description of the current system, but rather an attempt to highlight its most important features.

First, the final decision about which candidate becomes a party's presidential nominee is still made by the national conventions, which are usually held in mid- to late summer of the election year. Though the convention decision has become increasingly pro forma, much like the voting in the Electoral College, the ultimate goal of the candidates—the centerpiece of all their planning—is still to win a majority of the delegates to their party's national convention.*

Second, the national parties each promulgate general guidelines that specify how states are to select their national convention delegates and what sorts of things they must and must not do. As a general matter, national Democratic rules regulate the delegate selection process in considerable detail, the Republicans tend to give more discretion to states.

Third, the national rules in both major parties allow states to select their delegates in one of two ways: by primary or by a caucus-convention system. Primaries are elections, generally held under the auspices of state government, that are used to select or bind the national convention delegates. Caucuses are a multi-stage process, usually beginning with mass meetings held in each precinct or voting district, which select delegates to district and state conventions, which in turn select the national convention delegates. In recent years, the delegate selection process in both parties has clearly been dominated by primaries. In 2000, for example, 37 states held Democratic primaries, 42 states held Republican primaries.

Fourth, presidential primaries and caucuses both tend to be open to essentially any Democrat or Republican who wants to participate. Some states require participants to be a registered member of that party, but no further demonstration of past or future support for the party is required.

Fifth, besides choosing between caucuses and primaries, each state has considerable latitude in deciding when to select its delegates. In 2004, Republican rules require states to hold their primary or caucus between the first Monday in February and the third Tuesday in June; Democratic rules permit primaries and caucuses to be held between the first Tuesday in February and the second

---

*Today's party presidential nominating conventions are largely media events and typically take on the appearance of infomercials. The delegates come to the convention committed and bound to a particular candidate as the result of a series of late winter and early spring delegate selection contests—their formal vote at the convention is a foregone conclusion. Deliberation and bargaining among party leaders and delegates at the convention is no longer part of the process.

Tuesday in June, but provide specific exemptions for Iowa and New Hampshire. Within those "windows," the states themselves decide whether to select their delegates on, say, the first Tuesday in February or the third Tuesday in May.

The Criticisms

. . . The contemporary presidential nomination process has been criticized from a variety of perspectives. To many observers, perhaps the greatest single short-coming of the "reformed" system is that it has taken the nomination decision away from organized, institutional parties and entrusted it to ordinary voters who participate in primaries and caucuses. When compared to the system that preceded it, the current system gives substantially less weight to the views of party leaders and elected officials. Beginning in 1984, the Democrats made some attempt to rectify this problem by granting automatic delegate status to senators, governors, members of the House of Representatives and national committee members, but the number of "superdelegates" is probably not large enough to alter the system's fundamental dynamics.*

Another major criticism of the new process is simply that it is too long and too expensive. In the nomination races of the 1950s and 1960s, even the most ambi-tious presidential aspirants did not announce their candidacies until the beginning of the election year or the last few months of the year preceding the election. Today, major presidential candidates routinely launch their campaigns in the win-ter or early spring of the year before the election—more than a year before the na-tional conventions, and at least a year and a half before the General Election. For sitting senators and House members, such a long period of active campaigning almost inevitably requires presidential candidates to neglect their governmental responsibilities. It also, of course, increases the cost of running for president.

A third major criticism of the presidential nomination process concerns the outsized role that it gives to two small and not very representative states, Iowa and New Hampshire. Because these states hold the first caucus and first pri-mary, respectively, they see far more of the candidates than any other states, re-ceive substantially more press coverage, and have far more influence on the final outcome.[†] By contrast, California, which traditionally held its primary in

---

*In an effort to guarantee that elected public officials and party officials would be represented at the Democratic National Convention, the party developed a procedure whereby state conven-tions and congressional caucuses could select a portion of such officials as delegates. The origi-nal hope by some was that "super delegates" would have a moderating influence in the selection process, perhaps helping to counterbalance the impact of more extreme issue ac-tivists in choosing the nominee.

[†]Iowa and New Hampshire are especially unrepresentative on demographic grounds. For exam-ple, the percentage of African Americans in Iowa is 2.1 percent, while in New Hampshire the corresponding figure is 0.7 percent. Both states are far below the national average in terms of percentage of individuals below the government poverty line.

the first week in June, generally found that the nomination races were effectively over by the time that state selected its delegates.

Given all the advantages that accrue to early voting states, over the last two decades the delegate selection calendar has become increasingly front-loaded. Where primaries and caucuses were once spread out rather evenly over the delegate selection season, most primaries and caucuses now take place within a few weeks after the delegate selection season formally begins, with the result that the nomination races are effectively settled by early or mid-March.

Front-loading has a number of undesirable effects on the way we select our presidential candidates. First and most important, it greatly compresses the time that voters have to learn about the major candidates. Most voters do not start to pay attention to the nomination races until the delegate selection process begins. When the system was less front-loaded, this meant that the voters had three or four months to watch the candidates and learn more about their policies and personal abilities before reaching a final decision. Today, as the decision gets made more rapidly, the system has become less flexible, less deliberative, and less rational.

Front-loading also undermines both the extent and the quality of voter participation. As the primary and caucus calendar has become more front-loaded, it has become routine for nomination races to be settled in the early spring. Even with front-loading, this means that lots of states select their delegates at a time when everything of significance has already been decided. In 2000, for example, 25 states held their primaries after both Bill Bradley and John McCain had officially withdrawn. The result, not surprisingly, is that voter turnout in the presidential primaries declines quite substantially in the later stages of the race.

Proposed Remedies

If the contemporary nomination process is easy to criticize, it is a good deal more difficult to say what to do about it. Although a number of remedies have been proposed, it is not clear that any would solve all of the problems just discussed; many would probably carry significant negative consequences of their own. While it is impossible to do justice to all of the many proposals that have been made for changing the nomination rules, to get a sense of the difficulties and complexities of the problem, it is worth taking a look at two of the most talked-about proposals: a national primary and a system of regional primaries.

National Primary

Ever since the Progressive Era, many of those who were dissatisfied with the presidential selection system have wanted to scrap the current system, with its complicated pattern of the fifty distinct primaries and caucuses, and replace it with a single national primary. A national primary has two principal virtues: it is simple and straightforward; and it would treat all states equally. In particular, it would guarantee that no state had the kind of outsized, disproportionate role now played by Iowa and New Hampshire, and that no state would hold its primary after the effective nomination decision had already been made. In return for those benefits, however, a national primary has a number of severe problems that make it a highly questionable option.

Above all, a national primary would give an enormous advantage to early front-runners and candidates who were already well known and well financed. One advantage of having the current process start in small states like Iowa and New Hampshire is that it gives long-shots, outsiders, and insurgents a good venue in which to make the case for their candidacies. A full-scale campaign in both states can be mounted for a fraction of what it would cost to compete in a national primary. And, precisely because the total electorate in both states is so small, face-to-face, "retail" politics counts for a lot more than it would in a country with 200 million eligible voters. If the fierce scramble for campaign money is one of the less attractive features of the current system, it would only grow worse under a national primary.

Depending on how it is structured, a national primary might also lead to the nomination of a candidate who is supported by a small, highly committed minority, but is considered unacceptable by a large segment of that candidate's own party. If there are six or ten declared presidential candidates seeking a given party's nomination—which almost always occurs today except when an incumbent president is running for a second term—a candidate could win a national primary with as little as 25 or 30 percent of the vote. This might lead one or both parties to nominate someone totally inappropriate, who appeals to a very small minority.

To avoid such a problem, most recent national primary proposals have included a provision requiring the winner to receive some minimum percentage of the total vote (usually, 40 or 50 percent). If no candidate exceeds that threshold, there would be a runoff election between the top two finishers. Yet a runoff provision does not guarantee that at least one of the finalists will be minimally acceptable to most party voters. Nor is it clear that Americans would welcome the possibility of holding three national elections (two national primaries and then a General Election) within the space of three months.

Regional Primary

Though they differ in their details, regional primary proposals generally call for some central agency—usually either the national parties or the federal government—to divide the states up into a number of regions, each of which would hold a set of primary elections on a single date. In 1999, for example, the

National Association of Secretaries of State (NASS) put forward a plan that created four such regions—East, South, Midwest, and West. On the first Tuesday of each month between March and June, one of these regions would go to the polls, with the order rotating every four years.

Perhaps the principal advantage of a regional primary system, according to its supporters, is that it would make campaigning easier and more efficient, by cutting down on travel time and allowing candidates to advertise in media markets that cut across state lines. Regional primaries also hold out the hope of forcing candidates to confront the particular, often unique problems that confront each region.

There are also, however, a number of important disadvantages to regional primaries. Depending on how many regions are established, regional primaries might also give a huge advantage to early front-runners and those candidates with ample war chests. If the states are divided into just four regions, for example, every candidate would be forced to compete in twelve different states at the same time. Even with all the purported efficiencies of regional campaigning, long-shots and insurgents would almost certainly find it difficult to run a competitive race under such circumstances.

In addition, regional primaries would confer a significant advantage on any candidate who happened to be particularly strong in whatever region went first. Region is a very important variable in explaining primary outcomes: in almost every recent presidential nomination contest, at least one candidate has run significantly better in one region than in the others. Given the importance of momentum, this might mean that major-party nomination decisions would hinge on the essentially random factor of which region went first. In 1992, for example, Bill Clinton's candidacy would likely have been doomed if the southern states had voted last: for the first five weeks of that year's delegate selection season, Clinton didn't win a single primary or caucus outside the South.

Conclusion

In recent discussions of how to reform the presidential nomination process, a great deal of attention has generally been given to comprehensive reform proposals such as national or regional primaries, both of which would make significant, fundamental changes in the systems we currently use for selecting presidential candidates.

For those who are concerned about front-loading or the length and expense of the process, a better alternative might be to accept the basic framework that has now been in place for more than three decades, and look for incremental reforms that might alleviate some of its more pressing shortcomings.

For example, both parties already have rules that place broad limits on the timeframe during which primaries and caucuses can be held. Separately, or together, the parties might want to consider limiting the number of states that can vote prior to some specific date, or pushing back the entire delegate selection calendar so that it begins in March rather than January or February.

Then, too, many of the most criticized features of the current system are attributable, in whole or in part, to the difficulties that candidates frequently have raising the huge amount of money necessary to run a nationwide nomination campaign. Increasingly the contribution limits, or the federal matching fund ratio, might make the results of Iowa and New Hampshire less consequential by allowing losing candidates to stay in the race longer, and might give more successful candidates a better opportunity to expand their campaign to other states.

Finally, while the number of automatic delegate seats given to party and elected officials currently account for only one-sixth of all the delegates at the Democratic National Convention (and none of the Republican delegates), they do seem to have had the positive effect of giving the party leadership a somewhat greater voice in the presidential nomination process.

Incremental reforms such as those posited above, of course, will not resolve all of the shortcomings of the current nominating process. Still, while it is easy to appreciate some of the attractions of comprehensive reform proposals—in particular, they seem so much more "rational" and orderly than the current process—it is unlikely that any of these comprehensive reforms would actually make the system better. In substantial respects, they would probably make the system worse.

Questions for Discussion

1. Why is the current presidential nomination process so controversial? Do you believe that party and elected officials should have more influence in the process than they do now? Why or why not?
2. Many believe that having a national primary or a series of regional primaries to select party nominees for president would be far more democratic than the current process. What criticisms can be levied at such proposals? What kinds of candidates would be advantaged/disadvantaged by having a national primary or regional primary process for the selection of party presidential nominees? How would such changes affect the role of political parties?

7.2

McConnell v. The Federal Election Commission (2003)

In 2002, Congress passed the Bipartisan Campaign Reform Act (BCRA) in an effort to lessen the role of big money in federal elections. By the late 1990s, it had become clear to most observers that the campaign finance regulation system put in place in the early 1970s now had little meaning; the intent of the law was being widely disregarded. With its emphasis on limiting direct contributions to parties and candidate committees ("hard money") and extensive public disclosure of contribution sources, existing federal campaign law was being overshadowed by both party and group fund raising and spending not regulated by federal law and often hidden from public scrutiny.

The new campaign law had a variety of provisions, but two were especially prominent. Soft-money contributions to national party committees by individuals and organized interests were now prohibited. The parties had been raising and spending virtually unlimited amounts of money to influence federal elections, thanks largely to the soft-money contributions raised from interested individuals and groups that sometimes approached seven figures. The parties now were restricted to raising and spending only hard money, which was subject to federal contribution limits and source restrictions.

The BCRA also put forth a new standard concerning the *content* of election-related political communications and *when* interest groups could engage in issue advocacy electioneering. An "electioneering communication" is a broadcast, cable, or satellite communication that refers to a clearly identified candidate sponsored by corporations (including nonprofit corporations) and unions within thirty days of a primary election or sixty days of a general election; such ads were prohibited by the new law. Essentially, interest groups were no longer allowed to broadcast advertisements supporting or opposing a candidate close to Election Day.

The BCRA was so controversial that one of its provisions provided for a quick review of its constitutionality, first by a three-judge panel of the U.S. District Court for the District of Columbia, with appeals then to go directly to the Supreme Court. Congressional reformers passionately believed that big money in politics so corrupted the process, or at least created the appearance of corruption, that drastic measures were needed to control it. Opponents saw the issue largely in First Amendment terms; banning campaign ads by groups so close to an election, for example, denied them their basic First Amendment right of political expression.

In December 2003, the U.S. Supreme Court surprised many by upholding virtually all of the new law's provisions in a very contentious 5-to-4 decision, including the banning of soft-money contributions to the national parties and restrictions on campaign advertising by groups close to an election. Corporations and unions were banned from making or financing electioneering communications except through their political action committees (PACs).

The majority opinion, written by Justices John Paul Stevens and Sandra Day O'Connor, reflected an overwhelming, practical concern with the corrosive effects of soft money and the destructive influence of campaign advertising by organized interests so close to Election Day. The four dissenters on the court argued from a more philosophical perspective; they believed there was simply little good, hard, overwhelming evidence of the corrupting influence of money on the political system, certainly not enough to warrant the drastic suppression of free expression in elections.

What follows are excerpts from the Court decision.

For the Majority by Justices Stevens and O'Connor.

The question for present purposes is whether large soft-money contributions to national party committees have a corrupting influence or give rise to the appearance of corruption. Both common sense and the ample record in these cases confirm Congress's belief that they do. The F.E.C.'s allocation regime has invited widespread circumvention of F.E.C.A.'s [Federal Election Campaign Act of 1971] limits on contributions to parties for the purpose of influencing federal elections. Under this system, corporate, union and wealthy individual donors have been free to contribute substantial sums of soft money to the national parties, which the parties can spend for the specific purpose of influencing a particular candidate's federal election. It is not only plausible, but likely, that candidates would feel grateful for such donations and that donors would seek to exploit that gratitude.

The evidence in the record shows that candidates and donors alike have in fact exploited the soft-money loophole, the former to increase their prospects of election and the latter to create debt on the part of officeholders, with the national parties serving as willing intermediaries. Thus, despite F.E.C.A.'s hard-money limits on direct contributions to candidates, federal officeholders have commonly asked donors to make soft-money donations to national and state committees "solely in order to assist federal campaigns," including the officeholder's own. Parties kept tallies of the amounts of soft money raised by each officeholder, and "the amount of money a member of Congress raised for the national political committees often affected the amount the committees gave to assist the member's campaign." . . .

Even when not participating directly in the fund-raising, federal officeholders were well aware of the identities of the donors: national party committees would distribute lists of potential or actual donors, or donors themselves would report their generosity to officeholders.

For their part, lobbyists, C.E.O.'s and wealthy individuals alike all have candidly admitted donating substantial sums of soft money to national committees not on ideological grounds, but for the express purpose of securing influence over federal officials. For example, a former lobbyist and partner in a lobbying firm in Washington, D.C., stated in his declaration:

> You are doing a favor for somebody by making a large [soft money] donation and they appreciate it. Ordinarily, people feel inclined to reciprocate favors. Do a bigger favor for someone—that is, write a larger check—and they feel even more compelled to reciprocate. In my experience, overt words are rarely exchanged about contributions, but people do have understandings.

Particularly telling is the fact that in 1996 and 2000, more than half of the top 50 soft-money donors gave substantial sums to both major national parties, leaving room for no other conclusion but that these donors were seeking influence, or avoiding retaliation, rather than promoting any particular ideology. . . .

Plaintiffs argue that without concrete evidence of an instance in which a federal officeholder has actually switched a vote (or, presumably, evidence of a specific instance where the public believes a vote was switched), Congress has not shown that there exists real or apparent corruption. But the record is to the contrary. The evidence connects soft money to manipulations of the legislative calendar, leading to Congress's failure to enact, among other things, generic drug legislation, tort reform, and tobacco legislation. More importantly, plaintiffs conceive of corruption too narrowly. Our cases have firmly established that Congress's legitimate interest extends beyond preventing simple cash-for-votes corruption to curbing "undue influence on an officeholder's judgment, and the appearance of such influence." . . .

. . . To be sure, more political favoritism or opportunity for influence alone is insufficient to justify regulation. As the record demonstrates, it is the manner in which parties have sold access to federal candidates and officeholders that has given rise to the appearance of undue influence. Implicit (and, as the record shows, sometimes explicit) in the sale of access is the suggestion that money buys influence. It is no surprise then that purchasers of such access unabashedly admit that they are seeking to purchase just such influence. It was not unwarranted for Congress to conclude that the selling of access gives rise to the appearance of corruption.

In sum, there is substantial evidence to support Congress's determination that large soft-money contributions to national political parties give rise to corruption and the appearance of corruption.

Many years ago, we observed that "to say that Congress is without power to pass appropriate legislation to safeguard . . . an election from the improper use of money to influence the result is to deny to the nation in a vital particular the power of self-protection." We abide by that conviction in considering Congress's most recent effort to confine the ill effects of aggregated wealth on our political system. We are under no illusion that B.C.R.A. will be the last Congressional statement on the matter. Money, like water, will always find an outlet. What problems will arise, and how Congress will respond, are concerns for another day. In the main we uphold B.C.R.A.'s two principal, complementary features: the control of soft money and the regulation of electioneering communications.

From the dissent by Justice Scalia.

This is a sad day for the freedom of speech. Who could have imagined that the same court which, within the past four years, has sternly disapproved of restrictions upon such inconsequential forms of expression as virtual child pornography, tobacco advertising, dissemination of illegally intercepted communications, and sexually explicit cable programming would smile with favor upon a law that cuts to the heart of what the First Amendment is meant to protect: the right to criticize the government. For that is what the most offensive provisions of this legislation are all about. We are governed by Congress, and this legislation prohibits the criticism of members of Congress by those entities most capable of giving such criticism loud voice: national political parties and corporations, both of the commercial and the not-for-profit sort. It forbids pre-election criticism of incumbents by corporations, even not-for-profit corporations, by use of their general funds; and forbids national-party use of "soft" money to fund "issue ads" that incumbents find so offensive.

But what about the danger to the political system posed by "amassed wealth"? The most direct threat from that source comes in the form of undisclosed favors and payoffs to elected officials which have already been criminalized, and will be rendered no more discoverable by the legislation at issue here. The use of corporate wealth (like individual wealth) to speak to the electorate is unlikely to "distort" elections—especially if disclosure requirements tell the people where the speech is coming from. The premise of the First Amendment is that the American people are neither sheep nor fools, and hence fully capable of considering both the substance of the speech presented to them and its proximate and ultimate source. If that premise is wrong, our democracy has a much greater problem to overcome than merely the influence of amassed wealth. Given the premises of democracy there is no such thing as too much speech.

But, it is argued, quite apart from its effect upon the electorate, corporate speech in the form of contributions to the candidate's campaign, or even in the form of independent expenditures supporting the candidate, engenders an obligation which is later paid in the form of greater access to the officeholder, or indeed in the form of votes on particular bills. Any quid-pro-quo agreement for votes would of course violate criminal law, and actual payoff votes have not even been claimed by those favoring the restrictions on corporate speech. It cannot be denied, however, that corporate (like noncorporate) allies will have greater access to the officeholder, and that he will tend to favor the same causes as those who support him (which is usually why they supported him). That is the nature of politics—if not indeed human nature—and how this can properly be considered "corruption" (or "the appearance of corruption") with regard to corporate allies and not with regard to other allies is beyond me. If the Bill of Rights had intended an exception to the freedom of speech in order to combat this malign proclivity of the officeholder to agree with those who agree with him, and to speak more with his supporters than his opponents, it would surely have said so. It did not do so, I think, because the juice is not worth the squeeze. . . .

The first instinct of power is the retention of power, and, under a Constitution that requires periodic elections, that is best achieved by the suppression of election-time speech. We have witnessed merely the second scene of Act I of what promises to be a lengthy tragedy.

From the dissent by Justice Kennedy.

Our precedents teach, above all, that government cannot be trusted to moderate its own rules for suppression of speech. The dangers posed by speech regulations have led the court to insist upon principled constitutional lines and a rigorous standard of review. The majority now abandons these distinctions and limitations.

Until today's consolidated cases, the court has accepted but two principles to use in determining the validity of campaign finance restrictions. First is the anti-corruption rationale. The principal concern, of course, is the agreement for a quid pro quo between officeholders (or candidates) and those who would seek to influence them. The court has said the interest in preventing corruption allows limitations on receipt of the quid by a candidate or officeholder, regardless of who gives it or of the intent of the donor or officeholder. Second, the Court has analyzed laws that classify on the basis of the speaker's corporate or union identity under the corporate speech rationale. The court has said that the willing adoption of the entity form by corporations and unions justifies regulating them differently: their ability to give candidates quids may be subject not only to limits but also to outright bans; their electoral speech may likewise be curtailed. . . .

. . . The court . . . concludes that access, without more, proves influence is undue. Access, in the court's view, has the same legal ramifications as actual or apparent corruption of officeholders. This new definition of corruption sweeps away all protections for speech that lie in its path.

Access in itself, however, shows only that in a general sense an officeholder favors someone or that someone has influence on the officeholder. There is no basis, in law or in fact, to say favoritism or influence in general is the same as corrupt favoritism or influence in particular. By equating vague and generic claims of favoritism or influence with actual or apparent corruption, the court adopts a definition of corruption that dismantles basic First Amendment rules, permits Congress to suppress speech in the absence of a quid pro quo threat. . . . The generic favoritism or influence theory articulated by the court is at odds with standard First Amendment analyses because it is unbounded and susceptible to no limiting principle. . . .

The First Amendment underwrites the freedom to experiment and to create in the realm of thought and speech. Citizens must be free to use new forms, and new forums, for the expression of ideas. The civic discourse belongs to the people and Government may not prescribe the means used to conduct it. The First Amendment commands that Congress "shall make no law . . . abridging the freedom of speech." The command cannot be read to allow Congress to provide for the imprisonment of those who attempt to establish new political parties and alter the civic discourse. . . . The Court, upholding multiple laws that suppress both spontaneous and concerted speech, leaves us less free than before. Today's decision breaks faith with our tradition of robust and unfettered debate.

Questions for Discussion

1. Why, according to the majority of the Supreme Court in *McConnell* v. *The Federal Election Commission*, does money corrupt politics even if there is no hard evidence of "buying" votes? Do you agree?
2. Some have called BCRA an "incumbent protection" act. On what basis might this charge be made? In your view, is it wise to limit free expression in elections to reduce corruption or the appearance of corruption in elections?

7.3

Attack Ads Are Good for You

David Mark

A common criticism leveled by the press and much of the public during campaigns is that electioneering has become too negative because of its concentration on attacking or criticizing an opponent. Negative campaign advertising, which may involve pointing out opponents' character flaws, linking them to bad public policy, or warning of the catastrophic consequences of electing them, is alleged to increase cynicism and a lack of trust among the electorate, suppress voter turnout, and even discourage able candidates from running for public office. Ads can be mean, harsh, and misleading. A widely held view is that the public would be better served by positive messages, focusing on a candidate's own personal strengths and how he or she would address the pressing issues of the day, rather than talking about the opponent at all.

Research by political scientists addressing the issue of negative campaigning paints a much more mixed and puzzling picture of the consequences of negative advertising. Voters may be differentially impacted by negative ads. While the attack style of politics may suppress the vote in some instances, in others turnout may be enhanced. Levels of voter information and attention to campaigns may be actually elevated in the midst of a negative advertising campaign. One could also make the case that political accountability is enhanced when negative advertising focuses on incumbents—they are forced to aggressively defend their records.

In this selection, David Mark puts forth the argument that negative advertising gives the electorate valuable information with which to judge candidates that it would not have if campaigns were totally positive. Using three examples of the use of attack ads in congressional races during the 2006 election, Mark raises questions about the appropriateness and value of exposing the electorate to this type of information. The reader is left to make up his or her own mind.

David Mark is a freelance writer and occasional contributor to *Reason* magazine. He previously served as editor-in-chief at *Campaigns & Elections* magazine.

Michael Steele encountered tough financial times in the late 1990s. Though he earned a law degree at Georgetown in 1991, the Maryland Republican failed the bar exams in his home state and in Washington, D.C. As a result, his practice at a large international law firm in Washington was limited in the high-end work it could perform and in the fees it could charge.

Steele eventually struck out on his own, founding the Steele Group, a business and legal consulting firm in suburban Prince George's County, Maryland. It seems the business rarely made a profit; Steele says it encountered financial challenges when clients didn't pay their bills. The firm eventually dissolved, and Steele's personal debts mounted. By 2002, according to financial disclosure reports, he had borrowed $35,000 through a line of credit against his home.

A fuller picture of Steele's money situation at that time remains clouded, due to gaps in his résumé and his unwillingness to detail past finances. What is clear is that while his finances were plummeting, his political star was on the rise. He moved up quickly from local party activist to state Republican Party chairman and, in 2003, to lieutenant governor of Maryland, becoming the first black person of either party elected to statewide office.

Steele is now [fall 2006] a candidate for the U.S. Senate. When Democrats raise questions about his past personal money woes, he dismisses them as negative campaigning, suggesting his opaque financial past has no bearing on public policy decisions. "What does it matter to any voter whether or not you paid a bill on time?" Steele asked in a September 2005 radio interview, shortly before declaring his Senate candidacy. "There has to be, I think, a veil of privacy, even around public figures. The expectation is, to run for office doesn't mean I turn over everything I've ever done in my life for you to sit in judgment of. It's one of the reasons why it is very difficult to find individuals who are capable, competent, and committed to public service who want to get into this business."

Steele is hardly alone in his professed outrage at aggressive campaign tactics. Politicians routinely try to shift attention away from issues of public concern, playing the victim of unfair, invasive attacks. But is closely examining a candidate's questionable financial history wrong? Senators, after all, spend hundreds of billions of taxpayer dollars. Shouldn't potentially germane information about Steele's financial history be available to voters, who can decide for themselves whether it is relevant to his qualifications?

Negative campaigning is an issue across the country this fall [2006], in campaigns from Massachusetts to Hawaii and in races down the ballot from U.S. senator to county assessor. As wounded politicians whine that such speech is out of bounds, it's time to stand up in defense of the much-maligned attack ad. In this age of instantaneous information via blogs, round-the-clock cable coverage, and other media, political attacks can be swiftly countered. Any opinion offered about a candidate, no matter how mean, vile, or sinister, can be rebutted immediately and globally. Thanks to such exchanges, voters this year will know a lot about prospective elected officials if they are willing to process multiple sources of information and draw their own conclusions.

Voters Hate Negativity—Except When They Like It

Many people recoil at negative political ads. Indeed, *negative campaigning* has become a catch-all phrase that implies there is something inherently wrong with criticizing an opponent. It is one of the most bemoaned aspects of the American political system, particularly by academics and journalists who say it lowers the level of discourse and intensifies divisions among voters.

The dim academic view of negative campaigning was reflected in an influential 1999 *Political Science Review* study by Arizona State University political scientists Patrick J. Kenney and Kim Fridkin, titled "Do Negative Campaigns Mobilize or Suppress Turnout? Clarifying the Relationship Between Negativity and Participation." "Our most troubling finding is that negative or attack advertising actually suppresses turnout," Kenney and Fridkin wrote. "We would even go so far as to say that negative advertisements may pose a serious anti-democratic threat."

Journalists often reach similar conclusions. . . .

This conventional wisdom is dead wrong, argues the Vanderbilt political scientist John Geer, author of the 2006 book *In Defense of Negativity: Attack Ads in Presidential Politics.* "Journalists and academics think of negative campaigning as personal attacks," says Geer. "I don't particularly worry about it. It's going to take something a little more consequential to hurt this country than some rough 30-second spots."

Geer's research demonstrates that negative ads tend to be more substantive than positive spots, because to be credible they must be better documented and specific. His analysis of television campaign advertising from 1960 through 2004 found that nearly three-quarters of the claims in negative spots involved issues, not attacks on candidates' characters or values. "You can't just attack President Bush for being weak on the economy," Geer says. "You need to be more specific when you attack. You have to say why. For the attacks to work, they have to be based on fact."

There is considerable reason to believe the electorate appreciates negative campaigning. While studies . . . suggest the practice can turn voters off, voting participation statistics demonstrate that the toughest, most partisan races often bring more people to the polls. The 2004 presidential campaign was one of the most heated in recent memory, punctuated by thrusts and parries over Sen. John Kerry's Vietnam service, charges of deadly policy failure in Iraq, and warnings that electing the opposition could lead to further terrorist attacks. That same campaign produced a voter turnout of roughly 60 percent, the highest in 36 years. Kerry's vote total was up 16 percent from Vice President Al Gore's in 2000; President George W. Bush's vote total was 23 percent higher than it had been four years before.

Those numbers fit a historical pattern. Turnout rose during the years following the Civil War, when campaigns were very biting. This was a period when Republicans were accused of "waving the bloody shirt" from the military conflict of recent memory and Democrats were labeled "disloyal" for supporting the Confederacy, or at least being lukewarm on maintaining the Union. . . .

Ugly Truth Tellers

Few if any officeholders will openly admit to negative campaigning. To candidates, criticizing an opponent's voting record is properly called *comparative advertising*, and spotlighting a rival's marital infidelity is merely *raising character issues*. Campaign tactics that to one voter seem misleading, mean-spirited, or immoral can impart to another important and relevant information about how the candidate would perform under the pressures of public office. Negative campaigning, like beauty, is in the eye of the beholder.

Voter distaste for negative campaigning is understandable, if only because the form and content of political ads are so different from what people usually see in commercial spots. Anyone peddling breakfast cereal needs to be careful about criticizing competitors too overtly or else run the risk of turning off consumers. Rarely do product advertisements include direct comparisons to rival products, and when they occur the contrasts are usually mild and fleeting. As a result, viewers are often shocked at the stark criticisms offered in political ads, particularly when they're sandwiched between softer spots. . . .

Each race has its own local nuances, but some negative campaign themes are pervasive. Republicans contend their opponents are soft on terror and itching to raise taxes. Democrats portray Republicans as surrogates for President George W. Bush, trying to weigh them down with the burden of his low approval ratings; they cite the Iraq situation, high gas prices, stagnant wages, and scores of other issues. Republicans often try to neutralize such criticism by accusing the Democrats of "pessimism"—a charge heatedly denied by members of the minority party, who describe themselves as tellers of difficult truths.

The pessimism taunt is a time-honored way to duck fair questions, says William G. Mayer, a political scientist at Northeastern University. "This year, you will see a lot of Democratic ads talking about the failures of the Bush administration," he explains. "Some of those make quite valid points." Even in cases where charges contain only a kernel of truth, he argues, they raise important issues voters otherwise might not have considered. Positive ads, featuring happy family pictures and lists of accomplishments, do not provide enough information for voters to make informed decisions. What a candidate chooses not to discuss is usually as important as what he or she prefers to emphasize.

. . . Challengers in particular must go negative to demonstrate the flaws in the policies supported by the incumbent and show how they would do things differently.

Credit Crunch in Maryland

Although Michael Steele is not running as an incumbent, it's not surprising that Maryland Democrats would push hard to find information that reflected poorly on him as his Senate bid ramped up. Tall, suave, and debonair, Steele poses a potentially serious challenge to their party's hold on black voters, a crucial element of Democratic support whose defection would make it nearly impossible to win statewide elections.

Steele often shares his inspiring up-by-the-bootstraps personal story. Born at Andrews Air Force Base in Prince George's County, he was raised in a working-class family in Washington, D.C. His mother was a laundress who refused to go on welfare because she did not want the government raising her children.

Steele has said Ronald Reagan's 1976 insurgent candidacy for the GOP's presidential nomination led him to become a Republican. He spent three years in a Jesuit seminary after graduating from Johns Hopkins, then switched to a legal career. With his emphasis on entrepreneurship and his solidly conservative views on social issues, he quickly caught the notice of Republican higher-ups. In 1995 the state GOP selected him as Maryland State Republican Man of the Year. He worked on several political campaigns and served as an alternate delegate to the 1996 Republican National Convention in San Diego and as a delegate to the 2000 Regional National Convention in Philadelphia.

In December 2000 Steele was elected chairman of the Maryland Republican Party, becoming the first African American ever to lead a state GOP. Republican gubernatorial nominee Robert Ehrlich selected Steele as his running mate in 2002. They won, becoming the first Republican ticket in 36 years to occupy the state's top elected jobs.

But the campaign was often bruising. During that race Steele faced repeated questions about his financial past. He admitted that sometime during his career he had faced financial difficulties. But he was vague, and his biographies do not account for all the years between his college graduation, his time in seminary, his marriage, his law school graduation, the founding of his own business, and his time in office.

Questions about Steele's financial history became increasingly acute in fall 2002, when the Maryland Republican Party began paying him $5,000 a month in consulting fees shortly after his selection as Ehrlich's running mate. Democrats said the payments raised ethical questions, charging that the Republicans had essentially hired a candidate. State Republican Party officials defended the payments by saying Steele was being paid to continue performing his duties as party chairman because his replacement was not prepared to take over yet.

Similar questions were sure to emerge again during his Senate bid, which Steele made official in fall 2005, a few months after Democratic Sen. Paul Sarbanes announced he would retire. But Steele caught a lucky break through Democrats' clumsy attempts to dig up damaging information. In July 2005 Lauren B. Weiner, a researcher working for the Democratic Senatorial Campaign Committee (DSCC), illegally obtained a copy of Steele's credit report. *The Washington Post* reported that "sources familiar with the episode said Steele's credit report was obtained with the use of his Social Security number, which was found on a public court document." Weiner used Steele's Social Security number to obtain his credit report from TransUnion and used DSCC

Research Director Katie Barge's DSCC credit card to pay for the report. Weiner pleaded guilty to a misdemeanor charge of computer fraud and agreed to complete 150 hours of community service. Barge resigned.

Steele then went on the offensive, saying public figures deserve some privacy. He publicly warned fellow Republican Senate candidates around the country to beware of credit hackers and threatened a civil suit against the former Democratic operatives. The Democrats' ham-handedness has largely diffused outstanding questions about Steele's finances.

That's unfortunate. Obtaining a credit report under fraudulent auspices is wrong. But voters deserve to have the fullest possible accounting of candidates' financial backgrounds, which can shed light on their financial judgment. Steele was able to play the victim while deflecting important questions related to how he might spend taxpayer dollars.

All of this is not to say that Steele's past business woes and problems paying bills render him unqualified to serve in the Senate. Such a standard would sideline many intelligent, hard-working, well-intentioned people who have weathered money problems. But voters have the right to decide such information's relevance for themselves.*

A West Virginia Minefield

At the outset of the current [2006] election cycle, the race for West Virginia's 1st Congressional District didn't seem likely to yield much negative campaigning. In fact, it wasn't thought to be much of a campaign at all. The Democratic incumbent, Alan Mollohan, had a name that was political gold. His father, Robert Mollohan, had represented the district in the House from 1953 to 1957 and again from 1969 to 1983, and he had practically bequeathed the safe Democratic seat to his son upon retirement. Since then, Alan Mollohan had repeatedly won by wide margins. Moreover, as a longtime member of the House Appropriations Committee, he had proved himself a master at bringing home the bacon for the economically struggling northeastern regions of the Mountain State.

Though he operated behind the scenes for much of his congressional career, Mollohan in 2005 took on a more prominent role as the ranking Democrat on the House Committee on Standards of Official Conduct, popularly known as the Ethics Committee. There he criticized Republican efforts to allow then–House Majority Leader Tom DeLay to stay in his leadership post after being indicted by a Texas grand jury on state campaign finance violation charges. He blocked the Ethics Committee from organizing and beginning its work until the rule change was reversed.

---

*On Election Day Republican Steele lost his Senate bid to Democrat Martin O'Malley by a 54.6 to 43.9 percent margin.

Amid the Jack Abramoff and Duke Cunningham scandals, as Democrats assailed House Republicans for a "culture of corruption," GOP allies sought to neutralize the issue and target a prominent Democrat. Mollohan soon found himself in Republican crosshairs, thanks to allegations that through his Appropriations Committee position he gave millions of dollars in earmarks to groups staffed by his friends and business partners, while his personal wealth soared.

The conservative National Legal and Policy Center filed a 500-page ethics complaint with the U.S. Justice Department in February, accusing Mollohan of misrepresenting his assets on financial disclosure forms. The document noted, among other things, that Mollohan's real estate holdings and other assets jumped in value from $562,000 in 2000 to at least $6.3 million in 2004. The complaint also suggested that the congressman grossly undervalued assets, giving purported valuations which were a small fraction of the assets' true value.

Media outlets began digging into Mollohan's finances. In April *The Wall Street Journal* reported that Mollohan and Dale R. McBridge, CEO of FMW Composite Systems, jointly purchased a 300-acre farm along West Virginia's Cheat River. Mollohan had directed a $2.1 million government contract to McBridge's company to develop lightweight payload pallets for space shuttle missions.

More revelations about Mollohan's finances soon emerged, including news that the Federal Bureau of Investigation was looking into his dealings. House Minority Leader Nancy Pelosi pressured him to step aside from his Ethics Committee post. Republicans saw an opportunity to mount a competitive challenge for Mollohan's seat. State Del. Chris Wakim of Wheeling, previously an underdog with little backing from the national party, became a prominent GOP candidate.

Amid the well-documented allegations of using his public office for private gain, Mollohan refused to concede that any legitimate issues were being raised. Instead he tried to blame the whole episode on negative campaigning by Republican strategists. "It's payback time by Karl Rove," Mollohan told *The State Journal*. "They know my strength is in appropriations, my credibility is in appropriations. So that is where they are attacking my credibility. [They are] attacking everything that we've done in the region that's good and recasting it as bad."

What Mollohan failed to do was rebut the charges—other than denying generally any wrongdoing—or to concede that potential political corruption is a fair campaign issue. Even putative Democratic allies declared the business deals fair game in campaigning; the none-too-conservative editorial pages of *The New York Times* and *The Washington Post* called upon Mollohan to step down from his Ethics Committee post.

West Virginia voters will get their say on Mollohan's political fate come November.* . . .

---

*Despite the negative campaign against him, Democratic congressional incumbent Alan Mollohan easily defeated his Republican challenger Chris Wakim by an overwhelming 64.4 to 33.4 percent margin.

Absenteeism and Hypocrisy in Pennsylvania

Like Mollohan and Michael Steele, Republican Sen. Rick Santorum has tried to turn his opponent's negative campaigning against him. He has not had much success. Santorum has faced persistent questions about whether he and his family reside in Pennsylvania, as he claims. Actually, it would be more accurate to say he has persistently ducked those questions, declaring that such matters are not worth discussing.

Santorum did not always feel that way. When he first ran for the House of Representatives in 1990, he claimed that the longtime Democratic incumbent, Doug Walgren, did not live in the Pittsburgh district he represented. Instead, Santorum charged, the congressman kept his wife and kids with him in their home in D.C.'s Virginia suburbs. Walgren responded that he used his lifelong Pittsburgh residence for voting and taxes but that a member of Congress should keep his young family close to where he works. In a Pittsburgh debate Santorum, then a 32-year-old lawyer making his first bid for public office, said, "We're going to raise our family here."

Santorum won that race in an upset and was elected to the Senate four years later, again beating an incumbent Democrat. In the upper chamber Santorum quickly earned a reputation as a partisan brawler, stressing his opposition to same-sex marriage and abortion and championing other socially conservative issues of the day. . . .

Now, after a dozen years of Santorum's take-no-prisoners political combat, Democrats are in full battle mode against him. Santorum faces Democratic nominee Bob Casey Jr., son of a popular former governor, whose pro-life, anti–gun control, and economically populist positions dovetail with the views of most Pennsylvania voters. But public policy has been only one element in the campaign. The question of Santorum's residency is also a prominent issue. Critics contend that the senator, who did not hesitate to slam Walgren for pretending to live in Pennsylvania, does not reside at the suburban Pittsburgh address he claims.

It's valid to question whether a senator lives in the state he represents, especially if the senator in question has a history of arguing that the issue is important. Yet Santorum has tried to dismiss the matter as negative campaigning and has pointed his finger back at his accusers, turning the issue of residency into one of snooping on private property.

The controversy has been bubbling for two years, since Democrats began charging that Santorum actually lives in Leesburg, Virginia, with his wife and six children. Neighbors say they rarely see the senator or his wife and kids at their Penn Hills, Pennsylvania, house. Based on such reports, some Penn Hills residents objected to the local school district's paying for the senator's children to be enrolled in a cyber charter school.

Critics gathered more ammunition against Santorum in March, when the *Pittsburgh Post-Gazette* sent letters to the candidates seeking materials for its voter guide. A letter addressed to Santorum at his listed Penn Hills address came back with a note from the U.S. Postal Service saying "Not Deliverable as Addressed—Unable to Forward." The most recent contretemps over the residency issue began on May 16, the day of the primary elections, when Ed Vecchio, the husband of the Penn Hills Democratic Party chairwoman, said of Santorum: "He doesn't live here. The house that he's registered to vote out of is vacant—no curtains, furniture, nothing in there. It's abandoned for over a month."

Rather than confronting the merits of the charge, Santorum claimed that such information could be gleaned only by trespassing on his property. He fingered Vecchio as an operative of the Casey campaign, although there was no evidence of any coordination. He ran radio ads denouncing the alleged trespassing episode, or "windowgate," as local wags refer to it. Santorum's wife, Karen, then called Capitol Police, who protect members of Congress; the Capitol Police, in turn, contacted police in Penn Hills, who checked out the home and declared it safe. Democrats called the trespassing charge a diversionary tactic aimed at deflecting attention from the issue of the senator's residency.

As with Steele's Senate campaign, the questions about Santorum do not disqualify him from office. Voters can decide for themselves if their senator's main home should be in the state he represents. The issue is not clear-cut: Pennsylvania law anticipates that members of Congress will live out of state most of the year. Santorum and his wife both hold Pennsylvania driver's licenses and are licensed to practice law in the Keystone State. "The question Santorum faces is political, not legal," says [G. Terry] Madonna, . . . [a] Franklin & Marshall [College] political scientist. "What does it mean to live there? It's not been defined."

That's a question Pennsylvania voters will help answer in November. It's better that they have the fullest possible information when reaching a conclusion.*

Under Fire

. . . The history of political campaigns shows that when candidates present clear, stark differences between themselves and opponents, citizens are better able to judge whom to support. When those lines are drawn sharply in harsh, tough ads and attacks in the press, it's the voters who win.

---

*Incumbent senator Santorum was roundly defeated by Democratic challenger Robert Casey by a 58.7 to 41.3 margin.

Questions for Discussion

1. In the Maryland U.S. Senate race the Republican candidate Michael Steele said that his previous financial history was a private matter and had no bearing on his qualifications for the Senate. What do you think? Are there any guidelines that might be employed to determine what kinds of private matters should or should not be considered in the public evaluation of candidates?
2. According to Mark, "Negative campaigning is in the eye of the beholder." In your view, what kind of negative ads, if any, are most appropriate and useful? What characterizes those that are not? Do you believe the negative advertising style in many campaigns deters some people from seeking public office?

 Chapter 8

THE MASS MEDIA

Information is the lifeblood of a democratic system, and the communication of information is essential to democratic politics. Citizens need trustworthy, diverse, and objective information to perform their electoral role adequately. Decision makers need reliable information about the values, preferences, and opinions of citizens to respond intelligently to them. The mass media play a crucial role in the relationship between citizens and their government. Yet their potential impact on political life leaves many people feeling ambivalent.

On the one hand, the mass media have the potential to help the nation realize its democratic possibilities. They can expand the range of public debate and broaden the attentive audience, which creates an informed public. If they perform as a watchdog over elected officials, political accountability can be greatly improved.

On the other hand, the mass media's potential to propagandize and to manipulate the public could undermine the democratic process. In *Politics in the Media Age*, Ronald Berkman and Laura W. Kitch point out that even in the nineteenth century some people were worried that "by seeking the sensational and simplifying political matters," the mass media could "divert the attention of the masses, arouse irrational passions, and lower the level of political debate." In this century, government management of the news during both world wars exposed the danger that entire populations could be swayed. Government regulation of radio and television in our own period, as well as control over many of the sources of the news, raises concerns that the mass media are at best dependent on, and at worst captives of, the very institutions they scrutinize. The increasing concentration of media ownership, particularly in the last twenty years, suggests that diverse political information is hard to come by.

It is not surprising that media critics are found at both ends of the political spectrum. Social conservatives claim that violence and sexually suggestive material on television have undermined the American family and contributed to a decline in morals. Social liberals assert that television's depiction of women and minorities perpetuates unflattering stereotypes and limits social progress. Economic conservatives worry that the media's focus on business abuses and tight-fisted bankers will undermine the capitalist system. Economic liberals bemoan the fact that the media can never be a force for economic justice and equality because they draw their revenue from commercial sources.

Of course, when our nation was founded there was no such thing as the mass media. The newspapers that existed were partisan forums, directed toward narrow groups of elite supporters. Not until the Jacksonian era of the late 1820s and 1830s did American politics develop its mass character and the first mass circulation newspapers come into being.

Today the mass media are a fact of life. Most of what we know about politics and government comes from the media. A. C. Nielsen reports that 98 percent of American families own at least one television set and that the nation has more radios than people. Few of us acquire political information from other people; instead, strangers decide what information most of us receive.

Television is particularly pervasive. By the time the average American reaches eighteen years of age, he or she has probably spent more time in front of a TV set than in a classroom (roughly 15,000 hours). Television is highly credible because it utilizes both sight and sound. Although television is primarily an entertainment medium, many programs have either explicit or implicit political content. News programs and documentaries are obviously political, and entertainment shows that deal with, say, the police or education have some underlying orientation toward the institution in question. Even a show such as "Sesame Street" reveals strong values about politically relevant subjects such as race relations. Advertisements too are full of politically relevant content, particularly in the stereotypes they convey.

Because there are so many potential influences on political behavior and values, it is difficult to assess what effect such factors have. The mass media's impact is often inferred from their content, but the relationship is difficult to pin down. The one apparent truism is that the media exert the least influence when they attempt to affect people's views and preferences directly, especially through such devices as political endorsements. In 1936, for example, Republican Alf Landon was endorsed by more than 80 percent of the daily newspapers in the country, but Democrat Franklin Roosevelt achieved one of the biggest electoral landslides in U.S. history.

Media impact appears to be strongest in ambiguous, unstructured situations in which individuals have little prior information. Because most people know little about most political subjects, the media can set agendas, not so much by telling the public what to think as by telling it whom and what to think about. A good example is the presidential nomination process. By focusing citizens' attention on the actions of certain individuals and particular issues, the media can confer status (one candidate is "the strong frontrunner") and create disadvantage (another candidate "has little experience"). Audiences learn not only what the campaign issues are but how much importance to attach to them.

Research on the subject has yielded mixed results, suggesting the media are neither as benign as their supporters have argued nor as damaging as many critics have claimed. We need to distinguish among the various types of media and to specify the conditions under which they do influence political orientations and behavior. Their effect will remain controversial, as the selections in this chapter exemplify.

In the first selection, Joshua Meyrowitz makes a strong case that the electronic media have greatly affected our perceptions of political leadership, making it difficult for Americans to find leaders they respect and trust. The final two selections deal with media issues after the 9/11 terrorist attacks. Scott L. Althaus looks at where Americans got their news after 9/11, as he attempts to determine whether or not the crisis had a lasting impact on the public's news habits. He finds that within months Americans' attention to the news had returned to levels found before the devastating attacks and was again focused on domestic rather than foreign policy issues. Finally, Steven Kull evaluates how well the nation's press informed the public about the U.S. invasion of Iraq. He finds that, in a number of cases, the press contributed to a variety of factually incorrect views that the public held about the war.

8.1

Lowering the Political Hero to Our Level

Joshua Meyrowitz

Image has always been important in politics. Whether an individual is viewed as honest or untrustworthy, hard-working or lazy, tough or mean has much to do with that person's political success. Moreover, the use of the electronic media, particularly television, has dramatically altered how the public views political figures and has especially affected the image of elected leadership.

According to Joshua Meyrowitz, before the invention of the electronic media, the public held political leaders in awe. Politicians' images were based on mystification and careful management of public impressions. Political figures operated at a great distance from the public, who had limited access to them.

Radio and television, however, "reveal too much and too often." Television in particular appears to make politicians available for public inspection. This clouds the distinction between politicians' "onstage" and "backstage" behavior. Their human frailties are highlighted, as TV cameras show them sweating or reacting with anger or tears. National politicians no longer have the opportunity to test their presentations. They appear to the whole nation at the same time, and so they are more likely to make mistakes. Ill-chosen words or the inevitable inconsistencies that arise during a campaign are exaggerated, and call into question a politician's honesty and competence.

In the end, "the familiarity fostered by electronic media all too easily breeds contempt." According to Meyrowitz, mystification is necessary for an image of strong leadership, yet disclosure eliminates mystery. As a result, few contemporary political leaders are universally revered in their own lifetime.

A ll our recent Presidents have been plagued with problems of "credibility." Lyndon Johnson abdicated his office; Richard Nixon left the presidency in disgrace; Gerald Ford's "appointment" to the presidency was later rejected by the electorate; Jimmy Carter suffered a landslide defeat after

Joshua Meyrowitz is a professor of communication at the University of New Hampshire.

From Joshua Meyrowitz, *No Sense of Place: The Impact of Electronic Media on Social Behavior*, pp. 68–76. Copyright © 1985. By permission of Oxford University Press, Inc.

being strongly challenged within his own party; and even the comparatively popular Ronald Reagan has followed his predecessors in the now familiar roller coaster ride in the polls.*

We seem to be having difficulty finding leaders who have charisma and style and who are also competent and trustworthy. In the wish to keep at least one recent leader in high esteem, many people have chosen to forget that in his thousand days in office, John Kennedy faced many crises of credibility and ac-cusations of "news management."

During the 1990 campaign, *Newsweek* analyzed recent political polls and con-cluded that "perhaps the most telling political finding of all is the high degree of disenchantment voters feel about most of the major candidates."[1] Of course, every horse race has its winner, and no matter how uninspiring the field of candi-dates, people will always have their favorites. The obsession with poll percentage points and the concern over who wins and who loses, however, tend to obscure the more fundamental issue of the decline in the image of leaders in general.

There are at least two ways to study the image and rhetoric of the presidency. One is to examine the content and form of speeches and actions; in other words, to look at specific strategies, choices, and decisions. Another method is to examine the situations within which Presidents perform their roles. This second method requires a shift in focus away from the specific rhetorical strate-gies of individual politicians and toward the general environment that sur-rounds the presidency and is therefore shared by all who seek that office.

This [selection] employs the latter method to reinterpret the causes of the political woes of some of our recent national politicians and to shed some light on our leadership problem in general. I suggest that the decline in presidential image may have surprisingly little to do with a simple lack of potentially great leaders, and much to do with a specific communication environment—a com-munication environment that undermines the politician's ability to behave like, and therefore be perceived as, the traditional "great leader."

The Merging of Political Arenas and Styles

Before the widespread use of electronic media, the towns and cities of the country served as backstage areas of rehearsal for national political figures. By the time William Jennings Bryan delivered his powerful "cross of gold" speech to win the nomination for President at the 1896 Democratic convention, for example, he had already practiced the speech many times in different parts of the country.

The legendary oratory of Bryan and the treasured images of many of our other political heroes were made possible by their ability to practice and modify

---

*Ronald Reagan, especially after 1982 and before 1987, enjoyed levels of public regard that were exceptional among recent presidents and presidential contenders.

their public performances. Early mistakes could be limited to small forums, minor changes could be tested, and speeches and presentations could be honed to perfection. Politicians could thrill many different crowds on different days with a single well-turned phrase. Bryan, for example, was very fond of his closing line in the 1896 speech ("You shall not press down upon the brow of labor this crown of thorns, you shall not crucify mankind upon a cross of gold")—so fond, in fact, that he had used it many times in other speeches and debates. In his memoirs, Bryan noted his early realization of the line's "fitness for the conclusion of a climax," and after using it in smaller public arenas, he "laid it away for a proper occasion."[2]

Today, through radio and television, the national politician often faces a single audience. Wherever the politician speaks, he or she addresses people all over the country. Major speeches, therefore, cannot be tested in advance. Because they can be presented only once, they tend to be relatively coarse and undramatic. Inspiring lines either are consumed quickly or they become impotent clichés.

Nineteenth century America provided multiple political arenas in which politicians could perfect the form and the substance of their main ideas. They could also buttress their central platforms with slightly different promises to different audiences. Today, because politicians address so many different types of people simultaneously, they have great difficulty speaking in specifics. And any slip of the tongue is amplified in significance because of the millions of people who have witnessed it. Those who analyze changing rhetorical styles without taking such situational changes into account overlook a major political variable.

Many Americans are still hoping for the emergence of an old-style, dynamic "great leader." Yet electronic media of communication are making it almost impossible to find one. There is no lack of potential leaders, but rather an overabundance of information about them. The great leader image depends on mystification and careful management of public impressions. Through television, we see too much of our politicians, and they are losing control over their images and performances. As a result, our political leaders are being stripped of their aura and are being brought closer to the level of the average person.

The impact of electronic media on the staging of politics can best be understood by analyzing it in relation to the staging requirements of *any* social role. . . . Regardless of competence, regardless of desire, there is a limit to how long any person can play out an idealized conception of a social role. All people must eat, sleep, and go to the bathroom. All people need time to think about their social behavior, prepare for social encounters, and rest from them. Further, we all play different roles in different situations. One man, for example, may be a father, a son, a husband, an old college roommate, and a boss. He may also be President of the United States. He needs to emphasize different aspects of his personality in order to function in each of these roles. The performance of social roles, therefore, is in many ways like a multistage drama. The strength and clarity of a particular onstage, or "front region," performance depend on isolating the audience from the backstage, or "back region." Rehearsals, relaxations, and behaviors from other onstage roles must be kept out of the limelight. The need to shield backstage behaviors is especially acute in the performance of roles that rely heavily on mystification and on an aura of greatness—roles such as those performed by national political leaders.

Yet electronic media of communication have been eroding barriers between the politician's traditional back and front regions. The camera eye and the microphone ear have been probing many aspects of the national politician's behavior and transmitting this information to 225 million Americans. By revealing to its audience both traditionally onstage and traditionally backstage activities, television could be said to provide a "sidestage," or "middle region," view of public figures. We watch politicians move from backstage to onstage to backstage. We see politicians address crowds of well-wishers, then greet their families "in private." We join candidates as they speak with their advisors, and we sit behind them as they watch conventions on television. We see candidates address many different types of audiences in many different settings.

By definition, the "private" behaviors now exposed are no longer true back region activities precisely because they are exposed to the public. But neither are they merely traditional front region performances. The traditional balance between rehearsal and performance has been upset. Through electronic coverage, politicians' freedom to isolate themselves from their audiences is being limited. In the process, politicians are not only losing aspects of their privacy—a complaint we often hear—but, more important, they are simultaneously losing their ability to play many facets of the high and mighty roles of traditional leaders. For when actors lose parts of their rehearsal time, their performances naturally move toward the extemporaneous.

The sidestage perspective offered by television makes normal differences in behavior appear to be evidence of inconsistency or dishonesty. We all behave differently in different situations, depending on who is there and who is not. Yet when television news programs edit together videotape sequences that show a politician saying and doing different things in different places and before different audiences, the politician may appear, at best, indecisive and, at worst, dishonest.

The reconfiguration of the stage of politics demands a drive toward consistency in all exposed spheres. To be carried off smoothly, the new political performance requires a new "middle region" role: behavior that lacks the extreme formality of former front region behavior and also lacks the extreme informality of traditional back region behavior. Wise politicians make the most of the new situation. They try to expose selected, positive aspects of their back regions in order to ingratiate themselves with the public. Yet there is a difference between *coping* with the new situation and truly *controlling* it. Regardless of how well individual politicians adjust to the new exposure, the overall image of leaders changes in the process. The new political performance remains a performance, but its style is markedly changed.

Mystification and awe are supported by distance and limited access. Our new media reveal too much and too often for traditional notions of political leadership to prevail. The television camera invades politicians' personal spheres like a spy in back regions. It watches them sweat, sees them grimace at their own ill-phrased remarks. It coolly records them as they succumb to emotions. The camera minimizes the distance between audience and performer. The speaker's platform once raised a politician up and away from the people—both literally and symbolically. The camera now brings the politician close for the people's inspection. And in this sense, it lowers politicians to the level of their audience. The camera brings a rich range of expressive information to the audience; it highlights politicians' mortality and mutes abstract and conceptual rhetoric. While verbal rhetoric can transcend humanity and reach for the divine, intimate expressive information often exposes human frailty. No wonder old style politicians, who continue to assume the grand postures of another era, now seem like clowns or crooks. The personal close-up view forces many politicians to pretend to be less than they would like to be (and, thereby, in a social sense, they actually become less).

Some people were privy to a sort of "middle region" for politicians before television. Through consistent physical proximity, for example, many reporters would see politicians in a multiplicity of front region roles and a smattering of back region activities. Yet, the relationship between politicians and some journalists was itself a personal back region interaction that was distinguished from press accounts to the public. Before television, most of the news stories released were not records of this personal back region relationship or even of a "middle region." The politician could always distinguish for the press what was "on" the record, what was "off" the record, what should be paraphrased, and what must be attributed to "a high government official." Thus, even when the journalists and the politicians were intimates, the news releases were usually impersonal social communications. Print media can "report on" what happens in one place and bring the report to another place. But the report is by no means a "presentation" of the actual place-bound experience. The print reporters who interviewed Theodore Roosevelt while he was being shaved, for example, did not have an experience "equivalent" to the resulting news reports. Because private interactions with reporters were once distinct from the public communications released in newspapers, much of a politician's "personality" was well hidden from the average citizen.

Private press-politician interactions continue to take place, but electronic media have created new political situations that change the overall "distance" between politician and voter. With electronic coverage, politicians lose a great deal of control over their messages and performances. When they ask that the television camera or tape recorder be turned off, the politicians appear to have something to hide. When the camera or microphone is on, politicians can no longer separate their interaction with the press from their interaction with the public. The camera unthinkingly records the flash of anger and the shiver in the cold; it determinedly shadows our leaders as they trip over words or down stairs. And, unlike the testimony of journalists or of other witnesses, words and actions recorded on electronic tape are impossible to deny. Thus, while politicians try hard to structure the *content* of the media coverage, the *form* of the coverage itself is changing the nature of political image. The revealing nature of television's presentational information cannot be fully counteracted by manipulation, practice, and high-paid consultants. Even a staged media event is often more personally revealing than a transcript of an informal speech or interview. When in 1977, President Carter allowed NBC cameras into the White House for a day, the result may not have been what he intended. *As The New York Times* reported:

> Mr. Carter is a master of controlled images, and he is obviously primed for the occasion. When he isn't flashing his warm smile, he is being soothingly cool under pressure. But the camera ferrets out that telltale tick, that comforting indication of ordinary humanity. It finds his fingers nervously caressing a paperclip or playing with a pen. It captures the almost imperceptible tightening of facial muscles when the President is given an unflattering newspaper story about one of his sons.[3]

Some politicians, of course, have better "media images" than others, but few can manipulate their images as easily as politicians could in a print era. The nature and the extent of this loss of control become even clearer when back and front regions are not viewed as mutually exclusive categories. Most actions encompass both types of behavior. In many situations, for example, an individual can play a front region role while simultaneously giving off covert back region cues to "teammates" (facial expressions, "code" remarks, fingers crossed behind the back, etc.). . . . Because expressions are constant and personal, an individual's exuding of expressions is a type of ongoing back region activity that was once accessible only to those in close physical proximity. Thus, the degree of control over access to back regions is not simply binary—access/no access—but infinitely variable. Any medium of communication can be analyzed in relation to those personal characteristics it transmits and those it restricts.

Print, for example, conveys words but no intonations or facial gestures; radio sends intonations along with the words but provides no visual information; television transmits the full audio/visual spectrum of verbal, vocal, and gestural. In this sense, the trend from print to radio to television represents a shrinking shield for back region activities and an increase in the energy required to manage impressions. Further, Albert Mehrabian's formula for relative message impact—7% verbal, 38% vocal, and 55% facial and postural—suggests that the trend in media development not only leads to revealing more, but to revealing more of more. From the portrait to the photograph to the movie to the video close-up, media have been providing a closer, more replicative, more immediate, and, therefore, less idealized image of the leader. "Greatness" is an abstraction, and it fades as the image of distant leaders comes to resemble an encounter with an intimate acquaintance.

As cameras continue to get lighter and smaller, and as microphones and lenses become more sensitive, the distinctions between public and private contexts continue to erode. It is no longer necessary for politicians to stop what they are doing in order to pose for a picture or to step up to a microphone. As a result, it is increasingly difficult for politicians to distinguish between the ways in which they behave in "real situations" and the ways in which they present themselves for the media. The new public image of politicians, therefore, has many of the characteristics of the former backstage of political life, and many once informal interactions among politicians and their families, staff, reporters, and constituents have become more stiff and formal as they are exposed to national audiences. . . .

Most politicians, even Presidents, continue to maintain a truly private backstage area, but that area is being pushed further and further into the background, and it continues to shrink both spatially and temporally.

Writing and print not only hide general back region actions and behaviors, they also conceal the act of producing "images" and messages. Presidents once had the time to prepare speeches carefully. Even seemingly "spontaneous" messages were prepared in advance, often with the help of advisors, counselors, and family members. Delays, indecision, and the pondering of alternative solutions in response to problems were hidden in the invisible backstage area created by the inherent slowness of older media. Before the invention of the telegraph, for example, a President never needed to be awakened in the middle of the night to respond to a crisis. A few hours' delay meant little.

Electronic media, however, leave little secret time for preparations and response. Because messages *can* be sent instantly across the nation and the world, any delay in hearing from a President is apparent. And in televised press conferences, even a few seconds of thought by a politician may be seen as a sign of indecisiveness, weakness, or senility. More and more, therefore, the public messages conveyed by officials are, in fact, spontaneous.

Politicians find it more difficult to hide their need for time and for advice in the preparation of public statements. They must either reveal the decision process (by turning to advisors or by saying that they need more time to study the issue) or they must present very informal, off-the-cuff comments that naturally lack the craftsmanship of prepared texts. The new media demand that the politician walk and talk steadily and unthinkingly along a performance tightrope. On either side is danger: A few seconds of silence or a slip of the tongue can lead to a fall in the polls.

The changing arenas of politics affect not only the perceptions of audiences but also the response of politicians to their own performances. In face-to-face behavior, we must get a sense of ourselves from the ongoing response of others. We can never see ourselves quite the way others see us. On videotape, however, politicians are able to see exactly the same image of themselves as is seen by the public. In live interactions, a speaker's nervousness and mistakes are usually politely ignored by audiences and therefore often soon forgotten by the speaker too. With television, politicians acquire permanent records of themselves sweating, stammering, or anxiously licking their lips. Television, therefore, has the power to increase a politician's self-doubt and lower self-esteem.

Highly replicative media are demystifying leaders not only for their own time, but for history as well. Few leaders are universally revered in their own lifetime. But less replicative media allowed, at least, for greater idealization of leaders after they died. Idiosyncrasies and physical flaws were interred with a President's bones, their good deeds and their accomplishments lived after them. Once a President died, all that remained were flattering painted portraits and the written texts of speeches. An unusual speaking style or an unattractive facial expression was soon forgotten.

If Lincoln had been passed down to us only through painted portraits, perhaps his homeliness would have faded further with time. The rest of the Lincoln legend, however, including Lincoln's image as a dynamic speaker, continues to be preserved by the *lack* of recordings of his unusually high, thin voice, which rose even higher when he was nervous. Similarly, Thomas Jefferson's slight speech impediment is rarely mentioned. Through new media, however, the idiosyncrasies of Presidents are preserved and passed down to the next generation. Instead of inheriting only summaries and recollections, future generations will judge the styles of former Presidents for themselves. They will see Gerald Ford lose his balance, Carter sweating under pressure, and Reagan dozing during an audience with the Pope. Presidential mispronunciations, hesitations, perspiration, and physical and verbal clumsiness are now being preserved for all time.

Expressions are part of the shared repertoire of all people. When under control and exposed briefly, expressive messages show the "humanity" of the "great leader." But when they are flowing freely and constantly, expressive messages suggest that those we look up to may, after all, be no different from ourselves. The more intense our search for evidence of greatness, the more it eludes us.

There is a demand today for two things: fully open, accessible administrations and strong, powerful leaders. Rarely do we consider that these two demands may, unfortunately, be incompatible. We want to spy on our leaders, yet we want them to inspire us. We cannot have both disclosure *and* the mystification necessary for an image of greatness. The post-Watergate fascination with uncovering cover-ups has not been accompanied by a sophisticated notion of what will inevitably be found in the closets of all leaders. The familiarity fostered by electronic media all too easily breeds contempt.

Notes

1. David M. Alpern, "A Newsweek Poll on the Issues," *Newsweek*, 3 March 1980, 29.
2. William Jennings Bryan and Mary Baird Bryan, *The Memoirs of William Jennings Bryan, Vol. I*, Reprint of 1925 edition (Port Washington, New York: Kennikat, 1971), 103.
3. John J. O'Connor, "TV: A Full Day at the White House," *The New York Times*, 14 April 1977.

Questions for Discussion

1. Why does the author believe that "old style" political heroes are no longer possible?
2. It has been said that American voters prefer a "candidate of the people but not like the people." What does this mean? Would Meyrowitz agree with this assertion? Explain.

 8.2

American News Consumption During Times of National Crisis

Scott L. Althaus

Although there is evidence that the events of 9/11 sparked changes in the civic attitudes of citizens, it is far less clear that the terrorist attacks have resulted in changes in the civic behavior of citizens. In this selection, Scott L. Althaus attempts to determine whether or not the attention Americans pay to news of national and international affairs has changed since the attacks. He compares the viewing habits of the news audience during and after the 1990–1991 Persian Gulf War with that of the most recent crisis to determine whether the respective crises altered the levels of attention paid to the news.

Althaus documents a number of changes in news consumption, including the decline of attention paid to network news broadcasts and the increasing reliance on cable news sources. He suggests Americans appear to increasingly gravitate toward media that specialize in the "latest" news while reducing their reliance on new sources that emphasize in-depth reporting and provide context.

Within months after 9/11, Americans' attention to the news had returned to levels found before the terrorist attacks. Concern with the economy had displaced the war on terrorism as the most important problem facing the country in

Scott L. Althaus is an associate professor of political science and an associate professor of communications at the University of Illinois at Urbana–Champaign.

Scott L. Althaus, "American News Consumption During Times of National Crisis," *PS: Political Science and Politics* (September 2002): 517–521. Reprinted with permission of Cambridge University Press and the author.

the polls. And many Americans had come to view the war on terrorism as a domestic rather than a foreign policy issue. Althaus believes that the impact of 9/11 "seems to have left Americans' collective appetite for news largely undisturbed."

Have 9/11 and the ensuing war on terrorism sparked a reinvigoration of civic life in the United States? Opinion surveys show dramatic changes in the political attitudes of American citizens. . . . However, it remains unclear whether these changed attitudes have resulted in higher levels of civic activity.

If Americans today are more engaged in civic life than they were a year ago, we should see evidence of this change in the amount of attention they pay to news of national and international affairs. Unlike many other civic behaviors, watching or reading the news is relatively low in opportunity costs. Because the choice between viewing a *Simpsons* rerun or a national news broadcast is made so easily, the size of the audience for national news should be fairly sensitive to shifts in the perceived importance of public affairs. And like the proverbial canary in the mine shaft, changing levels of civic-mindedness are likely to be seen first in lower-cost behaviors like paying attention to news before they are seen in higher-cost activities like volunteering or joining a group.

This article looks at changes in the size of American news audiences during the 1990–91 Persian Gulf Crisis and the more recent period surrounding the 9/11 attacks. Like the current situation, the Persian Gulf crisis started suddenly, when Iraq launched a surprise invasion of Kuwait on August 2, 1990. Since there are clear starting points for both national crises, comparing the percentage of adults watching television news broadcasts before and after each precipitating event should show whether the respective crises prompted changes in levels of popular attention to the news.

Audience Trends for Network News Broadcasts

Weekly television-ratings data collected by Nielsen Media Research are available for both cases. Since the television audience grows in winter months, the time of year in which a precipitating event occurs can influence the apparent impact of the crisis. For this reason, I collected weekly ratings data from each case over 16-month periods starting the first week of January in the year the crisis began and ending the last week of April in the following year. To measure the combined total audience for nightly national news programs, I combined ratings for ABC's *World News Tonight*, CBS's *Evening News*, and NBC's *Nightly News*. To ease interpretation across the two cases, I translated these ratings data into the percentage of American adults that were tuning in to the nightly news.

One striking feature of these trends (Figure 1) is that the evening news audience today is only about half as large as it was a decade before. During the 1990–91 period, between 23% and 33% of American adults watched nightly network news broadcasts, depending on the time of year. Since January 2001, Nielsen data put the total size of nightly news audiences at between 11% and 16% of American adults (not counting the week of 9/11). It is unclear whether today's total audience for all forms of public-affairs content is any smaller than it was a decade before, but if it is, the falloff is likely to be slight. Instead, the once-larger broadcast news audience of 1990–91 is today spread out across a wider range of news products, with cable, the Internet, primetime news magazines, and local television news each attracting sizable portions of a national news audience that once was shared mainly by the three evening news programs.

Because news audiences have become increasingly fragmented, absolute differences in the percentage of adults watching network news during each crisis period are less telling than the relative changes in audience size within each trend. If we begin our analysis immediately before each precipitating event and follow the trends over the next several months, the two cases appear to reveal different patterns of audience response. In the Persian Gulf crisis, the Iraqi invasion of Kuwait immediately produced a four-percentage-point spike in the

Figure 1
Weekly Percentage of American Adults Watching Nightly Network News Broadcasts

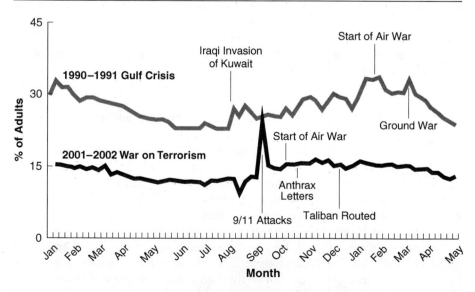

Source: Nielsen ratings data compiled from various media sources. These trends report the combined weekly audience for ABC's *World News Tonight*, CBS's *Evening News*, and NBC's *Nightly News*.

American news audience. The nightly news audience then grew steadily over the fall months as the American military buildup in Saudi Arabia signaled a looming confrontation with Iraq. Nearly a third of American adults were directly exposed to one of the three nightly news broadcasts in the weeks leading up to and immediately following the start of the air war, which began on January 17, as war against Iraq was vigorously debated in Congress and then witnessed live on television. The news audience shrank somewhat in early February before experiencing a three-percentage-point jump during the week of ground combat, which began on February 23. This rapid victory over Iraqi ground forces was followed by an abrupt turn away from the news, and the nightly audience dropped nearly 10 percentage points over the eight weeks following the close of the ground campaign.

Eleven years later, the tragedies of 9/11 had the immediate effect of more than doubling the size of the evening news audience, from 13% of American adults in the week of September 3–9 to more than 26% in the week of September 10–16. Nielsen Media Research later estimated that 79.5 million viewers were tuning into any of 11 broadcast or cable networks showing news coverage on the night of 9/11. As impressive as this level of attention seems, the January 2001 Super Bowl attracted about the same number of viewers. Moreover, the evening news audience just as swiftly contracted to 15% of American adults in the week of September 17–23 and never rose more than one-and-a-half percentage points above that level in the following seven months. In contrast to frequent event-driven surges in news attention throughout the Persian Gulf crisis, news attention in the post-9/11 U.S. held quite stable at about four percentage points above pre-9/11 levels for several months before declining steadily after the start of the new year in 2002. By the middle of April 2002, the size of the evening news audience had returned to the previous July's level of just 13% of adults.

When thus interpreting these postcrisis trends using the immediate precrisis period as a benchmark, it appears that the Persian Gulf crisis produced a gradual mobilization of adults into the television news audience, but that the present war on terrorism generated a smaller shock to the size of American news audiences that started decaying soon after it began. During the Persian Gulf crisis, the average size of the evening news audience grew by 13.8 million persons between the last week of July 1990, and the first week of January 1991. During the war on terrorism, the growth in the evening news audience between these two weeks was only half as large, amounting to 7.4 million more audience members in 2002.

However, this interpretation of postcrisis growth in the news audience requires us to ignore the left-hand side of Figure 1. The longer-term trends leading up to each precipitating event call into question whether either of these national crises fundamentally increased the size of the news audience. Once we take into account the cyclical shifts in the size of television news audiences, the apparent changes prompted by each crisis become harder to distinguish from normal seasonal movement. It seems impressive at first glance that 32.7% of American adults were following the evening news in a typical week during the critical month of January 1991, up from 23.2% for July 1990. However, this number loses some of its luster when we recognize that the evening news audience was nearly as large—31.4% of adults—in the previous January. Given the seasonal variation in the size of news audiences, a more appropriate way of measuring the impact of national crises is to calculate the size of the news audience after the precipitating event compared to its size from the same period in the previous year.

This comparison paints a very different picture. During the Gulf Crisis an average of approximately 2.4 million more adults per day were watching evening news broadcasts in the first four months of 1991 compared to the first four months of 1990. The same comparison for the war on terrorism produces a mean difference of just less than 900,000 more audience members per day in 2002 than in 2001. Seasonal-adjusted growth in the news audience was nearly three times as large during the Persian Gulf crisis as during the current war on terrorism, but in both cases the magnitude of growth was rather small, amounting to 0.4% of adults in 2001–2 and 1.3% in 1990–91. Seen from this perspective, the clearest impact of the Iraqi invasion of Kuwait was in increasing the amount of weekly variance around the seasonal mean rather than in shifting the mean itself. Similarly, 9/11 appears to have accelerated the seasonal growth curve for the evening news audience during the fall of 2001 without producing a substantive shift in its average size.

Where Else Are Americans Getting Their News?

The preceding analysis begs the question of whether Americans are still getting their news primarily from network news broadcasts. If people are turning instead to other sources for public affairs information, then an analysis of those sources might shed a more flattering light on levels of civic engagement in post-9/11 America.

According to surveys conducted by the Pew Center for the People and the Press (Figure 2), there have been some notable changes in the mix of news media used by Americans since 9/11. The questions from which I obtained these data allowed respondents to name up to three media as primary sources of news, so these survey data capture a potentially broad range of media involvement. In the first week of September 2001, newspapers were the most commonly mentioned source of information about public affairs. By the second week of January 2002, cable television news had become the most-cited news source, mentioned by over half of respondents.

All of the other pre- and post-9/11 differences are individually within the margins of sampling error for these surveys, but collectively they reveal some common patterns. First, there has been a decline in the percentage of Ameri-

Figure 2
Where Have People Been Getting Most of Their News About National and International Issues?

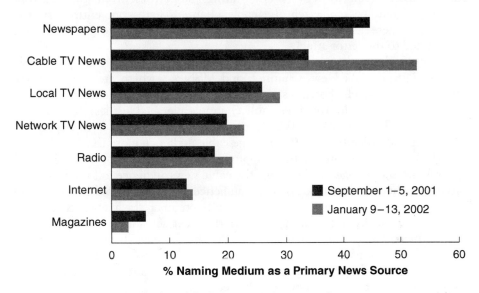

Source: Pew Center for the People and the Press surveys. Since up to three answers were accepted per respondent. . . , the sum for each survey adds up to well over 100%.

cans turning to print news since 9/11. . . . Second, the declining reliance on newspapers and news magazines seems to be offset by a shift toward electronic news sources. Aside from the obvious jump for cable television news, slightly higher percentages of Americans reported in January 2002 that they turn to local television news, network television news, radio, and the Internet for public affairs information. Taken together, these two changes suggest that Americans now seem to be more attentive to media that specialize in delivering the "latest" news even as they reduce their reliance on sources of news that emphasize in-depth reporting and providing context for understanding the current crisis. But how many people are actually tuning in to cable?

Audience Trends for Cable News

The Pew surveys suggest that many more people now rely on cable news outlets than before 9/11, and Nielsen ratings data confirm that the cable news audience has experienced a sizeable gain. Since cable news outlets provide continuous public affairs programming, Nielsen measures cable news audiences differently than network news audiences. Instead of estimating the average number of viewers for a particular program, Nielsen estimates for each cable channel the average number of viewers per minute in an entire day. While not directly comparable to network news ratings, since these averages mask how many different people watch the cable channels across an entire day, the change in these ratings before and after 9/11 clarifies how cable audiences have responded to the terror attacks.

Figure 3 shows the combined average audience per minute for the Cable News Network, Fox News Channel, and MSNBC, which are the top three cable news channels. For the six months leading up to September 2001, the combined audience for the three cable channels averaged just less than 0.4% of American adults, or about 800,000 persons. For the period from September 2001, through March 2002, the average cable audience more than doubled to nearly 1% of American adults, or approximately two million people. Figure 3 shows that the changes in the size of the cable news audience followed a similar course as that for the broadcast news audience. After a fourfold increase from 800,000 persons in August to 2.7 million in September, the average cable news audience gradually declined in size over the next several months. By March 2002, the combined per-minute audience for the three cable channels averaged 1.5 million viewers. While this is just half the size of the peak audience in September, it is also twice the size of the combined cable audience from a year before, indicating that cable news has indeed retained an appreciable number of new viewers.

Although Figure 3 appears to suggest that the cable audience remains far smaller than the broadcast news audience (and media reporters frequently interpret these numbers in this way), it is possible that the cumulative cable news audience—that is, the total number of unique viewers—could include a fairly large proportion of American adults on a given day. For example, the average per-minute cable news audience for November 2001, was 905,000 persons for CNN and 747,000 for Fox News. But the number of different people who watched at least 15 minutes of programming at some point during that same month was 93.4 million for CNN (or about 46% of American adults) and 58.5 million for Fox (or about 29% of American adults).

However, it is unclear whether these cable viewers are getting a mix of news comparable to that received by network audiences. A recent content analysis of primetime news programming on CNN, Fox, and MSNBC during late January of this year (News Hour 2002) found that cable news shows focused on a small number of "headline" stories, and that much of the primetime programming took the form of personal interviews or panel discussions rather than traditional news reporting. If the past behavior of cable audiences is any guide to the present, it is also likely that these new viewers constitute an irregular audience for cable news, tuning in to catch up with developing stories or breaking news, but otherwise relying primarily on noncable sources for their daily diet of news.

Figure 3
Average Percentage of American Adults Watching Cable News, March 2001 to March 2002

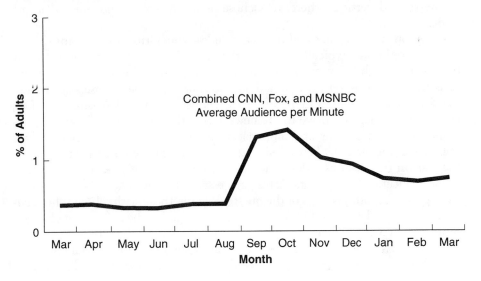

Source: Nielsen ratings data.

Consequences of Public Disengagement from the War on Terrorism

If 9/11 has founded a new era of civic-mindedness in the U.S., it seems to have left Americans' collective appetite for news largely undisturbed. The size of the network television news audience grew only slightly, and newspaper readership continued to decline after 9/11. While the average size of the cable news audience has doubled, it remains a small fraction of American adults, and the audiences for both network and cable news have diminished with each passing month.

It is too soon to identify any long-term implications for the public's limited attention to the early stages of this war, let alone to speculate whether the trends of the last year are likely to continue into even the near future. However, two consequences of the public's disengagement are already apparent.

First, many Americans consider the war on terrorism to be a domestic issue rather than a foreign-policy issue. The Pew Research Center for the People and the Press conducted a survey in January 2002, which asked two slightly different versions of the same question. The first read: "Right now, which is more important for President Bush to focus on: domestic policy or the war on terrorism?" A second version changed "the war on terrorism" to "foreign policy," but was otherwise identical. If Americans think about the war on terrorism as a foreign-policy issue, the percentages in both versions of the question should be nearly identical. Yet, the public's responses could hardly be more different. To the first version of the question, 33% of respondents answered domestic policy and 52% named the war on terrorism. These numbers were reversed in the second version, where 52% chose domestic policy and only 34% said foreign policy.

Question-wording effects of this magnitude—generating an 18-point shift in surveyed opinion—typically indicate that the mass public has insufficiently reasoned through its opinions. It is certainly understandable why many Americans see the war on terrorism as a domestic issue. Most paid close attention to news of the terrorist attacks in New York, Pennsylvania, and Washington, DC, but have been less attentive to the news during the Bush administration's subsequent military actions and diplomatic initiatives overseas. Further analysis of this wording effect by Pew researchers revealed that the tendency to think of the war on terrorism as a domestic policy issue was closely related to level of formal education: college graduates gave essentially the same mix of opinions in response to both versions of the question, while those with a high school education or less demonstrated the greatest sensitivity to these wording changes. Since people with higher levels of education also tend to be more attentive to the news, the tendency to see the war on terrorism as a matter of domestic policy may be a direct outgrowth of public disengagement from the news in the aftermath of 9/11.

A second consequence is that while opinion surveys reveal consistently high levels of support for American military action against countries and organizations suspected of sponsoring terrorism, the roots of this support may not run deep. This possibility is suggested in recent trends from Gallup polls that ask Americans to name "the most important problem facing the country today." Figure 4 shows how terrorism leaped onto the public's agenda following 9/11: nearly half of Americans named terrorism as the country's most important problem in an October Gallup poll (no data are available for the month of September). However, the ensuing months saw a rapid falloff in the percentage of the public concerned about terrorism, so that by January 2002, fewer than a quarter of Americans named terrorism as the country's most important problem. In contrast, unease with the state of the economy came to rival terrorism as the top issue of public concern in the first quarter of 2002. Given the impact of a shifting public agenda on evaluations of George Bush Sr.'s job performance in the aftermath of the Persian Gulf war, it is notable that the declining importance of terrorism and the increasing importance of economic concerns track George W. Bush's declining job-approval rating. Although President Bush has made it clear that the allied military campaign against terrorism is just beginning, fewer people today are likely to be evaluating him on the basis of his performance as commander in chief.

The rapid decline in public concern about terrorism is a sign that American support for U.S. military involvement abroad may be less firm than it seems. If

Figure 4

Percentages Naming Terrorism and the Economy as the "Most Important Problems," January 2001 to March 2002

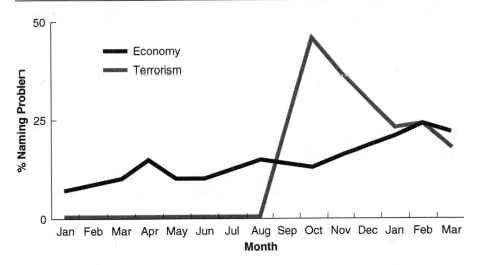

Source: Surveys by the Gallup Organization.

this American resolve is more closely tied to the dramatic events of 9/11 than to a new appreciation for the complexities of the post-9/11 geopolitical landscape, it becomes increasingly difficult to predict how Americans will respond to new developments or crises in the coming years of this war.

It remains to be seen whether this public disengagement has resulted from the stunning successes of the U.S. military campaign in Afghanistan, or from the secrecy in which the war on terrorism has necessarily been shrouded. But the public's steady retreat from opportunities for news exposure should give pause to military and political leaders pondering the next step in this solemn undertaking.

Questions for Discussion

1. What news sources do Americans use to learn about national and international issues? What sources are becoming more important? Less important? What factors underlie the increased importance of cable news sources in the aftermath of 9/11? What news sources do you use to learn about national and international issues?

2. Why have many Americans come to see the war on terrorism as a domestic rather than a foreign policy issue? What are the implications, if any, of this for public support for military involvement abroad?

The Press and Misperceptions About the Iraq War

Steven Kull

Citizen knowledge about government lies at the heart of a democracy, where decision makers must take into consideration public opinion and are held accountable for their actions through the ballot box. The nation's media ideally play a central "watchdog" role in the process, scrutinizing government actions, and helping to inform the public by uncovering and transmitting accurate and instructive information. The tendency of the government is to present itself in the best possible light and to obscure from public scrutiny anything that might create a negative image. This inherent tension between the press and the government is most pronounced on matters regarding foreign affairs and military activity, the very issues that create the most public reliance on the press for information. Unlike domestic matters, where the public may form impressions from their own experiences, on international matters the media may be the only source for information.

In this selection, Steven Kull raises a number of questions concerning the role of the press in its reporting about the Iraq War. Particularly disconcerting is the level of incorrect information many citizens had about the war even after exposure to news sources. After the U.S. invasion in 2003, a substantial portion of respondents in a national public opinion poll believed that Iraq and al-Qaeda were working together, that weapons of mass destruction had been found in Iraq, and that world public opinion favored the United States going to war, all factually in-

---

Steven Kull is director of the Program on International Policy Attitudes (PIPA) at the University of Maryland.

Steven Kull, "The Press and Public Misperceptions About the Iraq War," *Nieman Reports*, Vol. 58, No. 2, Summer 2004, pp. 64–66. Reprinted by permission.

correct positions. More than 60 percent of poll respondents had at least one of the three misperceptions. Kull finds that the level of respondent misperception, even after controlling for political bias and educational background, varied a great deal depending upon their primary source of news. Fox and CBS were the least likely to provide critical commentary, and their viewers had the highest levels of misperception; public radio and television listeners and viewers had the least number of misperceptions.

Kull believes that when the press are uneasy about challenging assumptions by government leaders, the media become "a means of transmission for an administration rather than serv(ing) as a critical filter for information." This passive role may have an effect on public policy and the outcome of elections.

When historians take a look back on this period, the Iraq War will surely stand out as a remarkable event. A major power went to war, overthrew another government, and occupied the nation on the basis of stated assumptions that turned out to be false. Equally striking, following the invasion, large portions of the public of this major power—a democratic one no less—failed to get accurate messages about what had occurred, which raises compelling questions about the role and practice of the press in a democratic society.

During the summer of 2003, the Program on International Policy Attitudes (PIPA) at the University of Maryland, together with the polling firm Knowledge Networks, conducted a large-scale study of U.S. public perceptions and misperceptions related to the Iraq War, with a special eye to determining what role the press might have played in this process. The polls were conducted from June through September with a nationwide sample of 3,334 respondents.

The study found three widespread misperceptions:

♦ 49 percent believed that the United States had found evidence that Iraq was working closely with al-Qaeda;
♦ 22 percent believed that actual weapons of mass destruction had been found in Iraq;
♦ 23 percent believed that world public opinion favored the United States going to war with Iraq.

Overall, 60 percent of those we polled had at least one of these three misperceptions.

Misperceptions and the Press

Naturally, this raises the question of how these misperceptions developed and persisted when no evidence of such links between al-Qaeda and Iraq had been found, no weapons of mass destruction had been located, and polls of world public opinion have found clear majority opposition to the U.S. war with Iraq. Was it simply a function of people seeking out information that confirmed their biases in favor of the war? Or did this represent some failure on the part of the press?

If these misperceptions were strictly a function of individual bias, then we would expect to find them distributed according to political preferences, no matter where respondents got their news. To find out if this was the case, respondents were asked about their primary source of news. It turned out that the frequency of misperceptions varied dramatically depending on respondents' primary source of news. As shown below, the percentage that had at least one of these misperceptions ranged from 23 percent among those who primarily got their news from National Public Radio (NPR) or PBS to 80 percent among those who primarily got their news from Fox News.

It would seem that such misperceptions might be derived from a failure to pay attention to the news. Indeed among those who primarily get their news from print sources (just 19 percent of our sample), misperceptions were lower among those who paid more attention. But overall, those who reported paying greater attention to the news were no less likely to have misperceptions. Most striking was a finding that among those who primarily watch Fox News, the people who paid more attention were *more* likely to have misperceptions.

Of course, this leads to the question of whether such variations are due to difference in the demographics of the audiences. However, when these demographics were controlled for, the effect remained. For example, when we looked only at Republicans, or only at Democrats, the same pattern of misperceptions between the various audiences was found. Extensive multivariate regression analyses that included numerous variables, including party identification, attitudes about the President, education and others, found that respondents' primary news source continued to be a very powerful predictor of the frequency of misperceptions. Clearly, this suggests Americans had these misperceptions not simply because of internal biases but because

Table 1

Frequency of Misperceptions by Respondent's Primary Source of News

Number of misperceptions per respondent	Fox	CBS	ABC	CNN	NBC	Print media	NPR/ PBS
None of the 3	20%	30%	39%	45%	45%	53%	77%
1 or more misperceptions	80%	70%	61%	55%	55%	47%	23%

of the important role being played by variations in the stimuli they received from their external sources of news.

Consequences of Bad Information

Such misperceptions can potentially have significant consequences: We found they were highly related to other attitudes. Among those with none of the misperceptions listed above, only 23 percent supported the war. Among those with one of these misperceptions, 53 percent supported the war, rising to 78 percent with those who have two of the misperceptions, and to 86 percent with all three of the misperceptions. While such correlations do not prove that these misperceptions caused the support for the decision to go to war with Iraq, it does appear likely that support for the war would be lower if fewer members of the public had these misperceptions. Such misperceptions are also highly related to the likelihood of voting for the President. Analyses suggest that if these perceptions changed, this could have a significant impact on voting decisions, apparently because they have an impact on perceptions of the President's honesty.

Earlier PIPA studies also suggest that during the run-up to the war misperceptions played a role in support for the decision to go to war. Before the war, approximately one in five Americans believed that Iraq was directly involved in the September 11th attacks, and 13 percent even said they believed they had seen conclusive evidence of it. Among those who believed that Iraq was directly involved in September 11th, 58 percent said they would approve if the President were to go to war without U.N. approval. Among those who believed that Iraq had given al-Qaeda substantial support, but was not involved in September 11th, approval dropped to 37 percent. Among those who believed that a few al-Qaeda individuals had contact with Iraqi officials, 32 percent were supportive, while among those who believed that there was no connection at all, just 25 percent felt that way. In polls conducted *during* the war, among those who incorrectly believed that world public opinion favored the United States going to war, 81 percent supported doing so, while among those who knew that the world public opinion was opposed only 28 percent supported going to war.

The Role of the Press

Such data lead to the question of why so many Americans have had these misperceptions, even after controlling for their political biases. The first and most obvious reason is that the Bush administration made numerous statements that could easily be construed as asserting these falsehoods. On numerous occasions the administration made statements strongly implying it had intelligence saying that Iraq was closely involved with al-Qaeda and was even directly involved in the September 11th attacks. The administration also made statements that came extremely close to asserting that weapons of mass destruction were found in postwar Iraq. On May 30, 2003, President Bush made the statement: ". . . for those who say we haven't found the banned manufacturing devices or banned weapons, they're wrong. We found them."

But the fact that misperceptions varied so greatly depending on their primary source of news strongly suggests that the way that the press reported the news played a role. This might be partly due to prominent reporting of official statements saying that it appeared that clear evidence of weapons of mass destruction had been found, while the later conclusions—refuting such assessments—were given little play. But it also appears that misleading assertions were often not challenged.

There is evidence that in the run-up to, during, and for a period after the invasion of Iraq, many in the press appeared to feel that it was not their role to challenge the administration. Fox News coverage of the invasion included a U.S. flag in the corner of the screen, and its correspondents and news anchors assumed the defense department's name for the war, "Operation Iraqi Freedom." Fox's reporting on Iraq during the occupation phase was conducted under the banner "War on Terrorism," implicitly confirming the administration's association between Iraq and al-Qaeda. When Fox News was criticized for taking a pro-war stance, one of its anchors, Neil Cavuto, replied: "You say I wear my biases on my sleeve. Better that than pretend you have none, but show them clearly in your work." Dan Rather of CBS News commented in an April 14, 2003 interview with Larry King: "Look, I'm an American. I never tried to kid anybody that I'm some internationalist or something. And when my country is at war, I want my country to win. . . . Now, I can't and don't argue that that is coverage without a prejudice. About that I am prejudiced."

A study conducted in 2003 by Fairness & Accuracy in Reporting (FAIR) tracking the frequencies of pro-war and antiwar commentators on the major networks found that pro-war views were overwhelmingly more frequent. In such an environment, it would not be surprising that the press would downplay the lack of evidence of links between Iraq and al-Qaeda, the fact that weapons of mass destruction were not being found, and that world public opinion was critical of the war.

When the press are reluctant to challenge what government leaders say, they can simply become a means of transmission for an administration, rather than serve as a critical filter for information. For example, when President Bush made the assertion that weapons of mass destruction had been found, the May 31, 2003 edition of The Washington Post ran a front-page headline saying "Bush: 'We Found' Banned Weapons."

There is also striking evidence that readiness to challenge the administration is a variable that corresponds to levels of misperception among viewers. The FAIR study found that the two networks notably least likely to present critical commentary were Fox and CBS. These are the same two networks whose viewers in the PIPA study were most likely to have misperceptions.

Clearly Americans had hoped and expected that once the United States went into Iraq, evidence of Iraq's link to al-Qaeda and of the development of weapons of mass destruction would be found, thus vindicating the decision to go to war as an act of self-defense. Perhaps, then, it is not surprising that many people have been receptive when the administration has strongly implied or even asserted that the United States has found evidence that Iraq was working closely with al-Qaeda and was developing weapons of mass destruction. However, there is also evidence that news outlets—some more than others—have allowed themselves to be passive transmitters of such messages.

Questions for Discussion

1. Why was much of the press so uncritical and unchallenging of Bush administration pronouncements after the invasion of Iraq? What consequences for public policy and elections may have resulted from the press's passive behavior?
2. Should the "watchdog" role of the press be different in the midst of a foreign conflict involving U.S. troops than it is in a peacetime context? Would a critical press that challenges an administration's actions undermine the war effort?

Chapter 9

INTEREST GROUPS

The United States has always been a nation of joiners, and more interest groups are active in our governmental affairs than in any other nation. Still, Americans have never been comfortable with special-interest politics. Ever since James Madison first warned of the "mischiefs of faction" in *The Federalist*, No. 10 (the first selection in this chapter), citizens, politicians, and scholars have debated the role of special interests in policymaking.

The conflict between special interests and the public interest has been especially evident when the government has seemed to be functioning ineffectively. During the Progressive era, for example, the influence of railroads, oil companies, and insurance firms drew the attention of scholars and the popular press; consequently, regulation of lobbyists became a major aim of the reformers. During the New Deal, in contrast, relatively little attention was paid to special interests. The dominant view of scholars during and after that period was pluralism—the belief that competition among groups is healthy for democracy.

By the 1960s, however, it had become obvious that such competition was highly distorted; some special interests almost always lost in the political process, and others—especially those with money, access, or inside information—usually won. The interest group universe had a blatant representational bias, as well; some interests, such as business, were well represented in the process, whereas others (minorities, the poor, and consumers) were seriously underrepresented.

Renewed attention to the role of interest groups grew stronger in the 1970s and 1980s. The tremendous expansion in the number of interest groups, the decline of political parties, and the heightened visibility of interest groups in the electoral and policymaking processes appeared to parallel government's inability to deal with economic and social problems. From the inability of Congress and the president to work together in recent years to the skyrocketing deficits and influence-peddling scandals that draw the attention of the media, interest groups have been accused of being at the heart of the problem of contemporary government.

Depending on one's perspective, the United States is either blessed or cursed with many special interests. The constitutional guarantees of free speech, free association, and petition are basic to group formation. Because political organizations often parallel government structure, federalism and the separation of powers have encouraged a multiplicity of groups as interests organize around various local, state, and national access points. Societal cleavages also help foster interest group development. Differences in economics, climate, culture, and tradition, and in racial, ethnic, and religious backgrounds, create ready-made interests within American life. Finally, our cultural values may well play a role. As Alexis de Tocqueville observed more than 150 years ago, values such as individuality and personal achievement underlie the propensity of citizens to join groups.

There is a difference, however, between the existence of special interests and the emergence of special interest groups—associations of individuals who share attitudes or goals and attempt to influence public policy. In a simple society there is little need for interest groups, because people have no political or economic reason to organize when they work only for their families. Not until the mid- to late-nineteenth century did interest groups start to appear regularly on the American political scene. As the nation became economically and socially complex, new interests were created and old ones redefined. Farming, for example, became specialized, commercialized, and dependent on other economic sectors. United States trade policies appeared to affect southern cotton farmers and midwestern grain producers, and it soon made sense for such people to organize.

Many political scientists argue that new interest groups are a natural consequence of a growing society. Groups develop both to improve individuals' positions and to protect existing advantages. For example, mobilization of business interests in the 1960s and 1970s often resulted from threats posed by consumer groups and environmentalists. The post–World War II era, especially since 1960, has witnessed a dramatic increase in the number of special interests that have organized for political purposes. New groups have crowded into areas such as business and agriculture, which already were well organized, but the most rapid expansion has taken place in areas that were poorly organized or not organized at all. Women, blacks, environmentalists, consumers, and other nonoccupational interests are now actively represented by groups.

Such changes have been so extensive that even the term *interest group* no longer seems appropriate. Much of the business lobbying in Washington, for example, is now done by representatives of individual companies as well as by "peak" associations, such as the National Association of Manufacturers, which represent groups of companies. Many institutions, even colleges and universities, have their own lobbyists. Some of the so-called groups operating in Washington are not mass membership organizations governed by a board of elected directors; one study of public interest groups discovered that 40 percent of the groups had fewer than one thousand members and 30 percent had no members at all. A large number of active groups are staff organizations, composed of a handful of individuals who are funded by foundation resources. Some are totally private concerns, like Ralph Nader's organization Public Citizen, which claims to lobby for all consumers.

Lobbying has become a growth industry. From 1975 to 1985, the number of registered lobbyists in Washington doubled; the number of attorneys more than tripled between 1973 and 1983, rising to more than 37,000. Washington now abounds with lobbying firms, which contract with companies and groups to represent their interests. Some have more than fifty clients, ranging from individual companies to entire nations. Some plan and manage political campaigns, as well as advise specialized interests.

New techniques of influence have also appeared as lobbyists have embraced technology. Orchestrated mass mailings to legislators or the president can be put in motion within minutes by some of the more sophisticated lobbies. The Campaign Finance Acts of 1971 and 1974 have made it possible for almost all groups to create political action committees (PACs) to coordinate financial contributions to candidates for public office. In 2000, over 4,500 PACs were registered.

To provide a sense of the controversy over interest groups and a flavor of today's environment, this chapter includes a diverse range of selections. *The Federalist*, No. 10, is a classic statement of the dilemma special interests posed to the framers, who sought to control the detrimental effects of factions, especially "majority factions." In the second selection, Jeffrey H. Birnbaum surveys the history of lobbying in America, focusing on some of the scandals that have given lobbyists an unsavory reputation. He suggests there is much improvement in how lobbyists conduct themselves today.

The final two selections look at the contemporary interest group universe and the influence of organized interests in both the electoral and policy processes. Theda Skocpol examines the factors underlying the decline of membership federations over the past half century and the recent proliferation of "associations without members" and attempts to assess the meaning of such trends for American democracy. In the final selection, Jim Drinkard looks at the activities of the pharmaceutical lobby as it attempts to sway decision makers in Washington. The wielding of substantial financial resources and unusual access to key congressional personnel together give drugmakers unparalleled clout in the policy process.

9.1

The Federalist, No. 10

James Madison

There is an inherent tension in any democratic society. Liberty demands that citizens be allowed to pursue their special interests, even if those interests are offensive and selfish; yet the pursuit of special interests may conflict with the public interest. The nation's founders were well aware of this dilemma and directed many of their efforts toward constructing a government that respected personal freedom but was capable of acting for the collective good.

This paper is perhaps the best statement of what the founders thought about special interests or factions. At base they feared all special interests, especially "majority factions," which had the potential to tyrannize the system. Madison realized, however, that special interests "are sown in the nature of man" and any attempt to eliminate them would involve the destruction of liberty, a remedy "worse than the disease." Madison's solution was to limit the effects of factions by promoting competition among them and designing a government with an elaborate system of checks and balances to reduce the power of any single, strong group, whether made up of a majority or a minority of citizens.

Among the numerous advantages promised by a well constructed Union, none deserves to be more accurately developed than its tendency to break and control the violence of faction.* The friend of popular governments, never finds himself so much alarmed for their character and fate, as when he contemplates their propensity to this dangerous vice. He will not fail therefore to set a due value on any plan which, without violating the principles to which he is attached, provides a proper cure for it. The instability, injustice and confusion introduced into the public councils, have in truth been the mortal diseases under which popular governments have every where perished; as they continue to be the favorite and fruitful topics from which the adversaries to liberty derive their most specious declamations. The valuable improvements made by the American Constitutions on the popular models, both ancient and

---

*Madison used the term *faction* to denote any special interest, including parties. Although interest groups did exist, they were not organized in the sense in which we think of them today. Interest "groups" representing special interests were not common until after the Civil War.

modern, cannot certainly be too much admired; but it would be an unwarrantable partiality, to contend that they have as effectually obviated the danger on this side as was wished and expected. Complaints are every where heard from our most considerate and virtuous citizens, equally the friends of public and private faith, and of public and personal liberty; that our governments are too unstable; that the public good is disregarded in the conflicts of rival parties; and that measures are too often decided, not according to the rules of justice, and the rights of the minor party; but by the superior force of an interested and over-bearing majority. However anxiously we may wish that these complaints had no foundation, the evidence of known facts will not permit us to deny that they are in some degree true. It will be found indeed, on a candid review of our situation, that some of the distresses under which we labor, have been erroneously charged on the operation of our governments; but it will be found, at the same time, that other causes will not alone account for many of our heaviest misfortunes; and particularly for that prevailing and increasing distrust of public engagements, and alarm for private rights, which are echoed from one end of the continent to the other. These must be chiefly, if not wholly, effects of the unsteadiness and injustice, with which a factious spirit has tainted our public administrations.

By a faction I understand a number of citizens, whether amounting to a majority or minority of the whole, who are united and actuated by some common impulse of passion, or of interest, adverse to the rights of other citizens, or to the permanent and aggregate interests of the community.

There are two methods of curing the mischiefs of faction: the one, by removing its causes; the other, by controlling its effects.

There are again two methods of removing the causes of faction: the one by destroying the liberty which is essential to its existence; the other, by giving to every citizen the same opinions, the same passions, and the same interests.

It could never be more truly said than of the first remedy, that it is worse than the disease. Liberty is to faction, what air is to fire, an aliment without which it instantly expires. But it could not be a less folly to abolish liberty, which is essential to political life, because it nourishes faction, than it would be to wish the annihilation of air, which is essential to animal life, because it imparts to fire its destructive agency.

The second expedient is as impracticable, as the first would be unwise. As long as the reason of man continues fallible, and he is at liberty to exercise it, different opinions will be formed. As long as the connection subsists between his reason and his self-love, his opinions and his passions will have a reciprocal influence on each other; and the former will be objects to which the latter will attach themselves. The diversity in the faculties of men from which the rights of property originate, is not less an insuperable obstacle to a uniformity of interests. The protection of these faculties is the first object of Government. From the protection of different and unequal faculties of acquiring property, the possession of different degrees and kinds of property immediately results: and from

the influence of these on the sentiments and views of the respective proprietors, ensues a division of the society into different interests and parties.

The latent causes of faction are thus sown in the nature of man; and we see
them every where brought into different degrees of activity, according to the different circumstances of civil society. A zeal for different opinions concerning religion, concerning Government and many other points, as well of speculation as
of practice; an attachment to different leaders ambitiously contending for pre-
eminence and power; or to persons of other descriptions whose fortunes have
been interesting to the human passions, have in turn divided mankind into parties, inflamed them with mutual animosity, and rendered them much more disposed to vex and oppress each other, than to co-operate for their common good.
So strong is this propensity of mankind to fall into mutual animosities, that
where no substantial occasion presents itself, the most frivolous and fanciful distinctions have been sufficient to kindle their unfriendly passions, and excite
their most violent conflicts. But the most common and durable source of factions, have been the various and unequal distribution of property. Those who
hold, and those who are without property, have ever formed distinct interests in
society. Those who are creditors, and those who are debtors, fall under a like discrimination. A landed interest, a manufacturing interest, a mercantile interest, a
monied interest, with many lesser interests, grow up of necessity in civilized nations, and divide them into different classes, actuated by different sentiments
and views. The regulation of these various and interfering interests forms the
principal task of modern Legislation, and involves the spirit of party and faction
in the necessary and ordinary operations of Government.

No man is allowed to be a judge in his own cause; because his interest would
certainly bias his judgment, and, not improbably, corrupt his integrity. With
equal, nay with greater reason, a body of men, are unfit to be both judges and
parties, at the same time; yet, what are many of the most important acts of legislation, but so many judicial determinations, not indeed concerning the rights
of single persons, but concerning the rights of large bodies of citizens; and what
are the different classes of legislators, but advocates and parties to the causes
which they determine? Is a law proposed concerning private debts? It is a question to which the creditors are parties on one side, and the debtors on the
other. Justice ought to hold the balance between them. Yet the parties are and
must be themselves the judges; and the most numerous party, or, in other
words, the most powerful faction must be expected to prevail. Shall domestic
manufactures be encouraged, and in what degree, by restrictions on foreign
manufactures? are questions which would be differently decided by the landed
and the manufacturing classes; and probably by neither, with a sole regard to
justice and the public good. . . .

It is in vain to say, that enlightened statesmen will be able to adjust these
clashing interests, and render them all subservient to the public good. Enlightened statesmen will not always be at the helm: Nor, in many cases, can such an
adjustment be made at all, without taking into view indirect and remote

considerations, which will rarely prevail over the immediate interest which one party may find in disregarding the rights of another, or the good of the whole.

The inference to which we are brought, is, that the causes of faction cannot be removed; and that relief is only to be sought in the means of controlling its *effects*.

If a faction consists of less than a majority, relief is supplied by the republican principle, which enables the majority to defeat its sinister views by regular vote: It may clog the administration, it may convulse the society; but it will be unable to execute and mask its violence under the forms of the Constitution. When a majority is included in a faction, the form of popular government on the other hand enables it to sacrifice to its ruling passion or interest, both the public good and the rights of other citizens. To secure the public good, and private rights, against the danger of such a faction, and at the same time to preserve the spirit and the form of popular government, is then the great object to which our enquiries are directed: Let me add that it is the great desideratum, by which alone this form of government can be rescued from the opprobrium under which it has so long labored, and be recommended to the esteem and adoption of mankind.

By what means is this object attainable? Evidently by one of two only. Either the existence of the same passion or interest in a majority at the same time, must be prevented; or the majority, having such co-existent passion or interest, must be rendered, by their number and local situation, unable to concert and carry into effect schemes of oppression. If the impulse and the opportunity be suffered to coincide, we well know that neither moral nor religious motives can be relied on as an adequate control. They are not found to be such on the injustice and violence of individuals, and lose their efficacy in proportion to the number combined together; that is, in proportion as their efficacy becomes needful.

From this view of the subject, it may be concluded, that a pure Democracy, by which I mean, a Society, consisting of a small number of citizens, who assemble and administer the Government in person, can admit of no cure for the mischiefs of faction. A common passion or interest will, in almost every case, be felt by a majority of the whole; a communication and concert results from the form of Government itself; and there is nothing to check the inducements to sacrifice the weaker party, or an obnoxious individual. Hence it is, that such Democracies have ever been spectacles of turbulence and contention; have ever been found incompatible with personal security, or the rights of property; and have in general been as short in their lives, as they have been violent in their deaths. Theoretic politicians, who have patronized this species of Government, have erroneously supposed, that by reducing mankind to a perfect equality in their political rights, they would, at the same time, be perfectly equalized and assimilated in their possessions, their opinions, and their passions.

A Republic, by which I mean a Government in which the scheme of representation takes place, opens a different prospect, and promises the cure for which we are seeking. Let us examine the points in which it varies from pure Democracy, and we shall comprehend both the nature of the cure, and the efficacy which it must derive from the Union.

The two great points of difference between a Democracy and a Republic are, first, the delegation of the Government, in the latter, to a small number of citizens elected by the rest: secondly, the greater number of citizens, and greater sphere of country, over which the latter may be extended.

The effect of the first difference is, on the one hand to refine and enlarge the public views, by passing them through the medium of a chosen body of citizens, whose wisdom may best discern the true interest of their country, and whose patriotism and love of justice, will be least likely to sacrifice it to temporary or partial considerations. Under such a regulation, it may well happen that the public voice pronounced by the representatives of the people, will be more consonant to the public good, than if pronounced by the people themselves convened for the purpose. On the other hand, the effect may be inverted. Men of factious tempers, of local prejudices, or of sinister designs, may by intrigue, by corruption or by other means, first obtain the suffrages, and then betray the interests of the people. The question resulting is, whether small or extensive Republics are most favorable to the election of proper guardians of the public weal: and it is clearly decided in favor of the latter by two obvious considerations.

In the first place it is to be remarked that however small the Republic may be, the Representatives must be raised to a certain number, in order to guard against the cabals of a few; and that however large it may be, they must be limited to a certain number, in order to guard against the confusion of a multitude. Hence the number of Representatives in the two cases, not being in proportion to that of the Constituents, and being proportionally greatest in the small Republic, it follows, that if the proportion of fit characters, be not less, in the large than in the small Republic, the former will present a greater option, and consequently a greater probability of a fit choice.

In the next place, as each Representative will be chosen by a greater number of citizens in the large than in the small Republic, it will be more difficult for unworthy candidates to practise with success the vicious arts, by which elections are too often carried; and the suffrages of the people being more free, will be more likely to centre on men who possess the most attractive merit, and the most diffusive and established characters.

It must be confessed, that in this, as in most other cases, there is a mean, on both sides of which inconveniencies will be found to lie. By enlarging too much the number of electors, you render the representative too little acquainted with all their local circumstances and lesser interests; and by reducing it too much, you render him unduly attached to these, and too little fit to comprehend and pursue great and national objects. The Federal Constitution forms a happy combination in this respect; the great and aggregate interests being referred to the national, the local and particular, to the state legislatures.

The other point of difference is, the greater number of citizens and extent of territory which may be brought within the compass of Republican, than of Democratic Government; and it is this circumstance principally which renders factious combinations less to be dreaded in the former, than in the latter. The smaller the society, the fewer probably will be the distinct parties and interests composing it; the fewer the distinct parties and interests, the more frequently will a majority be found of the same party; and the smaller the number of individuals composing a majority, and the smaller the compass within which they are placed, the more easily will they concert and execute their plans of oppression. Extend the sphere, and you take in a greater variety of parties and interests; you make it less probable that a majority of the whole will have a common motive to invade the rights of other citizens; or if such a common motive exists, it will be more difficult for all who feel it to discover their own strength, and to act in unison with each other. . . .

Hence it clearly appears, that the same advantage, which a Republic has over a Democracy, in controlling the effects of faction, is enjoyed by a large over a small Republic—is enjoyed by the Union over the States composing it. Does this advantage consist in the substitution of Representatives, whose enlightened views and virtuous sentiments render them superior to local prejudices, and to schemes of injustice? It will not be denied, that the Representation of the Union will be most likely to possess these requisite endowments. Does it consist in the greater security afforded by a greater variety of parties, against the event of any one party being able to outnumber and oppress the rest? In an equal degree does the encreased variety of parties, comprised within the Union, encrease this security? Does it, in fine, consist in the greater obstacles opposed to the concern and accomplishment of the secret wishes of an unjust and interested majority? Here, again, the extent of the Union gives it the most palpable advantage.

The influence of factious leaders may kindle a flame within their particular States, but will be unable to spread a general conflagration through the other States: a religious sect, may degenerate into a political faction in a part of the Confederacy; but the variety of sects dispersed over the entire face of it, must secure the national Councils against any danger from that source: a rage for paper money, for an abolition of debts, for an equal division of property, or for any other improper or wicked project, will be less apt to pervade the whole body of the Union, than a particular member of it; in the same proportion as such a malady is more likely to taint a particular county or district, than an entire State.

In the extent and proper structure of the Union, therefore, we behold a Republican remedy for the diseases most incident to Republican Government. And according to the degree of pleasure and pride, we feel in being Republicans, ought to be our zeal in cherishing the spirit, and supporting the character of Federalists.

Questions for Discussion

1. What is Madison's view of human nature? What factors led him to this conclusion?
2. According to Madison, what are the differences between a democracy and a
   republic? Would Madison's view on the subject be "popular" today?

 9.2

Lobbyists—Why the Bad Rap?

Jeffrey H. Birnbaum

Lobbying activity has a long history in the United States, protected by constitutional provisions that give citizens "the right to petition the government for a redress of grievances." At the dawn of the republic this right was often expressed
literally, as citizens signed and formally presented to elected representatives written petitions describing their problems. The petitioning process was all but forgotten shortly thereafter: Individuals quickly learned that traveling to Washington and
dealing directly with public officials was a much more effective way to influence
the new government on a range of concerns, from procuring jobs to policy. Today,
it is estimated that more than 80,000 lobbyists operate in Washington.

   In this selection, Jeffrey H. Birnbaum surveys the colorful history of lobbying in the nation's capital. He finds that many incidents of unethical, if not illegal, behavior by special-interest representatives in D.C. have contributed to
the unsavory stereotype of the Washington lobbyist. According to Birnbaum,
well-financed American business and manufacturing interests have long used
their resources to dictate public policy, their activities largely unregulated and
undisclosed.

Jeffrey H. Birnbaum is a senior correspondent for *Time* magazine. This selection is adapted
from his book *The Lobbyists* (Times Books, 1992).

Jeffrey H. Birnbaum. Reprinted from *The American Enterprise*, a Washington-based magazine of politics,
business, and culture.

Birnbaum believes that the relationship between lobbyists and public officials has changed in recent decades, "representing a complex symbiosis of lobbyists and politicians." Lobbyists still seek influence, and money is still important, but blatant bribery by those seeking favors is now uncommon. More common are attempts to influence legislators through devices such as campaign contributions. And often it is the legislators rather than the lobbyists who initiate contact in attempts to raise money for their re-election campaigns. Lobbying techniques have changed as well. Grassroots lobbying, which involves mobilizing a legislator's home constituents, has emerged as one of the most effective ways for special interests to influence public policy.

I n the past 10 years, the number of lobbyists in Washington has, by some estimates, more than doubled. This modern army of 80,000 uses techniques that are as old as the republic, but its forces wield influence with a precision and sophistication that is purely high tech. Right behind the commanders are divisions of specialists: economists, lawyers, direct-mail producers and telephone salespeople, public relations experts, pollsters, and even accountants, all marching to the time-honored First Amendment–guaranteed beat of petitioning the government for redress of grievances. What follows is a look at the history of lobbying, which lobbyists themselves concede has not always been commendable. It explains in short why lobbying has a bad rap.

Booze, Broads, and Bribes

Lobbying in the early days of the republic was not performed with a great deal of finesse. The first attempt at mass pressure on the U.S. government—during a meeting of the First Continental Congress in Philadelphia in 1783—featured fixed bayonets. Several hundred soldiers from the local garrison felt they were due extra compensation and threatened the assembled legislators with their rifles. The Congress disagreed with them but boldly adjourned to meet again to consider the aggrieved soldiers' requests—at a safe distance, in Princeton, New Jersey. Business interests of the time used more subtle lobbying tactics. After the Continental Congress concluded its meetings each day, hogsheads of wine and port flowed without restraint at sumptuous meals. Wealthy merchants picked up the check.

Blatant bribery was swiftly added to the lobbyists' repertoire. One of the new Congress's major debates was whether to fund the national debt and to assume the debts of the states. Some historians believe that Rep. John Vining of Delaware sold his deciding vote to the money changers who stood to profit most from the action. Rumor had it that the bribe was 1,000 English guineas, but Sen. William Maclay of Pennsylvania wrote in his journal that Vining's vote was probably purchased for a "tenth part of the sum."

The word "lobbyist" comes from Britain, where the journalists who stood in lobbies of the House of Commons waiting to interview newsmakers were so dubbed. It was first used in America in 1829 during Andrew Jackson's presidency when privilege seekers in New York's capital, Albany, were referred to as lobby-agents. Three years later, the term was abbreviated to "lobbyist" and has been heard frequently ever since, mostly as an expression of reproach.

President Jackson was the first of many American presidents to rail against lobbyists and their business patrons. He sought to deflate financier Nicholas Biddle's power by withdrawing federal deposits from his Second Bank of the United States. But Biddle was not without supporters, notably the illustrious Daniel Webster, who would go on to become secretary of state. The ardency of Webster's convictions on the issue was bolstered not so much by principle as by cash. On December 21, 1833, Webster, then senator from Massachusetts, wrote to Biddle: "If it is wished that my relation to the bank should be continued, it may be well to send me the usual retainers." After an especially eloquent speech by Webster, Biddle paid him $10,000. Webster received in total $32,000 in what would be seen as bribes today but was then considered business as usual.

Lobbying flourished as America grew. Washington was swarming with so many big-business lobbyists by 1852 that future president James Buchanan wrote to his friend, future president Franklin Pierce, that "the host of contractors, speculators, stockjobbers, and lobby members which haunt the halls of Congress . . . are sufficient to alarm every friend of this country. Their progress must be arrested." The influence of business was so strong that at the close of one congressional session, Sen. J. S. Morrill sarcastically moved to appoint a committee to inquire if the president of the Pennsylvania Railroad, skulking in the outer lobby, wanted Congress to consider any further legislation before adjournment.

One of the most heavy-handed corporate lobbyists at the time was Samuel Colt, the famous gun manufacturer. Colt paid a "contingent fee" of $10,000 to one congressman and probably many others to refrain from attacking a patent-extension bill that would have helped his company's sales. To supplement the effort, Colt's high-living lobbyist, Alexander Hay, distributed beautifully decorated revolvers to lawmakers. Other more attractive gratuities were also dispensed: to wit, three young women known as Spiritualists, who, according to one account, were very active in "moving with the members" of Congress on Colt's behalf. Other women of less spiritual natures called "chicks" were also available upon request.

Washington was flooded with even more lobbyists in the wake of the financial panic of 1857. "Everywhere," wrote historian Roy Franklin Nichols, "there was importunity." The most underhanded lobbying battle raged between railroad and steamship companies as lobbyists for each side fought bitterly to reduce government subsidies to the other. Commodore Cornelius Vanderbilt himself led the steamship companies' campaign, often from the gaming tables of a night spot called Pendleton's Gambling House. Hapless lawmakers would fall into debt there and be forced to surrender their votes under threat of exposure or demand for payment. Other times, lawmakers would be allowed to win—as long as they agreed to vote the right way.

The 1850s' most powerful lobbyist was an imposing man named Thurlow Weed. His diverse background included working as a printer and newspaper editor, crusading against the perfidy of corporate power. But for the price of $5,000, Weed switched allegiances and began to lobby for lower duties on wool for the Bay State Mills of Lawrence, Massachusetts. His predecessor had come to Washington armed with facts and figures and was laughed out of town: Weed came armed with cold cash and stayed for years. Weed also has the distinction of being the first lobbyist to hire a journalist in a lobbying campaign, David M. Stone of New York's *Journal of Commerce*.

The Court Steps In

Washington got a new "King of the Lobby," Samuel Ward, after the Civil War. He reigned for 15 years as the undisputed master of dinner-table deceit. "The way to a man's 'Aye' is through his stomach," he said. Ward's pedigree was impeccable: he was the great-great-grandson of Richard Ward, a colonial governor; the great-grandson of Samuel Ward, one of the framers of the Constitution, and the great nephew of General Francis Marion, the famous "Swamp Fox" of the Revolutionary War. His father headed the New York banking firm of Prime, Ward and King, and his sister, Julia Ward Howe, wrote "The Battle Hymn of the Republic."

Washington suited Ward's penchant for living well, and he quickly proved he could charm the natives for profit. With his balding pate, sweeping mustache, and diamond-studded shirts, he was a striking figure, hosting dinners and breakfasts of ham boiled in champagne and seasoned with wisps of newly mown hay.

Ward's clients ran the gamut. He was hired for $12,000 plus dinner expenses by Hugh McCulloch, an Indiana banker who later became President Lincoln's treasury secretary, to "court, woo, and charm congressmen, especially Democrats prone to oppose the war." He was also associated with Joe Morrissey, the lottery boss. It seemed incongruous, but Morrissey retained Ward to promote a bill that would impose a tax on lotteries. Morrissey believed that he could afford the levy but that it would drive his less prosperous rivals out of business.

Ward could be quite conniving, despite his elegant manners. He once wrote to his friend, Henry Wadsworth Longfellow: "When I see you again I will tell you how a client, eager to prevent the arrival at a committee of a certain member before it should adjourn, offered me $5,000 to accomplish this purpose, which I did, by having [the congressman's] boots mislaid while I smoked a cigar and condoled with him until they could be found at 11:45. I had the satisfaction of a good laugh [and] a good fee in my pocket."

When a congressional committee questioned Ward about his activities, he deflected their inquiries with erudition and humor. "Talleyrand says that diplomacy is assisted by good dinners," he responded. "At good dinners people do not talk shop, but they give people a right, perhaps, to ask a gentleman a civil question and get a civil answer." Ward insisted that he refused to take on issues that were meritless, but he also conceded that "the profession of lobbying is not commendable," a characterization still echoing today.

Under the weak presidencies that followed the Civil War, lobbying reached new heights—and depths. Two of the most jarring events were the Crédit Mobilier scandal in 1872, in which millions of federal dollars earmarked for a transcontinental railroad were diverted into the pockets of representatives, senators, and even a future president, James Garfield; and Jay Gould and Jim Fisk's attempt to corner the gold market in 1869. This latter effort, which ultimately failed, implicated the president himself.

The Supreme Court heard a rare case in 1875 involving a lobbyist, *Trist* v. *Child*, during Ulysses Grant's troubled presidency. The High Court refused to uphold the lobbyist's claim for payment after he had fulfilled his part of a contract to influence legislation. The ruling denied the payment on the ground that such an undertaking was contrary to "sound policy and good morals." The opinion continued: "If any of the great corporations of the country were to hire adventurers who make market of themselves in this way, to propose passage of a general law with a view to promotion of their private interests, the moral sense of every right-minded man would instinctively denounce the employers and employed as steeped in corruption and employment as infamous. If the instances were numerous, open, and tolerated they would be regarded as a measure of decay of public morals and degeneracy of the time. No prophetic spirit would be needed to foretell the consequences near at hand." Notably absent from the learned decision was the simple, telling observation that lobbyists and lobbying had become so enmeshed in the fabric of the government that an aggrieved lobbyist did not hesitate to go to the highest court in the land for redress.

That same year, lobbying moved further into the modern age with the first recorded instance of grass-roots lobbying. Instead of simply relying on individual adventurers in Washington, business interests began to reach back to the states and districts of congressmen for constituents to support their causes. The bellowing of home-state voices became so loud that Rep. George Frisbie Hoar forced a resolution through his Judiciary Committee requiring for the first time public disclosure by lobbyists about their activities. Hoar said he offered the resolution because four people from different parts of the country representing an important corporation had accosted and tried to sway four of his committee members. The resolution went nowhere, but grass-roots lobbying became a standard tool of the lobbyists' trade.

The first president to seriously challenge the business lobby was Woodrow Wilson, who had prominently featured its villainy in his 1912 campaign. Wilson had studied lobbyists' impact in Washington as a Princeton professor and concluded that it was dangerous. In a scholarly paper, he noted that special interests could not buy an entire legislature but could purchase individual committees, which was where the real power resided anyway. Such observations became grist for his presidential campaign speeches: "The masters of the government of the United States are the combined capitalists and manufacturers. It is written over every intimate page of the records of Congress; it is written all through the history of conferences at the White House. . . . The government of the United States is a foster child of the special interests. It is not allowed to have a will of its own."

Wilson told the lobbyists to get out of town when he took office in 1913, and for the most part, they did. A few diehards stayed, but according to Cordell Hull, they "became less pestiferous when they discovered just what our policy was and saw they could not influence us."

A story printed in the *New York World* by Martin M. Mulhall, the top lobbyist for the National Association of Manufacturers, soon demonstrated exactly why Wilson was so eager to banish lobbyists. Mulhall held no public title, but, as a powerful lobbyist, he had his own private office in the Capitol. He wrote that he paid the chief page of the House $50 a month and maintained a close association with Rep. John Dwight, the House minority leader, and with Rep. James T. McDermott, a Democrat from Chicago, whom he paid $1,500 to $2,000. These well-placed lawmakers gave him advance information about legislation and helped him dictate appointments to key committees.

Finis J. Garrett, a Tennessee Democrat and the House's minority leader, chaired a four-month inquiry into Mulhall's revelations that eventually censured McDermott. Garrett later proposed legislation that would require lobbyists to register with the clerk of the House and to disclose their employers. The bill passed the House but died in the Senate, not to become law, despite many intervening scandals, for another 33 years.

Lobbyists, scandals, and the harried congressional committees investigating them had all roared back by the 1920s. The Caraway Committee, launched in 1927 by Sen. Thaddeus Caraway (D-Ark.), rocked the city with the contention that most lobbying was simply fraud. Fully 90 percent of the nearly 400 lobbying groups listed in the Washington telephone directory were "fakes" whose primary aim was not to affect legislation but to bilk clients, said the committee.

At the end of the investigation, Caraway recommended yet another bill to register lobbyists. He wanted lobbying defined as "any effort in influencing Congress upon any matter coming before it, whether it be by distributing literature, appearing before committees of Congress, or seeking to interview members of either the House or Senate" and a lobbyist as "one who shall engage, for pay, to attempt to influence legislation or to prevent legislation by the national Congress." The Senate passed the stringent measure without dissent, but it died in the House because of lobbyists' pressure.

Former government and party officials began running on the cash-paved track of lobbying in the late 1920s and 1930s, setting a precedent that continues today. Women started to become full-fledged lobbyists during this time period, too. Mabel Walker Williebrandt, once assistant attorney general in charge of enforcing Prohibition laws, traded in her experience for bananas, oranges, apples, and cherries as counsel to Fruit Industries, Ltd. Quite simply, lobbying power resided with people who had personal connections to government.

According to journalist and lobbying historian Kenneth Crawford: "In the Hoover days, one who wanted to put on the fix saw James Francis Burke, secretary of the Republican National Committee; C. Bascom Slemp, who had been secretary to President Coolidge; or Edward Everett Gann, husband of the redoubtable social warrior, Dolly Gann, sister of Vice President Charles Curtis. Early in the Roosevelt administration, the men to get things done were Bruce Kremer, a friend of the attorney general; Robert Jackson of New Hampshire, long-time treasurer of the Democratic National Committee; Arthur Mullen, National Committeeman from Nebraska; and Joe Davies, later ambassador to Russia and Belgium."

Senator Hugo L. Black (D-Ala.) who was later a Supreme Court justice, introduced a bill to register and regulate lobbyists after a particularly egregious display of lobbying power in a debate over regulation of public utilities. This time, it passed both chambers of Congress—but it died in a House-Senate conference committee, thanks to the efforts of hundreds of lobbyists. Lobbyists didn't escape unscathed, however, and for the first time, utility lobbyists were required to make limited disclosure of their activities under terms of the final Public Utilities Holding Company Act.

Congress finally got around to regulating the business of lobbying as a whole in the 1930s and 1940s, starting with the vast and influential shipping industry. The Merchant Marine Act of 1936 required shipping agents to file disclosures with the Commerce Department before working to influence marine legislation or administrative decisions. Two years later, amid reports of Fascist and Nazi propaganda circulating in the United States, the Foreign Agents Registration Act was passed, requiring anyone who represented a foreign government or individual to register with the Justice Department.

In 1946, Congress passed the Federal Regulation of Lobbying Act as part of the Congressional Reorganization Act, requiring all lobbyists to register in Congress and report the amount and sources of their income from lobbying. There was no attempt to limit lobbying; that would violate the First Amendment's right to petition the government. It defined a lobbyist as a person or organization whose job is to influence the passage or defeat of legislation and who receives money for that purpose.

Like all previous lobbying strictures, the law was ignored at first. In 1950, spurred by complaints from President Harry Truman, a committee headed by Rep. Frank M. Buchanan, Democrat from Pennsylvania, investigated a wide range of lobbying abuses. The Congress of the time, the president complained, was "the most thoroughly surrounded . . . with lobbies in the whole history of this great country of ours. . . . There were more lobbyists in Washington, there was more money spent by lobbyists in Washington, than ever before." The committee requested detailed information about lobbying from 200 corporations, labor unions, and farm groups. The 152 organizations that replied said they had spent $32 million on lobbying from January 1, 1948, through May 31, 1950, and fewer than 50 of them had disclosed a single dime of it as required by the new lobbying law.

The Buchanan report also noted that lobbying had changed over the years. In effect, it said, lobbying had become less blatant and, in this view, more insidious. In 1948, there were 1,016 registered lobbyists. Two years later, the number had more than doubled to 2,047. Buchanan said the figures "reflect a significant picture of tremendous amounts of time and money being expended by pressure groups and pressure interests through the country in seeking to influence actions by Congress."

In the 1870s and 1880s, he continued, "lobbying meant direct, individual solicitation of legislators, with a strong presumption of corruption attached . . . [but] modern pressure on legislative bodies is rarely corrupt. . . . It is increasingly indirect, and [it is] largely the product of group rather than individual effort. . . . The printed word is much more extensively used by organizations as a means of pursuing legislative aims than personal contact with legislators by individual lobbyists."

The Buchanan Committee recommended strengthening the lobbying law, but no action was taken. Instead, in 1954, the Supreme Court weakened the already porous lobbying statute by exempting many types of lobbyists from the law's disclosure requirements. The Court decided that only those who solicited and collected money specifically with lobbying in mind need comply and that organizations need register only if they had lobbying as their "principal purpose" when they collected the funds. What's more, only direct contacts with legislators were considered lobbying; indirect pressure, such as the growing practice of grass-roots lobbying, was excluded.

A Complex Relationship

In the late 1940s and 1950s, it was "often hard to tell where the legislator [left] off and the lobbyist begins," according to lobbying expert James Deakin. Entire pieces of legislation were drafted by lobbyists. According to Rep. Arthur Klein, a Democratic member of the House Labor Committee, the primary author of the Taft-Hartley Act of 1947,* which restricted labor union activities, was neither Taft nor Hartley but William G. Ingles, a $24,000-a-year lawyer and highly

---

*The Taft-Hartley Act of 1947 was technically a series of amendments to the National Labor Relations (Wagner) Act of 1935, which many members of the business community felt was too pro-union. A major provision of the Taft-Hartley Act allowed states to pass right-to-work laws, which in effect banned "closed shop" requirements (which had made it mandatory for employers to hire only members of unions). Taft-Hartley also delineated various unfair labor practices by unions (the 1935 act only listed unfair labor practices by employers).

labor-dependent lobbyist for Allis-Chalmers, Fruehauf Trailer, J. I. Case, and Inland Steel.

The unprecedented expansion of government after the war was accompanied by a rapid growth in the number of lobbyists. Sensing their advantage, lawmakers began to play one off against the other. "Everything in Washington is a two-way street," Deakin wrote: "The legislators use the lobbyists as much as the lobbyists use them. A cocktail party—like an office conversation—may give the congressman information he needs. Or it may give him something he needs even more: cash. The Washington party has become an increasingly utilitarian institution. Invited to a reception, the lobbyist may find that he is giving more than he gets. The pressure boy is pressured. As he leaves, pleasantly oiled, his attention is directed to a hat in which he is expected to drop $50 or $100 for the congressman's campaign. . . . Washington is a very practical town, and money and votes mean more than liquor. In the final analysis, this is why bribes, blondes, and booze don't rank as high as they once did in the lobbyist's scheme of things. They just aren't as important to the congressman (to his political survival, which is his first law) as votes and money with which to get votes. The legislator may accept the lobbyist's entertainment, and gladly, but he is far more likely to do what the lobbyist wants if votes are involved."

The 1940s and 1950s were also the heyday of the brilliant, brash Thomas "the Cork" Corcoran, former law clerk to Oliver Wendell Holmes and President Franklin Roosevelt's chief legislative operative. Corcoran helped write much of the New Deal legislation, including the Securities and Exchange Act. He also supplied Roosevelt with the phrase, "This generation has a rendezvous with destiny." He made enemies when he tried to help Roosevelt pack the Supreme Court,* and he was blocked from the job he most coveted, becoming the U.S. solicitor general. He became instead a high-priced lobbyist for corporate interests, cementing what has since become a well-established route from White House adviser to Washington lobbyist.

Top executives of corporations were increasingly enlisted as lobbyists during the 1960s, but always under the strict guidance of their Washington consultants. Lobbying had come far since the early days of the republic, representing a complex symbiosis of lobbyists and politicians—but traditional, big-money lobbyists still wooed, and occasionally brought crashing down, lawmakers. The most famous victim of lawmakers' penchant for fancy living was Robert G. (Bobby) Baker, whose route from Pickens, South Carolina, to riches on the banks of the Potomac River was eased by lobbyists. Baker was secretary to the Democratic majority in the Senate. With a salary of $19,600 a year, he managed to accumulate assets of $2,166,886 in less than nine years.

---

*President Franklin Roosevelt, frustrated with the Supreme Court's reluctance to uphold major pieces of New Deal legislation, proposed a plan in 1937 to expand the size of the Court by appointing a new member for each sitting justice who had reached seventy years of age. If the plan had been approved, Roosevelt could have immediately appointed six justices, making the Court a fifteen-member body. Congress and the nation's press were strongly against the measure, viewing it as a thinly veiled attempt to "pack" the Court to create a liberal majority.

Improper contacts with lobbyists also helped bring down Richard M. Nixon's presidency. Investigations revealed that a number of corporations violated the federal law that prohibits them from contributing to the campaigns of federal office seekers. Some of those funds found their way into the hands of the Republican operatives who broke into Democratic Party headquarters in Washington's Watergate complex on June 17, 1972.

Foreign interests have increasingly hired Washington lobbyists in recent years. This foreign money led to the 1976 Koreagate scandal. The *Washington Post* reported that South Korean agents gave between $500,000 and $1 million a year in cash and gifts to members of Congress to help maintain a "favorable legislative climate" for South Korea. The Koreans, led by businessman and socialite Tongsun Park, sought to bribe U.S. officials and buy influence among journalists, funneling illegal gifts to as many as 115 lawmakers. In 1978, the House voted to reprimand three California Democrats for their part in the scandal, and Richard T. Hanna, a former California congressman, was sentenced to prison.

Subtlety Wields Influence

During the 1980s, lobbying was rarely so heavyhanded, yet it became astonishingly effective. Communications techniques reached new heights of sophistication and complexity, and with them lobbyists were able to mobilize thousands of ordinary citizens for the first time. When Congress was considering increasing milk price supports in 1980, for example, lawmakers heard not just from lobbyists for the dairy farmers who wanted the subsidy hiked but also from thousands of worried managers of fast-food restaurants spurred on by an "action alert" newsletter distributed by the fast-food industry's trade association.

The break-up of American Telephone & Telegraph spurred one of the decade's biggest grass-roots lobbying efforts. Legislators heard from thousands of telephone company managers and employees; not only had AT&T put out an action alert but so had the Communications Workers of America, 90 percent of whose members were AT&T employees. At the same time, a coalition of AT&T competitors stirred up its own pressure in favor of the break-up, mailing 70,000 envelopes bearing an imitation of the Bell System logo and this attention-grabbing warning: "Notice of Telephone Rate Increase Enclosed." The letter inside warned the reader that unless the recipient helped lobby in favor of the break-up, telephone rates would double.

Individual corporations also began using their employees and suppliers as lobbyists, a method previously used with great success by labor unions. The National Association of Home Builders—the 125,000-member trade association of the housing industry—developed one of the most comprehensive electoral strategies ever devised in the corporate world. Its 250-page manual, "Blueprint for Victory: Homebuilder's Political Offensive," outlined all aspects of what it called its G. I.

(Get Involved) Program. The manual detailed telephone or house-to-house can-vassing techniques, how to organize a "Victory Caravan" to transport campaign volunteers, and many other strategies previously reserved for political movements.

The Old and the New

In the postwar era, presidents continued to bash lobbyists. Harry Truman, whose presidency has been much discussed this campaign year, used these words: "There are a great many organizations with lots of money who maintain lobby-ists in Washington. I'd say 15 million people in the United States are repre-sented by lobbyists," he said. "The other 150 million have only one man who is elected at large to represent them—that is the president of the United States."

John F. Kennedy also attacked lobbyists, telling an audience at Ohio's Wit-tenberg College in 1960, "The consumer is the only man in our economy with-out a high-powered lobbyist in Washington. I intend to be that lobbyist." Yet throughout his presidency, he maintained a close friendship with one of Wash-ington's prominent lawyer-lobbyists, Clark Clifford, remarking jovially at one point that Clifford was not like other consultants who wanted rewards for their assistance to him. "You don't hear Clark clamoring," Kennedy said. "All he asked in return was that we advertise his law firm on the back of the one-dollar bills." That lighthearted quip told much about the power of lobbyists and the personal relationships that nurture the business.

Lobbyists remain an integral part of the Washington establishment, but the scandals of the past continue to stigmatize their standing. One lobbyist cap-tured the feeling: "My mother has never introduced me as 'my son, the lobby-ist.' My son, the Washington representative, maybe, or the legislative consultant. But never as the lobbyist. I can't say I blame her." This explains a paradox of Washington life. While lobbyists are highly compensated and influ-ential, they occupy a kind of underclass in the nation's capital. They are fre-quently left standing in hallways and reception areas for hours at a time. Theirs are the first appointments canceled or postponed when legislators are pressed by other business calls. Their activity suffuses the culture of the city, but their status suffers from a long history of lobbying scandals.

Questions for Discussion

1. How has Washington lobbying changed since the early days of the republic? What forces have brought about such changes? Is the negative image of lob-byists still warranted?
2. Why is it so difficult to regulate lobbying activity?

9.3

Associations Without Members

Theda Skocpol

Over the past half century, the interest group universe has experienced profound change. The number of organized interests in American politics has grown tremendously, as virtually every interest imaginable is now represented by a formally organized group. New voices have been heard, and the expansion of representation has had many positive consequences, including the expansion of rights for various categories of citizens.

In this selection, Theda Skocpol surveys the changes that have taken place in the style and substance of civic and association activities since the 1950s, and she speculates as to their consequences for a democratic polity. Particularly troublesome to Skocpol is the decline of "locally rooted and nationally active membership associations." Such groups have been replaced by "organizations without members," leadership-dominated advocacy groups with little democratic input. In Skocpol's view, the new groups are unable to mobilize mass support as well as the older membership organizations do, letting elites dominate policy-making and frustrating meaningful political reform.

I n just a third of a century, Americans have dramatically changed their style of civic and political association. A civic world once centered in locally rooted and nationally active membership associations is a relic. Today, Americans volunteer for causes and projects, but only rarely as ongoing members. They send checks to service and advocacy groups run by professionals, often funded by foundations or professional fundraisers. Prime-time airways echo with debates among their spokespersons: the National Abortion Rights Action League debates the National Right to Life Committee; the Concord Coalition takes on the American Association of Retired Persons; and the Environmental Defense Fund counters business groups. Entertained or bemused, disengaged viewers watch as polarized advocates debate.

Theda Skocpol is professor of political science at Harvard University.

"Associations Without Members" by Theda Skocpol. Reprinted with permission from *The American Prospect*, Volume 10, Number 45 (July 1, 1999): 66–73. The American Prospect, 11 Beacon Street, Suite 1120, Boston, MA 02108.

The largest membership groups of the 1950s were old-line and well-established, with founding dates ranging from 1733 for the Masons to 1939 for the Woman's Division of Christian Service (a Methodist women's association formed from "missionary" societies with nineteenth-century roots). Like most large membership associations throughout American history, most 1950s associations recruited members across class lines. They held regular local meetings and convened periodic assemblies of elected leaders and delegates at the state, regional, or national levels. Engaged in multiple rather than narrowly specialized pursuits, many associations combined social or ritual activities with community service, mutual aid, and involvement in national affairs. Patriotism was a leitmotif; during and after World War II, a passionate and victorious national endeavor, these associations sharply expanded their memberships and renewed the vigor of their local and national activities.

To be sure, very large associations were not the only membership federations that mattered in postwar America. Also prominent were somewhat smaller, elite-dominated civic groups—including male service groups like Rotary, Lions, and Kiwanis, and longstanding female groups like the American Association of University Women and the League of Women Voters. Dozens of ethnically based fraternal and cultural associations flourished, as did African-American fraternal groups like the Prince Hall Masons and the Improved Benevolent and Protective Order of Elks of the World.

For many membership federations, this was a golden era of national as well as community impact. Popularly rooted membership federations rivaled professional and business associations for influence in policy debates. The AFL-CIO was in the thick of struggles about economic and social policies; the American Legion and the Veterans of Foreign Wars advanced veterans' programs; the American Farm Bureau Federation (AFBF) joined other farmers' associations to influence national and state agricultural policies; and the National Congress of Parents and Teachers (PTA) and the General Federation of Women's Clubs were influential on educational, health, and family issues. The results could be decisive, as exemplified by the pivotal role of the American Legion in drafting and lobbying for the GI Bill of 1944.

Then, suddenly, old-line membership federations seemed passé. Upheavals shook America during "the long 1960s," stretching from the mid-1950s through the mid-1970s. The southern Civil Rights movement challenged white racial domination and spurred legislation to enforce legal equality and voting rights for African Americans. Inspired by Civil Rights achievements, additional "rights" movements exploded, promoting equality for women, dignity for homosexuals, the unionization of farm workers, and the mobilization of other nonwhite ethnic minorities. Movements arose to oppose U.S. involvement in the war in Vietnam, champion a new environmentalism, and further other public causes. At the forefront of these groundswells were younger Americans, especially from the growing ranks of college students and university graduates.

The great social movements of the long 1960s were propelled by combinations of grassroots protest, activist radicalism, and professionally led efforts to lobby government and educate the public. Some older membership associations ended up participating and expanding their bases of support, yet the groups that sparked movements were more agile and flexibly structured than pre-existing membership federations.

The upheavals of the 1960s could have left behind a reconfigured civic world, in which some old-line membership associations had declined but others had reoriented and reenergized themselves. Within each great social movement, memberships could have consolidated and groups coalesced into new omnibus federations able to link the grass roots to state, regional, and national leaderships, allowing longstanding American civic traditions to continue in new ways.

But this is not what happened. Instead, the 1960s, 1970s, and 1980s brought extraordinary organizational proliferation and professionalization. At the national level alone, the *Encyclopedia of Associations* listed approximately 6,500 associations in 1958. This total grew by 1990 to almost 23,000. Within the expanding group universe, moreover, new kinds of associations came to the fore: relatively centralized and professionally led organizations focused on policy lobbying and public education.

Another wave of the advocacy explosion involved "public interest" or "citizens" groups seeking to shape public opinion and influence legislation. Citizens' advocacy groups espouse "causes" ranging from environmental protection (for example, the Sierra Club and the Environmental Defense Fund), to the well-being of poor children (the Children's Defense Fund), to reforming politics (Common Cause) and cutting public entitlements (the Concord Coalition).

The Fortunes of Membership Associations

As the associational explosions of 1960 to 1990 took off, America's once large and confident membership federations were not only bypassed in national politics; they also dwindled as locally rooted participant groups. To be sure, some membership associations have been founded or expanded in recent decades. By far the largest is the American Association of Retired Persons (AARP), which now boasts more than 33 million adherents, about one-half of all Americans aged 50 or older. But AARP is not a democratically controlled organization. Launched in 1958 with backing from a teachers' retirement group and an insurance company, the AARP grew rapidly in the 1970s and 1980s by offering commercial discounts to members and establishing a Washington headquarters to monitor and lobby about federal legislation affecting seniors. The AARP has a legislative and policy staff of 165 people, 28 registered lobbyists, and more than 1,200 staff members in the field. After recent efforts to expand its regional and local infrastructure, the AARP involves about 5 to 10 percent of its members in (undemocratic) membership chapters. But for the most part, the AARP national office—covering an entire city block with its own zip code—deals with masses of individual adherents through the mail.

Four additional recently expanded membership associations use modern mass recruitment methods, yet are also rooted in local and state units. Interestingly, these groups are heavily involved in partisan electoral politics. Two recently launched groups are the National Right to Life Committee (founded in 1973) and the Christian Coalition (founded in 1989). They bridge from church congregations, through which they recruit members and activists, to the conservative wing of the Republican Party, through which they exercise political influence. Two old-line membership federations—the National Education Association (founded in 1857) and the National Rifle Association (founded in 1871)—experienced explosive growth after reorienting themselves to take part in partisan politics. The NRA expanded in the 1970s, when right-wing activists opposed to gun control changed what had traditionally been a network of marksmen's clubs into a conservative, Republican-leaning advocacy group fiercely opposed to gun control legislation. During the same period, the NEA burgeoned from a relatively elitist association of public educators into a quasi-union for public school teachers and a stalwart in local, state, and national Democratic Party politics.

Although they fall short of enrolling 1 percent of the adult population, some additional chapter-based membership associations were fueled by the social movements of the 1960s and 1970s. From 1960 to 1990, the Sierra Club (originally created in 1892) ballooned from some 15,000 members to 565,000 members meeting in 378 "local groups." And the National Audubon Society (founded in 1905) went from 30,000 members and 330 chapters in 1958 to about 600,000 members and more than 500 chapters in the 1990s. The National Organization for Women (NOW) reached 1,122 members and 14 chapters within a year of its founding in 1966, and spread across all 50 states with some 125,000 members meeting in 700 chapters by 1978. But notice that these "1960s" movement associations do not match the organizational scope of old-line membership federations. At its post–World War II high point in 1955, for example, the General Federation of Women's Clubs boasted more than 826,000 members meeting in 15,168 local clubs, themselves divided into representative networks within each of the 50 states plus the District of Columbia. By contrast, at its high point in 1993, NOW reported some 280,000 members and 800 chapters, with no intermediate tier of representative governance between the national center and local chapters. These membership associations certainly matter, but mainly as counterexamples to dominant associational trends—of organizations without members.

After nearly a century of civic life rooted in nation-spanning membership federations, why was America's associational universe so transformed? A variety of factors have contributed, including racial and gender change; shifts in the political opportunity structure; new techniques and models for building organizations; and recent transformations in U.S. class relations. Taken together, I suggest, these account for civic America's abrupt and momentous transition from membership to advocacy.

Society Decompartmentalized

Until recent times, most American membership associations enrolled business and professional people together with white-collar folks, farmers, and craft or industrial workers. There was a degree of fellowship across class lines—yet at the price of other kinds of exclusions. With only a few exceptions, old-line associations enrolled either men or women, not both together (although male-only fraternal and veterans' groups often had ties to ladies' auxiliaries). Racial separation was also the rule. Although African Americans did manage to create and greatly expand fraternal associations of their own, they unquestionably resented exclusion by the parallel white fraternals.

Given the pervasiveness of gender and racial separation in classic civic America, established voluntary associations were bound to be shaken after the 1950s. Moreover, changing gender roles and identities blended with other changing values to undercut not just membership appeals but long-standing routes to associational leadership. For example, values of patriotism, brotherhood, and sacrifice had been celebrated by all fraternal groups. During and after each war, the Masons, Knights of Pythias, Elks, Knights of Columbus, Moose, Eagles, and scores of other fraternal groups celebrated and memorialized the contributions of their soldier-members. So did women's auxiliaries, not to mention men's service clubs and trade union "brotherhoods." But "manly" ideals of military service faded after the early 1960s as America's bitter experiences during the war in Vietnam disrupted the intergenerational continuity of male identification with martial brotherliness.

In the past third of a century, female civic leadership has changed as much or more than male leadership. Historically, U.S. women's associations—ranging from female auxiliaries of male groups to independent groups like the General Federation of Women's Clubs, the PTA, and church-connected associations— benefited from the activism of educated wives and mothers. Although a tiny fraction of all U.S. females, higher-educated women were a surprisingly substantial and widespread presence—because the United States was a pioneer in the schooling of girls and the higher education of women. By 1880, some 40,000 American women constituted a third of all students in U.S. institutions of higher learning; women's share rose to nearly half at the early twentieth-century peak in 1920, when some 283,000 women were enrolled in institutions of higher learning. Many higher-educated women of the late 1800s and early 1900s married immediately and stayed out of the paid labor force. Others taught for a time in primary and secondary schools, then got married and stopped teaching (either voluntarily or because school systems would not employ married women). Former teachers accumulated in every community. With skills to make connections within and across communities—and some time on their hands as their children grew older—former teachers and other educated women became mainstays of classic U.S. voluntary life.

Of course, more American women than ever before are now college-educated. But contemporary educated women face new opportunities and constraints. Paid work and family responsibilities are no longer separate spheres, and the occupational structure is less sex-segregated at all levels. Today, even married women with children are very likely to be employed, at least part-time. Despite new time pressures, educated and employed women have certainly not dropped out of civic life. Women employed part-time are more likely to be members of groups or volunteers than housewives; and fully employed women are often drawn into associations or civic projects through work. Yet styles of civic involvement have changed—much to the disadvantage of broad-gauged associations trying to hold regular meetings.

The Lure of Washington, D.C.

The centralization of political change in Washington, D.C. also affected the associational universe. Consider the odyssey of civil rights lawyer Marian Wright Edelman. Fresh from grassroots struggles in Mississippi, she arrived in Washington, D.C. in the late 1960s to lobby for Mississippi's Head Start program. She soon realized that arguing on behalf of children might be the best way to influence legislation and sway public sympathy in favor of the poor, including African Americans. So between 1968 and 1973 Edelman obtained funding from major foundations and developed a new advocacy and policy research association, the Children's Defense Fund (CDF). With a skillful staff, a small national network of individual supporters, ties to social service agencies and foundations, and excellent relationships with the national media, the CDF has been a determined proponent of federal antipoverty programs ever since. The CDF has also worked with Democrats and other liberal advocacy groups to expand such efforts; and during periods of conservative Republican ascendancy, the CDF has been a fierce (if not always successful) defender of federal social programs.

Activists, in short, have gone where the action is. In this same period, congressional committees and their staffs subdivided and multiplied. During the later 1970s and 1980s, the process of group formation became self-reinforcing—not only because groups arose to counter other groups, but also because groups begot more groups. Because businesses and citizens use advocacy groups to influence government outside of parties and between elections, it is not surprising that the contemporary group explosion coincides with waning voter loyalty to the two major political parties. As late as the 1950s, U.S. political parties were networks of local and state organizations through which party officials often brokered nominations, cooperated with locally rooted membership associations, and sometimes directly mobilized voters. The party structure and the associational structure were mutually reinforcing.

Then, demographic shifts, reapportionment struggles, and the social upheavals of the 1960s disrupted old party organizations; and changes in party rules led to nomination elections that favored activists and candidate-centered efforts over backroom brokering by party insiders. Such "reforms" were meant to enhance grassroots participation, but in practice have furthered oligarchical ways of running elections. No longer the preserve of party organizations, U.S. campaigns are now managed by coteries of media consultants, pollsters, direct mail specialists, and—above all—fundraisers. In this revamped electoral arena, advocacy groups have much to offer, hoping to get access to elected officials in return for helping candidates. In low-turnout battles to win party nominations, even groups with modest mail memberships may be able to field enough (paid or unpaid) activists to make a difference. At all stages of the electoral process, advocacy groups with or without members can provide endorsements that may be useful in media or direct mail efforts. And PACs pushing business interests or public interest causes can help candidates raise the huge amounts of money they need to compete.

A New Model of Association-Building

Classic American association-builders took it for granted that the best way to gain national influence, moral or political, was to knit together national, state, and local groups that met regularly and engaged in a degree of representative governance. Leaders who desired to speak on behalf of masses of Americans found it natural to proceed by recruiting self-renewing mass memberships and spreading a network of interactive groups. After the start-up phase, associational budgets usually depended heavily on membership dues and on sales of newsletters or supplies to members and local groups. Supporters had to be continuously recruited through social networks and person-to-person contacts. And if leverage over government was desired, an association had to be able to influence legislators, citizens, and newspapers across many districts. For all of these reasons, classic civic entrepreneurs with national ambitions moved quickly to recruit activists and members in every state and across as many towns and cities as possible within each state.

Today, nationally ambitious civic entrepreneurs proceed in quite different ways. When Marian Wright Edelman launched a new advocacy and research group to lobby for the needs of children and the poor, she turned to private foundations for funding and then recruited an expert staff of researchers and lobbyists. In the early 1970s, when John Gardner launched Common Cause as a "national citizens lobby" demanding governmental reforms, he arranged for start-up contributions from several wealthy friends, contacted reporters in the national media, and purchased mailing lists to solicit masses of members giving modest monetary contributions. Patron grants, direct mail techniques, and the capacity to convey images and messages through the mass media have changed the realities of organization building and maintenance.

The very model of civic effectiveness has been up-ended since the 1960s. No longer do civic entrepreneurs think of constructing vast federations and recruiting interactive citizen-members. When a new cause (or tactic) arises, activists envisage opening a national office and managing association-building as well as national projects from the center. Even a group aiming to speak for large numbers of Americans does not absolutely need members. And if mass adherents are recruited through the mail, why hold meetings? From a managerial point of view, interactions with groups of members may be downright inefficient. In the old-time membership federations, annual elections of leaders and a modicum of representative governance went hand in hand with membership dues and interactive meetings. But for the professional executives of today's advocacy organizations, direct mail members can be more appealing because, as Kenneth Godwin and Robert Cameron Mitchell explain, "they contribute without 'meddling'" and "do not take part in leadership selection or policy discussions." This does not mean the new advocacy groups are malevolent; they are just responding rationally to the environment in which they find themselves.

Associational Change and Democracy

This brings us, finally, to what may be the most civically consequential change in late-twentieth-century America: the rise of a very large, highly educated upper middle class in which "expert" professionals are prominent along with businesspeople and managers. When U.S. professionals were a tiny, geographically dispersed stratum, they understood themselves as "trustees of community," in the terminology of Stephen Brint. Working closely with and for nonprofessional fellow citizens in thousands of towns and cities, lawyers, doctors, ministers, and teachers once found it quite natural to join—and eventually help to lead—locally rooted, cross-class voluntary associations. But today's professionals are more likely to see themselves as expert individuals who can best contribute to national well-being by working with other specialists to tackle complex technical or social problems.

Cause-oriented advocacy groups offer busy, privileged Americans a rich menu of opportunities to, in effect, hire other professionals and managers to represent their values and interests in public life. Why should highly trained and economically well-off elites spend years working their way up the leadership ladders of traditional membership federations when they can take leading staff roles at the top, or express their preferences by writing a check?

If America has experienced a great civic transformation from membership to advocacy—so what? Most traditional associations were racially exclusive and gender segregated; and their policy efforts were not always broad-minded. More than a few observers suggest that recent civic reorganizations may be for the best. American public life has been rejuvenated, say the optimists, by social movements and advocacy groups fighting for social rights and an enlarged understanding of the public good.

Local community organizations, neighborhood groups, and grassroots protest movements nowadays tap popular energies and involve people otherwise left out of organized politics. And social interchanges live on in small support groups and occasional volunteering. According to the research of Robert Wuthnow, about 75 million men and women, a remarkable 40 percent of the adult population, report taking part in "a small group that meets regularly and provides caring and support for those who participate in it." Wuthnow estimates that there may be some 3 million such groups, including Bible study groups, 12-step self-help groups, book discussion clubs, singles groups, hobby groups, and disease support groups. Individuals find community, spiritual connection, introspection, and personal gratification in small support groups. Meanwhile, people reach out through volunteering. As many as half of all Americans give time to the community this way, their efforts often coordinated by paid social service professionals. Contemporary volunteering can be intermittent and flexibly structured, an intense one-shot effort or spending "an evening a week on an activity for a few months as time permits, rather than having to make a long-term commitment to an organization."

In the optimistic view, the good civic things Americans once did are still being done—in new ways and in new settings. But if we look at U.S. democracy in its entirety and bring issues of power and social leverage to the fore, then optimists are surely overlooking the downsides of our recently reorganized civic life. Too many valuable aspects of the old civic America are not being reproduced or reinvented in the new public world of memberless organizations.

Despite the multiplicity of voices raised within it, America's new civic universe is remarkably oligarchical. Because today's advocacy groups are staff-heavy and focused on lobbying, research, and media projects, they are managed from the top with few opportunities for member leverage from below. Even when they have hundreds of thousands of adherents, contemporary associations are heavily tilted toward upper-middle-class constituencies. Whether we are talking about memberless advocacy groups, advocacy groups with some chapters, mailing-list associations, or nonprofit institutions, it is hard to escape the conclusion that the wealthiest and best-educated Americans are much more privileged in the new civic world than their (less numerous) counterparts were in the pre-1960s civic world of cross-class membership federations.

Mostly, they involve people in "doing for" others—feeding the needy at a church soup kitchen; tutoring children at an after-school clinic; or guiding visitors at a museum exhibit—rather than in "doing with" fellow citizens. Important as such volunteering may be, it cannot substitute for the central citizenship functions that membership federations performed.

A top-heavy civic world not only encourages "doing for" rather than "doing with." It also distorts national politics and public policymaking. Imagine for a moment what might have happened if the GI Bill of 1944 had been debated and legislated in a civic world configured more like the one that prevailed during the 1993–1994 debates over the national health insurance proposal put forward by the first administration of President Bill Clinton. This is not an entirely fanciful comparison, because goals supported by the vast majority of Americans were at issue in both periods: in the 1940s, care and opportunity for millions of military veterans returning from World War II; in the 1990s, access for all Americans to a modicum of health insurance coverage. Back in the 1940s, moreover, there were elite actors—university presidents, liberal intellectuals, and conservative congressmen—who could have condemned the GI Bill to the same fate as the 1990s health security plan. University presidents and liberal New Dealers initially favored versions of the GI Bill that would have been bureaucratically complicated, niggardly with public expenditures, and extraordinarily limited in veterans' access to subsidized higher education.

But in the actual civic circumstances of the 1940s, elites did not retain control of public debates or legislative initiatives. Instead, a vast voluntary membership federation, the American Legion, stepped in and drafted a bill to guarantee every one of the returning veterans up to four years of post–high school education, along with family and employment benefits, business loans, and home mortgages. Not only did the Legion draft one of the most generous pieces of social legislation in American history, thousands of local Legion posts and dozens of state organizations mounted a massive public education and lobbying campaign to ensure that even conservative congressional representatives would vote for the new legislation.

Half a century later, the 1990s health security episode played out in a transformed civic universe dominated by advocacy groups, pollsters, and big-money media campaigns. Top-heavy advocacy groups did not mobilize mass support for a sensible reform plan. Hundreds of business and professional groups influenced the Clinton administration's complex policy schemes, and then used a combination of congressional lobbying and media campaigns to block new legislation. Both the artificial polarization and the elitism of today's organized civic universe may help to explain why increasing numbers of Americans are turned off by and pulling back from public life. Large majorities say that wealthy "special interests" dominate the federal government, and many Americans express cynicism about the chances for regular people to make a difference. People may be entertained by advocacy clashes on television, but they are also ignoring many public debates and withdrawing into privatism. Voting less and less, American citizens increasingly act—and claim to feel—like mere spectators in a polity where all the significant action seems to go on above their heads, with their views ignored by pundits and clashing partisans.

From the nineteenth through the mid-twentieth century, American democracy flourished within a unique matrix of state and society. Not only was America the world's first manhood democracy and the first nation in the world to establish mass public education. It also had a uniquely balanced civic life, in which markets expanded but could not subsume civil society, in which governments at multiple levels deliberately and indirectly encouraged federated voluntary associations. National elites had to pay attention to the values and interests of millions of ordinary Americans.

Over the past third of a century, the old civic America has been bypassed and shoved to the side by a gaggle of professionally dominated advocacy groups and nonprofit institutions rarely attached to memberships worthy of the name. Ideals of shared citizenship and possibilities for democratic leverage have been compromised in the process. Since the 1960s, many good things have happened in America. New voices are now heard, and there have been invaluable gains in equality and liberty. But vital links in the nation's associational life have frayed, and we may need to find creative ways to repair those links if America is to avoid becoming a country of detached spectators. There is no going back to the civic world we have lost. But we Americans can and should look for ways to recreate the best of our civic past in new forms suited to a renewed democratic future.

Questions for Discussion

1. What factors led to a decline in importance of membership federations in the nation's civic and political life? What kinds of organizations have taken their place?
2. Although Skocpol believes that the number of organized interests represented in the interest group universe over the past half century has grown, she also believes that the political system may be less democratic than it had previously been. How can such a paradox be explained?

9.4

Drugmakers Go Furthest to Sway Congress

Jim Drinkard

Recent decades have witnessed a proliferation in the number of organized interests active in the political realm; the scope and intensity of organized interest efforts have increased as well. The expansion of government lawmaking and regulation has raised the stakes of politics, creating incentives for a multitude of such interests to pay continual attention to both elections and the policy process.

For many organizations, most notably those well endowed with financial resources, lobbying is a ubiquitous activity—one that lacks the traditional distinction between the electoral and policy processes. Further, lobbying is directed not only at decision makers, but targets the general public as well, in an effort to create the kind of public opinion that makes legislators take notice.

In this selection, Jim Drinkard profiles what arguably is the most sophisticated, comprehensive, and powerful lobby operating in Washington today, the pharmaceutical industry. Not only are drug companies among the biggest contributors to candidates and active in campaign advertising, the extent of their lobbying efforts on policy matters is unmatched by any other organized interest. Nearly 1,300 registered lobbyists are active in Washington on behalf of the pharmaceutical industry—more than two for every member of Congress. More than a third of the lobbyists are former federal officials, including forty former members of Congress. The pharmaceutical industry's return on its investment in the electoral and policy processes is indeed impressive—according to the article, "going up against them is more often than not a losing battle."

While Republicans no longer control the Congress in the wake of the 2006 elections, this selection represents an example of the apex of interest group influence in the halls of Congress under certain conditions. Interest group influence is potentially maximized under conditions where a symbiotic relationship evolves between a unified, majority legislative party seeking electoral advantage and a well-financed organized interest seeking support for its policy positions.

Jim Drinkard is a political campaign reporter for *USA Today*.

Jim Drinkard, "Drugmakers Go Furthest to Sway Congress," *USA Today*, April 25, 2005. Reprinted with permission.

W hen Sen. Bill Frist needed help in November [2006] for a quick tour celebrating the victories of newly elected Republican senators, he didn't have to look far. A Gulfstream corporate jet owned by drug-maker Schering-Plough was ready to zip the Senate majority leader to stops in Florida, Georgia and the Carolinas. Frist's political committee reimbursed the drugmaker $10,809, the equivalent of a first-class fare for the same trip on a commercial airline, as campaign rules require. The price, a fraction of the cost of a charter flight, was almost a wash for Frist; Schering had donated $10,000 to his committee in 2003–04. What he got was worth far more: the convenience, luxury and efficiency of flying on his own schedule.

The drug company's friendly gesture toward the Senate's most powerful member illustrates the political clout of the pharmaceutical industry. It will be needed in the months ahead as the industry faces the threat of increased federal regulation, brought on by mounting concerns about the safety of the nation's drug supply.

The drug companies' corporate planes have been made available not only to Frist, but also for dozens of trips taken by other powerful lawmakers. House Speaker Dennis Hastert, R-Ill., took at least four trips to GOP fundraising events in the past two years aboard Pfizer's Gulfstream.

Drug companies and their officials contributed at least $17 million to federal candidates in last year's elections, including nearly $1 million to President Bush and more than $500,000 to his opponent, John Kerry. At least 18 members of Congress received more than $100,000 apiece.

Figure 1

Top Spenders: Pharmaceutical Lobby Spending in Washington (in millions)

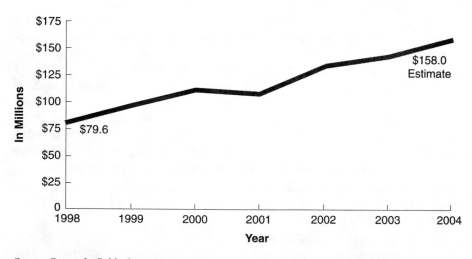

Source: Center for Public Integrity

The industry also liberally funds think tanks and patient-advocacy groups that don't bear its name but often take its side; the National Patient Advocate Foundation, for instance, receives financial support from at least 10 drug companies. And the industry isn't above playing hardball, according to David Graham, a Food and Drug Administration scientist who got on its bad side.

Since 1998, drug companies have spent $758 million on lobbying—more than any other industry, according to government records analyzed by the Center for Public Integrity, a watchdog group. In Washington, the industry has 1,274 lobbyists—more than two for every member of Congress.

"They are powerful," says Sen. Chuck Grassley, R-Iowa, chairman of the Senate Finance Committee. "You can hardly swing a cat by the tail in that town without hitting a pharmaceutical lobbyist."

Over the years those lobbyists have been very successful, demonstrating that the industry knows politics as well as it knows chemistry. Drug companies won coverage for prescription drugs under Medicare in 2003 while blocking the government from negotiating prices downward. They have so far kept out imports of cheaper medicines from Canada and other countries. And they have protected a system that uses company fees to speed the drug-approval process.

"They win more than they should," says James Love, an industry critic who is director of the non-profit Consumer Project on Technology. "The one thing they have going for them is money."

The industry's deep inroads into the government are rooted in its dependence on federal decisions. The government determines which products drug companies can market and how they're labeled. The government buys massive quantities of drugs through Medicaid, the Veterans Administration and other programs. Once the new Medicare prescription drug benefit takes effect in 2006, the government will be paying 41% of Americans' drug bills, up from 24% now.

Billy Tauzin, a former Republican congressman from Louisiana who now heads the Pharmaceutical Research and Manufacturers of America (PhRMA), serves as testament to the industry's power. He helped shepherd the Medicare prescription drug law to passage as chairman of the House Energy and Commerce Committee before joining PhRMA for a reported $1 million a year or more. PhRMA won't confirm his pay.

Tauzin says the lobbying presence is needed to protect the U.S. marketing system for prescription drugs. The United States "is probably the last place on Earth which encourages innovation and discovery," he says, contending that it costs about $1 billion to invent each new drug. In other countries, he says, government-controlled pricing has robbed drug manufacturers of the profits that finance new drug development.

But now, the industry faces the possibility of increased regulation. Grassley and Sen. Chris Dodd, D-Conn., are pushing legislation that would force drug developers to release data from all clinical trials of a new medicine—including negative ones the companies don't like to disclose. They also plan to introduce a bill that would strengthen the FDA's ability to protect patients if safety problems crop up after a drug has been approved for sale.

Friendly Skies

If Frist had chartered a jet for his victory lap last Nov. 3, it would have cost at least three times as much as he paid Schering. Many large companies make their planes available to lawmakers; campaign rules allow the lawmaker to pay the travel provider the relatively low cost of first-class airfare. In the days just before the election, Frist had been aboard Schering's jet one other time and had flown twice on the jet owned by another drugmaker, Abbott Laboratories.

Companies that provide their jets often send a lobbyist along to seize the chance for private time with a member of Congress. Schering spokeswoman Rosemarie Yancosek declined to say if that happened on Frist's trips. "We comply with all the laws regarding the use of the corporate jet," she said. Frist's office declined to comment on the flights.

As the gatekeeper for legislation that comes to the Senate floor, Frist, a Tennessee Republican and a heart surgeon, is a key lobbying target for the drug industry. Legislation to allow reimportation of lower-priced prescription drugs, previously passed by the House, faces its biggest test in the Senate. "If we ever get it to a vote in the Senate, it will pass," Grassley says.

Frist and Hastert are not the only lawmakers to take advantage of the convenience of drug companies' corporate jets. A spokesman for drugmaker Novartis, Sheldon Jones, confirmed that company lobbyists were aboard for three trips carrying lawmakers in 2003 and 2004. One, in June 2003, took Reps. Tom Reynolds, R-N.Y.; Mike Oxley, R-Ohio; and Mike Rogers, R-Mich., to a Republican fundraiser in New York City. Rep. Tom Davis, R-Va., and Sen. Chuck Hagel, R-Neb., also took trips on the Novartis Learjet.

Of the 1,274 people registered to lobby in Washington for drugmakers in 2003, according to the Center for Public Integrity, 476 are former federal officials—including 40 former members of Congress. "They are one of the strongest, most well-connected and most effective lobbies in Washington," says Amy Allina of the National Women's Health Network. "Going up against them is more often than not a losing battle."

Financing Other Groups

Lobbyists aren't the industry's only voice. When witnesses lined up last month for a Senate hearing on the FDA's drug-approval process, no representative from the pharmaceutical industry was present. But at least three witnesses on the six-member panel were from groups that get money from drugmakers.

The hearing was prompted by belated discoveries of health risks in drugs the agency had approved for sale: heart problems in patients taking Merck's Vioxx and other so-called COX-2 inhibitors, used to relieve pain; suicidal thoughts in adolescents taking antidepressants; and muscle damage from drugs that reduce cholesterol. The committee, under Sen. Mike Enzi, R-Wyo., wanted to know if the FDA needs additional regulatory authority to protect public health.

Leadoff witness Nancy Davenport-Ennis warned against any "overemphasis on safety" that might delay availability of new cancer drugs, a position in line with that of the pharmaceutical industry. Among the companies funding her National Patient Advocate Foundation: Pfizer, Merck and GlaxoSmithKline.

Davenport-Ennis says the drug company grants come with no strings attached and amount to "a whole bunch less than half" of the group's budget. "I don't think there is a patient-advocacy group in America that does not receive some level of funding from a pharmaceutical company," she says.

Witness Scott Gottlieb of the American Enterprise Institute (AEI), a conservative think tank, also cautioned Enzi's panel against lengthening the drug-approval process or making it more expensive. Veronique Rodman, an AEI spokeswoman, declined to say whether the organization gets drug-industry support. But one of Gottlieb's AEI colleagues, John Calfee, disclosed in a book review he wrote for the journal *Nature* last June that AEI does get drug-industry money.

A third witness, child and adolescent psychiatrist David Fassler, called for greater public access to clinical trial data for drugs. But he expressed concern that FDA action last year to require a "black-box warning" on antidepressants prescribed for children and adolescents might deter families from seeking medications.

Fassler personally receives no industry money, but he represented the American Psychiatric Foundation and the American Academy of Child and Adolescent Psychiatry, both of which receive drug-industry contributions. Mary Crosby, the academy's acting executive director, says drug-industry money accounts for about 12% of the group's funding but has no influence on what their witnesses say.

Tauzin says such outside groups are the industry's natural allies in the quest to cure more diseases. "This industry is doing a world of good for a lot of people, and they want to support us," he says.

More Money Channels

Health care consistently outspends other economic sectors on Washington lobbying, and the pharmaceutical industry makes up the largest component of that spending—$143 million in 2003.

Drugmakers also sell their message through TV advertising. Two of the top 10 ad spenders during the last session of Congress were pharmaceutical companies,

GlaxoSmithKline and Pfizer. A study by the Annenberg Public Policy Center at the University of Pennsylvania found they spent a combined $45.1 million on advertising in 2003–04, the largest chunk of it to promote the expansion of Medicare to cover prescription drugs.

In addition, the industry pours growing amounts into political campaigns, favoring Republicans—who control the White House and Congress—over Democrats by about 2 to 1. In last year's elections, the top Senate recipient of pharmaceutical campaign money was North Carolina GOP Sen. Richard Burr, a member of Enzi's panel. He got $288,684, according to a tally by the nonpartisan Center for Responsive Politics. In the House, Rep. Mike Ferguson, R-N.J., was the top recipient, with $264,560, roughly 10% of his total fundraising. He's a member of the House Energy and Commerce Committee; it has jurisdiction over the drug industry, which has a heavy presence in his state.

Pharmaceutical makers also were among top donors to the national conventions last year. They gave $4.7 million to help put on the GOP event in New York and $2.6 million for the Democrats' gathering in Boston.

Drug companies court lawmakers and their aides by paying for trips to industry meetings or to tour company plants and other facilities. Dozens of such trips took place last year, disclosure records filed in the House and Senate show. For example, a group of sponsors including PhRMA and GlaxoSmithKline paid $8,810 to take Rep. William Lacy Clay, D-Mo., to Brazil on a "fact-finding mission." GlaxoSmithKline paid $1,079 to fly Sen. Orrin Hatch, R-Utah, to Houston for a speech.

Other favors are routinely sprinkled on the policymakers who control the industry's fate. In 2003, when Congress worked late drafting the new Medicare prescription drug benefit, lobbyists sent in catered food. And when Bush was inaugurated on Jan. 20, AstraZeneca opened its fifth-floor offices overlooking Pennsylvania Avenue to select congressional staff for a parade-watching party.

Tougher Tactics

The industry also can present a harder edge. David Graham, the FDA drug-safety official whose research contributed to Merck's pain reliever Vioxx being taken off the market last year, says he was subjected to a whispering campaign in the days before he appeared at a Senate hearing in November [2006].

He says industry lobbyists and his FDA superiors planted suggestions on Capitol Hill that he was testifying to establish himself as a highly paid expert witness who could testify in liability suits against the drug's manufacturer. And he says they sought to undermine his credibility by alleging that his scientific conclusions were influenced by his devout Catholicism.

"It's really ridiculous," Graham says. His testimony, he says, was "a matter of conscience." . . .

There also is evidence that the industry's allies sought to dissuade Grassley from holding the Nov. 18 hearing. Grassley says he received entreaties from GOP colleagues worried about alienating an industry friendly to their party. He recalls: "I had one or two colleagues say to me, 'Why would you want to have that hearing? The pharmaceutical industry is so helpful.'"

Questions for Discussion

1. How is the switch in partisan control of Congress as a result of the 2006 elections likely to influence strategies of the pharmaceutical lobby? Are the fortunes of the lobby likely to be affected by having a Democratic majority in both houses?
2. Lobbying reform has been a recent concern of the Congress. Are there any lobbying practices discussed in this selection that you believe should be further regulated? What is the likelihood that any of your suggestions could become law? What interests would oppose changes in lobbying practices?

Chapter 10

CONGRESS

Of the three branches of government, the legislature is invariably the most open to scrutiny and influence. Members of Congress are directly accountable to their constituents. Even in a security-conscious age of metal detectors and concrete barriers, the U.S. Congress remains easily accessible to citizens who seek to influence their representatives and senators or merely to observe them in action. Just as the growth of government has affected the presidency and, to a lesser extent, the Supreme Court (see Chapters 11 and 13), Congress has changed greatly in the post–World War II era, especially since the mid-1960s.

Some of these changes are straightforward. For example, in 1947 members of Congress employed 2,030 staff aides in their personal offices. As of 2006, the total surpassed 7,200, and the overall cost of the legislative branch stood at more than $2 billion. Other developments have been more obscure, though no less important. The informal rules of legislative behavior have changed; today newcomers need not undergo a decade-long apprenticeship before wielding even a bit of power. Despite these and many other changes, however, contemporary legislators take on the same basic responsibilities as their predecessors: representing their constituents and making decisions about the major issues of the day.

Richard Fenno illuminates the complex nature of representation in selection 10.1, an essay entitled "If, As Ralph Nader Says, Congress Is 'the Broken Branch,' How Come We Love Our Congressmen So Much?" Rather than seeking to understand members of Congress through their Washington actions, Fenno tracked them at home and has provided a generation of students with the insights gleaned from this perspective.

Over the course of the American experience, Congress has received countless criticisms of its inefficiencies and its responsiveness to special interests. A bicameral (two-house) legislature is by nature difficult to control, even when a single political party holds majorities in both chambers. In addition, Congress often must face an executive branch whose interests run directly counter to its own. Differences in opinion between the two chambers or between Congress and the executive can and do produce deadlocks, especially when different parties control the different branches.

Similarly, the representative nature of Congress makes it an appropriate target for interest groups. Most legislators run expensive re-election campaigns. These require substantial contributions, which frequently come from the growing number of political action committees that represent a wide range of groups. The structure of Congress allows interest groups easy access to a hundred subcommittees that deal with very specific issues ranging from oil exploration to air traffic control to military construction. The small membership and narrow focus of most House and Senate subcommittees provide attractive opportunities for a seemingly limitless number of lobbyists to influence public policies.

The selections in this chapter emphasize both continuity and change in congressional politics. The days are gone when autocratic committee chairs could control the legislative agenda, a system that promoted the image of Congress as a body of tottering graybeards who relied on seniority and the power of their committee positions, rather than the strength of their ideas or intellect, to dominate the process.

By the early 1970s, congressional structure and personnel had undergone a dramatic transformation, especially in the House. After the 1982 elections, more than two-thirds of the 535 members of Congress (100 senators, 435 representatives) had arrived on Capitol Hill in 1974 or later. Accompanying this upheaval in personnel was a series of reforms that greatly dispersed power within the Congress. The changes of the 1969–1975 period profoundly affected the House of Representatives. Committee chairs lost much of their authority, and the big winners were the rank-and-file House members, especially the majority Democrats. These representatives demonstrated their new clout in 1975 by voting within the Democratic Caucus to oust three senior committee chairs.

Political scientist Kenneth A. Shepsle (selection 10.2) assesses these changes by first sketching the "textbook Congress" of the 1950s and then noting the various ways in which Congress has diverged from the conventional wisdom of that era. In particular, the decline of committees has led to more variability and uncertainty in congressional politics. The seeming equilibrium of the 1950s Congress gave way to a less predictable, less coherent legislative process within a fragmented House of Representatives by the 1980s. Changes in the way the House does business rest in large part on the replacement of veteran members with newcomers. Although this turnover slowed substantially during the 1980s as incumbents dominated electoral politics, 110 new representatives entered the House in the wake of the 1992 elections. Even more important was the group of 73 freshmen Republicans whose victories allowed the GOP to win control of the House in 1994. And in 2006, Democrats won control of both the House and Senate in an electoral reaction to Republican rule, and especially the Iraq War.

Changes have affected the Senate less profoundly than they have the House, because the upper chamber has always relied on informal cooperation among its members. Nevertheless, some senators have become increasingly adept at tying the body into knots by relying on rules and traditions that evolved to protect minority rights. Senators have often acted to obstruct the regular flow of legislative business, acknowledging that in so doing they will win no popularity contests among their colleagues. Indeed, obstructionism has made leading the Senate a formidable—and perhaps impossible—task. The greatest difficulty facing party leaders in the chamber derives from the profound individualism of the Senate. Given the power of a single senator to slow the legislative process, through filibusters and other means, each member must be accorded substantial respect, even deference, from the party leaders. Congressional scholar Barbara Sinclair (selection 10.3) addresses the central problem for the Senate in the modern era—how stronger party leadership can coexist with the historical strength of individual senators. This is no mean feat, in that unlike their House counterparts, Senate party leaders have few tools to maintain party discipline among their colleagues.

Congressional politics has always reflected continuing tensions between forces of centralization and decentralization. In the late 1970s, for example, decentralizing trends prevailed as subcommittees proliferated and individual legislators gained substantial personal resources, such as staff. Electoral competition for House seats has also declined, and most representatives are well insulated from any pressures that party leaders may seek to employ. Speakers Tip O'Neill, Jim Wright, and Thomas Foley instituted a strategy of "inclusive" leadership that gave large numbers of the majority Democrats an increased stake in the process. In addition, the memberships of the Democratic and the Republican parties in the House have become more homogeneous. As Republicans have gained an increasing number of seats in the South, moderate-to-conservative southern Democrats have lost much of their power. And fewer moderate Republicans have won elections, as conservatives have come to dominate their party.

These trends came together in 1994–1995, when Republicans captured control of the House for the first time since 1955. The House Republicans, led by Speaker Newt Gingrich and bolstered by seventy-three first-term insurgents, had to learn how to govern as a majority. Using the ten-point Contract with America as their script, the House acted on a host of major legislative initiatives in the first 100 (actually 93) days of the 104th Congress in early 1995 and subsequently confronted President Clinton on budget issues to the point of shutting down parts of the federal government in late 1995 and early 1996. The Republicans, who learned that they needed support in the Senate and the White House to accomplish much of their agenda, did eventually "learn to legislate" and maintained their majority status through 2006.

The Democrats' convincing victory in 2006, while related to the Iraq War, also reflected both the overall weakening of the legislative branch (as discussed by Thomas Mann and Norman Ornstein in selection 10.4) and the repudiation of the strong leadership style most firmly articulated by House Majority Leader Tom DeLay (R-Tex.), who was forced to resign from his seat in 2006 (see selection 10.5).

The key challenge for the Democratic majority will be to act as a unified force, while also allowing members to exercise more authority and to provide for a legislative process that is more open and accountable. In a highly partisan, highly polarized era, these tasks are formidable.

10.1

If, As Ralph Nader Says, Congress Is "the Broken Branch," How Come We Love Our Congressmen So Much?

Richard F. Fenno Jr.

Prior to Richard F. Fenno Jr.'s groundbreaking book *Home Style* (1978), congressional scholars focused most, if not all their attention, on legislative actions on Capitol Hill. What happened in Spokane, Savannah, or Schenectady was of little concern. The real action took place on the floor of the House or Senate in the back rooms of the legislative chambers. Fenno begged to differ, and in the 1970s he traveled to congressional districts across the country to examine what happened "out there."

Building upon the many instructive stories of representational styles honed by members back in their districts, Fenno argues persuasively that we can understand what happens on Capitol Hill *only* if we understand what takes place back in 435 separate constituencies, most of them far from the capital. In this 1975 essay, Fenno draws upon his visits to congressional districts to address the puzzle of why we almost always re-elect our individual representatives, while at the same time rating the overall Congress in relatively negative terms.

Fenno concludes that if we are to understand the Congress, we need to understand the individual members in that, "It is the Members who run Congress. And we get pretty much the kind of Congress they want. We shall get a different kind of Congress when we elect different kinds of congressmen or when we start applying different standards of judgment to old congressmen." This simple formulation was true in 1975, in the wake of Watergate, and it remains true today.

Richard F. Fenno Jr. is Distinguished University Professor and William R. Kenan Professor of Political Science at the University of Rochester.

Richard F. Fenno Jr., "If, As Ralph Nader Says, Congress Is 'the Broken Branch,' How Come We Love Our Congressmen So Much?" in Norman J. Ornstein, *Congress in Change: Evolution and Reform* (New York: Praeger, 1975), pp. 277–287. Reprinted by permission of Richard Fenno.

Off and on during the past two years [1970–1971], I accompanied ten members of the House of Representatives as they traveled around in their home districts. In every one of those districts I heard a common theme, one that I had not expected. Invariably, the representative I was with— young or old, liberal or conservative, Northerner, Southerner, Easterner, or Westerner, Democrat or Republican—was described as "the best congressman in the United States." Having heard it so often, I now accept the description as fact. I am even prepared to believe the same thing (though I cannot claim to have heard it with my own ears) of the members of the Senate. Each of our 435 representatives and 100 senators is, indeed, "the best congressman in the United States." Which is to say that each enjoys a great deal of support and approbation among his or her constituents. Judging by the election returns, this isn't much of an exaggeration. In the recent election, 96 percent of all House incumbents who ran were re-elected; and 85 percent of all Senate incumbents who ran were re-elected. These convincing figures are close to the average re-election rates of incumbents for the past ten elections. We do, it appears, love our congressmen.

On the other hand, it seems equally clear that we do not love our Congress. Louis Harris reported in 1970 that only one-quarter of the electorate gave Congress a positive rating on its job performance—while nearly two-thirds expressed themselves negatively on the subject. And we would not be here tonight if there were not considerable concern—dramatized recently by the critical Nader project*—for the performance of Congress as an institution. On the evidence, we seem to approve of our legislators a good deal more than we do our legislature. And therein hangs something of a puzzle. If our congressmen are so good, how can our Congress be so bad? If it is the individuals that make up the institution, why should there be such a disparity in our judgments? What follows are a few reflections on this puzzle.

A first answer is that we apply different standards of judgment, those that we apply to the individual being less demanding than those we apply to the institution. For the individual, our standard is one of representativeness—of personal style and policy views. Stylistically, we ask that our legislator display a sense of identity with us so that we, in turn, can identify with him or her—via personal visits to the district, concern for local projects and individual "cases," and media contact of all sorts, for example. On the policy side, we ask only that his general policy stance does not get too frequently out of line with ours. And, if he should become a national leader in some policy area of interest to us, so much the better. These standards are admittedly vague. But because they are locally defined and locally applied, they are consistent and manageable enough so that legislators can devise rules of thumb to meet them. What is more, by

---

*In the early 1970s, Ralph Nader undertook an extensive project to scrutinize the U.S. Congress. Nader's ambitious attempt was seen as generally hostile by many legislators and Capitol Hill insiders.

their performance they help shape the standards, thereby making them easier to meet. Thus they win constituent recognition as "the best in the United States." And thus they establish the core relationship for a representative democracy.

For the institution, however, our standards emphasize efforts to solve national problems—a far less tractable task than the one we (and he) set for the individual. Given the inevitable existence of unsolved problems, we are destined to be unhappy with congressional performance. The individual legislator knows when he has met our standards of representativeness; he is re-elected. But no such definitive measure of legislative success exists. And, precisely because Congress is the most familiar and most human of our national institutions, lacking the distant majesty of the Presidency and the Court, it is the easy and natural target of our criticism. We have met our problem solvers, and they are us.

Furthermore, such standards as we do use for judging the institutional performance of Congress are applied inconsistently. In 1963, when public dissatisfaction was as great as in 1970, Congress was criticized for being obstructionist, dilatory, and insufficiently cooperative with regard to the Kennedy programs. Two years later, Congress got its highest performance rating of the decade when it cooperated completely with the executive in rushing the Great Society program* into law. But by the late 1960's and early 1970's the standard of judgment had changed radically—from cooperation to counterbalance in Congressional relations with the Executive. Whereas, in 1963, Harris had found "little in the way of public response to the time-honored claim that the Legislative Branch is . . . the guardian against excessive Executive power," by 1968 he found that three-quarters of the electorate wanted Congress to act as the watchdog of the Executive and not to cooperate so readily with it. The easy passage of the Tonkin Resolution† reflects the cooperative standards set in the earlier period; its repeal reflects the counterbalancing standards of the recent period. Today we are concerned about Ralph Nader's "broken branch" which, we hear, has lost—and must reclaim from the Executive—its prerogatives in areas such as war-making and spending control. To some degree, then, our judgments on Congress are negative because we change our minds frequently concerning the kind of Congress we want. A Congress whose main job is to cooperate with the Executive would look quite different from one whose main job is to counterbalance the Executive.

Beneath the differences in our standards of judgment, however, lies a deeper dynamic of the political system. Senators and representatives, for their own

---

*The Great Society was the overall term used to characterize President Lyndon Johnson's ambitious set of domestic policy initiatives, which included education funding, Medicare/Medicaid, environmental reform, and the War on Poverty, among other initiatives.

†The 1965 congressional approval of U.S. military escalation in Viet Nam, passed in the wake of a disputed naval incident in the Gulf of Tonkin, off the Vietnamese coast.

reasons, spend a good deal more of their time and energy polishing and worry-
ing about their individual performance than they do working at the institution's performance. Though it is, of course, true that their individual activity is
related to institutional activity, their first-order concerns are individual, not
institutional. Foremost is their desire for re-election. Most members of Congress like their job, want to keep it, and know that there are people back home
who want to take it away from them. So they work long and hard at winning
re-election. Even those who are safest want election margins large enough to
discourage opposition back home and/or to help them float further political
ambitions. No matter what other personal goals representatives and senators
wish to accomplish—increased influence in Washington and helping to make
good public policy are the most common—re-election is a necessary means to
those ends.

We cannot criticize these priorities—not in a representative system. If we believe the representative should mirror constituency opinion, we must acknowledge that it requires considerable effort for him to find out what should be
mirrored. If we believe a representative should be free to vote his judgment, he
will have to cultivate his constituents assiduously before they will trust him
with such freedom. Either way we will look favorably on his efforts. We come
to love our legislators, in the *second* place, because they so ardently sue for our
affections.

As a courtship technique, moreover, they re-enforce our unfavorable judgments about the institution. Every representative with whom I traveled criticized the Congress and portrayed himself, by contrast, as a fighter against its
manifest evils. Members run *for* Congress by running *against* Congress. They
refurbish their individual reputations as "the best congressman in the United
States" by attacking the collective reputation of the Congress of the United
States. Small wonder the voters feel so much more warmly disposed and so
much less fickle toward the individuals than toward the institution.

One case in point: the House decision to grant President Nixon a spending
ceiling plus authority to cut previously appropriated funds to maintain that
ceiling. One-half the representatives I was with blasted the House for being so
spineless that it gave away its power of the purse to the President. The other
half blasted the House for being so spineless in exercising its power of the purse
that the President had been forced to act. Both groups spoke to supportive audiences; and each man enhanced his individual reputation by attacking the institution. Only by raising both questions, however, could one see the whole
picture. Once the President forced the issue, how come the House didn't stand
up to him and protect its crucial institutional power over the purse strings? On
the other hand, if economic experts agreed that a spending ceiling was called
for, how come the House didn't enact it and make the necessary budget cuts in
the first place? The answer to the first question lies in the proximity of their re-
election battles, which re-enforced the tendency of all representatives to think
in individualistic rather than institutional terms. The answer to the second

question lies in the total absence of institutional machinery whereby the House (or, indeed, Congress) can make overall spending decisions.

Mention of the institutional mechanisms of Congress leads us to a *third* explanation for our prevailing pattern of judgments. When members of Congress think institutionally—as, of course they must—they think in terms of a structure that will be most congenial to the pursuit of their individual concerns—for re-election, for influence, or for policy. Since each individual has been independently designated "the best in the United States," each has an equal status and an equal claim to influence within the structure. For these reasons, the members naturally think in terms of a very fragmented, decentralized institution, providing a maximum of opportunity for individual performance, individual influence, and individual credit.

The 100-member Senate more completely fits this description than the 435-member House. The smaller body permits a more freewheeling and creative individualism. But both chambers tend strongly in this direction, and representatives as well as senators chafe against centralizing mechanisms. Neither body is organized in hierarchical—or even in well-coordinated—patterns of decision-making. Agreements are reached by some fairly subtle forms of mutual adjustment—by negotiation, bargaining, and compromise. And interpersonal relations—of respect, confidence, trust—are crucial building blocks. The members of Congress, in pursuit of their individual desires, have thus created an institution that is internally quite complex. Its structure and processes are, therefore, very difficult to grasp from the outside.

In order to play out some aspects of the original puzzle, however, we must make the effort. And the committee system, the epitome of fragmentation and decentralization, is a good place to start. The performance of Congress as an institution is very largely the performance of its committees. The Nader project's "broken branch" description is mostly a committee-centered description because that is where the countervailing combination of congressional expertise and political skill resides. To strengthen Congress means to strengthen its committees. To love Congress means to love its committees. Certainly when we have not loved our Congress, we have heaped our displeasure upon its committees. The major legislative reorganizations, of 1946 and 1970, were committee-centered reforms—centering on committee jurisdictions, committee democracy, and committee staff support. Other continuing criticisms—of the seniority rule for selecting committee chairmen, for example—have centered on the committees.

Like Congress as a whole, committees must be understood first in terms of what they do for the individual member. To begin with, committees are relatively more important to the individual House member than to the individual senator. The representative's career inside Congress is very closely tied to his committee. For the only way such a large body can function is to divide into highly specialized and independent committees. Policy-making activity funnels through these committees; so does the legislative activity and influence of the individual legislator. While the Senate has a set of committees paralleling those of the House, a committee assignment is nowhere near as constraining for the career of the individual senator. The Senate is more loosely organized, senators sit on many more committees and subcommittees than representatives, and they have easy access to the work of committees of which they are not members. Senators, too, can command and utilize national publicity to gain influence beyond the confines of their committee. Whereas House committees act as funnels for individual activity, Senate committees act as facilitators of individual activity. The difference in functions is considerable—which is why committee chairmen are a good deal more important in the House than in the Senate and why the first modifications of the seniority rule should have come in the House rather than the Senate. My examples will come from the House.

Given the great importance of his committee to the career of the House member, it follows that we will want to know how each committee can affect such careers. . . .

Where a committee's members are especially interested in pyramiding their individual influence, they will act so as to maintain the influence of their committee (and, hence, their personal influence) within the House. They will adopt procedures that enhance the operating independence of the committee. They will work hard to remain relatively independent of the Executive Branch. And they will try to underpin that independence with such resources as specialized expertise, internal cohesion, and the respect of their House colleagues. Ways and Means and Appropriations are committees of this sort. By contrast, where a committee's members are especially interested in getting in on nationally controversial policy action, they will not be much concerned about the independent influence of their committee. They will want to ally themselves closely with any and all groups outside the committee who share their policy views. They want to help enact what they individually regard as good public policy; and if that means ratifying policies shaped elsewhere—in the Executive Branch particularly—so be it. And, since their institutional independence is not a value for them, they make no special effort to acquire such underpinnings as expertise, cohesion, or chamber respect. Education and Labor and Foreign Affairs are committees of this sort.

These two types of committees display quite different strengths in their performance. Those of the first type are especially influential. Ways and Means probably makes a greater independent contribution to policy-making than any other House committee. Appropriations probably exerts a more influential overview of executive branch activities than any other House committee. The price they pay, however, is a certain decrease in their responsiveness to noncommittee forces—as complaints about the closed rule on tax bills and executive hearings on appropriations bills will attest. Committees of the second type are especially responsive to noncommittee forces and provide easy conduits for outside influence in policy-making. Education and Labor was probably more receptive to President Johnson's Great Society policies than any other House committee; it successfully passed the largest part of that program. Foreign Affairs has probably remained as thoroughly responsive to Executive Branch policies, in foreign aid for instance, as any House committee. The price they pay, however, is a certain decrease in their influence—as complaints about the rubber-stamp Education and Labor Committee and about the impotent Foreign Affairs Committee will attest. In terms of the earlier discussions of institutional performance standards, our hopes for a cooperative Congress lie more with the latter type of committee; our hopes for a counterbalancing Congress lie more with the former.

So, committees differ. And they differ to an important degree according to the desires of their members. This ought to make us wary of blanket descriptions. Within the House, Foreign Affairs may look like a broken branch, but Ways and Means does not. And, across chambers, Senate Foreign Relations (where member incentives are stronger) is a good deal more potent than House Foreign Affairs. With the two Appropriations committees, the reverse is the case. It is not just that "the broken branch" is an undiscriminating, hence inaccurate, description. It is also that blanket descriptions lead to blanket prescriptions. And it just might be that the wisest course of congressional reform would be to identify existing nodes of committee strength and nourish them rather than to prescribe, as we usually do, reforms in equal dosages for all committees.

One lesson of the analysis should be that member incentives must exist to support any kind of committee activity. Where incentives vary, it may be silly to prescribe the same functions and resources for all committees. The Reorganization Act of 1946 mandated all committees to exercise "continuous watchfulness" over the executive branch—in the absence of any supporting incentive system. We have gotten overview activity only where random individuals have found an incentive for doing so—not by most committees and certainly not continuously. Similarly, I suspect that our current interest in exhorting all committees to acquire more information with which to combat the executive may be misplaced. Information is relatively easy to come by—and some committees have a lot of it. What is hard to come by is the incentive to use it, not to mention the time and the trust necessary to make it useful. I am not suggesting a set of reforms but rather a somewhat different strategy of committee reforms—less wholesale, more retail.

Since the best-known target of wholesale committee reform is the seniority rule, it deserves special comment. If our attacks on the rule have any substance to them, if they are anything other than symbolic, the complaint must be that some or all committee chairmen are not doing a good job. But we can only find out whether this is so by conducting a committee-by-committee examination. Paradoxically, our discussions of the seniority rule tend to steer us away from such a retail examination by mounting very broad, across-the-board kinds of arguments against chairmen as a class—arguments about their old age, their conservatism, their national unrepresentativeness. Such arguments produce great cartoon copy, easy editorial broadsides, and sitting-duck targets for our congressmen on the stump. But we ought not to let the arguments themselves, nor the Pavlovian public reactions induced by our cartoonists, editorial writers, and representatives, pass for good institutional analysis. Rather, they have diverted us from that task.

More crucial to a committee's performance than the selection of its chairman is his working relationship with the other committee members. Does he agree with his members on the functions of the committee? Does he act to facilitate the achievement of their individual concerns? Do they approve of his performance as chairman? Where there is real disagreement between chairman and members, close analysis may lead us to fault the members and not the chairman. If so, we should be focusing our criticisms on the members. If the fault lies with the chairman, a majority of the members have the power to bring him to heel. They need not kill the king; they can constitutionalize the monarchy. While outsiders have been crying "off with his head," the members of several committees have been quietly and effectively constitutionalizing the monarchy. Education and Labor, Post Office, and Interior are recent examples where dissatisfied committee majorities have subjected their chairmen to majority control. Where this has not been done, it is probably due to member satisfaction, member timidity, member disinterest, or member incompetence. And the time we spend railing against the seniority rule might be better spent finding out, for each congressional committee, just which of these is the case. If, as a final possibility, a chairman and his members are united in opposition to the majority part or to the rest of us, the seniority rule is not the problem. More to the point, as I suspect is usually the case, the reasons and the ways individual members get sorted onto the various committees is the critical factor. In sum, I am not saying that the seniority rule is a good thing. I am saying that, for committee performance, it is not a very important thing.

What has all this got to do with the original puzzle—that we love our congressmen so much more than our Congress? We began with a few explanatory guesses. Our standards of judgment for individual performance are more easily met; the individual member works harder winning approval for himself than for his institution; and Congress is a complex institution, difficult for us to understand: The more we try to understand Congress—as we did briefly with the committee system—the more we are forced to peel back the institutional layers until we reach the individual member. At that point, it becomes hard to separate, as we normally do, our judgments about congressmen and Congress. The more we come to see institutional performance as influenced by the desires of the individual member, the more the original puzzle ought to resolve itself. For as the independence of our judgments decreases, the disparity between them ought to grow smaller. But if we are to hold this perspective on Congress, we shall need to understand the close individual-institution relationship—chamber by chamber, party by party, committee by committee, legislator by legislator.

This is not counsel of despair. It is a counsel of sharper focus and a more discriminating eye. It counsels the mass media, for example, to forgo "broken branch" type generalizations about Congress in favor of examining a committee in depth, or to forego broad criticism of the seniority rule for a close look at a committee chairman. It counsels the rest of us to focus more on the individual member and to fix the terms of our dialogue with him more aggressively. It counsels us to fix terms that will force him to think more institutionally and which will hold him more accountable for the performance of the institution. "Who Runs Congress," asks the title of the Nader report, "the President, Big Business or You?" From the perspective of this paper, it is none of these. It is the members who run Congress. And we get pretty much the kind of Congress they want. We shall get a different kind of Congress when we elect different kinds of congressmen or when we start applying different standards of judgment to old congressmen. Whether or not we ought to have a different kind of Congress is still another, much larger, puzzle.

Questions for Discussion

1. Fenno talks about changing the Congress by changing its members; how has that applied to the Congress in the 1990s, and more recently, in the wake of the 2006 election? Is the Congress really different, or have we just replaced one set of leaders with another?
2. In citing Ralph Nader, Fenno uses the same term, "the broken branch," that Mann and Ornstein use for the title of their 2006 book. In what ways can the Congress be "broken"? What kinds of remedies might you propose to "fix" this institution?

 10.2

The Changing Textbook Congress

Kenneth A. Shepsle

Ordinarily, it takes a while for political scientists to agree that a certain article is a "classic" piece of work. For Kenneth A. Shepsle's "The Changing Textbook Congress," however, the recognition came quickly and virtually universally. A most imaginative and provocative theorist, Shepsle places congressional developments of the 1960s through the 1980s in a context of an institution that has changed profoundly since scholars painted their definitive portrait of the Congress of the 1940s and 1950s.

One of Shepsle's chief interests is determining how institutional equilibrium, or balance among forces, is established. Committees dominated the earlier era's equilibrium, but since the 1960s, committees have come under pressure from individual members, with their considerable staff and technology resources, and from party leaders, who have gained substantial powers through a series of reform efforts. Moreover, most House members must represent increasingly large and diverse districts, which makes coalition building all the more difficult.

Writing in the late 1980s, Shepsle does not identify a clear contemporary equilibrium within Congress. With large numbers of power centers and stronger individual members, we may be entering an era marked more by uncertainty and fluidity than by a well-defined equilibrium. Still, given increasing partisanship in the 1990s and beyond, the Congress may well be governed more by a strong party majority (either Democratic or Republican), at least in the House, than by a balance among a number of powerful members.

When scholars talk about Congress to one another, their students, or the public, they often have a stylized version in mind, a textbook Congress characterized by a few main tendencies and described in broad terms. This is not to say that they are incapable of filling in fine-grained detail, making distinctions, or describing change. But at the core of their descriptions and distinctions are approximations, caricatures, and generalities.

Kenneth A. Shepsle is professor of government at Harvard University.

Reprinted by permission from Kenneth A. Shepsle, "The Changing Textbook Congress," in John E. Chubb and Paul E. Peterson, eds. *Can the Government Govern?* (Washington, DC: Brookings Institution Press, 1989).

They are always incomplete and somewhat inaccurate, but still they consist of robust regularities. . . .

The textbook Congress I have in mind is the one that emerged from World War II and the Legislative Reorganization Act of 1946. Its main features persisted until the mid-1960s; its images remained in writings on Congress well into the 1970s. . . .

To illuminate the institutional dynamics of the past forty years, this [selection] describes some early signs of change in the textbook Congress in the 1950s, suggests how events of the 1960s and 1970s disrupted the equilibrium, and looks at some of the emerging features of a new textbook Congress, though I am not convinced that a new equilibrium has yet been established. The story I develop here is not a historical tour d'horizon [overview]. Rather it addresses theoretical issues of institutional development involving the capacity of Congress and its members to represent their constituencies, to make national policy, and to balance the intrinsic tensions between these tasks. . . .

The Textbook Congress: The Late 1940s to the Mid-1960s

Any portrait of Congress after World War II must begin with the member and, in a popular phrase of the time, "his work as he sees it." Then, as now, legislators divided their time between Washington and home, the relative proportions slowly changing in favor of Washington during the 1950s. In Washington they divided their time between chamber, committee, and personal office; all three demands grew from the 1940s to the 1960s as chamber work load, committee activity, and constituency demands increased.

In 1947, just after passage of the Legislative Reorganization Act, the average House member had three staff assistants and the average senator six. Because even these modest averages would be the envy of a contemporary member of the British Parliament or of most state legislatures, they indicate that by mid-century the American national legislature was a highly professional place. Nevertheless, by the mid-1960s congressional staffs had swelled even further: a typical House member now had twelve assistants and a typical senator eighteen. Committee staffs, too, grew dramatically from an average of ten to nearly thirty in the House and from fifteen to more than thirty in the Senate. These numbers do not include the substantial staffs of the nearly 400 offices of institutional leaders, informal groups, and legislative support agencies.

Since most committee staffers during these twenty years were in fact under the control of committee chairmen, some of the more senior legislators came to head sizable organizations. Indeed, if most legislators in the Eightieth Congress (1947–8) could be said to have headed mom 'n pop businesses with a handful of clerks and assistants, by the mid-1960s they had come to oversee major modern enterprises with secretaries, receptionists, interns, and a variety of legislative, administrative, and political professionals (typically lawyers). A

Chapter 10 ♦ Congress

committee chair or ranking minority member, who might also head a couple of subcommittees or party committees, might have a staff exceeding one hundred.

This growth transformed legislative life and work. In the 1940s the House had its norms and the Senate its folkways, perhaps even an inner club.* Hard work, long apprenticeship, restrained participation of younger members, specialization (particularly in the House), courtesy, reciprocity, and institutional loyalty characterized daily life in each chamber. Even if these norms of behavior were only suggestions, frequent contact among colleagues made them a reality. Undoubtedly, members who were neighbors in the same office building, who shared a committee assignment, or who traveled back and forth to Washington from the same state or region came to know each other exceedingly well. But even more distant relationships were based on familiarity and frequent formal or informal meeting.

By the mid-1960s this had all changed. The rubbing of elbows was replaced by liaisons between legislative corporate enterprises, typically at the staff level. Surrounded or protected by a bevy of clerks and assistants, members met other members only occasionally and briefly on the chamber floor or in committee meetings. And many of the norms supporting work and specialization eroded.

With limited time and resources, legislators of the 1940s and 1950s concentrated on only a few activities. They simply did not have the staffs or money to be able to involve themselves in a wide range of policy issues, manage a network of ombudsman activities back home, raise campaign finances, or intercede broadly and frequently in the executive branch's administration of programs. Rather, they picked their spots selectively and depended on jurisdictional decentralization and reciprocity among committees to divide the legislative labor, on the legislative party for voting cues inside the chamber, and on local party organizations for campaign resources and electioneering.

During the 1960s, as congressional offices gained staff and funding, members began to take on many new activities. Larger staffs in district offices, trips home, and franking privileges enabled them to develop a personal presence before their constituencies. This permitted them to orchestrate electioneering, polling, voter mobilization, and campaign finance activities themselves. They grew less dependent on organizations outside their own enterprises—local parties, for example—which previously performed such functions. The geographic constituency had, of course, always been important, but it had often been mediated by party, both local and national. By the mid-1960s the members' relationships with their constituencies were growing increasingly unmediated (just as the relationships between members were growing increasingly mediated). They were constant presences in their districts, had begun to develop personal followings, and consequently achieved a certain independence from their parties (and hence some insulation from party fortunes). As members made more

---

*The consensus view of the Senate of this era emphasized its dominance by a core of generally senior senators, who came disproportionately but not exclusively from the South.

trips home and allocated more staff to district offices and more Washington staff to constituency service and constituency-oriented legislation, calculations of how they would present themselves to the folks back home and explain their Washington activities took on added importance. Constituents' needs (the geographic imperative) began to compete with party as a guide to behavior.

Personal and institutional arrangements in Washington also changed. In the 1950s members, especially in the House, limited themselves to work on a few issues, determined to a considerable extent by their places in the committee system. Most members were able to land assignments to committees that were directly relevant to their constituencies. Much of their time, energy, and limited staff resources were devoted to work inside these little legislatures. By partitioning policy into committee jurisdictions, and matching member interests with those jurisdictions, legislative arrangements permitted members to get the most out of their limited resources. Aside from those with institutional ambitions, who hoped one day to be appointed to the Appropriations, Rules, or Ways and Means committees (Appropriations, Finance, Foreign Relations, or Armed Services in the Senate), most members had only limited incentives to become actively involved in policy areas outside their own assignments and were content to serve on legislative committees that had jurisdiction over the issues of central importance to their constituents. Thus, with limited means and incentives, members sustained a system of deference and reciprocity as part of the 1950s equilibrium, especially in the House.

Because of the growth of resources within their own enterprises in the 1960s, members began to acquire enhanced in-house capabilities. Deference to expert committee judgments on policy outside the jurisdiction of committees on which a member served was no longer so necessary. Members could now afford to assign some of their staff to track developments in other policy areas. The charge to the staffer became "Find something of interest for the boss, something that will help the district." Members were also no longer so dependent on party signals; with greater resources they were better able to determine their interests. In short, greater resources led to vertical integration—the absorption into the member enterprise of activities formerly conducted outside it—and with that, to member independence. Consequently, the relationship in which jurisdiction constrained both interest and activism began to fray as the 1960s came to an end.

Incentives for members to break away from the institutional niches in which they found themselves also multiplied. In both the 1960s and the 1970s, reapportionments,* along with economic and demographic changes, produced congressional districts that were neither so purely rural nor so purely urban as they

---

*The Constitution mandates reapportionment of House seats among the states every ten years. This requirement became especially significant in the 1960s and 1970s as the Supreme Court interpreted the Constitution to mean that districts should be drawn as equally in population as possible.

had been. Increasingly, the districts were mixed, often including a major city and a number of towns, as well as perhaps some rural areas. Member interests began to reflect this heterogeneity. Issues were also evolving in ways that cut across existing interest-group configurations and committee jurisdictions. Except in a few cases, one or two major committee jurisdictions could no longer encompass the interests of a district. Members thus had to diversify their portfolios of legislative activities. And this meant less specialization, less deference, less reciprocity.

Thus the limited resources and truncated policy interests characteristic of House members and to a lesser extent members of the Senate in the 1940s and 1950s began to give way in the 1960s and 1970s. Increased member resources and more diverse constituencies provided both the means and the incentives for members to break out of a now restrictive division and specialization of labor. Geographic imperatives were beginning to supersede considerations of party and seniority to become the principal basis on which members defined their responsibilities and work habits. Geography was also beginning to threaten jurisdiction as the principal basis on which the House organized its business.

These changes were less dramatic in the Senate only because it had traditionally been a much less specialized institution. Resources were more plentiful and constituencies more heterogeneous than in the House. And because the Senate was smaller, members had to have more diverse activities and interests. Yet even in the Senate the pressure toward less specialization was growing. Entire states were becoming more heterogeneous as a result of the industrialization of the South, the switch to a service economy in the North, and the nationalization of financial matters (so that even South Dakota could become a center for credit activities). And senators, like their House counterparts, were expanding their enterprises. By the end of the period the Senate, though less dramatically than the House, was also a less specialized place.

The argument I am making here is that geography, jurisdiction, and party hang together in a sort of equilibrium. The 1940s and 1950s represented one such equilibrium in which local parties helped the members get elected and legislative parties loosely coordinated committee activity. But the division of labor and committee dominance of jurisdiction were the central features of the textbook Congress. Committees both accommodated member needs and controlled agendas and decisionmaking. This arrangement "advantaged senior members, committees, and the majority party, with the chairmen of the standing committees sitting at the intersection of these groups." More heterogeneous constituencies and increased member resources upset this textbook equilibrium. Members have adapted by voting themselves even more resources and expanding their activities. By the 1970s parties both inside and outside the legislature had become considerably more submissive holding companies for member enterprises than had earlier been the case. Committees, too, had changed character. . . .

Beginning with the 1958 elections, however, and continuing throughout the 1960s, a new breed of legislator was coming to Washington, one more committed to legislative activism and policy entrepreneurship than in the past, one beginning to reflect demographic changes, and, most important, one that found ways to stay in office. By the early 1970s these legislators had accumulated considerable seniority. Thus the old equilibrium was disrupted and the stage set for institutional developments that would strike at the heart of the textbook Congress.

The Changing Textbook Congress: The 1970s and 1980s

An idiosyncratic historical factor had an important bearing on the institutional reforms of the 1970s that undermined the textbook Congress. For much of the twentieth century the Democratic party in Congress spoke with a heavy southern accent. In 1948, for example, more than 53 percent of the Democrats in the House and nearly 56 percent of those in the Senate came from the eleven Confederate states and five border states (Kentucky, Maryland, Missouri, Oklahoma, and West Virginia). These states accounted for only a third of all House and Senate seats. Beginning with the 1958 landslide, however, this distribution changed. In 1960 the same sixteen states accounted for just under 50 percent of Democratically held House seats and 43 percent of Democratically held Senate seats. By 1982 the numbers had fallen to 40 percent and 39 percent, respectively, and have held at that level. . . . Increasingly, Democrats were winning and holding seats in the North and West and, to a somewhat lesser extent, Republicans were becoming competitive in the South.

The nationalization of the Democratic coalition in Congress, however, was reflected far more slowly at the top of the seniority ladder.* Although between 1955 and 1967 the proportion of southern Democrats (border states excluded) in the House had dropped from 43 percent to 35 percent (46 percent to 28 percent in the Senate), the proportion of House committee chairs held by southerners fell from 63 percent to 50 percent, and rose from 53 percent to 56 percent in the Senate. Southerners held two of the three exclusive committee chairs in the House and two of the four in the Senate in 1955; in 1967 they held all of them.

The tension between liberal rank-and-file legislators and conservative southern committee chairs was important in the 1960s but had few institutional repercussions. True, Judge Howard Smith (Democrat of Virginia), the tyrannical chairman of the House Rules Committee, lost in a classic power struggle with Speaker Rayburn in 1961. But the defeat should not be exaggerated.

---

*Seniority means the number of consecutive terms a legislator has served on a committee. The most senior majority-party member would automatically become chair of the committee. This practice was modified but not eliminated in the 1970s.

Committees and their chairs maintained both the power to propose legislation and the power to block it in their respective jurisdictions. In 1967 southern Democrats George H. Mahon of Texas, William M. Colmer of Mississippi, and Wilbur D. Mills of Arkansas chaired the Appropriations, Rules, and Ways and Means committees, respectively, in a manner not very different from that of the incumbents a decade earlier. Although the massive legislative productivity of the Eighty-ninth Congress (1965–66) did much to relieve this tension, it relieved it not so much by changing legislative institutions as by managing to mobilize very large liberal majorities. After the 1966 elections, and with the Vietnam War consuming more and more resources and attention, the Eighty-ninth Congress increasingly seemed like a brief interlude in the committee dominance that stretched back to World War II, if not earlier.

By the end of the 1960s a Democratic president had been chased from office, and the 1968 Democratic convention revealed the tensions created by the war in Vietnam and disagreements over a range of domestic issues. Despite a Democratic landslide in 1964, Republican gains for the decade amounted to thirty-eight seats in the House and eight in the Senate, further accentuating the liberal cast of the Democratic rank and file in Congress. As the 1970s opened, then, liberal Democratic majorities in each chamber confronted a conservative president [Richard Nixon], conservative Republican minorities in each chamber, and often conservative southern committee chairmen of their own party who together blocked many of their legislative initiatives. The liberals thus turned inward, using the Democratic Caucus to effect dramatic changes in institutional practices, especially in the House.

The Age of Reform

Despite the tensions it caused, the mature committee system had many advantages. The division of labor in the House not only allowed for decisions based on expertise, but perhaps more important, it sorted out and routinized congressional careers. Committees provided opportunities for political ambitions to be realized, and they did so in a manner that encouraged members to invest in committee careers. In an undifferentiated legislature, or in a committee-based legislature in which the durability of a committee career or the prospects for a committee leadership post depended on the wishes and whims of powerful party leaders (for example, the Speaker in the nineteenth century House), individual legislators have less incentive to invest effort in committee activities. Such investments are put at risk every time the political environment changes. Specialization and careerism are encouraged, however, when rewards depend primarily on individual effort (and luck), and not on the interventions and patronage of others. An important by-product is the encouragement given talented men and women to come to the legislature and to remain there. The slow predictability of career development under a seniority system may repel the impatient, but its inexorability places limits on risks by reducing a member's dependence on arbitrary power and unexpected events.

Even Voltaire's optimistic Dr. Pangloss, however, would recognize another side to this coin. When a committee system that links geography and jurisdiction through the assignment process is combined with an institutional bargain producing deference and reciprocity, it provides the foundation for the distributive politics of interest-group liberalism. But there are no guarantees of success. The legislative process is full of hurdles and veto groups, and occasionally they restrain legislative activism enough to stimulate a reaction. Thus in the 1950s, authorizing committees, frustrated by a stingy House Appropriations Committee, created entitlements as a means of circumventing the normal appropriations process. In the 1960s the Rules Committee became the major obstacle and it, too, was tamed. In the 1970s the Ways and Means Committee, which lacked an internal division of labor through subcommittees, bottled up many significant legislative proposals; it was dealt with by the Subcommittee Bill of Rights and the Committee Reform Amendments of 1974. The solution in the 1950s had no effect on legislative arrangements. The solution in the 1960s entailed modest structural reform that directly affected only one committee. In the 1970s, however, the committee system itself became the object of tinkering.

The decade of the 1970s was truly an age of legislative reform. In effect, it witnessed a representational revolt against a system that dramatically skewed rewards toward the old and senior who were often out of step with fellow partisans. It is a long story, admirably told in detail elsewhere. Here I shall focus on the way reforms enabled the rise of four power centers that competed, and continue to compete, with the standing committees for political influence.

First, full committees and their chairs steadily lost power to their subcommittees. At least since the Legislative Reorganization Act of 1946, subcommittees have been a significant structural element of the committee system in the House. However, until the 1970s they were principally a tool of senior committee members, especially committee chairmen, who typically determined subcommittee structure, named members, assigned bills, allocated staff resources, and orchestrated the timing and sequence in which the full committee would take up their proposals and forward them to the floor. Because the structures were determined idiosyncratically by individual chairmen, committees could be very different. Ways and Means had no subcommittees. Armed Services had numbered subcommittees with no fixed jurisdictions. Appropriations had rigidly arranged subcommittees. In almost all cases the chairman called the tune, despite an occasional committee revolt.

During the 1970s a series of reforms whittled away at the powers of the committee chairmen. In 1970 chairmen began to lose some control of their agendas. They could no longer refuse to call meetings; a committee majority could vote to meet anyway with the ranking majority member presiding. Once a rule had been granted for floor consideration of a bill, the chairman could not delay consideration for more than a week; after seven days, a committee majority could move floor consideration.

In 1973 the Democratic members of a House committee were designated as the committee caucus and empowered to choose subcommittee chairs and set subcommittee budgets. During the next two years, committees developed a procedure that allowed members, in order of committee seniority, to bid for subcommittee chairmanships. Also in 1973 the Democratic Caucus passed the Subcommittee Bill of Rights, which mandated that legislation be referred to subcommittees, that subcommittees have full control over their own agendas, and that they be provided with adequate staff and budget. In 1974 the Committee Reform Amendments required that full committees (Budget and Rules excepted) establish at least four subcommittees, an implicit strike against the undifferentiated structure of Ways and Means. In 1976 committee caucuses were given the authority to determine the number of subcommittees and their respective jurisdictions. Finally, in 1977 the selection procedure for committee chairs was changed, allowing the party caucus to elect them by secret ballot.

Full committees and their chairs thus had had their wings clipped. A chair was now beholden to the committee caucus, power had devolved upon subcommittees, and standing committees were rapidly becoming holding companies for their subunits.

Another center of power was created by the growth of member resources. Through House Resolution 5 and Senate Resolution 60, members were able to tap into committee and subcommittee budgets to hire staff to conduct their committee work. Additional resources were available for travel and office support. Budgets for congressional support agencies such as the General Accounting Office, the Congressional Research Service, and the Office of Technology Assessment, which individual members could employ for specific projects, also increased enormously. In short, member enterprises were becoming increasingly self-sufficient.

Committee power was also compromised by increased voting and amendment activity on the floor. The early 1970s marked the virtual end to anonymous floor votes. The secret ballot was never used in floor votes in the House, but voice votes, division votes, and unrecorded teller votes had allowed tallies to be detached from the identity of individual members. This changed as it became increasingly easy to demand a public roll call, a demand greatly facilitated by the advent of electronic voting in 1973. Roll call votes in turn stimulated amendment activity on the floor. In effect, full committees and their chairs, robbed of some of their control of agendas by subcommittees, were now robbed of more control by this change in floor procedure.

Floor activity was further stimulated by the declining frequency with which the Rules Committee was permitted to issue closed rules, which barred floor amendments to legislation. The specific occasion for this change was the debate on retaining the oil depletion allowance. Because this tax break was protected by the Ways and Means Committee, on which the oil-producing states were well represented, efforts to change the policy could only come about through floor amendments. But Ways and Means bills traditionally were protected by a closed rule. The Democratic Caucus devised a policy in which a caucus majority could instruct its members on the Rules Committee to vote specific amendments in order. Applying this strategy to the oil depletion allowance, the caucus in effect ended the tradition of closed-rule protection of committee bills. This encouraged floor amendments and at the same time reduced committee control over final legislation. It also encouraged committees to anticipate floor behavior more carefully when they marked up a bill.

Finally, committee dominance was challenged by the increased power of the Democratic Caucus and the Speaker. For all the delegation of committee operations to subcommittees and individual members, the changes in the congressional landscape were not all of one piece. In particular, before the 1970s the Democratic Caucus was a moribund organization primarily concerned with electing officers and attending to the final stages of committee assignments. After these activities were completed in the first few days of a new Congress, the caucus was rarely heard from. In the 1970s, however, as committees and chairmen were being undermined by subcommittees, there was a parallel movement to strengthen central party leadership and rank-and-file participation.

The first breach came in the seniority system. In 1971 the Democratic Caucus relieved its Committee on Committees—the Democratic members of the Ways and Means Committee—of having to rely on seniority in nominating committee chairs. This had the effect of putting sitting chairs on notice, although none was threatened at the time. In 1974 it became possible for a small number of caucus members to force individual votes on nominees for chairs and later to vote by secret ballot. In 1975 the caucus took upon itself the right to vote on subcommittee chairs of the Appropriations Committee. In that same year three incumbent chairmen were denied reelection to their posts (a fourth, Wilbur Mills, resigned under pressure).

Next came the democratizing reforms. Members were limited in the number of committee and subcommittee berths they could occupy and the number they could chair. As the constraints became more binding, it was necessary to move further down the ladder of seniority to fill positions. Power thus became more broadly distributed.

But perhaps the most significant reforms were those that strengthened the Speaker and made the position accountable to the caucus. In 1973 House party leaders (Speaker, majority leader, and whip) were included on the Committee on Committees, giving them an increased say in committee assignments. The caucus also established the Steering and Policy Committee with the Speaker as chair. In 1974 Democratic committee assignments were taken away from the party's complement on Ways and Means and given to the new committee. In addition, the Speaker was given the power to appoint and remove a majority of the members of the committee and the Democratic members of the Rules Committee. In 1974 the Speaker also was empowered to refer bills simultaneously or sequentially to several committees, to create ad hoc committees, and, in 1977, to set time limits for their deliberations. Finally, in 1977 Speaker Thomas P. O'Neill started employing task forces to develop and manage particular policy issues. These task forces overlapped but were not coincident with the committees of jurisdiction and, most significant, they were appointed by the Speaker.

The caucus itself became more powerful. As mentioned, caucus majorities could instruct the Rules Committee and elect committee chairs and Appropriations subcommittee chairs. Caucus meetings could be called easily, requiring only a small number of signatories to a request, so that party matters could be thoroughly aired. In effect, the caucus became a substitute arena for both the floor and the committee rooms in which issues could be joined and majorities mobilized.

The revolt of the 1970s thus strengthened four power centers. It liberated members and subcommittees, restored to the Speakership an authority it had not known since the days of Joe Cannon,* and invigorated the party caucus. Some of the reforms had a decentralizing effect, some a recentralizing effect. Standing committees and their chairs were caught in the middle. Geography and party benefited; the division-of-labor jurisdictions were its victims. . . .

A New Textbook Congress?

The textbook Congress of the 1940s and 1950s reflected an equilibrium of sorts among institutional structure, partisan alignments, and electoral forces. There was a "conspiracy" between jurisdiction and geography. Congressional institutions were organized around policy jurisdictions, and geographic forces were accommodated through an assignment process that ensured representatives would land berths on committees important to their constituents. Reciprocity and deference sealed the bargain. Committees controlled policy formation in their respective jurisdictions. Floor activity was generally dominated by members from the committee of jurisdiction. Members' resources were sufficiently modest that they were devoted chiefly to committee-related activities. Constituencies were sufficiently homogeneous that this limitation did not, for most members, impose much hardship. Coordination was accomplished by senior committee members, each minding his own store. This system was supported by a structure that rewarded specialization, hard work, and waiting one's turn in the queue. Parties hovered in the background as the institutional means for organizing each chamber and electing leaders. Occasionally they would serve to mobilize majorities for partisan objectives, but these occasions were rare. The parties, especially the Democrats, were heteroge-

---

*Representative Joseph Cannon (R-Ill.) served as Speaker from 1903 to 1911. His power in this office was successfully challenged by a coalition of Democrats and dissident Republicans in 1910.

neous holding companies, incapable of cohering around specific policy directions except under unusual circumstances and therefore unwilling to empower their respective leaders or caucuses.

Something happened in the 1960s. The election of an executive and a congressional majority from the same party certainly was one important feature. Policy activism, restrained since the end of World War II, was encouraged. This exacerbated some divisions inside the Democratic coalition, leading to piecemeal institutional tinkering such as the expansion of the Rules Committee and the circumvention of the Appropriations Committee. At the same time the Voting Rights Act, occasioned by the temporarily oversized condition of the majority party in the Eighty-ninth Congress, set into motion political events that, together with demographic and economic trends, altered political alignments in the South. By the 1980s, Democrats from the North and the South were coming into greater agreement on matters of policy.

Thus the underlying conditions supporting the equilibrium among geographical, jurisdictional, and partisan imperatives were overwhelmed during the 1960s. The 1970s witnessed adjustments to these changed conditions that transformed the textbook Congress. Institutional reform was initiated by the Democratic Caucus. Demographic, generational, and political trends, frustrated by the inexorable workings of the seniority system, sought an alternative mode of expression. Majorities in the caucus remade the committee system. With this victimization came less emphasis on specialization, less deference toward committees as the floor became a genuine forum for policy formulation, and a general fraying of the division of labor.

One trend began with the Legislative Reorganization Act of 1946 itself. In the past forty years members have gradually acquired the resources to free themselves from other institutional players. The condition of the contemporary member of Congress has been described as "atomistic individualism" and the members themselves have been called "enterprises." The slow accretion of resources permitted members to respond to the changes in their home districts and encouraged them to cross the boundaries of specialization. These developments began to erode the reciprocity, deference, and division of labor that defined the textbook Congress.

The old equilibrium between geography and jurisdiction, with party hovering in the background, has changed. Geography (as represented by resource-rich member enterprises) has undermined the strictures of jurisdiction. But has the new order liberated party from its former holding-company status? In terms of political power the Democratic Caucus has reached new heights in the past decade. Party leaders have not had so many institutional tools and resources since the days of Boss Cannon. Committee leaders have never in the modern era been weaker or more beholden to party institutions. And, in terms of voting behavior, Democrats and Republicans have not exhibited as much internal cohesion in a good long while. Party, it would seem, is on the rise. But so, too, are the member enterprises.

What, then, has grown up in the vacuum created by the demise of the textbook Congress? I am not convinced that relationships have settled into a regular pattern in anything like the way they were institutionalized in the textbook Congress.

First, too many members of Congress remain too dissatisfied. The aggressive moves by Jim Wright* to redefine the Speaker's role are a partial response to this circumstance. Prospective changes in the Senate majority party leadership alignment in the 101st Congress convey a similar signal. The issue at stake is whether central party organs can credibly coordinate activities in Congress, thereby damping the centrifugal tendencies of resource-rich members, or whether leaders will remain, in one scholar's words, "janitors for an untidy chamber."

One possible equilibrium of a new textbook Congress, therefore, would have member enterprises balanced off against party leaders; committees and other manifestations of a specialized division of labor would be relegated to the background. Coordination, formerly achieved in a piecemeal, decentralized fashion by the committee system, would fall heavily on party leaders and their institutional allies, the Rules and Budget committees and the party caucuses. However, unless party leaders can construct a solution to the budgetary mess in Congress—a solution that will entail revising the budget process—the burden of coordination will be more than the leaders can bear. Government by continuing resolutions, reconciliation proposals, and other omnibus mechanisms forms an unstable fulcrum for institutional equilibrium.[†]

Second, any success from the continued strengthening of leadership resources and institutions is highly contingent on the support of the members. Strong leadership institutions have to be seen by the rank and file as solutions to institutional problems. This requires a consensus among majority party members both on the nature of the problems and the desirability of the solutions. A consensus of sorts has existed for several years: demographic and other trends have homogenized the priorities of Democrats; experience with the spate of reforms in the 1970s has convinced many that decentralized ways of doing things severely tax the capacity of Congress to act; and, since 1982, the Reagan presidency has provided a unifying target.

But what happens if the bases for consensus erode? A major issue—trade and currency problems, for instance, or war in Central America or the Middle East—could set region against region within the majority party and reverse the trend toward consensus. Alternatively, the election of a Democratic president could redefine the roles of legislative leaders, possibly pitting congressional and presidential factions against one another in a battle for partisan leadership.[‡]

---

*Jim Wright was Speaker from 1987 to 1989.

[†]Reconciliation proposals and continuing resolutions are budget-related bills that often combine many subjects in a catch-all (or omnibus) piece of legislation. Control by committees or other specialized groupings is rendered difficult by such practices.

[‡]As of 1994, that had not happened much in the Clinton administration, although House Democratic Whip David Bonior did lead the opposition to the Clinton-backed North American Free Trade Agreement in 1993.

The point here is that the equilibrium between strong leaders and strong members is vulnerable to perturbations in the circumstances supporting it.

. . . The member enterprises, however, will not go away. Members will never again be as specialized, as deferential, as willing "to go along to get along" as in the textbook Congress of the 1950s. For better or worse, we are stuck with full-service members of Congress. They are incredibly competent at representing the diverse interests that geographic representation has given them. But can they pass a bill or mobilize a coalition? Can they govern?

Questions for Discussion

1. How did the seniority system, which rewarded simple longevity rather than talent or political support, survive for so long? What are the advantages of promoting leaders based on seniority? The liabilities?
2. Why do you think legislators create strong "member enterprises"? Why might these undermine the committee system?

 10.3

The New World of U.S. Senators

Barbara Sinclair

The United States Senate has long been described as the "world's most exclusive club," where elegant, well-crafted, and civil debates take place, and where the great issues of the day are discussed and decided. Although this is true, to an extent, it has never been an accurate depiction of the Senate. Rather, each political era creates its own Senate, which operates with minimal rules and maximum flexibility for individual legislators. Even now, we often view the Senate through

Barbara Sinclair is the Marvin Hoffenberg Professor of American Politics at the University of California, Los Angeles.

Barbara Sinclair, "The New World of US Senators" in *Congress Considered*, 8e by Lawrence Dodd and Bruce Oppenheimer, 2006, pp. 1–22. Copyright © 2006 CQ Press, a division of Congressional Quarterly Inc. Reprinted by permission of the publisher, CQ Press.

the lenses of the 1950s, when elderly, white southern men dominated the chamber, and progressive legislation—especially civil rights—was laid to rest.

That may have been your grandfather's Senate, but it is not the Senate of today. Over the past forty years, the Senate has changed dramatically, and no one has chronicled and analyzed the collection of changes more acutely than political scientist Barbara Sinclair. In this selection, drawn from a 2006 essay, Sinclair argues that the Senate has become both more partisan and more individualistic (two seemingly incompatible trends) over time. As she develops these themes, Sinclair offers us an image of a modern, highly partisan institution that also willingly clings to past traditions that allow individual senators tremendous leeway in how they do their jobs. In the end, the Senate remains a bit of a club, with its 100 members, but it is also a venue for tough-minded, highly partisan politics that have become, more and more, the order of the day.

◆ A courtly older gentleman—probably a conservative southern Democrat, perhaps even white haired and clad in a white linen suit—working in committee behind closed doors

◆ A policy entrepreneur—Democrat or Republican, liberal or conservative— pursuing his cause singly or with a few allies on the Senate floor, aggressively using nongermane amendments and extended debate as his weapons

◆ A partisan warrior, acting as a member of a party team, dueling with his opposing party counterparts in the public arena and on the floor, using all the procedural and PR tools available

These three images capture the differences among the Senates of the 1950s, the 1970s, and the 1990s and beyond. To be sure, they are simplifications, and some elements of the 1950s Senate and many of the 1970s Senate still persist. Yet the Senate of the early twenty-first century is very different from the 1950s Senate, which fictional and some journalistic accounts still often depict as current, and appreciably different from the 1970s Senate.

The U.S. Senate has the most permissive rules of any legislature in the world. Extended debate allows senators to hold the floor as long as they wish unless cloture is invoked, which requires a supermajority of sixty votes. The Senate's amending rules enable senators to offer any and as many amendments as they please to almost any bill, and those amendments need not even be germane. The extent to which senators make full use of their prerogatives under the rules has varied over time. The Senate as it enters the twenty-first century is characterized by fairly cohesive party contingents that aggressively exploit Senate rules to pursue partisan advantage, but also by the persistence of the Senate individualism that developed in the 1960s and 1970s. . . .

Development of the Individualist, Partisan Senate

The Senate of the 1950s was a clubby, inward-looking body governed by constraining norms; influence was relatively unequally distributed and centered in strong committees and their senior leaders, who were most often conservatives, frequently southern Democrats. The typical senator of the 1950s was a specialist who concentrated on the issues that came before his committees. His legislative activities were largely confined to the committee room; he was seldom active on the Senate floor, was highly restrained in his exercise of the prerogatives the Senate rules gave him, and made little use of the media.

The Senate's institutional structure and the political environment rewarded such behavior. The lack of staff made it hard for new senators to participate intelligently right away, so serving an apprenticeship helped prevent a new member from making a fool of himself early in his career. Meager staff resources also made specialization the only really feasible course for attaining influence. Restraint in exploiting extended debate was encouraged by the lack of time pressure, which would later make extended debate such a formidable weapon; when floor time is plentiful, the leverage senators derive from extended debate is much less. Furthermore, the dominant southern Democrats had a strong, constituency-based interest in restricting and thus protecting the filibuster for their one big issue—opposition to civil rights.

The majority of senators, especially the southern Democrats, faced no imminent reelection peril so long as they were free to reflect their constituents' views in their votes and capable of providing the projects their constituents desired. The system of reciprocity, which dictated that senators do constituency-related favors for one another whenever possible, served them well. The seniority system, bolstered by norms* of apprenticeship, specialization, and intercommittee reciprocity, assured members of considerable independent influence in their area of jurisdiction if they stayed in the Senate long enough and did not make that influence dependent on their voting behavior. For the moderate-to-conservative Senate membership, the parochial and limited legislation such a system produced was quite satisfactory. The Senate of the 1950s was an institution well designed for its generally conservative and electorally secure members to further their goals.

Membership turnover and a transformation of the political environment altered the costs and benefits of such behavior and induced members to change the institution; over time, norms, practices, and rules were altered. The 1958 elections brought into the Senate a big class of new senators with different policy goals and reelection needs. Mostly northern Democrats, they were activist liberals, and most had been elected in highly competitive contests, in many cases having defeated incumbents. Both their policy goals and their reelection needs

---

*Norms are informal rules of the game that most legislators adhere to, most of the time.

dictated a more activist style; these senators simply could not afford to wait to make their mark. Subsequent elections brought in more and more such members.

In the 1960s, the political environment began a transformation. A host of new issues rose to prominence—first civil rights, then environmental issues and consumer rights, the war in Vietnam and the questions about American foreign and defense policy that it raised, women's rights and women's liberation, the rights of other ethnic groups, especially Latinos and Native Americans, of the poor, of the disabled, and by the early 1970s, gay rights. These were issues that engaged, often intensely, many ordinary citizens, and politics became more highly charged. The interest group community exploded in size and became more diverse; many of the social movements of the 1960s already had or spawned interest groups. So a horde of environmental groups, consumer groups, women's groups, and other liberal social welfare and civil rights groups joined the Washington political community and made it more diverse. Then, in response to some of these groups' policy successes—for example, on environmental legislation—the business community mobilized; in the 1970s, many more businesses established a permanent presence in Washington and specialized trade associations proliferated. The media—especially television—became a much bigger player in politics. . . .

By the mid-1970s the individualist Senate had emerged. The Senate had become a body in which every member, regardless of seniority, considered himself entitled to participate on any issue that interested him for either constituency or policy reasons. Senators took for granted that they—and their colleagues— would regularly exploit the powers the Senate rules gave them. Senators became increasingly outward directed, focusing on their links with interest groups, policy communities, and the media more than on their ties to one another.

The 1980 elections made Ronald Reagan president and, to almost everyone's surprise, brought a Republican majority to the Senate. As president, Reagan was more conservative and confrontational than his Republican predecessors of the post–World War II era, and his election signaled an intensification of ideological conflict that increasingly fell along partisan lines.

Realignment in the South, the Proposition 13 tax-cutting fever,* the rise of the Christian Right, and the development of the property rights movement were changing the political parties. In 1961 not a single senator from the eleven states of the old Confederacy was a Republican; by 1973, seven were, and by 1980 that number had risen to ten. In 2004 the number stood at thirteen, or 59 percent of the senators from the once solidly Democratic old South. As conservative southern Democrats were replaced by even more conservative

---

*Proposition 13 was a voter-sponsored initiative, which the California electorate approved in 1978 and which provided for drastic cuts on the state's soaring property taxes. Politicians in other states observed the support given this measure and embarked on various efforts to cut taxes across the country.

southern Republicans, the congressional Democratic Party became more homogeneously liberal and the Republican Party more conservative. Outside the South as well, Republican candidates and activists were becoming more ideologically conservative.

Voting on the Senate floor became increasingly partisan. In the late 1960s and early 1970s, a majority of Democrats opposed a majority of Republicans on only about a third of Senate roll call votes. By the 1990s, from half to two-thirds of roll calls were such party votes, and that continues today. The frequency with which senators voted with their partisan colleagues on party votes increased significantly as well. By the 1990s a typical party vote saw well over 80 percent of Democrats voting together on one side and well over 80 percent of Republicans on the other. In the 107th Congress (2001–2002), 89 percent of Democrats opposed 88 percent of Republicans on a typical party vote.

Partisan polarization has made participation through their parties more attractive to senators than it was when the parties were more heterogeneous and the ideological distance between them was less. Recent Senate party leaders have sought to provide more channels for members to participate in and through the party. Increasingly, senators of the same party are acting as a party team and are exploiting Senate prerogatives to gain partisan advantage.

Over this same time period, the Senate membership has become more diverse. Although most senators are still white men, the 108th Congress (2003–2004) did include fourteen women—an all-time high*—one Japanese American, one of Hawaiian and Chinese descent, and one Native American. By contrast, in the 85th Congress (1957–1958), every senator was white and only one was female. This greater diversity influences how the Senate operates, but its impact cannot compete with that of individualism and intense partisanship.

The Legislative Process in the Contemporary Senate

What effect has the combination of individualism and partisanship had on the legislative process in the Senate? Individualism changed how Senate committees work and altered even more floor-related legislative routines, complicating the Senate majority leader's job of floor scheduling and coordination. Intensified partisanship exacerbated the problems the majority leader faces in keeping the Senate functioning as a legislative body. . . .

Majority Leadership and the Senate Floor

In the contemporary Senate, floor scheduling is of necessity an exercise in broad and bipartisan accommodation. Although he is not the Senate's presiding

---

*In the 110th Congress (2007–2008), there are sixteen women in the Senate.

officer and lasks many of the powers the House Speaker commands, the Senate majority leader is as close to a central leader as the chamber has, and he is charged with scheduling legislation for floor consideration. To bring legislation to the floor, the majority leader uses his right of first recognition, a prerogative he has had under Senate precedents since the 1930s. The majority leader can move that a bill be taken off the calendar and considered, but the motion to proceed is a debatable—and thus filibusterable—motion. Or he can ask unanimous consent that the bill be taken off the calendar and considered, a request that can be blocked by any senator's objection. Clearly, any senator can cause problems for the majority leader.

How Senators Cause Trouble: The Strategic Use of Senate Rules.   Understanding the problems of legislative scheduling in the Senate and the routines that have developed requires a look at the strategic use of Senate rules by the individualistic and now also increasingly partisan Senate membership.

The filibuster, the use of extended debate to prevent a vote on a motion or measure unless a supermajority can be mustered, is certainly the best-known strategic use of Senate rules. With the development of the individualist Senate, the use of extended debate and of cloture* to try to cut it off increased enormously (see Table 1). To be sure, the data must be regarded with some caution. When lengthy debate becomes a filibuster is, in part, a matter of judgment. Furthermore . . . filibusters have changed their form in recent years, and threats to filibuster have become much more frequent than actual talkathons on the floor. As a consequence, cloture is sometimes sought before any overt evidence of a filibuster manifests itself on the floor. Nevertheless, experts and participants agree that the frequency of obstructionism has increased. In the 1950s filibusters were rare; they increased during the 1960s and again during the 1970s. By the late 1980s and the 1990s they had become routine, occurring at a rate of more than one a month—considerably more, if only the time the Senate is in session is counted. Cloture votes have increased in tandem, and more than one cloture vote per issue is now the norm. Cloture votes were, however, decreasingly likely to be successful through the late 1990s; in the early to middle 1980s, 43 percent got the requisite sixty votes to cut off debate; in the late 1980s and early 1990s, 39 percent did; in the period 1993–1998, only 28 percent did. In 1999–2002, the likelihood of a cloture vote being successful increased again to a bit more than half but only because more were taken after an agreement had been reached. Almost all of the winning cloture votes were very one-sided. When the parties split on a cloture vote, cloture was very unlikely to be imposed. The rate of successful cloture votes plunged to an all time low in 2003, when only one of twenty-three was successful.

---

*Cloture is the act of cutting off debate in the Senate; on most issues, 60 votes are required to enact cloture. Thus, the Senate often needs to have 60 votes in favor of a proposal to allow for its passage.

Table 1

The Increase in Filibusters and Cloture Votes, 1951–2002

Years	Congresses	Filibusters (per Congress)	Cloture Votes (per Congress)	Successful Cloture Votes (per Congress)
1951–1960	82nd–86th	1.0	0.4	0.0
1961–1970	87th–91st	4.6	5.2	0.8
1971–1980	92nd–96th	11.2	22.4	8.6
1981–1986	97th–99th	16.7	23.0	10.0
1987–1992	100th–102nd	26.7	39.0	15.3
1993–1998	103rd–105th	28.0	48.3	13.7
1999–2002	106th–107th	32.0	59.0	30.5

Sources: Data for 82nd–102nd Congresses: column 3, Congressional Research Service, comp., "A Look at the Senate Filibuster," in *Democratic Studies Group Special Report*, June 13, 1994, app. B; columns 4–5, Norman Ornstein, Thomas Mann, and Michael Malbin, *Vital Statistics on Congress 1993–1994* (Washington, D.C.: CQ Press, 1994), 162. Data for 103rd Congress: Richard S. Beth, "Cloture in the Senate, 103rd Congress," memorandum, Congressional Research Service, June 23, 1995. Data for 104th–107th Congresses: *Congressional Quarterly Almanac* for the years 1995–2002 (Washington, D.C.: Congressional Quarterly).

As filibusters became more frequent, the character of the filibusters and of the targeted legislation broadened. By the 1970s liberals as well as conservatives frequently used this weapon, and senators used it on all sorts of legislation, parochial as well as momentous. For example, as Congress was rushing to adjourn in October 1992, Sen. Alfonse D'Amato, R-N.Y., held the floor for fifteen hours and fifteen minutes to protest the removal from an urban-aid tax bill of a provision he said could have restored jobs at a New York typewriter plant. . . .

Nominations as well as legislation can be filibustered. . . . Senators now often block nominees they do not oppose in order to gain a bargaining chip for use with the administration. The nomination of William Holbrook as ambassador to the United Nations in 1999 was held up for months over matters having nothing to do with him. Sen. Charles Grassley, R-Iowa, wanted the administration to respond to his concerns about the treatment of a State Department whistleblower; Sens. Mitch McConnell, R-Ky., and Trent Lott, R-Miss., hoped to extract from the president a promise to appoint their candidate to the Federal Elections Commission. In 2003, Sen. Larry Craig, R-Idaho, placed holds on all Air Force promotions—which, of course, are normally approved routinely. Senator Craig had no objections to any of the Air Force personnel up for promotion; he wanted to force the Air Force to deliver on a promise he claimed it had made to station several planes at a base in Idaho. . . .

With the growth of partisan polarization, the minorities making use of Senate prerogatives are more often organized, partisan ones. In the 103rd Congress the minority Republicans used actual and threatened filibusters to deprive President Bill Clinton and the majority Democrats of numerous policy successes. Clinton's economic stimulus package, campaign finance and lobbying reform bills, and bills revamping the Superfund program, revising clean drinking water regulations, overhauling outdated telecommunications law, and applying federal labor laws to Congress were among the casualties. In the 104th and 105th Congresses, minority Democrats used extended debate to kill many Republican priorities, including ambitious regulatory overhaul legislation and far-reaching property rights bills. In the 103rd Congress, Republicans extracted concessions on many major Democratic bills—voter registration legislation ("motor voter") and the national service program, for example. Then, in the 104th Congress, Democrats used the same strategy to force concessions on product liability legislation, the Freedom to Farm bill, and telecommunications legislation, among others. In 2002 Republicans, then in the minority in the Senate, refused to allow a vote before the elections on the Democrats' version of the bill setting up the new Homeland Security Department; Democrats had the votes to pass a bill Bush disliked, and Republicans wanted to use a bill's not having passed as a campaign issue. At the end of the first session of the 108th Congress in 2003, minority Democrats refused Republicans an up-or-down vote on the conference report for the massive energy bill that Bush and most Republicans very much wanted to enact and many Democrats strongly opposed.

. . . Visible filibusters are now just the tip of the iceberg. The Senate's permissive rules have much more effect on the legislative process through filibuster threats than through actual filibusters. [These threats include the use of a "hold," which a knowledgeable participant explained as "a letter to your leader telling him which of the many powers that you have as a senator you intend to use on a given issue." Most holds, then, are threats to object to a unanimous consent agreement.*] Holds are the "lazy man's filibuster," a staffer complained. Sometimes placed by staff on their own initiative, sometimes at the instigation of lobbyists, holds require little effort on the part of senators, . . . and yet they enormously complicate the legislative process and not infrequently kill or severely weaken worthy legislation. . . .

Since holds are nowhere specified in Senate rules, why do Senate leaders condone and, in fact, maintain the hold system? "It's to the majority leader's advantage to have holds because it gives him information," a knowledgeable observer explained. "He's always trying to negotiate unanimous consent agreements, and he needs to know if there are pockets of problems, and holds do

---

*Unanimous consent agreements are understandings, often formalized in writing, hammered out by the majority and minority party leaders, who consult with their members and reach an agreement on how debate will proceed on a bill. The key word here is *unanimous*, in that all senators must be accommodated on procedures.

that." An expert concluded succinctly, "The only way you could get rid of holds would be to change the rules of the Senate drastically."

Critics often argue that leaders should be tougher and call the bluff of members more often. The threat to filibuster supposedly inherent in holds would, in many cases, prove to be empty rhetoric if put to the test, such critics claim. In fact, holds are not automatic vetoes. A hold cannot kill *must-pass* legislation such as appropriations bills, and in deciding how seriously to take a hold on less vital legislation, the leader weighs the reputation of the senator placing the hold; "some people are taken more seriously because it's just assumed they're willing to back it up," a leadership aide explained. . . .

Individualism, Partisanship, and Legislative Outcomes

How does the combination of individualism and intense partisanship that characterizes the contemporary Senate affect legislative outcomes? As shown in Table 2, the likelihood of a major measure becoming law is less in recent Congresses than in earlier ones. In the three 1990s Congresses and the first of the twenty-first century, all of which saw at least half of the major measures subject to some sort of filibuster problem, 42 percent of the major measures failed enactment. By contrast, in three earlier Congresses, characterized by lower filibuster activity, 27 percent of the major measures failed. Of course there are many steps in the legislative process, and these figures by themselves do not prove that the Senate is responsible for the increase in legislative failures. However, as also shown in Table 2, for the latter four Congresses, legislation

Table 2
Where Major Measures Failed

	Number of Failed Measures	
What Happened?	91st, 95th, and 97th Congresses	103rd, 104th, 105th, and 107th Congresses
Passed by neither House nor Senate	16	22
Passed by House but not by Senate	12	33
Passed by Senate but not by House	8	3
Passed by House and Senate	6	22
Total number of failed measures	42 (of 156 measures)	80 (of 192 measures)
Percentage of total measures that failed	27%	42%

Source: Author's calculations.

was much more likely to pass the House but fail in the Senate than the reverse; in the earlier Congresses, the difference was not very great.

Does the increasing frequency with which measures encounter extended-debate–related problems in the Senate explain this pattern? Filibuster problems do, in fact, depress a measure's chances of surviving the legislative process. Of those measures that did not encounter such a problem, either because senators chose not to use their prerogatives or because the measure enjoyed statutory protection, 74 percent were enacted; only 54 percent of those that did experience a filibuster problem became law. Since filibusters and filibuster threats are by no means always intended to kill legislation, those figures suggest a considerable effect. Filibuster problems are more likely to occur on partisan legislation, and when a measure is partisan at the committee level and also encounters a filibuster problem, its chances of enactment are significantly decreased. Less than half (46 percent) of such measures were successfully enacted, in contrast to 80 percent of the measures that were not partisan and did not experience an extended-debate–related problem, and 57 percent that had one but not both of these characteristics.

Thus, the combination of individualism and intense partisanship that characterizes the contemporary Senate does depress the likelihood of legislation successfully surviving the legislative process. Yet given the character of Senate rules and the ways in which senators currently exploit them, it is perhaps more surprising that the Senate manages to legislate at all. The Senate does pass a lot of legislation, both must-pass measures such as appropriations bills and other major bills. To be sure, some measures—budget resolutions and reconciliation bills, most importantly—are protected from filibusters and nongermane amendments by law, and that has been vital to the passage of some of the most important legislation of the last decade. But much legislation without such protection gets through the Senate as well.

Dodging Legislative Breakdown

Clearly, the Senate could not function if senators maximally exploited their prerogatives—if, for example, every senator objected to every unanimous consent agreement on any matter he or she did not completely support. What, then, keeps senators as individuals and as party teams from pushing their prerogatives over the limit and miring the Senate in gridlock?

Asked that question, senators, staff, and informed observers uniformly responded that almost all senators want to "get something done" and that they are aware that many senators' exploiting their prerogatives to the limit would make that impossible. As one knowledgeable insider phrased it, "I like to think of the Senate as a bunch of armed nuclear nations. Each senator knows he can blow the place up, but most of them came here to do something, and if he does blow things up, if he does use his powers that way, then he won't be able to do anything." Using one's prerogatives aggressively entails concrete short-run costs, most also argued. "If you do object [to a unanimous consent request], it's going to hurt someone and maybe more than one person," a senior staffer explained, "so the next time you want something, it may very well happen to you." In the Senate, individuals can exact retribution swiftly and often quite easily on those they believe have harmed them. Because of that, a junior senator and former House member reported, "In the Senate, you don't go out of your way to hack people off." In the House there is less such concern, he explained. The likelihood that some retaliation will be forthcoming forces the wise senator to be selective in the employment of his prerogatives. . . .

Similar considerations restrain senators as party teams and especially their leaders. The leaders are very much aware that as much as senators want to gain partisan advantage on the big issues, they also want, for both reelection and policy reasons, to pass bills. . . . The leaders are instrumental in maintaining the cooperation necessary to keep the Senate functioning. They do so by working together closely, by adeptly employing both procedural and peer pressure to encourage the recalcitrant to deal, and by accommodating to some extent all senators with problems. Although the procedural resources and the favors the leaders command are fairly meager, they do have one persuasive argument for inducing cooperation. As a knowledgeable insider put it, "[Senators] can use the powers they have to create chaos and confusion on the floor, in which case senators don't have a life. . . . where the floor debate goes on to all hours without any knowledge of when anything will happen, or they can defer to their leaders to create a structure with some predictability, and then they do have a life. And that's the bargain they have made." . . .

In its everyday functioning, the contemporary Senate exhibits a peculiar combination of conflict and cooperation, of aggressive exploitation of rules and accommodation. The hottest partisan legislative battles are studded with unanimous consent agreements. And the more intense the partisan fight, the more frequently the majority and minority leaders confer. On bills not at the center of partisan conflict, senators routinely cooperate across the partisan divide. As a senior aide expressed the consensus, "If you really want to move stuff, if it's not a big partisan matter, a big ideological issue, and you really want to move it, then you really have to be bipartisan. You've got to work out the difficulties, and you've got to work across the aisle." . . .

Thus senators' acute awareness of the weapons all senators command can work to produce cooperation and some restraint. Everyone knows that legislative breakdown is a very real possibility, and this seems to have a sobering effect. Yet, in an era of intensified partisanship combined with the continuing individualism that has characterized the Senate since the 1970s, the Senate legislative process is fragile. Senate party leaders are under considerable pressure from their members to pursue partisan advantage aggressively, and partisan battles aimed at electoral gain are zero-sum. The rewards of Senate individualism can be great, as John McCain's presidential candidacy demonstrated. Most of the time, the Senate manages to maintain the minimum restraint and cooperation necessary to avoid total gridlock, yet the chamber regularly seems to teeter on the precipice of legislative breakdown.

A Less Effective Senate?

Have individualism and partisanship and their impact on the legislative process made the Senate of today less effective than the Senate of the 1950s? Does the Senate play a less important role in our political life than it used to?

The contemporary Senate performs certain important functions well. It provides senators with an excellent forum for agenda setting, debate framing, and policy incubation. Using their prerogatives under Senate rules and their access to the media, senators as individuals, and now as party teams, publicize problems, promote solutions, speak for a wide variety of claimant groups, and provide a visible and legitimate opposition view—and increasingly an alternative agenda—to the president's. . . .

Furthermore, some scholars and journalists argue that Senate rules and the ways they are currently used actually give the Senate a bargaining advantage over other political actors. In particular, when the Senate and House meet in conference committee to resolve their differences over a bill, Senate conferees can, and sometimes do, use the fact that Senate approval effectively requires a supermajority to their advantage; if the conferees move the bill too far from the Senate version, a filibuster will block the bill in the Senate, they argue. Certainly, House members complain bitterly about such Senate "blackmail."

Finally, the enactment into law of nonincremental policy change seems considerably more a function of the external political environment than of the institutional structure within the legislative chambers. For example, in 1995–1996, Democrats and some moderate Republicans, using Senate rules, blocked much of Newt Gingrich's Contract with America that the House had passed. On the one hand, Senate rules were instrumental, but on the other, it is most unlikely that, had there been strong public support for the bills in question, senators would have been willing to incur the public's wrath and kill the legislation.

So the question, Is the Senate of today a less effective legislative body? has no simple answer. The Senate's nonmajoritarian rules as currently used greatly exacerbate the problems of building winning coalitions, and so the contemporary Senate is always at risk of legislative breakdown. If a legislature cannot respond to the problems that concern the people it represents, it loses legitimacy. That has not happened to the Senate yet, but the possibility is not farfetched.

Questions for Discussion

1. How has the Senate changed from the 1950s era described by Shepsle in "The Changing Textbook Congress" (selection 10.1)? Does it matter that there are sixteen women in the Senate as of 2007?
2. Sinclair emphasizes the continuing individualism in the Senate and its growing partisanship. Which do you think is the more profound force in shaping the Senate's actions? Why?

 10.4

The Broken Branch

Thomas E. Mann and Norman Ornstein

Those who study the Congress possess genuine affection for their chosen subject, perhaps more than those who study any other American political institution (the presidency, the Supreme Court, political parties, etc.). With 535 individualistic legislators, who represent widely differing states and districts, the U.S. Congress is continually surprising, frustrating, unwieldy, and ultimately the voice of the American people. The core representational linkage between the electorate and its rulers lies within the Congress. Over the course of the American experience, the bonds between the people and their representatives have often been frayed. The Congress, as a collective of ambitious and strongminded individuals, can be unresponsive to major issues, or may respond far too much to the parochial concerns of local constituencies. So it goes, and congressional scholars generally take these faults as the costs of representative democracy.

But the Congress can fail, especially when it does not effectively represent its own interests within the checks-and-balances system of American national politics. In particular, its failure is most serious when it does not stand up to a president

Thomas E. Mann is a senior fellow in governance studies at the Brookings Institution and Norman Ornstein is a resident scholar at the American Enterprise Institute.

who seeks to increase his own power, and that of the executive branch, at the expense of the Congress. In this selection, drawn from the introduction to a major critique of the Congress, Thomas Mann and Norman Ornstein argue that the legislative branch is indeed broken, largely because it has failed almost completely to limit the power of an overreaching president. Although their argument often uses partisan examples, given the Republican control of both branches from 2003 to 2006, Mann and Ornstein worry most about the power and legitimacy of the Congress as a whole; for them, a weakened legislative branch fatally injures our entire system of government.

The bill that brought House members to a fateful vote early on November 23, 2003, was not your average piece of legislation. It was the major social policy initiative of President George W. Bush and the top priority of his congressional leaders. Shortly before six o'clock in the morning on that Sunday, following a debate that began Saturday and a vote that began at 3 A.M., a House of Representatives described by the *New York Times* as "fiercely polarized" passed a bill to provide prescription drug benefits under Medicare. The 220 to 215 vote, begun under the normal procedure that routinely limits votes to fifteen minutes, took two hours and fifty-one minutes to complete; the *Times* piece said it took "an extraordinary bout of Republican arm-twisting to muster a majority."

Extraordinary it was. At exactly 3 A.M., Rep. Richard "Doc" Hastings (R-WA), presiding over the House, announced that the time for debate on the Medicare bill had expired. He said from the chair, "Members will have fifteen minutes to record their votes." As *Congress Daily* described it, the roll call opened at 3:01 A.M., with seventeen Republicans immediately voting no. The official time expired at 3:15 A.M. with no Democrats having voted for the bill, twenty-two Republicans against it, and the nays ahead. At 3:30, the vote still open, the official tally was 212 for and 214 against. At 3:40, Republican Dana Rohrbacher, after intense discussions at the back of the chamber with Speaker Dennis Hastert and fellow California Republicans David Dreier and Duncan Hunter, voted yes, moving the tally to 213 for and 214 against. By 3:48, the vote was 215 to 218; for the first time, the opposition to the bill had an absolute majority of the House on its side. The vote went on.

Over the next fifteen minutes, Speaker Hastert spoke directly to a few of the Republicans who had voted no: Marilyn Musgrave of Colorado, Ernest Istook of Oklahoma, and Nick Smith of Michigan. Musgrave waved the Speaker off; a lengthy conversation with Smith ended with Smith refusing to switch to yes. At 4 A.M., Democrat Ken Lucas changed from present to no. One minute later, after speaking with Hastert, Istook switched from no to yes, making the vote 216 for and 218 against. At 4:20 A.M., Speaker Hastert, joined by Health and Human Services (HHS) Secretary Tommy Thompson, returned to Nick Smith, who had announced his retirement from the House and was hoping his son would be able to succeed him. Hastert sat on one side of him, Thompson on the other, for an extended conversation.

At 5:30 A.M., with no movement in the preceding ninety minutes, Hastert and Ways and Means Committee Chairman Bill Thomas surrounded Nick Smith near the Republican entrance to the House chamber, joined by Thompson and others. He again declined to change. In the meantime, House Majority Leader Tom DeLay and other leaders gathered in the cloakroom with a group of GOP "no" voters, many of whom had been telephoned only a few minutes earlier by President Bush. At 5:53, DeLay emerged, smiling, having persuaded Reps. C. L. "Butch" Otter of Idaho and Trent Franks of Arizona to switch their votes, following which several other members also changed their votes (in both directions), leading to the final margin of 220 to 215. The gavel came down quickly.

Speaker Hastert and Majority Leader DeLay were delighted. House Democrats and some Republicans were outraged. "Never have I seen such a grotesque, arbitrary, and gross abuse of power," commented John Dingell (D-MI), dean of the House and a forty-eight-year veteran of the body. Said Democrat Jerrold Nadler of New York, "They grossly abused the rules of the House by holding the vote open. The majority of the House expressed its will, 216 to 218. It means it's a dictatorship. It means you hold the vote open until you have the votes." *Congress Daily* quoted one Republican who voted against the bill, "It was an outrage. It was profoundly ugly and beneath the dignity of Congress." Even a senior Republican aide acknowledged it was "winning ugly."

The ugliness did not end with the vote. In a newspaper column the day after the vote, Rep. Smith accused his own party's leaders of trying to bribe him. "Bribes and special deals were offered to convince members to vote yes," he wrote. Smith elaborated upon the charges in an interview with Michigan radio station WKZO, saying he had been "pressured by the 'leadership'" and they had offered "$100,000-plus in campaign contributions," and threatened "Some of us are going to work to make sure your son doesn't get to Congress" unless he "relented." Smith subsequently softened his charge, but there was more corroboration. The *Washington Post*'s Jeffrey Smith described a lunch held in the back room of a Capitol Hill restaurant two days before the House vote at which twenty conservative Republican congressmen, including Nick Smith, swapped tales of the pressure they faced on the vote. In this account,

> According to two other congressmen who were present, Smith told the gathering that House Republican leaders had promised substantial financial and political support for his son's campaign if Smith voted yes.

Rep. Tom Tancredo (R-CO), who was at the luncheon, also heard Smith report that someone suggested that if he were to vote for the bill, his son would be the "beneficiary . . . up to the tune of about $100,000." Tancredo believed, "If Nick Smith said it happened, it happened."

Strong feelings about the Medicare vote and questions about the tactics used on the House floor lingered. On December 8, the House ended the first session of the 108th Congress by rejecting, on a party-line, 207–182 vote, a resolution by Minority Leader Nancy Pelosi that condemned Republicans' handling of the Medicare vote. As part of an extraordinarily tense exchange on the floor, Pelosi and Minority Whip Steny Hoyer harshly denounced GOP tactics. To the dismay and scorn of Democrats, none of the top Republican party leaders, including Speaker Hastert and Majority Leader DeLay, showed up for the debate. Pelosi said, "The Medicare vote will be remembered as one of the lowest moments in the history of the House." When she mentioned the allegations of bribery involving Nick Smith, other Democrats shouted, "Shame, shame."

The allegations of bribery were taken up by the bipartisan House Ethics Committee in March 2004. At the end of September, the committee unanimously admonished Majority Leader Tom DeLay and Michigan Rep. Candice Miller for violating House rules. Their report said "Majority Leader DeLay offered to endorse Representative Smith's son in exchange for Representative Smith's vote in favor of the Medicare bill . . . it is improper for a Member to offer or link support for the personal interests of another Member as part of a *quid pro quo* to achieve a legislative goal." The Ethics Committee reached the same conclusion about Candice Miller, who made statements to Smith on the floor that Smith "fairly interpreted . . . as a threat of retaliation against him for voting in opposition to the bill."

The House vote on the Medicare prescription drug bill was the longest roll call in modern House history. As Rules Committee Chairman David Dreier said during the December 8 House debate, this was not, technically speaking, against the rules. House Rule XX, clause 2 (a) says that there is a fifteen-minute *minimum* for most votes by electronic device. There is no formal maximum. A vote is not final until the vote numbers have been read by the Speaker and the result declared. Indeed, after the November vote, Dreier had said in a radio interview that he saw nothing wrong with keeping a vote open for days.

But the norm for such votes was established and clear from the time electronic voting began in January 1973: fifteen minutes is the voting time. Votes have routinely been left open for a minute or two solely to accommodate members who were delayed getting to the floor; that practice was abused enough that successive Speakers, Democrat and Republican, warned members that the fifteen-minute limit would be imposed if they did not show more promptness.

In the twenty-two years that Democrats ran the House after the electronic voting system was put in place, there was only one occasion when the vote period substantially exceeded the fifteen minutes, and that was in 1987 when an important budget bill was one vote short of passage and one of the bill's supporters reversed his vote and left to catch a plane, unaware that his switch sank the bill. Speaker Jim Wright's daring action, . . . resulted in passage of the bill but infuriated Republicans.

Their reaction seems ironic in light of what would happen several years later: Then–Minority Whip Trent Lott of Mississippi referred to "Jim Wright and his goons." Then–Rep. Dick Cheney of Wyoming, later to become minority whip before becoming vice president, called Wright a "son-of-a-bitch" and denounced the action as "the most arrogant, heavy-handed abuse of power I've ever seen in the ten years I've been here."

In 1995, soon after the Republicans gained the majority, Speaker Newt Gingrich declared his intention to make sure that votes would consistently be held in the fifteen-minute time frame. The "regular practice of the House," he said, would be "a policy of closing electronic votes as soon as possible after the guaranteed period of fifteen minutes." The policy was reiterated by Speaker Hastert when he assumed the post.

The legislative process that preceded this Medicare floor vote in the House was no less offensive to congressional norms of deliberation and due process. The bill was considered and legislation drafted ("marked up") in the House Ways and Means Committee in a purely partisan fashion, with minority Democrats virtually left out of the process. When the bill went to a House–Senate conference committee to resolve differences between the two chambers, House Democratic conferees—like all conferees, formally elected by the House itself—were excluded from most of the deliberations and all of the negotiations, as were half the Senate Democratic conferees, including the Democratic leader.

The headlong rush in Congress to give the president a victory on Medicare prescription drugs had consequences that went beyond a simple violation of congressional norms and standards. The resulting law was criticized by conservative Republicans and liberal Democrats alike as based on faulty assumptions, filled with questionable cost estimates and flawed in many particulars, problems that came back to haunt the administration as the provisions of the new law began to be implemented.

Institutional Decline

It would be one thing if the Medicare vote was, like the 1987 budget vote, a singular exception driven by unique circumstances. But it was more a punctuation of a growing pattern in the House. Faced with a series of tough votes and close margins in recent years, Republicans have ignored their own standards and adopted a routine practice of stretching out the vote when they were losing until they could twist enough arms to prevail. On at least a dozen occasions before and after the Medicare issue, they went well over the fifteen minutes, sometimes over an hour.

The Medicare prescription drug vote—three hours instead of fifteen minutes, hours after a clear majority of the House had formally signaled its will—was thus not a unique exception to standard practice, but the extension of a now-common tactic that ended up descending into one of the most breathtaking breaches of the legislative process in the modern history of the House. The way in which the issue played out, and the vote itself, are far more a pattern of the House in the new century—a pattern that more closely resembles the House of the nineteenth century than that of the twentieth, of the Gilded Age more than the Cold War era. In its highly centralized leadership and fealty to the presidential agenda, the post–2000 House of Representatives looks more like a House of Commons in a parliamentary system than a House of Representatives in a presidential system.

The problems did not start with the Republican majority in 1995. Signs of institutional decline were much in evidence during the latter years of the longtime Democratic control of Congress. Under pressure from their increasingly ideologically unified members, Democratic leaders resorted to ad hoc arrangements that often circumvented the normal committee process, restrictive rules that limited debate and amendments on the House floor, and behemoth omnibus legislative packages that short-circuited the normal process, limited transparency, and rendered the majority less accountable. Sharp partisan differences on policy created an atmosphere in which the legislative ends could justify any procedural means. Tensions between the parties often reached a boiling point.

By the time the Republicans took control of both ends of Pennsylvania Avenue, it seemed almost natural for the House majority leadership to drive nearly every issue, controversial or not, in partisan ways. It did not take long before procedures guaranteeing adequate time for discussion, debate, and votes—known as "regular order"—in committee, on the floor, and in conference, which are essential if Congress is to play its critical deliberative role, were routinely ignored to advance the majority agenda. Wounds rubbed raw, civility was strained to the breaking point; in mid-2004, Republican Rep. and Hastert ally Ray LaHood of Illinois said, "It's as bad as I've seen it in my ten years in Congress."

The Democratic majority had in its final years begun to restrict debate and amendments on the House floor, but the practice accelerated sharply under Republican rule. Fewer bills were brought up under open rules, which allow members to offer amendments to the pending legislation. The Republican leadership resorted more frequently to totally closed rules on the House floor, shutting off all attempts at amendment. In the 103rd Congress, under the Democrats, 9 percent of bills came to the floor under closed rules. In both the 106th and 107th, under Republicans, the number went to 22 percent—and to 28 percent in the 108th, 2003–2004. Donald Wolfensberger, former Rules Committee staff director under Republican Chairman Gerald Solomon, has also noted the increased reliance by the GOP on "self-executing" rules, which alter bills automatically when they come to the floor, sometimes for technical corrections but often to accommodate the interests of majority members and leaders. Self-executing rules went from an average of 19 percent of all bills in the 101st–103rd Congresses to 29 percent in the 104th–107th. All of these practices, it should be noted, were roundly denounced by Republicans when they were in the minority.

Another change came with the behavior of the Speaker. The Speaker of the House is the first government official mentioned in the Constitution. Even though the practical reality is that the Speaker is selected by the majority party from its ranks and is its leader, the Speaker is elected by a vote of the whole House and represents the whole House. Underscoring their desire to have a Speaker above normal party politics, the framers established that the Speaker does not even have to be a member of the House. The Speaker rarely takes to the floor to speak on an issue and even more rarely votes. The Speaker does not lobby on the floor; that is supposed to be left to the party leaders—majority leader, majority whip, etc.—who are not elected by the whole House but chosen by their party members for that purpose.

Democratic Speaker Jim Wright was not shy about advancing an aggressive party agenda to challenge the Reagan administration during its last years in office. Nor was he reticent about engaging in personal diplomacy in Central America, actions his critics saw as infringing on the constitutional responsibility of the executive. Republicans in Congress certainly viewed Wright as a partisan, not an institutional leader, even if he mostly adhered to the norm of limiting his direct involvement on the House floor.

Fifteen years later, the Medicare prescription drug vote showed how far the House has strayed from that norm. Speaker Hastert actively lobbied and pressured members on the floor, over several hours. Moreover, by allowing Health and Human Services Secretary Tommy G. Thompson on the floor to twist arms during the vote, he violated a long-standing tradition of the House, whereby the floor was off limits to lobbying by outsiders. That he physically escorted Thompson onto the floor to perform a double team on Representative Smith and others was an unprecedented breach of House practice and ethics.

Restricted debate, loose interpretation of the rules, and a distortion of the role of Speaker are not the only problems with today's House. Unified party government threatens to sap the institution of any will to exercise its constitutional independence. Over a decade of Republican control, the House went from shrill opposition to a Democratic president, culminating in his impeachment, to reflexive loyalty to a Republican president, including an unwillingness to conduct tough oversight of executive programs or assert congressional prerogatives vis-à-vis the presidency—on matters ranging from the accessibility of critical information to war-making. The partisanship has bled over into areas where institutional norms have been particularly strong and resilient, such as the appropriations panels and the power of the purse.

The Senate managed in the 1990s to avoid much of the deeper division and acrimony that plagued the House, but it too has shown signs of institutional decline. The Senate evolved from a hierarchical institution that was shaped largely by the preferences of its senior conservative Democrats to one that spread the wealth to accommodate the interests—and whims—of every member. The parties in the Senate, just like the House, became more internally unified and ideologically polarized as voters realigned and turnover in the body accelerated. But Senate rules allowing unlimited debate and an open amendment process on the floor limited the degree of centralization and the power and resources given to party leaders.

The Senate became far more a bastion of individualism than the House. . . . The filibuster, which for decades had been limited to issues of great national significance, became a routine practice as leaders no longer brought the Senate to a halt for unlimited debate but simply raised the bar to two-thirds, and then sixty votes, not fifty, whenever a filibuster threat was raised. By the 1980s, it was used by the minority party as a core element of its legislative strategy on a wide range of bills.

. . . In the past few years of heightened partisanship and shared party stakes between the President and Congress, the Senate has begun to consider more radical steps to move away from its roots and toward the House model. The willingness of Republican Senate leaders to consider seriously a unilateral act to block filibusters on judicial nominations—the so-called nuclear option—was a sign of a breakdown in comity that could easily fracture any remaining bipartisan cooperation in that body.

Of course, a time traveler from the nineteenth century would laugh at the idea that the Congress has careened out of control. Partisan acrimony? How about a senator caned to within an inch of his life on the Senate floor by a House member who disagreed with his abolitionist positions. Highhandedness by a Speaker? Penny-ante compared to the arbitrary exercise of power by Speakers Thomas Brackett Reed and Joseph Cannon in the era from 1890–1910. But the rough-and-tumble of the first hundred years of American democracy, before Congress became institutionalized to meet the needs of an industrial society, should not minimize the difficulties to the American system caused by a broken Congress in the post-industrial age of terrorism, in a society with a GDP of over $12 trillion and a federal budget approaching $3 trillion.

It would also be a mistake to suggest that the problems facing Congress are all the result of the actions or misjudgments of a handful of Republican leaders. As we have noted, many of the larger problems plaguing Congress, including partisan tensions, the demise of regular order, and growing incivility, began years ago, when Democrats were in the majority and Republicans in the minority. Their roots, and the reasons they have gotten demonstrably worse, are firmly implanted in larger political dynamics.

The Rise of Partisan Polarization

Members, and leaders, have choices. But the performance of Congress is shaped powerfully by the broader context in which it operates. Political developments in the South over the past fifty years . . . profoundly changed the partisan dynamic in Congress and the ideological composition of the parties. The House of the 1930s through the 1970s had a Democratic majority populated by many Southern conservatives as well as Northern liberals. Conflicts on issues often crossed party lines, driven more by ideology and regional interests. The House lost virtually all of its Southern conservative Democrats, leaving a more homogeneous and left-of-center party. At the same time, the Republican Party, partly as a consequence of this secular realignment in the South, has become even more distinctively conservative, with an ambitious agenda revolving around tax cuts, an assertive national defense, and religious traditionalism.

This ideological sorting by party has now extended to voters, activists, and elected officials throughout the country, creating two rival teams whose internal unity and ideological polarization are deeply embedded in the body politic. Increasing geographical segregation of voters and successive waves of incumbent-friendly redistricting have contributed to this development by helping to reduce the number of competitive House seats to a few dozen. With the overwhelming majority of House seats safe for one party or the other, new and returning members are naturally most reflective of and responsive to their primary constituencies, the only realistic locus of potential opposition, which usually are dominated by those at the ideological extreme. This phenomenon has tended to move Democrats in the House left and Republicans, right.

Despite the fact that redistricting plays no role in the Senate, the same pattern of ideological polarization of the parties is present there, albeit shaped in part by politicians moving from service in the House to the Senate. Many senators brought with them to the chamber attitudes toward Congress that were shaped by the contentious combat in the House of the late 1980s and early 1990s.

In recent years a number of factors—the two parties at parity and ideologically polarized, a populist attack on Congress that has weakened its institutional self-defenses, a more partisan press and interest group alignment, and an electoral environment making legislative activity subordinate to the interests of the permanent campaign—have conspired to encourage a decline in congressional deliberation and a de facto delegation of authority and influence to the president. . . .

Questions for Discussion

1. Mann and Ornstein label the Congress "the broken branch." What do they mean? How should the Congress act to restore its power and status?

2. Is the Congress doomed to lose power to the president in this era of global-
   ization, in which the chief executive's role often seems to transcend domestic politics? Or can the Congress re-establish itself as a truly coequal branch
   of government by exercising its considerable powers, such as the power of
   the purse?

 10.5

Where the Republicans Went Astray

Evan Thomas

In 1994, after forty years in the wilderness, Republicans captured control of the
U.S. House of Representatives, as well as recapturing the Senate, which they
had held for six years during the 1980s. This new Republican era started with a
bang, as new Speaker Newt Gingrich (R-Ga.) led his House colleagues on a
ninety-three-day forced march to pass much of the "Contract With America," an
agenda that sought to address a mixed bag of reform and substantive issues.
After the initial burst of activity, congressional Republicans came to govern on
an increasingly partisan basis, often adopting the very tactics they had criticized
bitterly when exercised by Democrats in the past. This partisanship became
sharper after George W. Bush won the presidency in 2000 and chose to govern a
closely divided nation from the right, rather than seeking a more bipartisan path,
even after the 9/11 terrorist attacks. More and more, Republicans in the House
and Senate were left to defend increasingly unpopular policies, especially as the
Iraq War became a distinct political liability.

Writing in the immediate aftermath of the Democrats' 2006 takeover of both the
House and Senate, Evan Thomas offers a timeline of the Republicans' drift from
principle to polarized partisanship. Though Gingrich was effective first in his role
as opposition leader and then in the early days of his speakership, he could not
provide stable direction to a caucus that brought together old-line pragmatists
with younger revolutionaries. In the end, the wind went out of the sails of revolution, leaving Republicans with narrow majorities that required extensive deal-

---

Evan Thomas has been assistant managing editor at *Newsweek* since 1991.

making, often promoted by Majority Leader Tom DeLay, to remain intact. Thomas
details the ways in which the party leaders manipulated the legislative process to
pass major legislation and exclude the minority from most law-making tasks. In
the end, the Republican conservative movement was sacrificed in order to retain
power; coupled with the fiasco of Iraq and the support of an unpopular president,
it is no wonder that Democrats captured both houses of the Congress in 2006.
The remaining question, for Thomas and other observers, is whether Democrats
will seek partisan revenge or will chart a more moderate course.

This is how a revolution ends. Not with a bang, or a "thumping," as President George W. Bush called the 2006 Republican defeat at the polls, but with a misdirected phone call and a certain sinking feeling that even the most well-intentioned politicians can grow weary of rectitude and sell out their principles for the right price.

The scene happened almost 10 years ago, when the GOP revolution in the House of Representatives was still fresh, less than three years after Newt Gingrich and his promise of a Republican "Contract With America" had swept aside four decades of Democratic rule in the House. The House in that summer of 1997 was considering passage of its annual transportation bill, routinely a fat pork sausage of legislation, larded with goodies—bridges, tunnels, exit ramps, highway extensions—for individual congressmen to take home to their districts. A band of a dozen true believers from the Class of '94, the congressmen first elected under the Gingrich banner of reform, was meeting in a small room off the floor of the House. They were trying to plot some way to slow down or stop the pork-stuffed bill—to show that the GOP was still true to its campaign promises to cut profligate government spending.

The phone rang. According to one of the congressmen in the room, Joe Scarborough, another congressman—Steve Largent, a former NFL wide receiver and one of the leaders of the group—picked up the receiver and absentmindedly mumbled, "Yeah." At the other end of the line, Largent heard the voice of Elmer G. (Bud) Shuster, the all-powerful, all-beneficent chairman of the House Committee on Transportation and Infrastructure. Shuster, an unabashed practitioner of old-style politics, was notorious in the House for rounding up votes by dispensing highway projects to pliable congressmen. Shuster apparently did not recognize Largent's voice over the phone. The chairman thought he had instead reached a different congressman—who shall remain nameless in this retelling, but who was well known at the time, a stalwart figure who often spoke of "standing up against the Man." Dictating quickly at the other end of the line, Bud Shuster was in a hurry—like Santa Claus on Christmas Eve, he had a lot of deliveries to make. Without pausing for pleasantries, he ticked off five highway projects worth $70 million, the reward to the supposedly high-minded congressman for swallowing his scruples—

just this once!—and voting for the 1997 transportation bill. Package delivered, Shuster hung up.

Largent, the ringleader of the plotters, put down the phone and tried not to show his disappointment that one of their fellow do-gooders had apparently given in to temptation. Instead, as Scarborough recalls the story, Largent sardonically announced, "Well, I don't think [Congressman X] is going to be with us this time." The others in the room dryly laughed, but it was a demoralizing moment, recalls Scarborough. "You get beaten down," says the MSNBC talk-show host. . . . Scarborough . . . [said] that it became a "running joke" for members of the Class of '94 to say to each other, "Well, there goes the revolution," every time one of their Contract With America reforms—like imposing term limits on members of Congress—was abandoned by lawmakers intoxicated with power.

Was the fall of the Republican revolution as predictable as the fall of man? Did the GOP revolutionaries, like so many revolutionaries before them, have to become the very thing they had once vowed to change? Gingrich, the former House Speaker, who stepped down in late 1998 before he could be pushed out, blames his successors for taking the low road to disaster. With his fondness for alliterative lists, Gingrich cites four areas where the Republicans fell short or went astray: "Candor, competence, corruption and consultants." He specifically blames former majority leader Tom DeLay, who effectively replaced Gingrich as the GOP leader in the House from 1999 through 2005. In Gingrich's judgment, DeLay, as well as other Republican leaders, threw away the power of ideas in their narrow focus on self-preservation. "When an institution develops 'the Hammer' as a model, that's not the most intellectual form of leadership," says Gingrich, alluding to DeLay's nickname, earned for his skill at enforcing party loyalty in the handing out of favors to lobbyists and influence peddlers. . . .

But Gingrich deserves some of the blame himself for providing a grandiose and ultimately weak model of leadership. The story of the rise and fall of the Republican revolution in the House of Representatives is a timeless story of vanity and hubris—and a cautionary tale for incoming Speaker Nancy Pelosi and the new Democratic leaders, who would like to inaugurate another long period of their party's rule.

The Republican revolution hardly started with Gingrich. The seeds were planted by the GOP's failed but visionary 1964 presidential candidate, Barry Goldwater, and conservative prophet William F. Buckley; the Reagan landslide of 1980 brought the movement to power in the White House and the Senate, which the GOP held until 1986.

The House, however, long seemed a lost cause; it had not been in GOP hands since the first two years of Eisenhower's presidency. It was Gingrich who first saw a way to exploit growing public dissatisfaction with the old Democratic barons of big government in the House, Speaker Thomas P. (Tip) O'Neill of Massachusetts and his successor, Jim Wright of Texas. Gingrich, then an obscure Republican backbencher (O'Neill referred to him as a "stooge," as in the Three Stooges), used a new forum—C-Span—to rail against Democratic corruption. In 1989, somewhat surprisingly, he succeeded in forcing the resignation of Speaker Wright, who was implicated in a scheme to profit off book sales in violation of House rules.

Gingrich had been a bit of a joke even in his own party. The son of a military officer, he seemed to some lawmakers to be a Walter Mitty,* a soldier wanna-be who had missed Vietnam (student and family deferments). Gingrich spouted a kind of utopian futurism about the "opportunity society" and handed out tapes so other congressmen could learn, as the accompanying instructions put it, to "talk like Newt." Some congressmen made fun of the tapes. But others listened—and learned. The 1994 congressional campaign was a referendum on big government—Hillary Clinton had launched a massive health-care reform plan that wound up strangled by its own red tape. Gingrich mounted an attack on the "bureaucratic welfare state" that caught the public mood—and shocked the pundits and prognosticators by returning the Republicans with a 26-seat majority in the House.

Suddenly it was Speaker Gingrich. Irrepressible, he launched biting personal attacks on the First Lady, chortling, "We are a happy band of Vikings, who don't mind a fight!" More seriously, he led a campaign that summer to cut federal spending and succeeded in squeezing $50 billion out of the budget before he attacked the hardest nut: Medicare. Gingrich's attempt to trim spending on medical care for the elderly does not seem that extreme—he wanted to restrain the rate of growth from 10 percent a year to 7 percent over seven years. But he immediately ran into a political buzz saw.

. . . At first, President Bill Clinton seemed so diminished by the midterm humiliation that he had to argue that he was "still relevant" at a press conference in the spring of 1995. But by summer, after handling the tragic terror attack on the Murrah Building in Oklahoma City with grace, the president was secretly conferring with an old political consultant, Dick Morris, who was reminding his boss that governing was really a "permanent campaign." At Morris's urging, Clinton launched a demagogic but extremely effective advertising campaign accusing the Republicans of trying to "eliminate" Medicare.

In October '95, Clinton held a press conference at which he charged that the Republicans were cutting health care by $200 billion so that they could give the same amount of money back to the wealthy as tax breaks. Joe Scarborough was watching with some fellow freshman from the Class of '94. "I remember we broke out laughing, saying, 'That poor fool'," Scarborough recalled. The joke was on the Republicans. As the budget battle turned into a stalemate later that fall, the government shut down. Clinton blamed the Republicans, darkly

---

*Humorist James Thurber created this character in a short story, "The Secret Life of Walter Mitty," in which a meek, mild-mannered man becomes, in his fantasy life, an heroic figure.

warning that Social Security checks would no longer be mailed out. The president repeatedly outfoxed Gingrich. When Gingrich flew on Air Force One to the funeral of Israeli Prime Minister Yitzhak Rabin, Clinton declined to find and negotiate a budget solution (preferring, instead, to play hearts up front with business tycoon Mort Zuckerman). Gingrich threw a tantrum on their return—and the *New York Daily News* (owned by Zuckerman) ran a front-page cartoon of Gingrich in diapers (which the Democrats made into a poster and, in a mischievous violation of House rules, stuck on the Speaker's chair). Gingrich ultimately caved in and had to plead with his own hard-liners to reopen the government.

Clinton continued to outflank Gingrich, effectively stealing much of the Republican platform by being tough on crime and welfare and declaring that the era of big government was over. Worn down, Gingrich privately confessed, "I'm not a natural leader. I'm a natural intellectual gadfly." Even after Clinton was consumed by the Monica Lewinsky scandal in 1998, Gingrich was unable to lead; his own troops were already plotting to purge him.

Gingrich's resignation after the 1998 election (the Republicans lost five seats) brought on an interlude that could only be described as comic opera. At the height of the Clinton impeachment proceedings, the new House Speaker-designate, Rep. Robert Livingston of Louisiana, resigned after the publisher of *Hustler* magazine, Larry Flynt, placed an ad in *The Washington Post* offering up to a million dollars for information about sexual indiscretions by D.C. officials. After a story broke in the press, Livingston admitted to extramarital affairs in a dramatic speech on the floor of the House. Livingston did not run for Speaker and resigned his seat.

Stunned Republicans chose a blandly amiable former high-school wrestling coach, Dennis Hastert, as their next Speaker. But the real power belonged to DeLay, who rose from whip to majority leader in 2003. A former Houston pest exterminator and archfoe of the Environmental Protection Agency, DeLay gave off a cold, hard look that was the polar opposite of sunny Reaganism. He delighted in his "Hammer" nickname. From the beginning of Gingrich's tenure, the GOP's K Street offensive had warned lobbying firms along Washington's K Street corridor that they would be wise to hire Republicans if they wanted access. There was nothing especially new about such a partisan approach to the influence-peddling business. The Republicans had only to look across the aisle to study a past master at shaking the corporate tree—former representative Tony Coelho, the onetime chairman of the Democratic Congressional Campaign Committee. But DeLay brought a new brazenness to the game. Before long, lobbyists could be seen in committee rooms writing legislation. With corporate coziness came the abandonment of fiscal restraint. Committee chairmen now routinely handed out "earmarks," special provisions authorizing spending for members' pet projects. In 1987, President Ronald Reagan vetoed a highway bill because it had 152 earmarks. In 2005, President Bush signed a transportation bill with 6,371 earmarks.

The nadir of the DeLay era may have come in the early-morning hours of Nov. 23, 2003. The Republicans, who had once tried to cut back entitlement programs, were now voting to create a whole new one—a bill to provide prescription-drug benefits for the elderly. Normally, House members have 15 minutes to cast their votes. Instead, DeLay & Co. kept the voting open for three hours—until 6 a.m.—while they persuaded old-fashioned fiscal conservatives to abandon their scruples. The exact nature of the inducements has never been clear, but Rep. Nick Smith charged that "bribes and special deals were offered to convince members to vote yes." (For Smith's vote, the leaders allegedly offered financial and political support for the congressional race of Smith's son.) The House ethics committee, effectively neutered in recent years, gave DeLay a wrist-slap reprimand. DeLay accepted the committee's "guidance," adding that he "would never knowingly violate the rules."

The House took on a Darwinian feel. It was every man for himself as staffers and even lawmakers cashed in to become lobbyists. The number of registered lobbyists in Washington nearly doubled, to 37,000, between 2000 and 2006. About half of the 200-odd congressmen who left their seats after 1998 stayed in Washington to become lobbyists or consultants. They would use their privileges as retired congressmen to lobby in the House gym and even on the House floor.

It was perhaps inevitable that the culture of sleaze on Capitol Hill would produce a Jack Abramoff. With his two downtown restaurants and his skybox at the sports arena, Abramoff was a popular host to congressmen and staffers. He was positively gleeful about bilking his clients, ultimately liberating several Indian tribes of $82 million in fees. . . . When Abramoff finally pleaded guilty to fraud, he effectively took DeLay down with him. Several of DeLay's former staffers were caught up in the Abramoff scandal. DeLay was not charged with any wrongdoing, but he was embarrassed by an all-expenses-paid golfing trip to Scotland with Abramoff. Under indictment for campaign-money laundering in Texas in a weak but nagging case brought by a local prosecutor, DeLay gave up his seat in June [2006]. . . .

Hastert was never able to exercise the same iron control as DeLay. Nor was DeLay's successor as majority leader, John Boehner, able to bring real discipline to fractious House members who looked out primarily for their own political interests. The religious evangelicals became more demanding of the Republican leadership on Capitol Hill, leading to the deeply unpopular spectacle of the Terri Schiavo case. Last year [2005] Senate Majority Leader Bill Frist, eager to court religious conservatives for a possible presidential run, and the House leadership, sensitive to the religious right, intervened to try to keep the patient alive on a feeding tube, a questionable use of federal power, especially for a party that once stood for less government interference.

The GOP's evangelical base was shocked and demoralized this fall [2006] when Rep. Mark Foley of Florida was exposed for having sent salacious messages to congressional pages. House leaders blamed each other for not responding to warnings that Foley was a possible sexual predator. In early October, when Hastert was compelled to hold a press conference to announce that he would not step down as Speaker, it was clear that the GOP revolution was in its late Jacobin phase.*

Even so, the Republicans might have kept control of Congress had it not been for GOP overreaching on a different front—Iraq. In some ways, the hubris of Gingrich and DeLay was minor compared with the willful risk-taking of President Bush, backed by Vice President Dick Cheney, a former congressman from Wyoming.

History is full of accidents and what-ifs. Cheney was the second-ranking House Republican when he got the call to become Secretary of Defense in 1989, at the beginning of the George H. W. Bush administration. (Bush's original nominee to become SecDef, former senator John Tower of Texas, was disqualified by allegations that he was a tippling womanizer.) Had Tower not been blocked from taking office, and Cheney not chosen as his Pentagon replacement, Cheney probably would have stayed in the House—and become Speaker when the Republicans won in 1994. "If Cheney had stayed I never would have gone in the leadership," Gingrich [concluded]. Gingrich rated Cheney as a perhaps less imaginative but more politically shrewd lawmaker than himself. Had Cheney stayed in the House and not become a war-hawk adviser to both Presidents Bush, history might well have taken a different course. We will never know. But we do know this: Democrats who, in the glow of victory, now say that none of this could happen to them ignore the story of the last dozen years at their peril.

Questions for Discussion

1. In what ways did the Republican domination of congressional politics, especially in the House, contain the seeds for its own demise?
2. Why are congressional political parties strong? Do they contain groups of individuals who see the world in similar ways? Or do congressional leaders have great resources they can use to promote party discipline? Or is it some of each? Given that House Democrats, as of 2007, have fifty to sixty relative moderate-to-conservative members within their ranks, how will the process of building party positions differ for them?

---

*This refers to the most intense, bloodiest phase of the French Revolution, and it has frequently been used as a metaphor to describe the radicalization of a regime or movement.

Chapter 11

The Presidency

On the surface, the public knows far more about the president than it does about any other political figure. What the president does—whether traveling to a summit of world leaders or going to church—is news. Presidents have become highly public figures, to the point that the public often holds unrealistically high expectations for their performance. Yet we usually know relatively little about how the president makes decisions and even less about how the institution of the presidency operates on a day-to-day basis.

A generation ago, constitutional law scholar Alexander Bickel called the Supreme Court "the least dangerous branch" because of its inability to implement decisions. Today, we might consider the presidency the most dangerous branch, because the possibility of exercising immense power, especially in military matters and foreign policy, resides there. From the Korean War to the Iraq invasion, presidents have demonstrated their dominance. Indeed, the 9/11 attacks and the resulting military actions have extended this predominance. In domestic policy, on the other hand, the president is far more constrained by Congress and, occasionally, by the courts. This continuing difference between the domestic and foreign/military policy arenas has been aptly labeled the "two presidencies" phenomenon by political scientist Aaron Wildavsky.

The power of the president has long attracted the attention of presidential scholars. Without question the presidency has become much more powerful since Franklin Roosevelt recast its very nature in the 1930s. Even those presidents who have been most reluctant to increase the reach of the federal government, such as Dwight Eisenhower and Ronald Reagan, have sought to take advantage of the prerogatives of executive authority. At the same time, presidential power has still waxed and waned in the modern era. In large part it is dependent on the president's relationship with the legislative branch and capacity to retain substantial support from the public. And, as George W. Bush demonstrated, even the narrowest electoral victory can produce forceful presidential actions, given the right circumstances.

The presidencies of Lyndon Johnson, Richard Nixon, Gerald Ford, and Jimmy Carter all illustrated that Congress and the American people can impose major limitations on any president, even those, like Johnson and Nixon, who are eager to extend the limits of executive authority. Each of these presidencies was judged a failure, to a greater or lesser extent, by the public. These presidents were held accountable for actions and policies they could not completely control. As the presidency became more visible in the 1960s and 1970s, its occupants confronted an unwieldy Congress and an increasingly skeptical citizenry. Scholars, politicians, and journalists wondered whether the job had become impossible.

Then came the Reagan presidency. Its record will be the subject of debate for decades to come, but one thing is abundantly clear from the Reagan years: The presidency is not an unmanageable job. Reagan demonstrated that, even without working congressional majorities in both houses, the president can act authoritatively and maintain relatively high popularity ratings well into a second term. George H. W. Bush, his successor, consistently received strong job approval ratings, especially in the wake of the 1991 Gulf War.

In the end, however, President Bush lost much of his support for taking a principled action—he endorsed a tax increase in order to help balance the budget, thus contradicting his 1988 campaign pledge ("Read my lips . . .") of no new taxes. Most economists conclude that the 1990 budget agreement eventually helped turn budget deficits into surpluses. But the economy's short-term performance, along with Bush's broken promise, led to his defeat in 1992 by Arkansas governor Bill Clinton.

As Clinton's presidency ended in January 2001, evaluating the state of the office was difficult. In many ways, Clinton had learned a great deal about serving effectively as president in an era of divided government and narrow partisan majorities. The public gave him considerable credit, and he departed the White House with a higher job-approval rating than the highly popular Reagan. At the same time, Clinton left only modest policy legacies, aside from the considerable accomplishment of serving during the great turnaround from huge deficits to large budget surpluses. Most analysts believe that Federal Reserve chairman Alan Greenspan was as much (if not more) responsible for the state of the economy as Clinton was. And in international relations, Clinton could genuinely claim credit for some major successes (expanded trade, intervention in Bosnia), but he created no general policy blueprint for how the United States might act as the sole remaining superpower. Finally, his moral failings led many Americans to distrust him and allowed his opponents to pursue him with an unrelenting vengeance throughout his presidency. At the beginning of the twenty-first century, the role of the president remained strangely undefined, in the realms of both domestic and foreign policymaking. Well into the presidency of George W. Bush, uncertainty has remained, and even grown, over the proper presidential role.

The following selections examine the modern presidency from both institutional and psychological perspectives. Richard E. Neustadt (selection 11.1) offers his now classic formulation of presidential influence: Presidents must protect their reputations and popularity as they seek to persuade legislators and even their own administrative appointees to support their policy initiatives. Political scientist Robert A. Dahl (selection 11.2) dissects the notion of the presidential mandate as an element in the "pseudodemocratization" of the American presidency. Indeed, Dahl sees the contemporary presidency as representing exactly what the framers sought to avoid: an executive who obtains office by pandering to an ill-informed and malleable public that is incapable of producing a meaningful mandate for action. This has become all the more significant as presidents have adopted polling and other campaign strategies to frame and deliver their messages.

The George Bush presidency has not only used public relations techniques, but it has also expanded its reach through a truly historic, even radical, set of claims of executive authority. The post-9/11 setting provides much of the context here, but the Bush administration, led by Vice President Dick Cheney, has consistently pushed the limits of presidential power. Perhaps the sharpest attack on the Bush administration's expansion of presidential power has come from one of its nominal allies—the libertarian Cato Institute. In an extensive, sharply worded paper, Gene Healy and Timothy Lynch (selection 11.3) argue, "far from defending the Constitution, President Bush has repeatedly sought to strip out the limits the document places on federal power." Placing their analysis in a broader context than the war on terror, Healy and Lynch see the president as violating both the Constitution's words and its spirit, as he seeks to broaden the scope and extend the reach of executive power.

11.1

The Power to Persuade

Richard E. Neustadt

The American president generally is regarded as the most powerful elected official in the world. Some of this power derives from the presidential power of command. The president can order a wide range of policies to be carried out, especially when dealing with foreign affairs or defense issues. At the same time, any chief executive must confront the numerous obstacles to exercising presidential authority. Some of these are constitutional, such as the independent power bases of the Congress and the Supreme Court. Others are less formal but no less restrictive; for example, the bureaucracy often serves as a brake on presidential initiatives (see Chapter 12).

In this selection, political scientist Richard E. Neustadt fleshes out the nature of presidential power as the power to persuade—a classic formulation on which a generation of scholars has built. Not only are presidents obliged to persuade Congress of the virtues of their proposals; they must also persuade their own administrations, and often their top aides, that their proposals have merit, even after they have won legislative approval. (Although Neustadt added three chapters to his book *Presidential Power* in 1980, this excerpt appeared in the original edition, published in 1960, and is replete with references to the Truman and Eisenhower administrations.)

The limits on command suggest the structure of our government. The constitutional convention of 1787 is supposed to have created a government of "separated powers." It did nothing of the sort. Rather, it created a government of separated institutions *sharing* powers. "I am part of the legislative process," Eisenhower often said in 1959 as a reminder of his veto. Congress, the dispenser of authority and funds, is no less part of the administrative process. Federalism adds another set of separated institutions. The Bill of Rights adds others. Many public purposes can only be achieved by voluntary acts of private institutions; the press, for one, in Douglass Cater's phrase, is a

Richard E. Neustadt is professor emeritus of government at Harvard University.

"fourth branch of government." And with the coming of alliances abroad, the separate institutions of a London, or a Bonn, share in the making of American public policy.

What the Constitution separates our political parties do not combine. . . . The President and congressmen who bear one party's label are divided by dependence upon different sets of voters. The differences are sharpest at the stage of nomination. The White House has too small a share in nominating congressmen, and Congress has too little weight in nominating Presidents for party to erase their constitutional separation. Party links are stronger than is frequently supposed, but nominating processes assure the separation.

The separateness of institutions and the sharing of authority prescribe the terms on which a President persuades. When one man shares authority with another, but does not gain or lose his job upon the other's whim, his willingness to act upon the urging of the other turns on whether he conceives the action right for him.* The essence of a President's persuasive task is to convince such men that what the White House wants of them is what they ought to do for their sake and on their authority.

Persuasive power, thus defined, amounts to more than charm or reasoned argument. These have their uses for a President, but these are not the whole of his resources. . . . The status and authority inherent in his office reinforce his logic and his charm.

Status adds something to persuasiveness; authority adds still more. When Truman urged wage changes on his Secretary of Commerce while the latter was administering the steel mills, he and Secretary Sawyer were not just two men reasoning with one another.† Had they been so, Sawyer probably would never have agreed to act. Truman's status gave him special claims to Sawyer's loyalty, or at least attention. In [English political theorist] Walter Bagehot's charming phrase "no man can *argue* on his knees." Although there is no kneeling in this country, few men—and exceedingly few Cabinet officers—are immune to the impulse to say "yes" to the President of the United States. It grows harder to say "no" when they are seated in his oval office at the White House, or in his study on the second floor, where almost tangibly he partakes of the aura of his physical surroundings. . . .

A President's authority and status give him great advantages in dealing with the men he would persuade. Each "power" is a vantage point for him in the degree that other men have use for his authority. From the veto to appointments, from publicity to budgeting, and so down a long list, the White House now controls the most encompassing array of vantage points in the American

---

*From the vantage point of the present, Neustadt's language seems insensitive to gender. Remember, he wrote in 1960 when (1) there was little such sensitivity and (2) virtually all top-level appointees were men.

†In 1952, President Truman seized control of the steel industry to prevent a strike during the Korean War. The Supreme Court ruled his action unconstitutional.

political system. With hardly an exception, the men who share in governing this country are aware that at some time, in some degree, the doing of *their* jobs, the furthering of *their* ambitions, may depend upon the President of the United States. Their need for presidential action, or their fear of it, is bound to be recurrent if not actually continuous. Their need or fear is his advantage.

A President's advantages are greater than mere listing of his "powers" might suggest. The men with whom he deals must deal with him until the last day of his term. Because they have continuing relationships with him, his future, while it lasts, supports his present influence. Even though there is no need or fear of him today, what he could do tomorrow may supply today's advantage. Continuing relationships may convert any "power," any aspect of his status, into vantage points in almost any case. When he induces other men to do what he wants done, a President can trade on their dependence now *and* later.

The President's advantages are checked by the advantages of others. Continuing relationships will pull in both directions. These are relationships of mutual dependence. A President depends upon the men he would persuade; he has to reckon with his need or fear of them. They too will possess status, or authority, or both, else they would be of little use to him. Their vantage points confront his own; their power tempers his.

Persuasion is a two-way street. Sawyer, it will be recalled, did not respond at once to Truman's plan for wage increases at the steel mills. On the contrary, the Secretary hesitated and delayed and only acquiesced when he was satisfied that publicly he would not bear the onus of decision. Sawyer had some points of vantage all his own from which to resist presidential pressure. If he had to reckon with coercive implications in the President's "situations of strength," so had Truman to be mindful of the implications underlying Sawyer's place as a department head, as steel administrator, and as a Cabinet spokesman for business. Loyalty is reciprocal. Having taken on a dirty job in the steel crisis, Sawyer had strong claims to loyal support. Besides, he had authority to do some things that the White House could ill afford. . . . He might have resigned in a huff (the removal power also works two ways). Or, . . . he might have declined to sign necessary orders. Or, he might have let it be known publicly that he deplored what he was told to do and protested its doing. By following any of these courses Sawyer almost surely would have strengthened the position of [steel] management, weakened the position of the White House, and embittered the union. But the whole purpose of a wage increase was to enhance White House persuasiveness in urging settlement upon union and companies alike. Although Sawyer's status and authority did not give him the power to prevent an increase outright, they gave him capability to undermine its purpose. . . .

The power to persuade is the power to bargain. Status and authority yield bargaining advantages. But in a government of "separated institutions sharing powers," they yield them to all sides. With the array of vantage points at his disposal, a President may be far more persuasive than his logic or his charm could make him. But outcomes are not guaranteed by his advantages. There remain the counter pressures those whom he would influence can bring to bear on him from vantage points at their disposal. Command has limited utility; persuasion becomes give-and-take. It is well that the White House holds the vantage points it does. In such a business any President may need them all— and more.

I

This view of power as akin to bargaining is one we commonly accept in the sphere of congressional relations. Every textbook states and every legislative session demonstrates that . . . a President will often be unable to obtain congressional action on his terms or even to halt action he opposes. The reverse is equally accepted: Congress often is frustrated by the President. Their formal powers are so intertwined that neither will accomplish very much, for very long, without the acquiescence of the other. By the same token, though, what one demands the other can resist. The stage is set for that great game, much like collective bargaining, in which each seeks to profit from the other's needs and fears. It is a game played catch-as-catch-can, case by case. And everybody knows the game, observers and participants alike. . . .

In only one sphere is the concept [of power as give-and-take] unfamiliar: the sphere of executive relations. Perhaps because of civics textbooks and teaching in our schools, Americans instinctively resist the view that power in this sphere resembles power in all others. Even Washington reporters, White House aides, and congressmen are not immune to the illusion that administrative agencies comprise a single structure, "the" Executive Branch, where presidential word is law, or ought to be. Yet . . . when a President seeks something from executive officials his persuasiveness is subject to the same sorts of limitations as in the case of congressmen, or governors, or national committeemen, or private citizens, or foreign governments. There are no generic differences, no differences in kind and only sometimes in degree. The incidents preceding the dismissal of [General Douglas] MacArthur* and the incidents surrounding seizure of the steel mills make it plain that here as elsewhere influence derives from bargaining advantages; power is a give-and-take.

Like our governmental structure as a whole, the executive establishment consists of separated institutions sharing powers. The President heads one of these; Cabinet officers, agency administrators, and military commanders head others. Below the departmental level, virtually independent bureau chiefs

---

*A strong-willed commander of UN and American forces in South Korea and a prospective Republican presidential nominee, General MacArthur repeatedly challenged President Truman over Korean War strategies. Truman ultimately removed him from his command. This action reinforced the president's role as commander-in-chief, although MacArthur received much popular and legislative support upon his return to the United States.

head many more. Under mid-century conditions, Federal operations spill across dividing lines on organization charts; almost every policy entangles many agencies; almost every program calls for interagency collaboration. Everything somehow involves the President. But operating agencies owe their existence least of all to one another—and only in some part to him. Each has a separate statutory base; each has its statutes to administer; each deals with a different set of subcommittees at the Capitol. Each has its own peculiar set of clients, friends, and enemies outside the formal government. Each has a different set of specialized careerists inside its own bailiwick. Our Constitution gives the President the "take-care" clause and the appointive power. Our statutes give him central budgeting and a degree of personnel control. All agency administrators are responsible to him. But they *also* are responsible to Congress, to their clients, to their staffs, and to themselves. In short, they have five masters. Only after all of those do they owe any loyalty to each other.

"The members of the Cabinet," Charles G. Dawes used to remark, "are a President's natural enemies." Dawes had been Harding's Budget Director, Coolidge's Vice-President, and Hoover's Ambassador to London; he also had been General Pershing's chief assistant for supply in the First World War. The words are highly colored, but Dawes knew whereof he spoke. The men who have to serve so many masters cannot help but be somewhat the "enemy" of any one of them. By the same token, any master wanting service is in some degree the "enemy" of such a servant. A President is likely to want loyal support but not to relish trouble on his doorstep. Yet the more his Cabinet members cleave to him, the more they may need help from him in fending off the wrath of rival masters. Help, though, is synonymous with trouble. Many a Cabinet officer, with loyalty ill-rewarded by his lights and help withheld, has come to view the White House as innately hostile to department heads. Dawes's dictum can be turned around.

A senior presidential aide remarked to me in Eisenhower's time: "If some of these Cabinet members would just take time out to stop and ask themselves, 'What would I want if I were President?', they wouldn't give him all the trouble he's been having." But even if they asked themselves the question, such officials often could not act upon the answer. Their personal attachment to the President is all too often overwhelmed by duty to their other masters. . . .

Some aides will have more vantage points than a selective memory. Sherman Adams, for example, as the Assistant to the President under Eisenhower, scarcely deserved the appelation "White House aide" in the meaning of the term before his time or as applied to other members of the Eisenhower entourage. Although Adams was by no means "chief of staff" in any sense so sweeping—or so simple—as press commentaries often took for granted, he apparently became no more dependent on the President than Eisenhower on him. "I need him," said the President when Adams turned out to have been remarkably imprudent in the Goldfine case, and delegated to him even the decision on his own departure.* This instance is extreme, but the tendency it illustrates is common enough. Any aide who demonstrates to others that he has the President's consistent confidence and a consistent part in presidential business will acquire so much business on his own account that he becomes in some sense independent of his chief. Nothing in the Constitution keeps a well-placed aide from converting status into power of his own, usable in some degree even against the President—an outcome not unknown in Truman's regime or, by all accounts, in Eisenhower's.

The more an officeholder's status and his "powers" stem from sources independent of the President, the stronger will be his potential pressure *on* the President. Department heads in general have more bargaining power than do most members of the White House staff; but bureau chiefs may have still more, and specialists at upper levels of established career services may have almost unlimited reserves of the enormous power which consists of sitting still. As Franklin Roosevelt once remarked:

> The Treasury is so large and far-flung and ingrained in its practices that I find it almost impossible to get the action and results I want—even with Henry [Morgenthau] there. But the Treasury is not to be compared with the State Department. You should go through the experience of trying to get any changes in the thinking, policy, and action of the career diplomats and then you'd know what a real problem was. But the Treasury and the State Department put together are nothing compared with the Na-a-vy. The admirals are really something to cope with—and I should know. To change anything in the Na-a-vy is like punching a feather bed. You punch it with your right and you punch it with your left until you are finally exhausted, and then you find the damn bed just as it was before you started punching.[1]

. . . Real power is reciprocal and varies markedly with organization, subject matter, personality, and situation. The mere fact that persuasion is directed at executive officials signifies no necessary easing of his [the President's] way. Any new congressman of the Administration's party, especially if narrowly elected, may turn out more amenable (though less useful) to the President than any seasoned bureau chief "downtown." *The probabilities of power do not derive from the literary theory of the Constitution.*

II

There is a widely held belief in the United States that were it not for folly or for knavery, a reasonable President would need no power other than the logic of his argument. No less a personage than Eisenhower has subscribed to that

---

*Businessman Bernard Goldfine gave Sherman Adams, Eisenhower's top aide, the gift of a vicuna coat. When it became public, Adams's acceptance of the gift caused substantial embarrassment to the president, and Adams subsequently resigned.

belief in many a campaign speech and press-conference remark. But faulty reasoning and bad intentions do not cause all quarrels with Presidents. The best of reasoning and of intent cannot compose them all. For in the first place, what the President wants will rarely seem a trifle to the men he wants it from. And in the second place, they will be bound to judge it by the standard of their own responsibilities, not his. However logical his argument according to his lights, their judgment may not bring them to his view. . . . An able Eisenhower aide with long congressional experience remarked to me in 1958: "The people on the Hill don't do what they might *like* to do, they do what they think they *have* to do in their own interest as *they* see it. . . ." This states the case precisely.

The essence of a President's persuasive task with congressmen and everybody else, is *to induce them to believe that what he wants of them is what their own appraisal of their own responsibilities requires them to do in their interest, not his.* Because men may differ in their views on public policy, because differences in outlook stem from differences in duty—duty to one's office, one's constituents, oneself—that task is bound to be more like collective bargaining than like a reasoned argument among philosopher kings. Overtly or implicitly, hard bargaining has characterized all illustrations offered up to now. This is the reason why: persuasion deals in the coin of self-interest with men who have some freedom to reject what they find counterfeit.

III

A President draws influence from bargaining advantages. But does he always need them? . . . Suppose most players of the governmental game see policy objectives much alike, then can he not rely on logic (or on charm) to get him what he wants? The answer is that even then most outcomes turn on bargaining. The reason for this answer is a simple one: most men who share in governing have interests of their own beyond the realm of policy *objectives.* The sponsorship of policy, the form it takes, the conduct of it, and the credit for it separate their interest from the President's, despite agreement on the end in view. In political government, the means can matter quite as much as ends; they often matter more. And there are always differences of interest in the means. . . .

Adequate or not, a President's own choices are the only means *in his own hands* of guarding his own prospects for effective influence. He can draw power from continuing relationships in the degree that he can capitalize upon the needs of others for the Presidency's status and authority. He helps himself to do so, though, by nothing save ability to recognize the preconditions and the chance advantages and to proceed accordingly in the course of the choice-making that comes his way. To ask how he can guard prospective influence is thus to raise a further question: what helps him guard his power stakes in his own acts of choice?

Note

1. Quoted in Marriner S. Eccles, *Beckoning Frontiers* (New York: Knopf, 1951), 336.

Questions for Discussion

1. Why must presidents be able to "persuade" their own administrative appointees?
2. Can presidents *increase* their ability to persuade? How? By making good choices?

 11.2

Myth of the Presidential Mandate

Robert A. Dahl

The term *mandate* appears frequently in discussions of presidential elections. Presidents claim mandates—often broadly defined—in the wake of their victories. The people, they say, have spoken. After all, among elected officials only the president has a national constituency. The problem comes in interpreting what the people have to say. Many potential voters do not cast their ballots; in recent presidential contests, these individuals constituted almost 50 percent of the potential electorate. Moreover, many reasons lie behind the millions of votes that support a given candidate.

Political scientist and democratic theorist Robert A. Dahl argues that not until Woodrow Wilson's presidency did chief executives begin to claim mandates for their policies and goals. Such claims have become commonplace, but Dahl casts substantial doubt on their validity. Even with sophisticated sample surveys, Dahl finds the complexities underlying mandates exceedingly difficult to fathom. In addition, presidents frequently win by less than a majority of the popular vote and often receive only a bit more than a quarter of the ballots of all those eligible

Robert A. Dahl is professor emeritus of political science at Yale University.

"Myth of the Presidential Mandate" by Robert A. Dahl. Reprinted by permission of *Political Science Quarterly*, 105 (1990): 355–372.

to vote. In sum, although presidents may be eager to claim mandates for their actions, in most instances these claims are self-serving rather than based on adequate criteria or clear relationships between the candidate and the electorate.

O n election night in 1980 the vice president-elect [George H. W. Bush] enthusiastically informed the country that Ronald Reagan's triumph was

> . . . not simply a mandate for a change but a mandate for peace and freedom; a mandate for prosperity; a mandate for opportunity for all Americans regardless of race, sex, or creed; a mandate for leadership that is both strong and compassionate . . . a mandate to make government the servant of the people in the way our founding fathers intended; a mandate for hope; a mandate for hope for the fulfillment of the great dream that President-elect Reagan has worked for all his life.

I suppose there are no limits to permissible exaggeration in the elation of victory, especially by a vice president elect. He may therefore be excused, I imagine, for failing to note, as did many others who made comments in a similar vein in the weeks and months that followed, that Reagan's lofty mandate was provided by 50.9 percent of the voters. A decade later it is much more evident, as it should have been then, that what was widely interpreted as Reagan's mandate, not only by supporters but by opponents, was more myth than reality.

In claiming that the outcome of the election provided a mandate to the president from the American people to bring about the policies, programs, emphases, and new directions uttered during the campaign by the winning candidate and his supporters, the vice president elect was like other commentators echoing a familiar theory.

Origin and Development

A history of the theory of the presidential mandate has not been written, and I have no intention of supplying one here. However, if anyone could be said to have created the myth of the presidential mandate, surely it would be Andrew Jackson. Although he never used the word mandate, so far as I know, he was the first American president to claim not only that the president is uniquely representative of all the people, but that his election confers on him a mandate from the people in support of his policy. Jackson's claim was a fateful step in the democratization of the constitutional system of the United States—or rather what I prefer to call the pseudodemocratization of the presidency.

As Leonard White observed, it was Jackson's "settled conviction" that "the President was an immediate and direct representative of the people." Presumably as a result of his defeat in 1824 in both the electoral college and the House of Representatives, in his first presidential message to Congress, in order that "as few impediments as possible should exist to the free operation of the public will," he proposed that the Constitution be amended to provide for the direct election of the president.

> "To the people," he said, "belongs the right of electing their Chief Magistrate: it was never designed that their choice should, in any case, be defeated, either by the intervention of electoral colleges or by . . . the House of Representatives."

His great issue of policy was the Bank of the United States, which he unwaveringly believed was harmful to the general good. Acting on this conviction, in 1832 he vetoed the bill to renew the bank's charter. Like his predecessors, he justified the veto as a protection against unconstitutional legislation; but unlike his predecessors in their comparatively infrequent use of the veto he also justified it as a defense of his or his party's policies.

Following his veto of the bank's charter, the bank became the main issue in the presidential election of 1832. As a consequence, Jackson's reelection was widely regarded, even among his opponents (in private, at least), as amounting to "something like a popular ratification" of his policy. When in order to speed the demise of the bank Jackson found it necessary to fire his treasury secretary, he justified his action on the ground, among others, that "The President is the direct representative of the American people, but the Secretaries are not."

Innovative though it was, Jackson's theory of the presidential mandate was less robust than it was to become in the hands of his successors. In 1848 James Polk explicitly formulated the claim in a defense of his use of the veto on matters of policy, that as a representative of the people the president was, if not more representative than the Congress, at any rate equally so.

> "The people, by the constitution, have commanded the President, as much as they have commanded the legislative branch of the Government, to execute their will. . . . The President represents in the executive department the whole people of the United States, as each member of the legislative department represents portions of them. . . ." The President is responsible "not only to an enlightened public opinion, but to the people of the whole Union, who elected him, as the representatives in the legislative branches are responsible to the people of particular States or districts. . . ."

Notice that in Jackson's and Polk's views, the president, both constitutionally and as representative of the people, is on a par with Congress. They did not claim that in either respect the president is superior to Congress. It was Woodrow Wilson who took the further step in the evolution of the theory by asserting that in representing the people the president is not merely equal to Congress but actually superior to it.

Earlier Views

Because the theory of the presidential mandate espoused by Jackson and Polk has become an integral part of our present-day conception of the presidency, it may be hard for us to grasp how sharply that notion veered off from the views of the earlier presidents.

As James Ceaser has shown, the Framers designed the presidential election process as a means of improving the chances of electing a *national* figure who would enjoy majority support. They hoped their contrivance would avoid not only the populistic competition among candidates dependent on "the popular arts," which they rightly believed would occur if the president were elected by the people, but also what they believed would necessarily be a factional choice if the president were chosen by the Congress, particularly by the House.

In adopting the solution of an electoral college, however, the Framers seriously underestimated the extent to which the strong impulse toward democratization that was already clearly evident among Americans—particularly among their opponents, the anti-Federalists—would subvert and alter their carefully contrived constitutional structure. Since this is a theme I shall pick up later, I want now to mention only two such failures that bear closely on the theory of the presidential mandate. First, the Founders did not foresee the development of political parties nor comprehend how a two-party system might achieve their goal of insuring the election of a figure of national rather than merely local renown. Second, as Ceaser remarks, although the Founders recognized "the need for a popular judgment of the performance of an incumbent" and designed a method for selecting the president that would, as they thought, provide that opportunity, they "did not see elections as performing the role of instituting decisive changes in policy in response to popular demands." In short, the theory of the presidential mandate not only cannot be found in the Framers' conception of the Constitution; almost certainly it violates that conception.

No president prior to Jackson challenged the view that Congress was the legitimate representative of the people. Even Thomas Jefferson, who adeptly employed the emerging role of party leader to gain congressional support for his policies and decisions,

> was more Whig than . . . the British Whigs themselves in subordinating [the executive power] to "the supreme legislative power." . . . The tone of his messages is uniformly deferential to Congress. His first one closes with these words: "Nothing shall be wanting on my part to inform, as far as in my power, the legislative judgment, nor to carry that judgment into faithful execution."

James Madison, demonstrating that a great constitutional theorist and an adept leader in Congress could be decidedly less than a great president, deferred so greatly to Congress that in his communications to that body his extreme caution rendered him "almost unintelligible"—a quality one would hardly expect from one who had been a master of lucid exposition at the Constitutional Convention. His successor, James Monroe, was so convinced that Congress should decide domestic issues without presidential influence that throughout the debates in Congress on "the greatest political issue of his day . . . the admission of Missouri and the status of slavery in Louisiana Territory," he remained utterly silent.

Madison and Monroe serve not as examples of how presidents should behave but as evidence of how early presidents thought they should behave. Considering the constitutional views and the behavior of Jackson's predecessors, it is not hard to see why his opponents called themselves Whigs in order to emphasize his dereliction from the earlier and presumably constitutionally correct view of the presidency.

Woodrow Wilson

The long and almost unbroken succession of mediocrities who succeeded to the presidency between Polk and Wilson for the most part subscribed to the Whig view of the office and seem to have laid no claim to a popular mandate for their policies—when they had any. Even Abraham Lincoln, in justifying the unprecedented scope of presidential power he believed he needed in order to meet secession and civil war, rested his case on constitutional grounds, and not as a mandate from the people. Indeed, since he distinctly failed to gain a majority of votes in the election of 1860, any claim to a popular mandate would have been dubious at best. Like Lincoln, Theodore Roosevelt also had a rather unrestricted view of presidential power; he expressed the view then emerging among Progressives that chief executives were also representatives of the people. Yet the stewardship he claimed for the presidency was ostensibly drawn—rather freely drawn, I must say—from the Constitution, not from the mystique of the mandate.

Woodrow Wilson, more as political scientist than as president, brought the mandate theory to what now appears to be its canonical form. His formulation was influenced by his admiration for the British system of cabinet government. In 1879, while still a senior at Princeton, he published an essay recommending the adoption of cabinet government in the United States. He provided little indication as to how this change was to be brought about, however, and soon abandoned the idea without yet having found an alternative solution. Nevertheless, he continued to contrast the American system of congressional government, in which Congress was all-powerful but lacked executive leadership, with British cabinet government, in which parliament, though all powerful, was firmly led by the prime minister and his cabinet. Since Americans were not likely to adopt the British cabinet system, however, he began to consider the alternative of more powerful presidential leadership. In his *Congressional*

Government, published in 1885, he acknowledged that "the representatives of the people are the proper ultimate authority in all matters of government, and that administration is merely the clerical part of government." Congress is "unquestionably, the predominant and controlling force, the center and source of all motive and of all regulative power." Yet a discussion of policy that goes beyond "special pleas for special privilege" is simply impossible in the House, "a disintegrate mass of jarring elements," while the Senate is no more than "a small, select, and leisurely House of Representatives."

By 1908, when *Constitutional Government in the United States* was published, Wilson had arrived at strong presidential leadership as a feasible solution. He faulted the earlier presidents who had adopted the Whig theory of the Constitution.

> . . . [T]he makers of the Constitution were not enacting Whig theory. . . . The President is at liberty, both in law and conscience, to be as big a man as he can. His capacity will set the limit; and if Congress be overborne by him, it will be no fault of the makers of the Constitution—it will be from no lack of constitutional powers on its part, but only because the President has the nation behind him, and Congress has not. He has no means of compelling Congress except through public opinion. . . . [T]he early Whig theory of political dynamics . . . is far from being a democratic theory. . . . It is particularly intended to prevent the will of the people as a whole from having at any moment an unobstructed sweep and ascendancy.

And he contrasted the president with Congress in terms that would become commonplace among later generations of commentators, including political scientists:

> Members of the House and Senate are representatives of localities, are voted for only by sections of voters, or by local bodies of electors like the members of the state legislatures. There is no national party choice except that of President. No one else represents the people as a whole, exercising a national choice. . . . The nation as a whole has chosen him, and is conscious that it has no other political spokesman. His is the only national voice in affairs. . . . He is the representative of no constituency, but of the whole people. When he speaks in his true character, he speaks for no special interest. . . . [T]here is but one national voice in the country, and that is the voice of the President.

Since Wilson, it has become commonplace for presidents and commentators alike to argue that by virtue of his election the president has received a mandate for his aims and policies from the people of the United States. The myth of the mandate is now a standard weapon in the arsenal of persuasive symbols all presidents exploit. For example, as the Watergate scandals emerged in mid-1973, Patrick Buchanan, then an aide in the Nixon White House, suggested that the president should accuse his accusers of "seeking to destroy the democratic mandate of 1972." Three weeks later in an address to the country Nixon said:

> Last November, the American people were given the clearest choice of this century. Your votes were a mandate, which I accepted, to complete the initiatives we began in my first term and to fulfill the promises I made for my second term.

If the spurious nature of Nixon's claim now seems self-evident, the dubious grounds for virtually all such pretensions are perhaps less obvious.

Critique of the Theory

What does a president's claim to a mandate amount to? The meaning of the term itself is not altogether clear. Fortunately, however, in his excellent book *Interpreting Elections*, Stanley Kelley has "piece[d] together a coherent statement of the theory."

> Its first element is the belief that elections carry messages about problems, policies, and programs—messages plain to all and specific enough to be directive. . . . Second, the theory holds that certain of these messages must be treated as authoritative commands . . . either to the victorious candidate or to the candidate and his party. . . . To qualify as mandates, messages about policies and programs must reflect the *stable* views both of individual voters and of the electorate. . . . In the electorate as a whole, the numbers of those for or against a policy or program matter. To suggest that a mandate exists for a particular policy is to suggest that more than a bare majority of those voting are agreed upon it. The common view holds that landslide victories are more likely to involve mandates than are narrow ones. . . . The final element of the theory is a negative imperative: Governments should not undertake major innovations in policy or procedure, except in emergencies, unless the electorate has had an opportunity to consider them in an election and thus to express its views.

To bring out the central problems more clearly, let me extract what might be called the primitive theory of the popular presidential mandate. According to this theory, a presidential election can accomplish four things. First, it confers constitutional and legal authority on the victor. Second, at the same time, it also conveys information. At a minimum it reveals the first preferences for president of a plurality of votes. Third, according to the primitive theory, the election, at least under the conditions Kelley describes, conveys further information: namely that a clear majority of voters prefer the winner because they prefer his policies and wish him to pursue his policies. Finally, because the president's policies reflect the wishes of a majority of voters, when conflicts over policy arise between president and Congress, the president's policies ought to prevail.

While we can readily accept the first two propositions, the third, which is pivotal to the theory, might be false. But if the third is false, then so is the fourth. So the question arises: Beyond revealing the first preferences of a plurality of voters, do presidential elections also reveal the additional information that a plurality (or a majority) of voters prefer the policies of the winner and wish the winner to pursue those policies?

In appraising the theory I want to distinguish between two different kinds of criticisms. First, some critics contend that even when the wishes of constituents can be known, they should not be regarded as in any way binding on a legislator. I have in mind, for example, Edmund Burke's famous argument that he would not sacrifice to public opinion his independent judgment of how well a policy would serve his constituents' interests, and the argument suggested by Hanna Pitkin that representatives bound by instructions would be prevented from entering into the compromises that legislation usually requires.

Second, some critics, on the other hand, may hold that when the wishes of constituents on matters of policy can be clearly discerned, they ought to be given great and perhaps even decisive weight. But, these critics contend, constituents' wishes usually cannot be known, at least when the constituency is large and diverse, as in presidential elections. In expressing his doubts on the matter in 1913, A. Lawrence Lowell quoted Sir Henry Maine: "The devotee of democracy is much in the same position as the Greeks with their oracles. All agreed that the voice of an oracle was the voice of god, but everybody allowed that when he spoke he was not as intelligible as might be desired."

It is exclusively the second kind of criticism that I want now to consider. Here again I am indebted to Stanley Kelley for his succinct summary of the main criticisms.

> Critics allege that 1) some particular claim of a mandate is unsupported by adequate evidence; 2) most claims of mandates are unsupported by adequate evidence; 3) most claims of mandates are politically self-serving; or 4) it is not possible in principle to make a valid claim of a mandate, since it is impossible to sort out voters' intentions.

Kelley goes on to say that while the first three criticisms may well be valid, the fourth has been outdated by the sample survey,* which "has again given us the ability to discover the grounds of voters' choices." In effect, then, Kelley rejects the primitive theory and advances the possibility of a more sophisticated mandate theory according to which the information about policies is conveyed not by the election outcome but instead by opinion surveys. Thus the two functions are cleanly split: presidential elections are for electing a president, opinion surveys provide information about the opinions, attitudes, and judgments that account for the outcome.

However, I would propose a fifth proposition, which I believe is also implicit in Kelley's analysis:

> 5) While it may not be strictly impossible in *principle* to make a reasoned and well-grounded claim to a presidential mandate, to do so *in practice* requires a complex analysis that in the end may not yield much support for presidential claims.

---

*Sampling techniques allow a relatively small number of respondents (1,500 for a national sample) to accurately reflect the views of a much larger population (150 million adults).

But if we reject the primitive theory of the mandate and adopt the more so-phisticated theory, then it follows that prior to the introduction of scientific sample surveys, no president could reasonably have defended his claim to a mandate. To put a precise date on the proposition, let me remind you that the first presidential election in which scientific surveys formed the basis of an ex-tended and systematic analysis was 1940.

I do not mean to say that no election before 1940 now permits us to draw the conclusion that a president's major policies were supported by a substantial majority of the electorate. But I do mean that for most presidential elections before 1940 a valid reconstruction of the policy views of the electorate is impossible or enormously difficult, even with the aid of aggregate data and other indirect indicators of voters' views. When we consider that presidents or-dinarily asserted their claims soon after their elections, well before historians and social scientists could have sifted through reams of indirect evidence, then we must conclude that before 1940 no contemporary claim to a presidential mandate could have been supported by the evidence available at the time.

While the absence of surveys undermines presidential claims to a mandate before 1940, the existence of surveys since then would not necessarily have supported such claims. Ignoring all other shortcomings of the early election studies, the analysis of the 1940 election I just mentioned was not published until 1948. While that interval between the election and the analysis may have set a record, the systematic analysis of survey evidence that is necessary (though perhaps not sufficient) to interpret what a presidential election means always comes well after presidents and commentators have already told the world, on wholly inadequate evidence, what the election means. Perhaps the most famous voting study to date, *The American Voter*, which drew primarily on interviews conducted in 1952 and 1956, appeared in 1960. The book by Stan-ley Kelley that I have drawn on so freely here, which interprets the elections of 1964, 1972, and 1980, appeared in 1983.

A backward glance quickly reveals how empty the claims to a presidential mandate have been in recent elections. Take 1960. If more than a bare major-ity is essential to a mandate, then surely Kennedy could have received no man-date, since he gained less than 50 percent of the total popular vote by the official count—just how much less by the unofficial count varies with the counter. Yet "on the day after election, and every day thereafter," Theodore Sorenson tells us, "he rejected the argument that the country had given him no mandate. Every election has a winner and a loser, he said in effect. There may be difficulties with the Congress, but a margin of only one vote would still be a mandate."

By contrast, 1964 was a landslide election, as was 1972. From his analysis, however, Kelley concludes that "Johnson's and Nixon's specific claims of mean-ingful mandates do not stand up well when confronted by evidence." To be sure, in both elections some of the major policies of the winners were supported by large majorities among those to whom these issues were salient. Yet "none of these policies was cited by more than 21% of respondents as a reason to like Johnson, Nixon, or their parties."

In 1968, Nixon gained office with only 43 percent of the popular vote. No mandate there. Likewise in 1976, Carter won with a bare 50.1 percent. Once again, no mandate there.

When Reagan won in 1980, thanks to the much higher quality of surveys undertaken by the media, a more sophisticated understanding of what that election meant no longer had to depend on the academic analyses that would only follow some years later. Nonetheless, many commentators, bemused as they so often are by the arithmetical peculiarities of the electoral college, immediately proclaimed both a landslide and a mandate for Reagan's policies. What they often failed to note was that Reagan gained just under 51 percent of the popular vote. Despite the claims of the vice president elect, surely we can find no mandate there. Our doubts are strengthened by the fact that in the elections to the House, Democratic candidates won just over 50 percent of the popular vote and a majority of seats. However, they lost control of the Senate. No Democratic mandate there, either.

These clear and immediate signs that the elections of 1980 failed to confer a mandate on the president or his Democratic opponents were, however, largely ignored. For it was so widely asserted as to be commonplace that Reagan's election reflected a profound shift of opinion away from New Deal programs and toward the new conservatism. However, from this analysis of the survey evidence, Kelley concludes that the commitment of voters to candidates was weak; a substantial proportion of Reagan voters were more interested in voting against Carter than for Reagan; and despite claims by journalists and others, the New Deal coalition did not really collapse. Nor was there any profound shift toward conservatism. "The evidence from press surveys . . . contradicts the claims that voters shifted toward conservatism and that this ideological shift elected Reagan." In any case, the relation between ideological location and policy preferences was "of a relatively modest magnitude."

In winning by a landslide of popular votes in 1984, Reagan achieved one prerequisite to a mandate. Yet in that same election, Democratic candidates for the House won 52 percent of the popular votes. Two years earlier, they had won 55 percent of the votes. On the face of it, surely the 1984 elections gave no mandate to Reagan.

Before the end of 1986, when the Democrats had once again won a majority of popular votes in elections to the House and had also regained a majority of seats in the Senate, it should have been clear and it should be even clearer now that the major social and economic policies for which Reagan and his supporters had claimed a mandate have persistently failed to gain majority support. Indeed, the major domestic policies and programs established during the thirty years preceding Reagan in the White House have not been overturned in the grand revolution of policy that his election was supposed to have ushered in. For eight years, what Reagan and his supporters claimed as a mandate to reverse those policies was regularly rejected by means of the only legitimate and constitutional processes we Americans have for determining what the policies of the United States government should be.

What are we to make of this long history of unsupported claims to a presidential mandate? The myth of the mandate would be less important if it were not one element in the larger process of the pseudodemocratization of the presidency—the creation of a type of chief executive that in my view should have no proper place in a democratic republic.

Yet even if we consider it in isolation from the larger development of the presidency, the myth is harmful to American political life. By portraying the president as the only representative of the whole people and Congress as merely representing narrow, special, and parochial interests, the myth of the mandate elevates the president to an exalted position in our constitutional system at the expense of Congress. The myth of the mandate fosters the belief that the particular interests of the diverse human beings who form the citizen body in a large, complex, and pluralistic country like ours constitute no legitimate element in the general good. The myth confers on the aims of the groups who benefit from presidential policies an aura of national interest and public good to which they are no more entitled than the groups whose interests are reflected in the policies that gain support by congressional majorities. Because the myth is almost always employed to support deceptive, misleading, and manipulative interpretations, it is harmful to the political understanding of citizens.

It is, I imagine, now too deeply rooted in American political life and too useful a part of the political arsenal of presidents to be abandoned. Perhaps the most we can hope for is that commentators on public affairs in the media and in academic pursuits will dismiss claims to a presidential mandate with the scorn they usually deserve.

But if a presidential election does not confer a mandate on the victor, what does a presidential election mean, if anything at all? While a presidential election does not confer a popular mandate on the president—nor, for that matter, on congressional majorities—it confers the legitimate authority, right, and opportunity on a president to try to gain the adoption by constitutional means of the policies the president supports. In the same way, elections to Congress confer on a member the authority, right, and opportunity to try to gain the adoption by constitutional means of the policies he or she supports. Each may reasonably contend that a particular policy is in the public good or public interest and, moreover, is supported by a majority of citizens.

I do not say that whatever policy is finally adopted following discussion, debate, and constitutional processes necessarily reflects what a majority of citizens would prefer, or what would be in their interests, or what would be in the public good in any other sense. What I do say is that no elected leader, including the president, is uniquely privileged to say what an election means—nor to claim that the election has conferred on the president a mandate to enact the particular policies the president supports. . . .

Questions for Discussion

1. What is a mandate? Why is it so important, or at least useful, for a president to make such a claim in establishing a set of policy priorities?
2. In what ways does the idea of a presidential mandate violate the assumptions of the Constitution's framers?
3. Did George W. Bush have any possible mandate after the 2000 election? Did he claim one? How about after the 2004 election?

 11.3

Power Surge: The Constitutional Record of George W. Bush

Gene Healy and Timothy Lynch

For true believers in small government, and especially those with libertarian leanings, the presidency of George W. Bush has been an unmitigated disaster. Despite professing to be a small-government conservative, Bush has overseen a substantial growth of government and the extensive intrusion of the national government into traditionally local affairs. Moreover, after the 9/11 terrorist attacks, the Bush administration has acted to curb civil liberties in numerous ways, sometimes without consulting Congress. These incursions have made libertarians especially uneasy; indeed, some of the harshest attacks on the Bush administration's policies have not come from Democrats, but from libertarians who generally tend to side with a traditional Republican preference for smaller, less intrusive government.

In this article, originally published by the Cato Institute, Gene Healy and Timothy Lynch present a wide-ranging indictment of President Bush's systematic push to extend his presidential powers. Although issues surrounding the war on terror and the Iraq War receive understandable emphasis, the Healy-Lynch in-

Gene Healy and Timothy Lynch are senior staff members at the Cato Institute, in Washington, D.C.

Gene Healy and Timothy Lynch, *Power Surge: The Constitutional Record of George W. Bush*, 2006, pp. 2–23. Reprinted by permission of Cato Institute, www.cato.org.

dictment is far broader, with its focus on the nationalizing tendencies of the No Child Left Behind Act and the president's willingness to sign a campaign reform bill that limits political speech for independent groups. Healy and Lynch begin, interestingly enough, by examining the president's oath to uphold the Constitution. They stress the importance of the oath and argue that it has definite implications for the reach of presidential power.

Introduction

On March 4, 1793, George Washington stood before the assembled worthies in the Senate chamber in Congress Hall in Philadelphia and delivered his second inaugural address, still the shortest inaugural speech on record:

> Fellow citizens: I am again called upon by the voice of my country to execute the functions of its Chief Magistrate. When the occasion proper for it shall arrive, I shall endeavor to express the high sense I entertain of this distinguished honor, and of the confidence which has been reposed in me by the people of united America.
>
> Previous to the execution of any official act of the President, the Constitution requires an oath of office. This oath I am now about to take, and in your presence: That if it shall be found during my administration of the Government I have in any instance violated willingly or knowingly the injunctions thereof, I may (besides incurring constitutional punishment) be subject to the upbraidings of all who are now witnesses of the present solemn ceremony.

Washington's second inaugural is a model of presidential brevity, but it makes an important point. Fidelity to the constitutional oath of office should be a central factor in judging presidents; violation of that oath is just grounds for "upbraiding" them, and more. Unfortunately, our modern political culture treats the oath of office as little more than a ceremonial exercise. . . .

For the founding generation, however, such oaths had deep significance. . . . Indeed, the Framers of the Constitution considered the presidential oath important enough to specify the exact words that the president must speak before his ascendancy to office, as they did for no other position.

Thus, on January 20, 2005, at the West Face of the Capitol, George W. Bush raised his right hand, put his left on the Bible, and took the same oath he had taken four years previously, the same oath Washington and 40 other presidents had taken:

> I do solemnly swear that I will faithfully execute the Office of President of the United States, and will to the best of my Ability, preserve, protect and defend the Constitution of the United States.

. . . That the oath was not a mere formality—that it required independent constitutional judgment by the president—is clear from early historical practice. The leaders of the early Republic emphatically did not believe the judiciary held a monopoly on constitutional questions. As Thomas Jefferson said, explaining his decision to pardon those who had been convicted under the Sedition Act for exercising their right to free speech:

> The judges, believing the law constitutional, had a right to pass a sentence of fine and imprisonment; because the power was placed in their hands by the Constitution. But the Executive, believing the law to be unconstitutional, were bound to remit the execution of it; because that power has been confided to them by the Constitution. That instrument meant that its coordinate branches should be checks on each other.

Essential to maintaining those checks was the presidential veto. Our early presidents believed their oath of the office required them to veto unconstitutional legislation. Washington was the first president to veto a bill, and his first exercise of the Constitution's veto power was carried out explicitly on constitutional grounds. . . .

Though the Framers believed the oath of office imposed a solemn obligation on the president to uphold the Constitution and defend it from potential violations by coordinate branches, they were under no illusions about the oath's inviolability. The oath was merely the first line of defense in a system of checks and balances designed to restrain abuses of power. . . .

In a sense, George W. Bush campaigned on the sanctity of the oath of office. His signature move on the campaign trail in 2000 was to end his stump speech by pantomiming the oath of office, raising his right hand in the air, his left positioned as if on an imaginary Bible, declaring that he would "swear to not only uphold the laws of the land, but I will also swear to uphold the honor and the dignity of the office to which I have been elected, so help me God." Has he lived up to that promise "to uphold the laws of the land"? . . . The pattern that emerges is one of a ceaseless push for power, unchecked by either the courts or Congress, one, in short, of disdain for constitutional limits. That pattern should disturb people from across the political spectrum. . . .

The Free Speech Clause

The First Amendment's command, "Congress shall make no law . . . abridging the freedom of speech," enshrines the principle that "each person should decide for him or herself the ideas and beliefs deserving of expression, consideration, and adherence." That principle is a cornerstone of our political system. And it has given rise to a vibrant, dynamic, expressive culture—one that can, as Thomas Jefferson acknowledged in his first inaugural address, "[wear] an aspect which might impose on strangers unused to think freely and to speak and to write what they think."

The American constitutional tradition of free thought and free expression is nowhere more important than when it comes to criticizing those in power. For that reason, commentators from across the political spectrum have recognized that at the very core of the First Amendment lies the right to criticize elected officeholders. Unfortunately, President Bush has failed to protect that right.

Regulating and Rationing Political Speech

President Bush's decision to sign the McCain-Feingold campaign finance bill is as clear an example of willful violation of the constitutional oath of office as one is likely to find with this president or any other. That is because Bush first publicly acknowledged his constitutional duty to veto the proposed legislation because it violated the First Amendment—and then proceeded to sign it anyway.

In early 2000 Sen. John McCain (R-AZ), then-governor Bush's principal challenger for the Republican nomination, was one of the driving forces behind a legislative push to eliminate unregulated "soft money" donations to political parties and to severely restrict the ability of independent groups to run political advertisements. On ABC's *This Week* program on the morning of January 23, 2000, George Will asked candidate Bush for his views on such restrictions (having told him, prior to the show, that the question was coming). Governor Bush (1) agreed with Will that the president has an independent duty to judge the constitutionality of the legislation he signs, (2) acknowledged that the McCain-Feingold bill was unconstitutional, and (3) promised to veto it. . . .

Two years later, the McCain-Feingold bill, officially named the Bipartisan Campaign Reform Act of 2002 [BCRA], had passed both houses of Congress. And President Bush had changed his mind—not about the constitutional defects of the bill, but about the political merits of signing it. Asked at a news conference whether he'd hesitate to sign the bill, he wisecracked: "I won't hesitate. It will probably take about three seconds to get to the W., I may hesitate on the period, and then rip through the 'Bush.'" . . .

Media coverage of the signing ceremony tended to focus on the fact that President Bush did not invite Senator McCain to the scene of his legislative triumph. More interesting, however, was that President Bush acknowledged and conceded the constitutional objections to the bill even as he signed it. . . .

However, in President Bush's view, the ultimate responsibility lay with the judicial branch: "I expect that the courts will resolve these legitimate legal questions as appropriate under the law." But as President Bush had acknowledged on *This Week* two years earlier, judges are not the only officials who swear an oath to uphold the Constitution. They are merely the last line of defense against unconstitutional action. And when the president abdicates his constitutional responsibility, as President Bush did when he signed a bill he knew to be unconstitutional, there is no guarantee that the courts will act to uphold theirs.

In fact, the Supreme Court did not accept President Bush's invitation to strike down the offending portions of BCRA. In December 2003, in *McConnell v. Federal Election Commission*, the Court upheld all the major provisions of BCRA. . . .

And if, as candidate Bush agreed in January 2000, there is "no constitutionally significant difference between campaign contributions and expenditures" and both are "central to the First Amendment," one wonders why as president he signed a bill that restricts contributions to political parties. . . .

Also upheld by the Court was what President Bush referred to in his signing statement as "the broad ban on issue advertising." Title II of BCRA is a constitutional abomination, creating a new legal category called "electioneering communications," defined as "any broadcast, cable or satellite communication" that refers to a specific candidate for federal office, airs within 60 days of a general election (or 30 days of a primary), and is "targeted to the relevant electorate." Prior to BCRA, those ads could be funded as their sponsors saw fit. Unions, corporations, and nonprofits could give any sum they wished to support such political speech. After BCRA, the funding for such advertising had to be done within the strictures of federal campaign finance law, including its prohibitions and contribution limits. Unions and corporations—even nonprofit corporations—are prohibited from funding such advertisements from their general treasuries. . . .

How can a regulatory scheme that complex—a scheme openly designed to restrict political speech that incumbents find offensive—be squared with the First Amendment's clear command that "Congress shall make no law . . . abridging the freedom of speech"? It cannot. BCRA is, as Justice Antonin Scalia noted in dissent, "a law that cuts to the heart of what the First Amendment is meant to protect: the right to criticize the government." The travesty here is that President Bush knew that all along. He signed the bill into law nonetheless. . . .

Executive Power

The Framers sought an energetic executive, but a law-governed one. The Constitution instructs the president to "take Care that the Laws be faithfully executed." And as Justice Hugo Black noted, that clause "refutes the idea that he is to be a lawmaker." Perhaps most important, they left the decision about whether to go to war to the legislature. James Madison described the rationale for that allocation of power:

> In no part of the constitution is more wisdom to be found than in the clause which confides the question of war or peace to the legislature, and not to the executive department. . . . [T]he trust and the temptation would be too great for any one man. . . .

The Bush administration's view of executive power . . . amounts to the view that, in time of war, the president is the law, and no treaty, no statute, no coordinate branch of the U.S. government can stand in the president's way when, by his lights, he is acting to preserve national security. That is apparent in a series of startling claims the administration has made in official documents and public papers, which include the following:

♦ presidential power to ignore federal statutes governing treatment of enemy prisoners—as well as other federal laws that impinge on practices the president believes to be useful in fighting the war on terror;

♦ unilateral executive authority over questions of war and peace; and

♦ the power to designate American citizens "enemy combatants" and lock them up without charges for the duration of the war on terror—in other words, perhaps forever.

In a 1977 interview with David Frost, Richard Nixon described his view of the president's national security authority, "Well, when the President does it, that means it is not illegal." In the arguments it has advanced, both publicly and privately, for untrammeled executive power, the Bush administration comes perilously close to that view.

The Torture Memos

The Bush administration's view that the president, in time of war, is unrestrained by law is on display in a series of internal Justice and Defense Department memoranda written in 2002 and 2003 and publicly revealed in 2004. In those memos, Bush administration lawyers argued that Congress is powerless to interfere with the president's authority to order torture of enemy prisoners if the president decides such action will be useful in prosecuting the war on terror.

Much of the public discussion about the "torture memos" has focused on the narrowness of their definition of torture and the question of whether the Geneva Convention covers Al Qaeda and Taliban prisoners. Reasonable people can debate those issues, but what's perhaps most disturbing about the memos is their assertion that the president cannot be restrained by validly enacted laws. . . .

According to the memos, prohibiting torture infringes on the president's constitutional power as commander in chief. As an August 1, 2002, memo puts it, "Congress can no more interfere with the president's conduct of the interrogation of enemy combatants than it can dictate strategic or tactical decisions on the battlefield." The legal reasoning employed in the August 2002 memo resurfaces in a March 2003 Pentagon memo prepared for Secretary of Defense Donald Rumsfeld, which holds that "[a]ny effort by Congress to regulate the interrogation of unlawful combatants would violate the Constitution's sole vesting of the commander-in-chief authority in the President." Of the Pentagon memo, law professor Michael Froomkin says: "The Constitution does not make the President a king. This memo does."

The Constitution's text will not support anything like the doctrine of presidential absolutism the administration flirts with in the torture memos. It gives Congress powers that bear directly on the issue of military conduct and war crimes, including the power "To make Rules for the Government and Regulation of the land and naval Forces" and the power "To define and punish . . . Offences against the Law of Nations"—such as violations of international covenants against torture. And the president, in addition to his oath to uphold the Constitution, is commanded by that document to "take Care that the Laws be faithfully executed."

It's hard to divine anything in the administration's legal reasoning that would prohibit the seizure and torture of an American citizen on American soil, if the president concluded such action would be useful in fighting the War on Terror. After all, administration officials have argued repeatedly that the United States is as much a combat zone in that war as are the hills of Afghanistan. During oral argument in the *Padilla* case, Judge Luttig told Deputy Solicitor General Paul Clement that accusations that [U.S. citizen José] Padilla was an enemy combatant "don't get you very far, unless you're prepared to boldly say the United States is a battlefield in the war on terror." Clement replied, "I can say that, and I can say it boldly." . . .

Unreasonable Searches and Seizures

The Fourth Amendment to the Constitution provides, "The right of the people to be secure in their persons, houses, papers, and effects, against unreasonable searches and seizures shall not be violated, and no Warrants shall issue, but upon probable cause, supported by Oath or affirmation, and particularly describing the place to be searched, and the persons or things to be seized." The Bush administration has repeatedly sought to weaken the Fourth Amendment's limits on the government's power to arrest and search persons. Bush and his lawyers profess to adhere to the Constitution, but their actions belie their words.

Expanding the Power to Arrest

The arrest of a person is the quintessential "seizure" under the Fourth Amendment. In many countries around the world, police agents can arrest people whenever they choose, but in America the Fourth Amendment shields the people from overzealous government agents by placing some limits on the powers of the police. The primary "check" is the warrant application process. That process requires police to apply for arrest warrants, allowing for impartial judges to exercise some independent judgment with respect to whether sufficient evidence has been gathered to meet the "probable cause" standard set forth in the Fourth Amendment. When officers take a person into custody without an arrest warrant, the prisoner must be brought before a magistrate within 48 hours so that an impartial judicial officer can scrutinize the conduct of the police agent and release anyone who was illegally deprived of his or her liberty.

President Bush and his subordinates have undermined the Fourth Amendment's protections in three distinct ways. First, President Bush has asserted the authority to exclude the judiciary from the warrant application process by issuing his own arrest warrants. According to the controversial "military order" that Bush issued in November 2001, once the president determines that there is "reason to believe" that a noncitizen is connected to terrorist activity and that his or her detention is "in the interest of the United States," federal police agents "shall" detain that person "at an appropriate location designated by the secretary of defense outside or within the United States." . . .

Second, President Bush and the FBI have tried to dilute the "probable cause" standard for citizens and noncitizens alike. The Supreme Court has noted time and again that a person cannot be hauled out of his home on the mere suspicion of police agents—since that would put the liberty of every individual in the hands of any petty official. But in the days and weeks following September 11, the FBI arrested hundreds of people and euphemistically referred to the group as "detainees."

Many of those arrests were perfectly lawful, but it is also clear that many were not. . . . At bottom, this is an attempt to effect what Judge Richard Posner, in another context, has aptly called "imprisonment on suspicion while the police look for evidence to confirm their suspicion."

Third, federal agents misused an obscure federal statute, the material witness law, to detain suspects without having to charge them with a crime. The material witness law is designed to secure a potential witness's testimony so that it will not be lost in situations where the individual witness seems likely to ignore a summons and flee the jurisdiction. In the months following the September 11 attacks, federal agents used the law to incarcerate suspects, not witnesses. By "evading the requirement of probable cause of criminal conduct, the government bypassed checks on the reasonableness of its suspicion."

The Supreme Court has repeatedly rebuffed police and prosecutorial attempts to dilute the constitutional standard of probable cause, but President Bush and his lawyers keep trying to expand the power of executive agents. . . .

Expanding the Power to Eavesdrop

The Supreme Court has recognized that electronic surveillance, such as wiretapping and eavesdropping, impinges on the privacy rights of individuals and organizations and is therefore subject to the Fourth Amendment's warrant clause. President Bush claims that he can bypass the warrant application process and surveil the e-mail and phone conversations of Americans because he is the commander in chief of the U.S. military.

In December 2005 the *New York Times* broke a story about an eavesdropping program conducted by the National Security Agency. Shortly after the September 11 terrorist attacks, President Bush ordered the NSA to eavesdrop on Americans inside the United States to search for terrorist activity. Trying to detect the presence of terrorists inside the United States is, of course, a valid and important objective, but President Bush authorized the NSA to eavesdrop on Americans without the court-approved warrants that are ordinarily required for domestic spying. After the existence of this program was revealed, Bush made it plain that he would decide for himself whether to follow the Foreign Intelligence Surveillance Act and seek a warrant—or not.

President Bush's claim that he has the "inherent" power as commander in chief to order the secret surveillance of international e-mail and telephone conversations of persons within the United States raises a host of disturbing questions. For example, if the president can surveil international calls without a warrant, can he (or his successor) issue a secret executive order to intercept purely domestic communications as well? Can the president order secret warrantless searches of American homes whenever he deems it appropriate? Attorney General Alberto Gonzales has indicated that the president can order secret searches of American homes because President Bill Clinton deemed such break-ins "legal," as if that would bolster the validity of his claim.

Indeed, the president's lawyers have already informed the federal judiciary that they regard the entire world, including every inch of U.S. territory, a "battlefield." That outlandish claim has profound implications for the Bill of Rights because there are *no* legal rights whatsoever on the battlefield. . . . Bush trusts himself to do the right thing, but he does not seem to appreciate the fact that the precedents he is attempting to establish will not expire when he leaves the White House. Those precedents will open the door to abuses by future presidents in the years to come. Instead of fortifying the legal safeguards that protect the liberties of the American people, President Bush has weakened those safeguards considerably. Despite his protestations to the contrary, the president's actions exhibit a profound disrespect for the Constitution and the rule of law.

The "Great Writ" of Habeas Corpus

The most important constitutional issue that has arisen since the September 11 terrorist attacks has been President Bush's claim that he can arrest any person in the world and hold that person incommunicado indefinitely. According to the legal papers that Bush's attorneys have filed in the courts, so long as he has issued an "enemy combatant" order to his secretary of defense instead of the attorney general, it does not matter if the prisoner is a foreign national or an American citizen. And it does not matter if the prisoner was apprehended in Afghanistan or in some sleepy town in the American heartland. Under this sweeping theory of executive power, the liberty of every American rests on nothing more than the grace of the White House.

To fully appreciate the implications of the administration's "enemy combatant" argument, one must first consider the constitutional procedure of habeas corpus. The Constitution provides: "The Privilege of the Writ of Habeas Corpus shall not be suspended, unless when in Cases of Rebellion or Invasion the public Safety may require it." Since that provision appears in Article I of the Constitution, which sets forth the powers of the legislature, the implication is clear: Congress has the responsibility to decide whether or not the writ ought to be suspended. Notably, the Bush administration has not urged the Congress to suspend habeas corpus. Nor has President Bush asserted the claim that he can suspend the writ unilaterally. Bush's lawyers have instead tried to alter the way in which the writ operates when it is *not* suspended.

By way of background, the writ of habeas corpus is a venerable legal procedure that allows a prisoner to get a hearing before an impartial judge. If the jailor is able to supply a valid basis for the arrest and imprisonment at the hearing, the judge will simply order the prisoner to be returned to jail. But if the judge discovers that the imprisonment is illegal, he has the power to set the prisoner free. For that reason, the Founders routinely referred to this legal device as the "Great Writ" because it was considered one of the great safeguards of individual liberty.

The Bush administration's assault on the Great Writ was indirect but very real. It arose when a man challenged the legality of his imprisonment. Yaser Hamdi was initially captured in Afghanistan and was then transferred to the prison facility at Guantanamo Bay in Cuba. When the military authorities discovered that Hamdi was an American citizen, he was moved to a military brig in South Carolina. Because Hamdi was denied access to family and legal counsel, his father filed a writ of habeas corpus on his behalf in federal court. The Bush administration could have simply explained to the court its reasons for jailing Hamdi—that Hamdi was captured on an overseas battlefield—but it chose to respond to that petition by urging the district court to summarily dismiss the petition because, it argued, the court could not "second-guess" the president's "enemy combatant" determination. That assertion struck at the heart of habeas corpus. If the judiciary could not "second-guess" the executive's initial decision to imprison a citizen, the writ never would have acquired its longstanding reputation in the law as the Great Writ.

If Congress has not suspended the writ of habeas corpus, the law is clear. The prisoner must be able to meet with his attorney in order to adequately prepare for their "day in court." That day is significant because it may be the prisoner's only opportunity to persuade a judge that a mistake has been made or that an abuse has occurred. President Bush's attorneys tried to advance the astonishing notion that habeas corpus petitions could be filed—as long as they were all immediately thrown out of court. Bush's attorneys failed to persuade the Supreme Court that his "enemy combatant" policy was lawful. Writing for the Court, Justice Sandra Day O'Connor noted, "We have long since made clear that a state of war is not a blank check for the President when it comes to the rights of the Nation's citizens." Justice Antonin Scalia recognized that even though the president and his lawyers were well-intentioned, their legal arguments were profoundly misguided: "The very core of liberty secured by our Anglo-Saxon system of separated powers has been freedom from indefinite imprisonment at the will of the Executive."

Some conservative writers tried to downplay the significance of the president's stance by arguing that "only" a few Americans have been imprisoned on the "enemy combatant" theory. That argument misses the point completely. The American legal system is based on precedent. If the Bush administration is successful in claiming that it can imprison just one American citizen and deprive that person of habeas corpus protection, that precedent could be used against scores of citizens thereafter, whether by the present president or his successors. It is for that reason that Bush's attempt to undermine "the very core of our liberty" may be his most egregious failure to protect and defend our Constitution. . . .

Conclusion

One searches for bright spots in the Bush constitutional record. And there were at least two. Early on in the president's first term, Attorney General John Ashcroft made clear that it was the Bush administration's position that the Second Amendment guarantees a personal, individual right to bear arms. In two federal cases, the Bush administration argued in formal court papers that the "Second Amendment . . . protects the rights of individuals, including persons who are not members of any militia . . . to possess and bear their own firearms, subject to reasonable restrictions designed to prevent possession by unfit persons or . . . firearms that are particularly suited to criminal misuse." That was a significant, if symbolic, victory for those who believe that the Second Amendment means what it says, that "the right of the people" means an individual, personal right, just as it does in the First, Fourth, Fifth, and Ninth Amendments. The president has also appointed a number of federal judges who appear to take constitutional limits seriously and may be expected to look skeptically at broad claims of legislative power. However, whether the same judges will look skeptically at broad claims of executive power remains very much in doubt.

. . . The Bush constitutional record . . . is, overwhelmingly, one of contempt for constitutional limits. In its official papers and public actions, the

Bush administration has endorsed a vision of federal power that is astonishingly broad, a vision that includes

♦ a federal government empowered to regulate core political speech—and restrict it greatly when it counts the most: in the days before a federal election;

♦ a president who can launch wars at will, and who cannot be restrained from ordering the commission of war crimes, should he choose to do so;

♦ a president who can lock up American citizens at will and forever—without any meaningful oversight by the judiciary; and

♦ a federal government with the power to supervise all areas of American life, from education to marriage and through the end of life.

It is a vision, in short, unimagined by our Constitution's Framers.

On the campaign trail in 2000, then-governor Bush typically ended his stump speech with a dramatic flourish: he pantomimed the oath of office. But the oath is more than a political gimmick; for the founding generation it was a solemn pledge, designed to bind the officeholder to the country and the Constitution he serves. Throughout his tenure, President Bush has repeatedly dishonored that pledge. And because of that, he has weakened the constitutional order on which the American way of life depends.

Questions for Discussion

1. Healy and Lynch argue that George W. Bush has violated his oath of office by systematically expanding presidential powers. Does this argument hold water? If so, is this an impeachable offense?

2. Do you agree or disagree with Healy and Lynch's general assessment that the president has gone too far in asserting constitutional authority, or is it more reasonable to limit the analysis to elements of the war on terror?

Chapter 12

BUREAUCRACY

The terms *bureaucracy* and *bureaucrat* evoke negative images for most Americans. To many, *bureaucracy* is a synonym for red tape, rigidity, insensitivity, and long waiting lines, and *bureaucrat* suggests a faceless government drone sitting at a desk, pushing papers, and stamping forms. In fact, a bureaucracy is any complex organization that operates on the basis of a hierarchical authority structure with job specialization. Corporations are bureaucracies, as are educational institutions. The question is whether a bureaucracy complements democracy. On the one hand, it seems wise to have a government run by professionals whose jobs are not dependent on politics. But we may have created a class of government employees who are beyond the control of the voters.

In recent years, public officials and candidates for public office have nurtured the negative image of the public sector and those employed by it. Bureaucracy-bashing is good politics. Four recent presidents—Nixon, Carter, Reagan, and George W. Bush—were first elected during campaigns that made opposition to the Washington bureaucracy a central theme. Every election year congressional candidates remind the public that the federal government has paid $91 for three-cent screws or $511 for a sixty-cent light bulb. Contempt for the Washington bureaucracy may have reached a zenith during the Reagan presidency. Attorney General Edwin Meese once came to a cabinet meeting carrying a chubby, faceless, large-bottomed doll and announced that it was a bureaucrat doll—you place it on a stack of papers and it just sits there.

According to one student of American bureaucracy, Barry D. Karl, "the growth of the bureaucratic state may be the single most unintended consequence of the Constitution of 1787." The Constitution says little about the administration of government. It gives the president the appointment power and the obligation "to take care that the laws [are] faithfully executed," which suggests that the framers were well aware of the administrative needs of the new nation. But belief in limited government and fear of centralized power led them to envision a minimal role for the new federal government.

Thus, the administrative apparatus during the first few presidencies was very small. The State Department had only nine employees at its beginning, and the War Department had fewer than one hundred employees until 1801, at the start of the Jefferson presidency. Compared to Western European countries, the U.S.

bureaucracy experienced a rather late development, well after the growth of mass democracy under Andrew Jackson in the 1830s. By 1861, on the eve of the Civil War, roughly 80 percent of all federal personnel still worked for the Post Office Department.

The Civil War contributed substantially to the growth of American bureaucracy. Mobilization for the war effort led to the creation of many new agencies and the hiring of a large number of public employees. The establishment of a national economy and rapid industrialization after the war also had a profound effect on the size and functions of the federal government, which began to pay attention to particular constituencies. "Clientele" agencies such as the Department of Agriculture (1889) and the Department of Commerce and Labor (1903) were created to service increasingly organized interests.

This period also marked the beginning of the development of a professional bureaucratic class. Before 1883, all federal workers were patronage employees, appointed by the president. When presidencies changed hands, many government employees were out of a job. The assassination of President James A. Garfield in 1881 by an unsuccessful patronage applicant provided the impetus for passage of the Pendleton Act (1882), which established the civil service system. Only about 10 percent of government employees were initially covered by the act, but today more than 90 percent are; they receive their jobs on the basis of competitive merit, usually as the result of written examinations. Firing someone for political reasons is illegal.

The New Deal and mobilization for World War II gave the federal bureaucracy the basic form it has today. As the federal government took on an expanded social and economic role, myriad new agencies were created. Today there are more than a hundred federal government agencies, and the government employs almost 5 million people, 2.9 million of whom are civilians.

Despite the widely shared view that the federal bureaucracy has grown rapidly in recent decades, the number of federal employees has been relatively constant since 1945. Most of the growth in the public sector has been at the state and local levels. Nor do most federal bureaucrats work in or around the nation's capital. Only about 12 percent of federal employees work in Washington; 300,000, or 10 percent, work in California. Federal government employment as a percentage of the total work force decreased over the past two decades. "Big government" is more dollars and rules than it is huge numbers of federal bureaucrats. Indeed, political scientist Paul Light (selection 12.4) argued in 1999 that the "true size" of government through outsourcing and privatization is five to six times the actual number of federal employees, a trend that has accelerated over the course of the George W. Bush administration.

Whatever the size of the bureaucracy, its nature poses a dilemma. We need a bureaucratic organization and professional administrators so that government can carry out its basic functions without political interference. But the growth of a professional bureaucratic class has been considered at odds with American political values. Use of the term *civil servant* is an insistence that government employees serve the public, not their employer or themselves. Although Americans want state services, the fear of strong central government and administrative tyranny remains.

Because the U.S. government is involved in so many activities, almost everyone can view some aspect of bureaucracy as illegitimate and threatening. Conservatives generally disapprove of government's redistribution of income and regulation of business, viewing it as intrusive and at odds with traditional free-market philosophy. Liberals are concerned about the bureaucracy's intelligence gathering and domestic policing activities; the secrecy and potential violation of civil liberties raise concerns about "Big Brother" watching.

And the federal bureaucracy represents more than the passive administration of laws passed by the elected branches of government. Bureaucrats are given substantial authority: They issue rules, enforce compliance, allocate federal funds, and regulate economic activity. Because of their expertise, they often formulate policy, although the most successful bureaucratic policymakers work closely with Congress.

The American solution to the dilemma posed by the coexistence of bureaucracy and democracy is to keep the bureaucracy accountable through scrutiny by the other branches of government and by the nation's press. Congressional oversight of bureaucratic practices and spending, central direction in policymaking by the president and his staff, and judicial review of administrative processes and rule making are all important restraints on bureaucratic discretion.

The selections in this chapter are intended to convey a sense of the impact of the bureaucracy on American politics, the controversial nature of its activities, and the difficulties facing those who wish to reform it. Over the course of American history, both politicians and professional administrators have found themselves viewed with increasing skepticism, notes E. J. Dionne Jr. (selection 12.1). Ironically, we rely heavily on both political appointees and non-careerist bureaucrats to move policies from law to practice. Dionne expresses the fear that public service will become so costly and unattractive that it will not attract the necessary talent to govern effectively.

Selections 12.2 and 12.3 examine the challenges of bureaucratic culture. On a general level, James Q. Wilson focuses on the difficulties faced by managers of public organizations and how these can lead to flawed decisions. Then, Charles Peters examines how the specific bureaucratic culture of the National Air and Space Administration (NASA) contributed to the *Challenger* space shuttle disaster in 1986. He notes how problematic information flows can produce deadly consequences, arguing that the NASA bureaucracy bore some real responsibility for the tragedy.

 12.1

"Political Hacks" versus "Bureaucrats": Can't Public Servants Get Some Respect?

E. J. Dionne Jr.

American national government has always required citizens to enter into public service to serve the executive, administer laws, and respond to the demands from the electorate. Over the course of our history, two principal approaches to filling governmental jobs have evolved. As parties developed in the nineteenth century, so too did the "spoils system," in which the victorious party (for president, governor, mayor) would provide jobs for loyal partisans. The operating theory here was that any average citizen could handle most governmental jobs, thus party leaders should reward their followers when they won control of the government. This approach dominated much of the nineteenth century, but reformers sought a more professional approach to government after the expansion of the bureaucracy in the Civil War. Progressives and administrative science pioneers argued for a rational, professional approach to administration, freed from political considerations. Over the course of the twentieth century, the political and professional approaches to administration have fomented considerable debate and controversy.

E. J. Dionne Jr. takes a different tack in his discussion of both politicos and professionals. He argues that neither type receives the respect they have won in the past and almost certainly deserve today. Those who serve—whether as political appointees in the executive branch or as civil servants in the national bureaucracy—often make real sacrifices and generally work hard to produce good public policy. The public, however, has grown more cynical over the past forty years, and finds it difficult to accept the public sector as either interesting or challenging. Dionne's key point is that we rely on fresh faces—whether young idealists or experienced professionals—to fill demanding governmental positions.

E. J. Dionne Jr. is a regular columnist for the *Washington Post* and a senior fellow at the Brookings Institution.

E. J. Dionne Jr., " 'Political Hacks' versus 'Bureaucrats': Can't Public Servants Get Some Respect?" by E. J. Dionne Jr., from *Innocent Until Nominated: The Breakdown of the Presidential Appointments Process*, edited by G. Calvin Mackenzie (Washington, D.C.: Brookings Institution Press, 2001), pp. 254–264. Reprinted by permission of The Brookings Institution.

Allowing for creativity and real responsibility in these positions may be essential if public service is to remain one hallmark of American democracy.

The most moving moment at either party's national convention in 2000 was a resolutely nonpartisan speech that evoked a moment when taking a job in government was seen as far more than, well, just taking a job. "When my brother John and I were growing up," said Caroline Kennedy Schlossberg, "hardly a day went by when someone didn't come up to us and say, 'Your father changed my life. I went into public service because he asked me.'"

Note that lovely phrase, "public service." Schlossberg was not exaggerating or being unduly romantic about the spirit of John F. Kennedy's New Frontier, which both shaped its time and reflected it. Serving in a new administration, whether on the White House staff, in the cabinet, or in a less grand post, was not simply an obligation or, in the current ugly phrase, "a ticket to punch." It was also a source of excitement. And so, as Godfrey Hodgson put it in his biography of Daniel Patrick Moynihan, "a varied population of political and intellectual adventurers" descended on Washington in the winter of 1960 and 1961."

"They came," Hodgson writes, "from New York and San Francisco law firms, from state and city politics across the nation, from the growing world of foundations and pressure groups, and of course from the great graduate schools, swollen by the postwar demand for academic manpower." Hodgson understood that this crowd of adventurers were not saints, but neither were they mere opportunists: "The mood," he says, "was strangely blended from ambition and idealism, aggressive social climbing and a sense of youthful adventure."

The Diminished Promise of Citizen Service

No doubt many entered the Bush administration in 2001 with that same sense of vigor and adventure. Long lists of Republican office seekers, out of executive power for eight years, testified to the continuing lure of executive positions, from the highest posts to the lowest. Still, it is difficult to hear Schlossberg's speech and to read Hodgson's account and not sense a shift in the spirit of the times. Forty years after that winter of the New Frontier, public service in the executive branch retains its allure, but not quite the same sense of glamour or promise.

. . . [M]ost politicians who have won the presidency over the past quarter century did so by running against "the government in Washington." Bush was no exception. As a result, expressing an open desire to serve in that very government and an open belief that it might accomplish large things flies in the face of what is now deeply ingrained conventional wisdom. Those who want to serve in government in Washington have to bash government to get there. That cannot make a life in government service very attractive to those not yet committed to the venture.

Yet no country is as dependent as ours on "citizen service" in its national administration. None relies so heavily on people who might be called amateurs, as against career civil servants, to govern. From the beginning of the republic we have operated on the assumption that a professional ruling class is problematic and to be avoided. Government, according to this view, should be refreshed periodically by tides of new leaders with new ideas and untapped energy—the very spirit captured so well by Hodgson and Schlossberg. The assumption continues to prevail that citizen service is essential to the health of civil society—in this case, citizen service at the very highest levels—because citizen service links the government to the rest of the society in a way a purely professional bureaucracy could not.

Professionalism versus Politics

That is the theory, anyway. In truth, our attitude toward those citizen servants reflects an odd balance of ideas. Our history is one of ambivalence as between professionalism on the one side and politics on the other. We admire the independence and expertise of professionals, yet we regularly denounce them when they work for the government. It is no accident that the famous Republican campaign commercial of 2000 in which the word "rats" appeared ever so briefly on our television screens—conveying or not conveying a "subliminal" message, depending on whom you believed—was in fact depicting the word "bureaucrats" at that critical and controversial moment. However honored they might occasionally be, the day-to-day civil servants who make the American government run do not enjoy the honor or prestige of their counterparts in France or Germany, Britain or Japan.

Yet if we denounce bureaucrats, we also denounce political appointees. This is obvious from the normal parlance of politics and journalism. We condemn certain agencies of government as patronage dumping grounds. We say we dislike the political spoils system. We insist on praising independent, nonpartisan government. Indeed, this was the impetus behind the civil service reform that, from the 1880s forward, took the awarding of tens of thousands of jobs out of politics. The premise, as James Q. Wilson puts it in his classic work *The Amateur Democrat*, was that "the merit system and open competition should be extended to insure, insofar as is feasible, that general principles rather than private advantage govern the awarding" of government benefits.

These two traditions—a preference for political appointees over bureaucrats and a preference for civil servants over the beneficiaries of political patronage—are deeply rooted in our history. To understand the contradictions in our history is to understand our ambivalence today.

Jacksonian Rotation in Office

It is worth remembering that the idea of wholesale changes in the government following the defeat of an incumbent party in an election was originally seen as a "reform" by the advocates of Jacksonian democracy in the 1820s and 1830s. The followers of Andrew Jackson referred not to a spoils system but to a principle they held up as admirable and called "rotation in office." The Jacksonians believed their political foes had come to regard holding the appointive offices of government as a right that could not be disturbed even by the electorate. That is what Andrew Jackson was against. "Office is considered as a species of property," Jackson declared, "and government rather as a means of promoting individual interests than as an instrument created solely for the service of the people."

As Harry L. Watson summarizes Jackson's views in *Liberty and Power*, his admirable book on Jacksonian democracy, "No one in a republic had an inherent right to public office—so no one could complain if he lost a public job in favor of someone more honest, more competent, or more in agreement with elected officials who carried a popular mandate." Jackson . . . emphatically rejected the views of his former Federalist and soon-to-be Whig foes that "no one except a tiny elite had the training or experience to qualify for public office." As Jackson himself put it, "The duties of all public officers are, or admit to being made, so plain and simple that men of intelligence may readily qualify themselves for their performance." Jackson . . . was not arguing for the hiring of incompetents, but he did demand "that public duties be shared among the large body of qualified citizens to avoid the creation of an entrenched and corrupt bureaucracy."

The notion that rotation in office was a mighty weapon in the larger battle against privilege is nicely captured by historian Robert V. Remini in his study of Martin Van Buren. Remini notes that the Democrats' 1828 campaign placed heavy stress on the words "people" and "reform." "The precise direction all this 'reform' was to take," he writes, "was not explained. There was no need to. The people were simply banding together to take the national government out of the hands of the favored few. They were claiming what belonged to them. They were dispossessing 'the wise, the good, and the well born.' "

"Rotation in office" was more than just an excuse to appoint one's friends. "To Jackson the principle of rotation directly addressed the problem of how and by whom government should be run," Remini writes in *The Revolutionary Age of Andrew Jackson*. "Jackson believed that through rotation the federal government in Washington could be made to respond directly to the changing demands of the American people as expressed by their ballots. Thus, each new administration, elected by the people, should bring in its own corps of supporters to make sure the policies of that administration were honestly and fairly implemented."

Prefiguring, perhaps, the New Left's emphasis on participatory democracy, the Jacksonians thought, as Remini puts it, that "rotation meant that a great many more people would get an opportunity to serve the government. The more people actively involved in the affairs of the nation, the more democratic the system, and the more the problems of the nation get to be widely known and understood." The idea came from Jefferson: "Greater participation by the electorate in government safeguards the nation from arbitrary and dictatorial rule."

In other words, America's tradition of political appointments is rooted in a philosophical view of how democratic government can work best—and become more democratic in the process. If European democracies have a much shallower tradition of political nominations and a larger reverence for a career civil service, it is in part because none of the Western European democracies—many of which were not terribly democratic at the time—went through anything that quite resembled the Jacksonian revolution. Hard as it was for reformers to accept the idea later, the creation of a system of political patronage was originally seen as a way to foil both corruption and elitism. Despite abuses, Watson is correct in seeing rotation in office as "a solidly democratic principle that brought greater openness to government."

Civil Service Reform: Depoliticizing Public Service

But there were, indeed, abuses, and they grew over time. The Jacksonian system was "susceptible to political manipulation," as Watson acknowledges. As Remini, a sympathetic student of the Jacksonian principle, puts it, rotation "can be an easy excuse and justification for political head chopping, for regarding political jobs as 'spoils' won in a war in which enemies are punished and friends rewarded. . . . When rotation is administered by incompetents or thieves, then everyone suffers and the democratic system is dangerously compromised." It is precisely that sense of incompetence and thievery that helped unleash the other great American public service tradition—civil service reform combined with a preference for expertise. It reached high tide between the 1880s and 1920.

The historian Robert H. Wiebe picks up this thread in his excellent study of the period, *The Search for Order*. In contrast with the Jacksonians, the new reformers saw the removal of government jobs from the political realm as "democracy's cure." Wiebe notes that "by denying politicians the spoils of office, the argument ran, civil service would drive out the parasites and leave only a pure frugal government behind. The nonpartisanship inherent in civil service would permeate politics, and as party organizations withered away, the men of quality now excluded by the spoilsmen and unscrupulous businessmen would resume their natural posts of command."

It is also important to see that civil service reform and enhanced faith in a professionalized bureaucracy arose at a moment of growing faith in scientific rationality and a belief in the importance of expertise. The professionals of the period, Wiebe observes, "naturally conceived of science as a method for their disciplines instead of a set of universal principles."...

The importance of this view to American public life is described well by Moynihan himself in his famous 1965 essay, "The Professionalization of Reform." Moynihan cites Wesley C. Mitchell, of the National Bureau of Economic Research, who offered an almost perfect statement of [rationalism]: "Our best hope for the future lies in the extension to social organization of the methods that we already employ in our most progressive fields of efforts. In science and industry . . . we do not wait for catastrophe to force new ways upon us. . . . We rely, and with success, upon quantitative analysis to point the way; and we advance because we are constantly improving and applying such analysis."

Still a Healthy Tension?

Alas, it is not so clear how much we have advanced when it comes to making a joy in public service part of our political ethic. Where do our dueling traditions of political appointments and professionalized bureaucracy leave us today?

The professional view suffered body blows during the 1960s from left, right, and center. Moynihan predicted this in his original essay on the professionalization of reform: "a certain price will be paid and a considerable risk will be incurred." The price, said the man who journeyed to the New Frontier with such hope, "will be a decline in the moral exhilaration of public affairs at the domestic level." And so there was.

The rise of the idea of participatory democracy on the New Left suggested that the distant bureaucrat claiming vastly more knowledge than average citizens needed to be taken down a peg or two. The goal of Lyndon Johnson's War on Poverty, "maximum feasible participation," suggested that real expertise could be found only on the streets and in the neighborhoods. On the right, George Wallace's attacks on "pointy-headed bureaucrats with thin briefcases full of guidelines" nicely captured the conservative rebellion against experts— and, in the case of Wallace and his followers, especially those pushing for new programs of racial inclusion. But the resentments could not be explained simply by race.

As if this were not enough, the civil service bureaucracy also came under assault from the political center as a system that no longer worked—that no longer effectively delivered the very expertise and public-regarding ethos the civil service reformers at the turn of the century expected it to provide. Consider this thoughtful critique of the civil service offered in *The Public Interest.* Published in the summer of 1973, it was entitled, "The Civil Service: A Meritless System?" Its authors, E. S. Savas and Sigmund G. Ginsburg, [observe]: "The low productivity of public employees and the malfunctioning of governmental bureaucracies are becoming apparent to an increasing number of frustrated and indignant taxpayers. The problem shows up all over the country in the form of uncivil servants going through preprogrammed motions while awaiting their pensions."

. . . Too often, the result is mindless bureaucracies that appear to function for the convenience of their staffs rather than for the public whom they are supposed to serve. [Moreover,] "It is the system itself . . . rather than the hapless politician who heads it or the minions toiling within it that is basically at fault."

That system, they declare, "prohibits good management, frustrates able employees, inhibits productivity, lacks the confidence of the taxpayers, and fails to respond to the needs of citizens." The "worst feature of the promotion system," they continue, "is that an employee's chance of promotion bears no relationship to his performance on the job." At fault was "the rigor mortis of overdeveloped and regressive civil service systems."

. . . [T]his line of criticism, repeated often in subsequent years, led to what might be seen as a neo-Jacksonian call to replace parts of the civil service with political appointees, especially in city governments. The idea (it does, indeed, sound like rotation in office) was to give politicians more direct control over government—and to make governments more accountable to electorates. . . .

Indeed, this neo-Jacksonian reaction also encompassed a certain informed nostalgia in political science for the old political machine—the very institution upon which the civil service reformers had waged war. The problem with institutionalizing social benefits in national entitlement programs, says Calvin Mackenzie in his appropriately titled book, *The Irony of Reform*, was that doing so allowed their beneficiaries "to be less attentive to politics" and less active at election time. Why? Because "government had taken over control of the benefits that had once inspired so much political activity. What had long been the game of the political machines—the provision of material benefits in exchange for political support—soon became the game of government. And when it did, the machines ran out of fuel and shut down." As a result, "the parties and the traditional politics they represented began to wither." Never has patronage and "rotation in office" played as well among political scientists as it does now— after, of course, the machines (and, yes, their abuses) are gone.

But in truth, the spoils system and the political appointees who might be part of it play no better with the public than does the professional bureaucrat. . . . It is thus striking, and not surprising, that young people devoted to public service tend less than ever to carry out that service through government—in either civil service or political posts. As Paul C. Light has pointed out, the trend among young people oriented toward service is to seek to reform institutions and change society through the nonprofit sector rather than through government itself. Part of the problem . . . is the difficulty government has under current rules and practices in offering the flexibility and work opportunities available in the nonprofit sector. But it is also true that the idea of government service as an adventure . . . is about as fashionable as the now late, lamented Oldsmobile.

Another response to the discrediting of both civil servants and political nominees has been the rise in demands for the "privatization" of public services. As Light has shown, even as the formal numbers in some areas of government employment have fallen, many tasks once performed by government employees are taken on by employees of private companies—hired by the government. The merits of privatization can be debated—in general, government officials tend to make pragmatic rather than ideological judgments about which services should be performed by whom. But what is noticeable in much of the privatization rhetoric is the discrediting of government servants as efficient deliverers of public wants and the elevation of the market as the preferred mechanism for introducing responsiveness and productivity.

At its best, the American tradition of tension between the political and the professional control of government is highly productive. The Jacksonian instinct that elections should matter and that there should be a significant degree of political control—meaning democratic control—over the bureaucracy is correct. But the desire for genuine expertise in the right places is also correct. The president, and the people, need military strategists, research scientists, lawyers, economists, and environmental specialists who will feel free to tell the truth as they see it and inform decision making. A democratic government cannot be effective if it changes capriciously from one administration to another.

The American tradition creates a constant battle between the democratic impulse and the impulse for efficiency and predictability. This tension is not only useful but also necessary. The Jacksonian principle insists that in a democracy, there is not a bright line between "the government" on the one side and "civil society"—the array of communal institutions independent of government—on the other. If a government is not rooted in, and does not draw on, civil society, it can be neither democratic nor effective.

A Plague on Both Your Houses

It is not at all clear that the tension between our traditions is serving us well today. At most points in our history, at least one side of the government (the politicians or the professionals) enjoyed some claim on public esteem. Now it can be argued that neither does—and thus the tendency to want to farm government out as much as possible. The Jacksonians lifted up the political appointee to put a check on the arrogance of expertise. The civil service reformers lifted up expertise to put a check on political abuses. Now putting down both sides is the general rule.

The rise of a specifically presidential bureaucracy has in some ways divided the executive branch itself, aggravating its problems and the problems of those who work for it. As the political scientist Nelson Polsby has argued, one of the most interesting developments of the past half century "is the emergence of a presidential branch of government separate and apart from the executive branch." It is the presidential branch, Polsby writes, "that sits across the table from the executive branch at budgetary hearings, and that imperfectly attempts to coordinate both the executive and legislative branches in its own behalf."

In *The Presidency in a Separated System*, Charles O. Jones makes a parallel point: that "the mix of career ambitions represented by presidential appointees may well bring the outside world to Washington, but there is no guarantee that these officials will cohere into a working government." Jones sees the president as "somewhat in the position of the Olympic basketball coach. He may well have talented players but lack a team."

None of this means that George W. Bush or any future president will have trouble filling his (or, someday, her) government. None of it means that the country lacks the "practical idealists" of whom Al Gore liked to speak. But a government as peculiarly dependent as ours is on the willingness of citizens to interrupt the normal trajectory of their lives to devote themselves to government service needs to worry that it is not nourishing either of our great traditions of public service. When the political tradition has faltered, we have been able to call on our civil service tradition. When expertise falters, the politicos can step in to right the balance. But when both traditions fail, where do we turn?

We can privatize as much as we want, but government will never work if there is not a broadly accepted ethic that sees government service as honorable, productive, and creative—if there is not an ethic that views government service as public service. Nor will government work if young people see the independent sector as dynamic and the government sector as sterile and stolid. And, yes, it would help to have a president who drew people to public service because he asked them to do it and because he made it an adventure in which ambition and democratic idealism could coexist.

Questions for Discussion

1. In a federal work force of about 1.5 million civilians, how many of these positions should be based on political loyalty to the president and the president's party? A hundred? A thousand? Ten thousand? Currently the president can appoint about 3000 so-called Schedule C (political) appointees to full-time jobs. Do you think that is enough, given that the president has won a national election? Too many? What are your criteria for thinking about this?

2. One of Dionne's complaints is that many individuals choose public service to "get their tickets punched" before heading into the private sector to make a lot of money. Do you see anything wrong with this? Does it necessarily demean the idea of public service? What might you do to slow down the revolving door?

 12.2

Constraints on Public Managers

James Q. Wilson

Companies like AT&T or McDonald's rival in size and budget some of the largest government organizations and, on paper, are organized similarly, with a hierarchical authority structure and multiple layers of administration. They are bureaucracies in every sense of the term. Critics of government bureaucracy often point to the successes of such private sector organizations as efficient deliverers of services or products, in contrast to public bureaucracies that often are stereotyped as being bound by rules or red tape and staffed by unmotivated and unresponsive workers. Every election sees candidates committed to reforming government bureaucracies in an attempt to "run government more like a business."

Although government and private bureaucracies share many characteristics, they are different in fundamental ways, creating difficulties for those who aspire to make government agencies more like their private sector counterparts. In this selection, James Q. Wilson argues that all government agencies have certain characteristics that tend to make their management far more difficult than managing a business: "Government management tends to be driven by the *constraints* on the organization, not the *tasks* of the organization." Managerial control is particularly problematic because public managers have relatively little control over revenues, factors of production, and agency goals, which are "all vested to an important degree in entities external to the organization—legislatures, courts, politicians, and interest groups." One result is that public managers become "averse to any action that risks violating a significant constraint," rigidly interpreting rules and avoiding innovation.

B y the time the office opens at 8:45 A.M., the line of people waiting to do business at the Registry of Motor Vehicles in Watertown, Massachusetts, often will be twenty-five deep. By midday, especially if it is near the end of the month, the line may extend clear around the building. Inside, motorists

James Q. Wilson is professor of management and public policy at UCLA and past president of the American Political Science Association.

wait in slow-moving rows before poorly marked windows to get a driver's license or to register an automobile. When someone gets to the head of the line, he or she is often told by the clerk that it is the wrong line: "Get an application over there and then come back," or "This is only for people getting a new license; if you want to replace one you lost, you have to go to the next window." The customers grumble impatiently. The clerks act harried and sometimes speak brusquely, even rudely. What seems to be a simple transaction may take 45 minutes or even longer. . . .

Not far away, people also wait in line at a McDonald's fast-food restaurant. There are several lines; each is short, each moves quickly. The menu is clearly displayed on attractive signs. The workers behind the counter are invariably polite. If someone's order cannot be filled immediately, he or she is asked to step aside for a moment while the food is prepared and then is brought back to the head of the line to receive the order. The atmosphere is friendly and good-natured. The room is immaculately clean.

Many people have noticed the difference between getting a driver's license and ordering a Big Mac. Most will explain it by saying that bureaucracies are different from businesses. "Bureaucracies" behave as they do because they are run by unqualified "bureaucrats" and are enmeshed in "rules" and "red tape."

But business firms are also bureaucracies, and McDonald's is a bureaucracy that regulates virtually every detail of its employees' behavior by a complex and all-encompassing set of rules. Its operations manual is six hundred pages long and weights four pounds.[1] In it one learns that french fries are to be nine-thirty-seconds of an inch thick and that grill workers are to place hamburger patties on the grill from left to right, six to a row for six rows. They are then to flip the third row first, followed by the fourth, fifth, and sixth rows, and finally the first and second. The amount of sauce placed on each bun is precisely specified. Every window must be washed every day. Workers must get down on their hands and knees and pick up litter as soon as it appears. These and countless other rules designed to reduce the workers to interchangeable automata were inculcated in franchise managers at Hamburger University located in a $40 million facility. There are plenty of rules governing the Registry, but they are only a small fraction of the rules that govern every detail of every operation at McDonald's. Indeed, if the DMV manager tried to impose on his employees as demanding a set of rules as those that govern the McDonald's staff, they would probably rebel and he would lose his job.

It is just as hard to explain the differences between the two organizations by reference to the quality or compensation of their employees. The Registry workers are all adults, most with at least a high-school education; the McDonald's employees are mostly teenagers, many still in school. The Registry staff is well-paid compared to the McDonald's workers, most of whom receive only the minimum wage. . . .

Not only are the differences between the two organizations not to be explained by reference to "rules" or "red tape" or "incompetent workers," the differences call into question many of the most frequently mentioned complaints about how government agencies are supposed to behave. For example: "Government agencies are big spenders." The Watertown office of the Registry is in a modest building that can barely handle its clientele. The teletype machine used to check information submitted by people requesting a replacement license was antiquated and prone to errors. Three or four clerks often had to wait in line to use equipment described by the office manager as "personally signed by Thomas Edison." No computers or word processors were available to handle the preparation of licenses and registrations; any error made by a clerk while manually typing a form meant starting over again on another form.

Or: "Government agencies hire people regardless of whether they are really needed." Despite the fact that the citizens of Massachusetts probably have more contact with the Registry than with any other state agency, and despite the fact that these citizens complain more about Registry service than about that of any other bureau, the Watertown branch, like all Registry offices, was seriously understaffed. . . .

Or: "Government agencies are imperialistic, always grasping for new functions." But there is no record of the Registry doing much grasping, even though one could imagine a case being made that the state government could usefully create at Registry offices "one-stop" multi-service centers where people could not only get drivers' licenses but also pay taxes and parking fines, obtain information, and transact other official business. The Registry seemed content to provide one service.

In short, many of the popular stereotypes about government agencies and their members are either questionable or incomplete. To explain why government agencies behave as they do, it is not enough to know that they are "bureaucracies"—that is, it is not enough to know that they are big, or complex, or have rules. What is crucial is that they are *government* bureaucracies. . . . [N]ot all government bureaucracies behave the same way or suffer from the same problems. . . . But all government agencies have in common certain characteristics that tend to make their management far more difficult than managing a McDonald's. These common characteristics are the constraints of public agencies.

The key constraints are three in number. To a much greater extent than is true of private bureaucracies, government agencies (1) cannot lawfully retain and devote to the private benefit of their members the earnings of the organization, (2) cannot allocate the factors of production in accordance with the preferences of the organization's administrators, and (3) must serve goals not of the organization's own choosing. Control over revenues, productive factors, and agency goals is all vested to an important degree in entities external to the organization—legislatures, courts, politicians, and interest groups. Given this, agency managers must attend to the demands of these external entities. As a result, government management tends to be driven by the *constraints* on the organization, not the *tasks* of the organization. To say the same thing in other words, whereas business management focuses on the "bottom line" (that is, profits), government management focuses on the "top line" (that is, constraints). . . .

Revenues and Incentives

In the days leading up to September 30, the federal government is Cinderella, courted by legions of individuals and organizations eager to get grants and contracts from the unexpended funds still at the disposal of each agency. At midnight on September 30, the government's coach turns into a pumpkin. That is the moment—the end of the fiscal year—at which every agency, with a few exceptions, must return all unexpended funds to the Treasury Department. . . . Because of these fiscal rules agencies do not have a material incentive to economize: Why scrimp and save if you cannot keep the results of your frugality?

. . . When a private firm has a good year, many of its officers and workers may receive bonuses. Even if no bonus is paid, these employees may buy stock in the firm so that they can profit from any growth in earnings (and, if they sell the stock in a timely manner, profit from a drop in earnings). Should a public bureaucrat be discovered trying to do what private bureaucrats routinely do, he or she would be charged with corruption.

We take it for granted that bureaucrats should not profit from their offices and nod approvingly when a bureaucrat who has so benefited is indicted and put on trial. But why should we take this view? Once a very different view prevailed. In the seventeenth century, a French colonel would buy his commission from the king, take the king's money to run his regiment, and pocket the profit. At one time a European tax collector was paid by keeping a percentage of the taxes he collected. In this country, some prisons were once managed by giving the warden a sum of money based on how many prisoners were under his control and letting him keep the difference between what he received and what it cost him to feed the prisoners. Such behavior today would be grounds for criminal prosecution. Why? What has changed?

Mostly we the citizenry have changed. We are creatures of the Enlightenment: We believe that the nation ought not to be the property of the sovereign; that laws are intended to rationalize society and (if possible) perfect mankind; and that public service ought to be neutral and disinterested. We worry that a prison warden paid in the old way would have a strong incentive to starve his prisoners in order to maximize his income; that a regiment supported by a greedy colonel would not be properly equipped; and that a tax collector paid on a commission basis would extort excessive taxes from us. These changes reflect our desire to eliminate moral hazards—namely, creating incentives for people to act wrongly. But why should this desire rule out more carefully designed compensation plans that would pay government managers for achieving officially approved goals and would allow efficient agencies to keep any unspent part of their budget for use next year?

Part of the answer is obvious. Often we do not know whether a manager or an agency has achieved the goals we want because either the goals are vague or inconsistent, or their attainment cannot be observed, or both. Bureau chiefs in the Department of State would have to go on welfare if their pay depended on their ability to demonstrate convincingly that they had attained their bureaus' objectives.

But many government agencies have reasonably clear goals toward which progress can be measured. The Social Security Administration, the Postal Service, and the General Services Administration all come to mind. Why not let earnings depend importantly on performance? Why not let agencies keep excess revenues?

I am not entirely certain why this does not happen. To some degree it is because of a widespread cultural norm that people should not profit from public service. . . .

But in part it is because we know that even government agencies with clear goals and readily observable behavior only can be evaluated by making political (and thus conflict-ridden) judgments. If the Welfare Department delivers every benefit check within 24 hours after the application is received, Senator Smith may be pleased but Senator Jones will be irritated because this speedy delivery almost surely would require that the standards of eligibility be relaxed so that many ineligible clients would get money. There is no objective standard by which the tradeoff between speed and accuracy in the Welfare Department can be evaluated. . . .

The closest we can come to supplying a nonpolitical, nonarbitrary evaluation of an organization's performance is by its ability to earn from customers revenues in excess of costs. This is how business firms, private colleges, and most hospitals are evaluated. But government agencies cannot be evaluated by this market test because they either supply a service for which there are no willing customers (for example, prisons or the IRS) or are monopoly suppliers of a valued service (for example, the welfare department and the Registry of Motor Vehicles). Neither an organization with unwilling customers nor one with the exclusive right to serve such customers as exist can be evaluated by knowing how many customers they attract. When there is no external, nonpolitical evaluation of agency performance, there is no way to allow the agency to retain earnings that is not subject to agency manipulation. . . .

Critics of government agencies like to describe them as "bloated bureaucracies," defenders of them as "starved for funds." The truth is more complicated. Legislators judge government *programs* differently from how they judge government *bureaus*. Programs, such as Social Security, have constituencies that benefit from them. Constituencies press legislators for increases in program expenditures. If the constituencies are found in many districts, the pressures are felt by many legislators. These pressures ordinarily are not countered by those from any organized group that wants the benefits cut. Bureaucrats may or may not be constituencies. If they are few in number or concentrated in one legislative district they may have little political leverage with which to demand an increase in numbers or benefits. For example, expenditures on Social Security have grown steadily since the program began in 1935, but the offices, pay rates, and perquisites of Social Security administrators have not grown correspondingly.

If the bureaucrats are numerous, well-organized, and found in many districts (for example, letter carriers in the old Post Office Department or sanitation workers in New York City) they may have enough leverage to insure that their benefits increase faster than their workload. But even numerous and organized bureaucrats labor under a strategic disadvantage arising from the fact that legislators find it easier to constrain bureaucratic inputs than bureaucratic outputs. The reasons are partly conceptual, partly political. Conceptually, an office building or pay schedule is a tangible input, easily understood by all; "good health" or a "decent retirement" or an "educated child" are matters of opinion. Politically, legislators face more or less steady pressures to keep tax rates down while allowing program benefits to grow. The conceptual ambiguities combine neatly with the political realities: The rational course of action for a legislator is to appeal to taxpayers by ostentatiously constraining the budget for buildings, pay raises, and managerial benefits while appealing to program beneficiaries by loudly calling for more money to be spent on health, retirement, or education. (Witness the difficulty schoolteachers have in obtaining pay increases without threatening a strike, even at a time when expenditures on education are growing.) As a result, there are many lavish programs in this country administered by modestly paid bureaucrats working on out-of-date equipment in cramped offices.*

The inability of public managers to capture surplus revenues for their own use alters the pattern of incentives at work in government agencies. Beyond a certain point additional effort does not produce additional earnings. (In this country, Congress from time to time has authorized higher salaries for senior bureaucrats but then put a cap on actual payments to them so that the pay increases were never received. This was done to insure that no bureaucrat would earn more than members of Congress at a time when those members were unwilling to accept the political costs of raising their own salaries. As a result, the pay differential between the top bureaucratic rank and those just below it nearly vanished.) If political constraints reduce the marginal effect of money incentives, then the relative importance of other, nonmonetary incentives will increase. . . .

That bureaucratic performance in most government agencies cannot be linked to monetary benefits is not the whole explanation for the difference between public and private management. There are many examples of private organizations whose members cannot appropriate money surpluses for their own benefit. Private schools ordinarily are run on a nonprofit basis. Neither the headmaster nor the teachers share in the profit of these schools; indeed, most such schools earn no profit at all and instead struggle to keep afloat by soliciting contributions from friends and alumni. Nevertheless, the evidence is quite

---

*Elsewhere, government officials may enjoy generous salaries and lavish offices. Indeed, in some underdeveloped nations, travelers see all about them signs of public munificence and private squalor. The two may be connected.

clear that on the average, private schools, both secular and denominational, do a better job than public ones in educating children.[2]

Acquiring and Using the Factors of Production

A business firm acquires capital by retaining earnings, borrowing money, or selling shares of ownership; a government agency (with some exceptions) acquires capital by persuading a legislature to appropriate it. A business firm hires, promotes, demotes, and fires personnel with considerable though not perfect freedom; a federal government agency is told by Congress how many persons it can hire and at what rate of pay, by the Office of Personnel Management (OPM) what rules it must follow in selecting and assigning personnel, by the Office of Management and Budget (OMB) how many persons of each rank it may employ, by the Merit Systems Protection Board (MSPB) what procedures it must follow in demoting or discharging personnel, and by the courts whether it has faithfully followed the rules of Congress, OPM, OMB, and MSPB. A business firm purchases goods and services by internally defined procedures (including those that allow it to buy from someone other than the lowest bidder if a more expensive vendor seems more reliable), or to skip the bidding procedure altogether in favor of direct negotiations; a government agency must purchase much of what it uses by formally advertising for bids, accepting the lowest, and keeping the vendor at arm's length. When a business firm develops a good working relationship with a contractor, it often uses that vendor repeatedly without looking for a new one; when a government agency has a satisfactory relationship with a contractor, ordinarily it cannot use the vendor again without putting a new project out for a fresh set of bids. When a business firm finds that certain offices or factories are no longer economical it will close or combine them; when a government agency wishes to shut down a local office or military base often it must get the permission of the legislature (even when formal permission is not necessary, informal consultation is). When a business firm draws up its annual budget each expenditure item can be reviewed as a discretionary amount (except for legally mandated payments of taxes to government and interest to banks and bondholders); when a government agency makes up its budget many of the detailed expenditure items are mandated by the legislature.

All these complexities of doing business in or with the government are well-known to citizens and firms. These complexities in hiring, purchasing, contracting, and budgeting often are said to be the result of the "bureaucracy's love of red tape." But few, if any, of the rules producing this complexity would have been generated by the bureaucracy if left to its own devices, and many are as cordially disliked by the bureaucrats as by their clients. These rules have been imposed on the agencies by external actors, chiefly the legislature. They are not bureaucratic rules but *political* ones. In principle the legislature could allow the Social Security Administration, the Defense Department, or the New York

City public school system to follow the same rules as IBM, General Electric, or Harvard University. In practice they could not. The reason is politics, or more precisely, democratic politics.

The differences are made clear in Steven Kelman's comparison of how government agencies and private firms buy computers. The agency officials he interviewed were much less satisfied with the quality of the computers and support services they purchased than were their private counterparts. The reason is that private firms are free to do what every householder does in buying a dishwasher or an automobile—look at the past performance of the people with whom he or she previously has done business and buy a new product based on these judgments. Contrary to what many people suppose, most firms buying a computer do not write up detailed specifications and then ask for bids, giving the contract to the lowest bidder who meets the specifications. Instead, they hold conversations with a computer manufacturer with whom they, or other firms like them, have had experience. In these discussions they develop a sense of their needs and form a judgment as to the quality and reliability of the people with whom they may do business. When the purchase is finally made, only one firm may be asked to bid, and then on the basis of jointly developed (and sometimes rather general) guidelines.

No government purchasing agent can afford to do business this way. He or she would be accused (by unsuccessful bidders and their congressional allies) of collusion, favoritism, and sweetheart deals. Instead, agencies must either ask for sealed bids or for competitive written responses to detailed (*very* detailed) "requests for proposals" (RFPs). The agencies will not be allowed to take into account past performance or intangible managerial qualities. As a result, the agencies must deny themselves the use of the most important information someone can have—judgment shaped by personal knowledge and past experience. Thus, the government often buys the wrong computers from unreliable suppliers.[3]

Constraints at Work: The Case of the Postal Service

From the founding of the republic until 1971 the Post Office Department was a cabinet agency wholly subordinate to the president and Congress. As such it received its funds from annual appropriations, its personnel from presidential appointments and civil service examinations, and its physical plant from detailed political decisions about the appropriate location of post offices. Postal rates were set by Congress after hearings, dominated by organized interests that mail in bulk (for example, direct-mail advertisers and magazine publishers) and influenced by an awareness of the harmful political effects of raising the rates for first-class letters mailed by individual citizens (most of whom voted). Congress responded to these pressures by keeping rates low. . . . The wages of postal employees were set with an eye on the political power of the unions representing those employees: Congress rarely forgot that there were hundreds of organized letter carriers in every congressional district.

In 1971, the Post Office Department was transformed into the United States Postal Service (USPS), a semiautonomous government corporation. The USPS is headed by an eleven-member board of governors, nine appointed by the president and confirmed by the Senate; these nine then appoint a postmaster general and a deputy postmaster general. It derives its revenues entirely from the prices it charges and the money it borrows rather than from congressional appropriations (though subsidies still were paid to the USPS during a transition period). The postal rates are set not by Congress but by the USPS itself, guided by a legislative standard. . . . The USPS has its own personnel system, separate from that of the rest of the federal government, and bargains directly with its own unions.

Having loosened some of the constraints upon it, the Postal Service was able to do things that in the past it could do only with great difficulty if at all. . . . When it was still a regular government department, a small local post office could only be closed after a bitter fight with the member of Congress from the affected district. As a result, few were closed. After the reorganization, the number closed increased: Between 1976 and 1979, the USPS closed about twenty-four a year; between 1983 and 1986, it closed over two hundred a year.[4] . . . When the old Post Office, in the interest of cutting costs, tried to end the custom of delivering mail to each recipient's front door and instead proposed to deliver mail (at least in new suburban communities) either to the curbside or to "cluster boxes,"* intense pressure on Congress forced the department to abandon the idea. By 1978 the USPS had acquired enough autonomy to implement the idea despite continued congressional grumblings.[5] Because the USPS can raise its own capital by issuing bonds it has been able to forge ahead with the automation of mail-sorting procedures. It now has hundreds of sophisticated optical scanners and bar-code readers that enable employees to sort mail much faster than before. By 1986 optical character readers were processing 90 million pieces of mail a day. Finally, despite political objections, the USPS was slowly expanding the use of the nine-digit zip code.

In short, acquiring greater autonomy increased the ability of the Postal Service to acquire, allocate, and control the factors of production. More broadly, the whole tone of postal management changed. It began to adopt corporate-style management practices, complete with elaborate "mission statements," glossy annual reports, a tightened organizational structure, and an effort to decentralize some decisions to local managers.

Though Congress loosened the reins, it did not take them off. On many key issues the phrase *quasi-autonomous* meant hardly autonomous at all. Congress at any time can amend the Postal Reorganization Act to limit the service's

————

*A cluster box is a metal structure containing from twelve to one hundred mailboxes to which mail for a given neighborhood is delivered.

freedom of action; even the threat of such an amendment, made evident by committee hearings, often is enough to alter the service's programs. The nine-digit zip code was finally adopted but its implementation was delayed by Congress for over two years, thus impeding the efforts of the USPS to obtain voluntary compliance from the business community.

When the USPS, in a move designed to save over $400 million and thereby avoid a rate increase, announced in 1977 that it planned to eliminate Saturday mail deliveries, the service was able to produce public opinion data indicating that most people would prefer no Saturday delivery to higher postage rates. No matter. The House of Representatives by an overwhelming vote passed a resolution opposing the change, and the USPS backed down. It seems the employee unions feared that the elimination of Saturday deliveries would lead to laying off postal workers.[6]

Similarly, when the USPS in 1975–76 sought to close many rural post offices it had as an ally the General Accounting Office.* A GAO study suggested that twelve thousand such offices could be closed at a savings of $100 million per year without reducing service to any appreciable extent (many of the small offices served no more than a dozen families and were located within a few miles of other offices that could provide the same service more economically). The rural postmasters saw matters differently, and they found a sympathetic audience in Congress. Announcing that "the rural post office has always been a uniquely American institution" and that "service" is more important than "profit," senators and representatives joined in amending the Postal Reorganization Act to block such closings temporarily and inhibit them permanently.[7] As John Tierney notes, the year that the USPS timidly closed 72 of its 30,521 offices, the Great Atlantic and Pacific Tea Company closed 174 of its 1,634 stores, and "that was that.[8] . . ."

My argument is not that all the changes the USPS would like to make are desirable, or that every vestige of politics should be removed from its management. . . . Rather, it is that one cannot explain the behavior of government bureaucracies simply by reference to the fact that they are bureaucracies; the central fact is that they are *government* bureaucracies. Nor am I arguing that government (or more broadly, politics) is bad, only that it is inevitably (and to some extent desirably) sensitive to constituency demands. . . . For example, if Congress had been content to ask of the old Post Office Department that it deliver all first-class mail within three days at the lowest possible cost, it could have let the department arrange its delivery system, set its rates, locate its offices, and hire its personnel in whatever way it wished—provided that the mail

---

*The General Accounting Office (GAO), a research agency of Congress, has the broad mission of overseeing and investigating how executive branch agencies spend appropriated funds. Its activities, often controversial, range from investigating cost overruns in the Department of Defense to assessing the adequacy of environmental regulations. GAO typically initiates its activities at the request of congressional committee leaders.

got delivered within three days and at a price that did not lead mail users to abandon the Post Office in favor of a private delivery service. Managers then would be evaluated on the basis of how well they achieved these goals.

Of course, Congress had many goals, not just one: It wanted to please many different classes of mail users, satisfy constituency demands for having many small post offices rather than a few large ones, cope with union demands for wage increases, and respond to public criticism of mail service. Congress could not provide a consistent rank-ordering of these goals, which is to say that it could not decide on how much of one goal (e.g., keeping prices low) should be sacrificed to attain more of another goal (e.g., keeping rural post offices open). This inability to decide is not a reflection on the intelligence of Congress; rather, it is the inevitable consequence of Congress being a representative body whose individual members respond differently to different constituencies.

Neither Congress nor the postal authorities have ever supported an obvious method of allowing the customers to decide the matter for themselves—namely, by letting private firms compete with the Postal Service for the first-class mail business. For over a century the Post Office has had a legal monopoly on the regular delivery of first-class mail. It is a crime to establish any "private express for the conveyance of letters or packets . . . by regular trips or at stated periods over any post route."[9] This is justified by postal executives on the grounds that private competitors would skim away the most profitable business (for example, delivering business mail or utility bills in big cities), leaving the government with the most costly business (for example, delivering a Christmas card from Aunt Annie in Eudora, Kansas, to Uncle Matt in Wakefield, Massachusetts). In time the Post Office began to face competition anyway, from private parcel and express delivery services that did not deliver "by regular trips or at stated periods" (so as not to violate the private express statute) and from electronic mail and fund-transferring systems. But by then it had become USPS, giving it both greater latitude in and incentive for meeting that competition.

Faced with political superiors that find it conceptually easier and politically necessary to focus on inputs, agency managers also tend to focus on inputs. Nowhere is this more evident than in defense procurement programs. The Defense Department, through the Defense Logistics Agency (DLA), each year acquires food, fuel, clothing, and spare parts worth (in 1984) $15 billion, manages a supply system containing over two million items, and administers over $186 billion in government contracts.[10] Congress and the president repeatedly have made clear their desire that this system be run efficiently and make use of off-the-shelf, commercially available products (as opposed to more expensive, "made-to-order" items)[11] Periodically, however, the press reports scandals involving the purchase of $435 hammers and $700 toilet seats. Some of these stories are exaggerated,[12] but there is little doubt that waste and inefficiency occur. Congressional investigations are mounted and presidential commissions are appointed to find ways of solving these problems. Among the solutions offered are demands that tighter rules be imposed, more auditors be hired, and fuller reports be made.

Less dramatic but more common than the stories of scandals and overpriced hammers are the continuing demands of various constituencies for influence over the procurement process. Occasionally this takes the form of requests for special favors, such as preferentially awarding a contract to a politically favored firm. But just as important and more pervasive in their effects are the legal constraints placed on the procurement process to insure that contracts are awarded "fairly"—that is, in ways that allow equal access to the bidding process by all firms and special access by politically significant ones. For example, section 52 of the *Federal Acquisition Regulation* contains dozens of provisions governing the need to give special attention to suppliers that are small business (especially a "small disadvantaged business"), women-owned small businesses, handicapped workers, or disabled and Vietnam-era veterans, or are located in areas with a "labor surplus."*[13] Moreover, only materials produced in the United States can be acquired for public use unless, under the Buy American Act, the government certifies that the cost is "unreasonable" or finds that the supplies are not available in this country in sufficient quantity or adequate quality.[14]

The goal of "fairness" underlies almost every phase of the procurement process, not because the American government is committed heart and soul to fairness as an abstract social good but because if a procurement decision is questioned it is much easier to justify the decision if it can be shown that the decision was "fairly" made on the basis of "objective" criteria. Those criteria are spelled out in the *Federal Acquisition Regulation*, a complex document of over six thousand pages. The essential rules are that all potential suppliers must be offered an equal opportunity to bid on a contract; that the agency's procurement decision must be objectively justifiable on the basis of written specifications; that contracts awarded on the basis of sealed bids must go to the contractor offering the lowest price; and that unsuccessful bidders must be offered a chance to protest decisions with which they disagree.[15] . . .

To understand the bureaucratic significance of these rules, put yourself in the shoes of a Defense Logistics Agency manager. A decision you made is challenged because someone thinks that you gave a contract to an unqualified firm or purchased something of poor quality. What is your response—that in your

---

*For example, the law requires that a "fair proportion of the total purchases and contracts" shall be "placed with small-business enterprises" and that "small business concerns owned and controlled by socially and economically disadvantaged individuals, shall have the maximum practicable opportunity to participate in the performance of contracts let by any Federal agency" [15 *U.S. Code* 637(d)(i)]. In pursuance of this law, it is the government's policy "to place a fair proportion" of its acquisitions with small business concerns and small business disadvantaged concerns (*Federal Acquisition Regulation*, 19.201a). A "socially and economically disadvantaged individual" includes, but is not limited to, a black American, Hispanic American, Native American, Asian-Pacific American, or Asian-Indian American (ibid., 52.219.2).

judgment it was a good buy from a reliable firm? Such a remark is tantamount to inviting yourself to explain to a hostile congressional committee why you think your judgment is any good. A much safer response is "I followed the rules." . . .

If despite all your devotion to the rules Congress uncovers an especially blatant case of paying too much for too little (for example, a $3,000 coffeepot), the prudent response is to suggest that what is needed are more rules, more auditors, and more tightly constrained procedures. The consequence of this may be to prevent the buying of any more $3,000 coffeepots, or it may be to increase the complexity of the procurement process so that fewer good firms will submit bids to supply coffeepots, or it may be to increase the cost of monitoring that process so that the money saved by buying cheaper pots is lost by hiring more pot inspectors. . . .

Public versus Private Management

The late Professor Wallace Sayre once said that public and private management is alike in all unimportant respects.[16] This view has been disputed vigorously by many people who are convinced that whatever problems beset government agencies also afflict private organizations. The clearest statement of that view can be found in John Kenneth Galbraith's *The New Industrial State*. Galbraith argues that large corporations, like public agencies, are dominated by "technostructures" that are governed by their own bureaucratic logic rather than by the dictates of the market. These corporations have insulated themselves from the market by their ability to control demand (through clever advertising) and set prices (by dominating an industry). The rewards to the technocrats who staff these firms are salaries, not profits, and the goals toward which these technocrats move are the assertion and maintenance of their own managerial autonomy. . . .

Professor Galbraith's book appeared at a time (1967) when American businesses were enjoying such unrivaled success that its beautifully crafted sentences seemed to capture some enduring truth. But the passage of time converted many of those eloquent phrases into hollow ones. Within ten years, it had become painfully obvious to General Motors that it could not, in Galbraith's words, "set prices for automobiles . . . secure in the knowledge that no individual buyer, by withdrawing its custom, can force a change."[17] Competition from Toyota, Nissan, and Honda had given the individual buyer great power; coupled with an economic slowdown, that competition led GM, like all auto manufacturers, to start offering cash rebates, cut-rate financing, and price reductions. And still the U.S. firms lost market share despite the "power" of their advertising and saw profits evaporate despite their "dominance" of the industry.

But Galbraith's analysis had more serious flaws than its inability to predict the future; it led many readers to draw the erroneous conclusion that "all bureaucracies are alike" because all bureaucracies employ salaried workers, are enmeshed in red tape, and strive to insure their own autonomy. The large corporation surely is more bureaucratic than the small entrepreneur, but in becoming bureaucratic it has not become a close relative of a government agency. What distinguishes public from private organizations is neither their size nor their desire to "plan" (that is, control) their environments but rather the rules under which they acquire and use capital and labor. General Motors acquires capital by selling shares, issuing bonds, or retaining earnings; the Department of Defense acquires it from an annual appropriation by Congress. GM opens and closes plants, subject to certain government regulations, at its own discretion; DOD opens and closes military bases under the watchful guidance of Congress. GM pays its managers with salaries it sets and bonuses tied to its earnings; DOD pays its managers with salaries set by Congress and bonuses (if any) that have no connection with organizational performance. The number of workers in GM is determined by its level of production; the number in DOD by legislation and civil-service rules.

What all this means can be seen by returning to the Registry of Motor Vehicles and McDonald's. Suppose you were just appointed head of the Watertown office of the Registry and you wanted to improve service there so that it more nearly approximated the service at McDonald's. Better service might well require spending more money (on clerks, equipment, and buildings). Why should your political superiors give you that money? It is a cost to them if it requires either higher taxes or taking funds from another agency; offsetting these real and immediate costs are dubious and postponed benefits. If lines become shorter and clients become happier, no legislator will benefit. There may be fewer complaints, but complaints are episodic and have little effect on the career of any given legislator. By contrast, shorter lines and faster service at McDonald's means more customers can be served per hour and thus more money can be earned per hour. A McDonald's manager can estimate the marginal product of the last dollar he or she spends on improving service; the Registry manager can generate no tangible return on any expenditure he or she makes and thus cannot easily justify the expenditure.

Improving service at the Registry may require replacing slow or surly workers with quick and pleasant ones. But you, the manager, can neither hire nor fire them at will. You look enviously at the McDonald's manager who regularly and with little notice replaces poor workers with better ones. Alternatively, you may wish to mount an extensive training program (perhaps creating a Registration University to match McDonald's Hamburger University) that would imbue a culture of service in your employees. But unless the Registry were so large an agency that the legislature would neither notice nor care about funds spent for this purpose—and it is not that large—you would have a tough time convincing anybody that this was not a wasteful expenditure on a frill project.

If somehow your efforts succeed in making Registry clients happier, you can take vicarious pleasure in it; in the unlikely event a client seeks you out to thank you for those efforts, you can bask in a moment's worth of glory. Your colleague at McDonald's who manages to make customers happier may also derive some vicarious satisfaction from the improvement but in addition he or she will earn more money owing to an increase in sales.

In time it will dawn on you that if you improve service too much, clients will start coming to the Watertown office instead of going to the Boston office. As a result, the lines you succeeded in shortening will become longer again. If you wish to keep complaints down, you will have to spend even more on the Watertown office. But if it was hard to persuade the legislature to do that in the past, it is impossible now. Why should the taxpayer be asked to spend more on Watertown when the Boston office, fully staffed (naturally, no one was laid off when the clients disappeared), has no lines at all? From the legislature's point of view the correct level of expenditure is not that which makes one office better than another but that which produces an equal amount of discontent in all offices.

Finally, you remember that your clients have no choice: The Registry offers a monopoly service. It and only it supplies drivers' licenses. In the long run all that matters is that there are not "too many" complaints to the legislature about service. Unlike McDonald's, the Registry need not fear that its clients will take their business to Burger King or to Wendy's. Perhaps you should just relax. . . .

Notes

1. John F. Love, *McDonald's: Behind the Arches* (New York: Bantam Books, 1986), 140ff.
2. James S. Coleman, Thomas Hoffer, and Sally Kilgore, *High School Achievement* (New York: Basic Books, 1982).
3. Steven Kelman, *Procurement and Public Management* [Lanham: American Enterprise Institute, 1990].
4. John T. Tierney, *The U.S. Postal Service* (Dover, Mass.: Auburn House, 1988), 101–2.
5. Tierney, *U.S. Postal Service*, 94–97.
6. John T. Tierney, *Postal Reorganization: Managing the Public's Business* (Boston: Auburn House, 1981), 67.
7. Ibid., 68–73.
8. Ibid., 72.
9. 18 *U.S. Code* 1696.
10. General Accounting Office, *Progress and Challenges at the Defense Logistics Agency.* GAO report NSIAD-86-64, Washington, D.C., 1986, p. 2.
11. Wendy T. Kirby, "Expanding the Use of Commercial Products and 'Commercial-Style' Acquisition Techniques in Defense Procurement: A Proposed Legal Framework," Appendix H in President's Blue Ribbon Commission on Defense Management (the "Packard Commission"), *A Quest for Excellence: Final Report,* June 1986.
12. I discuss these matters in chap. 17.
13. Kirby, "Expanding the Use," 106–7.
14. 41 *U.S. Code* 10(a).
15. Kirby, "Expanding the Use," 82–83, 91.
16. Quoted in Graham T. Allison, Jr., "Public and Private Management: Are They Fundamentally Alike in All Unimportant Respects?" in Frederick S. Lane, ed., *Current Issues in Public Administra-*

tion, 2d ed. (New York: St. Martin's Press, 1982), 13–33. The academic literature on public-private differences is summarized in Hal G. Rainey, Robert W. Backoff, and Charles H. Levine, "Comparing Public and Private Organizations," *Public Administration Review* 36 (1976): 233–44.

17. Galbraith, *New Industrial State*, 46.

Questions for Discussion

1. According to James Q. Wilson, in what ways is managing a private organization different from managing a public one?
2. Wilson suggests that "red tape" is more often the result of democratic politics than the preferences of bureaucrats. What does he mean by this? Would increasing citizen and group participation in politics lead to more or fewer bureaucratic rules and regulations?

 12.3

From Ouagadougou to Cape Canaveral: Why the Bad News Doesn't Travel Up

Charles Peters

On January 28, 1986, seven crew members of the space shuttle *Challenger* were killed in a mid-flight explosion. The tragedy was caused by the disintegration of a type of seal called an O-ring, which led to failure in the joint between segments of one of the eight solid booster rockets. It can be argued, however, that the fundamental reason for the shuttle disaster was a communication failure within the hierarchy of the National Aeronautics and Space Administration (NASA). Private engineers on the project were aware of a history of problems with the O-rings and had advised certain mid-level NASA officials not to launch under certain conditions. Had top-level officials known of the problems, the launch might not have taken place.

Charles Peters is editor-in-chief of *The Washington Monthly*.

Charles Peters, "From Ouagadougou to Cape Canaveral: Why the Bad News Doesn't Travel Up," *The Washington Monthly* 19 (April 1986): 27–31. Reprinted by permission of *The Washington Monthly*.

In this selection, Charles Peters suggests that it is extremely difficult for top managers in a large organization to be aware of problems at various levels of a bureaucratic hierarchy. Officials at NASA were under tremendous political pressure to launch the shuttle, so negative information was suppressed within the chain of command. Peters suggests that this problem is common and can be blamed for a number of the government's recent flawed decisions. The remedies, he suggests, are more direct government oversight and an active press.

Everyone is asking why the top NASA officials who decided to launch the fatal Challenger flight had not been told of the concerns of people down below, like Allan McDonald and the other worried engineers at Morton Thiokol.*

In the first issue of *The Washington Monthly*, Russell Baker and I wrote, "In any reasonably large government organization, there exists an elaborate system of information cutoffs, comparable to that by which city water systems shut off large water-main breaks, closing down, first small feeder pipes, then larger and larger valves. The object is to prevent information, particularly of an unpleasant character, from rising to the top of the agency, where it may produce results unpleasant to the lower ranks.

"Thus, the executive at or near the top lives in constant danger of not knowing, until he reads it on Page One some morning, that his department is hip-deep in disaster."

This seemed to us to be a serious problem for government, not only because the people at the top didn't know but because the same system of cut-offs operated to keep Congress, the press, and the public in the dark. (Often it also would operate to keep in the dark people within the organization but outside the immediate chain of command—this happened with the astronauts, who were not told about the concern with the O-rings.)

I first became aware of this during the sixties, when I worked at the Peace Corps. Repeatedly I would find that a problem that was well-known by people at lower and middle levels of the organization, whose responsibility it was, would be unknown at the top of the chain of command or by anyone outside.

The most serious problems of the Peace Corps had their origins in Sargent Shriver's desire to get the organization moving.† He did not want it to become mired in feasibility studies, he wanted to get volunteers overseas and into action fast. To fulfill his wishes, corners were cut. Training was usually inadequate

*Morton Thiokol is the private engineering company that was in charge of the design and construction of the space shuttle booster rocket.

†Sargent Shriver—President Kennedy's brother-in-law—was the first director of the Peace Corps. The organization was set up to send American volunteers to help people in Third World countries. In 1972, Shriver was the Democratic vice-presidential candidate.

in language, culture, and technical skills. Volunteers were selected who were not suited to their assignments. For example, the country then known as Tanganyika asked for surveyors, and we sent them people whose only connection with surveying had been holding the rod and chain while the surveyor sighted through his gizmo. Worse, volunteers were sent to places where no job at all awaited them. These fictitious assignments were motivated sometimes by the host official's desire to please the brother-in-law of the president of the United States and sometimes by the official's ignorance of what was going on at the lower levels of his own bureaucracy.

But subordinates would not tell Shriver about the problems. There were two reasons for this. One was fear. They knew that he wanted action, not excuses, and they suspected that their careers would suffer if he heard too many of the latter. The other reason was that they felt it was their job to solve problems, not burden the boss with them. They and Shriver shared the view expressed by Deke Slayton, the former astronaut, when he was asked about the failure of middle-level managers to tell top NASA officials about the problems they were encountering. "You depend on managers to make a decision based on the information they have. If they had to transmit all the fine detail to the top people, it wouldn't get launched but once every ten years."

The point is not without merit. It is easy for large organizations to fall into "once every ten years" habits. Leaders who want to avoid that danger learn to set goals and communicate a sense of urgency about meeting them. But what many of them never learn is that once you set those goals you have to guard against the tendency of those down below to spare you not only "all the fine detail" but essential facts about significant problems.

For instance, when Jimmy Carter gave the Pentagon the goal of rescuing the Iranian hostages, he relied on the chain of command to tell him if there were any problems. So he did not find out until after the disaster at Desert One that the Delta Commandos thought the Marine pilots assigned to fly the helicopters were incompetent.*

In NASA's case chances have been taken with the shuttle from the beginning—the insulating thermal tiles had not gone through a reentry test before the first shuttle crew risked their lives to try them out—but in recent years the pressure to cut corners has increased markedly. Competition with the European Ariane rocket and the Reagan administration's desire to see agencies like NASA run as if they were private businesses have led to a speedup in the launch schedule, with a goal of 14 this year [1986] and 24 by 1988.

---

*In the spring of 1980, President Carter made a decision to have a U.S. commando force attempt to rescue the American hostages held in Iran. A number of reasons have been suggested for the failure of the mission. The helicopters chosen for the mission evidently could not operate successfully in the sand and wind of the Iranian desert. One crashed on takeoff, killing a number of soldiers, and the mission was aborted.

"The game NASA is playing is the maximum tonnage per year at the minimum costs possible," says Paul Cloutier, a professor of space physics. "Some high officials don't want to hear about problems," reports *Newsweek*, "especially if fixing them will cost money."

Under pressures like these, the NASA launch team watched Columbia, after seven delays, fall about a month behind schedule and then saw Challenger delayed, first by bad weather, then by damaged door handles, and then by bad weather again. Little wonder that [NASA's launch chief] Lawrence Mulloy, when he heard the warnings from the Thiokol engineers, burst out: "My God, Thiokol, when do you want me to launch? Next April?"

Mulloy may be one of the villains of this story, but it is important to realize that you need Lawrence Mulloys to get things done. It is also important to realize that, if you have a Lawrence Mulloy, you must protect yourself against what he might fail to do or what he might do wrong in his enthusiastic rush to get the job done.

And you can't just ask him if he has any doubts. If he's a gung-ho type, he's going to suppress the negatives. When Jimmy Carter asked General David Jones to check out the Iran rescue plan, Jones said to Colonel Beckwith: "Charlie, tell me what you really think about the mission. Be straight with me."

"Sir, we're going to do it!" Beckwith replied. "We want to do it, and we're ready."

John Kennedy received similar confident reports from the chain of command about the readiness of the CIA's Cuban Brigade to charge ashore at the Bay of Pigs and overthrow Fidel Castro. And Sargent Shriver had every reason to believe that the Peace Corps was getting off to a fabulous start, based on what his chain of command was telling him.

With Shriver, as with NASA's senior officials, the conviction that everything was A-OK was fortified by skillful public relations. Bill Moyers was only one of the geniuses involved in this side of the Peace Corps. At NASA, Julian Scheer began a tradition of inspired PR that endured until Challenger. These were men who could sell air conditioning in Murmansk. The trouble is they also sold their bosses the same air conditioning. Every organization has a tendency to believe its own PR—NASA's walls are lined with glamorizing posters and photographs of the shuttle and other space machines—and usually the top man is the most thoroughly seduced because, after all, it reflects the most glory on him.

Favorable publicity and how to get it is therefore the dominant subject of Washington staff meetings. The minutes of the Nuclear Regulatory Commission show that when the reactor was about to melt down at Three Mile Island,* the commissioners were worried less about what to do to fix the reactor than they were about what they were going to say to the press.

---

*Three Mile Island is the site of a Pennsylvania nuclear plant that experienced a serious accident in which the generator overheated. There were no injuries or deaths. Still, the incident helped contribute to growing public concern over the safety of nuclear power plants.

One of the hottest rumors around Washington is that the White House had put pressure on NASA to launch so that the president could point with pride to the teacher in space during his State of the Union speech. The White House denies this story, and my sources tell me the denial is true. But NASA had—and this is fact, not rumor—put pressure on *itself* by asking the president to mention Christa McAuliffe. In a memorandum dated January 8, NASA proposed that the president say: "Tonight while I am speaking to you, a young elementary school teacher from Concord, New Hampshire, is taking us all on the ultimate field trip as she orbits the earth as the first citizen passenger on the space shuttle. Christa McAuliffe's journey is a prelude to the journeys of other Americans living and working together in a permanently manned space station in the mid-1990s. Mrs. McAuliffe's week in space is just one of the achievements in space we have planned for the coming year."

The flight was scheduled for January 23. It was postponed and postponed again. Now it was January 28, the morning of the day the speech was to be delivered, the last chance for the launch to take place in time to have it mentioned by the president. NASA officials must have feared they were about to lose a PR opportunity of stunning magnitude, an opportunity to impress not only the media and the public but the agency's two most important constituencies, the White House and the Congress. Wouldn't you feel pressure to get that launch off this morning so that the president could talk about it tonight?

NASA's sensitivity to the media in regard to the launch schedule was nothing short of unreal. Here is what Richard G. Smith, the director of the Kennedy Space Center, had to say about it after the disaster: "Every time there was a delay, the press would say, 'Look, there's another delay . . . here's a bunch of idiots who can't even handle a launch schedule.' You think that doesn't have an impact? If you think it doesn't, you're stupid."

I do not recall seeing a single story like those Smith describes. Perhaps there were a few. The point, however, is to realize how large even a little bit of press criticism loomed in NASA's thinking.

Sargent Shriver liked good press as much as, if not more than, the next man. But he also had an instinct that the ultimate bad press would come if the world found out about your disaster before you had a chance to do something to prevent it. He and an assistant named William Haddad decided to make sure that Shriver got the bad news first. Who was going to find it out for them? Me.

It was July 1961. They decided to call me an evaluator and send me out to our domestic training programs and later overseas to find out what was really going on. My first stop was the University of California at Berkeley where our Ghana project was being trained. Fortunately, except for grossly inadequate language instruction, this program was excellent. But soon I began finding serious deficiencies in other training programs and in our projects abroad.

Shriver was not always delighted by these reports. Indeed, at one point I heard I was going to be fired. I liked my job, and I knew that the reports that I and the other evaluators who had joined me were writing were true. I didn't want to be fired. What could I do?

I knew he was planning to visit our projects in Africa. So I prepared a memorandum that contrasted what the chain of command was saying with what I and my associates were reporting. Shriver left for Africa. I heard nothing for several weeks. Then came a cable from Somalia: "Tell Peters his reports are right." I knew then that, however much Shriver wanted to hear the good news and get good publicity, he could take the bad news. The fact that he could take the bad news meant that the Peace Corps began to face its problems and do something about them before they became a scandal.

NASA did the opposite. A 1983 reorganization shifted the responsibility for monitoring flight safety from the chief engineer in Washington to the field. This may sound good. "We're not going to micromanage," said James M. Beggs, then the NASA administrator. But the catch is that if you decentralize, you must maintain the flow of information from the field to the top so that the organization's leader will know what those decentralized managers are doing. What NASA's reorganization did, according to safety engineers who talked to Mark Tapscott of the *Washington Times*, was to close off "an independent channel with authority to make things happen at the top."

I suspect what happened is that the top NASA administrators, who were pushing employees down below to dramatically increase the number of launches, either consciously or unconsciously did not want to be confronted with the dangers they were thereby risking.

This is what distinguishes the bad leaders from the good. The good leader, realizing that there is a natural human tendency to avoid bad news, traps himself into having to face it. He encourages whistleblowers instead of firing them. He visits the field himself and talks to the privates and lieutenants as well as the generals to find out the real problems. He can use others to do this for him, as Shriver used me. . . . But he must have some independent knowledge of what's going on down below in order to have a feel for whether the chain of command is giving him the straight dope.

What most often happens, of course, is that the boss, if he goes to the field at all, talks only to the colonels and generals. Sometimes he doesn't want to know what the privates know. He may be hoping that the lid can be kept on whatever problems are developing, at least until his watch is over, so that he won't be blamed when they finally surface. Or he may have a very good idea that bad things are being done and simply wants to retain "deniability," meaning that the deed cannot be traced to him. The story of Watergate is filled with "Don't tell me" and "I don't want to know."

When NASA's George Hardy told Thiokol engineers that he was appalled by their verbal recommendation that the launch be postponed and asked Thiokol to reconsider and make another recommendation, Thiokol, which Hardy well knew was worried about losing its shuttle contract, was in effect being told, "Don't tell me" or "Don't tell me officially so I won't have to pass bad news along and my bosses will have deniability."

In addition to the leader himself, others must be concerned with making him face the bad news. This includes subordinates. Their having the courage to speak out about what is wrong is crucial, and people like Bruce Cook of NASA and Allan McDonald of Thiokol deserve great credit for having done so. But it is a fact that none of the subordinates who knew the danger to the shuttle took the next step and resigned in protest so that the public could find out what was going on in time to prevent disaster. The almost universal tendency to place one's own career above one's moral responsibility to take a stand on matters like these has to be one of the most depressing facts about bureaucratic culture today.

Even when the issue was simply providing facts for an internal NASA investigation after the disaster, here is the state of mind Bruce Cook describes in a recent article in the *Washington Post*: "Another [NASA employee] told me to step away from his doorway while he searched for a document in his filing cabinet so that no one would see me in his office and suspect that he'd been the one I'd gotten it from."

It may be illuminating to note here that at the Peace Corps I found my most candid informants were the volunteers. They had no career stake in the organization—they were in for just two years—and thus had no reason to fear the results of their candor. Doesn't this suggest that we might be better off with more short-term employees in the government, people who are planning to leave anyway and thus have no hesitation to blow the whistle when necessary?

Certainly the process of getting bad news from the bottom to the top can be helped by institutionalizing it, as it was in the case of the Peace Corps Evaluation Division, and by hiring to perform it employees who have demonstrated courage and independence as well as the ability to elicit the truth and report it clearly.

Two other institutions that can help this process are the Congress and the White House. But the staff they have to perform this function is tiny. The White House depends on the OMB [Office of Management and Budget] to tell it what the executive branch is doing. Before the Challenger exploded, the OMB had four examiners to cover science and space. The Senate subcommittee on Space, Science and Technology had a staff of three. Needless to say, they had not heard about the O-rings.

Another problem is lack of experience. Too few congressmen and too few of their staff have enough experience serving in the executive branch to have a sense of the right question to ask. OMB examiners usually come aboard straight from graduate school, totally innocent of practical experience in government.

The press shares this innocence. Only a handful of journalists have worked in the bureaucracy. Like the members of Congress, they treat policy formulation as the ultimate reality: Congress passed this bill today; the president signed that bill. That's what the TV reporters on the Capitol steps and the White House lawn tell us about. But suppose the legislation in question concerns coal mine safety. Nobody is going to know what it all adds up to until some members of Congress and some members of the press go down into the coal mine to find out if conditions actually are safer or if only more crazy regulations have been added.

Unfortunately, neither the congressmen nor the press display much enthusiasm for visits to the mines. Yet this is what I found to be the key to getting the real story about the Peace Corps. I had to go to Ouagadougou and talk to the volunteers at their sites before I could really know what the Peace Corps was doing and what its problems were. I wasn't going to find out by asking the public affairs office. . . .

Because the reporters don't know any better, they don't press the Congress to do any better. What journalists could do is make the public aware of how little attention Congress devotes to what is called "oversight," i.e., finding out what the programs it has authorized are actually doing. If the press would publicize the nonperformance of this function, it is at least possible that the public would begin to reward the congressmen who perform it consistently and punish those who ignore it by not reelecting them.

But the press will never do this until it gets itself out of Larry Speakes's office. Woodward and Bernstein didn't get the Watergate story by talking to Ron Ziegler,* or, for that matter, by using other reportorial techniques favored by the media elite, like questioning Richard Nixon at a press conference or interviewing other administration luminaries at fancy restaurants. They had to find lower-level sources like Hugh Sloan, just as the reporters who finally got the NASA story had to find the Richard Cooks and Allan McDonalds.

Eileen Shanahan, a former reporter for the *New York Times* and a former assistant secretary of HEW, recently wrote "of the many times I tried, during my tenure in the Department of Health, Education and Welfare, to interest distinguished reporters from distinguished publications in the effort the department was making to find out whether its billion-dollar programs actually were reaching the intended beneficiaries and doing any good. Their eyes glazed over."

I have had a similar experience with reporters during my 25 years in Washington. For most of that time they have seemed to think they knew everything about bureaucracy because they had read a Kafka novel and stood in line at the post office. In their ignorance, they adopted a kind of wise-guy, world-weary fatalism that said nothing could be done about bureaucratic problems. They had little or no sense about how to approach organizations with an anthropologist's feel for the interaction of attitudes, values, and institutional pressures.

There are a couple of reasons, however, to hope that the performance of the press will improve. The coverage of business news has become increasingly sophisticated about the way institutional pressures affect executive and corporate behavior, mainly because the comparison of our economy with Japan's made the importance of cultural factors so obvious. And on defense issues, visits to the field are increasingly common as reporters attempt to find out whether this or that weapon works.

But these are mere beachheads. They need to be radically expanded to include the coverage of all the institutions that affect our lives, especially govern-

---

*Larry Speakes was Ronald Reagan's press secretary at the time this article was written. Ron Ziegler was President Nixon's press secretary. Bob Woodward and Carl Bernstein were the two *Washington Post* writers credited with unraveling the Watergate scandal.

ment. This may seem unlikely, but if the press studies the Challenger case, I do not see how it can avoid perceiving the critical role bureaucratic pressure played in bringing about the disaster. What the press must then realize is that similar pressures vitally influence almost everything this government does, and that we will never understand why government fails until we understand those pressures and how human beings in public office react to them.*

Questions for Discussion

1. What factors operate within large organizations to prevent top leaders from learning about organizational difficulties? How might a leader of an organization overcome such factors?
2. According to Peters, why don't congressional oversight and press scrutiny of the bureaucracy uncover problems? How could such oversight be improved?

---

*In 1990, NASA experienced another public relations disaster when its $1.5 billion Hubble Space Telescope failed to focus clearly. NASA's investigating panel fixed the blame for the telescope flaw in the same management climate that led to the fatal explosion of the space shuttle Challenger in 1986. As in the shuttle case, the report indicated that engineers working on the telescope as far back as 1980 and 1981 were discouraged from bringing potential problems to the attention of their superiors.

 12.4

The True Size of Government

Paul C. Light

In the 1990s, with a straight face, President Bill Clinton proclaimed, "The era of big government is over." Even though the number of federal employees shrank a bit in his tenure, Clinton and other presidents have played similar games to hold down the federal work force, even as the role of government grows larger and larger. For example, in late 2006, the United States had about 140,000 troops in Iraq; at the same time, approximately 100,000 private contractors were also there, providing everything from food to security to construction expertise. The number of civil servants actually fell between 1990 and 2002 (from 2.2 million to a bit more than 1.8 million); likewise, the military's numbers slipped to 1.44 million from 2.42 million in 1990. But private contract and grant jobs rose over this period and have skyrocketed in the wake of 9/11.

In this 1999 article (with a 2005 table, updating his findings), Paul Light simply counts the number of employees paid to do work for the federal government (the size of state and especially local governments has also grown substantially). Although President Clinton might have been technically correct in his pronouncement about the size of government, he scarcely dented the number of contract and grant employees. But the great leap in private employment by the federal government has come under George W. Bush, and by Light's calculations the "true size of government" has leapt by more than 3.5 million workers since 1999. In short, numbers can lie, if they are not complete, and executives have continuing incentives to farm out jobs and thus produce the appearance of a "lean" administration.

D espite declarations to the contrary from elected officials across the political spectrum, the federal government is much bigger, not smaller, than it was 30 years ago.

Only by using the narrowest possible definition of the true size of government—headcount in the federal civil service—could President Clinton declare that "the

Paul C. Light is the Paulette Goddard Professor of Public Service at New York University.

era of big government is over" in his 1996 State of the Union address. Although Clinton's declaration earned a roar of applause from both sides of the aisle, it was a partial truth at best, a false claim at worst. Counting all the people who deliver goods and services for Washington, while removing the masking effects of the huge Defense Department downsizing, Clinton would have been much more accurate to say that the era of big government was continuing pretty much unabated. And that is precisely what the vast majority of Americans want.

A more realistic headcount begins with the 1.9 million full-time permanent civilian federal workers who get their paychecks and identification cards from Uncle Sam. Add in the 1.5 million uniformed military personnel and 850,000 U.S. Postal Service workers who were counted in the federal workforce until their department became a quasi-government corporation in 1970, and the total full-time permanent federal workforce was just under 4.3 million in 1996, the last year for which good numbers are available on both the visible and shadow federal workforce.*

Add in the people who work under federal contracts and grants or mandates imposed on state and local governments and the illusion of smallness becomes clear. In 1996, the federal government's $200 billion in contracts created an estimated 5.6 million jobs, its $55 billion in grants created another 2.4 million jobs, and its array of mandates in such fields as air and water quality and health and safety regulation encumbered another 4.7 million jobs in state, county and municipal governments. Add these 12.7 million shadow jobs to the 4.25 million civilian, military and postal jobs, and the true size of government in 1996 expands to nearly 17 million, or more than eight times larger than the standard headcount of 1.9 million used by Congress and the President to declare the era of big government over. And the count does not even include the full-time equivalent employment of the people who work on a part-time or temporary basis for Uncle Sam—for example, the 884,000 members of the military reserves.

The Shadow of Government

The shadow government casts through its vast inventory of private, nonprofit and state and local partners is a blend of intent and accident. On the one hand, it reflects decades of perfectly appropriate contracting for impeccably commercial activities and non-inherently governmental functions. On the other hand, the shadow also reflects decades of personnel ceilings, hiring limits and unrelenting pressure to do more with less. Under pressure to create a government that looks smaller and delivers at least as much of everything the public wants, federal departments and agencies did what came naturally: They pushed jobs

---

*For the author's 2005 update to his findings, see Table 1 on page 450.

Table 1
The True Size of Government, 1990–2005

Measure	1990	1993	1999	2002	2005	Change 1992–2002	Change 2002–2005
1. Civil servants	2,238,000	2,157,000	1,820,000	1,818,000	1,872,000	–2,000	54,000
2. Contract jobs	5,058,000	4,884,000	4,441,000	5,168,000	7,634,000	727,000	2,466,000
3. Grant jobs	2,416,000	2,400,000	2,527,000	2,860,000	2,892,000*	333,000	32,000
4. Military personnel	2,106,000	1,744,000	1,386,000	1,456,000	1,436,000	70,000	–20,000
5. Postal service jobs	817,000	820,000	872,000	810,000	767,000	–62,000	–43,000
The True Size of Government	12,635,000	12,005,000	11,046,000	12,112,000	14,601,000	1,066,000	2,489,000

*Grant data are from 2004, the last year for which complete data were available at the time of this analysis.

From "Research Brief on the New True Size of Government," by Paul C. Light, p. 11. Reprinted by permission of the author.

outward and downward into a vast shadow that is mostly outside the public's consciousness.

That creates a truth-in-advertising problem. It is impossible to have an honest debate about the role of government in society if the measurements only include part of the government. The government also is increasingly reliant on non-federal workers to produce goods and services that used to be delivered in-house. Not only does the shadow workforce create an illusion of smallness that may mislead the public about the true size of government, it may create an illusion of merit as jobs inside government are held to strict merit standards, while jobs under contracts, grants and mandates are not. It may also create illusions of capacity and accountability as agencies pretend they know enough to oversee their shadow workforce when, in fact, they no longer have the ability to distinguish good product or service from bad.

The government knows virtually nothing about its shadow. Neither the Office of Personnel Management nor the Office of Management and Budget has ever counted the full-time-equivalent non-federal workforce, let alone analyzed its appropriateness.

Procuring such quasi-governmental labor allows politicians to say government is cutting employees. And at first glance—which is the glance that Congress and the President usually take—total federal employment (civilian and military) shrank by nearly 900,000 jobs between 1984 and 1996. (The year 1984 is used as the base because it's the first year for which good data are available on the contract and grant workforce; 1996 is the most recent year for which comparable data are available.)

At second glance, however, the Defense Department accounted for more than 100 percent of the decline. Subtract from the downsizing DoD's 260,000 cut in civilian employment and 670,000 cut in military personnel, and the non-Defense civilian workforce actually grew by 60,000 over the 12 years. Add in 145,000 new Postal Service jobs, and the non-Defense workforce grew by more than 200,000.

The masking effects of the Defense downsizing continue all the way back to 1960. Expressed in the aggregate, total civilian employment has declined steadily since reaching its post–World War II high in 1968 and is now smaller than it was in 1960. But remove Defense from the totals, and the civilian workforce grew by nearly half between 1960 and 1996, increasing from 760,000 employees to 1.1 million.

This is not to discount the very real downsizing that has taken place in many domestic agencies over the past five years. Civilian employment at non-Defense agencies fell by nearly 100,000 full-time-equivalent jobs during Clinton's first term, with particularly deep cuts coming at the General Services Administration, the departments of Housing and Urban Development and Interior, and OPM. Even so, non-Defense civilian employment is up, not down, since 1960, the starting point for the Clinton assertion that the U.S. government is smaller than it was when John F. Kennedy took office.

Turn next to the contract and grant workforce. Again at first glance, the shadow of government also shrank between 1984 and 1996, falling by 1.2 million jobs, including a 375,000 decline during Clinton's first term. But subtract Defense Department cuts once again, and the shadow actually grew over the 12 years by nearly 400,000 jobs, most of which were created through service contracts. Once again, absent the Defense downsizing, the shadow of government grew almost 15 percent between 1984 and 1996. As the Defense shadow declined, so did the purchase of products like tanks, guns, ammunition, boots and uniforms. In 1984, one out of two contract jobs involved products; by 1996, just one out of five did.

Unfortunately, the contract and grant data are so inconsistent prior to 1984 that there is no way to estimate the total shadow workforce. The only way to establish any meaningful trend line is to use the National Income and Product Account estimates of federal "consumption expenditures," which contain government purchases of goods and services. Calculated in constant 1990 dollars, these expenditures increased from $240 billion in 1960 to $357 billion in 1968, $393 billion in 1984 and $452 billion in 1988. They dropped to $449 billion in 1992 and $408 billion in 1996. Although these consumption expenditures include military and civilian civil service compensation, those costs have either declined (military) or remained relatively constant (civilian) over the period, suggesting that the federal government's contract workforce increased steadily during the 1960s and 1970s, only leveling off in the late 1980s and early 1990s with the Defense downsizing.

It is impossible to go back in time to estimate the total number of state and local employees who worked under federal mandates. It seems reasonable to conclude, however, that the number has increased dramatically as Congress and the President figured out how to encumber state and local governments at no cost to the federal Treasury.

The New Public Service

Whether the shadow of government is a problem depends very much on who is asking. Democrats will find ample support in the numbers for what Rep. Dennis Kucinich, D-Ohio, recently labeled a "piecemeal dismantling of our republic." Republicans, meanwhile, may well agree with Rep. Pete Sessions, R-Texas, that agencies should give over more work to private-sector competitors.

What few will dispute is that the federal government relies on a sizable shadow to do its job. "You can use any number you want," former OMB deputy director John Koskinen once admitted. "But whatever it is, it is a lot of people." Indeed it is. The shadow may not show up in the civil service headcount that allows presidents to claim that the era of big government is over, but it produces federal goods and services nonetheless. Given the personnel ceilings and freezes that have existed for the better part of a half-century, the federal government simply couldn't do its job without a large corps of contract, grant and mandate employees.

It is a fact already well understood by students at America's top schools of public policy and administration, who know that many of the nation's most challenging jobs are now to be found outside the civil service, not inside. At Harvard University's John F. Kennedy School of Government, for example, less than half of the class of 1997 took jobs in government, with nearly a quarter going to the nonprofit sector. "Training for the nonprofit sector is one area in which public policy schools need to redirect their focus," Kennedy School Dean Joseph Nye has written.

A recent survey by George Washington University's public administration department confirms the movement away from government. Asked to rank their preferred employers, 53 percent of the national sample of 1,000 public administration graduate students ranked government first, with the federal government the preference of 27 percent and state and local government of 26 percent. The rest of these future public servants hoped to serve in the shadow of government, with 27 percent looking to the private sector, 22 percent to nonprofits.

Some will object to defining private contractors as public servants. After all, contractors deliver their products for a price, while civil servants provide their labor for a wage. Yet, if headcount is to be used in measuring the true size of government, it only seems reasonable to count every head in the total.

Expanding the headcount would force Congress and the President to confront a series of difficult questions. Instead of engaging in an endless effort to keep the civil service looking small, they would have to ask just how many of the 16.9 million federal "producers" should be kept in-house and at what cost. One can easily argue that the answers would lead to a larger, not smaller, civil service, or at least a civil service very differently configured. There are many good reasons to hire a shadow employee, whether to improve government performance, protect taxpayer interests, or protect small business. But maintaining an illusion of smallness is not one of them.

Congress and the President would also have to ask tougher questions about who works in the shadow and under what conditions. It makes no sense, for example, to enforce a rule-bound merit system for one set of federal producers, while allowing an entirely different system for contractors, grantees, and state and local surrogates.

Counting all the jobs might also lead to a long-overdue discussion of public service in non-government settings. More than a third (4.7 million) of the federal government's 1996 shadow worked for state and local government, which makes them public employees, not private. Over a sixth (2.4 million) worked for grantees of one kind or another, including public and private universities, producing everything from knowledge to smoother highways. Almost a third

(4 million) worked for private contractors producing various services. Less than a tenth of the total (1.6 million) actually worked delivering products to government in the prototypical contractor relationship.

It is particularly difficult to draw lines between public and private when contractors and civil servants do the same jobs—often in the same office at the same time. Besides the size of the paycheck and the level of job security, there may be little discernible difference between the management analyst who works for the Commerce Department and the one who works for Arthur Andersen, the computer programmer who works for the Treasury Department and one who works for Unisys, the faculty member who teaches for the Agriculture Department Graduate School and one who teaches for Georgetown University, or the cancer researcher who works for the National Institutes of Health and the one who works for Upjohn. Again, there may be good reason for using contract, grant or mandate employees, not the least of which may be the federal government's inability to pay a competitive wage for key jobs. But civil servants and shadow workers can still share a common sense of service. Like identical twins raised apart, they may find themselves working in different sectors at different pay, but for very similar reasons.

Even if they don't share a common purpose, shadow workers still have public obligations. Just because they receive their paychecks and identification cards from private firms or nonprofit organizations does not mean they can be ignored as distant pieces of the federal public service. They may be motivated by profit, and may serve multiple customers, but they accept a public service obligation whenever they act on behalf of the federal government.

The Boeing employees who work on the space shuttle are no less obligated to do their jobs properly than the NASA employees who work at their side; the Lockheed Martin employees who administer state welfare programs are no less obligated to be fair and accurate than the employees they replace; the ICF-Kaiser employees who meet with concerned citizens at Superfund sites [designated by the government for hazardous waste cleanup] are no less obligated to be responsive than the Environmental Protection Agency employees they represent; the Westinghouse employees who clean up nuclear waste sites are no less obligated to protect public safety than the Energy Department employees who guide their contracts. The more the federal government relies on third parties to deliver public services, the more those third parties must recognize the public obligations of their private or nonprofit service.

Questions for Discussion

1. Why is the "size of government" important in the United States, both in terms of politics and policymaking?

2. In 2006, the press reported that there were more than 100,000 government-paid contractors in Iraq, doing everything from road building to serving meals to providing military-style protection to construction firms. What are the implications of this, given that at the same time the U.S. armed forces in Iraq numbered about 140,000?

3. What's the difference between having public services provided by public officials and those under private contract? Are there some services that should remain in the public sector? Which ones?

Chapter 13

THE SUPREME COURT

Barely outlined in the Constitution, the Supreme Court and the American judiciary have been forced, almost from the beginning of the republic, to define their own roles within the political system. Historically, this has meant that the Court has engaged in a long-term balancing act, adhering to the rule of law while remaining conscious of the political environment of the times. At the heart of the American court system is a central irony: We rely on a profoundly undemocratic institution to safeguard our democratic state as well as to check the likely excesses of popular rule.

The Court's major tool in its work has been the power of judicial review: The Court determines whether federal laws and regulations and state statutes are in accord with the Constitution and constitutional principles. Although the principle of judicial review was incorporated into American law with Chief Justice John Marshall's 1803 decision in *Marbury* v. *Madison* (see selection 13.2), the Court has not, over the course of two centuries, invalidated many federal laws. Indeed, there was a fifty-four-year gap between *Marbury* and the next such ruling, the 1857 *Dred Scott* decision, which struck down the Missouri Compromise. Since the New Deal, however, the Court has been somewhat more willing to overturn federal laws, especially when individual rights are at stake (see Chapter 3). State laws have received even more attention; close to a thousand such statutes have been declared unconstitutional. In a federal system, the power to strike down state legislation is essential, whereas the capacity to overrule national laws is less so.

It is surely conceivable that Congress or the executive branch could interpret the Constitution as well as the Court does. Still, the Supreme Court's role provides for a rough balance of power among the three branches. Lacking the authority to enforce its decisions, the Court can scarcely act in an arbitrary or capricious fashion. Nevertheless, it can have a major impact, as indicated by its decisions on subjects such as school desegregation, the rights of the accused, access to executive branch material (the Nixon tapes case), and the separation of powers (the *Chada* case, which invalidated legislative veto sections of approximately two hundred laws). In these and a host of other decisions, the Court clearly has acted in a policymaking role.

Despite the continuing controversy over whether the Supreme Court should make policy or merely interpret the Constitution in light of the framers' intent, the fact remains that it has consistently rendered policy decisions from its earliest days. It can hardly work in any other way. For example, in *Boyle* v. *United Technologies* (1988), conservative justice Antonin Scalia, writing for a 5-to-4 majority, argued that members of the military service could not sue the manufacturers of possibly defective military equipment (such as a helicopter that crashed). Scalia reasoned that allowing suits would ultimately increase the cost of defense material to the federal government and the American taxpayer. But as dissenting justice William Brennan observed, "the Court lacks both authority and expertise to fashion [a rule that exempts military contractors from civil suits], whether to protect the Treasury of the United States or the coffers of industry. . . . I would leave that exercise of power to Congress, where our Constitution places it." Justice Brennan, however, had previously written a broadly worded ruling that rendered the states almost superfluous in the face of federal power (*Garcia* v. *San Antonio Metropolitan Transit Authority*). In the end, both the conservative Scalia and the liberal Brennan have interpreted the Constitution expansively when doing so has suited their policy preferences. For further discussion of the question of intent and interpretation, see Richard A. Posner's article (selection 13.3) on the problematic notions of original intent and strict construction.

Mechanically, the Court sets its policy agenda by accepting a relatively small number of cases on which to rule. Although Congress and the president seem to have greater flexibility in setting their agendas, the Court can choose from among some 6,000 to 8,000 submitted cases in selecting the fewer than 100 that it will hear in its annual October-through-June session. In fact, its docket often includes controversies from which Congress and the president traditionally have shied away. The most notable example is school desegregation, which the Court addressed in 1954, a full decade before Congress passed a major civil rights bill. (See Chapter 3.)

Reprinted in this chapter, Alexander Hamilton's *The Federalist*, No. 78 (selection 13.1) and John Marshall's opinion in *Marbury* v. *Madison* (selection 13.2) provide the foundations for the Supreme Court's constitutional role. Hamilton articulates the classic formulation of the judiciary as "the least dangerous branch" because it "has no influence over either the sword [the executive] or the purse [the legislature]. . . . It may truly be said to have neither Force nor Will, but merely judgment; and must ultimately depend upon the aid of the executive arm even for the efficacy of its judgments." Marshall demonstrates the accuracy of Hamilton's observations in the *Marbury* decision, which involved a relatively trivial appointment but permitted Marshall to establish the principle of the judicial review of legislation.

In the next selection (13.3), federal appeals court judge Richard A. Posner, a prolific writer on an array of legal issues, addresses the ever-relevant issue of judicial activism. Although Posner is sometimes labeled a conservative, his intellect and range of interests make him difficult to classify. Most important, Posner does not sit as a judge merely to apply the Constitution in some rote manner or to determine what the framers' "original intent" might have been.

Nine justices, appointed for life, sit on the Supreme Court. Each has a single vote, but some exert more power than others. Although this power often flows from the quality of their arguments and thought, it can also derive from one's voting position on the Court. That is, if the justices are frequently divided equally on a set of issues, the one near their midpoint will exercise disproportionate authority. Between 1995 and 2005, that role was played by Justice Sandra Day O'Connor. A former Arizona state senator, the relatively conservative O'Connor often thought through major issues on narrow grounds, rarely being willing to break new constitutional ground if she could render a limited ruling. In the wake of O'Connor's retirement, Justice Anthony Kennedy has become the fulcrum for many Court decisions. David Cole (selection 13.4) outlines the results of the first Court session (2005–2006) without O'Connor and with two new Bush appointees, Chief Justice John Roberts and Associate Justice Samuel Alito. The Court as a whole has moved in a somewhat conservative direction, but it remains closely balanced on many issues, and Justice Kennedy sits at the center. Although the Court is ruling on fewer and fewer issues in the modern era, those that do reach its docket, such as the right to limit the scope of habeas corpus, strike at the very core of the American constitutional experience, as interpreted in the post-9/11 era. As usual, deciding hard cases defines the Court's role in our balance-of-powers system.

The Federalist, No. 78

Alexander Hamilton

Of the three branches of government, the judiciary is the least fully outlined in the Constitution. To an extent this vagueness reflects the framers' greater concerns with the legislature and the executive, but it also indicates their perception that the judiciary simply did not pose the dangers the other branches did. For Alexander Hamilton, the key problem was to ensure that the judiciary remained independent of the legislature and the executive. One way to provide for this separation was to make court appointments lifetime positions, with removal impossible as long as the incumbents maintained "good behaviour"—a purposefully vague term.

Hamilton also laid out the case for judicial review of legislation. He observed, "no legislative act . . . contrary to the Constitution can be valid." And it is the Supreme Court that makes the final judgment on constitutionality. This seemingly great grant of authority is tempered, however, by the Court's inability to enforce its decisions without cooperation from the executive.

*T*o the People of the State of New York: We proceed now to an examination of the judiciary department of the proposed government.

In unfolding the defects of the existing confederation, the utility and necessity of a federal judicature have been clearly pointed out. It is the less necessary to recapitulate the considerations there urged; as the propriety of the institution in the abstract is not disputed: The only questions which have been raised being relative to the manner of constituting it, and to its extent. To these points therefore our observations shall be confined.

The manner of constituting it seems to embrace these several objects—1st. The mode of appointing the judges. 2d. The tenure by which they are to hold their places. 3d. The partition of the judiciary authority between different courts, and their relations to each other.

First. As to the mode of appointing the judges: This is the same with that of appointing the officers of the union in general, and has been so fully discussed

Alexander Hamilton was the first secretary of the treasury and a consistent supporter of strong central government.

in the two last numbers, that nothing can be said here which would not be useless repetition.

Second. As to the tenure by which the judges are to hold their places: This chiefly concerns their duration in office; the provisions for their support; and the precautions for their responsibility.

According to the plan of the convention, all the judges who may be appointed by the United States are to hold their offices *during good behaviour,* which is conformable to the most approved of the state constitutions; and among the rest, to that of this state. Its propriety having been drawn into question by the adversaries of that plan, is no light symptom of the rage for objection which disorders their imaginations and judgments. The standard of good behaviour for the continuance in office of the judicial magistracy is certainly one of the most valuable of the modern improvements in the practice of government. In a monarchy it is an excellent barrier to the despotism of the prince: In a republic it is a no less excellent barrier to the encroachments and oppressions of the representative body. And it is the best expedient which can be devised in any government, to secure a steady, upright and impartial administration of the laws.

Whoever attentively considers the different departments of power must perceive, that in a government in which they are separated from each other, the judiciary, from the nature of its functions, will always be the least dangerous to the political rights of the constitution; because it will be least in a capacity to annoy or injure them. The executive not only dispenses the honors, but holds the sword of the community. The legislature not only commands the purse, but prescribes the rules by which the duties and rights of every citizen are to be regulated. The judiciary on the contrary has no influence over either the sword or the purse, no direction either of the strength or of the wealth of the society, and can take no active resolution whatever. It may truly be said to have neither Force nor Will, but merely judgment; and must ultimately depend upon the aid of the executive arm even for the efficacy of its judgments.

This simple view of the matter suggests several important consequences. It proves incontestibly that the judiciary is beyond comparison the weakest of the three departments of power; that it can never attack with success either of the other two; and that all possible care is requisite to enable it to defend itself against their attacks. It equally proves, that though individual oppression may now and then proceed from the courts of justice, the general liberty of the people can never be endangered from that quarter: I mean, so long as the judiciary remains truly distinct from both the legislative and executive. For I agree that "there is no liberty, if the power of judging be not separated from the legislative and executive powers." And it proves, in the last place, that as liberty can have nothing to fear from the judiciary alone, but would have every thing to fear from its union with either of the other departments; that as all the effects of such an union must ensue from a dependence of the former on the latter, notwithstanding a nominal and apparent separation; that as from the natural feebleness of the judiciary, it is in continual jeopardy of being overpowered, awed or influenced by its coordinate branches; and that as nothing can contribute so much to its firmness and independence, as permanency in office, this quality may therefore be justly regarded as an indispensable ingredient in its constitution; and in a great measure as the citadel of the public justice and the public security.

The complete independence of the courts of justice is peculiarly essential in a limited constitution. By a limited constitution I understand one which contains certain specified exceptions to the legislative authority; such for instance as that it shall pass no bills of attainder, no *ex post facto* laws, and the like.* Limitations of this kind can be preserved in practice no other way than through the medium of the courts of justice; whose duty it must be to declare all acts contrary to the manifest tenor of the constitution void. Without this, all the reservations of particular rights or privileges would amount to nothing.

Some perplexity respecting the right of the courts to pronounce legislative acts void, because contrary to the constitution, has arisen from an imagination that the doctrine would imply a superiority of the judiciary to the legislative power. It is urged that the authority which can declare the acts of another void, must necessarily be superior to the one whose acts may be declared void. As this doctrine is of great importance in all the American constitutions, a brief discussion of the grounds on which it rests cannot be unacceptable.

There is no position which depends on clearer principles, than that every act of a delegated authority, contrary to the tenor of the commission under which it is exercised, is void. No legislative act therefore contrary to the constitution can be valid. To deny this would be to affirm that the deputy is greater than his principal; that the servant is above his master; that the representatives of the people are superior to the people themselves; that men acting by virtue of powers may do not only what their powers do not authorise, but what they forbid.

If it be said that the legislative body are themselves the constitutional judges of their own powers, and that the construction they put upon them is conclusive upon the other departments, it may be answered, that this cannot be the natural presumption, where it is not to be collected from any particular provisions in the constitution. It is not otherwise to be supposed that the constitution could intend to enable the representatives of the people to substitute their *will* to that of their constituents. It is far more rational to suppose that the courts were designed to be an intermediate body between the people and the legislature, in order, among other things, to keep the latter within the limits assigned to their authority. The interpretation of the laws is the proper and peculiar province of the courts. A constitution is in fact, and must be, regarded by

---

*A bill of attainder is a legislative act that inflicts punishment without a judicial trial. Crimes are thus defined by statutes that are general in nature, and the courts interpret those statutes. An *ex post facto* law either makes an act illegal after the fact or removes the legal protection from behavior after that behavior has been performed.

the judges as a fundamental law. It therefore belongs to them to ascertain its meaning as well as the meaning of any particular act proceeding from the legislative body. If there should happen to be an irreconcileable variance between the two, that which has the superior obligation and validity ought of course to be preferred; or in other words, the constitution ought to be preferred to the statute, the intention of the people to the intention of their agents.

Nor does this conclusion by any means suppose a superiority of the judicial to the legislative power. It only supposes that the power of the people is superior to both; and that where the will of the legislature declared in its statutes, stands in opposition to that of the people declared in the constitution, the judges ought to be governed by the latter, rather than the former. They ought to regulate their decisions by the fundamental laws, rather than by those which are not fundamental.

This exercise of judicial discretion in determining between two contradictory laws, is exemplified in a familiar instance. It not uncommonly happens, that there are two statutes existing at one time, clashing in whole or in part with each other, and neither of them containing any repealing clause or expression. In such a case, it is the province of the courts to liquidate and fix their meaning and operation: So far as they can by any fair construction be reconciled to each other; reason and law conspire to dictate that this should be done. Where this is impracticable, it becomes a matter of necessity to give effect to one, in exclusion of the other. The rule which has obtained in the courts for determining their relative validity is that the last in order of time shall be preferred to the first. But this is mere rule of construction, not derived from any positive law, but from the nature and reason of the thing. It is a rule not enjoined upon the courts by legislative provision, but adopted by themselves, as consonant to truth and propriety, for the direction of their conduct as interpreters of the law. They thought it reasonable, that between the interfering acts of an *equal* authority, that which was the last indication of its will, should have the preference.

But in regard to the interfering acts of a superior and subordinate authority, of an original and derivative power, the nature and reason of the thing indicate the converse of that rule as proper to be followed. They teach us that the prior act of a superior ought to be preferred to the subsequent act of an inferior and subordinate authority; and that, accordingly, whenever a particular statute contravenes the constitution, it will be the duty of the judicial tribunals to adhere to the latter, and disregard the former.

It can be of no weight to say, that the courts on the pretence of a repugnancy, may substitute their own pleasure to the constitutional intentions of the legislature. This might as well happen in the case of two contradictory statutes; or it might as well happen in every adjudication upon any single statute. The courts must declare the sense of the law; and if they should be disposed to exercise WILL instead of JUDGMENT, the consequence would equally be the substitution of their pleasure to that of the legislative body. The observation, if it proved any thing, would prove that there ought to be no judges distinct from that body.

If then the courts of justice are to be considered as the bulwarks of a limited constitution against legislative encroachments, this consideration will afford a strong argument for the permanent tenure of judicial offices, since nothing will contribute so much as this to that independent spirit in the judges, which must be essential to the faithful performance of so arduous a duty. . . .

That inflexible and uniform adherence to the rights of the constitution and of individuals, which we perceive to be indispensable in the courts of justice, can certainly not be expected from judges who hold their offices by a temporary commission. Periodical appointments, however regulated, or by whomsoever made, would in some way or other be fatal to their necessary independence. If the power of making them was committed either to the executive or legislature, there would be danger of an improper complaisance to the branch which possessed it; if to both, there would be an unwillingness to hazard the displeasure of either; if to the people, or to persons chosen by them for the special purpose, there would be too great a disposition to consult popularity, to justify a reliance that nothing would be consulted but the constitution and the laws.

There is yet a further and a weighty reason for the permanency of the judicial offices; which is deducible from the nature of the qualifications they require. It has been frequently remarked with great propriety, that a voluminous code of laws is one of the inconveniences necessarily connected with the advantages of a free government. To avoid an arbitrary discretion in the courts, it is indispensable that they should be bound down by strict rules and precedents, which serve to define and point out their duty in every particular case that comes before them; and it will readily be conceived from the variety of controversies which grow out of the folly and wickedness of mankind, that the records of those precedents must unavoidably swell to a very considerable bulk, and must demand long and laborious study to acquire a competent knowledge of them. Hence it is that there can be but few men in the society, who will have sufficient skill in the laws to qualify them for the stations of judges. And making the proper deductions for the ordinary depravity of human nature, the number must be still smaller of those who unite the requisite integrity with the requisite knowledge. These considerations apprise us, that the government can have no great option between fit characters; and that a temporary duration in office, which would naturally discourage such characters from quitting a lucrative line of practice to accept a seat on the bench, would have a tendency to throw the administration of justice into hands less able, and less well qualified to conduct it with utility and dignity. In the present circumstances of this country, and in those in which it is likely to be for a long time to come, the disadvantages on this score would be greater than they may at first sight appear; but it must be confessed that they are far inferior to those which present themselves under the other aspects of the subject.

Upon the whole there can be no room to doubt that the convention acted wisely in copying from the models of those constitutions which have established *good behaviour* as the tenure of their judicial offices in point of duration; and that so far from being blameable on this account, their plan would have been inexcuseably defective if it had wanted this important feature of good government. The experience of Great Britain affords an illustrious comment on the excellence of the institution.

Questions for Discussion

1. Why might a lifetime term for judges and justices be considered a good policy? Why did the framers make officeholding contingent on continued "good behaviour" rather than on some more specific criterion?

2. Why did the framers consider the Supreme Court the weakest of the three branches of government? How can this be so if the Court has the final say over what the Constitution means?

 13.2

Marbury v. Madison (1803)

In March 1801, during the waning hours of his administration, President John Adams appointed William Marbury to be a justice of the peace in Washington, D.C. James Madison, the secretary of state under incoming president Thomas Jefferson, refused to deliver Marbury's commission, following Jefferson's instructions. Marbury subsequently applied to the Supreme Court to obtain the position.

This minor controversy offered a great opportunity to John Marshall, whom Adams had appointed chief justice in the last months of his tenure. Marshall, no friend of Jefferson's, found in this case a way to establish the Court's power to declare a federal law unconstitutional. Although Hamilton argued strenuously in favor of the judicial review of legislation in *The Federalist*, No. 78 (selection 13.1), the Constitution did not speak definitively on the topic. In this case Marshall ruled specifically that Marbury was entitled to his commission but the Court had no legitimate authority to order Madison to deliver it to him because the federal statute providing the Court with the power to provide the appropriate remedy was unconstitutional. In short, this decision answered the open question posed by the Constitution: Who has the authority to declare a statute unconstitutional? In *Marbury* v. *Madison*, Marshall won that power for the Supreme Court.

M r. Chief Justice Marshall delivered the opinion of the Court. At the last term on the affidavits then read and filed with the clerk, a rule was granted in this case, requiring the secretary of state to show cause why a *mandamus** should not issue, directing him to deliver to William Marbury his commission as a justice of the peace for the county of Washington, in the district of Columbia. . . .

In the order in which the court has viewed this subject, the following questions have been considered and decided.

1st. Has the applicant a right to the commission he demands?

2dly. If he has a right, and that right has been violated, do the laws of his country afford him a remedy?

3dly. If they do afford him a remedy, is it a *mandamus* issuing from this court? . . .

This . . . is a plain case for a *mandamus*, either to deliver the commission, or a copy of it from the record; and it only remains to be inquired,

Whether it can issue from this court.

The act to establish the judicial courts of the United States authorizes the supreme court "to issue writs of *mandamus*, in cases warranted by the principles and usages of law, to any courts appointed, or persons holding office, under the authority of the United States."

The secretary of state, being a person holding an office under the authority of the United States, is precisely within the letter of the description; and if this court is not authorized to issue a writ of *mandamus* to such an officer, it must be because the law is unconstitutional, and therefore absolutely incapable of conferring the authority, and assigning the duties which its words purport to confer and assign.

The constitution vests the whole judicial power of the United States in one supreme court, and such inferior courts as congress shall, from time to time, ordain and establish. This power is expressly extended to all cases arising under the laws of the United States; and, consequently, in some form, may be exercised over the present case; because the right claimed is given by a law of the United States.

In the distribution of this power it is declared that "the supreme court shall have original jurisdiction in all cases affecting ambassadors, other public ministers and consuls, and those in which a state shall be a party. In all other cases, the supreme court shall have appellate jurisdiction."

---

*A writ of *mandamus* is a binding directive, issued to individuals within the executive branch, that requires some action.

It has been insisted, at the bar, that as the original grant of jurisdiction, to the supreme and inferior courts, is general, and the clause, assigning original jurisdiction to the supreme court, contains no negative or restrictive words, the power remains to the legislature, to assign original jurisdiction to that court in other cases than those specified in the article which has been recited; provided those cases belong to the judicial power of the United States.

If it had been intended to leave it in the discretion of the legislature to apportion the judicial power between the supreme and inferior courts according to the will of that body, it would certainly have been useless to have proceeded further than to have defined the judicial power, and the tribunals in which it should be vested. The subsequent part of the section is mere surplusage, is entirely without meaning, if such is to be the construction. If congress remains at liberty to give this court appellate jurisdiction, where the constitution has declared their jurisdiction shall be original; and original jurisdiction where the constitution has declared it shall be appellate; the distribution of jurisdiction, made in the constitution, is form without substance.

Affirmative words are often, in their operations, negative of other objects than those affirmed; and in this case, a negative or exclusive sense must be given to them, or they have no operation at all.

It cannot be presumed that any clause in the constitution is intended to be without effect; and, therefore, such a construction is inadmissible, unless the words require it.

If the solicitude of the convention, respecting our peace with foreign powers, induced a provision that the supreme court should take original jurisdiction in cases which might be supposed to affect them; yet the clause would have proceeded no further than to provide for such cases, if no further restriction on the powers of congress had been intended. That they should have appellate jurisdiction in all other cases, with such exceptions as congress might make, is no restriction; unless the words be deemed exclusive of original jurisdiction. . . .

To enable this Court, then, to issue a *mandamus*, it must be shown to be an exercise of appellate jurisdiction, or to be necessary to enable them to exercise appellate jurisdiction. . . .

It is the essential criterion of appellate jurisdiction, that it revises and corrects the proceedings in a cause already instituted, and does not create that cause. Although, therefore, a *mandamus* may be directed to courts, yet to issue such a writ to an officer for the delivery of a paper, is in effect the same as to sustain an original action for that paper, and, therefore, seems not to belong to appellate, but to original jurisdiction. Neither is it necessary in such a case as this, to enable the court to exercise its appellate jurisdiction.

The authority, therefore, given to the supreme court, by the act establishing the judicial courts of the United States, to issue writs of *mandamus* to public officers, appears not to be warranted by the constitution; and it becomes necessary to inquire whether a jurisdiction so conferred can be exercised.

The question, whether an act, repugnant to the constitution, can become the law of the land, is a question deeply interesting to the United States; but, happily, not of an intricacy proportioned to its interest. It seems only necessary to recognise certain principles, supposed to have been long and well established, to decide it.

That the people have an original right to establish, for their future government, such principles as, in their opinion, shall most conduce to their own happiness is the basis on which the whole American fabric has been erected. The exercise of this original right is a very great exertion; nor can it, nor ought it, to be frequently repeated. The principles, therefore, so established, are deemed fundamental. And as the authority from which they proceed is supreme, and can seldom act, they are designed to be permanent.

This original and supreme will organizes the government, and assigns to different departments their respective powers. It may either stop here, or establish certain limits not to be transcended by those departments.

The government of the United States is of the latter description. The powers of the legislature are defined and limited; and that those limits may not be mistaken, or forgotten, the constitution is written. To what purpose are powers limited, and to what purpose is that limitation committed to writing, if these limits may, at any time, be passed by those intended to be restrained? The distinction between a government with limited and unlimited powers is abolished, if those limits do not confine the persons on whom they are imposed, and if acts prohibited and acts allowed, are of equal obligation. It is a proposition too plain to be contested, that the constitution controls any legislative act repugnant to it; or, that the legislature may alter the constitution by an ordinary act.

Between these alternatives there is no middle ground. The constitution is either a superior paramount law, unchangeable by ordinary means, or it is on a level with ordinary legislative acts, and, like other acts, is alterable when the legislature shall please to alter it.

If the former part of the alternative be true, then a legislative act contrary to the constitution is not law: if the latter part be true, then written constitutions are absurd attempts, on the part of the people, to limit a power in its own nature illimitable.

Certainly all those who have framed written constitutions contemplate them as forming the fundamental and paramount law of the nation, and, consequently, the theory of every such government must be, that an act of the legislature, repugnant to the constitution, is void.

This theory is essentially attached to a written constitution, and, is consequently, to be considered, by this court, as one of the fundamental principles of our society. It is not therefore to be lost sight of in the further consideration of this subject.

If an act of the legislature, repugnant to the constitution, is void, does it, notwithstanding its invalidity, bind the courts, and oblige them to give it effect?

Or, in other words, though it be not law, does it constitute a rule as operative as if it was a law? This would be to overthrow in fact what was established in theory; and would seem, at first view, an absurdity too gross to be insisted on. It shall, however, receive a more attentive consideration.

It is emphatically the province and duty of the judicial department to say what the law is. Those who apply the rule to particular cases, must of necessity expound and interpret that rule. If two laws conflict with each other, the courts must decide on the operation of each.

So if a law be in opposition to the constitution; if both the law and the constitution apply to a particular case, so that the court must either decide that case conformably to the law, disregarding the constitution; or conformably to the constitution, disregarding the law; the court must determine which of these conflicting rules governs the case. This is of the very essence of judicial duty.

If, then, the courts are to regard the constitution, and the constitution is superior to any ordinary act of the legislature, the constitution, and not such ordinary act, must govern the case to which they both apply.

Those, then, who controvert the principle that the constitution is to be considered, in court, as a paramount law, are reduced to the necessity of maintaining that courts must close their eyes on the constitution, and see only the law.

This doctrine would subvert the very foundation of all written constitutions. It would declare that an act which, according to the principles and theory of our government, is entirely void, is yet, in practice, completely obligatory. It would declare that if the legislature shall do what is expressly forbidden, such act, notwithstanding the express prohibition, is in reality effectual. It would be giving to the legislature a practical and real omnipotence, with the same breath which professes to restrict their powers within narrow limits. It is prescribing limits, and declaring that those limits may be passed at pleasure.

That it thus reduces to nothing what we have deemed the greatest improvement on political institutions, a written constitution, would of itself be sufficient, in America, where written constitutions have been viewed with so much reverence, for rejecting the construction. But the peculiar expressions of the constitution of the United States furnish additional arguments in favour of its rejection.

The judicial power of the United States is extended to all cases arising under the constitution.

Could it be the intention of those who gave this power, to say that in using it the constitution should not be looked into? That a case arising under the constitution should be decided without examining the instrument under which it arises?

This is too extravagant to be maintained.

In some cases, then, the constitution must be looked into by the judges. And if they can open it at all, what part of it are they forbidden to read or to obey?

There are many other parts of the constitution which serve to illustrate this subject.

It is declared that "no tax or duty shall be laid on articles exported from any state." Suppose a duty on the export of cotton, of tobacco, or of flour; and a suit instituted to recover it. Ought judgment to be rendered in such a case? Ought the judges to close their eyes on the constitution, and only see the law?

The constitution declares "that no bill of attainder or *ex post facto* law shall be passed."

If, however, such a bill should be passed, and a person should be prosecuted under it; must the court condemn to death those victims whom the constitution endeavours to preserve?

"No person," says the constitution, "shall be convicted of treason unless on the testimony of two witnesses to the same overt act, or on confession in open court."

Here the language of the constitution is addressed especially to the courts. It prescribes, directly for them, a rule of evidence not to be departed from. If the legislature should change that rule, and declare *one* witness, or a confession *out* of court, sufficient for conviction, must the constitutional principle yield to the legislative act?

From these, and many other selections which might be made, it is apparent, that the framers of the constitution contemplated that instrument as a rule for the government of *courts*, as well as of the legislature. . . .

It is also not entirely unworthy of observation, that in declaring what shall be the *supreme* law of the land, the *constitution* itself is first mentioned; and not the laws of the United States generally, but those only which shall be made in *pursuance* of the constitution have that rank.

Thus, the particular phraseology of the constitution of the United States confirms and strengthens the principle, supposed to be essential to all written constitutions, that a law repugnant to the constitution is void; and that *courts*, as well as other departments, are bound by that instrument.

Questions for Discussion

1. What was the precise legal issue at the core of *Marbury v. Madison*? Why is this case so important to the ultimate workings of the separation of powers?
2. Is it absolutely imperative that the Constitution be interpreted as the supreme law of the land? Why shouldn't the legislature's interpretation of what is constitutional be weighed equally?

 13.3

What Am I? A Potted Plant?

Richard A. Posner

Since the 1960s, there has been a continuing political debate over the appropriate amount of discretion that appeals court judges and Supreme Court justices should exercise in interpreting the Constitution. Liberals have generally argued for substantial leeway, noting that the framers could not have anticipated many key contemporary policy debates, such as those about abortion or the regulation of nuclear plants. By and large, conservatives have made a case for less discretion and a more literal interpretation of the Constitution. Nevertheless, some liberals, such as the late Supreme Court justice Hugo Black, have adopted a literalist position, while some conservatives, such as U.S. Court of Appeals judge Richard A. Posner, have taken a more discretionary approach.

Here, Posner reacts to the strict constructionist or "legal formalist" view, labeling it virtually impossible to carry out. "Judges," he notes, "have been entrusted with making policy from the start." Posner endorses this notion in large part because of his tendency to approach legal reasoning from an economic perspective—one that has little, if any, grounding in the Constitution or the ideas of the framers. What is clear from his point of view is that all judges make policy and that both liberals and conservatives can benefit from expanded judicial discretion.

Many people, not all of conservative bent, believe that modern American courts are too aggressive, too "activist," too prone to substitute their own policy preferences for those of the elected branches of government. This may well be true. But some who complain of judicial activism espouse a view of law that is too narrow. And a good cause will not hallow a bad argument.

This point of view often is called "strict constructionism." A more precise term would be "legal formalism." A forceful polemic by Walter Berns in the

---

Richard A. Posner is a judge on the U.S. Court of Appeals for the Seventh Circuit and a senior lecturer at the University of Chicago Law School. He served as a mediator in an unsuccessful attempt to resolve the Justice Department's antitrust lawsuit against Microsoft Corporation.
Richard A. Posner, "What Am I? A Potted Plant?" *The New Republic* (September 28, 1997): 23–25. Reprinted by permission of *The New Republic*.

June 1987 issue of *Commentary*—"Government by Lawyers and Judges"—summarizes the formalist view well. Issues of the "public good" can "be decided legitimately only with the consent of the governed." Judges have no legitimate say about these issues. Their business is to address issues of private rights, that is, "to decide whether the right exists—in the Constitution or in a statute—and, if so, what it is; but at that point inquiry ceases." The judge may not use "discretion and the weighing of consequences" to arrive at his decisions and he may not create new rights. The Constitution is a source of rights, but only to the extent that it embodies "fundamental and clearly articulated principles of government." There must be no judicial creativity or "policy-making."

In short, there is a political sphere, where the people rule, and there is a domain of fixed rights, administered but not created or altered by judges. The first is the sphere of discretion, the second of application. Legislators make the law; judges find and apply it.

There has never been a time when the courts of the United States, state or federal, behaved consistently in accordance with this idea. Nor could they, for reasons rooted in the nature of law and legal institutions, in the limitations of human knowledge, and in the character of a political system.

"Questions about the public good" and "questions about private rights" are inseparable. The private right is conferred in order to promote the public good. So in deciding how broadly the right shall be interpreted, the court must consider the implications of its interpretation for the public good. For example, should an heir who murders his benefactor have a right to inherit from his victim? The answer depends, in part anyway, on the public good that results from discouraging murders. Almost the whole of so-called private law, such as property, contract, and tort law, is instrumental to the public end of obtaining the social advantages of free markets. Furthermore, most private law is common law—that is, law made by judges rather than by legislators or by constitution-framers. Judges have been entrusted with making policy from the start.

Often when deciding difficult questions of private rights courts have to weigh policy considerations. If a locomotive spews sparks that set a farmer's crops afire, has the railroad invaded the farmer's property right or does the railroad's ownership of its right of way implicitly include the right to emit sparks? If the railroad has such a right, shall it be conditioned on the railroad's taking reasonable precautions to minimize the danger of fire? If, instead, the farmer has the right, shall it be conditioned on his taking reasonable precautions? Such questions cannot be answered sensibly without considering the social consequences of alternative answers.

A second problem is that when a constitutional convention, a legislature, or a court promulgates a rule of law, it necessarily does so without full knowledge of the circumstances in which the rule might be invoked in the future. When the unforeseen circumstance arises—it might be the advent of the motor vehicle or of electronic surveillance, or a change in attitudes toward religion, race, and sexual propriety—a court asked to apply the rule must decide, in light of information not available to the promulgators of the rule, what the rule should mean in its new setting. That is a creative decision, involving discretion, the weighing of consequences, and, in short, a kind of legislative judgment—though, properly, one more confined than if the decision were being made by a real legislature. A court that decides, say, that copyright protection extends to the coloring of old black-and-white movies is making a creative decision, because the copyright laws do not mention colorization. It is not being lawless or usurpative merely because it is weighing consequences and exercising discretion.

Or if a court decides (as the Supreme Court has done in one of its less controversial modern rulings) that the Fourth Amendment's prohibition against unreasonable searches and seizures shall apply to wiretapping, even though no trespass is committed by wiretapping and hence no property right is invaded, the court is creating a new right and making policy. But in a situation not foreseen and expressly provided for by the Framers of the Constitution, a simple reading out of a policy judgment made by the Framers is impossible.

Even the most carefully drafted legislation has gaps. The Constitution, for example, does not say that the federal government has sovereign immunity—the right, traditionally enjoyed by all sovereign governments, not to be sued without its consent. Nevertheless the Supreme Court held that the federal government has sovereign immunity. Is this interpolation usurpative? The Federal Tort Claims Act, a law waiving sovereign immunity so citizens can sue the government, makes no exception for suits by members of the armed services who are injured through the negligence of their superiors. Nevertheless the Supreme Court has held that the act was not intended to provide soldiers with a remedy. The decision may be right or wrong, but it is not wrong just because it is creative. The 11th Amendment to the Constitution forbids a citizen of one state to sue "another" state in federal court without the consent of the defendant state. Does this mean that you can sue your own state in federal court without the state's consent? That's what the words seem to imply, but the Supreme Court has held that the 11th Amendment was intended to preserve the sovereign immunity of the states more broadly. The Court thought this was implied by the federalist system that the Constitution created. Again the Court may have been right or wrong, but it was not wrong just because it was creative.

Opposite the unrealistic picture of judges who apply law but never make it, Walter Berns hangs an unrealistic picture of a populist legislature that acts only "with the consent of the governed." Speaking for myself, I find that many of the political candidates whom I have voted for have failed to be elected and that those who have been elected have then proceeded to enact much legislation that did not have my consent. Given the effectiveness of interest groups in the political process, much of this legislation probably didn't have the consent of a majority of citizens. Politically, I feel more governed than self-governing. In considering whether to reduce constitutional safeguards to slight dimensions, we should be sure to have a realistic, not an idealized, picture of the legislative and executive branches of government, which would thereby be made more powerful than they are today.

To banish all discretion from the judicial process would indeed reduce the scope of constitutional rights. The framers of a constitution who want to make it a charter of liberties and not just a set of constitutive rules face a difficult choice. They can write specific provisions, and thereby doom their work to rapid obsolescence or irrelevance; or they can write general provisions, thereby delegating substantial discretion to the authoritative interpreters, who in our system are the judges. The U.S. Constitution is a mixture of specific and general provisions. Many of the specific provisions have stood the test of time amazingly well or have been amended without any great fuss. This is especially true of the rules establishing the structure and procedures of Congress. Most of the specific provisions creating rights, however, have fared poorly. Some have proved irksomely anachronistic—for example, the right to a jury trial in federal court in all cases at law if the stakes exceed $20. Others have become dangerously anachronistic, such as the right to bear arms. Some have even turned topsy-turvy, such as the provision for indictment by grand jury. The grand jury has become an instrument of prosecutorial investigation rather than a protection for the criminal suspect. If the Bill of Rights had consisted entirely of specific provisions, it would have aged very rapidly and would no longer be a significant constraint on the behavior of government officials.

Many provisions of the Constitution, however, are drafted in general terms. This creates flexibility in the face of unforeseen changes, but it also creates the possibility of multiple interpretations, and this possibility is an embarrassment for a theory of judicial legitimacy that denies that judges have any right to exercise discretion. A choice among semantically plausible interpretations of a text, in circumstances remote from those contemplated by its drafters, requires the exercise of discretion and the weighing of consequences. Reading is not a form of deduction; understanding requires a consideration of consequences. If I say, "I'll eat my hat," one reason that my listeners will "decode" this in non-literal fashion is that I couldn't eat a hat if I tried. The broader principle, which applies to the Constitution as much as to a spoken utterance, is that if one possible interpretation of an ambiguous statement would entail absurd or terrible results, that is a good reason to adopt an alternative interpretation.

Even the decision to read the Constitution narrowly, and thereby "restrain" judicial interpretation, is not a decision that can be read directly from the text. The Constitution does not say, "Read me broadly," or, "Read me narrowly." That decision must be made as a matter of political theory, and will depend on such things as one's view of the springs of judicial legitimacy and of the relative competence of courts and legislatures in dealing with particular types of issues.

Consider the provision in the Sixth Amendment that "in all criminal prosecutions, the accused shall enjoy the right . . . to have the Assistance of Counsel for his defense." Read narrowly, this just means that the defendant can't be forbidden to retain counsel; if he can't afford counsel, or competent counsel, he is out of luck. Read broadly, it guarantees even the indigent the effective assistance of counsel; it becomes not just a negative right to be allowed to hire a lawyer but a positive right to demand the help of the government in financing one's defense. Either reading is compatible with the semantics of the provision, but the first better captures the specific intent of the Framers. At the time the Sixth Amendment was written, English law forbade a criminal defendant to have the assistance of counsel unless abstruse questions of law arose in his case. The Framers wanted to do away with this prohibition. But, more broadly, they wanted to give criminal defendants protection against being railroaded. When they wrote, government could not afford, or at least did not think it could afford, to hire lawyers for indigent criminal defendants. Moreover, criminal trials were short and simple, so it was not ridiculous to expect a person to defend himself without a lawyer if he couldn't afford to hire one. Today the situation is different. Not only can the society easily afford to supply lawyers to poor people charged with crimes, but modern criminal law and procedure are so complicated that an unrepresented defendant will usually be at a great disadvantage.

I do not know whether Professor Berns thinks the Supreme Court was usurping legislative power when it held in the *Gideon* case [selection 3.3] that a poor person has a right to the assistance of counsel at the state's expense. But his article does make clear his view that the Supreme Court should not have invalidated racial segregation in public schools. Reading the words of the 14th Amendment in the narrowest possible manner in order to minimize judicial discretion, and noting the absence of evidence that the Framers wanted to eliminate segregation, Berns argues that "equal protection of the laws" just means non-discriminatory enforcement of whatever laws are enacted, even if the laws themselves are discriminatory. He calls the plausible empirical proposition that "separate educational facilities are inherently unequal" "a logical absurdity."

On Berns's reading, the promulgation of the equal protection clause was a trivial gesture at giving the recently freed slaves (and other blacks, whose status at the time was little better than that of serfs) political equality with whites, since the clause in his view forbids the denial of that equality only by executive officers. The state may not withdraw police protection from blacks (unless by legislation?) but it may forbid them to sit next to whites on buses. This is a possible reading of the 14th Amendment but not an inevitable one, unless judges must always interpret the Constitution as denying them the power to exercise judgment.

No one really believes this. Everyone professionally connected with law knows that, in Oliver Wendell Holmes's famous expression, judges legislate "interstitially," which is to say they make law, only more cautiously, more slowly, and in more principled, less partisan, fashion than legislators.* The attempt to

*Oliver Wendell Holmes (1841–1935) served first on the Massachusetts Supreme Court and then on the U.S. Supreme Court between 1882 and 1932. He was labeled "the Great Dissenter," and many of Holmes's minority opinions became the fodder for subsequent Court majority reasoning.

deny this truism entangles "strict constructionists" in contradictions. Berns says both that judges can enforce only "clearly articulated principles" and that they may invalidate unconstitutional laws. But the power to do this is not "articulated" in the Constitution; it is merely implicit in it. He believes that the courts have been wrong to interpret the First Amendment as protecting the publication of foul language in school newspapers, yet the words "freedom of speech, or of the press" do not appear to exclude foul language in school newspapers. Berns says he deduces his conclusion from the principle that expression, to be within the scope of the First Amendment, must be related to representative government. Where did he get that principle from? He didn't read it in the Constitution.

The First Amendment also forbids Congress to make laws "respecting an establishment of religion." Berns says this doesn't mean that Congress "must be neutral between religion and irreligion." But the words will bear that meaning, so how does he decide they should be given a different meaning? By appealing to Tocqueville's opinion of the importance of religion in a democratic society. In short, the correct basis for decision is the consequence of the decision for democracy. Yet consequences are not—in the strict constructionist view—a fit thing for courts to consider. Berns even expresses regret that the modern Supreme Court is oblivious to Tocqueville's opinion "of the importance of the woman . . . whose chastity as a young girl is protected not only by religion but by an education that limits her 'imagination.' " A court that took such opinions into account would be engaged in aggressively consequentialist thinking rather than in strict construction.

The liberal judicial activists may be imprudent and misguided in their efforts to enact the liberal political agenda into constitutional law, but it is no use pretending that what they are doing is not interpretation but "deconstruction," not law but politics, because it involves the exercise of discretion and a concern with consequences and because it reaches results not foreseen 200 years ago. It may be bad law because it lacks firm moorings in constitutional text, or structure, or history, or consensus, or other legitimate sources of constitutional law, or because it is reckless of consequences, or because it oversimplifies difficult moral and political questions. But it is not bad law, or no law, just because it violates the tenets of strict construction.

Questions for Discussion

1. Can the notion of "original intent" be defended as a serious legal doctrine according to Posner? Why or why not?
2. Do all judges make policy at least part of the time?
3. Posner has frequently been mentioned as a prospective Supreme Court nominee. Do you think the sentiments articulated in this selection make his nomination and confirmation more or less likely? Why?

13.4

The "Kennedy Court"

David Cole

In the ten years following 1995, the Supreme Court's membership went unchanged, and Justice Sandra Day O'Connor represented the moderate midpoint of the Court's nine members. Although the Court was more conservative than in the 1960s, or even the 1970s and 1980s, Justice O'Connor, with a fine sense of both real-world and judicial politics, maintained a steady course as the reigning centrist. Such stability is unusual for the Court, given the average age of the Justices at any given time, but during the tumultuous days of the Republican takeover of the House, President Clinton's impeachment, and for much of the war on terror, the Court acted in a stable, incremental fashion.

This ended with O'Connor's 2005 retirement and the death, soon after, of Chief Justice William Rehnquist. President George W. Bush appointed, and the Senate confirmed, two fairly conservative, but well-qualified justices, John Roberts (as Chief Justice) and Samuel Alito. Although the jury is still out, so to speak, on how far the Court will tilt to the right with these additions, it's clear that O'Connor's centrist position has been assumed by Justice Anthony Kennedy. In this article, judicial scholar David Cole examines the first term of the post-O'Connor Court and speculates about the future, given Kennedy's new, pivotal role. Almost without question, on some of the issues in which he has sided with conservatives in the past (e.g., affirmative action), the Court will move in his direction; as the "swing" vote, he determines the Court's balance of power on a host of important issues.

The Supreme Court's 2005–06 term—the first to feature the newly confirmed Chief Justice, John Roberts Jr., and Justice Samuel Alito—began with a whimper and ended with a bang. The term's early months saw the Court issuing an unusually high number of unanimous opinions, even in such potentially controversial areas as abortion and gay rights, as the Court sought to decide cases extremely narrowly and thereby avoid controversy. But by the

David Cole is a professor of law at Georgetown University.

David Cole, "The Kennedy Court." Reprinted with permission from the July 31, 2006, issue of *The Nation*. For subscription information, call 800-333-8536. Portions of each week's *Nation* magazine can be accessed at www.thenation.com.

end of the term, controversy was front and center, as the Court divided sharply on its most significant cases, culminating in the stunning 5-to-3 decision, the last day of the term, declaring George W. Bush's military tribunals illegal.

In *Hamdan* v. *Rumsfeld*, the most important case of the term, the Court showed itself willing to do what neither Republicans nor Democrats in Congress have been able to do: Stand up to the President in the "war on terror." The Court's decision reaffirmed, as Justice John Paul Stevens put it, that "the Executive is bound to comply with the Rule of Law that prevails in this jurisdiction." The Court's capitalization of the "Rule of Law" underscored its effort to enforce the concept of legality on an Administration that has long since adopted the view that the law can impose little or no constraint on the President during wartime—whether it be the international laws of war, criminal prohibitions on torture and warrantless wiretapping of Americans, or the Uniform Code of Military Justice, a statute that establishes the rules for military trials.

But as much as *Hamdan* deserved celebration for rejecting the President's vision of unchecked power in the post-9/11 world, the term also showed just how close the country is to a system of government that has no meaningful checks and balances. Bush's two new appointees generally proved themselves reliable conservatives—if not exactly in the mold of Justices Scalia and Thomas, which Bush said he was striving for, at least very close. Justices Roberts, Alito, Scalia and Thomas proved a reliable four votes for conservative results, while Justices Stevens, Souter, Ginsburg and Breyer continued to be a fairly reliable four votes for moderate to liberal outcomes. (Long gone are the days of Justices William Brennan and Thurgood Marshall.)

That leaves Justice Anthony Kennedy smack dab in the middle, with the ability to cast the decisive vote in many of the Court's most contentious disputes. Before the term began, it was an open question whether Kennedy would be persuaded to join the conservative bloc by the less acerbic and more politic conservative voices of Roberts and Alito, or whether he would maintain a swing-vote presence in the center, a position he shared with Justice Sandra Day O'Connor until her retirement. Thus far, he has remained in the middle. Justice Kennedy sometimes voted with the conservative bloc, including in a case upholding a Kansas death penalty statute, but went his own way on such significant issues as the military tribunals, the reach of the Clean Water Act, the exclusionary rule, gerrymandering and the Voting Rights Act.

Kennedy's influence is perhaps best illustrated by the Court's review of the gerrymandered redistricting of Texas engineered by Tom DeLay. On the issue of whether the redistricting violated equal protection because it was too partisan, Kennedy joined the conservative bloc to rule that there was no constitutional violation. But on the separate question of whether one part of the redistricting contravened the Voting Rights Act by diluting Latino voting strength, Kennedy sided with the liberal bloc to find that a violation had occurred. As Kennedy went, so went the Court.

Where Kennedy sided with the conservatives, he often wrote separately to moderate the result. In *Hudson* v. *Michigan* the majority ruled that the prosecution can use evidence obtained illegally when police violate the constitutional requirement that they "knock and announce" before entering a home to execute a search warrant. In its decision the conservative bloc displayed open hostility toward the "exclusionary rule"* generally, but Kennedy concurred to specify that he supported the rule in general but simply did not think it justified for knock-and-announce violations. Similarly, in *Rapanos* v. *United States* the conservative bloc voted to restrict radically the reach of the Clean Water Act over "wetlands," but Justice Kennedy effectively saved the act, writing separately to say that while he agreed that the lower court had used the wrong standard, the act extends to any land with a "significant nexus" to a navigable body of water, and courts should generally defer to the environmental regulators on that judgment.

Kennedy's vote was also crucial in *Hamdan*. That case involved a challenge by Salim Hamdan, Osama bin Laden's bodyguard and driver, to the military tribunals Bush had created by executive order in November 2001 for trying foreign nationals accused of terrorism and war crimes. Under the rules set forth by the President, defendants could be tried, convicted and sentenced to death on the basis of hearsay evidence, testimony obtained through coercive methods or secret evidence that neither the defendant nor his civilian lawyer had any opportunity to confront. In addition, the Defense Secretary or his designate, instead of the presiding judge, was empowered to intervene in ongoing trials and decide issues.

After the Court agreed to hear the case, Congress passed a statute that appeared designed to strip the Court of its jurisdiction. But five members of the Court were undeterred. They ruled that the statute did not apply to pending cases and went on to decide that the President's military tribunals violated military law and the Geneva Conventions. The Court ruled that the Uniform Code of Military Justice requires that military tribunal procedures not vary from those of the courts-martial we use to try our own soldiers, unless court-martial procedures would be "impracticable"—and that the Administration had made no such showing.

More important, the Court declared that Congress had required the tribunals to adhere to the laws of war, and that the tribunals violated one such law in particular, Common Article 3 of the Geneva Conventions. Common Article 3 requires that detainees in conflicts "not of an international character" be tried by "a regularly constituted court affording all the judicial guarantees which are recognized as indispensable by civilized peoples." The Administration had insisted that this rule did not apply to the conflict with Al Qaeda, because it was an "international" conflict. But in its most significant holding, the Court

---

*The exclusionary rule is a legal principle holding that evidence collected or analyzed in violation of the U.S. Constitution is inadmissible for a criminal prosecution.

rejected that interpretation, ruling that the reference to conflicts "not of an international character" was intended to cover all conflicts not between sovereign nations, literally not inter-national. Since Al Qaeda is not a nation, our conflict with it is "not of an international character," and the conflict is therefore covered by Common Article 3. On July 11 the Administration acknowledged that the Court's ruling means that the Geneva Conventions govern its treatment of Al Qaeda detainees, but in typical fashion it insisted that this would require no change in its practices or policies.

In fact, the Court's Geneva Conventions ruling is significant for three reasons. First, it means that were Congress to enact a statute "overturning" *Hamdan* by authorizing the very procedures the Court found unauthorized, it would be sanctioning a violation of the laws of war. Second, Common Article 3 also bars any "humiliating and degrading treatment" of detainees, and any violation of Common Article 3 is a felony under the War Crimes Act. Thus, even though torture was not directly at issue in *Hamdan*, the decision in effect authoritatively bars any inhumane treatment of detainees—which would include most of what the CIA and Army interrogators have routinely been inflicting on Al Qaeda suspects. Third, and most important, the decision proclaims that the "war on terror" is not a law-free zone open to whatever rules ingenious White House lawyers can devise under cover of secrecy but must be subject to the international standards that govern all wars. In short, it refutes American exceptionalism.

All of this would not have been possible without Justice Kennedy's vote. But the voting alignment in *Hamdan* and many other important cases this term only illustrates how close the Court is to veering off in an extreme rightward direction. Its two oldest members are Justice Stevens, at 86, and Justice Ginsburg, at 73. If either retires while a Republican President is in office, the Court will likely be reliably conservative for several decades at least. On issues such as affirmative action, gay rights, states' rights, abortion, workers' rights, separation of powers and equal protection of the laws, the Court could become a rubber stamp for right-wing policies and an obstacle to progressive legislative reform—much as it was until midway through the New Deal. Perhaps never before has the power to appoint the next Justice been so potentially determinative of the course of constitutional law.

Meanwhile, the division on the Court will undoubtedly continue next year [2007]. The Court has already agreed to take up cases involving so-called "partial birth" abortion laws and efforts to maintain racial balance in public schools. On both issues Justice Kennedy has previously sided with conservatives. While he was in the majority that refused to overrule *Roe* v. *Wade* in *Planned Parenthood* v. *Casey*, he dissented passionately from the Court's application of *Casey* to strike down a "partial birth" abortion statute in 2000. And he has been an outspoken critic of affirmative action, voting to declare it unconstitutional in the University of Michigan's affirmative action cases just three years ago. This time next year, in other words, we may not be celebrating.

Questions for Discussion

1. Does an individual Justice like Anthony Kennedy, or Sandra Day O'Connor before him, hold too much power in a democratic system? Or, alternatively, might such a swing vote allow the Court to be a more responsive institution?
2. Why is the *Hamdan* decision so important? You may want to consider this in light of John Yoo's arguments about presidential power, made in selection 11.3.

Chapter 14

POLICYMAKING

The policymaking process brings together almost all of the elements in the structure of American politics. We can think of the Constitution as providing a framework within which policies are made—a framework that does not guarantee speedy action or governmental responsiveness to the wishes of the citizens. In addition, public opinion, as expressed through elections or interpreted in the media, is a basic element in policy formulation, yet it is often subject to change and adaptation. After all, presidents and legislators work diligently to generate public support for their own proposals.

The constitutional relationships outlined by the separation of powers and federalism impose serious limitations on policymakers. For example, education has traditionally been a state and local function in the United States; among national institutions, the Supreme Court, with its desegregation rulings, has affected local school districts more than the Congress or the president has.

Beyond these basic rules of the game, contemporary policymaking takes place within the context of a large and growing governmental establishment. Given an annual budget of roughly $2.8 trillion (an almost unimaginable sum), the permanent government of the federal bureaucracy is difficult for elected officials to control. In addition, the government extends its reach by providing guarantees in potentially risky undertakings (the banking industry, student loans, crop damage). The growth of government has produced two other hallmarks of contemporary policymaking: (1) the extensive use of regulation, which has generated substantial debate, and (2) the influence of annual budgetary actions on almost all domestic policy decisions.

Traditionally, students of public policy have focused much of their attention on the legislature and its decisions. But as the reach of government has grown and problems such as environmental pollution have become increasingly complex, Congress has delegated more and more policymaking authority to the bureaucracy and to independent agencies such as the Food and Drug Administration. In terms of the gross number of policies, regulations far outstrip legislation. Both Congress and the president have sought to control this proliferation. Congress has enacted large numbers of legislative veto provisions, which gave it the opportunity to review various regulations, but in 1983 the Supreme Court declared these vetoes an unconstitutional violation of the executive's authority under the separation of powers. The president has had greater success in monitoring regulation. Through the Office of Management and Budget, the executive reviews regulations to determine their consistency with existing policies.

Since the late 1970s, movements toward less new regulation and substantial deregulation have gained ground. Although the Reagan administration generally reduced the number of new regulations, the first moves toward deregulation came in the Carter administration, when economist Alfred Kahn, then chairman of the Civil Aeronautics Board (CAB), began action to curtail regulations within the airline industry. In the end, Kahn succeeded in eliminating the CAB. Increased fare competition among airlines was one short-term result of deregulation, although in the 1990s airline consolidation and higher fares seemed the order of the day. Still, as Pietro S. Nivola argues (in selection 14.2), despite high-profile deregulation, the overall impact of regulation for the society at large has steadily increased, much to the benefit of attorneys and targeted interests.

Although deregulation proved a mixed bag in the 1990s, two major governmental initiatives—eliminating budget deficits and reducing overall federal debt—were more successful. Building on an important 1990 budget deal, President Clinton adopted the elimination of budget deficits as a centerpiece of his economic planning. A second budget deal in 1993 and a strong economy allowed the budget deficit to decrease from $290 billion in 1992 to $200 billion-plus in 2001. Yet, with a post-2000 economic slump, the costs associated with terrorism and the Iraq War, as well as a decline in revenues due to tax cuts, the federal budget *deficit* grew to more than $500 billion in 2004, and has remained in the $200–$300 million range during the second term of the Bush administration.

No set of readings can adequately capture the diversity of domestic policymaking. In an excerpt from her book *Policy Paradox*, Deborah Stone describes how narratives—essentially stories—can define policy problems and possible solutions (selection 14.1). In a policymaking environment that is complex and filled to the brim with information from various sources, decision makers need stories to understand, and to help the public understand, how policies operate. Ironically, as we are faced with more and more information, the more valuable we will find narratives in allowing us to appear to understand complicated policies that respond to difficult problems like telecommunications reform or the impact of environmental regulations.

Of course, narratives can become obstructions to actual understanding. Nowhere is this truer than in health care in the United States, where more than 15 percent of the gross domestic product is spent. This crazy-quilt combination of private providers, governmental programs, and the insurance industry creates inefficiencies and anomalies in a system that produces a wide range of care, not necessarily tied to price or ability to pay. In his discussion of Medicare and the provision of drug benefits (selection 14.3), Eric Cohen considers how our largest program—Medicare—works and its impact on American health care. While praising the extension of drug benefits under Medicare D (for its controversial congressional enactment in 2003, see selection 10.4), Cohen sees both liberals and conservatives as viewing the program in different ways and thus allowing for many story lines to define Medicare, even as it remains in "permanent crisis."

Finally, we include two selections on the foreign policy and intelligence policy in the Bush administration. First, Ivo H. Daalder and James M. Lindsay make the argument in selection 14.4 that President George W. Bush, assisted by, but not dominated by, his advisors, has produced a revolution in American foreign policy. In particular, the United States has proven willing to act on its own, and in a preemptive manner, when its safety may be threatened. This major shift has come to define the Bush presidency and will almost certainly alter America's relations with most other countries around the globe. Directly related to the Bush administration's willingness to go it alone on Iraq, for the most part, has been its approach to the collection and use of intelligence. Former CIA analyst and administrator Paul Pillar makes a strong argument (selection 14.5) that the relationship between intelligence and policymaking is broken, in that policymakers have often compromised the intelligence gathering and reporting processes for their own political ends. Intelligence requires independence for those who gather and interpret information that comes in great volumes and myriad forms. Allowing policymakers to influence the intelligence process compromises both the information presented and its subsequent use, with potentially disastrous consequences, as the Iraq War has demonstrated.

 14.1

Stories

Deborah Stone

The context of policymaking in American politics has become increasingly complex over the past forty years. The government and its often-overlapping policies have grown steadily; regulations have increased; new rights have been created (by, for example, the Americans with Disabilities Act). And the number of interest groups has kept pace (see Chapter 9). Moreover, legislators, executives, and administrators are deluged with information—from the press, from organized interests, from think tanks, and increasingly from citizens using the Internet. In this "data smog" both decision makers and citizens must try to make sense of an almost incomprehensible world.

Although economists and some political scientists would willingly see the world in simplified economic terms, such simplification does not direct much policymaking (or explanations of policy decisions). Rather, as Deborah Stone points out, we often rely on stories to help us understand broad issues. In this selection, Stone briefly notes two common story lines that are used to justify decisions first to consider a certain problem and then to act on it. These "stories of decline" and "stories of control" are narratives used over and over in the discussion of why a certain issue needs to be addressed by government action. Data and information are included in these stories, but their power comes not from the information but from the construction of the stories themselves. And we may often enact policies in response that make little economic sense or do not improve the quality of societal life. Nevertheless, the narratives create their own realities that virtually demand some governmental response.

D efinitions of policy problems usually have narrative structure; that is, they are stories with a beginning, a middle, and an end, involving some change or transformation. They have heroes and villains and innocent victims, and they pit the forces of evil against the forces of good. The story line in policy writing is often hidden, but one should not be thwarted by the surface

Deborah Stone is the David R. Pokross Professor of Law and Social Policy at Brandeis University.
From *Policy Paradox: The Art of Political Decision Making* by Deborah Stone. Copyright © 1997, 1998 by Deborah Stone. Used by permission of W. W. Norton & Company, Inc.

details from searching for the underlying story. Often what appears as conflict over details is really disagreement about the fundamental story.

Two broad story lines are particularly prevalent in policy politics. One is a *story of decline*, not unlike the biblical story of the expulsion from paradise. It runs like this: "In the beginning, things were pretty good. But they got worse. In fact, right now, they are nearly intolerable. Something must be done." This story usually ends with a prediction of crisis—there will be some kind of breakdown, collapse, or doom—and a proposal for some steps to avoid the crisis. The proposal might even take the form of a warning: Unless such-and-such is done, disaster will follow.

The story of decline almost always begins with a recitation of facts or figures purporting to show that things have gotten worse. Poverty rates are rising, crime rates are higher, import penetration in U.S. markets is greater, environmental quality is worse—you have heard these all before. What gives this story dramatic tension is the assumption, sometimes stated and sometimes implicit, that things were once better than they are now, and that the change for the worse causes or will soon cause suffering. . . .

The story of decline has several variations. The *stymied progress story* runs like this: "In the beginning things were terrible. Then things got better, thanks to a certain someone. But now somebody or something is interfering with our hero, so things are going to get terrible again." This is the story told by every group that wants to resist regulation. In the 1970s and 1980s, the American Medical Association, fighting government cost-containment efforts, reminded us about the days of plagues, tuberculosis, and high infant mortality, and warned that government restrictions on the profession would undo all the progress doctors had brought us. Biotechnology firms, through their trade association known as "BIO," told a very similar story to fight President Clinton's medical cost-containment plans in the 1990s: biotechnology had brought us miracle medicine, but Clinton's planned regulation and price controls threatened the very survival of the nascent industry.[1] Manufacturing concerns, such as automakers, steel companies, and textile firms, tell a story of how minimum wage legislation, mandatory health benefits, and occupational safety regulations threaten to destroy America's once-preeminent position in the world economy. The CIA tells us that restrictions on its operating methods prevent it from maintaining the security it once could provide, and the Pentagon tells how budget constraints have undermined our once-dominant military position.

Another variant of the decline story is the *change-is-only-an-illusion* story. It runs like this: "You always thought things were getting worse (or better). But you were wrong. Let me show you some evidence that things are in fact going in the opposite direction. Decline (or improvement) was an illusion." Examples of the revisionist story are everywhere. Medical researchers tell us that the improved survival rates for cancer patients are really an artifact of measurement; it is only because we can now diagnose cancer at earlier stages that patients appear to live longer.[2] Child abuse (or rape or wife-battering) is not really on the rise; it only appears to have increased because we have more public awareness, more legislation, and more reporting.

The other broad type of narrative in policy analysis is the *story of helplessness and control*. It usually runs like this: "The situation is bad. We have always believed that the situation was out of our control, something we had to accept but could not influence. Now, however, let me show you that in fact we can control things." Stories about control are always gripping because they speak to the fundamental problem of liberty—to what extent do we control our own life conditions and destinies? Stories that purport to tell us of less control are always threatening, and ones that promise more are always heartening.

Much of the analysis in the areas of social policy, health and safety, and environment is a story of control. What had formerly appeared to be "accidental," "random," "a twist of fate," or "natural" is now alleged to be amenable to change through human agency. For example, much modern economic policy— the use of government fiscal and monetary tools to stabilize fluctuations in the economy—is based on a grand story of control. In the 1930s, when national economies had lurched into rampant inflation and disastrous depressions, they seemed to behave more like the weather than like social institutions. Lord Keynes* wrote a highly influential treatise whose central premise was that seemingly random fluctuations in economies are really manageable through government manipulation of spending and money supply.[3] The story of control governs in a vastly different policy area—public health—as well. Cancer, previously thought to strike victims unpredictably, now turns out to be related to diet, smoking, and chemicals—all things humans can control. Increasingly, cancer is linked to mutant genes, and though we cannot control our genes, the knowledge of genetic contributions to cancer can help us target screening and prevention programs, and may eventually help design genetically based therapies. Stories that move us from the realm of fate to the realm of control are always hopeful, and through their hope they invoke our support.

A common twist on the control story is the *conspiracy*. Its plot moves us from the realm of fate to the realm of control, but it claims to show that all along control has been in the hands of a few who have used it to their benefit and concealed it from the rest of us. Ralph Nader's famous crusade against automobile manufacturers was a story that converted car accidents into events controllable through the design of cars, and even willingly accepted by automakers. Advocates of industrial policy tell a story in which unemployment, thought to be intractable, is actually caused by "capital strike" (businessmen refuse to invest in new plants and ventures) and "capital flight" (businesses invest their capital in other regions or other countries). Conspiracy stories always reveal that harm has been deliberately caused or knowingly tolerated, and so evoke

---

*John Maynard Keynes's theories of state intervention in the economy dominated governmental policies and economic theories from the Great Depression until the Reagan-Thatcher era of the 1980s.

horror and moral condemnation. Their ending always takes the form of a call to wrest control from the few who benefit at the expense of the many.

Another variant of the control story is the *blame-the-victim* story.[4] It, too, moves us from the realm of fate to the realm of control, but locates control in the very people who suffer the problem. In one recent analysis of homelessness, "it was the fact that unskilled women not only married less but continued to have children that pushed more of them into the streets."[5] Homelessness, in this view, is the result of women's knowing choice between two alternatives:

> Few unskilled women can earn enough to support a family on their own. For many, therefore, the choices were stark. They could work, refrain from having children and barely avoid poverty, or they could not work, have children, collect welfare and live in extreme poverty. Many became mothers even though this meant extreme poverty.[6]

There are many versions of the blame-the-victim story. The poor are poor because they seek instant pleasures instead of investing in their own futures, or because they choose to live off the dole rather than work. Third World countries are poor because they borrow too eagerly and allow their citizens to live too extravagantly. The sick are sick because they overeat, consume unhealthy foods, smoke, and don't exercise. Women are raped because they "ask for it." Workers succumb to occupational diseases and injuries because they refuse to wear protective gear or to act with caution. Just as the conspiracy story always ends with a call to the many to rise up against the few, the blame-the-victim story always ends with an exhortation to the few (the victims) to reform their own behavior in order to avoid the problem.

What all these stories of control have in common is their assertion that there is choice. The choice may belong to society as a whole, to certain elites, or to victims, but the drama in the story is always achieved by the conversion of a fact of nature into a deliberate human decision. Stories of control offer hope, just as stories of decline foster anxiety and despair. The two stories are often woven together, with the story of decline serving as the stage setting and the impetus for the story of control. The story of decline is meant to warn us of suffering and motivate us to seize control.

Notes

1. "BIO" stands for Biotechnology Industry Organization. See Peter H. Stone, "Lost Cause," *National Journal*, Sept. 17, 1994, p. 2133.
2. Alvan R. Feinstein et al., "The Will Rogers Phenomenon: Stage Migration and New Diagnostic Techniques as a Source of Misleading Statistics for Survival in Cancer," *New England Journal of Medicine* 312, no. 25 (June 20, 1985): 1604–8.
3. John Maynard Keynes, *The General Theory of Employment, Interest and Money* (New York: Harcourt & Brace, 1936).
4. The phrase became a byword in social science after William Ryan's *Blaming the Victim* (New York: Random House, 1971).

5. Christopher Jencks, *The Homeless* (Cambridge, Mass.: Harvard University Press, 1994), p. 58.
6. Christopher Jencks, "The Homeless," *New York Review of Books*, April 21, 1994, p. 25.

Questions for Discussion

1. Relate Deborah Stone's discussion of "stories" to the other selections in this chapter. Why does the use of stories to think through complex issues seem so attractive?
2. Who gets to tell the stories that Stone alludes to: the public, the president, members of Congress, lobbyists, the media? How is the politics of getting our attention different from the politics of affecting decisions?

 14.2

Regulation: The New Pork Barrel

Pietro S. Nivola

Since the deregulation of air travel set off a spate of similar actions in banking, telecommunications, and other fields, the conventional wisdom has been that the United States has become a less highly regulated society. At the same time, although "pork" continues to be distributed in the legislative process, the conventional wisdom holds that there is less governmental "pork" than in years gone by. Regulations continue to be written, however, as legislators and administrators attack social ills ranging from toxic waste to deaths in automobile accidents. What has gone largely unnoticed, at least by the general public, is that many regulations confer benefits on particular groups (and costs on many others). In other words, "pork" lurking under the cover of "good policy" decisions may lessen the cost-effectiveness of policies.

Pietro S. Nivola is Vice President and Director of Government Studies at The Brookings Institution. He also holds the Douglas Dillon Chair at Brookings.

"Regulation: The New Pork Barrel" by Pietro S. Nivola, from *The Brookings Review*, Winter 1998, pp. 6–9. Reprinted by permission from The Brookings Institution.

In this selection, Brookings Institution scholar Pietro S. Nivola argues that many regulatory policies cost the government little or nothing but cost society at large a great deal, and he points out that these dispersed costs often funnel specific benefits to particular interests within society. The Superfund law, for example, has generated huge costs and substantial profits without doing much for the environment. Nivola recommends following the money to see who wins and who loses when the government decides to regulate an activity or require that certain standards be met. Not always, but often, the costs to society are substantial, and particular groups benefit from the regulatory requirements. The source of this type of "pork" may not be the old pork barrel from which legislators distributed benefits to their friends and supporters, but it does reflect a kind of politics that benefits organized interests (such as the waste disposal community) but does little for society at large (such as to improve environmental quality).

As the federal government's discretionary spending in the 1990s has become less lavish, so has the supply of old-fashioned lard in the U.S. budget. But if you think this means the era of big government is over, think again. Another pork barrel is burgeoning. Along with preferential micromanagement of the tax code, the bacon these days takes the form of unfunded mandates and regulatory programs and of public facilitation of private lawsuits.

Figure 1 tells most of the story. Led by robust military budgets during the late 1970s and the 1980s, discretionary spending increased. Until 1988 the estimated costs associated with federal regulatory activities declined in constant dollars as the economy realized tens of billions in savings from deregulation of the transportation and energy industries and from the Reagan administration's concerted efforts to curb costly new regulations. Afterward, however, regulatory costs turned up sharply and have been on the rise ever since. A profusion of new rules and legal liabilities increasingly bore down on business decisions about products, payrolls, and personnel practices. By the mid-1990s these costs were approaching $700 billion annually—a sum greater than the entire national output of Canada.

Explanations

Whatever else explains this trend, surely it demonstrates that fiscal constraints have not limited the ingenuity of politicians and their clients. Policies that are barely visible on the budget books can still intervene massively on behalf of special interests—and can do so, conveniently, without worsening the deficit or imposing transparent tax increases.

For instance, rules that have encouraged the use of ethanol (a fuel made from corn) are a kind of pork for corn farmers, only less obvious than, say, appropriating millions for irrigation projects in Corn Belt states. Often costing billions of dollars per cancer prevented, the Superfund law to remove carcinogenic toxins from waste dumps is charging society a small fortune. But Superfund's congressional appropriation is suitably modest, and the program is a gravy train for particular groups, like the thousands of lawyers engaged in cleanup litigation. Similarly, antidumping provisions in the trade laws, devised to regulate "unfair" foreign price competition, require small budgetary outlays to administer. At times, however, these regulations force consumers to pay markedly higher prices to protect a handful of domestic companies. The practice of crafting protections and preferences for selected groups in the name of civil rights is a relatively low-budget operation too. But this regulatory regime nonetheless reaches deep into the private sector, dispensing rewards to the regime's extensive vested interests. There is no shortage of examples of Washington's off-budget spoils system.

Though the regulatory pork barrel frequently serves well-organized constituencies, its scope tends to be broader than the traditional treats (a new post office here, a new road or sewer there) that members of Congress offered to their districts. In contemporary American politics, this difference is an added

Figure 1

Comparison of Federal Regulatory Costs and Discretionary Budget Outlays, 1977–1996

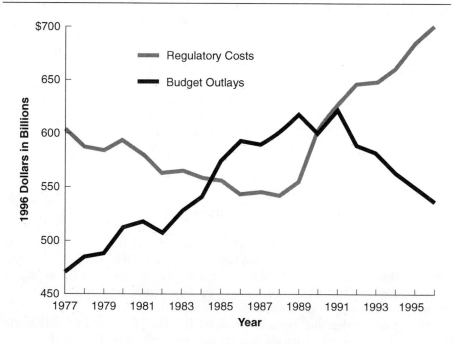

advantage for members of Congress who need increasingly to curry favor with *national* lobbies and pressure groups that provide valuable political backing. The pattern of influence and obligations is reflected in congressional campaign finance. Whereas candidates in House elections, for example, used to rely for support almost entirely on local constituents and state parties, now the winners draw almost 40 percent of their contributions from political action committees, that is, from the funding arms of national interest groups. Prosaic projects, reaching only hometown folks, do not satisfy many of these hungry organizations; they expect, instead, a diet rich in ubiquitous social mandates: more safety devices in *all* motor vehicles, pure water in *any* river, equality of athletic programs within virtually *every* university, prohibition of smoking from sea to shining sea, and so on.

The number and cost of such commandments also keep mounting because of the extraordinary legitimacy they are accorded. In part, this situation reflects the skill of their advocates and patrons at marshaling notions of fairness or rights. Thus, the trump card played by champions of rigid antipollution regulations is that all citizens have "an inherent right" to a pristine environment. The mandating of benefits for each new class of disadvantaged people reflexively summons the Fourteenth Amendment, rather than a plainspoken demand for government funding. The clinching argument in many product injury verdicts seems to be that buyers should bear no responsibility for the risks they run since consumers are entitled to be absolutely safe. The time-honored defense of antidumping regulations is that they uphold the economic rights of firms and workers victimized by foreign predators who employ "pauper labor."

Because regulatory pork barreling is presented not as a system of special favors, but as a means of honoring solemn legal claims, the claimants are often given a direct hand in enforcement. Many regulatory activities, in other words, gain momentum because they deputize vigilantes. Most environmental statutes and consumer protection laws invite citizen suits to ensure compliance. Of late, the employment laws have induced a surge of job-bias class actions. Various interests are parties to these lawsuits or become beneficiaries of them. Besides awarding significant sums to nonprofit advocacy groups, settlements have ordered a bevy of purchasing contracts and franchises to designated for-profit organizations and produced a billable hours bonanza for the contingency lawyers and for a cottage industry of diversity management consultants.

Concerns

Does all this pose a problem? A prosperous, civilized country should be expected to regulate harmful types of economic fraud and abuse, to reduce socially corrosive inequities, to bar morally repugnant forms of discrimination, and to protect the health and safety of its citizens. Despite the soaring costs of the policies produced by these exertions, their net worth is sometimes impossible to measure. Even though many of them advantage certain groups while disadvantaging others, society may have decided that such uneven outcomes are virtuous and just. And the fact that politicians pull in campaign funds and votes with the decisions does not, in itself, invalidate them. Pork, courtesy of other people's tax payments or of regulatory exactions, is a staple of politics. Without it, democratic government would lose some muscle as well as flab.

What is unsettling, however, is the seeming ease or insouciance with which current political arrangements seem to crank out expensive directives that invoke high principle to conduct . . . "public affairs for private advantage." The old pork barrel, stuffed as it was with federal bricks, mortar, and macadam, at least had to be paid for with tax dollars or with deficit spending. The favoritism was explicit, concrete (often literally), and visibly priced. Even the subtler fiscal delicacy, targeted tax relief, has had reasonably obvious budgetary implications, which sooner or later would alarm deficit hawks. Wasteful as these expenditures and tax measures frequently are, at least they have borne clearly the signatures of elected officials, who occasionally might be asked to answer for the consequences of their actions.

The new system is murkier. Its contents extend far beyond earmarked appropriations or tax breaks to a stack of selective legal strictures that appear budget-neutral and "tax free," and that are partly in the custody, so to speak, of unaccountable private attorneys general. In contrast to honest spending and tax bills, no consistent effort is made to score the economic impacts of the voluminous mandates, especially those that emanate from the executive branch. Hence, as [economists] Robert Hahn and Robert Litan recently reported, approximately half the federal government's social regulations issued between 1982 and mid-1996 generated costs plainly in excess of social benefits, yet remained unchallenged.

The rise of legal and regulatory burdens may seem of trivial consequence to America's formidable economy, but in fact the productivity and incomes of Americans would have grown more rapidly if the nation's cost-oblivious penchant for regulatory sanctions and suits had been brought under better control. As a conservative estimate, just ridding the *Federal Register* of the manifold rules since 1982 that flagrantly flunked an elementary cost-benefit test would have increased the size of the economic pie by almost $300 billion. Fixing countless other programs whose net benefits are not being maximized would "grow the economy" further. The penalty for not seizing these opportunities now while the going is good is likely to worsen substantially in the years ahead. In the next millennium, the competitive heat of the global marketplace will intensify and so will the incentives for firms to outsource across borders. Especially if encumbered by too many injudicious laws and lawsuits, more U.S. businesses will simply off-load more of their operations. In the course of this industrial upheaval, millions of American workers are likely to be sacked or, at a minimum, to see their wages stagnate.

Prudent Corrections

Not unaware of this prospect, the [1995–1996] 104th Congress made some tentative progress toward redressing abuses of the regulatory state. Legislation was passed requiring federal agencies to weigh the costs and benefits of major new mandates and to submit their studies to Congress for review. Narrower statutes were enacted eliminating zero-tolerance standards for health risks in some consumer goods (processed foods, for example) or at least requiring regulators to publish cost justifications for safety standards (as for drinking water). In an attempt to curb the excesses of what might be called privatized social regulation—in particular, the rampant civil litigation that purports to protect consumers—Congress succeeded in setting minimal limits on the rewards to shareholders and plaintiffs' attorneys for suing companies frivolously.

To call such steps anything but a bare beginning, however, would be a delusion. The shareholder "strike" suits bill should have, but didn't, clear the way for a broader legal reform proposal that would have restricted punitive damages in product liability cases generally. (President Clinton vetoed both bills, but only one of his vetoes was overridden.) So far, the new procedural requirements for the formulation of executive rules, in turn, have proved mostly exhortatory. In only one case, the Pipeline Safety and Partnership Act of 1995, is an executive bureau expressly enjoined from promulgating standards whose costs are unjustified by benefits. In the rest, administrators are only asked to consider and report their cost-benefit assessments and to explain any rule-making that discards them. The provisions for congressional oversight of proposed rules are constrained by tight statutory time-frames, presidential veto power over resolutions of disapproval, and too limited a role for the legislative branch's top economic analysts. (The 1995 Unfunded Mandates Reform Act authorizes the Congressional Budget Office to "score" regulatory acts of Congress, but not those of the executive. The latter's rules, according to the Small Business Regulatory Enforcement Fairness Act of 1996, are to be examined by the General Accounting Office, arguably under unrealistic deadlines.) Perhaps least satisfactory is the grandfathering* of existing laws and rulings. With a few notable exceptions—such as the Delaney clause, which barred any level of risk in food additives—old regulations, no matter how questionable, remain on the books.

Some of these deficiencies might be partially remedied by more fine-tuning. A pending bill, the so-called Regulatory Improvement Act authored by Senators Fred Thompson (R-TN) and Carl Levin (D-MI), would try to ensure, for instance, that agencies take seriously their evaluations and risk assessments of new rules by introducing a process of independent peer review. The bill would also extend methodically a similar review process to extant regulations.

---

*To "grandfather" a policy into law means that a current policy will be exempted from the impact of a newly enacted statute.

Even these corrections, however, will not suffice to sharpen the lines of political accountability for regulatory pork. A proliferation of agency analyses, peer committees, and reporting requirements is no substitute for democratic *choice*. Ultimately, the buck ought to stop with Congress itself, where members should have to cast transparent up or down votes on all the government's off-budget activism, just as votes are recorded on other important taxes and expenditures. But unless these decisions are well-informed, legislators will render them meaningless, if they render them at all. One way to minimize evasion might be to expand the capacity of the Congressional Budget Office to delineate for the legislature society's gains and losses from every major regulatory initiative, much as CBO performs this annual service with every big budgetary item. A joint report by the American Enterprise Institute and the Brookings Institution published last July suggested experimenting along these lines.

Beyond these institutional adjustments lie larger priorities. Sooner or later, policymakers in the United States will have to face the fact that inordinate legal contestation pervades the way this society seeks to regulate itself. Much of this punitive "adversarial legalism" . . . lines the pockets of lawyers and professional litigants while accomplishing little else. The resulting drag on American economic performance, though little noticed at the moment, may become considerably less affordable in time. Part and parcel of serious regulatory reform, therefore, has to be a reasonable contraction of federal enactments that stimulate, indeed sometimes sponsor, our seemingly insatiable appetite for litigation. This won't be easy, for it will mean rolling back an oversupply of suits everywhere, from the workplace to the doctor's office, as well as entertaining fewer complaints about sagging stock quotations, risky products, and many of life's hazards, misfortunes, and disappointments.

Questions for Discussion

1. The essence of traditional pork barrel politics has been the distribution of favors for political support (including, but not limited to, campaign contributions). What is the difference between what Nivola terms "regulatory pork" and traditional spending on roads, the military, or public works projects?
2. Implementing policy is a difficult and frequently unrewarding task. Does the new pork barrel regulation suffer from an absence of attention to how policies are implemented? How could oversight of such policies be improved?

14.3

The Politics and Realities of Medicare

Eric Cohen

More than any other domestic policy area, health care represents the most difficult set of challenges facing the American political system. And within the realm of health care, no single policy is more problematic than Medicare. Now more than forty years in operation, Medicare serves as the cornerstone of health care for the elderly; it has other provisions, but serving the elderly is its major mission. As more and more Americans reach age sixty-five, Medicare faces a mounting challenge to provide the care that it has promised. Moreover, Medicare did not cover prescription drugs when it first won congressional approval in 1965, largely because pharmaceuticals represented only a modest element of overall care. Over the past forty years, drug-based treatment has soared, as have costs, especially when insurance was unavailable.

In 2003, Congress narrowly passed Medicare D (as detailed in selection 10.4), which provided substantial subsidies for prescription drugs, albeit in a complex format. In this selection, Eric Cohen uses the 2003 Medicare Modernization Act (MMA) to illustrate the long-term issues facing a Medicare program that has come under increasing pressure—both in terms of maintaining levels of care and establishing firm financial footing. Using various elements of MMA to illustrate his argument, Cohen offers an evenhanded, if ultimately depressing, assessment of Medicare as in "permanent crisis." Perversely, Medicare's problems are those caused by its success, which "seems to bring its own novel miseries—whether dying alone in a nursing home, or living through a heart attack to suffer years of dementia." In the end, we have to pay the piper for desired treatments, Cohen notes, which represent "a cost we would be fools not to pay, but also fools to ignore."

Trying to understand the economics of Medicare is a difficult business, but nearly everyone agrees that things do not look good. In March 2004, the Medicare Board of Trustees issued its annual report on the financial

Eric Cohen is editor of the *New Atlantis* and director of the Project on Biotechnology and American Democracy at the Ethics and Public Policy Center.

Eric Cohen, "The Politics and Realities of Medicare," *The Public Interest*, No. 156 (Summer 2004): 37–50.

health of Medicare Part A, which funds primarily hospital expenses, and Medicare Part B, which funds outpatient care. The prognosis was grim: The Hospital Insurance (HI) "trust fund is projected to be exhausted in 2019— 7 years earlier than estimated in last year's report. . . . The long-range projections for HI continue to show a very substantial imbalance. . . . The Part B premium and corresponding general revenue transfers will need to be increased sharply for 2005 to match projected costs." To fix this "imbalance," the report concluded, "would require very substantial increases in revenues and/or reductions in benefits."

The Medicare Modernization Act (MMA), signed into law in December 2003, has no doubt made this financial crisis even worse. The new law provides partial prescription drug coverage for all desiring seniors—with an estimated cost between $395 billion and $534 billion over the next decade, before most of the drug-hungry baby boomers even retire. Many analysts believe these estimates are already far too low, and that policy makers have conveniently avoided discussing the benefit's costs in the second decade and beyond. The bill also includes a combination of other reforms. . . .

All of these additional measures are overshadowed by the new drug benefit that begins in 2006—the largest expansion of Medicare since the program was created in 1965. Specifically, the new benefit will cover 75 percent of drug costs between $250 and $2,250, provide no coverage between $2,250 and $5,100 (the so-called "hole in the doughnut"), and cover 95 percent of drug costs of $5,100 and over. Participation in the program is voluntary; the benefit will be administered by publicly approved private companies; and the premiums are estimated to cost $35 per month, with different private-sector plans competing to offer the best drug prices, and each plan required to offer drugs in every therapeutic category.

Not surprisingly, the debate over MMA was politically bitter and complex in legislative terms. It was pushed hard by the Bush administration, the Republican establishment, and some moderate Democrats—who saw it as the best way to give seniors the drug benefit they desire (a political plus), without breaking the bank or engineering a government take-over of the drug industry. The law was bitterly opposed by the majority of Democrats, who believe the drug benefits are too small and the "pay-off" to pharmaceutical companies too big; and it was attacked by many conservatives, who believe it will expand the grip of the welfare state and eventually lead to price controls, tax hikes, and a slowed economy.

MMA is a significant achievement, and in many ways an improvement. It corrects a genuine gap in Medicare, a program that was created before prescription drugs were a central part of modern medicine. And it significantly helps those seniors who are currently ineligible for Medicaid but still too poor to buy prescription drugs without economic hardship.

But one can also understand why so many people—Left, Right, and center— see the bill as irresponsible or inadequate, and why no one really believes it is what Medicare needs over the long-term. "We are building a new expansion onto a house that's teetering on a cliff," says Republican Senator Don Nickles. "It cynically uses the elderly's need for prescription drugs as a Trojan horse to reshape Medicare," says Democratic Senator Ted Kennedy. "Medicare has become pork barrel. It plays to retirees' desires and raises their discretionary income. The question of generational justice is nearly absent," says centrist columnist Robert J. Samuelson. The new law expands an entitlement that is already the fastest growing part of the federal budget. It leaves middle-class citizens with significant drug bills to pay, and thus invites future demands to "sweeten the benefits." And it punts the hardest social questions down the road—not only about the economics of Medicare, but about the intersection of modern medicine, an aging society, and the character of American society as a whole. These deeper questions are what lie at the core of the Medicare "crisis."

How Medicare Works

To understand the implications of the new Medicare bill and the political disagreements surrounding it, one needs to understand how Medicare works as a whole. This is no easy task, but a few salient points are worth noting.

First, Medicare is primarily a federally funded, third-party payer, fee-for-service program. In other words, when seniors get sick, they go to the doctor and the government pays most of the bill. Beneficiaries pay some premiums. . . . Seniors who participate in traditional Medicare (roughly 88 percent) have the freedom to see any doctor who will see them. This is generally wonderful for beneficiaries: They have access to all the care they desire. But it is problematic for society as a whole, since there are limited incentives for seniors to cut their own health-care costs, and there is limited room within the heavily regulated system for private insurers to improve efficiency by creating health-care networks or tailoring services to individual needs. This economic problem will only get worse, many believe, as expensive new medical technologies become available, as the percentage of the national population on Medicare increases, and as the average age of Medicare beneficiaries rises and their health deteriorates.

Second, Medicare is a major part of the "hidden subsidy" and "price control" system that now shapes American health care. The government sets the prices by fiat for all the medical services covered under Medicare—with different physician groups lobbying constantly for increases to the reimbursement rate for their own specialties, and the government trying constantly to keep up with ongoing changes in the nature of medical care. This system allows government to exert some control over Medicare costs—though reimbursement cuts in the past have often resulted in reduced access to care, reduced quality of care, or increased billing for a larger volume of services. And of course, government doesn't get the prices right. This means the system only works because those services that are over-reimbursed subsidize those services that are under-reimbursed—for example, over-payment for cancer drugs subsidizes under-payment for cancer treatment. This system of cross-subsidizing exists both *within* Medicare and *between* Medicare and private-sector health insurance.

Third, Medicare's system of government-controlled pricing also shapes *how* patients are treated, and not always for the better. In some cases, people seek not the best or cheapest treatments for a given condition but those treatments that are covered by Medicare. In other cases, avoiding inexpensive but uncovered therapies leads to expensive but covered emergencies in the future. . . .

Finally, the current Medicare system does not pay for long-term care. If someone suffers a stroke, for example, Medicare covers the expenses incurred in its immediate aftermath—hospital care, 21 days of skilled nursing care with no deductible, and 79 additional days of skilled nursing care for a subsidized rate of $109.50 per day. However, once the patient no longer requires skilled medical treatment but still requires constant personal care, Medicare pays nothing. This leaves individuals and families with a range of hard choices: family caretaking by a spouse or child; professional caretaking paid for out-of-pocket; or self-impoverishment until one qualifies for Medicaid, which does pay for long-term care, either by spending down one's assets or moving them in advance to one's children or siblings. The result is that a significant number of seniors who live to 65 end up on Medicaid—a welfare program—at some point before dying, including many who were self-sufficient throughout most of their lives. . . .

The Rich and the Poor

In trying to make sense of the significance of MMA, it is perhaps useful to begin with the two dimensions of the bill that have won nearly universal support: extra subsidies for low-income seniors to purchase prescription drugs and additional premiums for high-income seniors who participate in Medicare Part B. During the 2002 debate about prescription drug coverage, liberal commentator Michael Kinsley told policy makers the following: "When Congress takes up a drug benefit again, it should keep things simple and concentrate on the risk, approaching a certainty, that it wishes to prevent: people doing without drugs—or without food—because of the cost. That means concentrating on poor people."

In the MMA, Congress took his advice—about helping the poor, if not keeping things simple. Beginning in June 2004, the bill created a temporary "drug discount card" that aims to give all participating seniors a 10 to 25 percent discount and low-income seniors a $600 direct subsidy. The permanent drug benefit, which includes substantial out-of-pocket "cost-sharing" for middle-income and high-income seniors, requires only minimal cost-sharing for those below 150 percent of the poverty level. This includes roughly a third of all Medicare beneficiaries. . . .

No doubt the liberal and conservative reasons behind such support are not identical. Conservatives see subsidies for the poor as a way to limit the expansion of Medicare in general—by eventually making it a welfare program, not a universal entitlement. They believe that government action should be limited to helping those who cannot help themselves, while leaving individuals with middling means to plan, invest, and make choices in the marketplace. Liberals believe that society has a special obligation to help those who have been "left behind," and that the rich have a special obligation to support them. But both liberals and conservatives typically accept the notion that subsidizing the elderly poor (who are also chronically poor, with incomes likely to fall rather than rise) is a proper responsibility of the state. They disagree about whether MMA does this in the best possible way. Democrats believe that state-controlled drug prices are crucial to control costs, while Republicans believe America needs a subsidized voucher system that allows the poor to purchase drugs in the marketplace. But they both agree that drug benefits should be means-tested, with the poor paying less and everyone else paying more.

MMA also singles out wealthy seniors in a novel way by means-testing Medicare Part B benefits. Part B (also called "Supplementary Medical Insurance," or SMI) is a voluntary program, covering physician and outpatient care, in which nearly all seniors participate. At present, the premium is 25 percent . . . of the total cost of the benefit—the same for all seniors, regardless of health, income, or the amount of medical care they need (though patients pay roughly 20 percent co-insurance per doctor visit). In this way, Medicare has always been (in both Parts A and B) a universal entitlement, not a welfare benefit.

Beginning in 2007, however, Part B beneficiaries with incomes over $80,000 for individuals (or $160,000 for a married couple) will pay gradually escalating premiums, with individuals earning over $200,000 (or couples earning over $400,000) paying premiums of 80 percent. The cost savings of such a change are likely minor compared to the cost of Medicare as a whole, since the higher premiums will affect only an estimated 1.2 million seniors out of the 35 million now on Medicare. But the principle it establishes for future reform may be significant: namely, the idea that means-testing is a potential route for further cost-cutting. As liberal Democratic Senator Dianne Feinstein and the aforementioned conservative Senator Don Nickles wrote together in the *Washington Post*, "Why should low-income families pay 75 percent of the bill for Ross Perot to have a checkup?"

Of course, this idea still makes both sides a bit nervous—liberals because they fear the unraveling of Medicare as a universal entitlement, conservatives because they fear out-of-control taxes on successful wage-earners. But in such a bitter debate, this is a crucial point of consensus. It suggests that the real fights are not about the rich (who can take care of themselves) and the poor (who everyone agrees need public assistance) but the middle-class, whose prospects and obligations are more complex and ambiguous. And it suggests that the real disagreements are not about state subsidies for health care, which everyone agrees should exist, but how these subsidies should be spent and how health care should be delivered.

Liberals and Conservatives

The MMA debate also made clear that liberals and conservatives have fundamentally different ideas about the relationship between medicine, the state, and the elderly. They disagree both in their assumptions about how the world works and their priorities regarding what is most important. Neither side is finally happy with the Medicare bill as passed, but more conservatives than liberals perceived MMA as better than nothing and less disastrous than it could have been. It was, overwhelmingly, a Republican bill. That said, there were many exceptions—including conservative lawmakers who bitterly opposed the legislation as excessive, unnecessary, and misguided, and liberal lawmakers who supported it as a way to put a drug entitlement in place that could be expanded in the future.

The conservative idea of Medicare reform is rooted in three basic principles: First, government control over medical pricing and inadequate incentives for individuals to control their own health-care costs lead to waste and inefficiencies. Conservatives seek to replace traditional Medicare with a "premium support" system—which basically means giving all seniors vouchers, then allowing them to purchase the private-sector health-care plan that most suits their needs. They believe this will improve the "efficiency of health care delivery," . . . and thus maintain or improve the quality of care while both cutting costs and freeing resources for investment in new medical technologies.

Second, conservatives believe that government control over drug prices—whether by purchasing Medicare drugs directly or setting prices for drugs the way Medicare sets prices for physician services—would cripple the pharmaceutical industry. They argue that the price of many drugs is artificially high because such profits are necessary to recoup the money spent on past research failures and to make the investments necessary for finding more and better drugs in the future. If government sets drug prices too low, investors will pull out of the drug business for fear of making abnormally low returns. The result would be a great slow-down of medical progress.

Finally, conservatives believe that medicine must be balanced against other human goods—both by individuals and by society as a whole. They worry that the benign tyranny of medicine will crowd out other public necessities or limit other human aspirations. And they believe that a more privatized system would ensure adequate public resources for defense, education, and other priorities, and allow individuals to decide whether to put their own discretionary income toward marginally better health care or toward other goods (education for grandchildren, vacations, home improvements, for example) that give them a higher "subjective value." . . .

Liberals tend to share the same central goal as conservatives—better medicine for the elderly—but differ both in their priorities and their assumptions. First, they believe that only a government-run program can ensure that all seniors have access to quality care. A voucher system, they believe, would leave the poorest and sickest seniors worse off. Private plans would cherry-pick the healthiest seniors; premiums for the very sick would increase; and the poor would be left with great disruptions and great inadequacies in care—including high out-of-pocket costs, restrictions on doctors, and caps on certain therapies.

Second, liberals believe that government should use its buying power to demand lower drug prices and lessen the economic burden for poor seniors. They believe drug companies are both too profitable and too manipulative—charging too much for drugs, and producing drugs that promise advantages over generic alternatives that are often more fanciful than real. They point to lower drug prices in Canada and Western Europe—where state-run health-care systems negotiate the prices directly—and believe America should do the same. While they believe drug access in the present is more important than drug development in the future, most liberals do not accept that there is a trade-off between the two.

Finally, liberals see health care as a "right," and they are less likely to weigh it against other economic, civic, or human goods. They believe the real luxuries of life are enjoyed by a small percentage of wealthy Americans, and that raising their taxes would fund a more egalitarian and constantly improving health-care system for the elderly. They also believe valuable resources are squandered on unnecessary wars and corporate pork—money that could be used to pay for health care at home. When it comes to controlling rising health-care costs, they believe government can exert its buying power to reduce prices, and they do not believe this will lower the quality of care.

In the real world, of course, those who wish to govern must moderate their theories, and those who are in power have a much greater incentive to do so, since they can claim credit for "delivering the goods." In the MMA, neither conservatives nor liberals got their ideal reforms. Conservatives wanted open-ended competition between private plans and traditional Medicare, but they lost. Liberals wanted government-negotiated drug prices and drug benefits with virtually no deductibles, but they too lost. . . . For now, the major feature of the Medicare bill—the new drug benefit—. . . combines liberal and conservative elements, but satisfies the theoretical orthodoxies of neither. It includes a real, but limited, drug entitlement—with drug prices set in the marketplace, not by government fiat. It is a moderate, if expensive, reform. But whether it is prudent or addresses the deeper issues remains an open question.

Success or Failure?

The fact is that, if Medicare were being created from scratch, it would almost certainly include a prescription drug benefit. But there are also good reasons to believe that adding a universal drug benefit was unnecessary or unwise, and that the sense of urgency in doing so was more artificial than real—a battle for senior-friendly voters (young, not old) who presumed a crisis that never really existed. . . . A government survey of Medicare recipients in 2002 asked the following question: "In the last six months, how much of a problem, if any, was it to get the prescription medicine you needed?" The answers: 86.4 percent, not a problem; 9.4 percent, a small problem; 4.2 percent, a big problem. And so one could have imagined a targeted subsidy for low-income seniors in need, and national acceptance that drugs are just one of those things on which seniors will have to spend their own money.

But for the politically ambitious, drug coverage had already become a "must deliver" issue, and for the country, it had become a political expectation. Moreover, it is unclear how the above survey from 2002 meshes with other realities, such as the high number of low-income Medicare beneficiaries who will now be eligible for drug subsidies, or the deepening erosion of employee-based drug coverage for retirees. Clearly, there existed some real hardship, though hardly a national crisis. And clearly, both parties believed they needed to pass a prescription drug benefit in order to remain attractive to senior and senior-friendly voters.

Given these realities, there is a certain wisdom in the way MMA's drug benefit is designed. It establishes a baseline of coverage for all seniors, and thus assures universal access to at least the most urgently needed medications. It provides genuine insurance against catastrophic drug costs—that is, against suddenly losing all of one's financial resources in a desperate effort to stay alive. But MMA also establishes the principle that not everything can be paid for by government; that medicine must be balanced against other national priorities and other human goods; and that middle-class individuals will have to support their own middling drug bills. The "hole in the doughnut," for all the mockery it has received, is sensible in its guiding principles.

But in practice, of course, many unanswered questions remain. . . . Will it drive companies that offer drug benefits to retirees to stop doing so? Will it create an artificial demand for expensive drugs with limited medical benefits? Will the private-sector organizations that the drug benefit relies upon come into existence? Will the "doughnut hole" eventually be filled? Will government impose price controls if the cost of the new drug benefits far outstrips current expectations? Will the modest changes, like means-testing benefits and medical savings accounts, pave the way toward more fundamental reforms? How will increased access to prescription drugs affect the overall health of seniors and thus the trajectory of aging and death? Will the drug benefit reduce the costs of Medicare Part A and Part B by keeping seniors healthy? Or will it increase Medicare costs by preventing acute causes of death in favor of long, expensive, chronic diseases? . . .

Such questions—unanswerable for now, but important to ask—point to the grave shortcomings of the new law. MMA puts off any serious confrontation with the pending financial problems of Medicare as a whole, and it fails to reckon with the deeper human, generational, and medical realities that underlie our sense of impending "crisis." More deeply, it fails to grasp or even consider the novelty of the world to come: a world of aging baby-boomers, with fewer children, geographically scattered, with high rates of divorce, and a greater likelihood of living long enough to suffer diseases (like Alzheimer's) that create long-term states of dependence.

The hardest decisions about Medicare in the future may ultimately be faced by the middle-class members of the middle-aged generation—and specifically, by members of Generation X in their 40s and 50s. They will have to decide what they are willing to pay and what they are willing to give up, and they will have to balance the demands of aging parents and dependent children. When the financial balance finally hits, they may have to choose between higher taxes or lower benefits; between sending their child to Harvard or their parent to Sunrise Assisted Living; between raising their own retirement age or cutting funding for national defense; between forcing their proud father to become eligible for Medicaid or giving up their inheritance to pay for the nursing home.

The Dilemmas of Progress

Despite the bitter disagreements over Medicare, liberals and conservatives share two basic assumptions: the ideal of self-determination and the ideal of medical progress. They both want more choice for the aging, and they both believe that more drugs for more people is an unequivocal good, even if they disagree about how best to achieve these goals. And so they are both, in different ways, prone to utopianism, believing that the right policies will create a world where the Medicare crisis is largely solved. This is a fantasy shared by liberal and conservative thinkers alike, whether packaged in the rhetoric of new vouchers or new entitlements.

In reality, the Medicare crisis is permanent. So long as we continue to see aging and death as crises, we will feel the need to spend increasing amounts on the aging ill. Medicare confronts us with the impossibility of winning the war against time, and the limited capacity of rapidly improving medical technologies to fulfill our rapidly rising expectations. Our problems are largely those of success, and success seems to bring its own novel miseries—whether dying alone in a nursing home, or living through a heart attack to suffer years of dementia, or betraying our aging, declining parents to meet the demands of our growing children. This is the real human cost of our prescription-drug world—a cost we would be fools not to pay, but also fools to ignore.

Questions for Discussion

1. Look over the legislative circumstances of passing the Medicare Modernization Act as presented by Mann and Ornstein in selection 10.4. Does the political pressure exerted in that instance relate to the quality of the drug policy passed? More broadly, how does our legislative process (along with the role of the president) affect the kind of legislation we get?
2. Why is health care policy such a problem area within the United States? How does the MMA debate illuminate the differences between liberals and conservatives, broadly defined, on health care policy?

America Unbound: The Bush Revolution in Foreign Policy

Ivo H. Daalder and James M. Lindsay

Without a doubt the terrorist attacks of September 11, 2001, changed the United States policy toward the rest of the world, especially toward nations and forces we deemed dangerous. The subsequent Afghan and Iraq invasions demonstrate our newfound aggressiveness, even as we struggle to bring stability and democracy to those countries. One persistent question addresses whether our post-9/11 behavior has largely flowed out of a reaction to the attacks, or if there exists a more coherent, deeper set of policies, based on a coherent philosophy, which underlies our actions.

In this selection, Ivo H. Daalder and James M. Lindsay argue that just such a set of principles does exist and that it has been in place from the beginning of the Bush administration in 2001. Two basic tenets stand at the base of Bush's revolutionary approach to world affairs. First, America would not be constrained by other nations or by international agreements, as it sought to address the dangers in the world. Second, America should *use* its strength to change the status quo. Most observers would agree with these two basic points, but the authors go on to argue that changes in policy direction have come from President Bush himself, not his hawkish policy advisors. Such an interpretation downgrades the importance of his "neoconservative" advisors and offers a distinctive view of George W. Bush as a "revolutionary" leader, whose success will be determined long after he has left office.

When George W. Bush peered out the window of Air Force One as it flew over Baghdad in early June [2003], he had reason to be pleased. He had just completed a successful visit to Europe and the Middle

---

Ivo H. Daalder is a senior fellow in the Brookings Foreign Policy Studies Program. James M. Lindsay is the Tom Slick Chair for International Affairs and Director of the Robert S. Strauss Center for International Security and Law at the LBJ School of Public Affairs at the University of Texas–Austin.

Ivo H. Daalder and James M. Lindsay, "America Unbound: The Bush Revolution in Foreign Policy." *The Brookings Review*, Vol. 21, No. 4 (Fall 2003): pp. 2–6. Reprinted by permission of The Brookings Institution.

East. The trip began in Warsaw, where he had the opportunity to personally thank Poland for being one of the two European countries to contribute troops to the Iraq War effort. He then traveled to Russia to celebrate the 300th birthday of St. Petersburg. He flew on to Evian, a city in the French Alps, to attend a summit meeting of the heads of the world's major economies. He next stopped in Sharm el Sheik, Egypt, for a meeting with moderate Arab leaders, before heading to Aqaba, Jordan, on the shore of the Red Sea to discuss the road map for peace with the Israeli and Palestinian prime ministers. He made his final stop in Doha, Qatar, where troops at U.S. Central Command greeted him with thunderous applause. Now Bush looked down on the city that American troops had seized only weeks before.

Bush's seven-day, six-nation trip was in many ways a victory lap to celebrate America's triumph in the Iraq War—a war that many of the leaders Bush met on his trip had opposed. But in a larger sense he and his advisers saw it as a vindication of his leadership. During his first 30 months in office, the man from Midland had started a foreign policy revolution. He had discarded many of the constraints that had bound the United States to its allies and redefined key principles that had governed American engagement in the world for more than half a century. Like most revolutions, Bush's had numerous critics. Yet he now traveled through Europe and the Middle East not as a penitent making amends but as a leader commanding respect. America unbound was remaking the course of international politics. Bush was the rare revolutionary who had succeeded. Or had he?

The Bush Revolution

What precisely was the Bush revolution in foreign policy? At its broadest level, it rested on two beliefs. The first was that in a dangerous world the best—if not the only—way to ensure America's security was to shed the constraints imposed by friends, allies, and international institutions. Maximizing America's freedom to act was essential because the unique position of the United States made it the most likely target for any country or group hostile to the West. Americans could not count on others to protect them; countries inevitably ignored threats that did not involve them. Moreover, formal arrangements would inevitably constrain the ability of the United States to make the most of its unrivaled power. Gulliver must shed the constraints that he helped the Lilliputians weave.

The second belief was that an America unbound should use its strength to change the status quo in the world. Bush did not argue that the United States keep its powder dry while it waited for dangers to gather. Whereas John Quincy Adams—the only other son of a president later to occupy the White House—had held that the United States should not go abroad "in search of monsters to destroy," Bush argued that America would be imperiled if it failed to do just that. "Time is not on our side," he warned in the "Axis of Evil" speech, his 2002 State of the Union address. "I will not wait on events, while dangers gather. I will not stand by, as peril draws closer and closer. The United States of America will not permit the world's most dangerous regimes to threaten us with the world's most destructive weapons." That logic guided the Iraq War, and it animated Bush's efforts to deal with other rogue states.

These fundamental beliefs had important consequences for the practice of American foreign policy. One was a disdain for the sorts of multinational institutions and arrangements developed by presidents from Truman through Clinton and a decided preference for the unilateral exercise of American power. Unilateralism was appealing to Bush and his advisers because it was often easier and more efficient, at least in the short term, than multilateralism. In the Kosovo war, for example, Bush and his advisers believed that the task of coordinating the views of all NATO members greatly complicated the military effort. But in the Afghanistan war, Pentagon planners did not need to subject any of their decisions to foreign approval. This is not to say that Bush flatly ruled out working with others. Rather, his preferred form of multilateralism—to be indulged when unilateral action is impossible or unwise—involved building ad hoc coalitions of the willing, or what Richard Haass, a former adviser to Colin Powell, has called "multilateralism à la carte."

Second, preemption was no longer a last resort of American foreign policy. In a world in which weapons of mass destruction were spreading and terrorists and rogue states were readying to attack in unconventional ways, Bush argued in a report laying out his administration's national security strategy, "the United States can no longer solely rely on a reactive posture as we have in the past. . . . We cannot let our enemies strike first." Indeed, the United States should be prepared to act not just preemptively against imminent threats, but also preventively against potential threats. Vice President Dick Cheney was emphatic on this point in justifying the overthrow of Saddam Hussein on the eve of the Iraq War. "There's no question about who is going to prevail if there is military action. And there's no question but what it is going to be cheaper and less costly to do now than it will be to wait a year or two years or three years until he's developed even more deadly weapons, perhaps nuclear weapons."

Third, the United States should use its unprecedented power to change the regimes in rogue states. The idea of regime change was not new to American foreign policy. The Eisenhower administration engineered the overthrow of Iranian Prime Minister Mohammed Mossadegh; the CIA trained Cuban exiles in a botched bid to oust Fidel Castro; Ronald Reagan channeled aid to the Nicaraguan contras to overthrow the Sandinistas; and Bill Clinton helped Serb opposition forces get rid of Slobodan Milosevic. What was different in the Bush presidency was the willingness, even in the absence of a direct attack on the United States, to use U.S. military forces for the express purpose of toppling other governments. This was the gist of both the Afghanistan and the Iraq wars. It rested on the belief that if the United States pushed, nobody could push back.

September 11

The Bush revolution did not start, as many have suggested, on September 11. The worldview that drove it existed long before jet planes plowed into the Twin Towers and the Pentagon. Bush outlined his philosophy while he was on the campaign trail. Most commentators failed to notice what he was saying because they were concerned more with how much he knew about the world than with what he believed. Bush began implementing his ideas as soon as he took the oath of office. His belief in the need for an America unbound was behind his pursuit of missile defense. It was also behind his rejection of the Kyoto Protocol on climate change, the International Criminal Court, and a host of other multilateral agreements he criticized or abandoned during the first eight months of his presidency.

What September 11 provided was the motive to enact the Bush revolution rapidly and without hesitation. Foreign policy went from being a secondary priority of his presidency to being its defining mission. "I'm here for a reason," Bush told his chief political adviser, Karl Rove, shortly after the attacks, "and this is going to be how we're going to be judged." He told Japanese Prime Minister Junichiro Koizumi something similar. "History will be the judge, but it won't judge well somebody who doesn't act, somebody who just bides time here." The war on terrorism became an issue that boiled in his blood, and he intended to fight it in his fashion.

September 11 also gave Bush the opportunity to enact his revolution without fear of being challenged at home. Congressional displeasure with Bush's handling of foreign policy had grown throughout the summer of 2001. Some Democrats even thought it could be a winning issue for them in the midterm elections. In the wake of the attacks, however, congressional resistance to Bush's national security policies evaporated. Congress's deference partly reflected the enormity of the attacks and a principled belief that lawmakers should defer to strong presidential leadership in times of national crisis. But it also reflected a healthy dose of politics. Rather than blame the president for failing to anticipate the attacks, Americans rallied around him. Bush's new-found popularity translated into political power. Lawmakers may ignore the pleadings of an unpopular president, but they usually heed the demands of a popular one.

The Neoconservative Myth

By the end of the Iraq War, most commentators acknowledged that Bush had presided over a revolution in American foreign policy. They were doubtful, however, that the president was responsible for it. They instead gave the credit (or blame) to "neoconservative" thinkers within the administration, led by Deputy Secretary of Defense Paul Wolfowitz, who they said were determined to use America's great power to transform despotic regimes into liberal democracies.* One writer alleged that Bush was "the callow instrument of neoconservative ideologues." Another remarked on the "neoconservative coup" in Washington and wondered if "George W. fully understands the grand strategy that Wolfowitz and other aides are unfolding." A third thought the neoconservatives' victory was obvious. "Unless you live at the bottom of a well, you've probably noticed that 9/11 and Iraq have a transforming effect on the American Right. The short formulation is that so-called neoconservatism has triumphed."

This conventional wisdom was wrong on at least two counts. First, it fundamentally misunderstood the intellectual currents within the Bush administration and the Republican party more generally. Neoconservatives were more prominent outside the administration, particularly in the pages of Commentary and the Weekly Standard and in the television studios of Fox News, than they were inside it. The bulk of Bush's advisers, including most notably Dick Cheney and Defense Secretary Donald Rumsfeld, were not neocons. They were instead assertive nationalists—traditional hard-line conservatives willing to use American military power to defeat threats to U.S. security but reluctant as a general rule to use American primacy to remake the world in its image. Whereas neoconservatives talked of lengthy and expensive military occupation in Iraq, assertive nationalists spoke of a quick transition and leaving "Iraq for the Iraqis."

Although neoconservatives and assertive nationalists differed on whether the United States should actively spread its values abroad, both were deeply skeptical of the cold war consensus on the importance of the rule of law and the relevance of international institutions to American foreign policy. They placed their faith not in diplomacy and treaties, but in power and resolve. Agreement on this key point allowed neoconservatives and assertive nationalists to form a marriage of convenience in overthrowing the cold war approach to foreign policy even as they disagreed about what kind of commitment the United States should make to rebuilding Iraq and remaking the rest of the world.

The second and more important flaw with the neoconservative coup theory was that it grossly underestimated George W. Bush. The man from Midland was not a figurehead in someone else's revolution. He may have entered the Oval Office not knowing which general ran Pakistan, but during his first 30 months in office he was the puppeteer, not the puppet. He actively solicited the counsel of his seasoned advisers, and he tolerated if not encouraged vigorous disagreement among them. When necessary, he overruled them. George W. Bush led his own revolution.

---

*Neoconservativism is a conservative movement with roots in the traditional left of mid-century America. It has supported hawkish foreign policy positions.

Whither the Revolution?

Not all revolutions succeed. As Air Force One tipped its wings over Baghdad in a gesture of triumph, there were troubling signs of things to come for an America unbound. U.S. troops in Iraq found themselves embroiled in a guerrilla war with remnants of Saddam Hussein's regime. Anger overseas at what was seen as an arrogant and hypocritical America had swelled. Close allies spoke openly not of how best to work with the United States, but of how to constrain its ability to act. Washington was beginning to confront a new question: were the costs of the Bush revolution in foreign policy about to swamp the benefits?

Part of the problem with the Bush revolution lay in how Bush and his advisers conducted it. They declined to cloak the iron fist of American power in the velvet glove of diplomacy, preferring instead to express contempt for opinions different from their own. Donald Rumsfeld, as his dismissal of France and Germany as "old Europe" attested, had a particular zeal for insulting friends and allies. Not surprisingly, this attitude struck many outside the United States—and more than a few within it—as an arrogance born of power, not principle. They resented it profoundly.

The deeper problem, however, was that the fundamental premise of the Bush revolution—that America's security rested on an America unbound—was mistaken. For all the talk at the start of the 21st century of the United States being a hyperpower, the world was beyond the ability of any one country to control. Many of the most important challenges America faced overseas could be met only with the active cooperation of others. The question was how best to secure that cooperation.

Bush maintained that if America led, friends and allies would follow. True, they might grumble because they disliked how Washington intended to lead. Some might even decide to wait until they saw the benefits of American action. In the end, however, they would join forces with the United States in combating threats such as terrorism and weapons proliferation because they trusted America's motives and they shared its interests. Countries would not cut off their nose to spite their face.

Iraq exposed the flaw in this thinking. Most countries, including all members of the UN Security Council, shared a major interest in making sure Iraq did not possess weapons of mass destruction, especially nuclear weapons. But that common interest did not automatically translate into active cooperation in a war to oust Saddam Hussein—or even into support for such a war. A few countries actively tried to stop the march to war, and many others simply sat on the sidelines. Little changed after the toppling of Saddam Hussein's statue in Firdos Square. Although many countries believed that stabilizing postwar Iraq was vitally important—for regional stability, international security, and their own national safety—they did not rush to join the reconstruction effort. In July 2003, American troops constituted more than 90 percent of all forces supporting the Iraq operation—at an annual cost to the American taxpayer of $50 billion.

Britain provided most of the other forces. The remaining foreign contributions were insignificant. Hungary, for instance, agreed to provide 133 truck drivers but no trucks, mechanics, or anything else. In other cases, countries agreed to contribute troops only after Washington agreed to pay for them—giving a whole new meaning to the concept of burden sharing.

The lesson of Iraq, then, was that sometimes when America leads, few follow. This ultimately was the real danger of the Bush revolution. America's friends and allies seldom could stop Washington from doing as it wished, no matter how much some commentators opined to the contrary. However, America's friends and allies did not need to resist American policy to make Washington pay a price for its desire to play unbound by any rules. They could simply refuse to come to its aid when their help was most needed or desired. That, in turn, risked undermining not only what America could achieve abroad but also domestic support at home for engaging the world. Americans could rightly ask: if others are unwilling to bear the burdens of meeting tough challenges, why should we? In that respect, an America unbound could ultimately lead to a America that is less secure.

Questions for Discussion

1. Bush's "revolutionary" foreign policy disdains the use of multilateral institutions (such as the United Nations), according to Daalder and Lindsay. If that is so, what are the advantages for the United States? The disadvantages? Can this be effective as a long-term strategy?
2. What was the role of September 11 in the evolution of Bush's new foreign policy? Could that policy have been carried out absent the terrorist attacks? Explain.

 14.5

Intelligence, Policy, and the War in Iraq

Paul Pillar

As of 2007, the Iraq War looks like an unmitigated disaster, with its high costs, unachieved goals, and negative effect on the United States' relations with much of the world. Although many misjudgments were made, resulting in poor decisions, among the most serious systematic problems came in the relationships between the providers of intelligence and those who used the information that was produced. Perhaps the most troubling indictment of the Bush administration's decision process was that it had, in various ways, politicized the intelligence process, both in what information was gathered and how it was interpreted.

In this selection, Paul Pillar, a retired CIA officer, argues that on Iraqi issues a breakdown occurred in the separation of intelligence gathering and policymaking, a separation generally seen as critical to responsible, effective use of intelligence. In general, he sees the information gathered by the intelligence community and its initial analysis as responsible and broadly accurate in assessing Saddam Hussein's capabilities and actions. Subsequently, however, the Bush administration politicized the intelligence process by "cherry picking" bits of data that appeared to support their claims or by making requests of analysts to scrutinize particular items in hopes of finding evidence that would support the administration's preferred policies. As he illuminates various ways in which intelligence information and interpretation can be politicized, Pillar produces a profound indictment of a flawed process that led the United States into a war of choice in which the rationales for choosing were biased toward a given agenda. Such actions must be avoided in the future, he argues, and he suggests ways in which the intelligence community can be protected from serving political agendas.

Former CIA official Paul Pillar, who served as national intelligence officer for the Near East and South Asia between 2000 and 2005, currently teaches in the Security Studies Program of Georgetown University.

Paul R. Pillar, "Intelligence, Policy, and the War in Iraq." Reprinted by permission of *Foreign Affairs* (March/April 2006). Copyright 2006 by the Council on Foreign Relations, Inc.

A Dysfunctional Relationship

The most serious problem with U.S. intelligence today is that its relationship with the policymaking process is broken and badly needs repair. In the wake of the Iraq war, it has become clear that official intelligence analysis was not relied on in making even the most significant national security decisions, that intelligence was misused publicly to justify decisions already made, that damaging ill will developed between policymakers and intelligence officers, and that the intelligence community's own work was politicized. As the national intelligence officer responsible for the Middle East from 2000 to 2005, I witnessed all of these disturbing developments.

Public discussion of prewar intelligence on Iraq has focused on the errors made in assessing Saddam Hussein's unconventional weapons programs. A commission chaired by Judge Laurence Silberman and former Senator Charles Robb usefully documented the intelligence community's mistakes in a solid and comprehensive report released in March 2005. . . .

At the same time, an acrimonious and highly partisan debate broke out over whether the Bush administration manipulated and misused intelligence in making its case for war. The administration defended itself by pointing out that it was not alone in its view that Saddam had weapons of mass destruction (WMD) and active weapons programs, however mistaken that view may have been.

In this regard, the Bush administration was quite right: its perception of Saddam's weapons capacities was shared by the Clinton administration, congressional Democrats, and most other Western governments and intelligence services. But in making this defense, the White House also inadvertently pointed out the real problem: intelligence on Iraqi weapons programs did not drive its decision to go to war. A view broadly held in the United States and even more so overseas was that deterrence of Iraq was working, that Saddam was being kept "in his box," and that the best way to deal with the weapons problem was through an aggressive inspections program to supplement the sanctions already in place. That the administration arrived at so different a policy solution indicates that its decision to topple Saddam was driven by other factors—namely, the desire to shake up the sclerotic power structures of the Middle East and hasten the spread of more liberal politics and economics in the region.

If the entire body of official intelligence analysis on Iraq had a policy implication, it was to avoid war—or, if war was going to be launched, to prepare for a messy aftermath. What is most remarkable about prewar U.S. intelligence on Iraq is not that it got things wrong and thereby misled policymakers; it is that it played so small a role in one of the most important U.S. policy decisions in recent decades.

A Model Upended

The proper relationship between intelligence gathering and policymaking sharply separates the two functions. The intelligence community collects information, evaluates its credibility, and combines it with other information to help make sense of situations abroad that could affect U.S. interests. Intelligence officers decide which topics should get their limited collection and analytic resources according to both their own judgments and the concerns of policymakers. Policymakers thus influence which topics intelligence agencies address but not the conclusions that they reach. The intelligence community, meanwhile, limits its judgments to what is happening or what might happen overseas, avoiding policy judgments about what the United States should do in response.

In practice, this distinction is often blurred, especially because analytic projections may have policy implications even if they are not explicitly stated. But the distinction is still important. National security abounds with problems that are clearer than the solutions to them; . . . it is critical that the intelligence community not advocate policy, especially not openly. If it does, it loses the most important basis for its credibility and its claims to objectivity. When intelligence analysts critique one another's work, they use the phrase "policy prescriptive" as a pejorative, and rightly so.

The Bush administration's use of intelligence on Iraq did not just blur this distinction; it turned the entire model upside down. The administration used intelligence not to inform decision-making, but to justify a decision already made. It went to war without requesting—and evidently without being influenced by—any strategic-level intelligence assessments on any aspect of Iraq. . . .

Official intelligence on Iraqi weapons programs was flawed, but even with its flaws, it was not what led to the war. On the issue that mattered most, the intelligence community judged that Iraq probably was several years away from developing a nuclear weapon. The October 2002 NIE [National Intelligence Estimate] also judged that Saddam was unlikely to use WMD against the United States unless his regime was placed in mortal danger.

Before the war, on its own initiative, the intelligence community considered the principal challenges that any postinvasion authority in Iraq would be likely to face. It presented a picture of a political culture that would not provide fertile ground for democracy and foretold a long, difficult, and turbulent transition. It projected that a Marshall Plan-type* effort would be required to restore the Iraqi economy, despite Iraq's abundant oil resources. It forecast that in a deeply divided Iraqi society, with Sunnis resentful over the loss of their dominant position and Shiites seeking power commensurate with their majority status, there was a significant chance that the groups would engage in violent conflict unless an occupying power prevented it. And it anticipated that a foreign occupying force would itself be the target of resentment and attacks—including by guerrilla warfare—unless it established security and put Iraq on the road to prosperity in the first few weeks or months after the fall of Saddam.

---

*Named for Secretary of State George Marshall, the Marshall Plan provided $13 billion in aid (worth $130 billion in 2006 dollars) to rebuild European economies between 1947 and 1951. The program's overwhelming success has made it a standard for offering economic aid ever since.

In addition, the intelligence community offered its assessment of the likely regional repercussions of ousting Saddam. It argued that any value Iraq might have as a democratic exemplar would be minimal and would depend on the stability of a new Iraqi government and the extent to which democracy in Iraq was seen as developing from within rather than being imposed by an outside power. More likely, war and occupation would boost political Islam and increase sympathy for terrorists' objectives—and Iraq would become a magnet for extremists from elsewhere in the Middle East.

Standard Deviations

The Bush administration deviated from the professional standard not only in using policy to drive intelligence, but also in aggressively using intelligence to win public support for its decision to go to war. This meant selectively adducing data—"cherry-picking"—rather than using the intelligence community's own analytic judgments. In fact, key portions of the administration's case explicitly rejected those judgments. In an August 2002 speech, for example, Vice President Dick Cheney observed that "intelligence is an uncertain business" and noted how intelligence analysts had underestimated how close Iraq had been to developing a nuclear weapon before the 1991 Persian Gulf War. His conclusion—at odds with that of the intelligence community—was that "many of us are convinced that Saddam will acquire nuclear weapons fairly soon."

In the upside-down relationship between intelligence and policy that prevailed in the case of Iraq, the administration selected pieces of raw intelligence to use in its public case for war, leaving the intelligence community to register varying degrees of private protest when such use started to go beyond what analysts deemed credible or reasonable. The best-known example was the assertion by President George W. Bush in his 2003 State of the Union address that Iraq was purchasing uranium ore in Africa. U.S. intelligence analysts had questioned the credibility of the report making this claim, had kept it out of their own unclassified products, and had advised the White House not to use it publicly. . . .

The reexamination of prewar public statements is a necessary part of understanding the process that led to the Iraq war: But a narrow focus on rhetorical details tends to overlook more fundamental problems in the intelligence-policy relationship. Any time policymakers, rather than intelligence agencies, take the lead in selecting which bits of raw intelligence to present, there is—regardless of the issue—a bias. The resulting public statements ostensibly reflect intelligence, but they do not reflect intelligence analysis, which is an essential part of determining what the pieces of raw reporting mean. The policymaker acts with an eye not to what is indicative of a larger pattern or underlying truth, but to what supports his case.

Another problem is that on Iraq, the intelligence community was pulled over the line into policy advocacy—not so much by what it said as by its conspicuous role in the administration's public case for war. This was especially true when the intelligence community was made highly visible (with the director of central intelligence literally in the camera frame) in an intelligence-laden presentation by Secretary of State Colin Powell to the UN Security Council a month before the war began. . . .

But the greatest discrepancy between the administration's public statements and the intelligence community's judgments concerned not WMD (there was indeed a broad consensus that such programs existed), but the relationship between Saddam and al Qaeda. The enormous attention devoted to this subject did not reflect any judgment by intelligence officials that there was or was likely to be anything like the "alliance" the administration said existed. The reason the connection got so much attention was that the administration wanted to hitch the Iraq expedition to the "war on terror" and the threat the American public feared most, thereby capitalizing on the country's militant post-9/11 mood.

The issue of possible ties between Saddam and al Qaeda was especially prone to the selective use of raw intelligence to make a public case for war. In the shadowy world of international terrorism, almost anyone can be "linked" to almost anyone else if enough effort is made to find evidence of casual contacts, the mentioning of names in the same breath, or indications of common travels or experiences. Even the most minimal and circumstantial data can be adduced as evidence of a "relationship," ignoring the important question of whether a given regime actually supports a given terrorist group and the fact that relationships can be competitive or distrustful rather than cooperative.

The intelligence community never offered any analysis that supported the notion of an alliance between Saddam and al Qaeda. Yet it was drawn into a public effort to support that notion. To be fair, Secretary Powell's presentation at the UN never explicitly asserted that there was a cooperative relationship between Saddam and al Qaeda. But the presentation was clearly meant to create the impression that one existed. To the extent that the intelligence community was a party to such efforts, it crossed the line into policy advocacy—and did so in a way that fostered public misconceptions contrary to the intelligence community's own judgments.

Varieties of Politicization

In its report on prewar intelligence concerning Iraqi WMD, the Senate Select Committee on Intelligence said it found no evidence that analysts had altered or shaped their judgments in response to political pressure. The Silberman-Robb commission reached the same conclusion, although it conceded that analysts worked in an "environment" affected by "intense" policymaker interest. But the method of investigation used by the panels—essentially, asking analysts

whether their arms had been twisted—would have caught only the crudest attempts at politicization. . . .

The actual politicization of intelligence occurs subtly and can take many
forms. Context is all-important. Well before March 2003, intelligence analysts
and their managers knew that the United States was heading for war with Iraq.
It was clear that the Bush administration would frown on or ignore analysis
that called into question a decision to go to war and welcome analysis that supported such a decision. Intelligence analysts—for whom attention, especially
favorable attention, from policymakers is a measure of success—felt a strong
wind consistently blowing in one direction. The desire to bend with such a
wind is natural and strong, even if unconscious.

On the issue of Iraqi WMD, dozens of analysts throughout the intelligence
community were making many judgments on many different issues based on
fragmentary and ambiguous evidence. The differences between sound intelligence analysis (bearing in mind the gaps in information) and the flawed analysis that actually was produced had to do mainly with matters of caveat, nuance,
and word choice. The opportunities for bias were numerous, . . . [and] the effect
was probably significant.

A clearer form of politicization is the inconsistent review of analysis: reports
that conform to policy preferences have an easier time making it through the
gauntlet of coordination and approval than ones that do not. (Every piece of
intelligence analysis reflects not only the judgments of the analysts most directly involved in writing it, but also the concurrence of those who cover related topics and the review, editing, and remanding of it by several levels of
supervisors, from branch chiefs to senior executives.) The Silberman-Robb
commission noted such inconsistencies in the Iraq case but chalked it up to bad
management. The commission failed to address exactly why managers were inconsistent: they wanted to avoid the unpleasantness of laying unwelcome
analysis on a policymaker's desk.

Another form of politicization with a similar cause is the sugarcoating of
what otherwise would be an unpalatable message. Even the mostly prescient
analysis about the problems likely to be encountered in postwar Iraq included
some observations that served as sugar, added in the hope that policymakers
would not throw the report directly into the burn bag, but damaging the clarity
of the analysis in the process.

But the principal way that the intelligence community's work on Iraq was
politicized concerned the specific questions to which the community devoted
its energies. As any competent pollster can attest, how a question is framed
helps determine the answer. In the case of Iraq, there was also the matter of
sheer quantity of output—not just what the intelligence community said, but
how many times it said it. On any given subject, the intelligence community
faces what is in effect a field of rocks, and it lacks the resources to turn over
every one to see what threats to national security may lurk underneath. In an
unpoliticized environment, intelligence officers decide which rocks to turn

over based on past patterns and their own judgments. But when policymakers repeatedly urge the intelligence community to turn over only certain rocks, the process becomes biased . . . [and] leaves the impression that what lies under those same rocks is a bigger part of the problem than it really is.

That is what happened when the Bush administration repeatedly called on the intelligence community to uncover more material that would contribute to the case for war. The Bush team approached the community again and again and pushed it to look harder at the supposed Saddam-al Qaeda relationship—calling on analysts not only to turn over additional Iraqi rocks, but also to turn over ones already examined and to scratch the dirt to see if there might be something there after all. The result was an intelligence output that . . . obscured rather than enhanced understanding of al Qaeda's actual sources of strength and support.

This process represented a radical departure from the textbook model of the relationship between intelligence and policy, in which an intelligence service responds to policymaker interest in certain subjects (such as "security threats from Iraq" or "al Qaeda's supporters") and explores them in whatever direction the evidence leads. The process did not involve intelligence work designed to find dangers not yet discovered or to inform decisions not yet made. Instead, it involved research to find evidence in support of a specific line of argument—that Saddam was cooperating with al Qaeda—which in turn was being used to justify a specific policy decision.

One possible consequence of such politicization is policymaker self-deception. A policymaker can easily forget that he is hearing so much about a particular angle in briefings because he and his fellow policymakers have urged the intelligence community to focus on it. A more certain consequence is the skewed application of the intelligence community's resources. Feeding the administration's voracious appetite for material on the Saddam-al Qaeda link consumed an enormous amount of time and attention. . . . It is fair to ask how much other counterterrorism work was left undone as a result.

The issue became even more time-consuming as the conflict between intelligence officials and policymakers escalated into a battle, with the intelligence community struggling to maintain its objectivity even as policymakers pressed the Saddam–al Qaeda connection. The administration's rejection of the intelligence community's judgments became especially clear with the formation of a special Pentagon unit, the Policy Counterterrorism Evaluation Group. The unit, which reported to Undersecretary of Defense Douglas Feith, was dedicated to finding every possible link between Saddam and al Qaeda, and its briefings accused the intelligence community of faulty analysis for failing to see the supposed alliance.

For the most part, the intelligence community's own substantive judgments do not appear to have been compromised. . . . But although the charge of faulty analysis was never directly conveyed to the intelligence community itself, enough of the charges leaked out to create a public perception of rancor between the administration and the intelligence community, which in turn encouraged some administration supporters to charge intelligence officers (including me) with trying to sabotage the president's policies. This poisonous atmosphere reinforced the disinclination within the intelligence community to challenge the consensus view about Iraqi WMD programs; any such challenge would have served merely to reaffirm the presumptions of the accusers.

Partial Repairs

Although the Iraq war has provided a particularly stark illustration of the problems in the intelligence-policy relationship, such problems are not confined to this one issue or this specific administration. Four decades ago, the misuse of intelligence about an ambiguous encounter in the Gulf of Tonkin figured prominently in the Johnson administration's justification for escalating the military effort in Vietnam. Over a century ago, the possible misinterpretation of an explosion on a U.S. warship in Havana harbor helped set off the chain of events that led to a war of choice against Spain. The Iraq case needs further examination and reflection on its own. But public discussion of how to foster a better relationship between intelligence officials and policymakers and how to ensure better use of intelligence on future issues is also necessary.

Intelligence affects the nation's interests through its effect on policy. No matter how much the process of intelligence gathering itself is fixed, the changes will do no good if the role of intelligence in the policymaking process is not also addressed. Unfortunately, there is no single clear fix to the sort of problem that arose in the case of Iraq. The current ill will may not be reparable, and the perception of the intelligence community on the part of some policymakers—that Langley [CIA headquarters] is enemy territory—is unlikely to change. But a few steps, based on the recognition that the intelligence-policy relationship is indeed broken, could reduce the likelihood that such a breakdown will recur.

On this point, the United States should emulate the United Kingdom, where discussion of this issue has been more forthright, by declaring once and for all that its intelligence services should not be part of public advocacy of policies still under debate. In the United Kingdom, Prime Minister Tony Blair accepted a commission of inquiry's conclusions that intelligence and policy had been improperly commingled in such exercises as the publication of the "dodgy dossier," the British counterpart to the United States' Iraqi WMD white paper [an authoritative governmental report], and that in the future there should be a clear delineation between intelligence and policy. An American declaration should take the form of a congressional resolution and be seconded by a statement from the White House. Although it would not have legal force, such a statement would discourage future administrations from attempting to pull the intelligence community into policy advocacy. It would also give some leverage to intelligence officers in resisting any such future attempts. . . .

The legislative branch is the appropriate place for monitoring the intelligence-policy relationship. But the oversight should be conducted by a nonpartisan office modeled on the Government Accountability Office (GAO) and the Congressional Budget Office (CBO). Such an office would have a staff, smaller than that of the GAO or the CBO, of officers experienced in intelligence and with the necessary clearances and access to examine questions about both the politicization of classified intelligence work and the public use of intelligence. As with the GAO, this office could conduct inquiries at the request of members of Congress. It would make its results public as much as possible, consistent with security requirements, and it would avoid duplicating the many other functions of intelligence oversight, which would remain the responsibility of the House and Senate intelligence committees. . . .

The intelligence community should be repositioned to reflect the fact that influence and relevance flow not just from face time in the Oval Office, but also from credibility with Congress and, most of all, with the American public. The community needs to remain in the executive branch but be given greater independence and a greater ability to communicate with those other constituencies (fettered only by security considerations, rather than by policy agendas). An appropriate model is the Federal Reserve, which is structured as a quasi-autonomous body overseen by a board of governors with long fixed terms.

These measures would reduce both the politicization of the intelligence community's own work and the public misuse of intelligence by policymakers. It would not directly affect how much attention policymakers give to intelligence, which they would continue to be entitled to ignore. But the greater likelihood of being called to public account for discrepancies between a case for a certain policy and an intelligence judgment would have the indirect effect of forcing policymakers to pay more attention to those judgments in the first place.

These changes alone will not fix the intelligence-policy relationship. But if Congress and the American people are serious about "fixing intelligence," they should not just do what is easy and politically convenient. At stake are the soundness of U.S. foreign-policy making and the right of Americans to know the basis for decisions taken in the name of their security.

Questions for Discussion

1. What is the proper role of intelligence in relation to policymaking? Why is it so important to maintain a separation between these two activities? In the end, can these be separated?
2. How were the intelligence gathering and analysis processes on Iraq manipulated? What allowed this to occur? What actions and structures should be put in place to avoid these problems in the future?